1001 FOODS

TO DIE FOR

INTRODUCTION BY
CORBY KUMMER

An Andrews McMeel / Madison Press Book

**Andrews McMeel
Publishing, LLC**

Kansas City

Text, design, and compilation © The Madison Press Limited

Introduction © 2007 Corby Kummer

This edition published in 2007 by Andrews McMeel Publishing, LLC, an Andrews
McMeel Universal company, 4520 Main Street, Kansas City, Missouri 64111.

www.andrewsmcmeel.com

ISBN-13: 978-0-7407-7043-2
ISBN-10: 0-7407-7043-8

Library of Congress Control Number: 2007936143

Produced by
Madison Press Books
1000 Yonge Street, Suite 200
Toronto, Ontario
M4K 2K2

madisonpressbooks.com

Printed in Thailand by Imago Productions (F.E.) Ltd., Thailand.

Contents

Introduction

For those who think the unexamined meal not worth eating, this book will be a feast made up of many appetizing tidbits—the best way to eat and think about food at more or less every waking moment, as some of us do. Hunger may be the best sauce, but I would add that curiosity is the indispensable seasoning. It makes any bite either start or end up with a trip to a reference book (or, of course, to frequently unreliable websites). Why are langoustines known as scampi and Norway lobster and Dublin prawns? Why is Canadian bacon called "Canadian" (and do Canadians call it something else)? The answers, or a good start at them, are here.

When you stop at an unfamiliar restaurant, or roadside stand, or vendor's stall in a new city or country—a traveler's first obligation—this book will have many explanations about the foods you discover. The entries range all over the world, like any serious eater's appetite. They can serve as after-action reports or, given the many hunger-pang-inducing photographs, a cause to hunt for places that will serve, say, a Cuban sandwich oozing with mojo-sauce-soaked roast pork, cheese, ham, and sour pickles, squeezed together and warmed in a special press. Or beef bulgogi, Korean "fire meat," which may sound unpromising but looks like a must: pounded sirloin in a fragrant Asian marinade, stir-fried and sprinkled with toasted sesame seeds and red pepper.

Scanning the pages can be a reminder of the classic dishes we've relegated to a back shelf: sole Véronique, a simple but perfect dressing-up of delicately flavored flat-fish fillets in a cream sauce with white grapes, preferably perfumed muscat; a winy, impossibly deep-flavored soupe a l'oignon covered with melted, good gruyère, even if most restaurants now serve it diluted and debased. Why haven't the ubiquitous steakhouses opening in every city revived Châteaubriand, a better and more reliably delicious sign of sumptuous excess than the overused, over-fatty, overpriced kobe and wagyu beef? (You'll want to take the suggestion that the cattle's tummies are massaged with a grain of smoked salt, a prime duty of any curious eater.)

Odd names, a constant delight of food rambles, are amply represented here, and will inspire excursions, even if only around the corner to the local Chinese or Indian standbys, where we order what we already know. I want to try choo-chee shrimp the next time I'm in a Thai restaurant, named for the sound shrimp make when sizzled in a sauce of red-curry paste, coconut chiles, nam pla, and palm sugar. If I'm in an Indian restaurant, before I let myself lunge for hot, fresh-puffed naan (what breads are fresher or more tempting than Indian ones?), I'll look for the Kashmir lamb stew, spiced with cinnamon, ginger, garlic, cloves, cumin, and cayenne, with the irresistible name of rogan josh (and it's said to be a great dip for warm naan, if I can bring myself to leave any).

Even if the book's scope is worldwide, for me its chief attraction is as a guide to the mysteries of the British Isles. The meat chapter, the centerpiece of the book, explains the differences among Canadian, back, and other bacons, and those between gammon (cured, uncooked ham) and regular ham (cured, cooked), and between British and American cracklings, which the English call "scratchings." The British names are particularly irresistible. Take Cullen skink, a creamy, smoked fish chowder, from a Gallic word meaning "essence." Skink is not made with Arbroath smokies (small smoked haddock from the town of the same name in eastern Scotland), nor would it go well with Stinking Bishop cheese, which you might not run to the cheese shop to find. You might want to try your hand, though, at beef olives, pounded and rolled beef with a stuffing open to improvisation and even to olives, though the name is from the Old French word for lark, *alou* (think of veal birds).

Of course there are desserts we always want, like sundaes and crumbles and chocolate mousse and French apricot tart. But in the department of irresistible names, you'll be captivated by a lemon posset, a close cousin to the equally festively named syllabub. A posset entails whisking warm cream or milk, lemon, sugar, white wine or ale, and folding in beaten egg whites to make a warm, fizzy froth that is served in a special pot, preferably emblazoned with the family crest.

You'll hope to try one day the Canadian oat bar oddly called a "flapjack," and you'll instantly crave a slice of Victoria sandwich, a layered, golden, sponge cake filled with raspberry jam (the color photograph looks exactly like a Wayne Thiebaud painting). Come berry season, you'll seek out any version you can of the noblest dessert, the English summer pudding, though you won't want to call it by its old name, "hydropathic pudding."

1001 Foods is best seen as a kaleidoscope—the foods and cultures of the world all mixed up, appearing now in one light, now in another, bringing foods you never would have thought were related into new patterns. A lovely bonus are recipes from some of the greatest writers on food in English, which will send you to the books of Elizabeth David, Julia Child, and Marcella Hazan, and onward to more. So will the uncredited recipes, which assume varying degrees of experience.

But explorations into new lands, new markets, and new guides is what turns daredevil food adventurers into thoughtful ones—and it's that metamorphosis this book should inspire. The combination of unfamiliar foods and names, with generous, sometimes unbearably tempting photographs fulfills the chief obligation of any book on food: instilling curiosity and appetite in nearly equal measure.

—Corby Kummer

1 APPETIZERS AND SMALL FOOD

Albóndigas

Nearly all cuisines have a version of meatballs, and albóndigas are Spain's. The word is derived from the Arabic *al-bunduq* (hazelnut), which indicates that they were traditionally made small, and also suggests that they were a Moorish import to the Spanish kitchen.

They are usually fashioned from a mixture of ground beef (sometimes veal) and pork, bound with bread crumbs and olive oil, and gently seasoned. Eaten as part of a tapas spread, they are classically cooked and served in a rich tomato sauce, made by stewing down whole tomatoes with garlic and oregano. In a variant recipe, *albóndigas con picada de almendras*, the meatballs include a paste of crushed almonds and peas.

In Mexico, small albóndigas form the central component of a soup, *sopa de albóndigas*. A popular domestic dish throughout the country, this tends to be a fierier proposition than its Spanish antecedent. Chopped green chiles are added to the broth, and the meatballs are then simmered in it. An appreciative mention of albóndigas in Mexico often arouses knowing sniggers, as the word has passed into colloquial usage to denote part of the male anatomy.

Kofte

Kofte, or meatballs, feature in the cuisines of cultures from the Middle East to India, the eastern Mediterranean, and North Africa. Almost certainly first made in imperial Persia (now Iran) from ground lamb, their name probably derives from an old Persian word, *koofteh*, meaning "pounded or ground meat." From there, they migrated along trade routes to India, but also south and west to Turkey and the Balkan civilizations of southeast Europe.

There are inevitably numerous recipes for *kofte*, many based on other meats, some containing nuts, cheese, or dried fruits. They are very often highly spiced, and served in a thick, rich, often tomato-laden sauce. Cooking method varies from region to region, and includes shallow-frying, broiling, or stewing. Meatball or kofte size varies too: in Persia, they were the size of grapefruits or larger.

Lamb kofte adapt themselves obligingly to a range of different sauces, from creamy yogurt ones that offset the spicy heat in the meatballs, to fruity Moroccan ones that might contain apricots or preserved lemons.

Liptauer

Masala Dosai

An intense-flavored, cheesy dip from the mountains of central Europe, Liptauer is based on a soft sheep's-milk cheese called *bryndza* in the Slovak language. This is a strained curd cheese similar to quark, which has only a very unremarkable flavor in itself, but it is the other ingredients that make Liptauer so special. The young cheese is mixed to a thick paste with butter, and seasoned with paprika, caraway seeds, mustard, and chives. An even stronger version can be made containing anchovies, chopped onion, and capers. It is then spread onto thick slices of toasted whole-wheat bread or served as a dip. In Slovakia, where it probably originated, it is also often used as a filling for stuffed red bell peppers.

The dish probably came from the province of Liptov in the Tatra mountains, and was first made by sheep farmers. In its most rudimentary form, it would have been assembled on the plate, when the cheese would have been surrounded by little heaps of the flavoring ingredients. As Liptauer, it has traveled to neighboring regions of central Europe, including Hungary and Austria.

A *dosa* is southern India's answer to the pancake. Made predominantly around the state of Karnataka, it is a thin batter envelope made from lentils and rice, which are left to ferment overnight in water, and then mashed into a thin paste the next day. The batter is then ladled onto a flat iron griddle, and cooked in the ubiquitous Indian fat medium, ghee (clarified butter). When finished, it is folded around a filling, in the manner of a French *crêpe*. There is more interesting textural variation to a *dosa*, compared with the pancakes of other culinary traditions, the crisp exterior concealing a more doughy texture on the inside.

Masala dosai contain vegetable fillings, usually potatoes and fried onions, seasoned with a hot spice mixture (*masala*). They are served with soft chutneys, especially coconut, and are typically eaten as a breakfast dish. The Western palate being a little too fragile for an onslaught of spices first thing in the morning, dosai are more often eaten as an appetizer or midday snack outside India.

Taramasalata

One of two Greek purées that have become widely popular outside their country of origin, the other being hummus, taramasalata is made from preserved fish roe. Nearly always delicate pale pink in color, its principal ingredient was traditionally the dried roe sac of the gray mullet (known internationally by its Italian name, *bottarga*), but is now generally cod roe, the latter being the cheaper alternative. Increasingly, the lengthier drying process has been replaced by another preservation technique, smoking, giving the taramasalata a different kind of pungency. With cod itself now becoming an endangered species in waterways throughout the world, this too may change in time.

Taramasalata should be served very fresh, slightly chilled, and spread inside warm pockets of pita bread. Along with the fish roe, it often contains some finely minced onion, together with white bread crumbs as a bulking agent, olive oil, and lemon juice.

Hummus

Hummus is now widely known beyond Greece, perhaps because it has become a staple in many vegetarian diets. It is a thick, granular purée of garbanzos—sometimes known as chickpeas—tahini (a paste of crushed sesame seeds), garlic, lemon juice, and olive oil. Served in the centuries-old traditional manner, hummus is poured into a flat dish, a little red paprika mixed with olive oil is dizzled over the surface, and chopped fresh parsley is sprinkled on top.

Hummus is best served with gently warmed pita bread, but it is also good as a topping for various crispbreads, crackers, and even little pancakes.

This legume requires considerable preparation. Rarely eaten fresh, garbanzos are usually dried until they turn from their natural green to brown. From this preserved state, they need fairly lengthy soaking and cooking before they can be used. The occurrence of some form of hummus throughout eastern Mediterranean and Arabic cooking is explained by the need to use garbanzos in bulk.

Commercial hummus never replicates the appeal of homemade, often because a more neutral oil is used instead of olive, and also because the tahini in it has often begun fermenting by the time the product hits the supermarket shelf.

Skordalia

The English translation of the name of this dish—garlic sauce—may be a little misleading. Originating on Cephalonia, this is the Greek version of mashed potato. Recently, it has achieved international renown as a creamier, softer version of the northern European dish. Skordalia is best made with older winter potatoes, with their flourier texture. They are boiled in the traditional way, then mashed by hand with extra-virgin olive oil and steamed buttermilk. They are also seasoned with minced garlic and freshly chopped oregano, as well as salt and black pepper, and sometimes a little white wine vinegar.

This less bland mash may be served as a side dish to a meat or fish main course, but is also often part of a *mezedes* platter in Greek restaurants.

There are regional variations on skordalia in Greece. Some recipes use nuts—either almonds or walnuts—that are finely ground and then mixed in with the mashed potato. In this case, lemon juice is usually substituted for the wine vinegar.

Tzatziki ▷

More of a dip than a spread, some version of tzatziki is found throughout southeast Europe, in Greece, Turkey, Cyprus, and the Balkan countries. The main ingredient is strained yogurt (traditionally made from sheep's or goat's milk, rather than cow's) into which finely chopped cucumber is stirred, along with a little olive oil, white wine vinegar, and refreshing herbs, most notably mint or dill. More assertively flavored versions may contain minced onion and heroic quantities of garlic.

Aficionados of Indian cooking will recognize tzatziki as a distant cousin of *raita*, and it can perform the same function at a meal, being a cooling side dish to go alongside spicier or richer fare, such as *souvlaki* (chunks of pork or chicken cooked on skewers). In Greece, however, tzatziki is often served as a course on its own in a bowl, into which pieces of warm pita bread are dipped.

The Greek-Cypriot version of tzatziki tends to be lighter than the one eaten on the mainland, with the emphasis on mint rather than garlic, while versions in North America are often based on sour cream, which gives a richer result than yogurt.

Fried Cashews

Cashew nuts, which are distantly related to the mango, are many people's favorite nut. They are popular when eaten plain, perhaps even more so when bought roasted and salted in small, expensive packs. This Eastern treatment though, in which the raw nuts are deep-fried in peanut oil in a wok and spiced with chili powder and/or five spice, is best of all. They are eaten in this way as a very popular street snack throughout Southeast Asia, from Thailand to Malaysia.

In centuries gone by, cashews were first taken to the East Indies along the trade routes from South America, being originally native to Brazil. They grow on a fruit tree, which produces a tart, pear-shaped fruit called a cashew apple, at one end of which the nut grows. Cashew nuts have also found their way into many traditional dishes in Chinese and Indian cooking, either whole or ground with spices. More than any other nut, their rich, fatty flavor goes particularly well with spicy marinades.

Fried Cashews

2 cups raw cashew nuts

Oil for deep-frying

1 tsp salt

$1/2$ tsp freshly ground black pepper

$1/2$ tsp chili powder

Deep-fry the cashew nuts until they begin to turn light brown—a matter of minutes—then remove with a slotted spoon. Drop them straight into a hot frying pan with the remaining ingredients and stir-fry for a couple of minutes, coating the cashew nuts with the spices. Leave to cool before serving. *Makes 2 cups*

Guacamole

Hailing from Mexico, guacamole is a sharply seasoned blend of ripe avocado flesh, tomatoes, hot chiles, onion, garlic, cilantro, and citrus (usually lime) juice. (Contrary to myth, setting the avocado pit in the guacamole won't prevent browning of the avocado, but the lime juice does delay the reaction.) It is eaten at all times of day in its native land, including first thing in the morning.

Its origins date back to Aztec times, when the naturally high fat content of the fruit made the dish a useful dietary supplement. A traditional stone tool known as a *molcajete* is used to mash the avocado flesh, along the same principle as a mortar and pestle.

The name of the dish, which comes from Nahuatl, one of the indigenous Mexican languages, simply means "avocado sauce."

Guacamole has become a favorite party dip, especially scooped onto tortilla chips, but in Mexico, it is often a side dish accompanying almost any main course.

Guacamole

2 tbsp finely chopped white onion

2 serrano chiles to taste, finely chopped

3 heaped tbsp roughly chopped cilantro

Salt, to taste

3 large avocados

1 medium tomato, finely chopped

To serve:

1 heaped tbsp finely chopped white onion

2 heaped tbsp roughly chopped cilantro

Grind together the onion, chiles, cilantro, and salt to a paste. Cut the avocados into halves, remove the pits, and squeeze the flesh out of the shells and mash into the chile base to a textured consistency—it should not be smooth. Stir in all but 1 tablespoon of the tomatoes, adjust the seasoning, and top with the remaining chopped tomatoes, onion, and cilantro. Serve immediately at room temperature. *Makes 2⅓ cups*

Adapted from Diana Kennedy's *The Essential Cuisines of Mexico*

Bagna Cauda

With a name literally meaning "hot bath," bagna cauda is traditional to the Piedmont region of northwest Italy. It consists of a richly fatty and strong-flavored dip into which various vegetable cuts—raw or cooked—are dunked. The primary ingredients are anchovies, garlic, and walnut (or olive) oil, bulked with butter and, sometimes, cream. Favored vegetables for dipping are celery sticks, zucchini and carrot batons, red or yellow bell pepper strips, and scallions. Cooked baby artichoke hearts are also a good choice, although this dish is customarily eaten in the fall and winter, hence served hot.

In Italian homes, little forks are provided to spear the vegetables, and the dip-laden morsels are held over a piece of bread before being transferred to the mouth. The bread, liberally soaked with dip, is eaten in its turn. This is still a popular way to feed guests at a Christmas Eve gathering.

Italian migrants took the tradition with them to Argentina, where the dish is also popular as *bañacauda*.

Bagna Cauda

$1/2$ cup plus 2 tbsp extra-virgin olive oil

4–5 cloves of garlic, peeled, and Microplaned or minced

12 anchovies preserved in olive oil, drained, and chopped

$1/3$ to $1/2$ cup unsalted butter, cut into chunks

For dipping:

A variety of raw vegetables, including fennel, cauliflower, Belgian endive, sweet peppers, and zucchini

Put the oil in a pan with the garlic and anchovies, and cook over a low heat, stirring, until you have a melted, muddy mess. Everything should begin to meld together. Whisk in 6 tablespoons of butter, and as soon as it has melted, remove from the heat, and give a few more beats of your whisk so that everything is creamy and amalgamated. Taste, and if you feel you want this dipping sauce—which is meant to be pungent but not acrid—a little more mellow, whisk in the remaining 2 tablespoons of butter. Pour into a dish that, ideally, fits over a flame so that it does not get cold at the table.

Dip in the crudités and eat.

Adapted from Nigella Lawson's *Nigella Bites*

25 Best Nibbles to Eat with Champagne

Almonds

Walnuts

Salted pistachios

Toasted pumpkin seeds

Croutons topped with sour cream and
   salmon roe

Little rolls of cured (but not smoked) salmon

Plain oysters

Thinly sliced, lightly seared scallops

Shrimp with light mayonnaise

Shrimp vol-au-vents

Diced lobster on potato salad

Crab pâté on toast

Taramasalata on thin crackers

Anchovy straws

Light-textured chicken liver pâté on toast

Chicken and leek vol-au-vents

Sliced *boudin blanc* (white pork sausage)

Rolls of mortadella ham

Mini sausage rolls

Sliced quiche lorraine

Sliced *flamiche* (leek tart)

Goat cheese wrapped in Parma ham

Mini gougères

Mini potato tortilla

Cubes of crumbly white English cheese
   (Lancashire or Wensleydale)

Carpaccio

▷

Today's restaurant menus often refer to any ingredient that has been cut into large, wafer-thin slices as a form of carpaccio, but the original dish is slices of raw beef. Surprisingly, the dish does not hail from ancient tradition, but appears to have been invented in Harry's Bar in Venice in 1950, on behalf of an aristocratic customer whose doctor had forbidden her to eat cooked meat.

Although carpaccio can be made from the best cuts of beef, such as filet, a more flavorful cut is generally used. In some establishments, the joint of beef is kept in the freezer to make it easier to carve the wafer-thin slices, but many chefs claim this spoils the texture. A razor-sharp knife with a long, heavy blade is essential.

Beef Carpaccio

2 lb topside of beef

Freshly ground black pepper

2 oz Parmesan cheese

For the marinade:

½ cup balsamic vinegar

5 tbsp soy sauce

5 tbsp Worcestershire sauce

4 cloves garlic, chopped

1 bunch fresh basil

½ bunch fresh thyme

15 black peppercorns, crushed

1¼ cups dry white wine

2½ cups olive oil

1 tbsp coarse sea salt

Trim the beef of any fat and sinew. Mix together all the marinade ingredients, reserving a few basil leaves to finish the dish. Roll the beef in the marinade, cover, and steep in the refrigerator for 4 to 5 days to achieve the maximum taste. Turn the beef in the marinade every day.

Remove the meat from the marinade and wrap in plastic food wrap. Freeze for later use (slice from frozen on a slicing machine) or keep in the refrigerator and slice very thinly with a sharp knife as you want it. Push the marinade through a sieve to use as a dressing.

To serve: place very thin slices onto the serving plate, covering the whole surface. Chop the remaining basil leaves and add to the dressing. Brush this over the meat and twist on some freshly ground black pepper. Lay shavings of Parmesan on top or grate and serve the Parmesan separately. *Serves 8* **Adapted from Gary Rhodes'** *Rhodes Around Britain*

Chiles Rellenos

This traditional Mexican dish is an economical way of stretching a limited amount of meat, since it forms the filling for hot green poblano or ancho chiles. They can make either an appetizer or a main course, if served with rice and tortillas.

Chiles rellenos are prepared by first charring the outer skins of the chile peppers over a naked flame, so that they begin to blister and blacken. They are then transferred into a plastic food bag, where the trapped steam continues to cook the skin, which can then be gently rubbed off. The peppers are then slit, the seeds optionally removed (leaving them in makes for a hotter final result), and the filling pressed in. Two main fillings are traditional— ground beef fried with tomato and onion, and grated or cubed Monterey Jack cheese and chopped onion. Held together with toothpicks, they are then dipped in flour and an egg batter, before frying in corn oil.

When served, they are usually given a final dressing of mildly spiced tomato salsa, but there are many variants on this.

Wontons

Perhaps best known in the West as an ingredient in the eponymous soup, wontons are actually extraordinarily versatile. They emerged in China as part of the larger development of pasta some 2,200 years ago and can rightfully claim to be the direct antecedent of ravioli. Wonton wrappers are generally thin pieces of pasta dough cut into small squares and then stuffed with, or wrapped around, any number of ingredients. Usually, these are savory: ground meat, chopped seafood, or vegetables are common. That said, sweet wontons are also to be found in China and elsewhere. Once shaped and sealed, the wonton may be fried, producing a delightfully crispy shell. They may also be steamed, resulting in a silky texture and a favorite item at dim sum. And, of course, they may be used in soups, where the pasta absorbs the surrounding broth and swells with flavor.

Crab Wontons

¼ lb fresh crabmeat

1 tsp Worcestershire sauce

1 to 2 drops Tabasco

½ cup softened cream cheese

40 wonton skins

Oil for frying

Mix the crabmeat with the Worcestershire sauce, Tabasco, and cream cheese.

Place a small spoonful of the mixture in the center of a wonton skin. Brush the edges of the skin with water and press them together to seal.

Heat the oil in a large saucepan until it registers 350°F on a candy thermometer.

Fry the wontons until golden brown—in batches if necessary—and serve immediately with a dipping sauce of your choice.
Makes 40

Ceviche

A dish commonly found throughout Spanish-speaking Central and South America, ceviche is fresh fish marinated in citrus juices (either lemon or lime), olive oil, and spices, and served uncooked. It has become a significant feature on international restaurant menus in modern times, especially when made with sliced scallops. The acidity in the lemon or lime juice breaks down, or denatures, the protein bonds in the fish, thus mimicking the effects of cooking. Although it has not been subjected to heat, the fish is nonetheless, technically, no longer raw.

The dish appears to have originated in Peru in bygone centuries, and is also popular in neighboring Ecuador and increasingly in Mexico, where shrimp, lobster, and clams may be served in this way. Some recipes call for several hours of marinating, although modern kitchen practice has established that the requisite action of the citrus juices only takes a matter of minutes, thus allowing the fish to be served as fresh as possible.

Ceviche

2 lb firm, fresh red snapper fillets, cut into ½-in pieces, deboned

½ red onion, finely diced

3 tomatoes, peeled, seeded, and chopped

1 serrano chile, seeded and finely diced

2 tsp salt

Dash of Tabasco or a few grains of cayenne pepper

1 tsp oregano

½ cup fresh lime juice

½ cup fresh lemon juice

Bibb lettuce, to serve

Place the red snapper in a glass or ceramic dish. Add the onion, chopped tomatoes, chile, salt, Tabasco, and oregano. Pour on the lime and lemon juices. Cover the dish with plastic food wrap and place in the refrigerator. After 1 hour, stir the fish in the marinade so that all of the pieces of fish get covered in the citrus juices. Leave in the refrigerator for at least 6 hours to develop the flavors.

Arrange the Bibb lettuce leaves on a platter. Drain the fish from the marinade and arrange on the lettuce leaves. *Serves 6–8*

Caviar

One of the world's celebrated luxury foods, caviar is—for most people—a once-in-a-lifetime experience. With sturgeon now an endangered marine species, caviar's always sky-high price has been inflated even further in recent years due to controls on its export. Much is still illegally traded, making it one of the few food items in the worldwide trade in contraband.

Caviar is the salted roe of any of several members of the sturgeon family, a bottom-feeding species native to the Caspian Sea, where it is fished by Russia, Iran, and now Azerbaijan. Of the various grades, *beluga* (from the Beluga sturgeon) is the most highly prized. *Sevruga* is saltier and more pungent, and preferred by some connoisseurs. *Osetra* is an often golden-grained variety, while the price of the exceedingly rare albino caviar is off the dial. These names refer to different species of the fish. *Malassol* denotes any caviar with a lower salt content.

Caviar is traditionally eaten with blinis and sour cream, or sometimes unaccompanied. For serving, use a bone or plastic spoon, never a metal one, which tarnishes the flavor.

Chaat

Fiery chaat is the prime example of urban Indian street food, the small plates of snacks cooked by roadside stallholders in the major cities and towns. The word derives from a Hindi verb meaning "to lick."

There are many regional variations. Delhi chaat consists of dumplings of fried dough thickly coated in a mixture of hot chili sauce, chopped onions, yogurt, cilantro, tamarind, and mint. In vegetarian southern India, *dahi vada* are dough balls soaked in thin yogurt and then cooked with a spicy chutney, while Mumbai's *bhel puri* are made from a mixture of dried noodles and puffed rice, served with contrasting chutneys of hot chiles and sweet dates. The fish-based cuisine of the coast of Kerala offers spiced seafood pastries called *patri*.

A common ingredient in these snacks is *chaat masala*, the spice mix that forms the basis of their flavor range. The mix is usually composed of ground dried mango, chili powder, ginger, cumin, cloves, and mint.

Lox

Besides burying, drying, and salting, the other classic technique for preserving fish so that it could be eaten in the winter was smoking. Subjecting fresh fish to the pungent smoke rising from the embers of an almost extinguished wood fire not only denatures its proteins in a way that imitates the effect of cooking, it also imparts a salty, savory flavor to the fish.

Lox, or smoked salmon, was the most highly prized product of this preservation process. Over time, it became a luxury item, as salmon became a sought-after fish, and it ended up on the tables of well-to-do families as an elegant first course, served with brown bread and butter, a light dusting of freshly ground black pepper, and no more than a dribble of lemon juice. Its flavor was seen as too refined to need any other extraneous accompaniments.

Different food cultures developed divergent tastes for the amount of smoke flavor lox ought to have. What became known as the "London cure" was the most pungent, but Ashkenazi Jewish families preferred a lighter, more fugitive smoky hint, partnering it with cream cheese and bagels.

Hot- & Cold-Smoked Salmon

There are two techniques for smoking salmon, depending on whether the smoke is cool or hot. For traditional lox, the smoke is the tepid exudation of a wood fire that has been left to die right down. Known as cold-smoking, this method developed in English and Scottish smokehouses.

Hot-smoking is more traditional in the Scandinavian countries, and in Germany. The fires used in this type of preparation are much livelier, and the smoke is correspondingly hotter, often equivalent to the boiling point of water. This fiercer treatment results in fish with a firmer, drier texture, since it is slightly cooked. The smoked fish still keeps well, but the end product is distinctly different.

Hot-smoked salmon may be eaten cold, though it is sometimes served lightly warmed with stir-fried noodles in Pacific Rim cuisine. Due to its firmer texture, it is not usually sliced as thinly as lox, but is sold in thicker chunks.

Croque Monsieur

Don't call it toasted cheese. Croque monsieur is an altogether more sophisticated customer, for all that it is essentially a cheap French café or street snack, much favored by impoverished students on breaks between classes. Its name means "Munch, sir," which is good instruction on what to do with it.

Dating from the first decade of the 20th century, the true croque monsieur is a toasted sandwich: slices of Gruyère cheese and ham between two slices of white bread, which is broiled on both sides. Economical versions frequently omit the ham, or it may be replaced by chicken. For a more elaborate variant, seen at some Parisian street stalls, the croque monsieur is dipped in an egg batter and then fried in butter. This does not seem to add a great deal to the original recipe, other than an extra whack of cholesterol.

Croque madame, an innovation of the 1950s, comes topped with a fried egg, the name arising from the suggestive likeness of the egg to a woman's breast.

Crudités ▷

Derived from the French word *cru*, meaning "raw," these are one of the simplest, and yet most stimulating, appetizers. All you need are some good, fresh salad vegetables and a couple of tasty dips. Eaten outdoors with drinks, or served as appetite-whetters before lunch or dinner, crudités are not only healthy, they are easy to prepare. They make a fine picnic food, too.

The vegetables should be cut into manageable baton lengths where possible, so carrot, celery, cucumber, bell peppers, and scallions are all good, but crudités can also be baby plum tomatoes, whole radishes, pieces of fennel, even various types of mushroom. Not everything has to be raw—blanched asparagus or lightly steamed broccoli florets and baby corn are also good—but the vegetables should always be served cold.

Dips can be as simple as good mayonnaise, cream cheese with garlic, or sour cream with chives, or as elaborate as cocktail sauce, Thousand Island dip, variations on hummus (perhaps incorporating chiles or cheese), or puréed avocado and lemon.

Spring Rolls

Spring rolls are common to many of the national cuisines of east Asia, cropping up in one form or another in the cooking of China, Thailand, Vietnam, Laos, Singapore, and Malaysia. They are always formed of a thin wrapper, which turns crisp and brittle during deep-frying in corn oil, encasing a mixture of ingredients, and are usually served with a dipping sauce.

Chinese spring rolls can be filled with shrimp, small pieces of meat such as roast duck, or a traditional mixture of vegetables, perhaps carrot and scallion, but always with bean sprouts, too. Texturally, they are a satisfying appetizer (as long as they have been properly drained of excess oil) and are a very popular order in Chinese restaurants the world over. The dip that accompanies them should classically be sweet, sour, and hot all at once.

Why "spring" rolls? It was once the custom to celebrate the sowing of that year's corn by concocting fillings with new spring vegetables. Historically, they weren't cylindrical as they are now, but more of a round cake. A sweet version from the Shanghai region contains red-bean paste.

Spring Rolls

1/2 lb minced pork

1 tsp cornstarch, plus 2 tsp

1 tsp dark soy sauce

2 tbsp vegetable oil

1 cup shredded bamboo shoots

1 cup shredded carrots

1/4 cup chicken broth, plus 1/4 cup

8 oz baby shrimp

1/2 lb fresh bean sprouts

1 cup finely shredded Chinese cabbage

20 spring roll skins

1 egg, beaten

1 quart vegetable oil, for deep-frying

Combine the pork with 1 teaspoon of the cornstarch and the soy sauce and cook in 2 tablespoons of oil over medium heat. When the pork turns brown, add the bamboo shoots and carrots. Increase the heat, add 1/4 cup of the chicken broth, and stir until the liquid is reduced. Blend the remaining cornstarch and chicken broth and add to the wok along with the baby shrimp, bean sprouts, and Chinese cabbage. Cook, stirring for 1 minute, then remove from the heat and drain in a colander.

Once the filling has cooled, place a spring roll skin on your work surface, with one corner pointing toward you. Place a generous spoonful of the filling just above the bottom corner of the skin and shape to form a sausage.

Roll the skin over the filling from the bottom corner. Brush the edges and top corner with beaten egg and tuck the edges in before completing the roll.

Heat the oil for deep-frying in a wok until almost smoking. Cook the spring rolls in batches until crisp and golden. They should take about 2 minutes each. Remove with tongs and drain on paper towels before serving while still hot. *Serves 4–6*

Four Dim Sum

Chung Fun

Chung fun are made from rice-noodle dough, cooked to a delicate, slippery tenderness, before being wrapped around various fillings and either steamed or shallow-fried. They are then served with soy sauce and sesame oil, often added directly to the serving plate rather than offered separately. The fillings can be anything from roast pork (*char siu*) to whole small shrimp to crisp-fried dough (*ja leung*), and the chung fun are often garnished with a sprinkling of sesame seeds.

These are quite tricky to eat with chopsticks. They must be cut into individual slices and are extremely difficult to hold, as they are very slippery. Texturally, they are very satisfying, as the rice dough is softer than most pasta, and yet the fillings can be crisp or chewy.

In Chinese tradition, the length of the noodle dough that makes up chung fun symbolizes long life, and so they are always enthusiastically received as part of dim sum.

Guotie

A class of dumplings, or *jiaozi*, served on dim sum menus, *guotie* is Mandarin for these tasty morsels. The name literally means "pan-stick," which is how they got their North American name of "pot stickers." The whole point in preparing pot stickers, of course, is that they *shouldn't* stick to the pot, but these are undoubtedly the most hazardous type of dim sum for the novice cook to prepare. Other types of dumplings are boiled or steamed, but these have to be shallow-fried in oil first, and taken out before they have a chance to live up to their name.

As with other dumplings, the skin is a simple flour-and-water dough, which is wrapped around a usually meaty filling, such as ground pork with cabbage, and then crimped together to form a half-moon shape. They are quickly fried in oil to brown the underside, before chicken broth or water is added to complete the cooking of the fillings.

Xiao Long Bao

A feature of Shanghai cooking, these dumplings look like little money bags, gathered in at the top. They are cooked in a bamboo steamer until the dough goes almost transparent. The name means "little basket bun," denoting a small dumpling or bun, made to be steamed in a basket. The filling is usually comprised of ground meat and vegetables, seasoned with garlic and ginger, but the surprise component is a liquid broth or soup.

When the xiao long bao are made up cold, the soup element is incorporated in gelatinous form as aspic, which is then wrapped in the seasoned meat, so that the whole item remains solid until it is cooked.

They are not, it has to be said, the easiest items of dim sum for Westerners to eat, as the often red-hot soup floods out of them as soon as they are bitten into. They must be put in the mouth, not nibbled in half like a chocolate.

Shiu Mai

Shiu mai are made with a plain flour-and-water dough, allbeit a more delicate version than is used for pot stickers and are steamed not fried.

Unlike other types of dumpling, these are left open at the top, so that the filling is clearly visible on presentation. This also makes them much easier to assemble than, say, xiao long bao. In Chinese culinary lore, they are known as "cook and sell" dumplings, because they are so popular that you can always sell as many as you cook.

The filling is interesting in that—as with many other Cantonese recipes—it generally combines ground pork with finely chopped shrimp. The result is a balance of meat and salty seafood flavors, enhanced by soy sauce and oyster sauce. Other ingredients might include Chinese mushrooms, ginger, and the green part of scallions. A spoonful of crab roe is sometimes included on the top of the filling as a final colorful garnish.

Escargots au Beurre d'Ail

Synonymous, for many people, with traditional French home cooking, and possibly the first foreign ingredient the adventurous traveler in France tries out, snails have remained an acquired taste to the Anglo-American palate. Innovative restaurant chefs have tried using them in novel contexts, but they are undeniably most at home when served in the classic Burgundy manner—piping-hot with plenty of garlic butter.

If you don't like the thought of gathering snails from the garden, you can buy them in cans. They must be cooked in a poaching liquid of white wine and shallots until soft, then put back in their shells, which are then filled to the brim with a seasoned butter into which plenty of minced garlic and parsley have been beaten. Ideally, there should be enough garlic butter to first line the shell, then seal it, so that the snail is entirely encased. The escargots are then briefly baked or broiled until the butter is melted and bubbling, but not browned.

For the uninitiated, there is nothing alarming about the taste of snails, which is in itself quite bland (hence all that garlic). The texture is like one of the firmer-fleshed types of shellfish.

Gougères

It is impossible to eat only one gougère. Sometimes known as "cheese puffs," they are a doughy, cheese-flavored pastry served as a pre-dinner nibble or first course, or sometimes as an accompaniment to a glass of wine at a tasting.

Gougères are made from a savory version of choux pastry, the type that makes chocolate éclairs. The flour, milk, and butter dough must be cooked until it forms a solid ball, after which the eggs are incorporated into it, along with plenty of grated Gruyère, or other strong-flavored, hard cow's-milk cheese. It is then shaped into balls and baked in the oven under a final sprinkling of grated cheese, perhaps Parmesan, for extra richness. Like many such baked items, they are especially delicious if eaten when still slightly warm, but it is best to let them dry a little first.

For a fancier variation, the mixture might incorporate pieces of ham or sliced mushrooms, but the cheese element is always essential. Gougères originate from the Burgundy region, and a glass of the local Pinot Noir red wine is the perfect accompaniment to them.

Empanadas

Empanadas are Spain and South America's version of the portable, stuff-in-pastry formula that shows up in many other cultures: India has the samosa, Asia has spring rolls, even the simple sandwich is a variation. Made with pastry that envelops a savory filling, empanadas (the word literally means "covered in bread") are enjoyed throughout the Spanish-speaking world, with each country claiming its own version, depending on the availability of ingredients.

In Chile, for example, empanadas are larger, square-shaped, and filled with diverse items, including hard-boiled eggs.

In Colombia, smaller, triangular pockets stuffed with seasoned meat or cheese, or a combination of both, are deep-fried until crisp and hot.

In Argentina, similar-sized empanadas are baked. They are eaten in cafés as snacks, at parties as passed hors d'oeuvres, or small meals on the go.

Escabeche   ▷

For escabeche, often the fish is first cooked, then marinated, contrary to the usual marinate-then-cook approach. The technique is Spanish in origin, very probably from the Moorish period, as a version appears in certain North African cuisines as well, but it has also migrated into French cooking (*escabèche*), and even turns up in English cookbooks (*caveach*) as far back as the 17th century. Along with salting, smoking, and drying, it is a way of preserving fish.

The fish is fried or broiled, then pickled in a vinegar-based preserving liquid. Although the fish can be reheated, it is traditionally served cold as a first course or appetizer morsel. In centuries gone by, the serving style would combine sweet and sour elements, including dried fruits, but in the modern kitchen, escabeche comes with not much more than a vinaigrette dressing and herbs.

Escabeche of Tuna

2 oz tuna steak, cut into 1-in cubes

Juice and zest of 2 limes

1 tbsp olive oil

½ avocado (cut in half lengthwise)

Place the tuna in a glass or ceramic dish. Pour over the lime juice and cover with the zest. Finally, drizzle the olive oil over the tuna. To serve, remove the flesh from the avocado and fill the shell with the marinated tuna. *Serves 1*

Crostini

Crostini is the Italian word for croutons, denoting little pieces of toasted bread with various toppings, served at the outset of a multi-course meal, or as nibbly party food. They are, in a sense, the original Italian canapé, and eminently suitable as an accompaniment to drinks.

There are virtually as many crostini toppings as there are people who make them. Different kinds of spreadable pâté, or *spuma*, are commonly used, especially one made of chicken livers boldly seasoned with sage. Fried sliced mushrooms, salted fish, fresh tuna, anchovy paste, Parma ham, salami, and chopped tomatoes are all examples of everyday crostini. More unusual offerings include cured pork fat with garlic (*agliata*); veal spleen with capers, brandy, and butter; minced capers with pine nuts and raisins; and wilted black kale (*cavolo nero*) with garlic. The possibilities are limitless.

Any bread may be used for the base, but traditional Tuscan types such as *pane casalingo*, an unsalted bread, are often preferred. They are sometimes baked in novelty bread pans, so that the crostini are in the shapes of stars or playing-card suits.

Crostini

Extra-virgin olive oil as needed

1 loaf Italian bread or French baguette, cut into ½-in slices

Prepare a broiler or preheat the oven to 400°F. Lightly brush the oil onto both sides of each slice of bread. Broil or bake until grill lines appear or until golden and slightly crisp, about 10 minutes. Turning is unnecessary but doesn't hurt.

Garlic Crostini: Cut a clove of garlic in half and rub the bread with the cut side after broiling or baking. For a more subtle version, mince a couple of cloves of garlic and mix with the olive oil before brushing it on the bread. *Serves 8*

Adapted from Mark Bittman's *The Best Recipes in the World*

Bocadillo con Tomate

A bocadillo is a Spanish sandwich, eaten as a street snack or, sometimes, as an offering on a tapas menu. The bread is a crisp-crusted white roll, similar to a short French baguette, which is split in order to hold the filling. They are popular throughout Spain, often chosen as the late-afternoon snack that fills the gap between lunch and the traditionally very late evening meal.

The version made with tomato is the simplest recipe. The cut surfaces of the bread are lightly toasted, brushed with olive oil, and then covered with a purée of strained tomato, garlic, and olive oil. This can form the basis for other fillings, such as slices of Serrano or Iberico ham, slivers of manchego (sheep's-milk cheese), smoked salmon, anchovies, chorizo, green and black olive tapenade, even rolled potato tortilla.

Bruschetta

Italian bruschetta (pronounced "sk" in the middle, not "sh") came to general notice with the sudden Western fashion for Mediterranean cuisine that took root in the early 1990s. It is a long, flat slice of toasted bread rubbed with garlic, doused with extra-virgin olive oil, and served with a wide variety of toppings. These can be as simple as strips of seared red bell pepper slicked with olive oil, or a finely chopped, blanched plum tomato scattered with torn basil.

Known as *fettunta* in its heartland, the Tuscany region of north-central Italy, it has to be made in the proper Italian fashion for the true experience. The thickly sliced Italian country bread should be grilled over hot coals so the surfaces are slightly charred in places. In Italian homes now, the method is simulated with a special griddle pan called a *brustolina*, which has a perforated base. Set over gas burners, it toasts the bread on both sides. A charcoal-fired grill makes a good substitute.

The principal focus of bruschetta is neither the bread nor the toppings. This dish celebrates the first-pressed oil of the new olive harvest.

Foie Gras

Literally "fat liver," foie gras is the liver of either a goose or a duck that has been fattened to several times its natural size by overfeeding the bird. It is sold in many different forms: whole, raw preserved; partially cooked; or prepared as pâté or bloc and packaged in vacuum packs or cans, sometimes embedded with slivers of black truffle. Foie gras *d'oie* (goose) is more expensive, paler, and has a creamier flavor, but foie gras *de canard* (duck) is preferred by many chefs for its stronger, richer character.

For centuries, it has been regarded as a defining delicacy of classical French gastronomy, especially when eaten with plain toasted brioche as an hors d'oeuvre. Much foie gras is now imported into France, but two main centers of production remain: around Strasbourg in the northeastern region of Alsace and in the Gascon country of the southwest.

The technique for preparing foie gras was developed in classical antiquity, when the Romans fattened their poultry with figs. Today, corn is the preferred foodstuff, and although production has been mechanized in many places, the principle is essentially the same. It relies on exploiting a natural greed in the birds—they will happily consume as much food as is provided to them. Overfeeding massively distends the liver, which accumulates fatty tissue up to a standard weight of around two pounds in geese and about half that in ducks.

Much debate arises over whether force-feeding, or cramming (*gavage* in French), of the birds is ethically acceptable. On small farms, some rare artisanal production is still carried on by hand, with the feed gently massaged down the throats of the birds manually. The substantial demand for foie gras, in France and elsewhere, however, has made intensive production widespread, with feed pumped into the birds through a funnel as a daily regimen through the winter months. In some countries, campaigns urge importation bans of foie gras on animal welfare grounds.

Yet the divine, and decadent, allure of foie gras lives on. It is now often served as a whole lobe that is seared briefly and served with a fruit accompaniment, such as orange or figs, or with a sharply seasoned reduction sauce, perhaps based on balsamic vinegar. Its texture in this style is almost ethereally light, and yet it retains its almost overpowering richness.

Like other "once unaffordable" delicacies, foie gras is also gradually inveigling its way onto many restaurant menus as a reliable way of enriching a dish, thus winning it new converts.

Ploye à Champlain

Ploye à Champlain

For the ploye batter:

$^2/_3$ cup all-purpose flour

$^1/_2$ cup buckwheat flour

1 tsp baking powder

A pinch of salt

A pinch of sugar

2 eggs

$^3/_4$ cup milk, plus 2 tbsp

For the maple sauce:

$^1/_2$ cup minced onion

1 knob of butter

1 cup duck broth

1 cup maple syrup

$^1/_4$ cup vinaigrette

Salt

Freshly ground black pepper

For the egg in syrup:

$^3/_4$ cup maple syrup

1 egg

For the foie gras:

4 very thin slices bacon

1 potato, boiled and peeled, sliced into $^1/_4$-in pieces

4 slices 2-year-old Cheddar from the Ile-aux-Grues

4 ($3^1/_2$ oz; 1-in thick) slices foie gras

Freshly ground black pepper

To make the batter, place all of the dry ingredients in a bowl. Pour the liquid ingredients into the center of the bowl. Mix with a wooden spoon. Leave for 45 minutes.

To make the maple sauce, brown the onion in the butter in a skillet until slightly golden. Stir in the broth. Bring to a boil and reduce by half. Add the maple syrup and reduce until thick enough to coat the back of a spoon. Whisk in the vinaigrette and seasoning. Do not let the sauce boil—the vinaigrette may separate. Keep warm. To make the egg in syrup, reduce the maple syrup by one half in a saucepan. Crack the egg into the boiling syrup. Boil for 15 seconds, then lightly beat with a fork before it sets. Boil for another 15 seconds. Keep warm.

Preheat the oven to 450°F. Fry the bacon until crisp. Set aside. In another pan, make 4 small *ployes*, and transfer to serving plates. (*Ployes* are cooked on one side only.) Top each *ploye* with bacon, potatoes, and cheese. In a very hot pan, sear the slices of foie gras on both sides until golden brown. Place a slice of foie gras on each *ploye*. Place them in the oven for approximately 5 minutes to finish cooking the foie gras. Top the *ployes* with the sauce and garnish with the egg in syrup. Add black pepper and serve. *Serves 4*

Adapted from the restaurant menu at Au Pied de Cochon in Montreal

Pâté au Foie de Canard

Liver pâtés are very popular throughout the world, their most refined manifestation being pâté de foie gras, but a pâté made from ordinary (as opposed to fattened) duck livers is a rich and luxurious enough proposition in its own right.

In France, even commercial brands of duck liver pâté, sold in vacuum packaging or in cans, are generally of reliable quality, but nothing compares to the decadent richness of a house pâté eaten in a good restaurant.

The natural richness of the duck livers is augmented in many recipes with the addition of cream and cognac, and there may be some whole ingredient, such as green peppercorns, incorporated into the mixture to add textural variation. A top layer of clarified butter, or alcoholic jelly set with fruit pieces, makes a whole terrine of pâté look altogether majestic. Duck liver pâté is best eaten with thin toast or lightly broiled brioche. In France, it is considered vulgar to butter the toast, as the pâté is rich enough on its own.

Gravlax

Gravlax is a Scandinavian preparation of salmon, in which fillets are cured in salt, white pepper, sugar, and dill, and then sliced thinly and served with a sweet-sharp dressing of mustard, sugar, and dill. It is often mistakenly thought that the salmon in gravlax is smoked, because it looks the same color as lox, but it is only salt-cured.

Earliest records of gravlax date back to 14th-century Sweden, when its preparation

was quite different. The fish was buried in the ground for months to preserve it for the winter season, when fishing waters were frozen over. It gradually fermented, yielding a sour taste to the flesh. In modern times, the technique was developed of pressing two sides of filleted fish under a weighted board, with the curing mix encased in the middle. Home-produced gravlax is still made in this way, and—much like grilling in the English-

speaking world—has become a rare instance of culinary men's work.

Gravlax is traditionally eaten with a glass of cold aquavit on the side.

Gravlax

2 (2 lb) thick salmon fillets, skin on, scaled and pin bones removed

For the curing mix:

½ cup coarse rock salt

⅓ cup superfine sugar

1 tbsp white peppercorns, crushed

6 tbsp freshly chopped dill, plus 2 tbsp

For the dressing:

2 tbsp Dijon mustard

1 tbsp white wine vinegar

1 tbsp superfine sugar

1 egg yolk

½ cup vegetable oil

¼ cup freshly chopped dill

Salt

Freshly ground black pepper

Prepare the curing mix first. Combine the salt, sugar, and white pepper in a bowl. Add the 6 tablespoons of dill. Stir until well mixed.

You will need a large, shallow dish, big enough to hold the salmon. Line it with plastic food wrap. Spread a quarter of the curing mix over the base of the dish. Place one of the salmon fillets in the dish, skin-side down. Spread half of the remaining curing mix on top of the salmon fillet. Top with the second fillet skin-side up. Distribute the remaining curing mix on top of the second fillet. Wrap the dish in plastic food wrap and place some cans or weights on top. This weighs the fish down and removes excess liquid and moisture.

Place in the refrigerator. To allow the flavors to develop evenly, turn the salmon over every 6 hours. Preferably leave the salmon to "cure" in this way for 3 to 4 days.

On the day when you are going to serve the gravlax, you need to allow 6 hours for the final preparation stage. Rinse the curing mix off the fish and dry with paper towels. Place one salmon fillet, skin-side down, on a sheet of plastic food wrap. Sprinkle the 2 tbsp dill over the fillet and then place the second fillet, skin-side up, on top. Wrap the salmon tightly in the plastic food wrap and chill for 6 hours. Make the dressing in a large bowl. Whisk the mustard, vinegar, sugar, and egg yolk together. Slowly add the oil in a steady trickle, making sure it is well emulsified. Add the dill and stir well to combine. Add salt and pepper to taste.

To serve, cut the gravlax into thin slices and drizzle with the dressing. Serve rye bread on the side. *Serves 6*

Baba Ghanoush

A specialty of the Levantine cooking of the Middle East, baba ghanoush turns up in some form all around the eastern Mediterranean, Russia, North Africa, and as far afield as south Asia. The highly seasoned dip is traditionally served with an unleavened flatbread, such as pita. The common ingredient in all its manifestations is eggplant, which is sliced open and broiled, the brown flesh then being scooped out and mashed into a purée with olive oil. Chopped onion is generally added, as is diced tomato, and this mixture is seasoned strongly with garlic, ground cumin, lemon juice, and parsley.

Ideally, the finished dish should have a noticeable smoky flavor, derived traditionally from fire-roasting the eggplant. Scorching under the broiler and leaving on a little of the blackened skin when preparing the flesh can replicate the taste.

In the Egyptian version, tahini (sesame seed paste) is an important component, making the dish a distant cousin of Greek hummus. Russia's version is known, perhaps a little wishfully, as "eggplant caviar."

Baba Ghanoush

1 eggplant

¼ cup lemon juice

¼ cup tahini

2 tbsp sesame seeds

2 cloves garlic, minced

Salt

Freshly ground black pepper to taste

1½ tbsp olive oil

Preheat the oven to 400°F.

Lightly grease a baking sheet.

Prick the eggplant skin all over with a fork and place on the baking sheet. Roast for 30 to 40 minutes, turning occasionally, or until soft. Remove from the oven, and place in a plastic food bag for a few minutes. Remove and peel the skin off.

Place the eggplant, lemon juice, tahini, sesame seeds, and garlic in an electric blender, and purée. Season with salt and pepper to taste. Transfer the eggplant mixture to a mixing bowl, and slowly mix in the olive oil. Refrigerate for 3 hours before serving.

Makes 1½ cups

Tapenade

Most olives grown in the Mediterranean go into making oil, but some go into this delicious, highly seasoned black olive paste. Tapenade originates from the Provence region of southeast France, but a curiosity of its nomenclature is that it is derived from the Provençal word for caper, *tapeno*. It nearly always contains capers, but they are not the focal ingredient of tapenade.

As well as black olives and capers, this glossy, jet-black condiment usually includes anchovies and garlic, all pounded together with olive oil and lemon juice. Commercial brands of tapenade almost never replicate the oily, salty piquancy of the homemade version, ground with a mortar and pestle, using the ripest of the new season's olives.

It is an appetizing cracker spread, crudité dip, or condiment for meatier types of fish, such as tuna. Tapenade is also sometimes made with green olives.

Green Olive Tapenade

1 cup pitted Picholine olives

1 tbsp capers, rinsed

1 anchovy fillet

1 tsp Dijon mustard

About 3 tbsp extra-virgin olive oil

Cut the olives into very small, neat dice. Cut the capers and anchovy the same size. Combine the olives, capers, and anchovy in a small mixing bowl. Add the mustard and mix well. Gradually add enough oil just to bind the mixture. Serve or refrigerate for up to 3 days. *Makes ³⁄₄ cup*
Adapted from Tom Colicchio's *The Craft of Cooking*

Jamaican Patty

The patty, a baked pastry turnover with crimped edges, stuffed with a savory filling, isn't only native to Jamaica, despite its name. They are cooked on many other Caribbean islands, and have become popular throughout North America. Similar in appearance to an English pasty or South American empanada, the pastry tends to be heavier and the filling heartier.

Traditionally made with spiced ground beef seasoned with curry powder and turmeric and containing chopped fresh chiles, a Jamaican patty should be a fiery and satisfying mouthful. Not surprisingly, as it is such a simple formula, variations have been developed in recent years, including a chicken patty, seafood versions filled with shrimp or lobster, and vegetarian alternatives made with potato and cheese, or various mixtures of vegetables.

In Jamaica and other Caribbean islands, patties are the number one street food of choice, still outselling burgers and pizza, despite American influence.

Serrano Ham

Serrano occupies a position among the great cured meats of Europe, alongside Parma and Bayonne. The meat, which comes from the hind leg of various species of the white pig, is salted to draw out moisture and traditionally hung up to dry in pure mountain air. Its name is derived from the sierra, or mountain regions, of southwest Spain, where patient preparation of the meat takes place from the cold winter months through to the start of milder weather the following spring. Today, commercial drying facilities (*secaderos*) reproduce the effects of the mountain breezes, but the production is still closely regulated by the *Consorcio del Jamón Serrano Español*.

The ham is sold and eaten in its cured raw state, shaved into wafer-thin slices like Italian prosciutto. It has a superb flavor and a delicate, tender texture, and is often eaten as a tapas nibble.

A tradition in parts of Spain is to eat it on small pieces of bread that have been spread with strained tomatoes and olive oil. Depending on the size of the original leg, Serrano ham may be aged for up to 18 months before sale.

Parma Ham

Italy's most famous raw ham (or *prosciutto crudo*) comes from the countryside around the city of Parma, the same region that produces Parmesan cheese. Like Spain's Serrano, *prosciutto di Parma* is a salt-cured, dried ham matured over many months. It is always served uncooked in paper-thin slices, as an appetizer with drinks, or on its own as a first course.

After its initial salting, the pork leg is periodically pressed to expel all its moisture. This takes up to two months, whereupon it is hung up to continue its drying in the air.

As with its Spanish cousin, the air-drying begins during the cold season, when the winter winds are at their sharpest.

With the arrival of milder weather, the ham is rehung in a well-ventilated storage room to continue its maturation for up to 18 months.

The flavor of Parma ham is a little creamier than Serrano because the pigs are fed on whey from the production of Parmesan. It is a natural choice partnered with sweet, soft fruits, the two classic Italian preferences being musky, aromatic melon and pulpy, ripe figs.

FRANCE

Artichoke Vinaigrette

Possibly the most labor-intensive of all
vegetables to eat, the globe artichoke
(*Cynara scolymus*) is much prized around the
countries of the Mediterranean basin, where
it originated. A relative of the thistle family, it
has a large, unwieldy-looking head composed
of petal-like leaves, or bracts, mounted on
a thick stalk.

To serve it as an appetizer, it must be
boiled for 20 to 30 minutes, depending on
size. The diner picks off the leaves one by
one and dips them in the vinaigrette, which
is usually nothing more than seasoned
olive oil and wine vinegar (or lemon juice).
The tender tip of each leaf is nibbled off.
When all the leaves are gone, an inedible
bristly layer known as the "choke" is cut
away to expose the tender heart, the bottom
of the plant, which is the reward for all the
preceding effort.

The vinaigrette may be made more
assertive in flavor with the addition of a little
mustard. Some prefer to serve melted butter
instead. In the 19th century, the grandest sets
of tableware might include artichoke dishes,
which incorporated a central cup for the
vegetable, another for the dip, and a series
of recesses for the discarded leaves.

RUSSIA

Blinis with Sour Cream and Caviar

In the Russian Orthodox religious tradition,
meat is forbidden during the week before
Lent, but butter, milk, and eggs may still be
eaten, often in golden pancakes—symbols
of the sun—that, in the hands of an expert
cook, are so tender they melt in the mouth.
These pancakes, called blinis, are eaten
twice a day during Shrovetide, the Christian
festival that is celebrated at the same time
as the pagan festival Maslenitsa in one wild,
exuberant week to mark the end of winter.
Everyone indulges in parties and feasting
before embarking on the self-denial of Lent.

When blinis topped with caviar and
sour cream are eaten at any time of year,
the combination of salty bursts, smooth,
tangy cream, and rich crumbs can be akin
to a religious experience. These make
perfect appetizers when served as bite-sized
morsels accompanied by ice-cold vodka
in shot glasses.

Moong Dal Pancakes

A *dal* is a liquid-textured, granular soup made of pulses and legumes—typically various kinds of lentils and beans. *Moong dal* is made from the seed of the mung bean plant (*Vigna radiata*), which is native to India, but which has traveled into many other Asian cuisines, including Chinese. Unlike most other forms of legume, they require relatively little preparation to make them digestible.

Chiles, turmeric, and cumin are essential in the preparation of *moong dal*. In India, the spice mix often also includes *asafoetida*, a bitter, pungent spice made from the dried root of a member of the fennel family.

Moong Dal Pancakes

1 cup moong dal

3/4-in cube of gingerroot, roughly chopped (or more, to your taste)

3 cloves garlic

1 to 2 hot green chiles

1 small onion

Salt

1/4 tsp turmeric

1/4 tsp cumin

2 tbsp finely chopped cilantro

Vegetable oil for frying

Drain the dal. The easiest way to make the batter for these pancakes is in a food processor. Start the food processor and feed in the ginger, garlic, chile, and onion. Process until they are finely chopped. Add the dal and process until the ingredients are a paste-like consistency. Add just under 1/2 cup of water, a pinch of salt, the turmeric, and the cumin. Process again until the ingredients are well mixed and have the consistency of a thick batter. Transfer the batter to a bowl and stir in the cilantro.

This quantity of batter makes between 9 to 15 pancakes, depending on size. Heat a pan over medium heat (you can add a little oil if you're concerned about the pancakes sticking). Pour enough batter in the pan for 1 pancake, and spread it out with the back of a spoon. Cook until golden brown, then turn the pancake over and continue to cook until brown spots start to develop.

Remove to a warmed plate and continue cooking the remaining pancakes. Stir the batter well before each pouring, as the mixture will settle. Layer the cooked pancakes between parchment paper so they do not stick together. *Serves 6 to 8*

Nam Prik

One of Southeast Asia's classic condiments, nam prik is a ferociously spicy dipping sauce hailing from Thailand. In Thai homes, it would be as unthinkable not to have a dish of it on the table at mealtimes as the absence of ketchup would be in many Western households. It is used for dipping ingredients into, and also as a seasoning for whatever food is in your bowl.

The principal ingredient is roughly chopped red chile peppers of uncompromising heat, the smolder of which is accentuated by the seeds which are not discarded. To these are added garlic, lime juice, sugar, and *nam pla* (the traditional fermented salty fish sauce of Thai cooking).

A variant on the basic formula is nam prik pao (*pao* meaning "roasted"), in which the garlic and perhaps also some unpeeled shallots or small onions are heated briefly in a fatless, red-hot pan. Other additions to this semi-cooked version of nam prik might be shrimp paste, roasted peanuts, and pea eggplants, which are the tiniest relatives of the eggplant family, no bigger than a grape.

Okonomiyaki

Okonomiyaki are Japanese mix-and-match fast food, their name being best rendered as "grilled whatever." They consist of a fried pancake made from a flour, egg, and water batter, to which grated yam and cabbage are usually added, which forms the basis for a topping that can be pretty much anything that takes your fancy. Okonomiyaki stalls in the regions to which they are traditional—the provinces around Osaka and Hiroshima—display an array of various ingredients, the customer indicating whatever mixture he or she would like, much like a Western sandwich bar.

Typical toppings might be fried pork, seafood such as squid or octopus, pickled cabbage, thick noodles, even fried egg. In the Hiroshima tradition, the ingredients are built up in layers, whereas in Osaka, they tend to be spread over the surface in pizza fashion. Okonomiyaki sauce, a sweet-savory condiment of glutinous consistency, is the essential seasoning element. Some establishments offer tables fitted with hot-plates in the Korean style, where customers cook their own ingredients before loading them onto the pancakes themselves.

Hush Puppies

A delicacy of the southern states of the US, a hush puppy is a round or sausage-shaped fritter made of cornmeal and chopped onion, fashioned into a batter with milk and water, and deep-fried in oil that has been used for frying fish. They are cooked in batches, the temperature of the oil being judged correct when the fritter floats. Although they were developed sometime in the early 20th century as an accompaniment to fried fish, they are now commonly served as an appetizer or snack food throughout the United States. Their provenance may be much older, in that fritters of cornmeal are known to have been cooked in North America by European settlers in pre-Independence times.

The name reputedly derives from an incident at a Florida fish-fry, when the annoying barking of hungry dogs was silenced by throwing them one or two of these. Passing over the evident fact that almost any bit of food thrown to ravenous dogs will hush them momentarily, we can accept the legend as a picturesque piece of American food lore.

Olives

Arguably the single most important fruit tree in cultivation anywhere in the world, the olive (*Olea europae*) has a long and venerable history. As the source of one of the most widely used oils throughout the Middle East and the Mediterranean, it has been highly valued since pre-Egyptian antiquity. According to the Bible's *Old Testament*, when the dove that Noah releases from the ark comes back with evidence that the boat is nearing land, it is an olive twig that reassures the travelers that a return to civilization is at hand.

While the greater part of world olive production goes into oil, the fruits themselves are also eaten as a component of many dishes, as the basis for condiments like tapenade, or on their own as a table snack.

The fruits come in three colors: green, purple, and black. These are not distinct varieties, but have simply been picked at different stages of ripeness, although individual varieties have become associated with traditional presentations. Green olives are harvested in the fall in Europe, while those left on the tree into the winter months of December and January gradually turn black with continued ripening. Purple olives are an intermediate stage between these.

The flavors are quite different; green olives are often slightly bitter and astringent (although they are vigorously soaked in water to remove some of the bitterness), while the black have a rounder, fruitier, more pronounced taste. Green olives are often "cracked" prior to treatment, so that the liquid in which they are packed has a chance to penetrate and modify their flavor and soften their comparatively tough texture. Black olives often need nothing more than a slick of olive oil to show at their best.

Different countries have developed their own specialized varieties, known usually by regional names, which can be distinguished by aficionados much as grape varieties can be by wine connoisseurs. France has Picholine, Lucques, Niçoise, Cailletier, and Nyons, the latter sold black and dry-cured in salt. Spain's Manzanilla shares its name with a type of bone-dry sherry, with which it has a strong gustatory affinity, while Greece's Kalamata are small, purple-black, and intensely flavored. The Gaeta of Italy is black but surprisingly mild in taste, and is often treated with other flavorings such as garlic and herbs.

Sold as cocktail nibbles, olives are often marinated in their own oil, with the addition of herbs (such as rosemary, thyme, or fennel seed) or with slivers of hot chile pepper. Greek olives are often sold with cubes of feta cheese. Some are partially dried or salt-cured before packing. At their least appealing, they are packaged in cans or jars of brine, which should be discarded, and the olives themselves thoroughly rinsed before use. Stuffed olives are green specimens that have had a typically bright red plug of pimento inserted into them. Frowned upon by olive experts, they come into their own at cocktail hour, either as an accompanying nibble or as a garnish to the drinks themselves. A green cocktail olive is the indispensable addition for many to a classic dry martini. Not that long ago, cultures to which the olive tree wasn't native found olives an insuperable gastronomic challenge: they fell into that category of foods that virtually nobody liked. The wide dissemination of Mediterranean food culture toward the end of the 20th century was instrumental in transforming that.

Roti Prata

Vengaya Baji ▷

This is Singapore's entry in the world pancake stakes. It is a simple *crêpe* of butter, egg, flour, and water that can be customized—like Japan's *okonomiyaki*—with almost anything that the customer has a hankering for. There are sweet and savory versions, and some fast food outlets in Singapore have developed a special, translucently thin *prata* that is formed into a cone and sugared. The savory types are a common breakfast dish in their country of origin.

Traditionally, the roti prata is an accompaniment to a main dish, so they may well be sold at street stalls with a serving of chicken curry. However, the current fashion has been to incorporate a range of increasingly offbeat flavorings, such as spiced fried onions, melted cheese, various fruits (banana is a favorite), and even chocolate.

There are versions of roti throughout Southeast Asia and as far afield as the Caribbean. They all ultimately trace their origins back to the *roti* of India, a generic term for any of the hugely diverse range of breads.

One of the standbys of south Asian restaurant menus, the onion bhaji is seemingly everybody's favorite Indian appetizer. Formed from shredded onion, garlic, egg, and gram (garbanzo) flour, the bhaji has a crisp surface from being deep-fried in oil. In their Western manifestations, they are often spherical, sometimes bulked with mashed potato and even incorporating peas, but in vegetarian southern India, where they hail from, they are quite likely to be a simple flattened disk.

Indian bhaji tend to be forthrightly spiced, with chili powder, cumin, ginger, and cilantro, but a gentler version can be made using paprika instead of the chili. The traditional accompaniment to bhaji is *raita*, a thin yogurt into which chopped mint leaves have been stirred. This mitigates the spicy heat of the bhaji, so if you are making a milder version, spiced mango chutney may be a more complementary choice.

Bhaji used to be served as a garnish to a larger dish, but have become popular as a snack in their own right, similar to the Western battered and deep-fried onion ring.

Pissaladière

Pierogis

A Provençal specialty from the region around the port city of Nice, pissaladière is a baked snack consisting of anchovies, onions, and black olives on a base of either bread dough (like a pizza) or shortcrust pastry (like a quiche).

The base is coated with an anchovy paste, called *pissalat*, before being cooked. This is then topped generously with shredded onions that have been softened in olive oil, and garnished with anchovy fillets and pitted black olives. An important feature of good pissaladière is that the onion layer should be very deep, half as thick again as a bread base and as thick as a pastry shell. To a Provençal, anything less just isn't the real thing.

Sometimes spelled *pirozhki*, depending on where they are from, these are small Russian or Polish pastries stuffed with any one of a variety of savory or sweet fillings (the name comes from the Russian word for a pie, *pirog*). They are generally served as a hot first course or as part of a *zakuski* spread of savory nibbles, or bought as a street snack, but they originated as an accompaniment to soups.

Russian pierogis are traditionally filled with a salty seafood mixture, incorporating white fish and hard-boiled egg, but versions filled with cottage cheese and mushrooms, and various kinds of meat, are also popular. They are most often fashioned from unleavened pastry, which is crimped shut around the fillings, before being deep-fried in oil until they float to the surface. Versions made with lighter, flake pastry are baked.

Pierogis likely originated as an economical way of using up leftovers, and only later became a prized dish in their own right. Sweet fruit fillings were a subsequent development.

Rollmops

Herring, the staple fish of much of northern Europe, lends itself to various preparations, chief among them being rollmops. The peculiar name comes from the German, but the meaning is scarcely less peculiar in that native tongue: "rolled pug dog." The "rolled" part, at least, is straightforward enough, as the deboned fish are wrapped around a piece of pickled cucumber before curing in vinegar, to which chopped onion and capers may be added.

Cured herring is served as an appetizer throughout Germany, Scandinavia, and the Baltic states, but the rollmop tradition is specific to Germany and Denmark. The firm flesh of the herring lends itself well to sweet-and-sour treatments, tomato sauces, and mustard dressings, and its inherent flavor is somehow never overpowered.

As a finger food, rollmops are usually served skewered with a toothpick. When served as an appetizer, they may be accompanied by a sour cream dressing or potato salad.

Oysters

One of the most revered of seafoods, cultivated across a range of climates, oysters have come up in the world. In 19th-century England, they were a sure sign of a life reduced to indigence. To endure old age in Dickensian London on a diet of oysters was to have fallen on hard times indeed. Today, they command high prices, their value determined in part by the investment needed to establish and farm oyster beds, but also by their elevated gastronomic reputation.

The oyster is a saltwater bivalve mollusk that attaches itself to a firm surface, usually a rock, and filters gallons of sea water daily to extract its nutrients. It has many natural predators, making it commercially untenable to gather wild oysters. Instead, they are farmed on tiles or ropes, protected from harm's way until maturity.

There are several species. The European oyster (*Ostrea edulis*) is probably the most widely known in northwest Europe, on the Atlantic and North Sea coasts. In Brittany, Belon, known in England and Ireland as Native, is a sought-after variety.

In the 19th and early 20th centuries, oysters were commonly eaten cooked, as the central component of grand restaurant dishes such as oysters Rockefeller, or as an ingredient in stews and pies. In the 21st century, they are served on the half-shell, in sixes or dozens, with nothing more than a squeeze of lemon juice or a dash of Tabasco. In Ireland, they are classically eaten with Guinness, or other stout ale.

Mignonette Sauce

½ cup white wine vinegar

1 tbsp coarsely ground white peppercorns

2 tbsp finely chopped shallots

Salt to taste

Pour the vinegar into a medium bowl, add the remaining ingredients, and stir to combine.

Chill well before serving with fresh oysters on the half shell. *Makes ½ cup*

Tortilla de Patatas

Barely anything on the world menu is as improbably delicious as the Spanish potato tortilla. The improbability lies in its consisting only of ingredients of virtually Anglo-American blandness, yet it is an abidingly popular tapas and snack dish.

Not to be confused with the Mexican tortilla, Spain's omelette-style tortilla has slow-cooked sliced potato and onion added to beaten eggs, which are then cooked until firm. The finished product is left to go cold, then it is cut and served in wedges. Tortilla de patatas is often served in Spain as finger food, cut into small square pieces and eaten with a toothpick. A similar dish is known as frittata in Italy, and Denmark has its own version that is served hot directly from the pan.

Tortilla de Patatas

4 medium potatoes (russets are good for frying), peeled, washed, and dried

½ medium onion, finely chopped

1 tsp salt

Extra-virgin olive oil

4 eggs

Cut the potatoes in half lengthwise. Cut into very thin slices, about ⅟₁₆-inch thick. Place the potato slices in a bowl with the onion and salt. Stir to combine.

In a large frying pan, fry the potato slices and onion in a small amount of extra-virgin olive oil. Don't use too much oil and don't allow it to get too hot; you want the potato slices to be soft, not crispy. Cook for about 15 to 20 minutes, depending on the variety of potato that you are using.

Put the eggs in a large bowl and break them lightly with a fork. Do not overbeat.

Once the potatoes are cooked, tip them onto a plate, holding back as much of the oil as possible. Put into the bowl with the eggs and leave to rest for about 5 minutes.

Heat a very small amount of extra-virgin olive oil in a small frying pan. Pour the potato and egg mixture into the pan and spread it out to an even thickness. Cook for 10 to 15 minutes until it is golden underneath and almost set. Slide it out onto a plate. Hold the frying pan over the top and flip the tortilla back into the frying pan. Cook for a further 5 minutes or until browned.

When cooked, remove the tortilla from the pan. Leave to cool, then cut into wedges.

Serves 4

Patatas Bravas

Literally "ferocious potatoes," patatas bravas are a mainstay of the tapas menu, taking their place alongside albóndigas, manchego cheese, tortilla, anchovies, and so on. They are thickish slices or cubes of potato that are fried in olive oil until crisp on the surface but soft in the middle, and then coated with a chile-hot tomato sauce, for the promised ferocity.

The sauce is usually made from some combination of tomatoes, onion, garlic, chile peppers, paprika, and sugar, perhaps with a splash of white wine. Each restaurant or tapas bar in Spain prides itself on having its own proprietary recipe. A final sprinkling of parsley is considered de rigueur. The heat of the sauce is such that patatas bravas absolutely have to be accompanied by a cold drink—either a Spanish beer or a glass of white wine (or just iced water).

When all is said and done, this dish is not a million miles removed in concept from a plate of fries with ketchup, but in terms of taste, the distance is interplanetary.

Drunken Shrimp

"Drunken" dishes in eastern Chinese cooking denote cooking of the main ingredient in alcohol, namely *shao-xing* or rice wine. In the standard domestic recipe, large shrimp are marinated in wine, then steamed. A broth combining sharp, sour, and sweet seasonings, including ginger and chile, is prepared, and laced with more rice wine. Thickened with a little cornstarch and water, the resulting "soup" is poured over the cooked shrimp.

Drunken Shrimp

1 lb shrimp, preferably live

$1^1/_4$ cups Mei Kuei Lu Chiew, dry Gewürztraminer, or gin

If you are using live shrimp, leave the shells on and clean them thoroughly under cold running water. Place the shrimp in a bowl with 1 cup of the alcohol, cover, and refrigerate for 20 minutes.

Heat a wok or deep skillet over high heat, then add the remaining ¼ cup alcohol. When the alcohol is almost boiling, carefully ignite it, then immediately add the shrimp with its marinade. (If you are not comfortable igniting the alcohol, bring it to a rolling boil.) Cook the shrimp, stirring, until they turn pink, about 5 minutes. Remove from the heat and serve. *Serves 4*

Adapted from Mark Bittman's *The Best Recipes in the World*

Potted Shrimp

This is an excellent way of keeping a large quantity of shrimp if you happen to have been lucky with the day's catch. They are sautéed in generous quantities of gently spiced butter (mace, nutmeg, and cayenne pepper are typical seasonings), before being poured into small ramekins or "pots," and topped with a thin layer of clarified butter. In this state, they will keep for a surprisingly long time, rather as cooked meat can be preserved in fat by the *confit* method.

To eat, spread the potted shrimps on thin slices of buttered whole-wheat toast as a first course. Not only do they retain their flavor in this preservation method, but the seasonings enhance it. This is the English recipe, much prized when made with the small brown shrimp caught off the Lancashire coast in the northwest of the British Isles.

In the North American tradition, the cooked shrimp are usually blended in a food processor and more boldly flavored with cream cheese and horseradish. The resulting paste is pressed into small ramekins or a terrine pan, then served on toast as in the English style.

Saganaki

A *sagani* is a type of Greek frying pan with two handles and, in its diminutive form, gives its name to this dish of fried cheese. Any of the salty, sharply flavored Greek cheeses may be used for it, but the most popular is *kefalograviera*, a yellow-pasted cow's-milk cheese with holes in it. A much-admired sheep's-milk version of *graviera* is made in Crete. Traditional salt-brined feta is sometimes preferred, and in Cyprus, the first choice is *halloumi*.

The cheese is dipped in egg and flour, to give it a brittle coating as it cooks, then fried in olive oil. It is eaten as a first course with crusty country bread. A tradition has developed in US restaurants of flaming the cheese as it cooks. A potent spirit, very often Metaxa, a Greek brandy, is poured over it and set alight. After a few moments, the flames are extinguished by squeezing a lemon over them. This has become a performance dish in many restaurants, and is thought to have originated in Chicago.

Spanakopita

Spinach (*spanaki* in Greek) features prominently in Greek cooking. Here, it plays the starring role as a pastry filling. Spanakopita is a delicate pie containing masses of the leafy green vegetable with salty feta cheese, chopped onion, and parsley. It is much less substantial than many of the other baked, pastry-clad items of world cuisine, in that the pastry used is Greece's paper-thin phyllo.

Phyllo is made from flour and water only, and has to be hand-stretched until it is so thin that you can read the proverbial newspaper through it. Several layers are used in the creation of this dish, with butter or olive oil spread between them to moisten the final result. When baked, it forms a crackly, papery wrapping. Phyllo is almost certainly Turkish in origin.

Spanakopita can be made as a large pie, then sliced into portions to form a main course, or baked as smaller individual pies or rolls as an appetizer, often dressed with tzatziki.

Spanakopita

3 cups chopped onion

1/4 cup extra-virgin olive oil

2 lbs fresh spinach, washed and stems removed

1 large bunch fresh parsley, chopped

1 1/2 tsp fine salt

1 cup feta cheese, crumbled

1/4 tsp freshly ground black pepper

14 phyllo sheets

3/4 cup butter, melted

Preheat the oven to 375°F. Sauté the onion in olive oil until soft. Add the spinach, parsley, and salt, and sauté for a few minutes more. Remove from the heat and stir in the feta cheese and black pepper. Layer half of the phyllo sheets in a buttered 10-× 17-× 2-inch baking pan, brushing each with melted butter. Spoon in the spinach mixture and top with the remaining phyllo sheets, again brushing each with melted butter. Cut into squares, or diamonds if preferred, and bake for 30 minutes or until golden brown. *Serves 6–8*

◁ # Salsa

A salsa is any sort of dressing or dip that is made from roughly chopped or mashed fresh vegetables, classically tomatoes. Although the name simply means "sauce," it has passed into general usage now to denote a particular kind of sauce, typically the spicy tomato dip into which tortilla chips are dunked, so that some commercial products advertise themselves tautologically as "salsa sauce."

The chief characteristic that distinguishes salsa from other sauces is that its ingredients are raw. In this sense, its main influence is Mexican cooking, where dips and relishes of tomatoes, bell peppers, and tomatillos are prepared, mortar and pestle fashion, and used as everyday seasoning. Guacamole could be classed as an avocado salsa.

Mexican-style salsa should not be confused with the use of the term in Spanish and Italian cooking, where it generically denotes any type of sauce, including those that are cooked. The spicy relish added to patatas bravas, for example, is known as *salsa brava*.

Smörgasbord

Many cuisines have a name for a large spread of various small items that may be eaten at random as appetizers. India has its *thali*, southern China has dim sum, and Sweden has smörgasbord, a close relative of Russia's *zakuski*. An abundant repertoire of hot and cold items makes up a smörgasbord, which would once have been intended to serve as a buffet platter. In many homes it has now become a scaled-down starter dish, similar to French mixed hors d'oeuvres or Italian antipasti.

There was once a strict order in which the items on a smörgasbord were to be eaten. The all-important herring came first—pickled, smoked, or dressed in sour cream—followed by other seafood, such as salmon, dressed crab, and various roes. Cold meats ensued, whether in the form of roast beef, reindeer, or charcuterie products, then the final wave would consist of small portions of hot dishes, such as meatballs and sliced potatoes baked with anchovies, garlic, and cream.

In the neighboring Scandinavian countries, the various linguistic variants on this idea all refer to open sandwiches (*smörgasbord* means "sandwich table"), but only in Sweden, contrarily enough, do sandwiches have nothing to do with the concept.

Scallion Pancakes

These simple pancakes use a flour-and-water pancake batter, into which the white and green parts of scallions are mixed, to make a surprisingly satisfying snack dish. They are Chinese in origin, and are usually eaten in China accompanied by a strong dipping sauce of sweet chile, or of soy sauce and rice vinegar.

The trick to them is rolling the pancake dough firmly around the chopped scallions before cooking, so that they don't unravel while they are being fried. Alternatively, they can be cooked as one large pancake, which is then sliced into wedges like a pizza. Another favored technique is to brush the scallions with sesame oil for extra flavor.

Not surprisingly for such a simple recipe, local variations are virtually numberless. Chinese home cooks will add shredded carrot, thin strips of red bell pepper, or bean sprouts to the filling, or—more rarely—some cooked meat. Another variant has the same ingredients incorporated into beaten egg, to make a kind of scallion omelette.

Scallion Pancakes

2 cups all-purpose flour
1 cup boiling water
$\frac{1}{2}$ cup vegetable oil
$\frac{1}{2}$ cup scallions, thinly sliced
Salt
Freshly ground black pepper

In a large bowl, combine the flour and enough boiling water to form a soft dough. Leave to rest for 30 minutes, covered with a damp cloth. Roll out the dough very thinly on a floured surface and brush generously with oil. Sprinkle the scallions over in an even layer and season well with salt and pepper.

Carefully roll up the dough like a pancake, then cut the roll in half. Roll out each half into a round, brush with oil and fry over medium-high heat until brown and crispy, about 5 minutes. Repeat with remaining dough. Cut the pancakes into wedges to serve. *Serves 4*

Suppli di Riso

Italy's rice dumplings make a hearty winter appetizer—a substantial, carbohydrate-rich dish to ward off the advancing chill. Their main ingredient is any variety of risotto rice (arborio, vialone nano, or carnaroli). The rice is cooked and seasoned with Parmesan, before being shaped into balls that are filled with a fortifying mixture of diced ham, provolone or mozzarella cheese, and bread crumbs, coated in a flour-and-egg batter, and then shallow-fried in oil. Eaten as a fast food, they often have a tangy tomato sauce poured over them, like Spanish albóndigas. At one time, these were more often served as the accompaniment to a main dish. Their savory appeal made them a considerably more tasty alternative to a piece of bread. They have now become a course or snack in their own right.

Another name for this dish in Italian is *arancini*, literally "oranges" of rice, which doesn't refer to any ingredient, but simply to the shape of the dumplings and, possibly once, their size.

Dolmades

Dolmades are a celebrated Greek *meze* dish, although similar preparations are found in Turkish and other eastern Mediterranean cuisines, and even in Swedish cooking. There are several popular variations, with the best known made of edible vine leaves wrapped around a filling of rice, pine nuts, spinach, currants, cinnamon, and mint. They are eaten cold. A hot version with a meat-based filling—usually ground lamb—is a lesser-known alternative.

The name may come from the Turkish *dolma*, meaning "stuffed," or the Greek *dolm*, meaning "vine leaf."

Dolmades

2¼ cups rice

2 tsp salt

½ cup raisins

½ cup pine nuts

2 tsp dried mint

1 pack of brined vine leaves

1 tbsp olive oil

Juice of half a lemon

Cook the rice, with salt, according to the packet instructions and stir in the raisins, pine nuts, and mint while the rice is still warm.

Rinse the vine leaves and blanch in boiling, unsalted water for 3 minutes. Drain the leaves and allow to cool.

Place a leaf on your work surface, stem end toward you and underside of leaf facing up. Drop a tablespoonful of filling just above the stem, and roll the leaf away from you, tucking in the sides as you near the top. You should have a neat, oblong package. Repeat with the remaining leaves, adjusting the amount of filling to the size of leaf.

Place the dolmades, seam-side down, in a steamer, packing them tightly to prevent them unfurling. Bring a pan of water to a rolling boil and set the steamer over the top. Cover and steam for about an hour, topping the water up now and again.

Once cooked, allow to cool slightly. Combine the olive oil and lemon juice, sprinkle over the vine leaves, and serve at room temperature. *Serves 6*

Four Tapas

Gambas al Ajillo

Garlic shrimp are one of the more luxurious items on the tapas menu: large shrimp sautéed in olive oil with plenty of minced garlic and usually a little chopped red chili pepper. Like other sizzling tapas dishes, they come to the table in their cooking pot, generally a flat heavy-bottomed cast-iron pan.

Like the best seafood recipes, the success of this dish depends on quick cooking. Once the shrimp hit the hot oil, they need only about three minutes or so, just enough time to turn pink.

No Spaniard would be seen without a piece of crusty bread in hand when eating garlic shrimp. It is essential for soaking up the deliciously aromatic cooking juices.

Pimientos

This simple preparation consists of strips of skinned red bell pepper lightly cooked in olive oil with garlic, parsley, and perhaps some chopped red chile pepper, then marinated in jars with oil and wine vinegar. They are often seen on the shelves of traditional-style Spanish tapas houses, where their enduring presence assures diners that the business of lengthy in-house marination is taken seriously.

A favorite ingredient for this dish is Piquillo peppers, sweet red peppers that are roasted over wood until they acquire a charred, smoky taste. Packaged in jars of vinegar-sour marinade and found in specialty food stores and delicatessens, they are usually of reliable quality. Excellent with fish and seafood dishes, they are also great on their own with just a trickle of olive oil.

Manchego

The least elaborate of all tapas is manchego cheese, cut into thin triangles and served plain. Manchego is the hard, creamy sheep's-milk cheese that originated in La Mancha, the vast, arid plateau of central Spain. Graded, and sold according to age, like Parmesan, the oldest manchego has the strongest, most mouth-filling flavor. The milder varieties are more commonly served in tapas houses today.

Manchego canapés have a spoonful of some relish on top, typically a mixture of black olives, Piquillo peppers and anchovies pounded in olive oil.

Traditional aging involves keeping the cheese in large glass flagons of olive oil, which imparts the flavor and moistens the paste of the cheese. Practiced to a lesser extent now, it is still done in rural parts of Spain. Ideally, the manchego you order from the tapas menu will have been cured in this way, and will have an oily surface as proof.

Pimientos de Padron

Born in Padron, a small town in Galicia, in Spain's northwest, these tiny green peppers are now also cultivated in California, in response to the many North American Hispanophiles who crave them. They make for wonderful summertime bar food, best enjoyed as a tapa with cold beer or a crisp white wine. Pimientos de Padron are prepared in a hot pan with a generous splash of rich olive oil. As they cook, they shrivel and char, and concentrate their distinctive flavor. Once plated, they receive a sprinkle of coarse salt before serving. But there is more. Many commentators have compared eating them to culinary Russian roulette. While most of them are mild, sweet, and somewhat nutty, every tenth one or so is as hot as a jalapeño. There's no means of telling which peppers will pack the punch, so finding one is always a surprise, either pleasant or painful, depending on the eater's tolerance for spice.

Championes Rellenos

English food writer and novelist Shirley Conran once declared, "Life is too short to stuff a mushroom." She cannot have been thinking of championes rellenos. A tapas menu favorite, large open-cap mushrooms, stalks removed, are stuffed with a mixture of minced onion and garlic, perhaps with some chopped bell pepper, and a little diced chorizo (spicy Spanish sausage) added. The filling ingredients are fried in olive oil and the loaded mushrooms are then baked briefly until browned.

Stuffed Mushrooms

3 slices firm white sandwich bread

2 tbsp olive oil

$1/2$ tsp salt

$1/4$ tsp freshly ground black pepper

20 large (2 to 2 $1/2$ inches in diameter) white mushrooms

2 tbsp unsalted butter

1 medium onion, finely chopped

1 stalk celery, finely chopped

2 cloves garlic, finely chopped

$1/2$ tsp dried oregano, crumbled

2 tbsp freshly grated Parmesan cheese

1 medium bunch fresh parsley, finely chopped

Preheat the oven to 400°F.

Blitz the bread in a blender until you have coarse crumbs. Transfer them to a bowl and toss with oil and half the salt and pepper. Spread in a shallow baking pan and bake in the middle of the oven until golden, 6 to 8 minutes. Transfer to a bowl.

Remove the stems from the mushroom caps and chop. Lightly oil the baking pan and lay the mushroom caps in a single layer, stem side down. Bake for about 10 minutes, then remove from the oven.

While the mushroom caps are baking, melt the butter in a large, heavy skillet over medium to high heat and sauté the chopped stems for about 5 minutes. Add the onion, celery, garlic, oregano, and remaining salt and pepper and sauté for a further 5 minutes. Allow the vegetables to cool slightly before adding them to the bread crumbs along with the cheese and parsley. Stir well to combine.

Spoon the filling into the mushroom caps and bake in the middle of the oven until the mushrooms are tender and the stuffing is golden brown, about 20 minutes. Melt cheese on top, if desired. *Makes 20*

Vol-au-Vents

Tacos

Once the "must have" at any party occasion with pretensions to sophistication, the vol-au-vent is a puff pastry shell with a lid that is hollowed out after baking and filled with some sauce-based savory mixture, then baked again for a few minutes before serving. As its name indicates, it should be so light that it might fly away in the wind when removed from the oven.

Fillings can be as daring or as mainstream as you like. In the 1970s, nearly all were shrimp or sliced mushrooms in creamy sauces. In France, chefs who aimed higher produced versions based on spiced chicken, veal sweetbreads, foie gras, puréed meats or shellfish, salmon, lobster, and creamed black truffles.

The North American fast-food taco chain version bears only a passing resemblance to the genuine Mexican taco (the word means "plug"). There, a soft corn tortilla is the base or holder for any one of a huge variety of meaty fillings. Tacos in the US have crisp shells, which have been deep-fried to form rigid containers for the filling. There is some historical precedence for this version of the taco among the people who once inhabited Mexican California, but the taco in Mexico is definitely the soft and pliable type.

Roadside taco stands (*taquerias*) in Mexico do a roaring trade, and the fillings are more likely to be various parts of a cow's head, including the brain, thin-sliced pork steak, pig tripe (stomach lining), or the Mexican version of chorizo. Accompaniments are guacamole, whole salted red turnips, and sliced cucumber. California or Texas innovations include the breakfast taco—containing sausage, bacon, and fried egg.

Vegetable Samosa

A street snack in India, a vegetable samosa
is a crisp deep-fried pastry traditionally made
from gram (garbanzo) flour, formed into a
triangular shape around a potato-based filling
that usually also contains peas and onion.
The filling is mildly spiced, with a strong
yellow hue if turmeric is in part of the spice
mix. They are eaten with relishes such as
cilantro or tamarind chutney.

Non-vegetarian versions of samosas
feature meaty fillings, most commonly spiced
ground lamb.

Vegetable Samosa

4 cups all-purpose flour

1/2 tsp nigella seeds

1/2 tsp salt

2 tbsp vegetable oil, plus 3 to 4 cups for frying

3 potatoes, peeled

1 medium bunch scallions (white and green
parts), chopped

2 fresh green chiles, such as jalapeños, seeded
and minced, optional

1 medium bunch fresh cilantro, chopped

1 tsp whole cumin seeds

1/2 tsp ground cumin

1/2 tsp chili powder

1/2 tsp salt

Plain yogurt for serving

Whisk the flour, nigella seeds, and salt
together in a large bowl. Add 2 tablespoons
of oil and use your fingertips to blend the
mixture until it resembles fine bread crumbs.
Add 3/4 cup warm water and mix with a fork
to bring the dough together. Knead the dough
on a lightly floured surface until smooth
and elastic, about 10 minutes. Put the dough
in a large, greased bowl, cover with a towel,
and leave to rest for 30 to 40 minutes.

Put the potatoes in a large saucepan and
cover with cold water. Bring to a boil, reduce
the heat, and simmer, covered, until tender.
Drain and leave to cool. Dice the potatoes
and put them in a large bowl along with the
scallions, chiles (if using), cilantro, cumin
seeds, ground cumin, chili powder, and salt.
Mix with a fork to combine.

Divide the dough into 12 equal balls,
rolling out each on a floured surface to a
6-inch circle. Cut the circle in half, then shape
it into a cone with a 1/4-in wide overlapping
seam. Fill with 2 tablespoons of the potato
mixture, and seal the open edge. Repeat with
remaining dough and filling.

Heat 2 inches of oil in a heavy, deep skillet
over medium heat. Working in batches, fry
the samosas in the hot oil until golden
brown—1 to 2 minutes per side. Drain on paper
towels, before serving warm with yogurt.
Serves 4–6

Tamales

A popular street snack in Mexico and many South American countries, especially for breakfast, tamales are filled rolls of cornmeal dough. The wrapping is made of *masa*, a simple batter of corn-flour and water. The tamale is traditionally wrapped in a corn husk before cooking. Fillings usually consist of cooked meat—either chicken or pork—which is dressed in a red or green salsa or *mole*. The rolled tamales are then cooked in a steamer, or *tamalera*.

As with all such wrapped items, tamales are subject to wide local variation. They became a staple convenience food many centuries ago because they could be carried by people on the move and heated up as needed. Sweet versions are made by adding sugar to the cornmeal and using dried fruits, pineapple, or coconut as fillings.

In the United States, tamales have taken on a whole divergent tradition of their own. Beef is a favored filling, often in the form of Texas-style chili con carne, and creamed corn fillings echo the main component of the wrapping.

Zatar

Produced in Turkey, the Near East, and North Africa, zatar is comprised of toasted sesame seeds, ground sumac with thyme (the Arabic word for which gives the dish its name), and salt. The ingredients are pounded together in a mortar and pestle. Like Morocco's harissa, it can be used as a seasoning in meat or vegetable dishes, but it is also often mixed with olive oil and eaten with flatbread. A piece of bread is dipped first in oil, then in the zatar.

There are many regional variations on the basic recipe, but all contain sumac, the ground dried berries of a Middle Eastern shrub. In Syria and Jordan, zatar is sprinkled on bowls of *labneh* (a yogurt-based soft cheese), while in Lebanon, it is spread like pizza topping onto a bread-dough base, which is then baked and eaten as a breakfast food called *manakish bil-zatar*.

Beet Salad

Beloved for their earthy flavor and vibrant color, beets star in a diverse range of salads. From the first tiny bulbs pulled in spring to the hearty specimens from the root cellar, beet salads are enjoyed year-round.

Every country in Eastern Europe has a cherished beet salad. In Poland, cooked beets are grated with apple to make *buraczki*, a simple dish and an Easter staple. Estonians love their *rosolje*, a violet-colored salad of potatoes, beets, apple, pickles, herring, and onion dressed with mayonnaise and sour cream. In Scandinavia, pickled beets with caraway seed are often put out with just a sprinkling of dill as a tasty side dish. Beets also star in a hearty French bistro salad with mâche, walnuts, and goat's cheese.

Of the various flavorings, beets have a natural affinity for orange, ginger, tarragon, and horseradish. From the brilliant golden beet to the candy-striped chioggia, there are many colorful varieties to create a dramatic presentation. When beets come attached to their greens, the leaves can be boiled and added to the salad, balancing the sweetness and adding a new layer of texture and flavor.

Soupa Avgolemono

In Greek, *avgolemono* means "egg-lemon" and
it is also the name given to a popular soup
starring these ingredients. Soupa avgolemono
is a simple affair, starting with just chicken
broth and rice. Cooked vegetables and meat
are sometimes included to make it more of
a meal. Eggs and lemon juice are the finishing
touches, added at the end of cooking to
thicken the soup.

The egg mixture must be carefully
incorporated to prevent it from scrambling.
It is first tempered with a ladleful of the hot
broth before being whisked into the soup
over the gentlest heat. The eggs add richness,
the lemon sharpens the flavors, and the soup
turns a beautiful creamy yellow. It should
never return to a boil or it will curdle.

In summer, soupa avgolemono is served
chilled, without the rice, as a refreshing
first course. In colder months, the soup is
prized for its restorative powers, dispensed
by Greek mothers at the first sign of a cold.
And following an ouzo-filled night, a steaming
bowl of soupa avgolemono is the perfect
hangover cure. It's no wonder the soup is
known as Greek penicillin.

Soupa Avgolemono

6 cups chicken broth

¼ cup rice

3 eggs

¼ cup fresh lemon juice

1 lemon, thinly sliced

Bring broth and rice to a boil in a large
saucepan. Cover and simmer until the rice is
tender, about 15 minutes. Remove from the
heat. In a bowl, beat the eggs until fluffy,
then beat in the lemon juice. Whisk the egg
mixture vigorously as you slowly add about
2 cups of the hot soup. Return to the soup
pot and continue whisking until slightly thick.
Garnish each serving with a lemon slice.
Serves 6

GREECE

Faki Soupa

Lentils are an important part of the Greek diet, as they are both economical and a delicious source of protein. During Lent, when it is forbidden to eat meat, lentils are featured in simple, yet satisfying faki soupa.

Also called fakes soupa, this soup is about as easy as it gets. In fact, the hardest part is searching through the tiny legumes for stones! Brown lentils are the color of choice. Picked over and rinsed, they are put in the pot with water, onion, garlic, and a bay leaf. When it reaches a simmer, chopped tomatoes, olive oil, and a pinch of dried oregano are added. The soup is cooked until the lentils are soft and the mixture is thick. A splash of wine vinegar added at the end cuts the starchiness of the lentils and highlights their earthy flavor.

Greeks aren't the only ones who love faki soupa. Both vegetarians and vegans have adopted this gratifying dish as their own.

GREECE

Fassolada

From a garlicky dip made from yellow peas to giant white beans cooked with tomato, legumes feature prominently in Greek cuisine. It's no wonder, then, that the national dish of Greece is a hearty bean soup.

Fassolada is peasant food at its best. Made from just beans, vegetables, herbs, and olive oil, this matronly soup has raised countless generations of Greeks.

It starts with some type of white bean, usually cannellini. The beans are soaked overnight in water then placed in a pot with onions, carrot, celery, and bay leaves. After this mixture has simmered for a while, tomatoes are added, giving the soup its characteristic color while adding sweetness and acidity. A pinch of dried oregano and a lavish splash of olive oil round things out. Once ladled into bowls, fassolada gets a sprinkle of chopped parsley and more of that fine olive oil.

Like the Greek lentil soup, faki soupa, this meatless dish is a Lenten staple. In keeping with tradition, fassolada should be eaten with crusty bread, feta cheese, and black olives. Of course, a glass of rustic red wine wouldn't hurt, either.

Fattoush

While the ubiquitous tabbouleh can be found in falafel shops around the world, its close cousin, fattoush, is relatively unknown. Interestingly enough, the two salads are almost interchangeable: substitute the bulgur in tabbouleh with pieces of toasted pita bread and you've got fattoush!

In the same spirit as Italy's panzanella, fattoush is a delicious way to use up stale bread. It may start with chopped green pepper, cucumber, scallions, parsley, and mint dressed with olive oil, garlic, and lemon juice. Some versions include purslane, a fleshy salad green, and sumac, a ground, dried berry that imparts a citrusy tang. The salad is tossed with diced tomato and toasted pita just before serving, which allows the tomatoes to hold their shape and the pita to remain crisp. In the Syrian version, the pita is fried in olive oil before being added to the dish.

Cool cucumber, juicy tomato, aromatic herbs, and crunchy pita provide an array of textures and flavors. Fattoush is served as a side dish to grilled meats, and is a colorful addition to *meze*, the Middle Eastern antipasto table.

Fattoush

½ to 1 flat pita bread
Juice of 1 to 2 lemons
1 large cucumber
3 to 4 firm tomatoes, chopped
1 medium-sized mild onion, chopped
1 bunch fresh parsley, finely chopped
2 tbsp finely chopped fresh mint
3 tbsp chopped fresh cilantro
2 cloves garlic, crushed
6 to 8 tbsp olive oil
Salt
Freshly ground black pepper

Open the pita bread, place in a hot oven or under the broiler until it is crisp and brown, then crunch it into little pieces in your hands. Place the broken pieces of toast in a bowl and moisten with a little cold water or lemon juice. Mix with the remaining ingredients. Taste and adjust the seasoning. *Serves 6*
Adapted from Claudia Roden's *A New Book of Middle Eastern Food*

◁ # Black Bean Soup

Fava Beans and Prosciutto

Black turtle beans are prized all over South America for their meaty texture, earthy flavor, and dramatic color. Not surprisingly, there are dozens of soups made from this tasty little bean.

Because of their unparalleled flavor, black bean soups are often water-based, as the liquid the beans are cooked in rivals any meat broth. For this reason, these soups have long been a vegetarian favorite.

The most famous black bean soup is *feijoada*, Brazil's national dish. This orange-scented stew is packed with pork, sausage, and beef and served with collard greens and rice. Cuba is known for its *sopa de frijoles negros*, zinged with cumin and chile and garnished with raw onion. In the Oaxaca region of Mexico, black bean soup is perfumed with an aromatic herb called *hierba de conejo* (Indian paintbrush) and served with plump corn dumplings.

Black bean soup has also become the darling of southwestern American chefs. The purplish-black liquid acts as a canvas for such colorful Tex-Mex garnishes as creamy avocado, spicy tomato salsa, and crispy strips of corn tortilla.

In Italy, fava beans are the true harbinger of spring. Prized for their rich texture and nutty flavor, there is no better way to eat favas than with the sweet, silky prosciutto (cured ham) from Parma.

Cultivated for millennia, they must first be shucked from their swollen green pods. How they are prepared depends on when they are picked. The first tender beans of spring—no bigger than a fingernail—can be eaten raw. Called *baccelli* by Tuscans, they are served in a simple salad with ribbons of prosciutto, sharp pecorino cheese, and a drizzle of peppery extra-virgin olive oil.

Later in summer, when the beans are starchier, they need to be popped out of their tough outer skin—a time-consuming process and true labor of love. The plump beans are then braised with olive oil and garlic. Mixed with slivers of prosciutto, the cooked beans are served at room temperature as an antipasto-type salad. Hot or cold, spring or summer, fava beans and prosciutto are a Tuscan delight.

Borscht

It would be hard to think of a more popular dish in Eastern European cuisine than borscht. While the variations are endless, it always contains beets, which give the soup its vibrant purple-red hue.

Since beets grow easily and thrive in the root cellar, borscht is consumed year-round. In cooler months, it is a hearty affair brimming with root vegetables and meat such as beef, pork, sausage, or duck. Beef broth is traditionally used, though vegetarian versions are made with mushroom broth. As the temperature rises, borscht is simplified down to cooked beets and broth, and is served cold. The monochromatic nature of borscht welcomes contrasting garnishes such as sour cream and chopped dill.

Borscht is the national dish of Ukraine, where it is said to have originated. There, it usually contains beef and arrives at the table with a basket of *pampushky* (little garlic buns). Russian cooks add cabbage and potatoes to their borscht and occasionally make it with *kvass*, a type of low-alcohol beer. In Poland, borscht is spelled *barszcz*, and is a favorite at Christmas Eve, when it is served with delicate mushroom dumplings called *uszka*.

Borscht

1 medium celery root, chopped

1 medium parsley root, chopped

2 medium carrots, chopped

1 medium leek, chopped

1 medium onion, chopped

1 large parsnip, chopped

4 medium red beets, thinly sliced

10 black peppercorns

1/8 tsp allspice

2 bay leaves

1½ cups red wine

Juice of 2 lemons

1 tsp sugar

2 garlic cloves, crushed

Salt

Freshly ground black pepper

Heat 6 cups of water in a large pot. When it boils, add the celery and parsley root, carrots, leek, onion, and parsnip. Simmer for 20 minutes. Place the beets in a separate pan with 2 cups of water, the peppercorns, allspice, and bay leaves. Simmer, uncovered, for 30 minutes.

Strain the liquid from both pans into one large saucepan and discard the vegetables. Return the borscht to the heat and add the red wine, lemon juice, sugar, and garlic. Simmer for 20 minutes and season to taste. *Serves 4*

Bird's Nest Soup

In China, bird's nest soup is prized for its rich nutrient content and purported health benefits. Made from the unique nests of a certain species of swift, this rare soup is one of the priciest delicacies in Chinese cuisine.

The nests are composed of the birds' saliva and are formed high up in caves around Southeast Asia. Harvesters must scale bamboo trellises to retrieve the nests, which is a difficult and risky operation. Once cleaned, the hard, golden nests look like a small bowl. Costing thousands of dollars a kilogram, they are one of the most expensive foods in the world. It's no wonder they're called "white gold"!

To make bird's nest soup, the nests are simmered for hours in chicken broth until they take on a gelatinous texture. To let the star ingredient shine, little else is added, usually just some ginger, egg, and a few slivers of Yunnan ham. Bird's nests can also find their way into *tong shui*, a sweet Cantonese soup eaten for dessert.

Treasured since the Ming dynasty, there is no higher honor one can bestow upon a guest than serving them bird's nest soup.

Broccoli and Stilton Soup

Despised by kids and pushed around on plates, much-maligned broccoli deserves more respect. Transformed into a thick green soup flavored with Stilton cheese, it should finally start earning it.

This traditional British soup is a great way to use up oft-discarded broccoli stems— though they must be peeled first. It is a simple blend of onions, broccoli, and a little potato cooked in vegetable broth and puréed in a food processor, but not too smoothly, so the soup retains some texture. It is finished with cream and just a modicum of Stilton so the pungent cheese doesn't overpower the soup's delicate flavor.

Blue cheese is not to everyone's taste, but since broccoli gets along with most sharp cheeses, this soup is equally delicious made with aged Cheddar, Parmesan, or salty pecorino.

Whether from a can or mom's kitchen, broccoli and Stilton soup will always hold a special place in British hearts and bellies.

Carrot and Cilantro Soup

Making soup without carrots is almost unthinkable. Whether it is to add sweetness to chicken broth or give color to minestrone, the humble carrot is happy in just about any soup pot. Promoted to star ingredient, carrots are transformed into a sweet, velvety purée. Combined with the strong, citrusy flavor of fresh cilantro, this soup is sublime.

Carrot soup follows the basic formula for any puréed soup. Sliced onions are sautéed in butter or olive oil until soft, but not brown, as you don't want to dull the carrot's brilliant orange color. A light vegetable broth is added with the carrots and a few potatoes to give the soup body. Ginger is a popular flavoring, as are hot chiles. The soup is gently simmered until the vegetables are soft, then whizzed in a blender to achieve a creamy texture without cream. A gentle squeeze of lime juice magically brightens the flavors and balances the sweetness.

For an elegant presentation, a stark white bowl provides the perfect frame. Whole cilantro leaves, tossed with a few drops of oil, sparkle front and center in this truly stunning soup.

Caesar Salad

From roadside diners to temples of gastronomy, Caesar salad is the darling of the North American restaurant. And judging by the array of bottled dressings, salad kits, and boxed croutons, the almighty Caesar rules the home kitchen as well.

The salad is said to be the invention of Caesar Cardini, an Italian restaurateur living in San Diego, who owned an eponymous hotel across the border in Tijuana. Created sometime in the 1920s, the original salad contained romaine lettuce, croutons, garlic, Parmesan, coddled eggs, olive oil, lemon juice, and Worcestershire sauce. Tossed tableside with great showmanship, the barely-cooked eggs created a luscious dressing that enrobed the sturdy greens. The lettuce leaves were left whole to be eaten with the fingers, a practice still in evidence today. The addition of Dijon mustard, bacon bits, and anchovy would come later, though many chefs continue to make an authentic Caesar that would do Cardini proud.

At its best, Caesar salad is a delight—juicy, tender romaine hearts cloaked in a bold, creamy dressing with crisp croutons and nutty Parmesan cheese. Of course, there should be just enough garlic to keep the vampires at bay.

Callaloo

Callaloo, the legendary Caribbean soup, must contain some type of leafy green vegetable to earn its lyrical name. With as many different recipes as there are cooks who make it, the verdant soup is cherished from Puerto Rico to Brazil.

Basic callaloo is flavored with garlic, herbs, and fiery Scotch bonnet peppers. It usually contains okra, brought over by African slaves who created the dish. Other popular ingredients include salt pork, bacon, crab, and coconut milk. The type of greens used depends on the country of origin. In Trinidad, where callaloo is considered a national treasure, they use the fan-shaped leaves of the starchy taro root, called *dasheen* in the West Indies. Jamaican cooks also use *dasheen* in addition to salt beef, calling their version pepper pot. The red-veined leaves of the amaranth plant often find their way into callaloo. Outside of the Caribbean, spinach is a common substitute.

No matter who is making callaloo, it is always cooked low and slow until dark green and thick. Served on its own or as a side dish to a Sunday roast, legend has it that serving callaloo is a surefire way for a woman to extract a marriage proposal.

Caldo Verde

A simple soup made with just a handful of ingredients, caldo verde exemplifies the best of Portuguese peasant cooking. From home kitchens to fancy restaurants, this "green soup" is loved by one and all.

There is little variation from recipe to recipe, and it can be quickly mastered by even the most novice cook. First, onions and garlic are sautéed in olive oil. Potatoes and water are added to the pot and simmered until tender. To keep the soup rustic, this mixture is left in its chunky state or gently crushed with a potato masher. For a more elegant version, a blender transforms it into a velvety purée. The *verde* comes in the form of a leafy green vegetable, most commonly kale, though collard greens or cabbage can be used. For a truly authentic caldo verde, the greens must be finely shredded. Thin slices of chorizo sausage are often added, which give the soup a hit of *umami*, the savory fifth taste.

Whether served as a first course or a light meal, it's best eaten with a hunk of *broa*, Portugal's dense corn bread. Smooth potato, hearty greens, and smoky sausage: caldo verde packs a lot of punch for such a humble soup.

Carrot and Cumin Salad

Sweet carrots have a natural affinity for
the robust flavor of cumin, and this happy
marriage can be found in salads from
Morocco to Lebanon. These bright orange
salads are often part of the room-temperature
spread of appetizers popular throughout the
southern Mediterranean.

Carrot and cumin salads rarely involve
anything more than a handful of ingredients,
but how they are prepared can vary greatly. In
Morocco, where the salads are sold by street
vendors, the carrots are usually cut into sticks,
boiled until tender-crisp, and tossed with a
dressing made from olive oil, garlic, cumin,
and lemon juice. The Tunisian version is very
similar, but gets a flavor boost from harissa
(hot sauce) and chopped cilantro. A crunchier
rendition finds grated raw carrot mixed with
a cumin-scented dressing that is marinated
for a few days to let the flavors mingle.

Cooked carrot salads are also popular in
Israel, where they are traditionally served on
Rosh Hashanah (Jewish New Year) to represent
the sweetness of the year to come.

Carrot and Cumin Salad

1 lb carrots, peeled and grated into fine shreds

For the dressing:

2 oranges, juiced

1 lemon, juiced

2 tbsp extra-virgin olive oil

1 tsp ground cumin, or to taste

Salt

Freshly ground black pepper to taste

Put the grated carrots in a large bowl. Combine
the orange and lemon juice with the olive oil
and add cumin, salt, and pepper to taste. Pour
the dressing over the grated carrots, toss lightly,
and refrigerate for at least 1 hour to blend the
flavors. Toss again and serve. *Serves 4*

CHINA

◁ # Egg Drop Soup

Chicken broth plays an essential role in Chinese cuisine. It's used as a base for sauces, braising liquids, and, of course, every soup from humble wonton to luxurious bird's nest.

One of the easiest chicken soups in the Chinese canon is egg drop soup. Its simplicity demands strong homemade chicken broth perfumed with ginger, garlic, and scallions. The broth is brought to a simmer and seasoned with salt. An egg or two is beaten with soy sauce and sesame oil and poured into the hot broth in a thin stream. With a pair of chopsticks, the eggs are swirled into the soup in a figure-8 motion and are instantly transformed into short, silky strands.

Whipped up in a matter of minutes, egg drop soup is the perfect medicine for a cold or a sensitive stomach. The delicate egg threads floating on the surface of the broth are said to resemble flower petals, hence its alias of egg flower soup.

KOREA

Samgyetang

Surely as every country has a flag, they also boast of a national chicken soup. In Korea, this is samgyetang.

Also known as chicken ginseng soup, samgyetang uses a whole baby chicken, preferably 5 to 7 months old. It is stuffed with glutinous rice and simmered in an aromatic broth with fresh ginseng, jujubes, and garlic. Ginseng is a slim, licorice-flavored rhizome that is prized both as a restorative and a stimulant. Jujubes—also called Chinese dates—are dried, purplish-red berries that give the soup a touch of sweetness and are said to relieve stress. Samgyetang is cooked in a heavy clay pot called a *tukbaege*, which is brought straight to the table still bubbling and giving off puffs of fragrant steam.

Like most chicken soups, samgyetang is treasured for its curative powers. But what makes this soup unique is that it's a summer dish, traditionally eaten on the three hottest days of the year for energy and stamina.

Ajiaco

The national dish of Colombia is a hearty chicken soup called ajiaco. It is popular all over the country, but the most famous version comes from the capital city of Bogotá. Ajiaco Bogotano starts off by simmering pieces of chicken in broth flavored with onion, garlic, and cilantro. In addition to chunks of corn, three varieties of potatoes are added, most importantly the native Papa Criolla, a yellow-fleshed spud that breaks down and thickens the soup. When the chicken is cooked, it is shredded and returned to the pot. The secret ingredient is *guasca*, a local herb that gives the soup its characteristic grassy flavor. Without *guasca*, it is not an authentic ajiaco.

Once it has been ladled into bowls, the soup receives three garnishes: a drizzle of cream, slices of ripe avocado, and a teaspoon of briny capers.

While ajiaco is enjoyed all year round, it is traditionally served as part of a Colombian Christmas celebration.

Chicken Soup with Kreplach ▷

Chicken soup, in its many guises, is a cornerstone of Jewish cuisine. It's a fixture at the Shabbat dinner table, used to celebrate holidays, and owing to its reliable healing properties, it is fondly known as Jewish penicillin.

In a Jewish kitchen, chicken soup will float everything from fluffy matzo balls to egg noodles to a few coins of carrot. But for special occasions—the night before Yom Kippur, for example—chicken soup is served with meat-stuffed pasta called kreplach.

The dough for kreplach is a mixture of flour and eggs that is thoroughly kneaded by hand. It is rolled thin, cut into squares, and stuffed with a filling of cooked onion and ground meat. It is folded to form a triangle and boiled in salted water before being added to the soup.

Chicken soup with kreplach bears a striking resemblance to a popular Chinese soup: hence its nickname of "Jewish wonton soup."

Cazuela

Celeriac Remoulade

In Spanish, *cazuela* means casserole or stew, and in South America, it means a favorite one-pot meal.

Cazuelas vary greatly from country to country. In Argentina, *cazuela de cordero* finds lamb and vegetables in rich cumin-scented broth that is thickened with eggs. Also from Argentina is *cazuela gaucho*, a hearty chicken stew that was originally cooked over campfires by local cowboys. *Cazuela de mariscos* is a Colombian-style bouillabaisse, brimming with seafood with a splash of coconut milk. In the mountains of Peru, cazuela sometimes means alpaca stew!

Cazuela is tremendously popular in Chile. *Cazuela de vaca*, the national beef stew, was modeled after *cocido*, the hearty boiled dinners of Spain. The cornerstones of this Chilean cazuela are beef, pumpkin, and corn, all cut into large pieces. Other vegetables include onions, potatoes, and peppers, with a pinch of oregano. The broth is thickened with cornmeal and finished with fresh cilantro. In the bowl, the meat is placed front and center, flanked by the bright orange pumpkin and golden corn. The succulent meat paired with tender veggies and a heady broth is Chile's answer to the French pot-au-feu.

Celeriac, or celery root, is not the most popular of root vegetables, but when sliced into thin strips and mixed with a tangy mayonnaise dressing, it is transformed into remoulade, a French bistro classic.

Peeling its tough, knobby skin reveals snowy white flesh that tastes mildly of celery. It is cut into juliennes with a sharp knife—though a French mandoline is a more efficient tool for the job—and tossed with a generous squeeze of lemon juice to prevent discoloration.

The dressing dates back to 19th-century France. Considered to be the precursor to tartar sauce, it was originally mayonnaise flavored with garlic, anchovy, capers, and parsley. In Louisiana, Cajun-style remoulade is still the sauce of choice with fried seafood. Celeriac remoulade, however, is nothing more than thick mayonnaise fortified with strong Dijon mustard. Once the toothsome celeriac meets the creamy sauce, it is allowed to sit for a few hours to soften and develop flavor.

Celeriac remoulade can be served on its own as a hearty first course. It is an amazingly diverse side dish, complementing everything from poached salmon to roast pork. An elegant substitute for creamy coleslaw, it would not be out of place alongside fish and chips.

Soupe au Pistou

In the Provençal dialect, *pistou* means "pounded." It is also the name given to a fragrant sauce of basil, tomato, garlic, and olive oil pounded in a mortar—a French spin on Genovese pesto. Mixed with grated Parmesan, pistou can be spread on bread or tossed with pasta, though it is most commonly used as a condiment for a soup that shares its name.

Soupe au pistou is a summer vegetable soup similar to Italian minestrone. It is traditionally vegetarian, made with dried navy or kidney beans, onions, potatoes, carrots, zucchini, and green beans. If fresh shell beans are available, they're used in place of dried, as the soup is traditionally a way of celebrating the bean crop harvest. Carnivores will pump up the flavor with bacon or smoked ham, and adding pasta makes it more of a meal.

Just before serving comes the herbaceous flourish that gives the soup its name. A dollop of the verdant pistou is swirled into the bowl, invigorating the soup with a blast of sweet basil, pungent garlic, and nutty cheese.

Soupe au Pistou

⅓ cup dry white navy beans, soaked overnight

For the pistou:

2 cloves garlic

3 tbsp extra-virgin olive oil

1 medium bunch fresh basil, leaves only

1 cup freshly grated Gruyère or Parmesan cheese

For the soup:

8 cups chicken broth

2 small red potatoes, skins on, diced

1 large carrot, diced

1 small onion, diced

1 small zucchini, diced

1 small yellow crookneck squash, diced

1 stalk celery, peeled, diced

1 large tomato, peeled, seeded, and diced

1 cup green beans, diced

Salt and freshly ground black pepper

Place the beans in a small saucepan and cover with a generous amount of water. Bring to a boil and cook, covered, until tender, about 1 hour. Drain and reserve.

For the pistou, purée garlic, olive oil, and a few basil leaves in a blender. Gradually add the remaining basil leaves until smooth. Transfer to a small bowl, add the grated cheese, and stir. Set aside.

In a large pot, bring the chicken broth to a boil. Add the white beans, potatoes, carrot, and onion. Return to a boil, reduce to a simmer, then cook, uncovered, for 15 minutes. Add the remaining vegetables and bring back to a boil. Reduce to a simmer, and cook for an additional 10 minutes, uncovered. Season to taste. Serve soup with a dollop of pistou in each bowl. *Serves 4*

Bouillabaisse

Originally from Marseilles, this fish stew has earned an international reputation. Like any classic French dish, however, there is heated debate over what makes it authentic.

First, a selection of firm-fleshed fish such as rascasse (rock fish) and monkfish are filleted and cut into pieces. A broth made from the bones provides the soup's base. Sliced onions are stewed in olive oil and combined with fresh tomato and the fish broth. What distinguishes bouillabaisse from other fish soups is the flavor triumvirate of saffron, fennel seed, and orange peel. The fish is simmered in this aromatic broth along with clams, mussels, and squid. The cooked seafood is removed to a large serving platter and the broth is boiled—bouillabaisse is derived from *bouillir*, the French word for boil—which emulsifies the oil with the broth and concentrates the flavors.

Bouillabaisse is traditionally served in two stages. The heady soup is ladled into bowls over slices of toasted bread rubbed with garlic. The fish and shellfish are served separately with a side of *rouille*, garlicky mayonnaise zinged with chile. At this point, all that's needed is crusty bread, chilled rosé, and a festive group of friends to enjoy it with.

La Potée

Spring Vegetable Soup

Visit any farmhouse in France during winter, and chances are you'll find a hulking pot of potée simmering on the stove. Packed with pork and hearty root vegetables, this rustic soup is meant to satisfy the most ravenous of appetites.

Potée is popular in every corner of rural France. It varies from region to region, but it usually contains three basic ingredients: pork (fresh, salted, or smoked), cabbage, and potatoes.

In addition to its famous quiche, the Lorraine region in northeastern France is renowned for a potée brimming with pork shoulder, ham, smoked sausages, leeks, and crinkly savoy cabbage.

Up in the French Alps, potée is served somewhat like classic pot-au-feu. The vegetables are left whole or cut into large pieces, and boiled with a charcuterie full of sausages. The cooked meats and veggies are arranged on a platter, and the broth is poured over.

Another classic potée comes from the Champagne region, where it includes bacon, salt pork, turnips, carrots, and celery root. Served to the field hands during harvest, it is fondly known as grape pickers' potée.

Springtime brings a cornucopia of green soups. Italy has *minestrone verdissima*, the French have *potage printanière*, and just about every restaurant in the West puts asparagus soup on their menu.

Lebanese cooks also take advantage of this verdant time of year to make a very green soup. This chunky staple starts with a pot of simmering broth that's soon brimming with vegetables. Leeks, celery, peas, fresh fava beans, artichoke hearts, and the first tiny zucchini of the season are all welcome additions, along with chopped garlic for flavor.

What makes this soup uniquely Lebanese is the one-two punch of lemon juice and dried mint. The lemon gives the broth a sour bite while sharpening the flavors, and the dried mint makes a much bolder statement than fresh. Other popular Lebanese spices, such as cumin, are left on the shelf to keep the soup light and delicate. Poured over a bowl of white rice, it is a delicious way to celebrate spring.

Red and White Clam Chowder

The cold waters of the North Atlantic yield sweet clams that, for more than a century, have been the heart and soul of the all-American clam chowder. But with two popular versions of this maritime soup—tomato-based red and creamy white—chowder fans are split along the red/white divide.

New England (white) clam chowder is packed with potatoes, onions, and steamed clams. It's thickened with a flour-butter roux and enriched with milk or cream. A little salt pork or bacon goes into the pot, which complements the briny bivalves. Whether it's by the cup or bowl, this hearty, stick-to-your-ribs soup is always served with a package of saltines or oyster crackers.

Manhattan (red) clam chowder is said to have originated in 19th-century Rhode Island. Made by Portuguese immigrants, this dairy-free chowder was distinguished by the addition of tomatoes, peppers, and herbs. This became the chowder of choice in New York, and was called Coney Island chowder or Fulton Fish Market chowder before the Manhattan name stuck.

If they were to hold a popularity contest, white clam chowder would win hands down. But the red version still has its legions of fans. As long as you don't live in a red or white state, it's okay to like both.

Red Clam Chowder

4 slices bacon, cut into 1-in pieces

2 tbsp olive oil

4 cloves garlic, minced

1 cup chopped onion

1 cup chopped green bell pepper

4 cups diced potatoes

2 cups diced carrots

1½ cups diced celery

1 (10-oz) can sweet corn

1 (28-oz) can crushed tomatoes

2 tbsp tomato paste

2 (6-oz) bottles clam juice

1 cup white wine

4 cups water

½ tsp oregano

¼ tsp thyme

Freshly ground black pepper

2 tsp chopped fresh parsley

2 bay leaves

4 lb fresh clams

Brown the bacon in a large saucepan over medium heat. Add the olive oil and sauté the garlic and onion until golden brown. Add all remaining ingredients except the clams. Stir well, bring to a boil, and reduce to a simmer. Cook for 1 hour. Add the clams and cook for 15 minutes more before serving. *Serves 10*

Classic Green Salad

With its crisp, just-picked lettuces glistening with perfectly balanced vinaigrette, a simple green salad is one of life's great pleasures.

The secret to a classic green salad is choosing the right mix of lettuces, taking into account color, flavor, and texture. Ruffled leaf lettuces, while mild, give the salad bulk. Peppery arugula and watercress add spice, while baby spinach provides substance. Finally, chicories such as Belgian endive and radicchio assert their bitterness along with contrasting colors. Even a few sprigs of delicate herbs such as basil and dill are a fragrant addition to any green salad.

The dressing should be freshly made using only the finest ingredients. Extra-virgin olive oil, perhaps, sharpened with lemon juice and perfumed with garlic. Or walnut oil blended with sherry vinegar and Dijon mustard. The vinaigrette should be added judiciously, just enough to make the leaves sparkle.

Of course, the best way to enjoy green salads is to plant your own lettuce. Many varieties will re-sprout as you pick the leaves, allowing you to enjoy homegrown salads all summer long.

Classic Green Salad

2 tsp sherry vinegar

½ tsp Dijon mustard

1 small clove garlic, minced

¼ tsp coarse sea salt

Freshly ground black pepper

¼ cup extra-virgin olive oil

7 oz loosely packed mixed salad greens, torn in bite-size pieces

Put the vinegar, mustard, garlic, and salt and pepper to taste in a medium bowl and whisk until blended. Slowly add the olive oil, whisking constantly until thickened. Add the greens and toss well to coat with dressing. Serve immediately. *Serves 4*

Cobb Salad

Mystery shrouds the origins of many popular dishes, but not the Cobb salad. Invented by Robert H. Cobb in 1937, this all-American classic lives on today.

Cobb owned the Brown Derby restaurant in Los Angeles, California, a celebrity hangout during Hollywood's Golden Age in the thirties and forties. One night he decided to raid the huge walk-in fridge and fix himself a snack. Gathering lettuce, avocado, tomato, roast chicken, hard-boiled eggs, bacon, and blue cheese, he chopped up all the ingredients and doused them with vinaigrette. Sid Grauman, owner of the landmark Chinese Theater,

happened to be with Cobb on the fateful night and was so impressed with the creation that he requested a "Cobb salad" the next day. It was added to the menu and the rest is history.

There have since been endless variations, but an authentic Cobb salad contains four kinds of lettuce—iceberg, watercress, curly endive, and romaine. The ingredients are always cut into small pieces and lined up in rows on top of the lettuce with the dressing on the side. Crisp lettuce, juicy tomato, silky avocado, succulent chicken, and smoky bacon—this hearty meal-in-a-bowl is like a club sandwich without the bread.

Coconut and Cilantro Soup

Any dish made with coconut milk benefits from the citrusy flavor of fresh cilantro. This one-two punch is employed in an array of exotic soups.

Coconut and cilantro feature prominently in the cuisines of Southeast Asia. The coconut milk tempers boldly-spiced dishes and the cilantro gives a fresh, herbaceous kick at the end. The most famous coconut and cilantro soup from this region is Thailand's *tom kha gai*, a fragrant chicken soup perfumed with galangal, lemongrass, and kaffir lime leaf. The cilantro is added just before serving, as the heat will dissipate its flavor. Malaysia's famous curry *laksa* is a rich, fiery noodle soup that also takes advantage of this dynamic duo.

The most interesting soup using coconut and cilantro comes from the Bahia region of Brazil. *Vatapá* is an African-inspired seafood stew flavored with a paste of dried shrimp and peanuts.

Vegan cooks have also embraced this fragrant soup. Coconut milk adds creaminess without dairy, while the cilantro complements many spicy soups in the vegan repertoire.

Coconut and Cilantro Soup

3½ cups coconut milk

1 cup water

2 tbsp fresh galangal root, sliced

1 fresh lemongrass stem, cut into 1-in lengths

4 kaffir lime leaves, torn in half

2 fresh Thai chiles, halved

1 lb chicken, skinned, boned, and diced

1 tsp salt

3 tbsp fish sauce

1 tsp palm sugar

⅓ cup fresh lime juice

2 tbsp roughly chopped cilantro leaves

Pour the coconut milk and water into a saucepan and bring to a boil over medium heat. Reduce the heat, add the galangal, lemongrass, kaffir lime leaves, and chile halves. Cook for a few minutes longer, stirring occasionally. Now add the chicken, salt, fish sauce, sugar, and lime juice. Cook until the chicken is done. Serve sprinkled with cilantro leaves. *Serves 4*

SCOTLAND

Cock-a-Leekie Soup

Unlike such cryptically named Scottish dishes
as *rumbledethumps* (potatoes mashed with
cabbage) and *clootie* (steamed pudding),
there is no mystery behind what goes in cock-
a-leekie soup. Also known as "cocky-leeky,"
it's a simple soup of just chicken and leeks.

The recipe starts with a chicken, often an
old boiling fowl, simmered in water with fresh
herbs. The cooked meat is removed from the
bones and cut into bite-sized pieces. Leeks
are sliced and stewed in butter or chicken
fat until soft, before joining the chicken in its
broth. A little salt and pepper goes into the
pot and voilà, it's ready. Barley is sometimes
added to thicken the soup and give it body.
Prunes are a traditional, though optional,
garnish added near the end for sweetness.

This simple, yet satisfying union of tender
chicken and sweet leeks is often dispensed
as a panacea during winter. It is also an old
standby on Robbie Burns Night, served as a
first course before Scotland's most famous
dish, the much-maligned haggis.

FRANCE

Consommé

Crystal clear and deeply flavored with nary
a drop of fat, a perfectly made consommé
is a thing of beauty. It's no wonder this classic
French soup is considered to be a true test
of a chef's skill.

An exacting process, consommé starts
with a pot of homemade beef broth to
which ground beef, finely chopped *mirepoix*
(carrot, celery, and leek), and egg whites are
added. As the mixture slowly comes to a
boil, the solids clump together and float to
the top, forming a "raft." As it gently simmers,
the meat and vegetables flavor the soup
while any impurities cling to the egg whites.
When it is done, the raft is discarded and
the consommé is carefully strained through a
double layer of cheesecloth to ensure perfect
clarity. Lastly, the dark amber bouillon must
be assiduously skimmed of any traces of fat.

Consommé is usually served at the
beginning of a meal, and there are dozens
of optional additions, each with a special
name. *Consommé celestine* is garnished with
a julienne of herbed crêpes, while *consommé
brunoise* floats a tiny dice of carrot, turnip,
and celery cooked in butter.

Beef does not hold the monopoly on this
luxurious broth. Consommé now refers to
any strong, clear soup, whether it's made from
chicken, lobster, or even tomato.

Coleslaw

Cucumber and Yogurt Soup

What do fish and chips, barbecue, and fried chicken have in common? They all taste better with a side of coleslaw. It's no surprise, as the crunchy, refreshing cabbage plays the perfect foil to rich, heavy foods.

This quintessentially American salad is derived from the Dutch word *koolsla*, which means cabbage salad. In the US, the name is often shortened to just slaw. Coleslaw is usually little more than shaved or chopped cabbage with a bit of carrot. Depending on the dressing, it is split into two camps. Mayonnaise-based (creamy) coleslaw is the most popular, and is the slaw of choice at most supermarket deli counters and New England clam shacks. Tangy coleslaw made with a sharp vinaigrette reigns supreme at Jewish delicatessens and barbecue joints.

Outside the US, there are some interesting riffs on coleslaw. Salvadoran *curdito* is a spicy slaw made with pickled cabbage, while the Lebanese mix cabbage with olive oil, lemon juice, garlic, caraway seeds, and mint.

Coleslaw also pulls double duty as a condiment. In North Carolina, slaw adds welcome crunch to a pulled pork sandwich, and in Montreal, Canada, an all-dressed hot dog is always crowned with a tangle of slaw.

From the Balkans down to the Middle East and over to the Indian subcontinent, cucumber and yogurt soup is loved by one and all. Served ice cold, it does battle with gazpacho for favorite summer soup.

The most famous cucumber and yogurt soup is Bulgarian *tarator*. The star ingredients are puréed with water, garlic, and dill, with a few walnuts and some olive oil to balance the sharpness of the yogurt. Iran has a similar soup, though it is showered with fresh herbs and sweetened with plump raisins.

Turkish *cacik* is another renowned cucumber soup that is flavored with dried mint. Served in small bowls, with a drizzle of fine olive oil, *cacik* is the perfect accompaniment to grilled meats and rice pilaf.

In India, cucumber *raita* is most commonly served as a side salad to tame a spicy curry. Spiced with cumin and chili, *raita* can be thinned with water to become a tasty soup.

No matter where it is eaten, cucumber and yogurt soup is a warm-weather staple. The cool cucumber refreshes while the tangy yogurt stimulates the appetite. When the heat is unbearable, a few ice cubes in the bowl provide an invigorating garnish.

Crab and Corn Soup

There are a few Chinese dishes conceived in the West, and crab and corn soup is certainly one of them. In the United States, a land of swaying cornfields and bulging crab traps, this soup is an old favorite.

At a cheap and cheerful Chinese takeout joint, it means creamed corn from a can and imitation crab. At a more upscale Cantonese restaurant, crab and corn soup becomes something far more delicate.

Like all good Chinese soups, it starts with golden homemade chicken broth. Raw corn kernels are scraped from the cob and puréed in a food processor. This "creamed" corn thickens the soup and adds richness without dairy. Cooked crab is then shredded and added to the pot. Whole corn kernels may be added for crunch. Finally, egg whites become feathery strands as they are whisked into the simmering broth.

Juicy corn kernels play against silky crab in a smooth, velvety broth perfumed with a hint of ginger. It's the perfect start to a Chinese-American feast.

Quick Crab and Corn Soup

4½ oz crabmeat

½ tsp minced fresh gingerroot

2 egg whites

3 to 4 tbsp milk

1 tbsp cornstarch mixed with 1 tbsp water

2 cups good chicken broth

1 (8-oz) can creamed corn

Salt

Freshly ground black pepper

Finely chopped scallions to garnish

Flake the crabmeat and mix with the ginger. Beat the egg whites until frothy, then add the milk and cornstarch paste. Beat again until smooth. Blend in the crabmeat. Bring the broth to a rolling boil, add the creamed corn and return to a boil. Stir in the crab-and-egg-white mixture, adjust the seasoning, and stir gently until well blended. Serve hot, garnished with scallions. *Serves 4*

Cream of Celery Soup

While celery joins onion and carrot as a flavor base for many soups—the French call this trio *mirepoix*—it is rarely allowed to shine on its own. One exception is cream of celery soup.

Making cream of celery soup is quite simple. Onions and celery (along with its flavor-packed leaves) are first cooked in butter, then simmered in vegetable broth. The soup could be thickened with a roux, though potato does the same job without any added fat. Once the vegetables are soft, the soup is puréed in a blender, which helps break down the fibrous strings that run along the stalks. A generous dollop of cream helps temper celery's assertive herbal character.

In keeping with the theme, the soup could be garnished with a few deep-fried celery leaves, or even a seared scallop.

Cream of Mushroom Soup

Mushrooms and cream go together like peanut butter and jelly. When combined in a soup, the sweet, rich cream softens the meaty mushroom flavor.

These days, cream of mushroom soup has come to mean the condensed variety from a can, which in turn is used as a base for a host of recipes from meatloaf to tuna casserole.

True cream of mushroom soup has its roots in classical French cooking. It was traditionally made with a *velouté*, light chicken broth thickened with a flour-butter roux. The soup was further enriched by a liaison of egg yolks and cream.

Today, chefs take a much lighter approach to mushroom soup, eschewing the heavy *velouté* in favor of a simple purée finished with a touch of cream.

Mushrooms also have an affinity for grape-based libations. A last-minute splash of sherry, madeira, or brandy gives the soup character while playing off the mushrooms' earthy flavor.

A final garnish of snipped chives and a few choice mushrooms sautéed in butter make this soup an elegant start to any meal.

Cream of Tomato Soup

Whether it's clear consommé or chunky gazpacho, tomatoes are generally associated with the chilled soups of summer. But come fall, with the evenings cooling off and plenty of fruit still hanging from the vines, tomatoes shine in a soothing cream soup.

To ensure a smooth texture, the tomatoes must be liberated from their tough skins and seeds. Dropped into boiling water for 20 seconds (or peeled with a serrated peeler), the skins slip off easily. Cut in half, the seeds can be squeezed into a fine mesh strainer over a bowl to catch the tasty juices.

Cream of tomato soup should be simple; some onion cooked gently in butter, a bit of carrot to boost the color, and a light vegetable broth as the base. Cream should be added with a restrained hand, just enough to soften the tomato's acid, but not enough to make it cloyingly rich. Basil is a natural garnish, especially in the form of summer pesto from the freezer.

Ladled into bowls and served with a grilled cheese sandwich, this maternal lunch is American comfort food at its best.

Cream of Tomato Soup

3 tbsp unsalted butter

1 tbsp extra-virgin olive oil

1 medium onion, chopped

1 medium carrot, chopped

1 stalk celery, chopped

2 cloves garlic, chopped

4 lb vine-ripened tomatoes, seeded and chopped

¼ cup all-purpose flour

1 cup chicken or vegetable broth

4 stalks fresh parsley

2 sprigs fresh thyme

2 bay leaves

1 tbsp sugar

2 cups heavy cream or milk

Salt

Freshly ground black pepper

Heat the butter and the olive oil in a large pot on medium heat. Sauté the onion, carrot, celery, and garlic for 5 minutes, stirring occasionally. Add the tomatoes and simmer for another 5 minutes. Stir in the flour and cook for another 5 minutes.

Slowly add the broth along with the parsley, thyme, bay leaves, and sugar. Bring to a boil and simmer, uncovered, for 30 to 40 minutes, until vegetables are tender.

Remove the bay leaf and thyme, and pass the soup through a food mill or rub through a fine mesh sieve, pressing down on solids with the back of a spoon.

Return the soup to the pot and reheat gently with the cream or milk. Season to taste and serve. *Serves 4*

Cullen Skink

Cullen skink is a prime example of the Scottish penchant for bestowing strange monikers on their native dishes. Hailing from the town of Cullen on the northeast coast of Scotland, this hearty fish chowder gets its name from the Gallic word for "essence."

Like most traditional Scottish cooking, Cullen skink is simple, rib-sticking fare made from a handful of ingredients. It starts with a smoked haddock, known locally as finnan haddie. The fish is gently poached in milk with onions, then flaked. The bones may go back into the pot for simmering to make the base of the soup. The strained broth is then thickened with mashed potato, a delicious way for a cook to use up last night's leftovers. Once the desired consistency has been reached, the fish is returned to the pot along with a touch of cream.

In the bowl, a pat of butter may be floated on top with a pinch of chopped parsley for color. The sweetness of the milk balances the smoke, while the delicate flakes of haddock give texture to the smooth, creamy soup. With the North Sea winds rattling the windows, there is comfort in a bowl of Cullen skink.

Cullen Skink

2 medium onions
2 cloves
4 cups whole milk
1 bay leaf
⅓ cup Finnan smoked haddock

4 tbsp butter

¾ lb potatoes, cut into ½-in dice

⅓ cup heavy cream

Salt and freshly ground black pepper

2 tbsp roughly chopped fresh parsley

Peel one of the onions, cut in half, and stud each half with one of the cloves. Put into a pan with the milk and bay leaf, bring just to a boil, and simmer for 5 minutes. Add the fish and simmer for 4 to 5 minutes or until just firm and opaque.

Transfer the fish to a plate and strain the liquid through a fine sieve into a bowl. When the fish is cool enough to handle, remove and discard the skin and bones. Flake the fish into large pieces and set aside.

Peel and finely chop the remaining onion. Melt the butter in a large pan, add the onion, and cook over gentle heat for 5 minutes, until softened but not browned. Add the reserved milk and diced potatoes. Bring to a boil, then simmer gently for 10 minutes, until the potatoes are cooked but still just firm.

Blend half the soup in a blender until smooth. Return to the pan with the cream and flaked haddock. Season with a little salt and pepper and warm through for 1 to 2 minutes. Serve in a warmed soup tureen, sprinkled with the chopped parsley. *Serves 4*
Adapted from Rick Stein's *Fruits of the Sea*

Cucumber Raita

No connoisseur of Indian cuisine would think of eating a fiery curry without a side of cucumber raita. This refreshing salad of cucumber and yogurt plays the perfect foil to India's many boldly-spiced dishes.

A good raita starts with rich, full-fat yogurt. The cucumbers are usually peeled, but the skin can be left on for a more verdant result. They are thinly sliced or grated and added to the yogurt with fresh cilantro or mint. When served with extra spicy dishes, raita is generally left plain. But some cooks like to zip it up with cayenne pepper and garam masala, a fragrant spice blend that includes cumin, cloves, and cinnamon.

Like the Greek tzatziki, raita can double as a dip for grilled meats and flatbreads. A thin, smooth raita becomes a tasty chilled soup in summer.

Of course cucumber does not have the monopoly on raitas. Other versions of this creamy salad include eggplant, tomato, and a sweet one made with banana and cardamom. Whether it's a salad, soup, condiment or dip, cucumber raita is always a welcome addition to an Indian feast.

Duck Soup

Despite playing second fiddle to chicken, duck offers a range of tasty soups.

In Chinese cuisine, duck soup is a delicious way for a thrifty cook to use up the leftover carcass from a barbecued Peking duck. The bones of the lacquered bird impart a smoky-sweetness to the broth, and all that's needed is a handful of noodles and some sliced napa cabbage. For an important guest, a few elegant slices of barbecued duck breast could be floated on top along with a few enoki mushrooms.

Duck plays an important supporting role in *garbure*, the hearty cabbage and bean soup from southwest France. Duck confit is popular in this region, and the less attractive pieces are chopped up and added to this substantial soup. Even the salty gelatin at the bottom of the confit pot contributes a blast of duck flavor.

One of the most interesting duck soups comes from Poland. *Czarnina* is a sweet-and-sour duck soup brimming with dried fruit and scented with allspice and cloves. A traditional Easter dish, it is served with either egg noodles or potato dumplings. The secret ingredient in *czarnina* is duck's blood, which thickens the soup. Not for the faint of heart!

Duck and Kale Soup

1 tbsp olive oil

½ medium onion, diced

1 clove garlic, diced

1 medium bunch kale

1¾ cups chicken broth

½ duck breast, cooked and sliced

⅓ cup heavy cream

Salt

Freshly ground black pepper

1 oz brie cheese

Heat the oil in a pan and sauté the onion and garlic for 2 to 3 minutes. Stir in the kale and heat for a further 2 minutes. Pour in the broth and add the duck and cream. Bring to a boil, then reduce the heat and simmer gently for 10 to 12 minutes.

Transfer to a blender or use a hand-held blender and purée until smooth. Return to the heat and season with salt and pepper. Stir in the cheese over gentle heat until melted. *Serves 1*

Assam Laksa

Malaysia's culinary claim to fame is a spicy noodle soup called *laksa*. Most versions are enriched with coconut milk, but on the northern island of Penang, *laksa* is based on a heady fish broth flavored with the tart pulp of tamarind fruit. Since *assam* is the Malay word for tamarind, this rendition is called assam laksa.

Making this popular soup is a labor-intensive process that starts with poaching whole fish, usually mackerel, then flaking the cooked flesh. The simmering broth is given a flavor boost from a pungent paste of garlic, shallots, lemongrass, galangal, and chiles. Tamarind gives it a sour kick, while sugar softens the edges. The rich, aromatic soup is poured over a bowl of slippery rice noodles and topped with the cooked fish. A kaleidoscope of garnishes includes pineapple, cucumber, red onion, mint, and sliced ginger flower buds, which add sweetness, heat, and crunch. Some people up the ante with *haeko*, a sweet, molasses-like condiment made from shrimp.

In Georgetown, Penang's capital, *laksa* fans flock to the epicurean boardwalk along Gurney Drive, where each vendor offers his own unique spin on the popular dish. Eaten for lunch or dinner, assam laksa is a fireworks of tastes and textures in a bowl.

Beer Soup

Best known as a thirst-quenching libation, beer is also the star ingredient in an eponymous soup. In fact, in the days before coffee and tea, many Europeans started their day with a steaming bowl of beer soup.

In Germany, *Biersuppe* is spiced beer thickened with a roux (flour and butter) and enriched with egg yolks and cream. This soup bears some resemblance to eggnog, which in turn evolved from a hot drink called *posset*, made from spiced milk and ale.

In Alsace, France, *soupe à la bière* is a savory purée of chicken broth, onions, bread, and the local brew with a pinch of nutmeg. Beer soup is also a legendary hangover cure in Denmark, where it is made from dark ale, pumpernickel, lemon, sugar, and cream.

Beer plays a supporting role in many other soups. Since it pairs nicely with sharp cheeses, beer is the liquid of choice in a hearty potato and Cheddar soup. The bitterness of a pale ale helps balance the onion's sweetness in French onion soup. And Belgium's beloved beer joins its favorite mollusk in mussel soup.

Of course, some say beer soup always goes best with a cold glass of the same brew that went in the pot.

Ajo Blanco

Ajo blanco, which means "white garlic," is the famous chilled soup from Malaga in southern Spain. Also known as white gazpacho, it predates the popular tomato-based version by hundreds of years.

The first ajo blanco dates back to pre-Roman times, when it was made by pounding bread, garlic, water, olive oil, vinegar, and salt in a mortar. The Moors, who ruled Andalusia from the 8th to the 13th centuries, introduced almonds to Spain, which were then incorporated into the soup. The rich nuts transformed it into a creamy, white emulsion that earned the dish its name.

Today, ajo blanco is whizzed in a blender, achieving a silky, smooth texture unattainable with a mortar and pestle. It is traditionally garnished with peeled green grapes or thinly sliced apple, though modern chefs love to jazz up the stark white soup with colorful flourishes such as edible flowers and infused oils.

Ajo blanco is best appreciated during the dog days of summer. The almonds provide sustenance, the vinegar stimulates the appetite, and the cold soup offers welcome relief from the dry heat.

Ajo Blanco

2 cups day-old bread, crusts removed

1 cup blanched almonds

3 cloves garlic

½ cup extra-virgin olive oil

¼ cup sherry vinegar

2 tsp salt

2-2½ cups water

12 green grapes, halved and seeded

Put the bread in a bowl and add water to cover. Let soak for 5 minutes, until softened. Squeeze out the water from the bread and set aside.

Meanwhile, put the almonds and garlic in a blender or food processor and pulse until finely ground. Add the bread and blend to a smooth paste. With the motor running, slowly add the oil followed by the vinegar and salt. If the mixture is too thick, thin with ½ cup water.

Transfer the mixture to a pitcher and add 2 cups water. Season to taste, adding more salt or vinegar if necessary to make the soup tangy. Chill. Stir before serving and garnish with the halved grapes. *Serves 4*

Fennel, Watercress, and Orange Salad

The licorice flavor of fennel combined with sweet orange is a match made in heaven. In Italy, this dynamic duo is featured in a favorite winter salad.

Fennel and orange salad is usually made from just that: shaved, raw fennel and peeled, sliced oranges. All that's needed is a drizzle of extra-virgin olive oil, a sprinkling of sea salt, and a few grinds of the pepper mill. To balance the sweetness of the fruit and add color to the plate, the salad can be augmented with a number of garnishes. Thinly sliced red onion gives it piquancy, arugula adds peppery notes, and radicchio lends its bitterness along with a splash of crimson. In Sicily, an island dotted with olive and orange groves, briny black olives are often sprinkled on top. Finally, the feathery fennel fronds can be used like an herb, adding another layer of anise flavor. Of course when blood oranges are in season, they turn this salad into a Mediterranean sunset.

Fennel and orange salad is a delicious first course, especially when paired with skewers of grilled shrimp. It can also be savored at the end of a meal as a palate cleanser. The crunchy fennel and juicy oranges are the perfect antidote to winter's rich, heavy foods.

Fennel, Watercress, and Orange Salad

1 large fennel bulb

2 bunches watercress

1 large juicy orange

¼ cup thick natural yogurt

Salt

Freshly ground black pepper to taste

Olive oil

Slice the fennel bulb in half, then into thin slices; they need not be paper thin. Rinse in cold running water, then shake dry. Rinse the watercress under the cold water tap, then cut off roots and the toughest stalks. Put in a bowl with the fennel. Peel the orange, then cut in half from stalk to navel. Slice the orange halves crosswise to give semi-circles of orange flesh. Add to the fennel. Mix the yogurt with salt, black pepper, and a little olive oil, about 1 tablespoon, whisking with a fork. Tip it over the salad and toss gently. Serve soon, before the watercress goes limp. *Serves 2*
Adapted from Nigel Slater's *Real Cooking*

Soupe à l'Oignon

Of all the comforting dishes to come out of a bistro kitchen, there are few more satisfying than French onion soup. The readied spoon quivers with anticipation as it arrives at the table, puffs of fragrant steam escaping through the molten roof of cheese.

The secret to good French onion soup lies in the onions. First they must be sliced thinly, then cooked gently in butter for hours, until the sugars caramelize and the mixture turns a deep mahogany brown. A rich broth made from roasted beef bones provides the base of the soup along with wine, cognac, or beer. Seasonings rarely go beyond salt, pepper, and thyme, plus a few drops of vinegar to balance the onions' sweetness.

Once the soup has been ladled into heatproof bowls, a toasted bread round is floated on top to support the cheese, usually Gruyère or Emmenthaler. It is popped under a hot broiler until the cheese is bubbling and golden brown.

The gooey cheese yields to soft, luscious bread with soothing onion-packed broth. It's like a soup and a sandwich rolled into one!

Soupe à l'Oignon

¼ cup butter

1 tsp sugar

3 medium onions, thinly sliced

1 tbsp all-purpose flour

5 cups beef broth

½ cup red wine

4 baguette slices, cut 1-in thick

8 oz Swiss cheese, thinly sliced

Melt the butter in a large saucepan on medium heat. Stir in the sugar. Cook the onions for 10 to 15 minutes, or until golden brown. Stir in the flour until well blended. Add the broth and wine; bring to a boil. Reduce heat to low, cover and simmer for 10 minutes, until the onions are tender.

Meanwhile, preheat the oven to 325°F and toast the bread slices until just browned, about 10 minutes. Raise the heat to 425°F.

Arrange four 12-oz ovenproof bowls on a baking sheet. Ladle the soup into the bowls and top each with 1 slice of toasted bread. Top the bread with cheese slices, folded to fit.

Bake for 10 minutes, or just until the cheese melts. *Serves 4*

Garlic Soup

As curative soups go, chicken will always be number one. But running a close second is garlic soup. Light, yet flavorful, with an egg added for substance, garlic soup is the perfect medicine for anyone feeling frail.

The two most popular garlic soups come from the western Mediterranean. *Aïgo buido* means "boiled water" in the Provençal dialect. As the name promises, this simple garlic soup is made by boiling smashed garlic cloves in water with a bay leaf and sage. The broth is poured over toasted stale bread and garnished with chopped herbs, olive oil, and freshly ground pepper. *Aïgo buido* can also be enriched with egg yolks and Parmesan cheese.

Spain's *sopa de ajo* is similar in spirit to the French garlic soup with a few Iberian twists. In the Spanish version, the garlic cloves are browned in olive oil, paprika lends its reddish-orange hue, and a poached egg is perched on top of the toasted bread.

Garlic Soup

5 cups water

10 cloves garlic

1 bay leaf

2 sprigs fresh thyme

5 egg yolks

3 tbsp freshly grated Parmesan

3 tbsp extra-virgin olive oil

1/4 loaf country-style bread, torn in pieces

In a saucepan bring the water, garlic, bay leaf, and thyme to a boil. Cover and simmer for 45 minutes. Discard the bay leaf and thyme sprigs, and force the mixture through a sieve or food mill into another saucepan. In a large bowl whisk together the yolks, Parmesan, and 2 tablespoons of the oil until well combined. Add 1/2 cup of the hot garlic broth to the yolk mixture in a slow stream, whisking, then whisk the yolk mixture into the remaining hot garlic broth. Cook the soup over moderately low heat, whisking constantly, until slightly thickened and a thermometer registers 170°F, about 10 minutes. Do not boil.

Divide the bread among 4 soup bowls. Ladle the broth over the bread and garnish with the remaining 1 tablespoon of oil. *Serves 4*

Gazpacho

Gumbo ▷

Gazpacho is Spain's greatest gift to the culinary world. As soon as summer arrives, various renditions of this chilled Andalusian soup make their way onto menus across the globe.

The history of gazpacho goes back millennia. Shepherds in pre-Roman times made the first version from bread, garlic, olive oil, vinegar, and water. When tomatoes and peppers were brought back from the New World in the 15th century, Andalusian farmers eventually incorporated them into the soup. This new vegetable-based gazpacho provided a light, yet fortifying meal while working the hot fields.

Modern gazpacho is made by puréeing tomatoes, cucumbers, and peppers in a blender or food processor. Garlic lends its trademark bite, olive oil adds richness, and sherry vinegar gives it a refreshing edge. Stale bread is a traditional thickener, turning the soup a beautiful coral pink, but it is rarely used outside Spain. Gazpacho can be served with croutons and diced vegetables, or straight up in a tall glass with a straw.

Salmorejo, the hearty gazpacho from Cordoba, is much thicker and can double as a dip for raw vegetables. Served in an earthenware cazuela, *salmorejo* is garnished with sliced hard-boiled eggs and diced *jamón*, cured Spanish ham.

In Louisiana, nothing says party like a big pot of gumbo. Brimming with seafood, meat, and vegetables, fragrant with Creole spices, gumbo is a Mardi Gras celebration in a bowl.

There are as many versions of gumbo as there are cooks who make it. The only agreement seems to be the inclusion of okra, as gumbo is derived from an African word for this gelatinous green vegetable.

Classic gumbo starts with a roux, a mixture of flour and butter that is cooked slowly until it turns mahogany brown. This dark roux will both thicken the stew and impart a rich, nutty flavor. Gumbo's character comes from onion, celery, sweet peppers, tomatoes, garlic, and Cajun spices. The main ingredients depend on the cook. Chicken, duck, quail, andouille sausage, shrimp, oysters, and crayfish are all welcome additions to the pot. Once the gumbo is cooked, a light sprinkling of *filé* powder (ground sassafras leaves) helps thicken the stew while imparting a woodsy flavor. To serve, the gumbo is ladled over a bowl of steaming hot white rice.

Vegetarians needn't feel left out—meatless *gumbo z'herbes*, made with hearty greens, was once a popular Lenten dish. But no matter what goes into the pot, there is only one important gumbo rule: always make enough to feed a crowd.

Greek Salad

Left in the wrong hands, a Greek salad has come to mean a soggy pile of iceberg lettuce showered with cheap feta and garnished with a wedge of unripe tomato. To a connoisseur, this salad has no business calling itself Greek.

An authentic Greek salad—known as *horiatiki*, or the "village salad"—has very little in common with its various impostors. First of all, there is no lettuce in a real Greek salad. It starts with chunks of ripe tomato, cool cucumber, sweet bell pepper, and sharp red onion. The veggies are dressed with little more than extra-virgin olive oil and dried oregano, though some cooks like the acidic kick of fruity wine vinegar. Tangy sheep's-

milk feta is crumbled overtop with a handful of plump Kalamata olives. The salty cheese and briny olives play the foil to the juicy, raw vegetables.

In addition to being a refreshing summer treat, this colorful salad is a feast for the eyes. Serve with warm pita or crusty bread to mop up the lovely juices pooled at the bottom of the bowl. Once you've tasted an authentic Greek salad, there's no going back.

Greek Salad

2 cups seeded and diced tomatoes

2 cups peeled, seeded, and diced cucumber

1 cup diced red bell pepper

¼ cup pitted Kalamata or other brine-cured black olives, halved

¼ cup diced red onion

3 tbsp chopped fresh Italian parsley

3 tbsp extra-virgin olive oil

1½ tbsp red wine vinegar

½ tsp dried oregano

¼ cup crumbled feta cheese

Salt

Freshly ground black pepper

In a medium bowl, toss all the ingredients except the cheese to blend. Gently mix in the cheese; season to taste. Greek salad can be made 2 hours ahead; let sit at room temperature before serving. *Serves 4*

Harira

This hearty soup of meat, beans, and vegetables is Morocco's favorite meal in a bowl. Fragrant with saffron, ginger, turmeric, and cinnamon, harira showcases the deft spicing that is the hallmark of North African cuisine.

While no two recipes are the same, harira follows a basic formula. Meat, usually lamb or chicken, is simmered in water with onion, tomatoes, garbanzos, lentils, and spices. Once the meat and pulses are tender, rice or broken vermicelli noodles are added to the pot. An herbaceous mound of chopped parsley and cilantro goes in, along with flour to thicken. To further enrich the soup, some cooks swirl in a beaten egg just before serving. A last-minute squeeze of lemon gives the soup a slight sour edge while brightening the flavors. Spice fans can jack up their harira with harissa, a garlicky hot sauce.

Harira is commonly eaten during the Muslim holy month of Ramadan. Observant Moroccans, who do not eat from sunup to sundown, will break the fast each evening with a steaming bowl of harira—or as they like to call it—Ramadan soup.

Harira

1 lb lamb shoulder, cut in small cubes

1 tsp turmeric

1 tsp freshly ground black pepper

1 tsp cinnamon

¼ tsp dried ginger

2 tbsp butter

¾ cup chopped celery with leaves

2 medium onions, chopped

½ cup each chopped fresh parsley and cilantro

2 (8-oz) cans tomatoes, juice reserved

Salt

¾ cup lentils

1 cup cooked garbanzo beans

¼ cup vermicelli noodles

2 eggs, beaten with 1 tbsp lemon juice

Put the lamb, spices, butter, celery, onion, and herbs in a large stockpot and stir over low heat for 5 minutes. Add the tomatoes and continue cooking for 10 to 15 minutes, breaking them up with the back of a spoon. Add a little salt.

Add the reserved tomato juice with the lentils and 7 cups of water. Bring to a boil, reduce the heat, and simmer, partly covered, for two hours.

At serving time, add the garbanzos and the noodles, and simmer for 5 minutes. With a wooden spoon, stir the lemony eggs into the stock. Stir slowly and continuously until the eggs create long strands and thicken the soup. Season to taste and ladle into bowls. If desired, serve extra lemon juice at the table.

Serves 8

Hot-and-Sour Soup

While many Asian cuisines boast of a hot-and-sour soup, China's is the most renowned. Hailing from the western province of Szechuan—whose cuisine is synonymous with spicy—hot-and-sour soup has become a staple in Chinese restaurants around the world.

The soup starts with chicken broth, though meatless versions will use vegetable broth. A cornucopia of ingredients is employed, providing the soup with an impressive range of tastes and textures. Dried Chinese and tree ear mushrooms lend their earthy flavor; slivers of pork, cubed tofu, and slippery glass noodles give the soup substance; and bamboo shoots add some crunch. The "hot" comes from a generous grinding of pepper, while rice vinegar provides the "sour" component. Additional seasonings include soy sauce, scallions, and ginger. Finally, a beaten egg is transformed into delicate threads by the hot broth, while cornstarch acts as a thickener, giving the piquant soup its trademark gloss.

Once it has been ladled into bowls, fire-eaters will turn up the heat with a crimson drizzle of chili oil. Spicy, nourishing, and packed with flavor, it's no wonder this invigorating soup is used to fight colds.

Hot-and-Sour Soup

4 oz lean boneless pork, finely shredded

For the marinade:

1 tsp light soy sauce

1 tsp Shaoxing rice wine or dry sherry

½ tsp sesame oil

½ tsp cornstarch

A pinch of salt

A pinch of sugar

1 oz dried Chinese shiitake mushrooms

½ oz dried "tree ear" mushrooms

2 eggs, beaten with a pinch of salt

2 tsp sesame oil

For the soup:

5 cups chicken broth

2 tsp salt

9 oz fresh bean curd, drained and shredded

1½ tbsp light soy sauce

1 tbsp dark soy sauce

1 tsp freshly ground white pepper

6 tbsp Chinese white rice vinegar or cider vinegar

2 tsp sesame oil

1 tbsp chili oil

2 tbsp finely chopped fresh cilantro

Combine the pork with the soy sauce, Shaoxing rice wine or dry sherry, sesame oil, cornstarch, salt, and sugar. Mix well and set aside. Soak the mushrooms in warm water for 20 minutes. Drain and squeeze out any excess liquid. Discard the stems and finely shred the caps. In a small bowl, combine the eggs and salt with the sesame oil and set aside.

Bring the broth to a simmer in a large pan and add the salt. Stir in the pork and simmer for 1 minute. Then add the mushrooms and bean curd and continue to simmer for 2 minutes. Add the egg mixture in a very slow, thin stream. Using a chopstick or fork, pull the egg slowly into strands. Remove the soup from the heat and stir in the soy sauces, pepper, and vinegar.

Give the soup a good stir, then finally stir in the sesame oil, chili oil and fresh cilantro. Ladle into a large soup tureen or individual bowls and serve. *Serves 4*
Adapted from Ken Hom's *Illustrated Chinese Cookery*

Kartoffelsalat

German potato salad is a far cry from the mayo-bound American version. For one thing it includes bacon, and for another it's served warm.

The potatoes must be waxy, which hold their shape better than floury varieties. They are boiled in salted water with the skins left on to keep the insides firm and dry. While the potatoes are cooking, diced bacon and onions are browned in a pan and then seasoned with oil, vinegar, and mustard seeds. The cooked potatoes are drained, peeled, and cut into chunks. Tossed with the hot bacon dressing along with scallions and parsley, the salad is ready to eat.

This tangy salad is the ideal accompaniment to rich Bratwurst or any of the other delectable sausages found hanging in German butcher shops. With a frothy stein of beer, it's the perfect Oktoberfest lunch. Kartoffelsalat is also traditionally served at lunch on Christmas Eve with Bockwurst, a white sausage made of veal and pork.

While Kartoffelsalat is meant to be served warm, leftovers taste just as good cold the next day.

Hochzeitssuppe

Warm Liver Salad

In Germany, the traditional first course at a wedding is a bowl of Hochzeitssuppe. A rich beef broth with a flotilla of intricate garnishes, this "wedding soup" is a symbol of wealth for the bride and groom.

The broth is made from simmering beef bones and root vegetables in water. To show off the elegant garnishes, the amber soup is carefully strained and skimmed to ensure perfect clarity. What goes into today's Hochzeitssuppe often depends on where it is made. A simple version might include a few tiny meatballs and some flour dumplings.

A more luxurious "wedding soup" comes from the Swabe region, where it is a proud specialty. There could be buttery diamond-shaped biscuits, rich dumplings made from liver or bone marrow, or delicate ribbons of crêpe. The most decadent garnish is Maultaschen, a German spin on ravioli stuffed with spinach and meat—also called Swabian pockets. A pinch of minced chives adds a final splash of color before the soup joins the matrimonial celebration.

When it comes to cooking chickens, French chefs use everything but the cluck. The necks and feet go into the stockpot; hearts and gizzards are preserved in duck fat; and the livers can be used to make pâtés, terrines, and an old bistro favorite, hot duck or chicken liver salad.

The green part of this salad should be a sturdy lettuce that can handle a bit of wilting under the hot livers. Spinach, arugula, and escarole, or a combination of all three, would work well.

The livers should be very fresh and from a healthy free-range bird that spent a happy life roaming around a farm. Once seasoned, the livers are seared in sizzling butter until crusty on the outside and pink and juicy on the inside, then transferred to the waiting greens. A red wine vinaigrette is then swirled into the hot pan, deglazing the tasty brown bits. The warm dressing is poured over the salad et voilà, lunch is ready! All that's missing is a glass of Beaujolais and a warm baguette.

With its soft, gamey livers contrasting with the crisp greens, some believe this salad celebrates the best part of the chicken.

Kimchi

Kimchi refers to a group of pickled vegetables that is an essential part of every Korean meal. It is most commonly made with napa cabbage, though daikon radish and cucumber are also used.

The history of kimchi goes back thousands of years, but it didn't earn its trademark color and bite until the 1600s, when traders from the New World introduced fiery red chile peppers to Korea.

Basic kimchi is made by layering leaves of salted napa cabbage between leeks, garlic, ginger, chiles, and salted fish. The cabbage is bundled together, packed into a large earthenware jar, and covered with brine. As it ferments, the lactic acid produced imparts a unique sour flavor to the pickle, similar to German Sauerkraut.

Kimchi is most commonly eaten as a side dish, though it can be used to spice up a pork stew called *kimchi jigae*. Hot, crunchy, and beyond piquant, kimchi has gained an international reputation and has become synonymous with Korean cuisine.

Kimchi

10 cups water

2 cups coarse sea salt

2 heads napa cabbage, trimmed and cut in half lengthwise

1 cup red chili powder

⅓ cup reconstituted dried shrimp, chopped; reserve juice

1 daikon radish

10 cloves garlic, chopped

1 large scallion, cut in ¾-in lengths

3 thin scallions, cut in ¾-in lengths

2-in piece gingerroot, chopped

3 fresh shelled oysters

⅓ bunch watercress

¼ bunch Indian mustard leaf, cut in ¾-in lengths

¼ cup salt

Make a brine with the water and 1 cup of the coarse sea salt and soak the cabbage in it for 3 to 4 hours. Drain, sprinkle with some of the remaining salt, and let sit. When the cabbages are well salted and a bit limp, rinse thoroughly in cold water and drain. Meanwhile, mix the red chili powder well with the ¼ cup shrimp juice. Cut one-third of the radish into thin strips, then stir into the chili mixture until the reddish color is set. Add the chopped shrimp, garlic, scallions, ginger, oysters, watercress, and mustard leaf. Mix well and season with salt. Cut the remaining radish into large pieces and mix it with the seasoned mixture. Pack this mixture between each leaf of the wilted cabbage. Place the stuffed cabbages and radish pieces in a large crock and cover with cabbage leaves. Weigh it down with a clean, heavy stone and let it sit for several days to ripen. *Makes 16 cups*

Cioppino

Stroll along Fisherman's Wharf in San Francisco and you will undoubtedly be treated to the aroma of boiling crabs, fresh-baked sourdough bread, and the city's beloved seafood stew.

Cioppino was first made by Italian-immigrant fishermen, who used the maritime soups of their homeland as a blueprint. The name is derived from *ciuppin*, the Ligurian word for seafood soup. Before it became the luxurious dish it is today, cioppino was a rustic soup consisting of a coarse vegetable purée cooked with whatever the fisherman hadn't sold that day.

Today, cioppino is more on par with French bouillabaisse, using only the choicest catch of the day. Clams, mussels, shrimp, crab, fish, and squid are cooked in a hearty white wine and tomato broth perfumed with garlic and fennel. Like many Italian peasant soups, it is poured over a thick slice of toasted bread—sourdough, of course—which soaks up the rich soup. In an authentic cioppino, the shells and bones are left on, which makes for a more flavorful broth, not to mention a visceral dining experience. In fancier restaurants, the shells and bones are removed in the kitchen, earning it the nickname "lazy man's cioppino."

Lentil Soup

When it comes to soup, lentils have one advantage over all other legumes: they don't need to be soaked. Forget advanced planning— a quick raid of the pantry and lentil soup can be ready in under an hour. Packed with earthy flavor, not to mention a rich source of protein, the humble lentil is a favorite soup ingredient around the world.

Lentil soups are especially popular in the Muslim world, where they are eaten to break the daily fast at sunset during the holy month of Ramadan. In Turkey, black lentils are cooked with wheat berries in *alaca çorba*, a hearty soup perfumed with the anise flavor of dried tarragon.

Red lentils often find their way into the soup pot. Since their seed coats have been removed, they dissolve into a thick purée. In Lebanon, red lentils combine with rice for *makhlouta*, a rustic soup spiced with cumin and coriander and served with wedges of toasted pita bread.

When the *soupe du jour* at a French bistro is lentil, the bowl will be brimming with leeks, carrots, bacon, smoked sausage, and the prized green Puy lentils. A pinch of cloves highlights this enduring marriage of pork and beans.

Lobster Bisque

Thick with cream, perfumed with cognac, and tasting like the very essence of the sea, lobster bisque is the definition of decadence.

The term bisque was originally used to describe soups made from game birds. It now almost always refers to a luxurious pink purée of shellfish—shrimp, crab, crayfish, or lobster.

Lobster bisque can only be found on menus at fancy restaurants, as it is both costly and labor-intensive. First, live lobsters are cooked in wine, broth, and water. The meat is removed and the shells are returned to the pot to make the base for the soup. Aromatic vegetables are cooked in butter, then combined with the lobster broth and rice, which thickens the soup. Tomatoes, paprika, and cayenne boost the color and give it some zip. The reserved lobster meat is added at the last minute, and the soup is puréed and finished with cream and cognac.

As for garnishes, a soup of this pedigree doesn't need much gussying up. Chunks of sweet lobster meat and a few wispy tarragon leaves complete the long journey from ocean floor to silver spoon.

EASTERN EUROPE

Matzo Ball Soup

When it comes to Jewish comfort foods, matzo ball soup is number one. Whether it's to cure all that ails or celebrate Passover, matzo ball soup holds a special place in every Jewish heart.

Essentially just broth and dumplings, this soup can only shine if both components are made with love. The chicken broth must be homemade, a slow simmer of chicken bones, onions, carrots, celery, and herbs in water. Jewish grandmothers from the old school use chicken feet, which add unparalleled flavor and gelatin. The soup is usually made a day in advance so the hardened fat can be easily removed from the chilled broth.

This rendered fat—called schmaltz—is then used to make the matzo balls. For a texture lighter than clouds, the eggs must be separated with the whites beaten to soft peaks. The fat is melted, mixed with the yolks, and the matzo meal (ground matzo) and foamy whites are folded in. Formed into balls, the dumplings are boiled in water until tender.

At dinnertime, the broth and matzo balls are brought to a simmer and seasoned aggressively with salt. The homey aroma of chicken soup wafts into the dining room as guests clutch their spoons, giddy with anticipation.

UNITED STATES

Maryland Crab Soup ▷

Chesapeake Bay is famous for its sweet blue crabs. In the state of Maryland, these succulent crustaceans usually find their way into one of two dishes: plump crab cakes or spicy Maryland crab soup.

While a few chefs might add their signature to Maryland crab soup, it follows a basic formula. More than anything, it is a chunky vegetable soup packed with onions, carrots, celery, potatoes, green beans, corn, peas, and lima beans. The broth is often water-based and flavored with canned tomatoes, Worcestershire sauce, and Old Bay Seasoning, an all-American spice mix that includes celery salt, mustard powder, bay leaves, and paprika.

The crabs can be cooked right in the soup, then removed and picked. But since blue crabs are quite small, this arduous process is often bypassed in favor of using picked lump crabmeat. Of course, this soup is a great way to use up leftovers from a Maryland crab feast. The crabmeat always goes in right at the end to preserve its silky texture.

This dish could easily be made with Dungeness crabs from the west coast. Just don't call it Maryland crab soup!

Migas

Migas—which translates as crumbs—is essentially a salad of fried croutons. One of Spain's oldest peasant dishes, it was conceived by shepherds who cooked chunks of stale bread in rendered sheep fat for their morning meal.

Migas is still popular all over Spain, loved by rich and poor. Like all national dishes, it varies from region to region, but it always contains one important ingredient—stale bread, preferably four days old. The bread is cut into cubes and moistened with salted water before being fried in olive oil or lard until brown and crisp.

In pork-loving Extremadura, migas is flavored with garlic, hot paprika, and salty bits of cured ham—a delightful tapa washed down with cold *cerveza*. In Aragon, migas is a hearty affair mixed with smoky chorizo sausage and topped with fried eggs and grapes.

For the sweet tooth, *migas canas* is made from bread moistened with milk and deep-fried before being dusted with cinnamon sugar. Not to be outdone, *migas negras* is drizzled with melted chocolate. Stale bread never tasted so good!

Mulligatawny Soup ▷

Mulligatawny was conceived in India during the British occupation. As soups do not play a big role in Indian cuisine, mulligatawny was created for those homesick colonialists who missed a good bowl of soup.

The strange name is derived from the Tamil words *milagu thanni*, which translates as "pepper water." Originally a sauce, it would evolve into a spicy chicken and vegetable soup.

Early recipes for mulligatawny call for little more than simmering chicken with onions and curry powder. It has now become a much heartier affair with tomato, vegetables, rice, and cream. Tart apple is also popular, as it complements the bold curry flavors. Vegan versions of mulligatawny substitute lentils for chicken and coconut milk for cream, which inadvertently gives the soup a south Indian twist. With or without meat, chopped fresh cilantro is a natural garnish to further enliven this comforting soup.

Mulligatawny is a great cold-weather lunch, especially when served with warm Indian flatbread such as naan or chapati. Like chicken tikka masala and other Anglo-Indian specialties, mulligatawny is an Indian dish with a British heart.

Minestrone

Minestrone is the granddaddy of vegetable soups. Although Italian in origin, people the world over have adopted this comforting soup as their own.

There are as many versions of this hearty vegetable soup as there are Italian towns. It changes with the seasons and almost always contains some type of bean. The broth may be made with meat or vegetables, or the liquid left over from cooking dried beans.

Minestrone verde, for example, is a celebration of spring, brimming with tiny fava beans, peas, asparagus, spinach, and baby zucchini. In winter, the soup relies on the pantry and root cellar for dried legumes, canned tomatoes, cabbage, potatoes, and carrots.

In Tuscany, minestrone is flavored with pancetta, rosemary, and tomato and poured over slices of broiled bread. *Minestrone alla Genovese*, like the French *soupe au pistou*, is garnished with a dollop of garlicky pesto. In Milan, minestrone is distinguished by the addition of rice. In summer, it is served at room temperature with chopped basil.

One secret ingredient for minestrone is the crust from a piece of Parmesan cheese. It is simmered with the soup and discarded at the end, highlighting the Italian flair for never wasting a crumb.

Minestrone

¼ cup olive oil

2 medium onions, chopped

3 medium carrots, chopped

3 stalks celery, chopped

2 large potatoes, diced

2 small green or yellow zucchini, diced

½ lb green beans, sliced

½ head small green cabbage, shredded

2 cups water

5 cups beef broth

1 (28-oz) can and 1 (14½-oz) can diced tomatoes, undrained

1 bay leaf

1 sprig thyme

Salt

Freshly ground black pepper

Heat the oil in a large pot on medium heat, add the onions and cook until translucent and golden. Add the carrots and cook for 2 to 3 minutes, stirring occasionally. Add the remaining vegetables one at a time. Stir in the water, broth, tomatoes, bay leaf, and thyme. Bring to a boil, reduce the heat, cover, and simmer for about 1 hour, until the vegetables are tender. Season to taste. *Serves 6*

◁ Miso Soup

It would be hard to imagine starting a Japanese meal without miso soup. This light, simple soup takes the edge off while stimulating the appetite for the dishes to come.

The two basic components of miso soup are *dashi* and *miso*. *Dashi* is the all-purpose broth made by boiling *kombu* (kelp) and *katsuobushi* (smoke-dried tuna) in water. *Miso* is a salty fermented paste of soybeans plus rice or barley that is aged anywhere from three months to three years. It varies in color from white to dark brown, though the lighter varieties are more commonly used for soup. Packed with protein and vitamins, miso seasons the *dashi* and imparts a sweet fruity flavor. It also gives the soup a hit of *umami*, what the Japanese call the fifth savory taste.

Garnishes reflect the season and are chosen to balance color, texture, and flavor. One combination might include cubes of silky tofu, toothsome *wakame* (seaweed), and a few slivers of shiitake mushroom.

Traditionally served in lacquered bowls, the cloudy broth is sipped straight from the dish and the solids are eaten with chopsticks. Not only is miso soup a tasty beginning, it is a breakfast staple eaten with rice.

Osumashi

A bowl of cloudy miso soup is a familiar sight at any Japanese restaurant. But one way to tell if you are in for an authentic dining experience is if osumashi soup is also on the menu.

Unlike miso soup, osumashi is perfectly clear, which allows the chef to show off his or her artistic flair with the carefully prepared garnishes. The base is *dashi* broth, made by boiling *kombu* (kelp) in water. Once off the heat, the broth is briefly infused with shavings of dried tuna, which lend its smoky flavor.

Solid ingredients for the soup are chosen to balance taste, texture, and color, and always reflect the season. Mushrooms are popular in osumashi, especially matsutake, prized for its meaty texture and spicy perfume. Other authentic garnishes might include slices of *fu*, a gluten cake that absorbs the tasty broth.

Osumashi is often served as part of a multi-course dinner, and always arrives in a red or black lacquered bowl fitted with a lid. When placed in front of the diner, the lid is removed, releasing the tantalizing aroma. The beautiful bowl and clear soup frame the vivid garnishes like a work of art.

Oyster Soup

Oysters are delicious raw, steamed, grilled, or fried. They also feature prominently in a range of tasty soups, particularly in the US.

In Louisiana, the briny bivalves are combined with artichokes, cream, and herbs for an elegant first course. They are also paired with chicken in a spicy gumbo that celebrates both land and sea. In New England, a rich oyster stew made with onion, celery, and cream is often served before the turkey at Thanksgiving dinner.

The secret to oyster soup is to shuck your own over a bowl to catch the precious juices. This salty liquid will flavor and season the soup. Both the oyster and its liquid must be carefully checked for sand and bits of shell so you don't end up with a gritty soup. Most importantly, oysters should only be added right at the end just to heat through so they don't end up rubbery.

Of course, oysters don't need to be served in a hot soup. Some chefs float raw oysters in a spicy gazpacho topped with freshly grated horseradish. Raw or cooked, oysters are always at home in soup.

Oxtail Soup ▷

Oxtail is tough, fatty, and full of bones. But when cooked slowly and gently in a soup or stew, it becomes one of the tastiest cuts of beef available.

Oxtail soup is popular all over China, where epicures appreciate its sticky, lip-smacking qualities. In Szechuan province, sections of oxtail are simmered in water and rice wine perfumed with ginger and Szechuan peppercorns. The succulent meat is liberated from the bones with chopsticks and dipped in chili sauce, while the broth is sipped straight from the bowl.

Oxtail is also revered in the Caribbean, where it is usually featured in hearty stews. In Jamaica, it is simmered with garlic, tomatoes, thyme, and lima beans. *Rabo encindidio*—which means "tail on fire" in Spanish—is a spicy Cuban specialty served with fried plantains.

Whether it's a soup or stew, the secret to any oxtail dish is making it a day in advance. The considerable fat rendered by the oxtail can be effortlessly lifted from the soup once it has been refrigerated. Besides, braised meat dishes always taste better the next day.

Panzanella

Whether it's to make garlicky bread crumbs to sprinkle on pasta or to help thicken hearty soups, Italian cooks are ingenious at using up leftover bread. The crown jewel of these peasant dishes is panzanella, a summery bread salad from Tuscany.

Panzanella can't be made with just any old bread. It must be a rustic loaf with a sturdy crumb—ciabatta is ideal—or it will disintegrate into a soggy mess. For the same reason, the bread must be good and stale, preferably four days old.

At its simplest, panzanella combines cubes of bread, ripe tomatoes, and basil with a dressing made from extra-virgin olive oil, red wine vinegar, and garlic. Absorbing both the vinaigrette and tomato juices, the bread is transformed from something destined for the garbage bin to a gastronomical delight. To make panzanella more of a meal, not to mention a feast for the eyes, chefs add roasted peppers, anchovies, capers, and olives. These piquant garnishes play off the sweetness of the tomatoes.

The squishy bread, juicy tomatoes, fragrant basil, and fruity olive oil are a summer celebration in a bowl. Panzanella is so good that it's worth buying extra bread and letting it go stale.

Panzanella

3 stale ciabatta loaves, cut into thick pieces

2¼ lb fresh plum tomatoes

4 cloves garlic, crushed to a paste with a little coarse sea salt

Coarse sea salt and freshly ground black pepper

1 cup Tuscan extra-virgin olive oil

2 tbsp red wine vinegar

3 red bell peppers, roasted and cut in eighths

3 yellow bell peppers, roasted and cut in eighths

2 red chiles, roasted and finely chopped, optional

1 cup salted capers, rinsed

4 oz salted anchovies, soaked in 2 tbsp red wine vinegar

1 cup black olives, pitted

1 large bunch basil, chopped

Place the bread slices in a large bowl. Skin, halve, and seed the tomatoes into a sieve over a bowl to retain their juice. Season the juice with the garlic and some black pepper, then add the olive oil and red wine vinegar. Pour the seasoned tomato juice over the bread and toss until it has absorbed all the liquid. In a large dish, layer the soaked bread with the remaining ingredients. The final layer should have the peppers, tomatoes, capers, and anchovies all visible. Leave for an hour at room temperature before serving. *Serves 6*
Adapted from Rose Gray's and Ruth Rogers' *The River Café Cookbook*

Ribollita

Tuscan cuisine is renowned for its hearty vegetable soups that pour as thick as porridge. The most revered is ribollita, a cold weather staple at any Tuscan trattoria. The ingredients depend on the season and the cook, but three are essential for an authentic ribollita: white beans, black kale, and stale rustic bread.

The beans are first cooked in water, which will become the base of the soup. Onion, carrot, celery, garlic, and herbs are gently stewed in olive oil, then added to the pot along with tomatoes, kale, the beans and their liquid. Other veggies such as potatoes and cabbage might be added, and the soup is simmered gently until everything is soft. When removed from the heat, chunks of stale bread are stirred in.

Ribollita means "reboiled" in Italian, and refers to the fact that this soup is always made in advance and reheated the next day. This process intensifies the flavors and ensures a thick consistency. Once the soup is ladled into shallow, wide-rimmed bowls, it is drizzled with peppery Tuscan olive oil—as much as your conscience will allow.

Ribollita

2 tbsp extra-virgin olive oil

4 cloves garlic, finely chopped

4 bay leaves

1 large onion, finely chopped

2 large carrots, peeled and diced

1 stalk celery, diced

8 cups vegetable broth

1 cup dried navy beans, presoaked overnight

3 cups shredded red cabbage

2 large tomatoes, chopped

2 tsp chopped fresh thyme

½ tsp salt

¼ tsp freshly ground black pepper

½ loaf Italian bread, cut into ½-in slices

½ cup freshly grated Parmesan cheese

Heat the olive oil in a large saucepan over medium heat. Sauté the garlic and bay leaves for 3 minutes. Add the onion, carrot, and celery and cook for 4 minutes, or until softened. Add the vegetable broth and beans, and bring to a boil. Reduce the heat and simmer for 40 minutes, or until the beans are tender. Stir in the cabbage, tomatoes, thyme, salt, and pepper. Simmer for 5 minutes, then remove the bay leaves. In the meantime, preheat the oven to 350°F. Toast the bread slices for 15 minutes, or until lightly browned.

Pour a third of the bean mixture into a 13-x-9-inch baking dish. Top with half of the bread slices. Repeat the layers, ending with the bean mixture and making sure all the bread is moistened. Sprinkle with Parmesan. Bake for 45 minutes. *Serves 8*

Adapted from Massimo Capra's *One Pot Italian*

◁ # Minted Pea Soup

Royal Game Soup

Most pea soups are made from the dried variety. But as surely as spring turns to summer, fresh garden peas will find their way into a smooth, emerald soup flavored with mint.

Since the natural sugars in peas start converting to starch the moment they leave the vine, the key to this soup is fresh-picked peas. A trip to a farmers' market is a must, or even better, growing your own. The purest garden pea soup is little more than peas cooked in a light vegetable broth made from their pods. It is whizzed in a blender and seasoned with salt and a pinch of white pepper. The mint, sliced into a fine chiffonade, is added when the soup is in the bowl.

One of the admirable characteristics of pea soup is its flexibility. It can be served hot on a cool June night or chilled during the dog days of July. Garnishes range from a few tendrils of baby pea shoots to such luxurious splashes as lobster, caviar, and truffle oil.

Preserved at the peak of freshness, frozen peas work well in this soup. In fact, frozen are preferable to less-than-perfect fresh. Of course, frozen peas let you enjoy this early summer treat all year long.

Scotland is considered to have some of the finest game in the world, which has become an integral part of its cuisine. In addition to roasts and stews, game will often find its way into a royal soup.

Like most of Scotland's famous dishes, royal game soup is a hearty, cold weather favorite. An economical version will use the leftover carcass from a roasted game bird, such as partridge or pheasant, and its giblets. Once the bones are liberated of every last shred of meat, they are simmered in wine and broth to make the base. Onion, carrot, and turnip may be added, perhaps with some barley and the meat scraps at the end. A luxurious version of this soup can be made with fresh game birds, venison, and hare, but to a frugal Scottish cook, this would be a waste of perfectly good game.

Of course, you don't have to go hunting to enjoy this royal soup. Delicious renditions are available in British supermarkets, and the only weapon you'll need is a can opener.

Pozole

Psarosoupa

Pozole is a traditional stew made from pork, hominy, and chiles from Mexico's Jalisco state. Its popularity reaches all the way down into Central America and up into the southwestern United States.

The main ingredient is hominy, kernels of dried white corn. Hominy is often bought in a can, but for pozole, it is best to cook your own and use the flavorful cooking liquid.

Pozole comes in a variety of colors depending on the region. The original red pozole gets its hue from dried chiles, while green pozole from the state of Guerrero is made with green pumpkin seeds, tomatillos, and cilantro. Plain *pozole blanco* is the stew of choice in Guadalajara.

Garnishes are served on the side, allowing diners to jazz up their own soup. Fresh, crunchy additions such as onions and radishes contrast the stew's slow-cooked flavors. Cilantro, cheese, lettuce, and avocado are also popular, while fried pork cracklings are favored in Guerrero.

While pozole is enjoyed any time of year, it is traditionally served at Christmas—fitting for a soup that can be red, green, or white.

While most Mediterranean fish soups require a long day in the kitchen, not to mention a major investment at the fishmonger, this Greek favorite is refreshingly simple. No pot full of fish, crustaceans, and bivalves here: in fact, this humble dish calls for just one kind of fish.

Psarosoupa requires a firm, white-fleshed fish such as grouper, snapper, or rockfish— oily fish are too strong for this delicate soup. If the fish is a manageable size it is left whole, otherwise it is cut into steaks. It is poached in water with onion, carrot, celery, potato, and a bit of tomato for flavor.

Once the fish and vegetables are cooked, the soup can be served as is. Like bouillabaisse, however, psarosoupa can be served in two courses. The strained fish and vegetables are arranged on a platter and dressed with extra-virgin olive oil and a squeeze of lemon. The broth is cooked with rice and thickened at the end with *avgolemono*, a tart, creamy mixture of eggs and lemon juice.

Fresh ingredients prepared without a lot of fuss—psarosoupa is a perfect example of authentic Greek cooking.

Shabu-Shabu

Similar in spirit to fondue, Japanese shabu-shabu is a do-it-yourself dining experience that is healthy, delicious, and loads of fun.

Also known as hotpot, shabu-shabu is like *sukiyaki*, except the bite-sized pieces of meat and vegetables are cooked in a central pot of broth instead of on a grill. The broth is a simple stock made by boiling dried seaweed in salted water. The main ingredient is usually thin slices of beef sirloin with a supporting cast of cubed tofu and vegetables such as napa cabbage, leeks, and shiitake mushrooms. At upscale restaurants, luxurious ingredients such as richly marbled Kobe beef, lobster, and foie gras are not uncommon.

The diner pinches a morsel of food between chopsticks and immerses it in the simmering broth, briefly swishing it back and forth—shabu-shabu is derived from the "swish-swish" sound it makes. When the item is cooked, it can be dipped in salty-sour *ponzu* or a creamy sesame sauce called *goma-dare*.

Once the food is enjoyed, the now richly flavored broth can be consumed on its own or mixed with noodles. Dip, swish, dip—there is an entire world of Japanese food beyond sushi.

Shabu-Shabu

2 slices *kombu*

7 cups *dashi* broth

1 lb sirloin, very thinly sliced

8 shiitake mushrooms

3 cups enoki mushrooms

1 (1 lb) Chinese cabbage, shredded

1 lb tofu, cut in 1-in cubes, pressed and drained

To serve at the table, prepare the shabu-shabu in a fondue pot or similar, portable, range. Place the *kombu* in the bottom of the pot and cover with the *dashi* broth. Heat the broth, and remove the *kombu* just before boiling point. Keep the broth simmering gently to serve.

Arrange the remaining ingredients on a large platter and allow people to serve themselves, simply by dipping the food into the shabu-shabu and swishing it around in the hot liquid until cooked—a matter of seconds for the beef; minutes for the vegetables. Serve with a dipping sauce and hot steamed rice, if desired. *Serves 6*

Russian Salad

Invented in Moscow in the 1860s by French chef Lucien Olivier, of the renowned Hermitage restaurant, Russian salad is still popular all over Europe. In its original form, it was a luxurious mix of game, tongue, crayfish, caviar, pickles, and eggs bound in a secret mayonnaise dressing. Called "salade Olivier," it became the restaurant's signature dish.

Over the years, a much humbler version of Russian salad evolved from the decadent original. Now it is more of a vegetable medley that includes cooked potatoes, turnips, carrots, and peas along with chicken, ham, and hard-boiled eggs. Of course, everything should be evenly diced. The dressing is still mayonnaise-based, though some cooks mix it with sour cream.

For years, Russian salad was a staple at elaborate hotel buffets all over France, where it was often molded into an aspic-lined bowl and garnished with slivers of pickled tongue and black truffle.

Today, the popularity of this creamy salad shows no signs of waning. In Italy, *insalata russa* is still an essential part of any summer antipasto spread. *Ensaladilla rusa* is also a familiar sight at tapas bars all over Spain, where it gets a Mediterranean twist of tuna and green olives.

Ramen ▷

In Japan, ramen borders on religion. This noodle soup has inspired everything from the universally loved instant noodles to the Japanese cult film *Tampopo*, an entertaining story about a truck driver who helps a young widow revive her struggling ramen house.

While the instant variety, introduced to the US in 1970, has hijacked the name, authentic ramen is an epicurean delight. Ramen are based on Chinese wheat noodles—*lamian* is the word for stretched noodles, while *lo-mein* translates as boiled noodles. This rich broth falls into four basic categories: *shio* (clear chicken); *tonkatsu* (cloudy pork); *shoyu* (seasoned with soy sauce); and *miso* (flavored with fermented soybean paste).

Not only does ramen vary from region to region in Japan, it can change from district to district within a city. For example, the legendary ramen from the Hakata ward of Fukuoka is a *tonkatsu*-style soup garnished with sliced pork, pickled ginger, scallions, and sesame seeds.

Whether it's from a packet, a street vendor, or a bustling noodle joint, most dining etiquette goes out the window when eating ramen. After all, noodle soup can only truly be enjoyed with a cacophonous medley of sipping and slurping.

Salade Niçoise

From a rustic mélange of vegetables to an haute composition of quail eggs, fingerling potatoes, and rare tuna, salade Niçoise is a chameleon of a dish. Interestingly enough, an authentic version does not necessarily include tuna.

The first recorded recipe for this salad from Nice, in Provence, combined artichoke hearts, peppers, tomatoes, olives, and anchovies in an herb vinaigrette. Today's Niçoise is a much heartier dish that includes boiled potatoes, green beans, hard-boiled eggs, and, yes, tuna.

Whatever goes into a Niçoise, it should be made only in summer. The tomatoes must be sweet and juicy and the green beans are preferably svelte *haricots verts*. Tiny Niçoise olives are ideal, but any briny black olives will do. Anchovies, though an acquired taste, have a happy relationship with both tomato and green beans. A few basil leaves could also join the party. The dressing is a simple blend of olive oil, red wine vinegar, Dijon mustard, and garlic. If tuna is included, it should be packed in olive oil, or even better, a hunk of the fresh stuff seared in a hot pan.

Tuna or no tuna, an authentic Niçoise should taste like the Provençal summer sun cooled with a salty Mediterranean breeze.

Salade Niçoise

1 large handful thin French beans

1 small head romaine lettuce, torn

2 hard-boiled eggs, peeled

4 medium tomatoes, peeled and quartered

6 preserved artichoke hearts, drained
and quartered

8 salted anchovies, rinsed

12 black olives

2 tbsp chopped fresh parsley

For the dressing:

2 tbsp red wine vinegar

1 tsp Dijon mustard

2 small cloves garlic, peeled and crushed

⅓ cup extra-virgin olive oil

Salt

Freshly ground black pepper

Cook the beans briefly in salted boiling water until tender-crisp.

Meanwhile, put torn lettuce in a shallow bowl and arrange eggs, vegetables, anchovies, and olives on top. Sprinkle with parsley.

Whisk the vinegar, mustard, and garlic, then slowly drizzle in the olive oil. Season to taste, pour over the salad, and serve with crusty bread. *Serves 2*

Rasam

Fried snacks, grilled meats, and bold curries—Indian cuisine is known for a lot of things, but soup is not one of them. A big exception is rasam, a spicy lentil soup.

Lentils play an important role in Indian cuisine, especially in the south, where vegetarianism has a long history. Rasam is made with golden *toor dal*—hulled and split pigeon peas. They are cooked in water with tomatoes and tart tamarind, which give the soup its dark color and sour edge. The spice comes from rasam powder, a fiery blend of red chiles, whole cumin, coriander, and black mustard seeds, as well as black peppercorns that have been toasted in a dry skillet and finely ground. The secret ingredient is *asafetida*, a pungent spice made from the dried sap of a wild fennel plant. It adds flavors of onion and garlic and is said to temper the windy properties of dried legumes.

Rasam is usually served at the beginning of a meal, especially when heavy meat dishes and coconut-milk curries are on the menu. The sour soup awakens the palate from its slumber and helps us digest the rich food to come.

Shark's Fin Soup

Shark fins are among the most coveted and costly foodstuffs in Chinese cuisine. And like bird's nests, these fins make a very expensive bowl of soup.

Shark fins are either the dorsal, tail, or pectoral, and are usually dried before being shipped to market. Before it is transformed into a delicacy, the dried fin must be thoroughly soaked in warm water to remove the fishy smell. It is then gently simmered in chicken broth with ginger and scallion for at least 6 hours. It is basically tasteless, but the cartilage takes on a slippery and gelatinous texture prized in Chinese cuisine. It also thickens the broth as if cornstarch has been used. The fin is pulled into long, silky strands and often combined with chicken, Yunnan ham, dried scallop, and abalone.

Shark fins are classified as "strengthening" foods and are said to boost virility. It is no coincidence that shark's fin soup is an essential part of a Chinese wedding banquet.

Scotch Broth   ▷

Scotch broth exemplifies the best of traditional Scottish cooking. This rib-sticking soup is simple, hearty, and economical, making use of locally-grown vegetables and a frugal cut of meat. And unlike the infamous haggis, Scotch broth is loved the world over.

Scotch broth starts with meat—lamb or mutton is traditional, though beef is commonly used. Most importantly, it should be an inexpensive cut suitable for braising—neck, shoulder, or shank all work well. The meat is simmered in water for a few hours and the fat is carefully skimmed from the broth. Barley helps thicken the soup to a porridge-like consistency. In addition to the usual root cellar suspects, rutabaga is an essential part of Scotch broth; the Scots fondly refer to these giant yellow turnips as "neeps."

Traditionally, the meat was served separately from the soup. These days it is removed from the bone, chopped, and returned to the pot. Scotch broth can also be made with chicken, and vegetarian versions substitute split peas for the meat. Just before serving, the final touch is a wee pinch of chopped parsley.

In a country known for its cold, blustery weather, one can take solace in a steaming bowl of Scotch broth.

Sopa de Picadillo

Snert ▷

The Andalusia region of southern Spain is known for its chilled soups: *ajo blanco*, *salmorejo*, and the international star, gazpacho. These soups are refreshing in summer, but when there's a nip in the air, Andalusians turn their spoons to sopa de picadillo.

Meaning "soup of little things," sopa de picadillo is essentially just that: a rich meat broth with a host of little garnishes. The liquid base could be chicken broth or a more complicated bouillon made from the bones of chicken, beef, and ham. Depending on the cook, this soup can range from light to hearty. At its simplest, sopa de picadillo is a bowl of broth garnished with diced ham, hard-boiled egg, and fresh mint. A heftier version will include chicken, potatoes, rice, and Andalusia's favorite legume, garbanzo beans. A last-minute splash of dry sherry lends its nutty, floral flavor.

Sopa de picadillo is a frugal cook's way of using up the leftover bone from a cured ham. The bits of meat lurking in the crevices are scraped and chopped up for garnish.

Erwentsoep, the Dutch word for pea soup, is difficult to pronounce if you don't speak the language. Luckily, this beloved dish is more commonly known as "snert."

Making snert is not difficult, though it does take a while to cook. Dried split peas go into a pot with water, a smoked ham hock, and a pig's foot or two. The peas and the pork simmer gently while the cook chops and adds onion, carrot, celery, potatoes, and celery root. Once the meats are tender, they are removed, diced, and returned to the pot. The final addition is smoked sausage, preferably a plump Dutch rookworst. Snert should be made a day ahead, to intensify the flavors and ensure a porridge-like consistency. According to tradition, the finished soup must be thick enough to stand a spoon in.

The arrival of cold weather signals the start of snert season. It is enjoyed at homes and restaurants, and sold from stands along canals in winter as a post-skating snack. Thick pea soup brimming with root vegetables, smoked pork, and sausage—nothing shakes off the winter blahs like a bowl of rib-sticking snert.

Stracciatella

Greeks have avgolemono, Jews have matzo ball soup, and when Italians feel frail, chances are they'll be prescribed a bowl of stracciatella.

A Roman specialty, stracciatella is basically egg drop soup with an Italian twist. It starts with a simmering pot of homemade chicken broth. An egg is beaten with semolina flour, finely grated Parmesan, and a pinch of nutmeg. Whisked into the hot broth, the egg mixture is transformed into fluffy rags that give the soup its name—*straccetti* is the Italian word for rag. The soup is poured into bowls, garnished with a pinch of chopped parsley, and served piping hot.

The aromatic broth, delicate egg threads, and nutty cheese form a light, yet satisfying soup that is the perfect medicine for an upset stomach or a lingering cold. In addition to its role as Italy's Jewish penicillin, stracciatella is the ideal first course before a rich, heavy meal.

Sorrel and Spinach Soup

When the first spear-shaped leaves of sorrel break through the ground in gardens all over Europe, spring has arrived. Early in the season, while the temperature is still cool, a bowl of tangy sorrel soup is the perfect way to celebrate.

Sorrel is slightly bitter and has a distinct sour, lemony flavor that comes from the presence of oxalic acid in the leaves. To temper its sharp taste, it is often combined with spinach, which in turn imparts its dark green character to the soup. Potatoes, which have a natural affinity for sorrel, also mellow the tartness while adding body. Sorrel and spinach soup is almost always puréed and served with a swirl of crème fraîche.

Sorrel is not just a spring treat. The fleshy leaves grow straight through summer and can be savored equally in a chilled soup. In Latvia, where sorrel grows in nearly every home garden, chilled sorrel soup is a warm-weather staple. Ashkenazi Jews have also long enjoyed *schav*, a cold sorrel soup thickened with eggs and garnished with sour cream.

Tom Yum

Pad Thai may be Thailand's best-known dish, but running a close second is tom yum soup. *Tom* means "boil", *yum* means "mix," and together they make an invigorating hot-and-sour soup.

Tom yum can be made with everything from chicken to mushrooms, but the most common star ingredient is shrimp (*tom yum goong*). As soups go, tom yum is easy to make and ready in minutes. Fish or shrimp broth is first brought to a boil. Lengths of lemongrass, kaffir lime leaves, and blistering bird's eye chiles are bruised and added to the broth. These aromatics flavor the soup, but are not to be eaten—especially the chiles.

The minute peeled shrimp dropped into the broth turn pink, the soup is removed from the heat and seasoned with freshly squeezed lime juice and pungent fish sauce. In the bowl, cilantro leaves lend their cool, citrusy flavor while doubling as a verdant garnish. To turn up the heat and add a splash of red, some cooks swirl in a spoonful of *nam prik*, a piquant condiment made from chiles, shallots, garlic, and dried shrimp.

Hot, sour, salty, and perfumed with exotic herbs—tom yum soup showcases the exuberant flavors of Thai cuisine.

Tabbouleh

Tabbouleh is a ubiquitous presence at falafel shops around the world. What makes this refreshing salad so unique? It's all about the herbs.

Hailing from the mountains between Lebanon and Syria, tabbouleh is primarily a parsley salad. Heaps of the stuff are chopped along with a handful of mint leaves. Thinly sliced scallions assert their presence, diced cucumber provides the cool factor, and fine bulgur lends it bulk. The dressing can be as simple as olive oil and lemon juice, though some cooks spice it up with cinnamon and aleppo pepper, a hot chili powder from Syria.

When to dress the salad depends on the cook. Some like to toss it the night before, so the bulgur absorbs the tasty juices. Others prefer to mix it *à la minute*, which prevents the acid in the lemon juice from dulling the green herbs. But everyone agrees that the diced tomato should be incorporated just before serving so it doesn't turn to mush.

Tabbouleh is traditionally served as part of *meze*, the Middle Eastern spread of appetizers. The bowl may be garnished with leaves of romaine lettuce, the perfect utensil for scooping up this verdant treat.

Tabbouleh

1½ cups bulgur

1⅔ cups boiling water

⅓ cup olive oil

⅓ cup lemon juice

1 medium bunch scallions, chopped

1 medium bunch fresh parsley, chopped

1 medium bunch fresh mint, chopped

3 medium tomatoes, chopped

1 cucumber, peeled, seeded, and chopped

Salt

Freshly ground black pepper

Place the bulgur in a bowl and pour in the boiling water. Cover the bowl with plastic wrap and set aside for one hour. Stir in the remaining ingredients, seasoning to taste. Cover and chill before serving. *Serves 6*

Tortellini in Brodo

Home to prosciutto, mortadella, and Parmigiano Reggiano cheese, Emilia-Romagna is widely considered to be the gastronomical heart of Italy. In Bologna, the region's capital, a legendary soup is made starring all three of these ingredients.

Tortellini in brodo is part soup and part pasta, though it technically falls into the latter category, as it is served as a pasta course. The tortellini filling starts with chicken and veal cooked in butter and white wine. This mixture is puréed in a food processor with the prosciutto and mortadella. Finally, an egg, grated cheese, and a pinch of nutmeg are mixed in. A spoonful of filling is placed on each small square of fresh pasta, which is folded to make a triangle. The two bottom corners are pinched together around a finger, forming the ring-shaped tortellini.

While tortellini are labor-intensive, the soup should not be an afterthought. After all, pasta of this caliber deserves only the finest homemade meat broth.

Sipping deeply-flavored soup alternating with rich, yet delicate tortellini, you can taste the love that goes into this Bolognese delicacy. Legend has it that the golden rings were inspired by Venus's navel. A sexy soup indeed!

Insalata Caprese

Like Caesar and Greek, you don't have to be an epicure to know what goes into a Caprese salad. But with so many imposters out there, an authentic Caprese is hard to come by.

Hailing from the island of Capri, the classic Neapolitan dish is a celebration of summer. And like all simple dishes, Caprese salad is only as good as its ingredients. The tomatoes must be sweet, juicy, and picked at the peak of ripeness. The cheese is ideally *mozzarella di bufala*, made from water buffalo milk in the Campania region of Italy, though artisanal mozzarella made from cow's milk called *fior di latte* is a perfectly acceptable substitute.

The dish's co-stars are thickly sliced or cut into chunks, showered with whole basil leaves, drizzled with fruity extra-virgin olive oil, and seasoned with sea salt and freshly ground pepper. If the tomatoes are just short of perfect, a few drops of aged balsamic vinegar will bring out their sweetness.

Of course, Caprese salad must be served with crusty bread to wipe the plate clean of the heavenly blend of tomato juices, olive oil, and the buttery milk that oozes from the cheese. Coincidentally, this salad shows off the red, white, and green of the Italian flag. It's a patriotic dish and one of Italy's gastronomic gifts to the world.

Tuscan Bean and Vegetable Soup

Tuscans are so fond of beans that they are known throughout Italy as *mangiafagioli* or "bean eaters." They put them on crostini, toss them with pasta, and cook them in a flask with olive oil and sage for *fagioli al fiasco*. Of course, beans also star in a host of rustic Tuscan vegetable soups.

The bean of choice for soup in Tuscany is the fat, white cannellini bean. The most famous of these soups is *ribollita*, a "reboiled" soup of beans and black kale thickened with hunks of stale bread. Another hearty bean soup, popular all over Italy, is *pasta e fagioli*. The Tuscan version is flavored with tomato, rosemary, and pancetta. Small pasta shells are added at the end along with a healthy grating of Parmesan cheese. (In the United States, this soup is affectionately known as "pasta fazool.")

Some bean soups are little more than beans cooked in water with garlic and tomato. Tuscans also like to put whole *farro* grains in bean soups, which turns it into a thick, hearty meal.

Whatever bean and vegetable soup you happen to be eating, the Tuscan seal of authenticity comes in the form of a lavish drizzle of peppery extra-virgin olive oil.

Vichyssoise

Since the potato arrived in Europe from the New World, leek and potato soups have been a staple of French country cooking. But it wasn't until 1917 that Louis Diat, chef of the Ritz-Carlton in New York, decided to serve a cream-enriched version of this soup cold. Based on the hot potato and leek soup of his childhood, Diat named this refreshing soup vichyssoise after Vichy, a town near his birthplace in France.

Vichyssoise is essentially a purée of onions, leeks, potatoes, chicken broth, and cream. To keep the color pure white, only the whites of the leeks are traditionally used. But since leeks are the priciest of alliums, many chefs also employ the light green part as well, resulting in an emerald soup. Vichyssoise should be served ice cold with a sprinkle of finely sliced chives, another Diat touch.

Once the chilled soup of choice, vichyssoise was usurped by gazpacho decades ago. It remains, however, a warm-weather staple at bistros around the world. Of course, vichyssoise can be served hot in winter, when it goes by the name of *potage Parmentier*.

Waldorf Salad

While chefs and restaurateurs get credit for most famous dishes, a maitre d' invented the Waldorf salad. Oscar Tschirky, head waiter at the Waldorf Hotel in New York, first mixed the unique blend of diced apples, celery, and mayonnaise sometime in the 1890s. It quickly caught on and became a fashionable salad at hotel dining rooms around the world.

The Waldorf shows off the natural pairing of apples and celery. Mayonnaise is the ideal dressing, as its creaminess tames both the tart apples and the herbal character of celery. The addition of walnuts would come a few decades later, adding richness and crunch. Some chefs include halved grapes, raisins, or chopped dates for a sweet touch. These days celery root is often used in place of celery, as it has a milder flavor and its dense texture contrasts with the juicy apple.

Since Tschirky tossed the first Waldorf salad, there have been countless mutations using everything from bananas to yogurt. Some crafty parents even top it with marshmallows as a way of getting their kids to eat their veggies.

Waldorf Salad

- ⅔ cup golden raisins
- 1 cup boiling water
- ½ cup mayonnaise
- 3 tbsp sour cream
- 2 tbsp lemon juice
- 1 tsp sugar
- 4 Granny Smith apples, cut in ½-in cubes
- 1⅓ cups thinly sliced celery
- 1⅓ cups red seedless grapes, halved
- Salt
- Freshly ground black pepper
- Romaine lettuce leaves
- 1 cup walnut halves

Soak the raisins in boiling water until softened, about 10 minutes. Drain.

In a large bowl, whisk the mayonnaise, sour cream, lemon juice, and sugar. Add apples, celery, grapes, and raisins. Toss, season to taste, and toss again. Arrange the lettuce on a platter and the mound of salad on top. Sprinkle with walnuts. *Serves 6*

Wonton Soup

Hailing from southern China, wonton soup has been North America's favorite Chinese soup for decades. Wonton is derived from *yun tun*, Mandarin for "swallowing clouds." Peer into a fragrant bowl of clear chicken broth floating plump, billowing wontons, and it all makes perfect sense.

Chinese chicken soup is as simple as boiling a chicken in water with a few slices of ginger. The whole bird creates a rich, deeply-flavored soup, while the cooked meat can be used in everything from noodle dishes to fried rice.

The wonton filling is made from ground pork seasoned with scallions, rice wine, sesame oil, and soy sauce. Chopped shrimp and crunchy bits of water chestnut may be folded in. This mixture is wrapped in delicate skins of flour, egg, and water, and then boiled in water so they won't cloud the soup.

A sip of ginger-scented broth followed by a bite of a juicy wonton will transport you back to your first meal at a Chinese restaurant. Wontons may have lost some ground to hot-and-sour over the years, but a soup that tastes of childhood will never go out of style.

Wonton Soup

8 oz ground pork

1 scallion, chopped

$\frac{1}{4}$ tsp ground ginger

$\frac{1}{2}$ tsp cornstarch

24 wonton skins

5 cups water

8 cups chicken broth

1 tbsp soy sauce

1 cup spinach or watercress, torn in pieces

In a large bowl, mix the pork, scallion, ginger, and cornstarch. Cook until the pork loses its pink; drain off fat. When cool, place 2 teaspoons of filling in the center of each wonton skin. Moisten the edges with water. Fold each in half to form a triangle and press edges together. Then moisten the outside points of each triangle and pinch together. Cover and refrigerate for up to 1 day.

In a large pot, bring the water to a boil. Add the wontons. Return to a boil, reduce the heat, and simmer, uncovered, for 2 minutes, or until the dumplings float to the top. Drain.

Heat the broth and add the soy sauce and spinach. Bring just to a boil and remove from the heat. Place 3 wontons in each soup bowl and ladle the hot broth on top. *Serves 6*

Waterzooi

Zarzuela

While waterzooi does not enjoy the same international reputation as *carbonnades flamandes* (beef stew) and *moules frites* (mussels and French fries), this rich, creamy stew is the culinary pride of Belgium.

What goes into an authentic waterzooi is still an ongoing debate. Is it chicken or fish? Food historians believe it originated in Ghent and was made with freshwater fish—perch, carp, and eel—caught in the surrounding canals. Since these waterways are no longer fished, *waterzooi à la Gantoise* is now more commonly made with seafood such as turbot, mussels, and shrimp. You are as likely to find chicken in today's waterzooi as you are fish, though Belgian epicures insist it must be a free-range bird.

Be it chicken or fish, the meat is poached in wine and broth with a julienne of onion, carrot, and leek. Seasonal delicacies may also be employed: perhaps svelte spears of white asparagus in spring, or wild mushrooms in fall. The finished broth is enriched with a liaison of egg yolks and cream, then showered with herbs such as chervil and tarragon.

Waterzooi is a rich and gratifying stew, yet the flavors are delicate and light. With a glass of crisp blonde ale, this is Belgian dining at its best.

Brimming with seafood and perfumed with garlic, zarzuela is a popular stew from the Catalan coast of Spain. This maritime dish gets its name from a type of variety show, a medley of music, comedy, and dance popular in the 19th century. Hence, zarzuela is sometimes called a "seafood operetta."

While there is no exact formula for zarzuela—spelled *sarsuel* in Catalan—it always begins with a *sofregit*, a mixture of onions, garlic, and tomato gently stewed in olive oil. Then paprika, saffron, and bay leaves are added, which give the dish its characteristic color, flavor, and aroma. White wine, dry sherry, or fish broth provide the liquid base—sometimes a combination of all three. The type of seafood depends on what is fresh and available, though in Catalonia it usually includes monkfish, shrimp, squid, clams, and langoustines (a small variety of lobster). Some chefs like to thicken zarzuela with *picada*, a paste made from fried bread, garlic, and almonds.

While zarzuela is enjoyed all over the world, it is best savored at one of the seafood restaurants in Barceloneta, a beachfront neighborhood in the Catalan capital. With a cold glass of *cava*, the local sparkling wine, this seafood operetta will make your taste buds sing.

3 NOODLES AND RICE

Udon Noodles

Udon is a thick, wheat noodle at the heart of Japanese cuisine. The noodles are white and possibly the thickest of noodles, measuring nearly a quarter of an inch in diameter. They are usually served hot in a noodle soup of udon, *dashi* (fish broth), soy sauce, and mirin (sweet rice wine) topped with chopped shallots. The broth flavorings vary from region to region. In eastern Japan, it's likely to be made with dark soy sauce, while light soy sauce is preferred in western Japan.

Udon soup may also include tofu pockets, or thin slices of *kamaboko*, a half-moon-shaped fish cake. Udon is also popular in Korea, where it is known as *udong*.

Dried, boiled, and fresh udon are available. Because cooking times vary, it is best to follow the instructions on the package. Udon noodles can be eaten hot or cold, and slurping is encouraged—when you're in Japan. It's best to keep the distance between the bowl and your mouth small in order to avoid splashing. If a ceramic spoon is not provided, lift the bowl to your mouth to drink the soup.

Ants Climbing Trees

While the term "ants climbing trees" may lack gourmet appeal, it does accurately describe this simple and tasty dish from Szechuan province. It's named for the bits of cooked ground pork—the ants—which appear to climb up the noodle "branches" when a mouthful is picked up with chopsticks. The pork is marinated and cooked in a red-hot chili sauce, then tossed with thin vermicelli made from mung beans, which become translucent when soaked. Because it is simple and inexpensive to make, ants climbing trees is a favorite among Chinese college students.

Ants Climbing Trees

For the marinade:

1 tbsp light soy sauce

1 tbsp sugar

1 tsp sesame oil

$\frac{1}{2}$ lb ground pork

For the noodles:

4 oz transparent bean thread noodles

Oil for stir-frying

1 small red chile, seeded and chopped

2 (1-in) slices gingerroot, finely chopped

2 scallions, chopped, green and white part

$\frac{1}{2}$ tsp to 1 tbsp chili sauce

$\frac{1}{4}$ cup water

Combine the marinade ingredients in a shallow dish and marinate the ground pork for about 10 minutes. Meanwhile, without removing the string, put the noodles in a shallow bowl and cover with hot water. Let stand for about 5 minutes, or until pliable. Drain well and break into short pieces before removing the string.

Heat the oil in a wok or large frying pan. Sauté the chile, ginger, and scallions for 1 minute, then add the pork and any marinade. Cook until the pork changes color, then stir in the chili sauce and the noodles. Add the water, cover, and cook until most of the liquid has been absorbed and the noodles are tender. Serve hot. *Serves 4*

Bean Thread Noodles

Bean thread noodles are thin noodles made from ground mung beans or (the cheaper version) mung-bean flour. The slender gelatinous noodles are widely used throughout China in soups, stir-fries, salads, desserts, and even drinks.

Before use, they must be soaked in hot water for about 7 minutes, until they become soft and slippery, springy, and translucent. Known by a multitude of alternative names, including cellophane noodles, silver noodles, and Chinese vermicelli, they are flavorless and take on the taste of their accompanying sauce or broth. The dried noodles can also be deep-fried to make a crunchy garnish or a bed for sauces. Whether deep-frying or stir-frying, cutting the mung bean noodles crosswise before cooking makes them easier to handle.

The Japanese have their own version of bean thread noodle, *harusame* or rice vermicelli, and the Koreans have sweet potato vermicelli. They are made from potato or sweet potato starch and can be used in the same way as their Chinese relative.

Rice Noodles

Rice noodles are commonly eaten throughout east and Southeast Asia. They can be bought fresh, frozen, or dried, and in various shapes, sizes, and thicknesses. As well as rice they may contain other ingredients such as tapioca or cornstarch.

In Malaysia, Singapore, Sri Lanka, and southern India, a soft form of rice noodle called *idiappam* (also known as "stringhoppers" or *noolputtu* in some parts of Kerala), is often served at breakfast or dinner, along with a range of spicy or sweet side dishes.

Idiappam can be made with many types of grain apart from rice. In Tamil Nadu in India, *sevai* (known as *santhaka* in the Coimbatore region), is very popular. This type of rice noodle differs from *idiappam* in that it is steamed and because it contains little or no oil. *Sevai*, meanwhile, is generally believed to be more easily digested than other types of rice noodles.

Yakisoba

Mee Goreng

These stir-fried Japanese noodles originated from the Chinese dish chow mein. *Yaki* is the Japanese word for fried, while *soba* in this case refers to a wheat-flour noodle. The key ingredient is the special sauce. This delicious fast food is the Japanese version of a burger or hot dog. In fact, it's occasionally piled into a bun that's sliced down the middle and garnished with mayonnaise and pickled ginger.

Yakisoba is available in all types of restaurants, and street vendors sell it to those stressed *sarariman* (office workers), and to late-night partygoers as a snack on their way home.

To prepare yakisoba at home, simply stir-fry Chinese egg noodles (*chuka-men*) with diced pork or vegetables such as cabbage, onions, or carrots. Season with yakisoba sauce, *tonkatsu* sauce, or Worcestershire sauce and garnish with seaweed powder, shredded pickled ginger, or fish flakes. This dish takes just 10 to 15 minutes to make, and the ingredients are easily available in Asian food stores.

Those seeking traditional Malaysian dishes need look no further than mee goreng. The ubiquitous dish is found at *mamak* stalls throughout Malaysia and "hawker" stalls in Singapore. It is popular with the young people who congregate at these markets to socialize and enjoy this cheap and cheerful dish washed down with a cup of hot *teh tarik*, the local, dark, and frothy "pull tea."

Essentially a tempting pile of fried, thin yellow noodles, mee goreng is made robust and nutritious by the addition of egg, vegetables, onions, chile, and tomatoes. Tofu is used for a vegetarian version. In more upmarket eateries, this dish aspires to greater gastronomic heights with the inclusion of chicken breasts—lightly wok-fried in chili sauce—shrimp and a dollop of oyster sauce. This is a truly delectable, highly addictive dish, which may spoil the palate for blander versions.

Pho

Steeped in history spanning a century, legend has it that pho (rhymes with "duh") began life as a humble boiled beef and noodle broth in the back streets of Hanoi in North Vietnam.

Today pho is the most popular Asian noodle soup in North America and Australia. In fact, wherever Vietnamese immigrants settle throughout the world, there will be pho. The hot, pungent beef broth, fragrant with star anise, is poured over softened, opaque white noodles nestling in the base of large, wide bowls, to which thin, tender pieces of beef are added.

Many eateries today present pho as a "do-it-yourself" soup, allowing customers to choose chicken, pork, shrimp, or tofu. An array of garnishes such as Thai basil leaves, bean sprouts, chopped chiles, or scallions allows guests to customize their soup.

Pho Bo

2 lb beef bones

1 gallon water

2 yellow onions, quartered, plus 1 yellow onion, very thinly sliced

1 tsp salt

2 (1-in) pieces gingerroot

5 cardamom pods

3 star anise

1 cinnamon stick

1 lb beef brisket

2 tbsp fish sauce (*nuoc mam*)

1 lb fresh rice sheet noodles

8 oz beef tenderloin or sirloin, frozen and sliced paper-thin

4 scallions, finely chopped

White pepper for sprinkling

Put the bones in a large saucepan with the water, 1 quartered onion, salt, 1 piece of ginger, the cardamom pods, star anise, and cinnamon. Broil the remaining quartered onion and ginger until skins are burnt, add to the broth, and bring to a boil. Skim off any froth that rises, add the brisket, bring to a boil, and skim again. Add the fish sauce and simmer for 4 hours.

Remove the brisket and slice half of it very thinly. Strain the broth into a bowl or saucepan. Cut the rice noodles into ½-inch strips and put in a large bowl. Cover with boiling water and soak for 20 seconds, gently separating noodles with a pair of chopsticks. Drain and divide the noodles among 6 bowls along with 3 or 4 slices of brisket, raw steak, a few onion slices, and chopped scallion.

Bring the broth to a boil, ladle over the meat and noodles, and sprinkle with white pepper. Serve with lime wedges, chopped, fresh cilantro, and/or bean sprouts. *Serves 6*

Adapted from Terry Durack's *Noodle*

Pad Thai

Visitors to Bangkok flock to the omnipresent food carts dotting city streets to sample the umpteen variations of this national street food. Pad thai translates as "Thai-style frying." The best examples are dry and light, with a fresh, complex, balanced flavor. Many Thai restaurants in the West produce a poor imitation—oily, heavy-tasting, and too red in color. Though a simple dish, cooking the perfect pad thai requires some skill. Rice noodles are soaked in broth or water until just flexible and solid, not expanded and soft.

A wok is used briefly to stir-fry all the ingredients, except the rice, in extremely hot oil. And the last tricky bit? Beaten egg is slowly drizzled into the hot mixture, forming fine ribbons as it cooks.

A generous scattering of fresh shrimp and bean sprouts adds the finishing touch to this mouthwatering dish.

Dry-Fried Beef Noodles

Singapore Noodles

The intense heat of the food in China's Szechuan province is provided by the Szechuan peppercorn. This small, dry, rusty-brown pod is quite different from the familiar chile pepper or black peppercorn. Cooking techniques such as dry-braising, dry-stewing, and quick-frying also set Szechuan's cuisine apart from that of other provinces.

Beef, which is abundant in the region, is usually dry-braised. It is cut into slivers, heated in an iron pot, and stirred continuously in very little oil until completely dry. Seasonings, including the characteristic pepper, are added at the end. The dish is ready when it is dry, piquant, crisp yet soft.

A Cantonese variation exists, originating in Guangzhou, in which strips of dried beef are combined with *hofun* noodles. The essence of this dish is the flavor that develops from the charring and searing of beef strips in the wok at a very high heat. While the finished dish can be greasy, it is bursting with flavor.

While there are dozens of famous noodle dishes to be found in Singapore, from the street hawkers to the stylish restaurants, Singapore noodles is not one of them. Like English muffins and Danish pastries, this golden stir-fried tangle of thin curried rice noodles, vegetables, seafood, chicken, and barbecued pork is named in honor of the country, yet the name is not used by its citizens. European Chinese restaurants made this dish famous, and it was introduced to the United States in the 1980s. Its lack of geographic authenticity, however, does not detract from this wonderful, simply prepared dish, which offers Chinese, Malay, and Indian influences on one plate. Served as a main course, snack, or appetizer, it's essentially an Asian way to clear out the refrigerator.

Chicken Chow Mein

In China, *mein* (noodles) are served in as many ways as Italian pasta dishes are, but chow mein (fried noodles) is one of the most popular outside China, particularly in the United States. In China, chow mein are a staple teahouse food, being quick to prepare and comforting to eat, especially in the winter months. Almost any quick-fried food can be added to chow mein; but the best are vibrant mixtures of flavors and textures. Chicken is always popular, and it is the combination of the very thin, quickly fried strips, the crunchy vegetables, and bean sprouts, and then other succulent items such as abalone, shrimp, or oysters, all soused in a rich, savory sauce of soy, broth, and rice wine, that makes this dish so irresistible.

Chicken Chow Mein

10 oz dried egg noodles

2 tbsp soy sauce

1 tbsp Shao Xing rice wine or dry sherry

1$\frac{1}{2}$ tbsp cornstarch

2 tsp grated gingerroot

7 oz boneless chicken, cut into thin strips

5 oz pork loin, cut into thin strips

6 stems choy sum (flowering cabbage), cut into 2-in pieces

3 tbsp peanut oil

6 dried shiitake mushrooms, soaked in hot water for 1 hour, sliced in to thin strips

4 scallions, cut into 1-in pieces, plus 2 scallions, green part only, thinly sliced

2 tsp sesame oil

$\frac{1}{2}$ cup chicken broth

Cook the noodles in boiling water for 3 to 4 minutes, or until tender. In a large bowl, combine 1 tablespoon soy sauce, the rice wine, 1 tablespoon cornstarch, and the ginger. Add the strips of meat and marinate for 30 minutes.

Put the thicker choy sum stems into boiling water and cook for 1 minute. Add the thinner stems and leaves and cook for another 30 seconds. Drain and refresh with cold water.

Heat 2 tablespoons of peanut oil in a hot wok and stir-fry the meats for 1 minute. Add the choy sum, mushrooms, and scallion pieces and cook for 2 minutes. Remove from the wok. Add the remaining tablespoon of peanut oil to the hot wok and stir-fry the noodles for about 3 minutes. Return the meat and vegetables to the wok, along with the sesame oil and remaining tablespoon of soy sauce. Toss well. Add the chicken broth and remaining cornstarch, mixed to a paste with a little cold water. Transfer to a large serving plate and sprinkle with sliced scallions. *Serves 4*
Adapted from Terry Durack's *Noodle*

Tagliatelle al Tartufo Bianco

The white truffle, *Tuber magnatum*, is one of the world's most expensive foods and a symbol of luxury in league with caviar, champagne, and foie gras. Its powerful fragrance has been likened to mold, garlic, smelly cheese, onions, and cabbage, it resembles a dusty old gnarled potato, and yet it easily commands a price of $1,500 a pound.

More rare and expensive than the French black winter truffle from Périgord, the white tuber grows in Italy and northern Croatia. The best, it is generally agreed, hails from the Piedmont region of Italy, particularly around the town of Alba, home of Barolo and Barbaresco reds and the sparkling Asti Spumante.

From mid-October to December, truffle hunters furtively search their secret spots in the forest with highly-trained dogs (pigs were once used but tended to gobble them up) to unearth the fungus, which grows underground next to the roots of poplar, oak, and hazel trees.

Tagliatelle, the classic pasta of Italy's Emilia-Romagna region, are long, flat ribbons inspired, according to culinary legend, by the hairstyle of Lucrezia d'Este on the occasion of her marriage in 1487.

Tagliatelle al Tartufo Bianco

14 oz tagliatelle

Salt

1/4 cup butter

3 tbsp finely grated Parmesan cheese

Freshly ground black pepper

Freshly grated nutmeg

1 white truffle, very thinly sliced

Bring a large pan of salted water to a boil. Cook the tagliatelle for 8 to 10 minutes, until just tender, and drain, leaving about 1 tablespoon of the cooking water in the pan.

Return the drained pasta to the pan and add the butter and cheese. Season with pepper and nutmeg to taste and toss well to coat the pasta. To serve, transfer the pasta to warm bowls and sprinkle with the thinly-sliced truffle. *Serves 4*

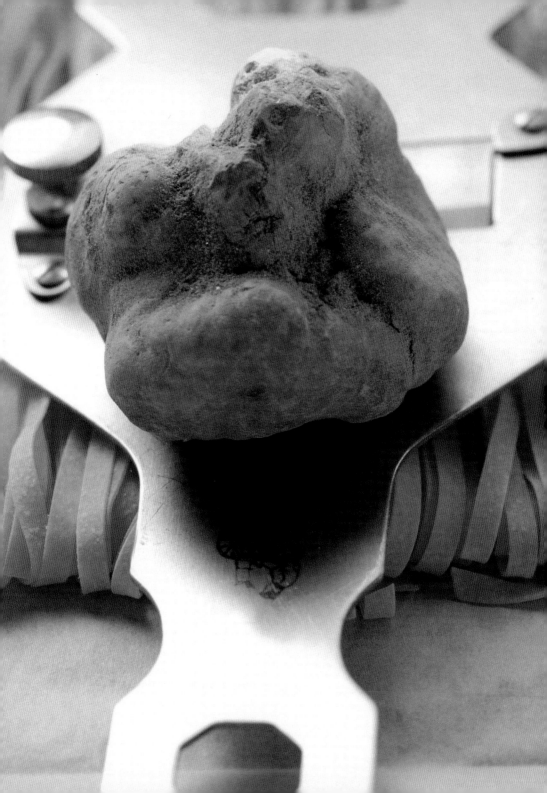

Pasta e Fagioli

Every country has its comfort food, but Italy proudly boasts of discovering, and perfecting, the universal comfort dish in the form of hearty pasta and bean soup. Using the traditional cannellini or white kidney bean, this Italian stalwart forms the base for a tremendous number of local variations on the theme.

Most Italian dishes are simple, but well prepared. In this one the beans (white or red will do) are cooked with pancetta, garlic, and seasonings until soft and may be puréed with tomatoes. Vegetable broth is then added and brought to a boil. At this point any short pasta, such as *maltagliati*—small pieces of soft broken lasagne noodles—or small elbow pasta is added and cooked al dente. Served in bowls with crunchy croutons and a bottle, or two, of zesty red wine, this is a wholesome treat.

Pasta e Fagioli

$1/4$ cup extra-virgin olive oil

2 tbsp chopped onion

3 tbsp chopped carrot

3 tbsp chopped celery

3 or 4 pork ribs

4 tomatoes, peeled and chopped

2 lb fresh cranberry beans

3 cups meat broth

Salt

Freshly ground black pepper

$1/2$ lb small macaroni

2 tbsp butter

2 tbsp freshly grated Parmesan cheese

Put the olive oil and chopped onion in a soup pot and turn on the heat to medium. Cook the onion, stirring it, until it becomes colored a pale gold. Add the carrot and celery, stir once or twice to coat them well, then add the pork. Cook for about 10 minutes, turning the meat and the vegetables over from time to time with a wooden spoon.

Add the chopped tomatoes and their juice, adjust the heat so that the juices simmer very gently, and cook for 10 minutes. Shell the beans, rinse them in cold water, and put them in the soup pot. Stir 2 or 3 times to coat them well, then add the broth. Cover the pot, adjust the heat so that the broth bubbles at a steady, but gentle boil, and cook for 45 minutes to 1 hour, until the beans are fully tender.

Scoop up about ½ cup of the beans and mash them through a food mill back into the pot. Add salt, a few grindings of black pepper, and stir thoroughly. Check the soup for density: it should be liquid enough to cook the pasta in. If necessary, add more broth. When the soup has come to a steady, moderate boil, add the pasta. Taste for doneness after a few minutes and stop the cooking when the pasta is tender, but still firm to the bite. Before turning off the heat, swirl in the butter and the grated cheese. Pour the soup into a large serving bowl or into individual plates, and allow to settle for 10 minutes before serving. It tastes best when eaten warm, rather than piping hot. *Serves 6* **Adapted from Marcella Hazan's** *Essentials of Italian Cooking*

Pesto

Pasta lovers the world over wax lyrical over
the delicate blend of fresh basil, olive oil,
and garlic that is pesto.

From gardens and farmlands that cling
to the Ligurian hillsides of northern Italy,
basil flourishes in abundance. With its faint
clove-like scent, this intensely green and
fragrant herb is so versatile, hardly an Italian
dish exists without its inclusion—to a greater
or lesser degree of taste.

The basic ingredients of pesto are common
to most dishes: fresh basil leaves, garlic,
olive oil, pine nuts, salt, and pepper. While
traditionalists will insist upon it all being
pounded by hand in a mortar and pestle, a
modern electric blender simplifies the job.

A favorite sauce of the Genovese, it is
sharp and pungent and served with ravioli
filled with veal and cheese. But the sauce
is not confined to use in pasta dishes—it is
often added to chunky minestrone or fish
soup and is an excellent accompaniment to
grilled chicken, meat, and fish. The inclusion
of pesto in an Italian ham and cheese
sandwich (prosciutto and fresh mozzarella),
meanwhile, is considered a gourmet delight.

Penne all'Arrabbiata

There is nothing shy about the flavors of this
zesty sauce smothering the smooth tubular
shapes of penne pasta. *Arrabbiata* means
"angry" in Italian and succinctly describes
the fiery heat of the ingredients.

Originally a Roman pasta dish, there is
now great diversity throughout Italy in the
preparation of this sauce. It is essentially a
combination of extra-virgin olive oil, garlic,
plum tomatoes (canned or fresh), red chile
peppers, and the ubiquitous basil.

To create the rich smooth version of penne
arrabbiata—most often served in expensive
Italian restaurants—the cooked sauce is
pushed through a mesh strainer, before being
mixed with the pasta and sprinkled with
grated pecorino cheese.

The country version is a more wholesome
and rugged affair: cooked chicken or Italian
sausage is added to the sauce, along with
chunky strips of bell pepper, mushroom, and
onion, or vegetables of choice.

Whatever the version, have pitchers of
water nearby to put out the fire!

Bucatini all'Amatriciana

This classic pasta specialty hails from Amatrice, a town on the border northeast of Rome. It is made with a thick, hollow, spaghetti-shaped pasta called bucatini, made from hard durum wheat flour and named for *buco*, or "hole" in Italian. The classic *amatriciana* sauce comprises pancetta or *guanciale* (unsmoked bacon), and tomatoes.

Bucatini all'Amatriciana

1¼ cup extra-virgin olive oil

12 oz thinly sliced guanciale, pancetta, or good bacon

1 red onion, sliced into ¼-in thick half rings

3 cloves garlic, sliced

1½ tsp hot red chile flakes

2 cups basic tomato sauce

1 lb bucatini

Freshly grated Pecorino Romano

Bring 6 quarts of water to a boil in a large pot and add 2 tablespoons salt. Combine the olive oil, guanciale, onion, garlic, and red chile flakes in a 10- to 12-inch sauté pan set over low heat, and cook until the onion is softened and the guanciale has rendered much of its fat, about 12 minutes. Drain all but ¼ cup of the fat out of the pan. Add the tomato sauce, turn up the heat, and bring to a boil, then lower the heat to a simmer and allow to bubble for 6 to 7 minutes. While the sauce simmers, cook the bucatini in the boiling water for about a minute less than the package instructions, until still very firm; drain. Add the pasta to the simmering sauce and toss for about 1 minute to coat. Divide the pasta among four heated bowls and serve immediately, topped with freshly grated pecorino. *Serves 4*

Adapted from Mario Batali's *Molto Italiano*

Linguine al Ragù di Funghi

Here is a splendid combination of classic Italian ingredients. The ragout—*ragù* in Italian—is a hearty sauce that is usually meat-based, like the bolognese sauce so often served with spaghetti. In this recipe the meat is replaced with the king of dried mushrooms, the porcini (or cepe), prized for its strong nutty flavor.

The ingredients common to all ragouts, however, are the sofritto—a sautéed mixture of chopped onions, celery, carrots, and seasonings—and a slowly simmered tomato sauce. The slow cooking provides the characteristic intense flavor.

Linguine—one of the long flat pastas—means "little tongues" and originates in the Campania region of southern Italy.

Fettuccine Alfredo

Throughout Italy and increasingly in North America, freshly made pasta, such as tagliatelle, fettuccine, tortellini, and ravioli, can be bought in the local supermarket to cook at home. In Rome, homemade egg fettuccine is a specialty, particularly when combined with a luxurious creamy Alfredo sauce.

This dish was created by an inspired cook named Alfredo di Lelio, who created the dish at his restaurant in Rome in 1914. It is said that he tossed egg fettuccine with Parmesan cheese and butter for his wife, who had lost her appetite during pregnancy.

Made well, the unctuous sauce of butter, cream, and cheese, slowly melted together, before being tossed with the golden pasta ribbons and showered with grated Parmesan cheese is perfect for special occasions.

Bolognese Meat Sauce

What most of the world outside of Italy considers spaghetti sauce is, in fact, a simpler version of bolognese sauce, the city of Bologna's culinary gift to the world. Naturally, it has undergone many changes, but the basic meat sauce fundamentally remains the same. Luckily, the *Accademia Italiana della Cucina* has set the rules. According to the Academy, authentic bolognese sauce consists of beef, pancetta, onions, carrots, celery, tomato paste, meat broth, white wine, and milk. Onions, carrots, and celery form the aromatic base and are sautéed in oil with the meat until softened. The pan is deglazed with white wine and then broth is introduced until the liquid has reduced. The whole lot is thickened with a dollop of tomato paste and, after a long simmer, finished with milk. International versions, found in Italian restaurants around the world, tend to emphasize tomatoes and may include only ground beef, as opposed to the finely chopped meat preferred by traditionalists.

Bolognese Meat Sauce

1 tbsp vegetable oil

3 tbsp butter, plus 1 tbsp for tossing the pasta

$1/2$ cup chopped onion

$2/3$ cup chopped celery

$2/3$ cup chopped carrot

$3/4$ lb ground beef

Salt

Freshly ground black pepper

1 cup whole milk

Whole nutmeg

1 cup dry white wine

$1^1/2$ cups canned imported Italian plum tomatoes, cut up, with their juice

$1^1/4$ to $1^1/2$ pounds pasta

Freshly grated Parmesan cheese at the table

Put the oil, butter, and chopped onion in the pot, and turn the heat on to medium. Cook and stir the onion until it has become translucent, then add the chopped celery and carrot. Cook for about 2 minutes, stirring the vegetables to coat them well.

Add the ground beef, a large pinch of salt, and a few grindings of pepper. Crumble the meat with a fork, stir well, and cook until the beef has lost its raw, red color.

Add the milk and let it simmer gently, stirring frequently, until it has bubbled away completely. Add a tiny grating—about

¼ teaspoon—of nutmeg, and stir. Add the wine, let it simmer until it has evaporated, then add the tomatoes and stir thoroughly to coat all ingredients well. When the tomatoes begin to bubble, turn the heat down so that the sauce cooks at the laziest of simmers, with just an intermittent bubble breaking through to the surface.

Cook, uncovered, for 3 hours or more, stirring from time to time. While the sauce is cooking, you are likely to find that it begins to dry out and the fat separates from the meat. To keep it from sticking, continue the cooking, adding a little water when necessary.

At the end, however, no water at all must be left and the fat must separate from the sauce. Taste and correct for salt. Toss with cooked drained pasta, add the remaining tablespoon of butter, and serve with freshly grated Parmesan on the side. *Serves 6*
Adapted from Marcella Hazan's *Essentials of Italian Cooking*

Spaghetti Marinara

Spaghetti is the versatile, thin, string pasta that is popular throughout the country and, indeed, much of the world. It is frequently served with a tomato sauce, which may contain a variety of herbs, including oregano and basil, and the cooked spaghetti with its sauce may be topped with several hard cheeses, such as Pecorino Romano or Parmigiano Reggiano. Some versions of spaghetti are colored red (tomato flavored), green (spinach flavored), and white, to reflect the colors of the Italian flag.

The tomato-based marinara sauce ("the sauce of the mariners") is meatless with a high acid content. Its resistance to spoiling meant that it was widely used on sailing ships before the advent of refrigeration. Mashed garlic is sautéed in olive oil to which chopped fresh tomatoes are added and simmered for 10 minutes. One of the most famous tomato-based sauces was featured in the film *The Godfather*, in 1972. Meat, tomato paste, wine, and sugar were simmered with the basic tomato recipe before ladling over spaghetti.

Spaghetti all'Aglio e Olio

This is a dish for those addicted to garlic. When the spaghetti is cooked, olive oil is barely warmed and into it is stirred a quantity of finely chopped garlic. The garlic-steeped oil is then stirred into the drained spaghetti. Chopped parsley or any other herb and grated Parmesan can be added.

Sophia Loren famously claimed that "Spaghetti can be eaten successfully if you inhale it like a vacuum cleaner." In truth, much is made of the technique for eating spaghetti. Those who fork the food into the bowl of a spoon, or who dare to cut the 8-inch strands before eating, are considered fraudsters. The *only* way to eat spaghetti is by twirling the fork in the center of the dish and hoping for a neat, mouth-sized bundle.

Spaghetti alla Carbonara

This sauce is quick and very easy to make. The name derives from *carbone*, meaning coal, suggesting it was originally a coalminer's dish. The specks of coarse-grained black pepper that are ground over the prepared dish resemble coal dust.

Spaghetti alla Carbonara

9 slices bacon, chopped

1 tbsp butter

$^1/_2$ cup heavy cream

$^1/_2$ cup grated Parmesan cheese, plus extra for sprinkling

4 egg yolks

12 oz spaghetti

Salt

Freshly ground black pepper

Combine the bacon and butter in a large heavy frying pan over medium heat. Sauté until the bacon is brown and crisp. With a slotted spoon, transfer the bacon to paper towels and drain. In a medium bowl, whisk the cream, cheese, and egg yolks to blend, then whisk in 2 tablespoons of drippings from the pan. Discard any remaining drippings.

Cook the pasta in a large pot of boiling salted water until just tender but firm to the bite, stirring occasionally. Drain the pasta and return it to the same pot.

Add the cream mixture and toss over medium-low heat until the sauce cooks through and coats the pasta thickly, about 4 minutes. Do not boil. Mix in the bacon and season to taste with salt and pepper. Divide up the pasta and pass extra cheese at the table.

Serves 6

Tortellini with Prosciutto

This stuffed, ring-shaped egg pasta and its larger version, *tortelloni*, originate in the Emilia region of Italy, in particular around the cities of Bologna and Modena. The stuffing is typically a mixture of meats or cheeses of the region—prosciutto from Parma, rotund mortadella sausage from Bologna, ground pork and Parmesan cheese—and the tortellini are traditionally served in a homemade broth. Their shape is said to be inspired by a woman's navel, espied through a keyhole by an innkeeper. The possessor of the navel is, in one account, Lucrezia Borgia and in another the goddess, Venus, both of whom apparently visited the region.

To make the famous Parma ham, or prosciutto, pigs are fattened on whey from the making of Parmigiano Reggiano cheese. The resulting high-quality meat is salt-cured and air-dried but not smoked. It takes up to 12 months of aging to produce this silky-textured raw ham with its distinctive nutty flavor. The best prosciutti come from the village of Langhirano.

Cannelloni

Cannelloni are squares or tubes of cooked pasta that are stuffed, rolled, and baked in a béchamel or cheese sauce. They are sometimes known as *pasta pipiera*, or "big pipes." In the United States, the pasta is more commonly known as manicotti, which are traditionally rolled on the diagonal while cannelloni are rolled on the square.

The all-important filling may be made from ground meat or sausage, seafood, ricotta and spinach, even wild mushrooms. It must be fresh and delicate and the tubes filled with a light hand to avoid a dense, heavy final result.

The pasta is boiled briefly then drained carefully to avoid breakage. When cool, each square is spread with some filling and rolled up. The "pipes" are then arranged side by side in an ovenproof dish, covered with thick sauce and a layer of grated Parmesan cheese, and baked.

Though Italians serve cannelloni as a small portion before the main course, internationally it is more likely to be served as a main course.

Macaroni and Cheese

Ancient Greeks and Romans may have been the first to combine these two comfort foods. In medieval Italy, pasta recipes called for grated cheese mixed with spices. The dish migrated from Italy to the court of English King Richard II in the 14th century, as evidenced by a recipe for "macrows." After boiling the pasta, the recipe says, "take cheese, and grate it, and butter, cast beneath, and above...and serve it forth." An 18th-century English recipe from one Elizabeth Raffald layers the pasta with Parmesan cheese and cream. American recipes of the 1800s also use the layering technique, while a recipe from 1915 melts the cheese into a sauce before adding it to the pasta.

The pasta shapes, meanwhile, called *maccheroni* in Italian, may be related to the Greek *makaria*, a kind of barley broth. Or they might come from the Latin *macerare*, to bruise or crush, referring to the crushing of the wheat to make pasta. This comforting everyday dish is also known as "mac 'n' cheese" in the United States, while in Britain it is called "macaroni cheese."

Macaroni and Cheese

6 tbsp butter

6 tbsp all-purpose flour

4 cups milk

1$\frac{1}{2}$ tsp dry mustard

Salt

Freshly ground black pepper

1 lb elbow macaroni

3 cups grated Cheddar cheese

1$\frac{1}{3}$ cups freshly grated Parmesan cheese

Preheat the oven to 350°F.

Melt the butter in a saucepan over moderately low heat. Add the flour and cook for 1 to 2 minutes, stirring continuously. Add the milk in a steady stream, whisking to blend with the butter. Bring the sauce to a boil, still whisking, and add the dry mustard, salt, and pepper to taste. Continue to cook over low heat until the sauce thickens, about 2 minutes.

Cook the macaroni according to the package instructions. Drain well, and combine with the sauce, the Cheddar, and 1 cup of the Parmesan. Transfer the mixture to a buttered shallow baking dish. Sprinkle the remaining Parmesan over the top and bake in the preheated oven for 25 to 30 minutes. The top should be browned and bubbling. *Serves 6*

Lasagne

There is a first-century mention of *lagana* in Roman writings, referring to pasta strips layered with meat and fish. Horace and Cicero both mention a liking for it, and the word *lagane* survives in central and southern Italy today. Medieval lasagne was typically creamy, sweet, and layered with cheese, often eaten during Lent. Since it required a baking oven, it was only to be found in the kitchens of the wealthy. In fact, for most of Italian history, this comforting dish of fresh pasta sheets layered with meat, vegetables, or seafood was considered a lavish one. Today we know it as a protein-rich ground meat, tomato, and pasta dish with an egg-and-cheese béchamel sauce. It takes time to make the dish at home, but the rewards are rich and filling enough for a comforting main course. If you are lucky, there will be leftovers, which always taste better the next day.

Maultaschen

A large German form of ravioli, Maultaschen are a specialty of Swabia in Baden-Württemberg, southern Germany. Four of them make an ample serving for one. The pasta pockets are filled with spinach and ground meat (veal, pork, beef, bacon, or sausage) and a liberal helping of parsley.

Translated as "nosebags," these dumplings were originally eaten toward the end of Lent, possibly to conceal the fact that meat was on the menu, which would explain its other local name *Herrgottsbscheißerle* (God cheaters). The monks of Maulbronn Abbey are said to have come up with this ingenious idea. To ring in the changes during Holy Week, the Maultaschen were served in a broth on Holy Thursday and sliced and fried with onions on Good Friday. Any leftovers could be baked on Saturday with a little cheese.

Lochshen

These flat, wide egg noodles belong to Eastern European and Jewish cuisines. A typical example is lochshen soup, our familiar chicken noodle soup or "Jewish penicillin," believed to benefit the sick by 12th-century rabbi, physician, and philosopher Maimonides. Carrots, onions, celery, parsnips, and dumplings are added to the chicken broth to make this splendid noodle soup.

Lochshen kugel is a baked sweet pudding. *Kugel* is Yiddish for "ball," a reference to its puffed shape. The lochshen are boiled, mixed with cinnamon, beaten eggs, and sugar, and then baked. Apples and raisins are sometimes added. Kugel is a mainstay of festive meals in Ashkenazi Jewish homes, particularly on the Jewish holy days. Some Hasidic Jews believe that eating kugel on the Jewish Sabbath brings special spiritual blessings.

Ravioli

The most common forms of ravioli are rectangular or circular pasta sheets wrapped around a meat or cheese-based filling. In fact, the word ravioli comes from *ravvolgere*, the Italian verb "to wrap." In the last century, ravioli made use of meat left over from festive meals. Cheese or vegetable fillings were often used by the poor and by richer families during traditional periods of denial such as Lent or on Fridays. Ravioli is frequently served with a tomato sauce, pesto, or cream sauce.

Although thought of as an Italian dish, ravioli, along with other pasta, was introduced to Italy from China via the Silk Road in the medieval period. They would not have been served with a tomato sauce as tomatoes were unknown in Europe at that time. The Chinese version of ravioli is *jiaozi*—thinly rolled dough sealed around ground meat or vegetables and served with a soy-based dipping sauce. Many countries have their own version of ravioli. In Palestine and Lebanon, *shishbarak* is pasta stuffed with ground beef and cooked in a hot yogurt sauce, whereas the Tibetan *momo* (filled with various types of meat) can be steamed, cooked in broth, and fried or served in soup.

Tortellini with Spinach and Ricotta

The subtle, delicate flavors of spinach and ricotta marry well when mixed together—neither one overpowering the other. The combination is popular in Italian cuisine and is seen again and again in regional dishes, including a non-meat version of lasagne and spinach-ricotta gnocchi. Teamed up in tortellini, they make a smooth, fresh, and creamy filling that is delicious served simply with olive oil and grated Parmesan cheese, or topped with a fresh homemade tomato sauce.

Ricotta, though termed a cheese, is strictly a by-product of cheese-making, made from the whey of such Italian cheeses as mozzarella and provolone. The word means "re-cooked," a reference to the two heating processes used in its production. White, creamy, and slightly sweet with a fine, grainy texture, ricotta is naturally low in fat and salt. Since it's unripened, the cheese must be refrigerated in a well-sealed container, and is best eaten fresh and as soon as possble.

Polenta

Cornmeal porridge is popular in many parts of the world, from Africa to central Europe to South America and the southern US. In northern Italy it vies with pasta in popularity. Once a rather bland peasant staple, it is now dressed up in many guises to form an important ingredient in the regional cuisine of Friuli, Lombardy, Piedmont, and the Veneto. The yellow cornmeal is traditionally cooked for an hour or more, stirred constantly in a copper cauldron or *paiolo*.

The resulting creamy soft mass can be mounded in a bowl, perhaps with added cheese. Otherwise it is poured onto a surface, where it solidifies as it cools and before reaching the edge.

Uses for the firm polenta are myriad—formed into patties or balls and fried or broiled to accompany meat; sliced and topped with meat or fish; cooked with cheese and butter or various sauces; or incorporated into stews. The Corsicans have a sweet version they call *pulenta*, made with sweet chestnut flour.

Polenta

8 cups water

1¼ tsp salt

3 cups coarse yellow cornmeal

Bring the water and salt to a boil. Lower the heat and slowly add the cornmeal a handful at a time, whisking constantly. Beware of splashes. Turn up the heat, just until bubbles rise and burst on the surface, and cook for 40 to 50 minutes, stirring constantly from the bottom up. When ready, the polenta should come away from the sides of the pot. Serve immediately, with condiments.

For a more firm polenta, smooth the surface, place a wooden board over the pot, and briskly turn the pot upside down. Cool, cut into portions, and serve. *Serves 4*

Knödel

Knödel is the name for dumplings in Austria and southern Germany. They can be made from potatoes (*Kartoffelknödel*), or from stale bread with milk and egg yolks (*Semmelknödel*) and are cooked like pasta in boiling water. Bakers grind their day-old *Semmel* or breakfast bread rolls into crumbs or cut them into cubes and sell them for dumpling-making. The cooked dumplings are rolled in bread crumbs and replace potatoes as a side dish.

Dumplings are also typical of the Czech Republic, Poland, and other parts of Germany. Potato dough was a Bohemian specialty that spread throughout the Austro-Hungarian Empire. In Germany, Knödel are most commonly served with roast pork while Austrians add chopped bacon to the plain potato dumpling to make *Speckknödel,* which can be added to soup. Knödel can also be stuffed with a plum or an apricot and tossed in bread crumbs, then heated with butter, sugar, and cinnamon to make a sweet dumpling.

Kreplach

Kreplach are the dumplings served in chicken soup in Ashkenazic Jewish cuisine, a hearty style of cooking that reflects centuries of residence in the cold climate of central and Eastern Europe. Traditionally prepared for the feast of Purim (the Feast of Lots), kreplach are now enjoyed on other holy festivals as well, such as Hoshannah Rabbah (the Seventh Day of the Festival of Booths), or on the day before Yom Kippur (the Day of Atonement).

Originally, the dumplings were a thrifty peasant food, made with leftover cooked meat—for example the flesh of the boiling fowl used to make the chicken soup—which was ground up, mixed with grated onion, and made into dumplings to stretch the meal further. Cooked potato was another filler.

Today, egg pasta dough is rolled out and cut into squares, filled with a fresh, ground meat mixture, folded into triangles, and boiled. If the kreplach are to be served separately, they can be sautéed in oil until golden brown. They are sometimes referred to as Jewish wontons, the Jewish version of a Chinese dumpling.

Gnocchi

Pronounced "nyò-ki," these small oval dumplings come from the Italian word *gnocco*, or lump. They are made with potato, semolina, or all-purpose flour, and can be flavored—ricotta cheese and spinach are a popular choice.

Gnocchi can be purchased fresh in vacuum-sealed packages. Like fresh pasta, they are quickly boiled and have an affinity with tomato or cheese sauces, which cling well to the little pillows with their fork-etched grooves. As a side dish, they are an excellent accompaniment to meat or poultry.

In South American countries where Italian cuisine is popular, there was a tradition for eating gnocchi on the 29th day of each month, the day before payday when people needed a cheap and hearty meal. Florentines call them *topini* (field mice), because the homemade dumplings resemble little mice, although in other Italian regions this may not be a familiar name.

Ricotta and Spinach Gnocchi

Gnocchi are one of the more historic Italian foods. The ricotta and spinach variety is a specialty of an area east of Florence, the Casentino, where spinach grows wild on the hillsides.

Ricotta and spinach gnocchi have several alternative names, such as *malfatti* (badly made), *ravioli nudi* (naked ravioli), or *topini verdi* (little green mice). The name *ravioli nudi* refers to the fact that these little morsels are essentially mounds of ravioli filling.

To prepare the gnocchi, spinach is boiled until just wilted and added to a mixture of egg, flour, and cheese to make a soft dough. Lightly flattened balls of dough are boiled for a few minutes and served with a sauce of melted butter and Parmesan.

Ricotta and Spinach Gnocchi

1 lb spinach, trimmed and washed

8 oz ricotta cheese

$1/3$ cup all-purpose flour

2 tbsp grated Parmesan cheese

1 egg

Freshly grated nutmeg

Salt

Freshly ground black pepper

Flour for dusting

For the sauce:

$1/2$ cup olive oil

1 small onion, chopped

1 clove garlic, chopped

6 tomatoes, skinned, seeded, and chopped

Juice of $1/2$ a lemon

3 tbsp chopped fresh basil

In a large pan, cook the spinach with just the water clinging to its leaves until wilted. Drain in a colander. When cool, squeeze out excess moisture and chop. Transfer to a large bowl and add the cheeses, flour, egg, and nutmeg. Mix well. Add salt and pepper to taste, then refrigerate for at least 1 hour, until firm.

Place a 12-inch sheet of parchment paper on a clean counter. Have a bowl of flour nearby. Dip both hands in the flour and roll a small piece of the chilled spinach mixture into a ball about the size of a walnut. Place on the paper. Repeat with remaining spinach mixture, dusting hands frequently. Cover and refrigerate until ready to cook.

Just before serving, heat the oil and sauté the garlic and onions until tender, about 15 minutes. Add the tomatoes and cook for a further 5 minutes. Keep warm. Meanwhile, bring a large pot of salted water to a boil. Drop in the spinach balls, in batches if necessary, and cook until they float to the surface. Transfer the gnocchi to warm shallow bowls and spoon the sauce overtop. Garnish with basil and Parmesan shavings. *Serves 4*

Moros y Cristianos

For more than 500 years, Spain and its former New World colonies have celebrated the triumph of Spanish Catholicism over its enemies in festivals, re-enacting the medieval battles between Christians and the Moorish invaders in dance and drama.

In Spain, such events are staged throughout the year up and down the country, from January (the Feast of the Holy Child in Cuenca) to December (the festival of the Moorish King in Alicante). In Mexico, battles with the Aztecs have been incorporated into this tradition.

The dark-skinned Moors and light-skinned Christians have been translated in culinary terms into a single dish of black beans and white rice. It is particularly popular in Cuba where it is known as *congri*. Red beans are sometimes substituted for black. A simple dish to make, onions and bell peppers are first sautéed with spices, the soaked beans are added along with tomatoes and seasonings, followed by the rice and broth. The resulting mixture is simmered for half an hour. Sometimes bacon is added for extra flavor. The dish frequently accompanies meat or fish.

Cuban tradition says Moros y Cristianos bring good luck if eaten on New Year's Day.

Moros y Cristianos

$2/3$ cup black beans, soaked overnight

$1/2$ medium onion

2 cloves garlic

2 bay leaves

$1/2$ cinnamon stick

Zest of $1/2$ orange

Juice of $1/2$ orange

3 tbsp olive oil

$1/2$ bunch fresh flat-leaf parsley, roughly chopped

$1/2$ cup white rice

Sea salt

Freshly ground black pepper

Drain the beans and place in a large saucepan with at least 6 times their volume of cold water. Add the onion, garlic, bay leaves, and cinnamon stick. Bring to a boil, reduce the heat to a simmer, and skim off any scum. Cook for 1 to 2 hours until tender. Pour off the cooking liquid until level with the beans, season with salt and pepper, orange zest, orange juice, olive oil, and parsley; set aside. Simmer the rice in lightly salted boiling water until firm but not chalky (about 10 to 15 minutes), and drain. When you are ready, serve the rice, then spoon the beans and a little of their juice on top, so you can see both the black and the white. *Serves 4*

Adapted from Sam and Sam Clark's

Moro: The Cookbook

Hominy Grits

No self-respecting breakfast is complete
without hominy grits—a creamy, crunchy
concoction of cooked ground corn kernels.
The word grits comes from the old English
grytta meaning any coarse meal, while
hominy (or *sampe*) refers to corn with the
grain. In America, the early English colonists,
baffled by this strange new grain, enlisted
the help of Native Americans to make the
tough corn kernels edible. Today the process
is much improved and less labor-intensive.

The appeal of grits, apart from being
inexpensive, simple, and easily digested, is
in their versatility. In the southern states and
Mexico, "big hominy" (whole kernels) is used
in the preparation of *posole*—a rich hearty
stew. The smaller ground kernels or "little
hominy" are ground even finer for use as
tamale and tortilla dough.

Variations of hominy grits can be found
around the world. Italy's golden cornmeal
polenta is a popular side dish, while in
Barbados a blend of cornmeal and okra,
called *cou cou*, is served with flying fish.

Rice and Lentils

Rice and lentils are eaten around the world.
In some countries, such as Nepal, it is the
staple daily diet for most of the population.
Typically, the *dhal* (lentils) are boiled with
spices for about 30 minutes, with fried onions,
chiles, and garlic added for the last few
minutes. The rice is served separately. A south
Indian recipe involves frying mustard seeds,
curry leaves, and onions in oil, then adding
tamarind juice and water. This is brought to
a boil before adding lentils, rice, and masala
paste. When cooked, the rice and lentils are
garnished with cilantro leaves and may be
served with a tangy pickle. To make Lebanese
m'jadrah, the rice and lentils are cooked
together with fried onions and salt as
flavoring, and served as a side dish to fish
or meat, or with salad as a main course.
A hearty stew from the mountainous region
of Valencia in Spain includes vegetables
such as chard, potatoes, and turnip and is
often flavored with tomatoes, garlic, and bell
pepper. The vegetables and lentils are cooked
together first, with the rice added during the
last 20 minutes to absorb the liquid.

Dirty Rice

The Cajun rice of the southern states of
Louisiana and Mississippi is a simple dish that
makes use of some decidedly unfashionable
yet full-flavored ingredients such as dried
chicken livers and gizzards. Cooked and finely
chopped, these tiny pieces give the rice a
"dirty" look, though the flavor is delicious.

The rice is boiled until just tender, while
garlic, onions, and green bell peppers are
sautéed separately in oil until soft, then
seasoned. Meanwhile, in a third pan, the livers
and gizzards are simmered for 30 minutes
in water. The cooked, diced ingredients are
added to the rice and simmered on low heat
for a further 30 minutes to combine the
flavors before serving.

Wild Rice

This sacred food of Native Americans is
technically not rice at all, but an aquatic
cereal grass, *Zizania*, producing slender hard
black grains. It is now commercially produced
in California and several midwest US states,
although it is native to the Great Lakes area.
The cooked grain has a chewy texture, and
with its nutty taste makes a robust base for
salads, stuffings, and pilafs.

Wild rice is prepared like rice, and
benefits from a thorough cleaning in a bowl
of water to remove any debris. It takes about
30 minutes to cook, which allows the hard,
dense grains to reveal their starchy white
interior. It is high in protein and fiber and a
good source of minerals and vitamins.

Wild rice was once an important grain in
ancient China gathered from the wild. It is
expensive, but combines well with white rice,
brown rice, or bulgur wheat.

Hoppin' John

Believed to have been a staple food of slaves during the American Civil War, hoppin' John is today a popular dish in the southern states. It consists of soaked black-eyed peas, ham-flavored rice, and piquant seasonings. This time-honored dish is served in the South on New Year's Day. The notion that, once eaten, good luck will prevail throughout the year, is one of many well-loved stories handed down through generations.

Native to Africa, the black-eyed pea is a subspecies of the cowpea and is named for its prominent black spot. It was first introduced to the West Indies before migrating north. The local dish in Trinidad is known quite simply as "peas and rice," and immortalized in a popular calypso tune.

The origins of the name hoppin' John are obscure. However, one apocryphal story tells of a one-legged waiter (a slave) who successfully hopped around the tables while serving. One evening he produced a meal of rice and black-eyed peas, which delighted the diners so much they named the dish for him.

Couscous

Couscous is a staple of North African cuisine and the national dish of Morocco. It consists of tiny balls of semolina grain coated with a fine layer of flour before their lengthy steaming. The balls are formed by sprinkling the semolina and the flour with a little salted water, then rolling them with the palm of the hand against the sides of a wide shallow straw bowl.

The grains are steamed in a *couscousière*, a special two-piece pot that resembles a perforated metal colander set over a large pot. The cooked semolina is heaped in the top half while the meat and vegetables are placed in the bottom. As they cook, the rising steam infuses the grain with flavor.

In Morocco, couscous is never served as a side dish as is common in the West. Instead, it is accompanied by meat and vegetable broth, chicken and raisins, or even fish in tomato sauce. It is always served at the end of a banquet to ensure that no guest goes hungry.

Moroccan families traditionally sit down on Friday to a steaming meal of couscous served with its many garnishes.

Couscous

2³/₄ cups water

¹/₄ tsp salt

1¹/₂ cups couscous

Bring the water to a boil in a large saucepan. Add the salt and stir in the couscous. Remove from the heat, cover, and let sit for about 5 minutes, or until the water is absorbed. Fluff with a fork. *Serves 6*

Arroz con Coco

This sweet coconut rice pudding, rich with grated coconut, is served along the Caribbean coast of Colombia and Venezuela. It is also popular in Puerto Rico and Cuba.

Traditionally, the coconut flesh is extracted from the kernel and grated, then pressed to obtain the milk, which is then strained. The pulp is cooked fiercely to extract the oil, which is then added to the cooking liquid for the short-grain rice, along with liberal amounts of sugar. The whole mixture is cooked for about 30 minutes until the water is absorbed.

A simpler way to prepare this delicious dessert is to cook the rice in store-bought coconut milk blended with whole milk and shredded coconut. Lemon peel may also be used as a flavoring. Cooked slowly for an hour over low heat, the rice becomes sticky as it absorbs the milk. Heavy cream is gently stirred into the cooked rice. Before serving, the pudding is sprinkled with cinnamon.

Arroz con Pollo

This popular Cuban dish makes any meal special. The use of short-grain Valencia-style rice (Italian arborio is a good substitute) makes it similar in style to paella. Unlike the Spanish baked rice dish, however, which gets its golden glow from saffron, Cuban cooks use annatto oil to give this dish its distinctive yellow color.

A cut-up chicken is sautéed in hot oil until golden brown, then set aside while onion, pepper, garlic, and saffron are sautéed until softened. The chicken is returned to the pan and cooked with tomatoes, wine (or beer), and a bay leaf. Rice and water are added and brought to a boil, then the dish is covered and cooked on top of the stove or in the oven until the rice is tender. Just before serving, green peas and red bell peppers are stirred in for color and flavor.

Green Rice

Rice and Spinach ▷

Rice is so versatile that adding practically
any ingredient automatically guarantees
it a mention among specialty dishes. So it
is with green rice.

Mexico's visually intriguing contribution
combines rice with poblano chile peppers,
parsley, peas, and cilantro. The vegetables are
puréed with garlic and onion and added while
the rice is cooking. Green peas are added
just before serving. A Thai variation omits the
garlic but adds creamed coconut, gingerroot,
and cinnamon sticks to the mix, producing a
delicious and fragrant dish.

The Italians, meanwhile, create a rice pie
for spring—*torta primavera*. Originating
in Italy's Piedmont region, it is made with
chopped spinach, (collard greens or young
nettles do equally well), chives, celery leaves,
and minced sautéed pancetta. Halfway
through cooking, the rice is allowed to cool.
The eggs, herbs, and cheese are then added
and the mixture turned out into a buttered
pan. It is baked for 10 minutes, flipped over
onto a serving dish, cooled, and cut into
wedges. The taste is exquisite, or *squisito*!

With rice being a staple food for many
people, and with spinach being a good source
of vitamins and vital antioxidants, it is not
surprising that rice and spinach in one form
or another make a popular combination.
Frozen spinach is a good alternative to fresh,
as it is ready to use and has not lost its
nutritional value through prolonged storage.

One of the most famous traditional recipes
is *spanakorizo*, a side dish from Greece.
Onions are fried in a little olive oil over
medium heat until soft and golden. Spinach
is added to cook for a few minutes, followed
by tomatoes and water. Seasonings include
dill and parsley. Brought back to a boil,
the rice is added and cooked until tender.
The dish is often served at room temperature,
garnished with a little feta cheese and freshly
squeezed lemon juice.

Arroz a la Tumbada

Mexico's gulf coast, where this dish originates, is naturally influenced by the sea that lines its shores. The country's oldest and largest city, Veracruz, is a lively port renowned for its seafood dishes. Similar to a paella or risotto, arroz a la tumbada presents a variety of seafood (recipes may include shrimp, clams, calamari, crab, or whitefish) cooked with rice that itself has been cooked slowly in fish broth. Traditionally, it is prepared and served from a thick clay pot called a *cazuela*, accompanied by fresh corn tortillas and a bowl of chili sauce.

Arroz a la Tumbada

1 cup fruity olive oil

1¹/₂ lb medium shrimp, unshelled

Salt

2 cups finely chopped tomatoes

³/₄ cup finely chopped white onion

1 small red bell pepper, seeded and thinly sliced

2 cloves garlic, finely chopped

1¹/₂ cups long-grain unconverted white rice, rinsed and drained

5 cups fish broth

1/2 cup roughly chopped cilantro

2 tbsp roughly chopped chives

2 tbsp roughly chopped mint

1 tsp dried oregano

Heat the olive oil in an ovenproof casserole about 5 inches deep. Add the shrimp and a good sprinkle of salt, and stir-fry over high heat for about 1 minute. Remove with a slotted spoon and set aside. In the same oil, fry the tomatoes, onions, pepper, and garlic over medium heat until well mixed—about 5 minutes.

Stir in the rice, add the broth with salt to taste, and bring to a boil. Cover the pan and cook over medium heat for about 8 minutes. Add the shrimp and herbs, and continue cooking, covered, still over medium heat, until the rice is tender—about 10 minutes.

The consistency is between a soup and a rice dish—very moist and juicy. You may need to add a little more broth. *Serves 4*
Adapted from Diana Kennedy's *The Essential Cuisines of Mexico*

Jambalaya

Originating in the American South—on the banks of Louisiana's bayous—the quaintly named jambalaya (possibly derived from the Spanish *jamón*, meaning ham, or its French equivalent, *jambon*) is a fusion of European, African, and American influences dating from the late 18th century.

Traditionally made in one pot with meats, vegetables, and rice, the method of including the rice during cooking often denotes a particular ancestry.

The African jambalaya calls for gentle cooking of meats, chicken, and sausage, along with vegetables and tomatoes (often referred to as "red jambalaya"). Seafood features frequently. The rice and chicken broth are then added in equal proportions and simmered for an hour.

The Louisiana "Cajun" version of jambalaya, which has its roots in French provincial cooking and bears more than a passing resemblance to Spanish paella, requires a cast-iron pot to first brown all the meats— the bits stuck to the bottom create the dish's rich brown color. The "trinity" of onions, green bell peppers, and celery are sautéed in oil. The meat is returned to the pot with chicken broth and seasonings and simmered for an hour. After coming back to a boil, the rice is added to steam and soak up the juices.

Pamplona Rice

Pamplona, capital of Navarra in northeastern Spain, is famous for its annual Running of the Bulls, part of the festival of San Fermin and one of the country's most famous (if foolhardy) events. The great American writer, and one-time resident of Spain, Ernest Hemingway, loved this high-spirited spectacle.

Pamplona rice, essentially a rice and fish dish, has wide appeal not only to the vegetarian palate, but also to those of carnivorous persuasion. As with most rice dishes in this area, onions and peppers, both fancy and fiery, are sautéed to form a base sauce for the addition of chunks of cod or whatever fresh fish is available. For color and taste, tomatoes are added with the rice and seasoned with black pepper and turmeric.

Anchovies and green olives garnish this robust meal, much welcomed after a day of dodging stampeding bulls—perhaps just a bit too close for comfort.

Paella

This food originated in Valencia, Spain. *Paella* is the word for "frying pan" and both the dish and the flat, round, shallow pan used to cook it in are given the same name. This typical Spanish rice dish is invariably eaten on a Sunday. Such is its popularity that at large gatherings in Valencia, festivals and protests alike, an enormous paella is prepared—in specially-commissioned pans— to feed the masses.

Curiously, the traditional pan used for this dish, with two large handles on either side, has dimples in the center like the surface of a golf ball. It's still used today in the oven or over an open flame.

The preparation of paella is simple and based on three main ingredients—rice, saffron, and oil. Any additions of chicken, meat, vegetables, and seasonings are fried until lightly browned, then gently stewed in hot water or broth poured to the brim of the pan. The rice is then added to the mixture and cooked over high heat until all the liquid has been absorbed. Get out your wooden spoons and dig in!

Jewel of Persia

As the name suggests, this regal-sounding rice dish is native to the Islamic Republic of Iran—formerly known as Persia. Locals call it *javaha pole* and consider it the prince of Persian culinary fare. It is traditionally featured as a stunning centerpiece at wedding feasts, which include dishes such as yogurt and cucumber dips, chicken, eggplant, and zucchini, and end with sweet baklava pastry and mint tea.

To create this gilded illusion of wealth and riches, the rice is first simmered in chicken broth flavored with curry powder, turmeric, and several strands of exotic saffron—prized for its deep yellow color. The golden grains of rice are then studded with orange peel, almonds, red berries, and green pistachio nuts—artfully masquerading as rubies, emeralds, and other fine jewels.

Saffron is considered the world's most expensive spice—truly a fitting tribute to this royal dish.

Saffron Rice

Saffron is the world's most expensive spice—ounce by ounce more valuable than gold. It's no wonder, as its production is extremely labor-intensive. The spice comes from yellow-orange pistals of the small purple crocus (*Crocus sativus*). Each flower provides just three stigma, which are hand-picked and dried. In fact, it takes at least 14,000 of these tiny stigmas for each ounce of saffron.

The precious spice can be purchased in powder form or in threads (the whole stigmas). The threads should be crushed before use, and you only need a tiny amount to flavor an entire dish, a fact many chefs ignore.

In ancient times, saffron was used to dye cloth a deep yellow, and was prized for its medicinal qualities. It is frequently mentioned in the Bible. The Phoenicians could not live without their saffron and took it with them on their voyages, which explains the saffron buns of Cornwall, England.

Today the aromatic spice is used to flavor and tint food and is integral to dishes such as bouillabaise, risotto Milanese, and paella.

Saffron rice is a tasty recipe that goes well with a wide variety of dishes from the Indian subcontinent. The rice looks marvelous—each grain separate and a tempting yellow-brown with flecks of saffron.

Saffron Rice

1 1/2 cups long-grain rice

2 tbsp vegetable oil

1 (3-in) cinnamon stick

7 whole cloves

5 cardamom pods

2 1/4 cups water

1 tsp salt

1/4 tsp crumbled saffron threads

2 tbsp milk

In a large bowl, wash the rice in several changes of cold water until the water runs clear. Drain in a fine sieve. In a large heavy saucepan heat the oil over medium-high heat until it is hot but not smoking. Add the cinnamon, cloves, and cardamom pods. Stir-fry the spices for 30 seconds, or until the cloves puff slightly. Add the rice and stir for 1 minute, or until it is opaque. Add the water and salt and bring to a boil. Reduce the heat to low and cook, covered, for 15 minutes or until the rice is tender.

While the rice is cooking, set a heat-proof bowl over a small pan of simmering water. Add the saffron and heat for 3 to 4 minutes, or until brittle. Add the milk and heat, stirring occasionally, until bubbles form around the edges. Remove from the heat and let stand, covered, for 5 minutes before stirring into the cooked rice, and serving. *Serves 6*

Forbidden Rice

Forbidden rice is one of several varieties of black rice. Its dark husk is high in fiber, rich in iron, and has a nutty taste. Unlike other black rice from Asia, it is not glutinous or rough.

This striking rice turns a brilliant purple when cooked, suggesting the presence of phytonutrients. In Indonesia, black rice is cooked in coconut milk and served as a breakfast porridge. Ancient Chinese emperors prized black rice for its nutritional value. It may have earned its "forbidden" status because it was reserved for the emperor's table and was probably shared with his consorts and other members of the court only at his discretion.

Another theory has it that when the Greeks conquered the Middle East, they banned the nutritious rice, believing it was aiding their enemies in battle.

When cooked, black rice smells like freshly popped popcorn. It's delicious served with swordfish, pork, or shellfish.

Forbidden Rice

1 medium onion, finely chopped
3 tbsp butter
2 cloves garlic, minced
1 cup short-grain forbidden rice
2 cups chicken broth or water
Zest of 1 lime (reserve lime)

In a hot pan, sauté the onion in the butter until translucent. Add the garlic and cook for 1 minute. Add the rice, broth, and the peeled lime, pith removed, and cut in quarters, and bring to a boil. Reduce to a simmer and cook for about 50 minutes, or until the rice is soft and creamy but not mushy, like a risotto. If the rice dries out during cooking, add more liquid. Fluff the cooked rice and add the lime zest to taste. The rice should be creamy like a black risotto. *Serves 4*

Pilau Rice

The variations of this international dish are as numerous as its names: pilaw, pilaf, pulau, and *plov*. The latter originates from what is now Uzbekistan in eastern Iran, where it is considered to be one of the oldest preparations of rice, dating back to the 1600s.

Whatever the name, the basis of this rice dish is well cooked basmati rice, flavored with fragrant spices including cardamom, cinnamon, cloves, and saffron. It may also contain meat and vegetables. Over the years, pilau became standard fare in the Middle East. It took hold in Britain in the 18th century with the spread of the British Empire into India. Its introduction into the United States maximized the potential of the southern states' prolific rice crops and the influence of the spice trade made it a popular dish.

A south-Asian variant, *pulau*, holds great appeal for its high energy value, being prepared with peas, potato, mutton, or chicken. In India and Pakistan a close relative is *biryani*—a dish, now so successfully absorbed into Britain's culinary scene that it is neck and neck with traditional English fish and chips in the popularity sweepstakes.

Muri

In many areas of India and Bangladesh, puffed rice or *muri* (also known as *mur mure* in some parts and as *churmuri* or *kurlu* in Tulu) is a staple food. Typically, it is made by heating rice kernels in a sand-filled oven. The result is less perishable than the unprocessed rice and is incorporated in many recipes including the popular *bhelpuri*, where it forms part of the savory base topped with tomatoes, onions, chiles, garbanzo beans, cilantro leaves, and lime. This is usually accompanied by green chile chutney and sweet date or tamarind chutney. Commonly used as a *chaat* dish, this savory snack is often sold at the roadside from stalls or carts.

Gun puffing is one method used to make puffed rice on a commercial scale. Rice with optimum moisture content is heated under pressure. When the pressure is released very quickly, the kernel puffs out, making it spongy in the process, ideal for use in breakfast cereals and rice cakes.

Bhelpuri

3 cups puffed rice

¼ cup roasted, salted peanuts

2 boiled potatoes, cut into tiny cubes

1 large onion, finely chopped

1 large tomato, finely chopped

½ bunch cilantro, finely chopped

2 green chiles, finely chopped

Tamarind chutney

Green chile chutney

A handful of coarsely crushed *papdi* (savory biscuits)

Mix the puffed rice, peanuts, potato, onion, tomato, cilantro, and green chiles in a large bowl. Add the two chutneys to taste. Mix well and garnish with lots of papdi.

Serve immediately. *Serves 6*

Kedgeree

This quintessential English dish with its un-English sounding name was a stalwart of the 19th and 20th century country-house breakfast table. The name originates from India, then a colony of the British Empire. Kedgeree is derived from the dish *khichri*—consisting of rice, lentils, and sliced hard-boiled eggs spiced with turmeric powder—a favorite Bombay breakfast dish often served with fried fish.

In the days of the Raj, fish was regularly eaten for breakfast, as in the heat, fresh fish caught early in the morning would not be palatable by evening. The British adopted kedgeree as their own. On its arrival in Britain, catering to the blander palate prevailed, turmeric was omitted and the strong salty flavor of smoked haddock was added—or, as the Scots would say, "finnan haddie." The name originates from the Scottish coastal town of Findon—whose cottage industry was the smoking of haddock.

Kedgeree

$1/4$ cup butter

3 scallions, chopped

2 tsp curry powder

1 cup basmati rice

2 cups chicken broth

5 oz smoked haddock, cubed

2 tbsp cream

$1/4$ cup chopped fresh parsley

Melt the butter in a large saucepan and sauté the scallions until soft. Add the curry powder and rice and stir well to coat. Stir in the broth. Bring to a boil, then reduce the heat and simmer, covered, for 12 minutes, or until just tender. Remove from the heat and stir in the fish, cream, and parsley. Cover and let sit 5 minutes to heat through. Serve hot. *Serves 2*

Biryani

Biryani is a fragrant and delicious Indian concoction of spices, basmati rice, meat or vegetables, and yogurt. Favorite spices include cloves, cardamom, cinnamon, bay leaves, coriander, mint, onion, garlic, and ginger. A superior biryani is dyed gold with a few strands of expensive saffron. It can be made with beef, lamb, chicken, even goat. Fish, quail, deer, even hare are also used. A vegetarian biryani usually comprises cauliflower, peas, carrots, and potatoes.

Preparing this dish requires delicate timing. The meat is marinated and the rice parboiled before both are fried separately. Rice, meat, or vegetables are layered in an earthen cooking pot known as a *dum*.

Biryani is traditionally served with *raita* (a yogurt and cucumber sauce), *korma* (a mild curry), or *brinjal* (eggplant).

It is said that the Nawabs, the governors of an Indian province, would match their turbans to the variety of biryani on which they were to dine.

Butter Rice with Onion

Although the cuisine of Myanmar has been influenced by China, India, and Thailand, it retains its own flavors and preparation techniques. Daily fare consists of a wide range of meat, fish, and vegetable dishes eaten with steamed sticky rice. Breakfast might be a warm noodle soup flavored with coconut.

One favorite dish is rice cooked in butter or coconut milk and combined with dried grapes, cashew nuts, and cinnamon. This fragrant dish is scattered with shredded, fried golden onion before serving. It often accompanies chicken curry.

At the table, the eldest diners are traditionally served first before the rest join in. When the Burmese elders are absent, the first morsel of rice from the pot is set aside for them out of respect.

Banana Leaf Rice

Colorful, hot, and spicy, this Indian rice specialty has become an institution in Malaysia. It dates from colonial times when Indians migrated to Malaysia to work on the rubber plantations. Southern Indian food soon became part of the gastronomic landscape.

Banana leaf rice is served for lunch or dinner. It comprises supremely fresh, fluffy rice served on placemats of green, glossy, veined banana leaves instead of plates.

Several types of curry and dhal are poured over the rice, along with other items such as dried, salted chile peppers, diced cucumbers, pineapple, cabbage, or spinach. Locals usually eat the rice with the fingers of their right hand, but you can also request a fork and spoon.

Once you've finished eating, simply fold your banana leaf in half. But here's the fun part. If the food is good, fold the leaf from the top down. If it's not so good, fold the leaf from the bottom up. By folding one corner down, you're telling the waiter that you alone will settle the bill!

Nasi Uduk

Jakarta, Indonesia's capital, is the home of this intriguing steamed rice. Similar to the Malaysian *nasi lemak*, it is made by mixing rice with coconut milk, grated nutmeg, cinnamon, lemongrass, galangal, and ginger. All the ingredients are placed in a saucepan and brought to a boil. The heat is turned off and the mixture is left to stand for 15 minutes until the rice has absorbed all the coconut milk. The rice is then steamed, using a bamboo steamer, for another 20 minutes. A sprinkling of fried shallots on top enhances the flavor. Uduk will often be accompanied by cucumber, lettuce, and tomatoes in a fresh salad. It may also be served with fried chicken or beef boiled in a spice-infused broth.

Nasi Goreng

Indonesia, a chain of islands large and small between the Pacific Ocean to the north and the Indian Ocean to the south, is the home of this breakfast dish, which simply means "fried rice." It is often prepared from the boiled rice left over from the previous evening's meal. This simple, yet wholesome breakfast combines the rice with fried onions, garlic, *sambal*, or minced chile, and shrimp paste, tossed until all the grains are coated. Soy sauce adds the characteristic orange-red tinge. Cooked meat or shrimp may be added at the end.

For an extra treat, the rice is topped with a lightly fried egg, cucumber slices, and *kerupuk* (shrimp crackers).

Nasi goreng has also become a culinary mainstay in Holland. It is said that during the time of the Dutch East Indies—when trade was plied between the two countries—the Dutch adapted the dish with spices to suit their own taste, replacing the hot chiles with less fiery curry powder.

Egg-Fried Rice

Egg-fried rice is just one of many variations of fried rice beloved in Chinese restaurants. The eggs are usually fried separately, then tossed with the rice in the frying pan or wok until the rice is flecked with yellow. A little salt is all that's needed for seasoning.

The method of quick-frying cold, leftover rice and adding any number of ingredients was created by necessity in the Tang Dynasty as a speedy method of cooking to save precious fuel, at the same time creating a way to use up leftover ingredients.

Egg-fried rice rose to international fame when the Chinese began opening their restaurant doors to the world. It was created for, and became a favorite among, the non-Chinese clientele and has remained a popular choice ever since.

Glutinous Rice

White sticky rice (*kao niow*) is also known as glutinous or sweet rice. This starchy grain is steamed dry after prolonged soaking to yield a sticky, chewy texture. It is popular in China and northern Thailand, where it is cultivated on hillsides and high plateaus, since it requires less water to grow than the wet rice of the central lowlands.

To prepare the short-grain rice, a special bamboo steamer that resembles a woven hat-like basket is set over a pot. The rice can also be steamed or boiled the same way as regular rice, allowing the grains to become soft and mushy. Though the grains remain whole, steamed sticky rice clings together in a lump, enabling it to be pulled off in bite-sized chunks by hand and eaten. These chunks, or balls, can be dipped in a spicy sauce or pulled together with accompanying meat, fish, or vegetables. In Thailand's poorest and most traditional region, Isahn, a local song likens the people's togetherness to the sticky rice they eat, saying that the people "stick" together and help each other.

Risotto Nero

Despite an unsavory black appearance, risotto made with squid or cuttlefish ink (sometimes called black risotto) is a popular seafood dish. It originated in Venice, but versions appear around the Mediterranean where squid are plentiful.

The squid must be purchased fresh, as the frozen variety does not contain the ink sac. Preparation closely follows that of any other risotto: aromatics and arborio rice are cooked slowly in a combination of liquids. In this case, the seafood calls for white wine (a zesty sauvignon blanc would be suitable) and fish broth. The rice absorbs the liquids and releases its own starch, making the individual grains slightly sticky.

The meat is the squid itself, which has a delicate, almost neutral flavor. The role of the ink, which is added toward the end of the cooking, is key. Not only does it turn the otherwise milky dish a uniform black color, it also adds a subtle yet distinct flavor. Because of this subtlety, squid-ink risotto should not be finished with Parmesan cheese.

Risotto al Tartufo Bianco

The white truffle is the star of an annual fair held in the medieval Piedmontese city of Alba in October. Since this is also the season for wild mushrooms and chestnuts, game, frogs, and snails, as well as the grape harvest, fall is a time when cooking in this region really comes into its own.

From October to December, fine slivers of highly scented, raw, white truffle are shaved onto dishes using a special slicer. Though it may not look like much, when cut open, the tan, veined interior of this revered delicacy releases an intoxicating scent. At the high prices paid for them it is fortunate that just a little will flavor a dish sufficiently.

The marriage of the white truffle with risotto is inspired, raising the status of an otherwise humble dish to one of melt-in-the-mouth extravagance. A simple risotto is prepared, first frying onion in butter, then adding the arborio rice and stirring well to coat each grain. Slowly cooked in a rich beef broth and perhaps a glass of white wine, the risotto gradually reaches al dente stage. The pan is removed from the heat and a generous handful of freshly grated Parmesan is stirred into the rice, which is then served, topped with a few shavings of the pungent truffle.

Risotto Milanese

This is the classic among Italian risottos. It was in the northern city of Milan that the first risotto is said to have been prepared when Charles V made his son Duke of Milan in 1535, heralding 200 years of Spanish rule. The dish bears a marked resemblance to Spanish paella. Northern Italy was, and remains, the rice bowl of the peninsula and it was an earlier Duke of Milan who had pioneered in Italy the growing of rice in flooded fields, against strong opposition prompted by the fear of malaria.

The flavor of risotto Milanese comes from the bone marrow, wine, meat broth, and Parmesan cheese, while the saffron added near the end of cooking adds its distinctive yellow color. Risotto Milanese is sometimes served as an accompaniment to the veal dish osso buco but is normally a first course dish.

Risotto Milanese

4 cups chicken broth

2 tbsp olive oil

2 tbsp butter, plus $1/4$ cup

1 medium onion, finely chopped

1 tsp saffron threads

2 cups arborio or carnaroli rice

$1/2$ cup white wine

$1/2$ cup freshly grated Parmesan cheese

Bring the chicken broth to a simmer. In a heavy-bottomed pot, heat the oil and 2 tablespoons of the butter over medium heat. Add the onion and cook until softened and translucent, 8 to 10 minutes. Add the saffron and cook, stirring, for 1 minute. Add the rice and stir with a wooden spoon until the rice is well coated and opaque, 3 to 4 minutes. Add the wine, then add $1/2$ to $3/4$ cup of warm broth. Cook, stirring constantly, until all the liquid is absorbed. Continue adding the broth a little at a time, adding more when the liquid is completely absorbed. After about 20 minutes, begin to taste the rice. It is ready when tender and creamy, but still a little firm to the bite. Stir in the $1/4$ cup butter and cheese and mix well. Serve immediately. *Serves 4*

Risotto con Funghi

Rice was introduced to Italy by the Arab invaders and, by Renaissance times, the Italians had developed their own way of serving it—combining it with other ingredients during cooking. The fertile plain of the River Po in Lombardy in northern Italy favors cultivation of all kinds of rice. Arborio and carnaroli, both superfine, short-grain varieties, are the best suited for risotto because their grains are less likely to break during cooking and the rice absorbs plenty of liquid while retaining firmness and bite. Rice is more popular in the north of the country than the south, where pasta still holds sway.

Common to all risottos is the method of turning the rice in hot butter or oil before pouring in the wine and then gradually ladling in hot broth to produce a creamy consistency. Normally served as a "primo," or first course, in Italy, risotto can also take center stage, especially when enriched with additional ingredients, such as the wild mushrooms in the recipe here. The porcini is the favorite mushroom among Italian chefs, who use them either fresh or dried to impart a strong woodsy flavor to risotto, pasta, and casseroles.

Risotto con Funghi

$1/3$ oz dried porcini mushrooms

$3/4$ cup warm water

6 tbsp butter

1 small onion, finely chopped

$2^1/2$ cups arborio or carnaroli rice

6 cups beef or chicken broth

$1/2$ cup freshly grated Parmesan cheese

Crumble the mushrooms and soak in the warm water for 20 minutes. Strain through a fine sieve to remove any grit and reserve the soaking liquid. Meanwhile, heat the butter in a heavy pot. Rinse mushrooms briefly and set aside. Add the onion and sauté over medium-low heat for 5 minutes. Add the rice and stir for about 2 minutes. Stir in $1^1/2$ cups of the broth and the mushroom water. Cook, stirring, for about 20 minutes, gradually adding 1 cup of broth at a time as the liquid is absorbed. The risotto should be creamy, but the individual rice grains should be slightly al dente. Stir in the Parmesan cheese and serve immediately. *Serves 4*

Risotto Primavera

This dish made its debut at Le Cirque 2000 in midtown Manhattan as a rice version of the popular pasta primavera (spaghetti in cream sauce with spring vegetables). Pasta primavera was devised by the restaurant's owner Sirio Maccioni in 1976 when, making pasta at a friend's house, unexpected guests turned up. Instead of simply adding cheese as planned he threw in some vegetables to stretch the meal.

Unlike the Milanese, then, this risotto boasts bulky ingredients such as asparagus tips, peas, squash, zucchini—fresh and colorful vegetables which make a filling and healthy dish indeed.

Heat the oil in a large pot and sauté the onion and carrots until tender-crisp. Stir in the rice and cook, stirring, until it begins to brown. Add ½ cup broth and cook, uncovered, stirring occasionally, until liquid is absorbed.

Continue cooking and stirring for 10 to 15 minutes, adding broth ½ cup at a time, until the rice is tender and creamy. With the last ladle of broth, add the broccoli, peas, and zucchini. Sprinkle with Parmesan cheese and serve immediately. *Serves 2*

Risotto Primavera

2 tsp olive oil

1 medium onion, chopped

2 medium carrots, cut into julienne strips

1 cup arborio rice

3 cups chicken broth

2 cups broccoli florets

1 cup green peas

2 small zucchini, cut into julienne strips

3 tbsp grated Parmesan cheese

Sushi

It's not often that a food from a single culture not only takes the world by storm, but also influences the direction of food in other cultures. Yet in the past decade, Japanese sushi has evolved into a unique international art form. The word "sushi" refers to rice flavored with a rice vinegar mixture. The hot cooked rice is stirred and fanned until cool and forms a glossy sheen.

To make the sushi, a square sheet of crisp nori seaweed is placed on a bamboo mat, then covered with a thin layer of the now-sticky rice. Various items such as raw tuna, salmon, pickles, julienned vegetables, or tofu are placed in a line crosswise across the rice, and the whole thing is tightly rolled into a cylinder with the help of the mat. The chef then deftly slices the long roll into individual rounds. The rolls are served on a wooden board or a beautiful plate accompanied by a smudge of fiery green wasabi paste and thin slices of pink-dyed pickled ginger, plus a small dipping bowl for soy sauce.

Great care is taken in the creation of different types of sushi. In Japan, becoming a sushi chef is a tremendous honor that requires years and years of training.

There are different types of sushi, depending on how the item is presented.

They are:

Chirashi-sushi: Usually a bowl or box of sushi rice topped with a variety of raw seafood.

Inari-sushi: A fried tofu pouch stuffed with sweet sushi rice.

Nigiri-sushi: Fingers of rice topped with wasabi paste and raw or cooked fish.

Temaki-sushi: Cones of sushi rice, fish, and vegetables wrapped in nori.

Maki-sushi: Rice and nori rolls with fish and/or vegetables.

The rolls each have a name depicting their style:

Futomaki (thick rolls); *Hosomaki* (thin rolls); *Uramaki* (inside-out rolls).

Zong Zi

The story of celebrated poet and scholar Qu Yuan gave rise to the legend of these sticky rice dumplings, a Chinese specialty enjoyed during the annual Dragon Boat Festival (*Duan Wu*) in his honor. According to the tale, villagers rushed to throw rice dumplings into the river when they heard the poet had drowned himself. One day, the spirit of Qu Yuan appeared before them, crying out that he was starving because a river dragon had eaten the rice. To prevent the dragon from stealing them, Qu Yuan ordered the balls to be wrapped in reed leaves and tied with thread. Today's zong zi is made similarly. The fillings vary from region to region, and may be savory with meat or sweet with red-bean paste or Chinese dates. Every type of zong zi has its own flavor, shape, and wrapping—the way in which the string is wound and knotted indicates the ingredients to be found inside. The dumplings may be four-sided with pointed or rounded ends, cylindrical, or pyramid-shaped. They are steamed or boiled for several hours before serving.

Congee

Rice congee is a type of porridge widely eaten in Asia, often as breakfast or a late-night meal but also at other times, depending on the region. As it is easily digested, congee is an ideal food for invalids, with ingredients chosen for their therapeutic value as well as flavor.

In China's southern Guangdong province, the rice is typically boiled for many hours in a large amount of water until the rice breaks down to a viscous consistency.

Accompaniments include fried dough sticks, salted duck eggs, bamboo shoots, or thousand-year-old eggs, and the dish is seasoned with white pepper and soy sauce. A sweet dish is made by adding red beans and sugar. In Japan, rice congee is called *okayu*. It is cooked for less time and has a thicker consistency than the Chinese version. Chicken broth or eggs are often added, and typical toppings include salmon, roe, or ginger. A traditional version served at Japanese New Year is *nanakusa-gayu* or seven-herb porridge, with the herbs selected to protect against evil and invite good luck and longevity. The Phillipine version, *lugao*, is boiled with ginger and often topped with scallions and crispy fried garlic.

Agemochi

Whereas in Europe and North America rice cakes are widely made with puffed rice and treated as a health food, in east Asia they are made from glutinous rice, which is steamed, ground into a paste, molded, and sometimes cooked again. Throughout east Asia, the rice cake is a ceremonial dish traditionally eaten at New Year. The Japanese rice cake (*mochi*) is particularly sticky and is sprinkled with soy flour, or dipped in soy sauce and then rolled in dried seaweed. There are many regional variations eaten in China where it is called *nianga*. In Shanghai, the rice cake is rolled into a long rod, then sliced and stir-fried or added to soup. A sweeter version is found in Guangzhou where the paste is sweetened with sugar, poured into a cake pan, and steamed. This gives the cake the consistency of cheese. It can be eaten like this or pan-fried so that it is crispy on the outside and soft in the middle. The sweet mixture is sometimes flavored with rosewater or red-bean paste and then steamed until solid, before serving in thick slices.

4   FISH AND SEAFOOD

Angels on Horseback

A savory dish for serving at the end of dinner, angels on horseback are oysters wrapped in bacon, usually served on thin slices of toast. They are threaded on a skewer for cooking over a fire, or else individually held together on cocktail sticks and cooked in the oven. As such, they are one of the few traditional recipes for cooked oysters to have survived from the Victorian era, when angels on horseback was a working-class dish.

Various recipes for enriching the basic formula have surfaced over the years. One suggests spreading the toast with a blend of butter, anchovy paste, and parsley, while another proposes egging and crumbing the bacon-rolled oysters, seasoning with Worcestershire sauce, and frying in butter. A fashionable spin on the dish involves substituting scallops for the oysters.

Although in Victorian England, oysters were an everyday staple of the diet of poor families, angels on horseback is considered to be more of an indulgence in North America, where oysters have been elevated to the status of a delicacy.

Abalone

The abalone is a marine gastropod much prized in east Asian and South American cooking in particular. There are many different subspecies, but they all have in common a hard, nacreous (mother-of-pearl) inner shell, pierced with several holes, enclosing a large, fleshy, but very firm, edible adductor muscle. They use this powerful muscle to cling to rocks deep beneath the surface of the coastal waters in which they live.

Abalone is used in Chinese, Japanese, and Southeast Asian cooking, and to a lesser extent on the Iberian peninsula. A black-shelled species known regionally as *loco* is particularly revered along the Pacific coast of Chile. In the Channel Islands, it is known as "ormer." As it tends to be fairly tough when raw, abalone usually needs some tenderizing with something resembling a steak mallet before it can be eaten.

In Japanese cuisine, abalone is either lightly broiled or steamed, or, for tougher specimens, tenderized but raw, with a dipping sauce to accompany. In many countries, abalone is sold dried or canned. Worldwide stocks are dwindling, and abalone-gathering is subject to strict limits in most jurisdictions.

Anchoïade

Anchoïade is a Provençal preparation made from anchovies pounded in a mortar and pestle with olive oil, garlic, and wine vinegar. It can be served either as a dip with crudités or spread on slices of bread that are then cooked briefly in a hot oven. In this form, it is often eaten as a savory at the end of a meal. Anchoïade will keep well for a few days in the refrigerator under a layer of olive oil.

The fish that goes into this condiment has been important in Mediterranean cooking since the classical era. It was the basis of *garum*, the fermented fish sauce that was an indispensable seasoning in the Roman kitchen. Since it lives in vast, gregarious shoals, it is easily fished, with most of the catch going to the canning industry. Anchovies canned in olive oil are quite suitable for anchoïade, but they should be drained first and split lengthways to remove the flimsy dorsal bone.

It is possible to come across fresh anchovies on seafood stalls or in restaurants along the Mediterranean coasts of Spain or France. They are generally served marinated as a tapas dish (*boquerones*) or grilled on beachside barbecues like sardines.

Salmon Rillettes

Originally rillettes were a method of preparing pork, duck, or other meat in which the meat was cooked in its own fat and then pounded into a rough, fibrous purée. When applied to salmon, the result is more delicate, but the principle is much the same.

The fresh salmon is gently poached in a cooking liquid over low heat, and left to cool. It is then flaked and seasoned with condiments such as mustard and chili flakes, before being bound with mayonnaise. This can be done in an electric blender or simply with a fork for a rougher texture. Pieces of shredded smoked salmon are then incorporated into the mixture, as are beads of salmon roe in some versions. If the roe is used, fold it in very gently so as not to break the eggs.

Salmon rillettes can be made ahead and stored in the refrigerator until needed. It is traditional to serve the rillettes by shaping them into *quenelles* between two spoons and accompanying them with thin strips of unbuttered toast.

Salmon Rillettes

2 cups water

1 cup white wine

1 medium onion

$\frac{1}{2}$ celery stalk

4 sprigs fresh thyme

1 bay leaf

1 lb skinless fresh salmon fillet

1 lb smoked salmon, chopped fine

$\frac{1}{2}$ cup unsalted butter, at room temperature

$\frac{1}{3}$ cup finely minced onion

$\frac{1}{3}$ cup chopped fresh parsley

2 tbsp fresh lemon juice

2 tsp Dijon mustard

2 tsp capers

2 tsp brandy

2 tsp freshly grated lemon zest

Salt

Freshly ground black pepper

$\frac{1}{3}$ cup salmon roe

Put the water, wine, onion, celery stalk, thyme, and bay leaf in a large shallow pan and bring to a boil. Add the fresh salmon, reduce the heat to a low simmer, and poach the salmon, turning once, for about 8 minutes or until opaque in the center. Transfer the salmon to a bowl and cool.

With a fork, shred the fresh salmon. Add the smoked salmon, butter, minced onion, parsley, lemon juice, mustard, capers, brandy, lemon zest, and salt and pepper to taste.

Stir the mixture until it's well combined. Gently fold in the salmon roe and pack into a 1-quart terrine or bowl. Rillettes may be made 4 hours ahead and kept chilled, covered.

Serves 6

Three Ways with Salmon

Salmon en Croûte

Salmon en croûte has long been a staple of the Anglo-Saxon kitchen, but it is French in origin, as its name indicates. In its original manifestation, it involved baking a whole skinned salmon in puff pastry (*feuilleté*), which was marked along the sides to show where the individual portions should be cut.

The trick to good salmon en croûte is making sure that the fish remains moist as it cooks. The pastry is often given a lining of seasoned butter that spills out as the slices are cut, and sometimes other flavoring elements are also incorporated in it. Herbed cream cheese, spinach, even currants and ginger have been used in variant recipes. The pastry should always be rolled as tightly as possible around the fish to seal in the flavors.

This dish has become a favorite of mass catering at wedding banquets and large-scale functions, where it can easily be made to look quite grand in glazed latticed pastry. It is also quite palatable if served cold, although it loses the moistening effect of the melted butter in that form.

Salmon Sashimi

Salmon lends itself beautifully to the Japanese technique of expertly cut raw fish (*sashimi* means "pierced flesh"). Not only is absolute freshness a prerequisite, but it is also important that the salmon is caught when its natural oils are at their greatest—generally in the summer months.

The different presentations of sashimi depend on how thinly the raw fish is sliced. Wafer-thin slices are usually served with a *ponzu* sauce, which is a mixture of Japanese *shoyu* (soy), lemon juice, mirin (light rice wine), and dried bonito flakes. If the sashimi is sliced to about half an inch thick, it is traditional to serve it with a more robust dipping sauce, combining *shoyu* with finely grated wasabi, or wasabi paste, and paper-thin slices of gingerroot.

Other garnishes for salmon sashimi are small salad leaves (Japanese shiso leaves lend the presentation an air of authenticity, but watercress would do), and slices of daikon, the mild Japanese white radish.

Confusingly for Westerners, the Japanese word for salmon is the same as the word for the traditional rice wine, *sake*.

Poached Salmon with Hollandaise

One of the most appealing ways of serving cooked salmon is to poach fillets in a court-broth (seasoned fish stock and white wine), then serve them warm draped in a light hollandaise sauce.

Usually the fillets are cooked in a large pan on top of the stove, but they can also be put in an ovenproof dish (a fish kettle was once the required utensil) and cooked in the oven. Either way, the fish should be sitting in a shallow bath of the cooking liquid. Some confusion has arisen lately regarding the term poached, with many stretching the meaning to include fish that has been wrapped in foil and cooked in the oven. This method is in fact baking and tends to produce a drier result.

Hollandaise sauce is classically made by warming egg yolks in a double boiler, and then whisking in cold butter, a cube at a time. The sauce is seasoned, then sharpened with lemon juice, and must be used as soon as it is ready, to guard against coagulation. In *The Curious Cook* (1990), food scientist Harold McGee reveals that hollandaise can simply be made by gently heating all the ingredients in a pan at the same time.

Baby Octopus

The octopus is a member of the cephalopod family and is native to both Atlantic and Pacific Oceans. It is caught along both seaboards of the Americas, and also in Southeast Asia and southern Europe, where it is a relatively important seafood item.

We tend to think of the octopus as being fearsomely large, yet most are only a foot or two in length from the top of the head to the ends of the tentacles. The baby octopus is no larger than a small squid and has something of the same texture. It requires no tenderizing, but can be briefly broiled or stir-fried, perhaps after marinating for a short time.

In Spain, octopus is baked inside empanadas, those savory pies, or served *à la gallega* (boiled, then eaten cold dressed in paprika and olive oil). The Portuguese like to eat it with rice. In Italian coastal areas, it finds its way into pasta dishes, where it may be cooked—as here—in a rich, spicy, tomato-based ragout.

Thai cooks marinate baby octopus in soy sauce with garlic and pepper before barbecuing or else boil it for use in a seafood soup.

Baby Octopus Ragout

¼ cup olive oil

1 lb tiny octopus, blanched

1 medium onion, chopped

4 cloves garlic, chopped

1 cup white wine

2 tbsp tomato paste

2 cups plum tomatoes, peeled, seeded, and chopped

Heat the olive oil in a saucepan. Add the octopus and sauté until the flesh wrinkles, about 2 minutes. Some browning isn't a problem.

Add the onion and garlic, stirring to prevent burning. Add the wine and cook until it evaporates. Stir in the tomato paste and cook until it dries, 3 to 5 minutes. Add the tomatoes, season to taste, and simmer for 15 to 25 minutes or until the octopus is fork tender. *Serves 4*

Adapted from Massimo Capra's *One Pot Italian Cooking*

Fish and Chips

Still seen as the national dish of Great Britain, fish and chips have been an institution of the takeaway food industry since the Victorian era. Although British tastes have wandered off in search of the cooking of sunnier climes in the postwar period, fish and chips remain a cheap and cheerful standby.

The origins almost certainly lie in a shop opened in the East End of London by one Joseph Malin in 1860. He seems to have been the first to partner the Jewish tradition of fried fish, imported from Spain and Portugal at least a century earlier, with the probably Belgian innovation of deep-frying sticks of potato in oil. The second fish-and-chip shop, a wooden hut, was opened by John Lees in the market at Mossley in Lancashire three years later. Between them, these entrepreneurs established the twin traditions of fish and chips as the food of both Cockneys and northerners.

Fresh fish cooked in non-hydrogenated vegetable oil, together with hand-cut chips that are fried twice to crisp and puff them up, are the holy grail of this dish. Sadly, the fish traditionally used—cod, haddock, and plaice—are all currently on the endangered list.

Fish and Chips

$4\frac{1}{2}$ cups vegetable oil

4 potatoes, peeled and cut into thick wedges

Coarse sea salt

2 cups flour

Salt

$1\frac{1}{2}$ cups beer (preferably ale)

4 (6- to 7-oz) monkfish or haddock fillets, cut into thick slices

Preheat the vegetable oil in a deep pan to 350°F or until a 1-inch cube of bread browns evenly in 1 minute when added to the oil. Deep-fry the potatoes in batches for 6 to 8 minutes or until they are tender. Drain on paper towels and set aside.

In a bowl, make the batter by whisking together the flour, salt, and beer. Add the fish slices and coat them in the batter.

Cook the fish in batches in the hot oil for 5 to 6 minutes, depending on the size of the fish. Drain on paper towels. Plunge the potatoes back into the hot oil for 2 to 3 minutes to make them crisp and golden.
Serves 4

PORTUGAL

Bacalhau

The tradition of preserving fish by salting
and drying derives from the days of strict
Christian observance, when on Fridays and
certain saints' days it was customary not
to eat meat. Large quantities of fish were
therefore consumed, and a way had to be
found to keep it without it spoiling.

Of these preparations, bacalhau, to give
it its Portuguese name, is one of the most
revered. It is salt cod, made by dry-salting
the fresh fish, and then drying it to reduce
its moisture content still further. It is sold
in hard white blocks that can be cut to the
customer's specifications. Salt cod needs
up to 24 hours' soaking in several changes
of water to mitigate its saltiness before it
is ready to eat.

There is reputedly a bacalhau recipe for
every day of the year in Portugal. It can be
stewed with tomatoes and onions; served
with sautéed potatoes, scrambled eggs,
or green vegetables; and fried in batter.
Bacalhau com Todos is literally "salt cod
with everything," a plentiful mixture of
vegetables and hard-boiled egg, dressed in
oil and vinegar.

Salt cod is also popular in Spain, Italy,
and France.

SPAIN

Bacalao a la Vizcaina

This recipe hails from the Basque region
in the northern part of Spain, around the city
of Bilbao. Cod is found as far south as the
northern part of the Bay of Biscay, after which
the region of Vizcaya is named, and the
tradition of producing salt cod is almost as
tenacious here as it is in Portugal.

Bacalao prepared in the regional fashion
is fried in olive oil with garlic and is then
dressed in a colorful, hearty, spicy sauce. This
consists of diced potato cooked with white
and red onions, garlic, tomatoes, and dried
hot red choricero peppers, which are all
stewed down into a rich, chunky consistency.

Bilbao chef, Jenaro Pildain, prepares a
grand version of this dish, in which the sauce
contains cubes of ham, as well as the more
traditional ingredients, although, curiously
enough, no tomatoes. It is fortified with beef
broth before being passed through a blender
and then dabbed with butter.

Cod with Puy Lentils

This is very much a contemporary classic combination of fish with an accompaniment more traditionally associated with meat. The firm texture of the cod is robustly offset by a bed of Puy lentils.

In the version of it given in Lindsay Bareham's recipe book *The Fish Store*, the cod is poached in lemon juice and water, while the lentils are simmered in chicken broth with a whole onion, a bay leaf, and cloves. The fish is served over the lentils, and the whole composition is set off with a chunky salsa verde made from parsley, mint, and basil, with anchovies, capers, garlic, mustard, and olive oil.

Puy lentils are considered the best variety of this legume. Originally grown in the volcanic soils of the Velay region of south-central France (though also cultivated in North America now), they are slender and green, have a wonderful flavor, and possess the obliging characteristic of not breaking up before they have finished cooking.

Cod with Puy Lentils

1 cup dried Puy lentils

1 onion

1 bay leaf

For the salsa verde:

1 large clove garlic, chopped

¼ tsp salt

1 tbsp Dijon mustard

2 tbsp chopped capers

½ cup chopped flat-leaf parsley

¼ cup lemon juice

¼ tsp black pepper

1 cup olive oil

For the fish:

4 (5- to 6-oz) pieces cod fillet, ¾ to 1 inch thick

½ tsp salt

⅛ tsp black pepper

1 tbsp unsalted butter

1 tbsp olive oil

Put the lentils, the onion, and the bay leaf in a pan and cover them with cold water. Bring to a boil. Simmer, uncovered, until lentils are just tender, 12 to 25 minutes. Drain, reserve ½ cup of the cooking liquid, and transfer the lentils to a bowl. Discard the onion and bay leaf.

To make the salsa, stir all the ingredients together.

To cook the fish, pat it dry and sprinkle it with salt and pepper.

Heat the butter and oil in a frying pan over moderately high heat, then sauté the fish, turning it over once, until browned and just cooked through, 6 to 8 minutes.

Serve the fish on a bed of lentils and spread the salsa verde on the fish. Garnish with lemon wedges and parsley if desired. *Serves 4*

Baked Bream with Potatoes

Barbecued Whole Fish　　▷

Versions of this dish are known in both
Spanish and Italian cooking, where it is
described respectively as *al horno* and *al
forno*. It involves oven-cooking a whole
gutted and descaled fish on a layer of
overlapping, wafer-thin potato slices. The
surface of the fish is sometimes covered with
a layer of bread crumbs seasoned with garlic,
parsley, and paprika, or the fish may be simply
garnished with whole garlic cloves, onion
rings, and lemon slices.

There are many different subspecies of
bream found in Mediterranean waters alone.
The red bream, known to Spanish speakers
as *besugo*, is particularly favored for this
dish and has long been a special tradition
of Christmas Eve feasting. Another prized
member of the same noble family is the
gilt-head bream, or *dorada*, recognizable for
the distinctive golden arc between its eyes.
The black bream, or *chopa*, also makes a
good baking fish, but the flesh of others may
be too delicate to withstand this treatment.

A festive variation on the dish involves
layering the potato slices on top of the fish
so that it looks as though it is done up in its
Sunday-best jacket.

Although many people see steaks, chops,
and sausages as the essential barbecue foods,
there is an established tradition of barbecuing
whole fish in those countries where the
climate permits open-air cooking. This might
seem surprising at first, until one remembers
that the heat source in a barbecue is relatively
gentle, and the slow cooking that it makes
possible is perfect for many species of fish.

The barbecuing of fish is a specialty of
the Caribbean islands, where the technique
may be used for fish such as red snapper,
sea bream, or bass. East Asian cooking also
features barbecued fish and extends the
treatment to the larger and meatier varieties
of shellfish too.

To cook a whole fish by this method, it
should be cleaned and descaled. Make two
or three diagonal slashes along the flank, and
fill them, if you wish, with a garnish (perhaps
a mixture of chopped peppers, minced onion,
garlic, and chili flakes). Brush the fish with
oil, and then clamp it between a pair of fish
tongs, or fish racks, and cook it slowly, turning
it occasionally. The blackened skin should
be crisp and edible, with the flesh still
moist and tender.

Cod Cheeks

Herb-Crusted Cod

In those parts of the world where cod is considered the "king of fish"—rather than a staple of the deep-fryer—the cheeks are a special delicacy. On the Atlantic seaboard of Canada and in parts of northwest Europe, they are extracted from the whole fish and cooked separately as a dish in their own right. They have the same full flavor as the body, but the texture is notably less flaky.

Cod cheeks should be quickly fried in oil or butter. When cooked, they can resemble the white meat of crab and can take a reasonably rich sauce. In Chinese cooking, they are steamed like other white fish and dressed in oil, scallions, and ginger, while Newfoundland cooks give them a light flour coating, before frying them in pork fat. In Belgium, there is a dish called *kaaksjes en keeltjes*, literally "cheeks and tongues" of cod. (The tongues referred to are actually the fish's throat muscle.) The cheeks also lend themselves well to cooking in curries.

One lamentable by-product of the overfishing of cod has been for the cheeks to become a rarity because too many fish are being caught too young to yield a sizeable cheek.

As cod is one of the firmer-fleshed species of fish, it has a natural affinity with quite meaty culinary treatments. One of these is herb-crusted cod, in which the upper surfaces of fillets of the fish are coated in a finely chopped mixture of parsley, chives, maybe some cilantro and garlic, before being either baked or broiled.

The topping for the fish binds together better if the herbs are mixed with bread crumbs. Lemon zest and chopped capers help to deepen the flavor. What makes the dish a success is the textural contrast between the crunchy topping, which will have crisped up on exposure to the heat, and the soft, moist flesh of the dish.

Cod cooked in this way will take a fairly robust sauce too. Roasted tomatoes and garlic are a good combination with it, as is a classic French *beurre blanc*, made by reducing white wine vinegar with herbs and peppercorns, and then emulsifying it with butter. Otherwise, a homemade tartar sauce once more comes into its own.

Catalan Fish Stew

The traditional *zarzuela de mariscos a la catalana*—Catalan fish stew—is a bounteous stew of fish and seafood, all cooked in white wine, Spanish brandy, tomato paste, peppers, and almonds, and served with plenty of crusty bread for sopping up the juices. These are much more piquant and colorful than are found in, for example, French versions of fish stew, as they are seasoned with paprika and saffron. Sauces such as *romesco* (an almond-thickened relish of bread crumbs and red peppers) are used as thickening agents in dishes like *zarzuela* and are generally freshly pounded for the purpose in a pestle and mortar.

Typical marine ingredients for the *zarzuela* will be sea bass, monkfish, squid, clams, mussels, shrimp, and scampi, but it is one of those dishes that can be adapted to accommodate whatever looks freshest and most inviting when you get to market or to the fishmonger's.

Some recipes incorporate a salty meat ingredient too, perhaps bacon or diced chorizo. Some recipes even use chocolate.

The name *zarzuela* originally referred to a form of musical theater, a kind of comic opera of great colorfulness and vivacity. Its application to this dish indicates the eclectic variety of its ingredients.

Catalan Fish Stew

6 tbsp olive oil

1 large onion, chopped

1 red chile pepper, finely chopped

2 cloves garlic, crushed

$1/2$ tsp smoked paprika

1 tbsp fresh thyme leaves

1 tsp saffron strands

3 bay leaves

3 medium tomatoes

$1/3$ cup fish broth or water

$1/2$ cup white wine

A dash of sherry vinegar

1 lb mussels, cleaned

$1^1/2$ lb cod (or other firm white fish)

$3/4$ cup toasted almonds, ground

Heat the olive oil in a large pan and sauté the onion, chile, and garlic for a few minutes. Add the paprika, thyme, saffron, bay leaves, and tomatoes and cook until the sauce has thickened. Add the fish broth, white wine, and vinegar and bring to a simmer. Add the mussels and cook until they all open. Discard any that have not opened.

Put the fish into the stew and stir in the almonds. Heat gently for about 5 minutes, just long enough for the fish to cook through.
Serves 6

Boquerones Fritos

Bonito Flakes

Although the vast majority of anchovies consumed around the world are preserved in some way, usually by salting and canning or bottling, they have always also been used fresh in Mediterranean cooking, especially in northeastern Spain and the south of France. Boquerones fritos is a Spanish dish of fried fresh anchovies, served either as a first course or as a tapas dish.

The anchovies require little in the way of preparation. They usually have the heads removed, before being split open to extract the backbone. After being lightly coated in egg and flour to create a brittle batter surface, they are quickly fried in red-hot olive oil. They are traditionally served with nothing more than a wedge of lemon for squeezing or a little pot of *alioli*, Spain's garlic mayonnaise.

In Catalonia, it is customary to eat a plate of boquerones fritos with a bottle of very cold beer, although a crisp, dry white wine is also appropriate.

A central ingredient in Japanese fish cuisine, bonito flakes (or *katsuobushi*) are fragments of dried and smoked bonito, otherwise known as the skipjack tuna. They are used as a seasoning ingredient in the dip known as *ponzu* sauce, often used with sashimi, or in *dashi*, the broth that forms the basis for miso soups, or used as a filling in *onigiri* (rice balls).

Now largely sold in packets, bonito flakes used to be literally shaved off a curved block of the fish and bear a strong resemblance to wood shavings. (In Chinese, they are known by a name that translates as "firewood fish.") When shaved paper-thin, they are known as *hanakatsuo* and are used as a garnish topping for hot dishes such as the Japanese pizza equivalent, *okonomiyaki*. A fascinating aspect of this presentation is that the heat of the dish agitates the flakes on its surface, causing an effect known in Japanese tradition as "dancing fish flakes."

Further down the convenience food chain, dried bonito is now also sold in granular form, like instant gravy.

Choo-Chee Shrimp

Calamari

This is a Thai dish in which shrimp or large prawns are cooked in a hot mixture of red curry paste, coconut milk, chiles, *nam pla* (the fermented fish sauce of Thailand), palm sugar, and water. The sauce should properly be thickened by the coconut milk before the shrimp are introduced into it, so that it coats the shellfish in a kind of paste, rather than a liquid dressing. When served, the dish should be garnished with leaves of Thai basil. It is generally eaten with rice.

Although shrimp (*goong* in Thai) is a favored ingredient for a choo-chee dish, the sauce can also be used with most other types of seafood, including scallops, squid, mussels, clams, or any crisp-fried white fish.

The name of the dish is a bit of Thai onomatopoeia, as "choo-chee" is the sound the sauce makes when it is cooking in the pan, which should be so hot that the sauce seethes and sizzles.

Calamari is the culinary name for squid, much eaten throughout the world, from the waters of the Mediterranean to those of east Asia. Squid lends itself to a wide variety of cooking techniques, including stir-frying, stuffing (the cleaned body sac making an obvious receptacle for other ingredients), or stewing in the Spanish fashion with tomatoes, onion, chorizo, and white wine.

The dish generally referred to simply as calamari, however, consists of squid sliced into rings that are then battered and shallow-fried. This preparation is found throughout southern Europe, from Italy to Greece and Turkey, and is also popular in North America. They are often served with some sort of dip, perhaps garlic mayonnaise, a tomato and garlic salsa, or—in southeast Europe—tzatziki. In Italian restaurants, a wedge of lemon is often the only accompaniment to a first-course dish of *calamari fritti*.

A distant eastern cousin of European calamari is Chinese salt-and-pepper squid, in which the chopped squid is coated in a batter seasoned with Szechuan and black peppercorns, deep-fried, and then sprinkled with chili salt.

Coulibiac

Originally a Russian dish, coulibiac made its way into French haute cuisine in the 19th century. In its Russian homeland, it is effectively a sort of grand pierogie, or pie, while a French cook of the era of the Second Empire might have recognized it as a variant of salmon en croûte.

Strictly speaking, it can be prepared with any fish, or even chicken, but it has become traditional to use salmon. The fish is baked in a wallet of yeasted dough, which is also filled with rice, mushrooms, onions, and chopped hard-boiled egg, the various fillings usually built up in layers. A common alternative to rice in the Russian kitchen was *kasha*, or buckwheat porridge. In the dish's French manifestations, it became traditional to cook and serve coulibiac in a fish-shaped dish, with an outer wrapping of a lighter, egg-washed puff pastry.

A once indispensable finishing touch to the filling was a sprinkling of *vesiga*, the dried marrow of the spinal cord of the sturgeon, which added an incomparably rich and pungent savory flavor to the dish.

Coulibiac

2/3 cup rice
A pinch of turmeric
1/3 cup butter
1 medium onion, finely chopped
3 cups button mushrooms, roughly chopped
1 lb salmon fillets, cooked and shredded
1 tbsp chopped fresh parsley
1 tbsp chopped fresh tarragon
2 hard-boiled eggs, chopped
Salt
Freshly ground black pepper
9 oz frozen puff pastry, thawed
1 egg, beaten

Preheat the oven to 400°F.

Put the rice in a pan of boiling water with a pinch of turmeric and cook for 15 to 17 minutes, or until just done but still firm, then drain.

Melt the butter in a frying pan and sauté the onion for 4 to 5 minutes, until soft. Add the mushrooms and sauté for 3 to 4 minutes, or until softened. Add the cooked rice, salmon, parsley, tarragon, eggs, and salt and pepper to taste.

Roll out half the pastry dough to a 12-×-18 inch rectangle on a clean flat surface. Set it on a greased baking sheet. Spoon the salmon mixture over the pastry to within 1 inch of the edge. Brush some beaten egg around the edge. Roll out the remaining dough and place it ontop, crimping the edges to seal firmly.

Brush the pastry all over with the remaining beaten egg, then bake for 40 minutes, or until it is hot throughout and crisp and golden all over. *Serves 6*

Clams with Manzanilla

Another of those dishes that proves a perennial favorite of the tapas menu, this simple way of cooking shellfish brings out the best in them. Garlic and onion are briefly sweated in olive oil, before the pale dry manzanilla sherry is poured in. The clams are then cooked in this broth for a few minutes until they have opened and are then taken out while the sauce is reduced. Popular additional elements may be some finely chopped chile pepper, or even snippets of ham, which makes a good match with the clams.

The clam is a bivalve mollusk with a hinged, tightly shut shell (from which we derive our metaphors about reticent people "clamming up"). Clams have long been hugely popular in the United States, where the clambake of New England derived from Native American traditions. Dozens of different species are eaten throughout the world.

Manzanilla, the proper liquor for this dish, is a pale sherry produced in and around the coastal town of Sanlúcar de Barrameda in southern Spain. It is absolutely bone-dry with a nutty taste, and aficionados claim it has something of the tang of salty sea air about it.

Clams with Manzanilla

$^3/_4$ cup manzanilla sherry

A pinch saffron threads

$^1/_4$ cup olive oil

3 cloves garlic, thinly sliced

5 lb clams, rinsed well

A bunch of parsley, leaves torn

3 oz serrano ham or prosciutto, thinly sliced

Mix the sherry and saffron together in a small bowl. In a large wide pan, heat the oil over medium heat, then add the garlic and cook for 1 minute, until it begins to color.

Add the sherry mixture and simmer until reduced by half. Add the clams, cover, and cook for 35 minutes, or until clams open. Toss with the parsley and ham. Serve with lemon wedges and bread. *Serves 6*

Cockles, Whelks, and Winkles

A class of shellfish that was once a standby of the diet of coastal communities in northern Europe, these marine treats have shown a sharp decline in popularity. Cockles are found in mudflats on the Atlantic shorelines, but also farther south, around the Mediterranean.

The whelk lives in a whorled shell and is a ferocious carnivorous predator. The flesh is extremely tough and, unlike cockles, cannot be eaten raw. Ten minutes of boiling is necessary to pry them out of the shell.

Winkles are among the tiniest and most mildly flavored of shellfish, so small that they need to be coaxed out of the shell with a pin.

Fresh cockles should have tightly closed shells and be left in a bucket of lightly salted water for about 1 hour to remove the sand. To prepare them for cooking, scrub the shells thoroughly under cold running water, then cook them in a large pan with a little water. Heat them gently, shaking the pan, until the shells have opened, about 5 minutes. Drain well and serve.

To prepare live winkles and whelks, put them in boiling water, then simmer for about 5 minutes. Shell the whelks before serving but winkles are left in the shell; serve them with vinegar, salt, and pepper.

To eat winkles, use a pin to remove each winkle from its shell. Sprinkle with vinegar and season with salt and pepper.

Arbroath Smokies

Fish-Head Curry

An Arbroath smokie is a world away from the yellow-dyed smoked haddock often seen in the fishmonger's display. This small smoked haddock comes from the town of Arbroath in eastern Scotland and has a smooth, rounded, salty, and smoky flavor, the pearly-white flesh encased in a deep brown exterior. The smokies are first salted and dried, before being hung up by their tails in pairs to hot-smoke for an hour or so over a hardwood fire.

Smokies originated in the clifftop village of Auchmithie, around 3 miles away from Arbroath, where their preparation was perfected by communities of Norse fishermen. The smoke pits over which the fish were cured were constructed on shelves in the cliff face. In the early years of the 19th century, some families uprooted themselves and moved to the boom town of Arbroath, where the tradition was carried on and the fish gained their present name.

The best Arbroath smokies are made by small family producers rather than the bigger factories. They are best eaten in situ straight off the barrel or as a half-time treat at Arbroath soccer ground. Otherwise, warm them in the oven for a few minutes for a true Scots breakfast.

Fish-head curry appears to have originated in Singapore in the mid-20th century, when a thrifty cook decided that the waste of discarding the heads of fish before cooking was too awful to contemplate. It has since risen virtually to the status of a national dish. There is no particular tradition in Indian cooking of eating the heads of fish separately, so this would appear to be a regional specialty, but it is also found in Malaysia.

There are various presentations. In Singapore, it is quite common for restaurants to cook the single head of one large species, usually the red snapper, and serve it with a red-hot spicy sauce on a banana leaf. Grouper or even salmon head may also be used. In other versions, many heads of smaller fish are cooked in a curry sauce.

This is one of those dishes that will attract only the bravest Western diner. All parts of the head are eaten by Singaporeans, including the spiny lips and the giant, milk-white eye. Accompaniments usually include okra, eggplant, tomatoes, and shallots, while the spicing is based on red and green chiles, turmeric, and tamarind juice.

Fish-Head Curry

10 cloves garlic

20 shallots

10 dried Thai red chiles

1 piece gingerroot, sliced into 2-in lengths

$1/2$ tsp ground turmeric

1 lemongrass stalk, sliced

2 tbsp oil, plus 2 tbsp

$1^3/_4$ lb fish heads

2 tbsp tamarind pulp

20 curry leaves

3 tbsp curry powder

1 cup water, plus 1 cup

2 cups coconut milk

5 small okras

1 Chinese or Japanese eggplant, cut into 6 pieces

1 tsp salt

1 tbsp sugar

Sliced scallions

Sliced tomatoes

In a food processor, blend into a paste the garlic, shallots, chiles, ginger, turmeric, lemongrass, and 2 tablespoons of oil.

In a saucepan filled with boiling water, blanch the fish heads for about 3 minutes, then soak them in ice water for a few minutes. Drain and set aside. Soak the tamarind pulp in water and strain, reserving the juice.

Heat the remaining 2 tablespoons of oil in a large pan over low heat. Add the garlic mixture with the curry leaves, and cook, stirring frequently until fragrant, about 5 minutes. Add the curry powder and continue stirring for 1 minute. Add 1 cup of water and simmer for about 3 minutes. Add the remaining cup of water, tamarind juice, coconut milk, fish heads, okra, and eggplant. Bring to a boil over medium heat and simmer, uncovered, until the fish is cooked, about 5 minutes. Stir in the salt and sugar. Garnish with the scallions and tomatoes.

Serves 6

Crab Cakes

Fried crab cakes with a sharply seasoned butter sauce are a traditional dish of New England cooking, particularly of the state of Maryland. In the most popular version, the white meat of crab, ideally from Chesapeake Bay, is mixed with crushed crackers or bread crumbs, and bound with mayonnaise, Worcestershire sauce, mustard, and lemon juice, rolled into patties like flying saucers, and then quickly fried in hot oil until lightly browned and crisp on the surface. The dressing can be something like a tarragon butter, but is usually a firmer dip, such as red pepper mayonnaise or tartar sauce.

Farther south, the recipe gets typically spicier, so that the crab cakes of Louisiana may be seasoned with Tabasco and cayenne pepper, while the mixture incorporates green bell pepper, celery, and onion. A fashionable spin on crab cakes in recent years is to cook them in a Southeast Asian style, with scallions, lime zest, and cilantro mixed into them.

Crab Linguine

Crab Cakes

5 handfuls fresh white bread crumbs

13 oz crabmeat

$\frac{1}{2}$ tsp cayenne pepper

3 tbsp grain mustard

1 tbsp Worcestershire sauce

3 scallions, chopped

4 heaped tbsp mayonnaise

5 tbsp chopped parsley

Juice of half a lemon

Peanut oil

Mix together all the ingredients except the oil and season with salt and pepper. Leave in the refrigerator for at least 20 minutes. With heavily floured hands, gently (and I mean gently) shape the mixture into 9 round patties. The less you handle them, the easier the job will be. As you shape each one, put it onto a floured plate.

Heat a little peanut oil in a frying pan—just enough to cover the bottom. When it is hot, put the patties in (you will probably need to do this in 2 lots, adding new oil to do the second batch). Fry for 2 minutes on the first side, then turn and cook for 3 minutes longer. Drain on paper towels and eat with halves of lemon for squeezing and a watercress salad.

Serves 3

Adapted from Nigel Slater's *Real Cooking*

For this hearteningly simple, but superbly tasty, pasta dish, the only effort that might be involved is in starting with a whole live crab. If your culinary skills don't fully extend to slaughtering and anatomizing such a creature, start instead with some fresh (not canned) white and brown crabmeat.

Aromatize some olive oil by sweating off some minced garlic and finely chopped red chile, then add the crabmeat. Keep moving it around in the pan to prevent scorching while you cook it for a few minutes. Deglaze the pan with dry white wine, and leave it to simmer until it has reduced by about half. Season with salt, pepper, and parsley, then toss the mixture in freshly cooked linguine. Finely grate some Parmesan cheese over the dish if you like.

Some versions of crab linguine add cream with the wine, but the dish doesn't strictly require it, as the crab has such a wonderfully rich flavor of its own. Serve it with a good young Soave.

Crayfish

Although they have become something of
a rarity in European cuisine, crayfish are still
a popular seafood item in North America,
especially in the south and in the Pacific
northwest, and in Australia, where different
subspecies go by the names of marrons and
yabbies. They are a relatively small crustacean,
related to the lobster, but living in freshwater
habitats rather than the sea.

Crayfish should have the gut removed
before cooking. They are generally best
poached or broiled and are ready when the
shells turn red. If served as a first course on
their own, or with garlic butter for dipping,
they are eaten with the fingers. They should
shell as easily as prawns. Most of the flesh is
in the tails, although with larger specimens,
extracting the claw meat with shellfish
crackers is worth the effort too.

A plague all but wiped out the European
species in the late 19th and early 20th
centuries, but stocks recovered with American
imports, much to the indignation of certain
French chefs, who consider the American
varieties inferior. The shells have long been
used as an integral ingredient in the
preparation of classic creamy shellfish sauces.

Dover Sole

Until it became an over-exploited species, the
Dover sole was considered a prince among
flatfish. Oval in shape, it is brownish-gray
on its upper surface and white underneath.
It got its name from the fact that it was once
plentiful in the English Channel, much of it
being landed in the port town of Dover in
Kent, but it is also native to the North Sea,
the Baltic, and the Atlantic.

Sole has a delicate but much esteemed
flavor, lending itself to the gentlest of
treatments for white fish. Light poaching
or steaming suit it best, and it is usual to
serve it fairly plain, if the whole fish is being
offered, with nothing more than melted
butter and a squeeze of lemon. If a fillet or
two is to be served as an intermediate fish
course, they can be given a light, wine-based
cream sauce.

Sole is a very easy fish for the diner to
fillet. The two fillets on each side are pushed
gently away from the central dorsal bone
without carrying smaller bones with them.
Paupiettes of sole were once a fashionable
gastronomic dish and entailed rolling the
fillets around some filling, often seasoned
creamed mushrooms.

Fishcakes

Fishcakes crop up in one form or another in many of the world's cuisines. Thai fishcakes (*tod mun*) are thin and crisp, bound with curry paste, and usually served with a hot chili relish. The kind that are most popular in the English-speaking world, though, are the kind featured in this recipe.

Originating as an economical means of stretching fresh fish when supplies were scarce, fishcakes are made from flakes of white fish, mixed with mashed potato and parsley, and given a bread crumb coating. They are then fried or broiled, and more often than not served with fries, despite the fact that they already contain potato. More upmarket versions might be made with salmon or smoked fish such as haddock, or might incorporate shrimp.

During times of privation, the fish-and-chip shops of England turned to fishcakes, making fish go further. They remain on the menu at most such places to this day, as a cheaper alternative for those whose budget doesn't quite stretch to a whole piece of fish.

Old-Fashioned Fish Cakes with Creamed Spinach

4 potatoes, peeled

1 lb cod, hake, or haddock, skinned

1 cup milk

A large fistful of parsley, chopped

12 anchovy fillets, rinsed

2 tbsp butter

Flour (enough to cover a plate), seasoned with salt and cayenne pepper

Oil

2 big handfuls of baby spinach leaves

1/2 cup heavy cream or crème fraîche

A lemon

Cut the potatoes into chunks, put them in a saucepan, and cover with water. Bring to a boil, add a teaspoon of salt, turn down the heat, and simmer till tender, about 25 minutes. While they are cooking, put the fish in a shallow pan, almost cover with milk, and cook at a gentle bubble until the fish turns opaque and can be pulled apart in big fat flakes. A matter of 8 to 10 minutes.

Put the chopped parsley in a mixing bowl. Chop the anchovy fillets and add half of them to the parsley. Lift the fish out of the milk with a slotted spoon and add to the bowl. Break up the flakes gently, removing any bones as you go and taking care not to smash the fish up too much. Season with salt and black pepper.

The spuds should be done by now. Test them with a skewer. Drain them and mash them with the butter. Mix the mash lightly with the seasoned fish. There should be large flakes of fish and flecks of green in the potato. Shape into 8 flat cakes by patting them gently in your hand. Don't overdo this or they will lose their rough texture. Pat them in the seasoned flour, turning them over to cover both sides.

Heat a little oil in the frying pan. A non-stick one might be the best bet. When it starts to shimmer, add the floured fish cakes. Cook for 2 minutes on each side, turning them carefully with a spatula. Serve with creamed spinach and lemon quarters for squeezing.

Wash the spinach and tear it into small shreds. Put the wet leaves into a shallow pan with the remaining anchovies and cover with a lid. Cook for a minute or two until the leaves have wilted but are still a vivid emerald green. Pour in the cream, add a little salt and some black pepper. Leave to bubble for a couple of minutes. Serve at the side of the fish cakes, with quarters of lemon.

Serves 4

Adapted from Nigel Slater's *Real Cooking*

Goujons of Sole with Tartar Sauce

This dish is made up of strips of sole fillet coated in a seasoned bread crumb layer, deep-fried, and served with tartar sauce for dipping. It is essentially one of the many spinoffs of the fried-fish tradition, but one that enjoys a slightly more elevated reputation than fish and chips.

Tartar sauce can be made at home by mixing a good mayonnaise with capers, chopped gherkins, parsley, and seasonings, and will always be much better than the ready-made commercial product. It has an appealing piquancy that suits fish perfectly. In classical French cooking, *sauce tartare* contained only onion, chives, and chopped hard-boiled egg with the mayonnaise, but the version suggested here is now what is expected of this dressing.

Although the dish may be made with the best sole in French gastronomy, it is a less than delicate way of treating what is after all a rather delicate fish. The tendency these days is to make it with lemon sole, which isn't related to the sole species proper, but is nonetheless a good fish. It has the advantage of being less expensive and is therefore better suited to this treatment.

Fisherman's Pie

Pure comfort food on a chilly winter's day, a fisherman's pie is also a very satisfying dish to make. It is constructed of a mixture of fish—generally a white fish such as cod, along with smoked haddock, and sometimes shrimp or anchovies—with a green vegetable (perhaps broccoli florets, French beans, or peas) in a creamy béchamel sauce, topped with mashed potato and baked in the oven.

Fisherman's pie (sometimes just called fish pie) is a British dish, although whether it originated in England or Scotland is hard to say. It is a close cousin to many another potato-topped "pie," such as cottage pie (made with minced beef) and shepherd's pie (minced lamb), none of which actually involves pastry.

Some recipes suggest gratinéeing the surface of the mashed potato with grated Cheddar, but this isn't essential. What does seem essential, and will always be in evidence when this dish is ordered in a British pub, is that the surface of the mash should have a pattern of wavy lines all over it, made by dragging a fork across it.

Fantastic Fish Pie

5 large potatoes, peeled and diced into 1-inch squares

Salt and freshly ground black pepper

2 large free-range eggs

2 large handfuls fresh spinach

1 onion, finely chopped

1 carrot, halved and finely chopped

Extra-virgin olive oil

1⅓ cups heavy cream

2 good handfuls grated mature Cheddar or Parmesan cheese

Juice of 1 lemon

1 heaping tsp English mustard

1 large handful flat-leaf parsley, finely chopped

1 lb haddock or cod fillet, skin removed, pin-boned, and sliced into strips

Fresh nutmeg, optional

Preheat the oven to 450°F.

Put the potatoes into salted boiling water and bring back to a boil for 2 minutes.

Rape al Ajillo

Carefully add the eggs to the pan and cook for a further 8 minutes until hard-boiled, by which time the potatoes should also be cooked. At the same time, steam the spinach in a colander above the pan. This will only take a minute. When the spinach is done, remove from the colander and gently squeeze any excess moisture away. Then drain the potatoes in the colander. Remove the eggs, cool under cold water, then peel and quarter them. Place to one side.

In a separate pan slowly fry the onion and carrot in a little olive oil for about 5 minutes, then add the heavy cream and bring just to a boil. Remove from the heat and add the cheese, lemon juice, mustard, and parsley. Put the spinach, fish, and eggs into an appropriately sized earthenware dish and mix together, pouring over the creamy vegetable sauce. The cooked potatoes should be drained and mashed—add a bit of olive oil, salt, pepper, and a touch of nutmeg if you like. Spread on top of the fish. Don't bother piping it to make it look pretty—it's a homely hearty thing. Place in the oven for about 25 to 30 minutes until the potatoes are golden. Serve with some nice peas or greens, not forgetting your baked beans and tomato ketchup. Tacky but tasty and that's what I like. *Serves 6*
Adapted from Jamie Oliver's *The Return of the Naked Chef*

This Spanish preparation for monkfish (also known as angler-fish) means "monkfish with garlic." The traditional way to prepare it is to buy a large piece of monkfish tail, which can be roasted in one piece in a large ovenproof dish. Incisions are made across the fish and cloves of garlic stuffed into them. The fish is further seasoned with lemon juice and herbs, doused with olive oil, and then cooked in the oven for no more than about 20 minutes.

When the cooking is finished, the surface of the fish should be lightly browned, and the garlic cloves nicely softened. If you like, you can throw in a whole bulb of garlic, sliced across laterally, to cook alongside the fish, but it may be as well to parboil it first. Some recipes call for the fish to be basted with white wine vinegar while it cooks, to guard against the flesh becoming dry.

The texture and flavor of monkfish are sufficiently dense and rich that it was once sold by fishmongers as the "poor man's lobster." In the last 20 to 30 years, it has become increasingly voguish in kitchens throughout the English-speaking world, a trend that has caused its price to rise accordingly.

Goan Fish Curry

Fresh Mackerel

The province of Goa on the southwest coast of India was, for 450 years, a Portuguese enclave, and its cooking reflects the mingled influences of Portugal and native tradition. Being a coastal region, its cuisine is centered on fish, with the pomfret—a local species—being one of the main ingredients.

The sauce for this curry is based on tamarind, tomatoes, onions, and some combination of garlic, ginger, hot chiles, turmeric, coriander seed, cardamom, and cumin, all mashed together into a paste. An essential element in nearly all Goan dishes is coconut, and a fish curry to feed a family will probably contain the grated flesh of a whole coconut. The fish is cut into bite-sized pieces and then cooked gently in this mixture. The finished dish is served with plain rice.

Some recipes use coconut milk as well as coconut flesh for extra creaminess, but this is always offset by the sour tang of tamarind (some use vinegar too). When pomfret isn't available, tuna makes a good substitute.

Mackerel is a very distinctive fish, found in large quantities in the waters of the North Atlantic, around northern Europe and the Mediterranean. It is characterized by its silvery skin and greenish-blue back. During the winter months, from November to March, it tends to congregate close to shorelines, making it a good winter catch.

Although a lot of mackerel is sold hot-smoked or even dried, it is much underrated as a fresh fish. It is high in omega-3 fish oils, which makes it one of the healthier choices; this oiliness means it favors acidic accompaniments. In English cooking, a dressing made of sour fruits—especially gooseberries—was traditional in the past, and a cooking liquid of vinegar and water (soused mackerel) suits it well for the same reason.

Mackerel is best if quickly broiled, but it can also be fried, poached, or barbecued. Its high oil content means that it tends to degrade quickly, so it is all the more important that freshly caught fish be cooked the same day. The danger with fishing for them is that, as they live in such densely packed shoals, more will be caught than can be used promptly.

Le Grand Aïoli

Aïoli is the garlic mayonnaise of Provence, considered by Provençals to be the finest vehicle for garlic ever invented. Indeed, so ceremonially is it revered that lavish festivals are held each year to celebrate the new season's garlic crop, at which huge quantities of aïoli are consumed, either in the broiling midday sun of early summer or on the night before Christmas.

"Le grand aïoli" is just such an occasion. Served perhaps two or three times a year, it is a spectacular spread of many different cooked and raw items, from boiled meats to stewed vegetables and crudités, but always including a show-stopping fish dish. This could be poached salmon, fried large shrimp, or—most authentically—the local version of salt cod, either poached or boiled. Other seafood items at a grand aïoli might include octopus or squid and broiled white fish such as sea bass.

Aïoli is a portmanteau word encompassing the names for garlic (*ail*) and oil (*oli* in the local dialect). It also crops up over the border in Catalan cooking as *allioli*.

Le Grand Aïoli

2 lb salt cod

6 small gold or red beets (or a combination)

6 fingerling potatoes

1 lb small carrots

1 lb green beans

6 young artichokes

2 small heads cauliflower

12 plum tomatoes

6 hard-boiled eggs, shelled

A large pinch of coarse sea salt

4 cloves garlic (garlic lovers can add up to 9)

2 egg yolks

2 cups olive oil

Juice of 1/2 lemon

Prepare the platter ingredients. Soak and poach the salt cod. Wrap the beets individually in foil and bake at 350°F for 45 to 60 minutes, until tender. Cook the potatoes in boiling salted water for about 30 minutes, until tender. Cook the carrots in boiling salted water for 10 to 15 minutes, until tender. Parboil the green beans in salted water for 10 to 15 minutes. Trim the artichokes and cook in boiling salted water for about 20 minutes, until tender. Separate the cauliflower into florets and parboil in salted water for 2 to 3 minutes until tender-crisp. Peel the tomatoes.

To make the aïoli, crush the sea salt and garlic cloves in a mortar. Pound it into a paste. Transfer the paste to a bowl and add the egg yolks, working them in well.

Add the olive oil by pouring it in a slow trickle down the side of the bowl, whisking and drawing in the oil. As the sauce begins to thicken, increase the flow of the oil, whisking constantly. When the mixture has started to become very thick, usually after about half the oil has been added, add the lemon juice, continuing to whisk. Whisk in the remaining oil. If the mixture is too stiff, add a little water to thin it.

Arrange the fish, vegetables, and eggs on a platter and serve with the aïoli. *Serves 6*

Greek Baked Fish

Since Greece is almost entirely surrounded by the Mediterranean and Aegean Seas, the fact that Greek cuisine features plenty of fish and seafood should come as no surprise. Many varieties of small shellfish are eaten, but perhaps the grandest, and simplest, fish preparation is the serving of a whole fish that has been baked in the oven (*psari sto fourno*) with nothing more than a few herbs and some lemon.

Virtually any available fish can lend itself to such a treatment, but large sea bass or bream are best suited for a family occasion, while red snapper and red mullet are regional specialties. The fish is cleaned and descaled, brushed with olive oil, and a couple of incisions are usually made in the side. Into each slit is pushed some mixed herbs—perhaps parsley, thyme, rosemary, and bay—and then the fish is wrapped in foil and baked. It is served with lemon for squeezing (this too may have been cooked in the oven), or with a dressing of olive oil and lemon juice.

Alternatively, the fish may be laid on a bed of sautéed onions and tomato, and doused in white wine, before cooking.

Greek Baked Fish

Olive oil

8 small potatoes, wiped and cut into wedges

1 onion, roughly sliced

2 large, juicy cloves garlic, peeled and sliced

1 whole white fish, weighing about 1 lb

4 tomatoes, halved

Oregano, mint, or dill—a handful of chopped leaves

Juice of a large lemon

Salt

Freshly ground black pepper

Preheat over to 350°F.

Heat enough olive oil in a shallow roasting pan to cover the bottom generously. Add the wedges of potato, onion, and the garlic and cook them over moderate heat. After 10 minutes or less, they will be soft and lightly colored. Put them in the oven for 10 minutes. Shake them about a bit, then put the fish on top of them and surround with the tomatoes. Add the herbs, lemon juice, and some salt and pepper. Bake for about 35 minutes. If you need to, you can keep the dish warm for a while without it drying up by covering it with a lid and keeping it in a very low oven. It comes to no harm when the Greeks do it. *Serves 2*

Adapted from Nigel Slater's *Real Cooking*

Broiled Red Mullet in Vine Leaves

Another Greek recipe, this is an excellent preparation for the much prized red mullet, a Mediterranean fish with a good flavor and attractive silvery-pink skin. The fish is usually stuffed after gutting with a mixture of preserved lemon, chiles, and parsley, and is then wrapped up in a vine leaf, of the kind that can be bought in packs and used for making dolmades.

The prepared fish is then broiled or grilled and dressed in olive oil and lemon juice before serving. Each diner peels away the vine leaf before eating the fish. It is usual to wrap the fish in the leaf so that it looks as though it is wearing a jacket, that is, with its head and tail exposed, but some cooks use up to three vine leaves to completely cover it.

As an alternative approach, the mullet need not be stuffed, but can simply be marinated in a mixture of olive oil, lemon juice, garlic, and herbs, which is then brushed on to the fish immediately before cooking.

The dish should be served with plain steamed rice.

Grilled Stingray

The stingray is a member of that family
of flatfish that also includes rays and skates.
It is native to tropical waters throughout
the world and is a popular food fish. Its long
tail-spine is the stinging bit, and the creature
secretes a venom that it uses on its prey,
feeding as it does on the seabed. In common
with the everyday skate stingray, it has no
bones as such, but only a cartilage structure,
from which the cooked flesh parts with
obliging ease.

Grilling stingray is a popular treatment
wherever it is fished but is perhaps best
known in Malaysian cooking as the dish *ikan
bakar*. The name means "burned fish," because
the technique is actually a form of chargrilling
using charcoal. After being rubbed with a
hot spice mixture, the fish is set on a banana
leaf on the hot grill.

The best parts of the stingray are the wings,
the large pectoral fins with which the fish
propels itself through the water. The cheeks
and the liver are also valued.

Grilled Sardines   ▷

Fresh sardines make a wonderful appetizer
dish, especially if simply grilled. They need
very little in the way of preparation and are
usually given only a little minced garlic and
lemon juice, along with olive oil, seasonings,
and perhaps some finely chopped onion.
The emphasis is on what should be the
impeccable freshness of the just-caught fish.

Apart from gutting, the fish needs no
other treatment before grilling. Diners will
fillet them for themselves as they eat them,
and leaving on the head makes it easier to
turn the whole fish on the griddle without
them breaking up.

The sardine is a relative of the herring
family and is so named because it was once
copiously fished from the waters around the
Italian island of Sardinia. They are at their
best toward the end of the summer, when
they have grown quite large and plump and
won't look anything like the little fellows
that come in cans.

Hake in Salsa Verde

Hake is nowhere in the world more highly valued than it is in Spain and Portugal, and this dish, from the Basque region of northern Spain, is one of the most popular methods of preparing it. Hake steaks are pan-fried in olive oil with garlic, and then simmered in white wine until cooked, whereupon they are liberally scattered with handfuls of chopped flat-leaf parsley. In many recipes, the dish also has clams added to it.

The hake (*Merluccius merluccius*) is a near relative of the cod and has the same firm flesh, but a notably milder flavor. This flavor provides a neutral background to the other ingredients and it is perhaps because of this that this dish works so well. In French cooking, the hake is nowhere near so highly esteemed and, although it lives in waters from the Mediterranean all the way up to northern Europe, it hasn't ever found great favor in England either.

The usual accompaniment to hake in salsa verde is plain boiled potatoes, but it goes especially well with asparagus too. A good wine to accompany it is Txacoli de Guetaria, a light, dry white produced in the Basque region.

Hake in Salsa Verde

Oil

1 medium onion, sliced

4 cloves garlic, finely chopped or sliced

4 (7-oz) hake steaks

Flour for dusting

1 cup fish broth

A handful of parsley, well chopped

Salt

Freshly ground black pepper

Heat the oil in a shallow heatproof dish over medium heat. Cook the the onion and garlic in the oil until they begin to turn golden.

Wash the fish and dry it, then coat it with the flour. Add the steaks to the dish and brown them lightly. Pour the broth into the dish, then add the parsley, salt, and pepper. Simmer and stir until the sauce thickens and the fish is just tender. The fish can be served in the dish, garnished with hard-boiled eggs and some asparagus tips. *Serves 4*

Bombay Duck

Kippers ▷

Bombay duck is not a type of duck, but is a species of lizard fish, so called because its head resembles a lizard. It is native to the Arabian Sea, the Bay of Bengal, and the South China Sea, and is variously known in the south Asian languages by such names as *bamaloh* (Bengali) or *bumla* (Gujarati). It appears to have gained its misleading English name during India's days under British colonial rule, when the odor of the fish was said to resemble the smell of the mail trains, known as *daks*, that served Mumbai (then called Bombay).

The strong smell arises when the fish is salted and sun-dried for preservation. Rather like certain French cheeses, it may not be carried on public transport unless it is sealed inside an airtight container. It is generally used as a seasoning element in curries or incorporated into a pickle, but when fresh, it can be deep-fried in spicy batter.

In Thai cooking, they are often cooked in the form of deep-fried fish balls. One of the obliging features of the Bombay duck is that its bones are very soft, so it needs no filleting.

The kipper is a smoked herring, traditional to the British kitchen, where it has often been eaten as a breakfast dish. Although legend insists that the technique of cold-smoking herring was discovered when a batch of fresh herring was accidentally left overnight in a room with a smoking stove—said to have happened in a house in the fishing port of Seahouses in Northumberland, northeast England, in the mid-19th century—the basic method is in reality much older than that.

The smoking of herring has been carried on in the Scandinavian countries and on the Baltic coast of Germany for many centuries, and kippers are the British offshoot of that tradition. They are butterflied during the gutting process, before being salted and cold-smoked. The smoking is what gives kippers their deep reddish-brown color. Some of the best come from the coastal town of Craster in Northumberland. Scotland and the Isle of Man (Manx kippers) are notable producers too.

Kippers are best either broiled or warmed in the oven. They should be left in until the flesh is cooked and eaten with nothing more than a little melted butter.

Mojama

Mojama is another of the techniques for drying fish, in this case tuna. It is meat taken from the back of the fish, which is then dried and salted, acquiring in the process a tough, chewy texture not unlike cured meats. The process is an ancient one, having been transmitted to the indigenous peoples of the Iberian peninsula by the Phoenicians.

The tuna are filleted at sea, with two fillets being cut lengthways from either side of the back of each fish. These are stacked and then shoveled over with coarse salt. After a couple of days under salt, which draws out much of the natural moisture content of the fish, the salt is washed away, and the fillets are put into wire clamps to be hung up for air-drying. This is now done in special drying rooms, where, over about three weeks, the tuna turns a deep red, and its flavor becomes intensely concentrated.

Mojama is often served as a tapas dish, when it is thinly sliced like Serrano ham, sprinkled with olive oil, and served on pieces of bread smeared with sieved tomato. It can also be grated over main-course fish dishes to add extra savory kick.

Merluza a la Gallega

The phrase *a la Gallega* in Spanish dishes means that the dish is cooked in the style of Galicia, the province in the northwest corner of Spain. *Merluza* is the Spanish word for the nation's favorite fish, the hake.

In this dish, which should be cooked in the traditional shallow, handled earthenware pot known as a *cazuela*, a layer of onions cooked in garlic and paprika is topped by sliced potatoes, along with chopped sweet red peppers. These are simmered in white wine and water until the potato is nearly cooked, and then the seasoned fillets of hake are placed on top, where they are effectively poached. The dish continues cooking until the fish is done.

The one variation in the technique is that some cooks transfer the dish to the oven once the fish is put in. Those who feel that no Spanish dish is complete without chorizo will be pleased to know that little chunks of the spicy sausage can also be incorporated with the onion, the sauce being quite red anyway from the peppers and paprika. The middle cut of hake is the best part of the fish for this dish.

Lobster Roll

A lobster roll is the size and shape of a hot-dog bun, but there all similarities end. Instead of containing a frankfurter, the split roll is filled with a lobster salad mixture. Cold pieces of cooked lobster meat are bound with mayonnaise and chopped scallions and piled into the roll, which should be buttered, toasted, and lined with lettuce. Garnishes such as dill pickles or potato chips are optional add-ons.

This is a specialty of New England, where much of North America's lobster is caught. The preeminent state for lobster has always been Maine, with Massachusetts and Connecticut not far behind, and the dish is often sold locally as Maine Lobster Roll. It originated in the mid-20th century in the fishing ports of New England, where it was sold from simple wooden shacks on the waterfront.

Variations on the preparation often involve adding some extra flavoring ingredient to the filling, perhaps finely chopped fresh tarragon or thin slivers of celery. The point, however, is not to mask the fresh, rich flavor of the lobster itself.

Some restaurants offer versions made with French brioche but, whatever the medium, sticklers for authenticity insist that the roll should be top-heavy with its filling.

Lobster Américaine

The most highly valued marine crustacean of them all, the European or American lobster has long been viewed as a luxury food. Whatever outlandish prices it commands at market and on restaurant menus reflect the labor-intensive process involved in catching and shipping it. It must be coaxed into "pots" and then transported live in conditions that don't impair its vigor.

The meat is concentrated in the seven-sectioned abdomen and tail, and also in the principal claws and highly developed pincers. It is densely textured and full of flavor, its natural richness often enhanced by any of the classic ways of preparing it in cooked dishes. Its deep blue-black color turns vividly orange-pink when cooked.

Lobster Américaine is a typically complex dish that is based on a reduction sauce made using fragments of the shell, along with cognac, white wine, tomatoes, garlic, and herbs. The sauce is thickened at the end of cooking by adding *beurre manié* (butter and flour mashed to a paste). *Larousse Gastronomique* says that it should also be enriched by adding the coral (or roe) and liver to it. The lobster is arranged on a platter, anointed with the sauce, and served with rice.

Lobster with Chile and Black Bean Sauce

Lobster makes for as grand a dish in Chinese cooking as it does in the Western kitchen. This Cantonese recipe from southern China maximizes the richness of its flavor without the traditional Western resort to dairy fats.

The lobster tail is cut into sections with the shell left on. It is deep-fried until the shell has turned pink. The sauce is made by first frying some pounded black beans with garlic, then stir-frying scallions and ginger with chopped chiles and ground pork. The liquid ingredients are added—usually a combination of soy sauce, rice wine, and chicken broth—and the lobster pieces are introduced to the pan. It is all thickened up in the traditional fashion with a mixture of cornstarch and water, and the final addition is beaten egg.

It is up to the diner to pick the meat from the shell when eating the dish. This may seem messy to convenience-fixated Western diners, but cooking the lobster in its shell enhances the flavor of the sauce (the classic French lobster sauce also depends for its color and flavor on cooking the shell to make the basic broth).

Lobster Thermidor

The Thermidor preparation is named indirectly after one of the months of the French revolutionary calendar created in 1793 (roughly mid-July to mid-August). The dish itself wasn't conceived then, but was created a century later at a Paris restaurant called Maire's, situated near the Comédie Française theater, which at the time was staging a long-forgotten play entitled *Thermidor*.

This is possibly the most time-consuming lobster recipe of them all. It is based on an extremely rich mixture of cooked lobster meat bound with béchamel sauce and flavored with mustard, Parmesan, cognac, and tarragon. It is classically served in the two hollowed-out halves of the lobster shell, sprinkled with more grated Parmesan, and given a browned surface by being flashed under the broiler. The shells themselves should be prepared by lining them with a little of the mustard sauce before the rest of the mixture is packed in.

There are simpler, short-cut recipes, in which the lobster meat is simply cooked in slices and then laid on a layer of cream sauce in the shell, before being baked in the oven, but no Thermidor purist would accept this as the genuine article.

Marmitako

Langoustines

The Basque name for a fish stew known across northern Spain, marmitako is a traditional way of cooking tuna. In the neighboring region of Cantabria, its name is marmita, both names deriving from the pot in which the stew is cooked—a deep, two-handled, metal or earthenware dish originally set over a fire. In French, it is known as a *marmite*.

The tuna is cooked slowly in a rich, chunky mixture of potatoes, plum tomatoes, green or red bell peppers, and onions, cooked in white wine or just water, and usually given a little bite with capers, paprika, and garlic. Its consistency should be quite thick and soupy, an effect enhanced by the indispensable potato in it. The stew minus the tuna can be cooked ahead of time and reheated when needed, with the tuna cooked in it at the last minute.

These days, marmitako appears on upscale restaurant menus, but it was originally eaten— and still is—by fishermen on the tuna boats. An alternative recipe uses salmon in place of the tuna, but this is decidedly less authentic.

The langoustine is a marine crustacean that looks something like a miniature lobster (also known as the Norway lobster and the Dublin Bay prawn). Native to European waters from Scandinavia to the Mediterranean, it has a pink shell even before cooking, with white-tipped legs and claws. Although they are often eaten whole in France and the Mediterranean countries, many recipes call only for the meaty tail.

Langoustines lend themselves to many of the same techniques used for cooking crayfish and shrimp or lobster. If served whole, they can be boiled for a few minutes in a wine-based broth before cooking and serving with a mustard and mayonnaise mix.

Langoustines en Brochettes

For each person have half a dozen tails of freshly boiled Dublin Bay prawns. Take them from their shells without breaking them, season them with pepper and lemon juice, paint them with just melted butter, thread them onto small skewers, putting a whole mushroom head, also seasoned and buttered, between each. Broil them gently, turning the skewers as round once or twice. Serve on a bed of cooked rice or with béarnaise, hollandaise, or bretonne sauce.

Adapted from Elizabeth David's *French Provincial Cooking*

Monkfish Wrapped in Parma Ham

The affinity of certain firm-fleshed species of fish with meats has been long established. Spanish cooking often mixes chorizo and fish in the same dish, while combinations of ham and anchovies are typical in Italy. The technique of wrapping monkfish in Parma ham is one such dish that has become a modern classic.

Thick cuts of monkfish tail, the best, most succulent part of the fish, are tightly bound in strips of Parma ham, and then cooked in the oven. The ham helps to season the fish and also prevent it from becoming too dry in the cooking, and the combination of the two flavors, and the counterpointing textures of crisp ham and softer fish is highly appealing.

Monkfish has the benefit of having only one central bone, so no filleting is required, and its meaty texture and pronounced flavor are very satisfying.

Monkfish Wrapped in Parma Ham

1 tbsp finely chopped parsley

1 tbsp finely chopped oregano

6 tbsp olive oil

Salt

Freshly ground black pepper

2 (5-oz) monkfish tail fillets, skinned, all membrane removed

8 slices Parma ham

1 cup shredded baby spinach

For the sauce:

1 small onion, finely chopped

1 tbsp butter

1 tbsp white wine vinegar

²/₃ cup white wine

1 cup vegetable broth

Salt

Freshly ground black pepper

Preheat oven to 400°F. Mix the parsley, oregano, and olive oil together to make a marinade, adding salt and pepper to taste. Put the monkfish in a bowl and cover with the marinade. Let sit for 20 minutes.

Lay half the slices of the ham on the work surface so that they are overlapping. Scatter half the baby spinach over the ham. Set one of the marinated fillets on the ham, and roll up the ham around the fish. Repeat with the other fillet, remaining spinach, and the rest of the ham, and place on a baking tray. Bake for 12 to 15 minutes.

To make the sauce, fry the onion in the butter until soft. Add the vinegar and boil until almost dry, then add the wine and reduce to about a quarter. Add the broth and reduce by about half. Pour the sauce through a sieve and season to taste. To serve, slice the cooked fillet, arrange the slices on the plate, and drizzle with the sauce. *Serves 2*

Moules Frîtes

If you see moules frites on a menu in Belgium (and you will, everywhere you look), what you will get is mussels and fries. These are eaten all over Belgium, and indeed have become such a popular dish elsewhere that chain restaurants serving them have opened in many English-speaking countries too. The mussels are simply cooked until they open, and then served with crunchy fries, which the Belgians—like the Dutch—love to dip in mayonnaise (which makes for a happier marriage with the shellfish than ketchup would!).

The absolutely authentic accompaniment to moules frites is a glass of richly flavored Belgian beer.

Mussels themselves may also be fried, as in the traditional French recipe that also bears this name. They should be briefly boiled to open them and then set aside to cool. Once cooled, they are marinated in a mixture of olive oil, lemon juice, parsley, and seasonings, before being coated in batter and shallow-fried. They can be served as a first course with lemon or as a canapé speared on cocktail sticks.

Moules Marinière

The marinière method may be applied to any shellfish, but is most classically associated with mussels in French cuisine. It essentially involves making something more of the liquid that the shellfish are cooked in than simply boiling them in water.

The mussels are poached in dry white wine, along with very finely chopped shallots, a bay leaf, a little thyme, white wine vinegar, and butter. When the mussels have all opened, they are removed from the pan, and the sauce is very slightly reduced with a little more butter, or perhaps some thin cream, added to it. Each diner receives a bowl of mussels in the shells, with the thin sauce poured over it like a soup. Chunks of crusty bread usually accompany the dish.

The beauty of serving shellfish in the shells is that they make a perfect implement for scooping up the sauce. This dish is best accompanied by a glass of chilled Muscadet, the bone-dry white wine of Brittany that is good with nearly all shellfish dishes.

Moules Farcies

The mussel is a bivalve mollusk found all around the world and in many different species. Most have an oval, convex shell, which may be darkly striped, enclosing an oval body that is either gray or orange in color. Mussels should always be bought tightly closed, and any that fail to open during cooking need to be thrown away.

The many recipes for mussels are all about enhancing their fresh flavor. Great care should be taken not to overcook them, as they become rubbery and unpleasant.

In this classic French recipe for stuffed mussels, the shellfish are cooked and then carefully removed from their shells. The empty half-shells are lined with garlic butter, and the mussels are put back in and covered over with more of the garlic butter. They are sprinkled with fine bread crumbs and browned briefly in a hot oven or under a broiler until the filling is nicely bubbling. They are served simply with lemon for squeezing.

Moules Farcies

4 lb large mussels

$3/4$ cup butter, cut into small pieces

$3/4$ cup dry bread crumbs

3 shallots, finely chopped

2 cloves garlic, finely chopped

1 medium bunch parsley, chopped

1 tsp freshly ground black pepper

Parsley for garnish

Wash and debeard the mussels, discarding any that are broken or are not closed.

In a large pot, steam them over high heat in about a cup of water for 3 to 4 minutes, shaking the pot now and then. Drain the mussels. Remove the empty half-shell from each mussel and discard it, leaving the mussel attached to the other half-shell.

Mix the butter with the bread crumbs, shallot, garlic, parsley, and pepper. Top each mussel with some of the stuffing, then transfer the mussels to a baking dish. Broil until brown. Garnish with parsley and serve immediately. *Serves 4*

Jellied Eels

This traditional English dish relies on the abnormally high fat content shared by all the various species of eel. The eel pieces are cooked to encourage their fat to exude and then are allowed to cool. As they do so, the cooking juices solidify into a kind of aspic, the process sometimes catalyzed by the addition of gelatin. They are usually eaten cold, seasoned with salt and chili vinegar.

Jellied eels were once a staple of the pie-and-mash shops of the East End of London, eaten alongside mashed potato and often accompanied by a parsley sauce. Much declined in popularity now, the dish arose from the abundance of eels that could be easily caught in the waters of the Thames estuary and brought to the London markets in barrels. They were also traditionally sold from stalls in the English coastal resorts, as a snack treat on a day out at the seaside.

The life cycle of the European eel is a testament to its hardiness. After living contentedly in European coastal waters until they attain sexual maturity (around ten years old), they embark on a journey to the Sargasso Sea in the Caribbean region, where they spawn and then perish of exhaustion.

Jellied Eels

2 lb eels, skinned and boned
Grated nutmeg
Juice and zest of ½ lemon
A handful of parsley, chopped
A handful of chervil, chopped
2½ cups fish broth
1 medium onion, finely chopped
1 medium carrot, finely chopped
1 celery stalk, finely chopped
1 bouquet garni
1 tbsp gelatin

Sprinkle the eels with some grated nutmeg, grated lemon zest, and chopped herbs. Cut eels into 4-inch lenghs, then roll up each piece and tie it with string. Put the broth, onion, carrot, celery, bouquet garni into a saucepan and bring to a boil. Add the eels and simmer gently for 15 minutes or until tender.

Remove the eels from the pan (set the hot broth aside). Take the string off the eels and put them in a shallow bowl. Measure the broth and add enough water to make 2 cups.

Dissolve the gelatin in the lemon juice, then add the gelatin to the hot broth, stirring to dissolve it completely. Strain the broth over the eels and leave to set. When the jelly is firm, turn it out of the dish for serving.

Serves 6

Oysters Charentais

The oyster beds of the Charente-Maritime
department of western France are justly
renowned all over the country. They produce
some of the most succulent oysters in
all of Europe, from areas such as Marennes,
Chateau-d'Oléron, and La Tremblade.
Marennes have a distinctive green shell, which
they acquire from the presence of algae in
the waters. It is traditional, as with all oysters
of the northern hemisphere, to eat them in
months that have an "r" in them, that is, from
September to April.

The cooking of the Charente region prides
itself on being an unrefined rustic idiom,
which is why it should come as no surprise
to learn that a favored way of eating oysters
in these parts is with an accompaniment
of broiled spicy sausages. What works most
winningly about this dish is precisely the
combination of the hot, paprika-laden, fatty
sausage with the salty, sea-clean flavor of
the raw oysters. The contrast in textures is
also fascinating. Opinions vary as to whether
the sausage is best chased down with the
oyster, or the other way around. Either way,
this is a dish to remember.

Oysters Rockefeller

There are many dishes in the classical French
repertoire named after one scion or another
of the Rockefeller oil dynasty. Most involve
luxuriously expensive ingredients, as one
would expect, but this has to be the simplest,
gaining its association with opulence from
the sumptuousness of the bivalves themselves
and the richness of their filling.

It is reputed to have originated in a
restaurant called Antoine's in the French
quarter of New Orleans at the end of the
19th century, but nobody knows the precise
formula. Approximations of it, though,
involve cooking down some spinach with
bread crumbs, parsley, Tabasco, pastis, and
seasonings, and then puréeing the cooked
mixture. This is then used to spread over the
oysters in their shells, which are flashed under
the broiler until the topping has browned.

More elaborate recipes add other green
vegetables, such as fennel, scallions, leeks,
and celery, to the basic mixture, along with
Worcestershire sauce and tomato ketchup.
The liquor used should properly be a
Louisiana pastis called Herbsaint, but Pernod
does very well as a substitute.

Moroccan Fish Tagine

A tagine is the generic name for any of a range of aromatic stewed dishes in Moroccan cuisine. They are often meat-based, especially with lamb or chicken, but a fish version is quite common too. The tagine should ideally be cooked in a pot of the same name, which has a pointed lid, over a gentle charcoal fire. Long, slow cooking is essential to allow the main ingredients to cook tenderly, and for all the aromatic spices to impart their flavors.

The main condiment in a tagine, as in much of Moroccan cooking, is harissa, a spice paste made from red chile, garlic, coriander seed, cumin, turmeric, cinnamon, and lemon zest, all pounded together in oil. In addition to the fish, which should be chunks of firm white fish such as hake, cod, or monkfish, the stew should contain tomatoes, black olives, bell peppers, and another standby of the North African kitchen, preserved lemon chopped into small pieces.

Traditionally, the dish is served directly from its cooking pot, accompanied by steamed couscous with a sprinkling of chopped cilantro.

Razor Clams

Two species of razor clam are known throughout North America, one on the eastern seaboard (the Atlantic jack-knife clam, *Ensis directus*), the other on the western (the Pacific razor clam, *Siliqua patula*). They both look quite different from the ordinary round clam by having, as their name indicates, a long, knifelike appearance, something like a jack-knife or a cut-throat razor. They live in the mud of tidal estuaries and are expert diggers, bedding themselves down in the ooze at a rate that often exceeds the prospective clam-fisher's speed of reaction.

In the United States and Canada, clams are traditionally lightly floured or coated in a cracker batter, before being rapidly cooked in hot oil. Like many other shellfish, they go rubbery with even a few seconds of overcooking, so it is important to be brief.

When they are done, they can be eaten whole. The shells can be used to make a good broth for fish chowder.

A separate species found in Asian waters is used in Chinese cuisine. The European variant, known in Italian as *cannolicchi*, are prized above ordinary clams and form the main ingredient of a rich soup.

Pepper Crab

A Singaporean dish that makes the most of the rich flavor of crabmeat by coating it in a mixture of savory and spicy seasonings, pepper crab has become particularly fashionable in Asian restaurants in North America. The recipe is generally prepared with hard-shelled crab, but the soft-shell crabs favored by Eastern cuisines work well too, and don't, of course, need shelling.

Garlic, ginger, and chile peppers are heated in a buttered wok. Oyster sauce, soy sauce, and sugar are added, and then a large quantity of ground black pepper. The trick to the dish is the dry-frying of the black pepper beforehand, which concentrates its fire and brings out all its assertive flavor. The crab, which has been deep-fried first, is then added to the pan and stirred vigorously to get it well coated with the spice mixture.

This dish is relatively new to Singapore itself, having become a staple of the street-food stalls only since the 1980s. The original recipe is said to have been invented at a restaurant chain called Long Beach Seafood in the late 1950s. Some places use white pepper instead of black, or perhaps a blend of the two.

Rock Mussels in Cilantro Foam

From the world of what has become known as "molecular gastronomy," this dish was created at El Bulli restaurant at Rosas in Catalonia by the chef-proprietor Ferran Adrià. The movement is all about scientific techniques to cooking to discover unexpected potentials for new flavor and textural combinations.

Adrià had been experimenting in the early 1990s with creating foams and froths as airy garnishes for dishes, which concentrated their flavors in a much lighter way than the rich sauces of traditional haute cuisine. They are created in a machine equipped with nitrogen cartridges and consist only of the main ingredient plus air.

In 1994, Adrià discovered the creative culinary potential of matching the flavors of marine mollusks such as clams, scallops, and mussels with acidic fruits, pairing clams with lychees, scallops with red currants, and—in this dish—using a blood orange reduction in a dish of rock mussels garnished with a foam created from cilantro.

Gambas al Ajillo

This Spanish dish, literally "shrimp with garlic," hails from Catalonia and consists of large shrimp cooked in sherry with flaked dried red pepper, chile, lemon juice, parsley, and of course plenty of coarsely minced garlic. It is often seen on tapas menus, but may also be served as a first course with crusty bread to mop up the cooking juices.

In Spanish restaurants, the dish will nearly always be served still sizzling in the pot in which it has been cooked, a flat, shallow, earthenware dish called a *cazuela*: the idea is that the shrimp finish their last minute or so of cooking at the table. An alternative name for the dish is *gambas al pil-pil*, the latter term being suggestive of the sputtering oil in the dish. Many people tear into pieces the bread served with it and throw them into the oil, too, to take up its flavors.

A good accompaniment to this dish is a young Rias Baixas, an aromatic white wine made from the Albariño grape in Galicia, northwest Spain.

Shrimp Wontons

Wontons are the rough Chinese equivalent of tempura, although they are wrapped in a thicker coating. The same crisp dough that is used to wrap spring rolls is used on wontons. It is simply folded around a whole shelled shrimp, glued together with beaten egg, and deep-fried in oil. They are served with a dipping sauce. Thick red chili and garlic sauce is a favorite Chinese condiment.

The word *wonton* in Mandarin simply means something like "misshapen dumpling," but its Cantonese variant, *yuntun*, more poetically suggests the idea of "swallowing clouds." Wontons may be fried until crisp and eaten as a snack or dim sum item, or they may be steamed and added to soups. In this latter form, though, they are more likely to contain a ground mixture of pork and shrimp, rather than a whole shrimp.

Chinese home cooks rarely use the kind of deep-fat fryer familiar to Western kitchens. They deep-fry in the all-purpose wok, which is deep enough to contain sufficient oil to submerge the food. If you are going down this route, it is as well to invest in a splash-guard to fit over the surface of the oil, to prevent painful spattering.

Shrimp Tempura

Japanese tempura are the prime example of dishes classed as *agemono*—deep-fried items. They are said to have originated when Portuguese missionaries brought the tradition of tempuras with them in the 17th century. These were fried foods that were to be eaten on days when the religious calendar forbade the consumption of meat, and so were always either fish or vegetables.

The tempura batter is an ethereally light, thin coating made of egg, flour, and water, in which anything from lengths of zucchini to whole small fish are covered, before being deep-fried in either a neutral vegetable oil or, for a more pronounced flavor, sesame oil. They are very popular at Japanese fast-food outlets, where they are made to order and presented to the customer to be eaten at once. Shrimp lend themselves well to the tempura treatment. Indeed, they appear in one battered form or another in a spectrum of Eastern cuisines, from Chinese through Thai to Vietnamese. In Japan, they are always eaten with a soy-based dipping sauce containing *dashi* (fish broth), rice wine, and shavings of daikon (white radish) and ginger.

Scallops

Scallops are found all over the world and come in several subspecies. They are highly revered almost wherever they are found, except for Southeast Asia, where they are eaten but considered rather humdrum. They all have a broad, nearly flat, attractive shell with deep grooves along it in the form of the spines of a fan. The mollusk itself is a pure white color, is relatively firm, and is often sold with its crescent-shaped, bright orange roe attached to it. Opinion differs sharply as to whether the roe is worth eating.

Scallops must be cooked very briefly, either by poaching or searing in hot oil. Even a few seconds' overcooking will leave them dry and rubbery.

Seared Scallops and Crispy Prosciutto with Roasted Tomatoes and Smashed White Beans

4 large ripe plum tomatoes, quartered

Salt and freshly ground black pepper

A pinch of dried oregano

Olive oil

8 slices of prosciutto

1 small clove garlic, finely chopped

1 to 2 small dried red chiles, crumbled to taste

4 to 6 anchovy fillets, chopped

1 (15-oz) can of cannellini beans or flageolet beans, drained

Extra-virgin olive oil

12 to 16 scallops, trimmed with roe on or off to your preference

A small handful of peppery leaves (arugula or watercress)

For the olive oil and lemon juice dressing:

5 tbsp olive oil

2 tbsp fresh lemon juice

Preheat the oven to 475°F.

Season the tomatoes and sprinkle with the oregano. Drizzle with olive oil and roast in the oven, skin side down, for about 10 to 15 minutes. Place the prosciutto slices beside the tomatoes and continue to roast for a further 10 minutes until the tomatoes are juicy and the prosciutto is crisp. In a pan, fry the garlic, chiles, and anchovies in a lug of olive oil for a

Scallops Bercy

minute or so. Add your beans and cook for a couple of minutes before adding a wine glass of water. Bring to a boil, then lightly mash to a coarse purée. Loosen the purée with a little more water if need be. Finish the flavor off with some peppery extra-virgin olive oil, salt, and freshly ground black pepper.

Season the scallops, then sear them in a frying pan with a touch of olive oil for 2 minutes without touching them. Check and continue to fry until they have a lovely sweet caramelized skin—turn them over and allow the other side to do the same. Don't overcook them. Remove to a bowl. In a glass or an empty jam jar, mix together the olive oil, lemon juice, and some seasoning, to taste. Coat the scallops with the dressing. Put some smashed-bean purée on each plate, scatter over the tomatoes, prosciutto, and scallops, and finish off with some peppery leaves.

Serves 4

Adapted from Jamie Oliver's *The Return of the Naked Chef*

The refined white sauce served with the scallops in this classical French first course is named after a sector of Paris where there was once a huge wine market. It isn't surprising, therefore, to find wine a central ingredient in the sauce. Sauce bercy is a type of velouté, that is, a sauce based on a broth—in this case, fish broth—that has been thickened with a flour-and-butter roux.

Finely diced shallots are sweated in butter in a pan that is then deglazed with white wine (or a mixture of wine and wine vinegar). When this has reduced until almost dry, the velouté is added, along with more butter, lemon juice, fresh parsley, and seasonings. The sauce should be used immediately. It can accompany almost any fish dish, but in this case is poured over scallops, which may be served on the half-shells, with the sauce poured into them.

Bercy sauce is not to be confused with bercy butter, which is a straightforward reduction of white wine, shallots, and beef marrow, not based on a velouté, and which is usually served with meat.

Squid in its Own Ink

Stargazy Pie

Some marine species, notably octopus, cuttlefish, and squid, contain a sac beside the intestine, filled with a black, inky fluid. This liquid is released in emergencies to confuse predators, creating a billowing black "smokescreen" in the water.

The ink plays a part in culinary preparation too, especially in Mediterranean cuisines. Spanish cooking has a dish called *calamares en su tinta*, in which the ink forms the basis of a jet-black, sea-savory sauce. Ink can be bought separately in packets if you don't feel up to anatomizing the squid yourself, but it should always be diluted with water before being added to the sauce.

There is also *arroz negro* ("black rice"), but it is more usual to cook that with cuttlefish ink, which is slightly less concentrated in its pigment than squid ink. In Italian cooking, squid ink may be used to dye the rice in certain risotto dishes or, alternatively, to blacken pasta in which seafood is to be cooked (it makes a very attractive combination with the pink flesh of salmon). In all these dishes, the ink is simply added to the water in which the rice or pasta are cooked.

This is a traditional dish of Cornwall, in the southwest of England. It is a fish pie with a pastry crust, made with small whole fish such as pilchards or sardines. Its distinguishing feature is not so much its ingredients as the novelty of its presentation, which involves standing a number of the whole fish up in the pie filling, so that their head ends are poking up through the crust—gazing at the stars, indeed.

The filling for the pie is a mixture of bacon and chopped onion, bound with egg or a béchamel-style white sauce, while the crust should be made of light flaky pastry. It is traditionally served on December 23, in honor of a local fisherman called Tom Bawcock of Mousehole, who once set out in his boat in foul conditions on this date to save his community from going without food at Christmas.

The fish should be gutted and filleted while leaving the heads and tails intact for ease of eating. Some recipes show the heads peeping out of one side of the pie, with the tails at the other. The top crust itself can be decorated with little star shapes.

Steamed Fish Curry

In this Thai recipe (known as *ho mok pla* in Thailand), it is the whole curry dish that is steamed, not just the fish. A curry paste is made by pulverizing red curry paste, coconut milk, *nam pla* (Thailand's fermented fish sauce), eggs, and peanuts, with cilantro, lime leaves, and lemongrass. Pieces of white fish or salmon, with perhaps some shrimp as well, are added to this mixture, which is spooned into banana leaves or bamboo steamers and cooked over boiling water. When the curry is ready, it can be garnished with a little more coconut milk and some chopped red chile and served with boiled jasmine rice.

Other whole ingredients that can be added to the curry, alongside the fish, include chopped red bell pepper, mushrooms, and bamboo shoots.

If banana leaves are available, you will need two for the dish, one to hold the curry and one to cover it. The edges should be sealed with skewers (stapling works well enough), and the whole arrangement suspended over the pot of water.

Steamed Fish Curry

3 tbsp fish sauce

1 chile pepper, finely chopped

Juice of 1 lime

1 tbsp finely shredded kaffir lime leaves

10 Thai basil leaves

$1/2$ lb fish fillets, sliced

$1/2$ cup coconut milk

2 eggs

8 banana leaves

8 Thai basil leaves

Preheat the oven to 375°F.

Make the curry paste by mixing in a small blender the fish sauce, chile, lime juice, kaffir lime leaves, and basil leaves. Mix the paste with the fish, then stir in the coconut milk and eggs.

Form the banana leaves into cups (or use ramekins). Put a few tablespoons of the fish mix in the bottom, top with a leaf or two of the basil. Put another banana leaf on top and seal the outside with staples or bamboo skewers.

Steam the parcels for about 5 minutes or until cooked. If you are using ramekins, set them in a baking dish and pour some water into the dish, to a depth about halfway up the sides of the ramekins. Bake in the preheated oven for about 45 minutes. *Serves 4*

Coquilles St. Jacques Mornay

Although *coquilles Saint-Jacques* is the French name for scallops themselves, it is customary in other culinary cultures to use it to refer to a specific scallop dish the French would call Coquilles Saint-Jacques Mornay, which is scallops poached and then cooked on the half-shell with mushrooms under a gratinéed topping of cheese sauce. Alternatively, a creamy sauce is poured into the shell, and then a bread-crumb topping sprinkled generously with grated Parmesan makes a browned, crisp surface.

Coquilles St. Jacques Mornay

1 lb scallops

3/4 cup water

1 bouquet garni

Salt

Freshly ground black pepper

3 tbsp butter

1 cup sliced mushrooms

3 tbsp flour

1/2 cup milk

1/3 cup bread crumbs

1/3 cup grated Parmesan cheese

Preheat the oven to 400°F.

Put the scallops in a saucepan with the water, bouquet garni, and salt and pepper. Bring to a boil, lower the heat, cover, and simmer for 5 minutes. Drain the scallops, reserving the broth and discarding the bouquet garni.

In a saucepan, over medium heat, melt the butter. Add the mushrooms, and cook over low heat for about 5 minutes. Blend in the flour, stirring constantly. Slowly add 1 cup of the broth, stirring constantly. Add the milk and cook, stirring, until the sauce is thickened. Add the scallops and remove from the heat.

Fill scallop shells (or use small heatproof bowls) with the scallop mixture.

Mix the bread crumbs and cheese and sprinkle over the filling. Put under a broiler for about 10 minutes. *Serves 4*

Sea Bass with Fennel

The sea bass is another of those fishes that works well when served whole. Its flesh is relatively firm and not too full of pin bones, so that it can easily be portioned when it comes off the grill or out of the oven. It has a juicy texture if not overcooked and is full of flavor, making it a good choice with strong savory accompaniments.

In the traditional recipe of the Provençal kitchen, the whole fish is baked in the oven on a bed of finely sliced fennel, sliced onion, and garlic, with pastis poured over it. It is cooked until the flesh flakes nicely from the bone, and then is served with the vegetables with which it has been cooked. In restaurants in Nice and environs, the dish is often flambéed in the pastis at the table, creating a momentarily diverting spectacle for the whole dining room.

The flavors of aniseed and licorice in the liqueur echo the aniseed taste of the fennel. Flaming burns off most of its alcohol, which some find makes the cooking juices a gentler accompaniment to the fish, but sea bass doesn't exactly need the kid-glove treatment.

Broiled Sea Bass with Fennel

There are two or three slightly varying versions in the presentation of this dish, but the main elements are red mullet or sea bass and dried fennel stalks.

Get the fishmonger to clean the fish. Make 2 deep crosswise incisions on each side of the fish. Stick 2 or 3 short pieces of fennel in the incision through which the intestines were removed. Paint the fish all over with oil, and broil each side for about 7 minutes, turning them over once only. On a long flameproof serving dish arrange a bed of dried fennel stalks, remove the grid with the fish on it from under the broiler and place it over the fennel. In a soup ladle, warm a small glass of Armagnac or brandy; set light to it; pour it flaming into the dish. The fennel catches alight and burns, giving out a strong scent, which flavors the dish.

The fennel-burning performance can be carried out either in the kitchen or at the table under the noses of the guests. In either case it is advisable to have a second hot dish in readiness to receive the fish and its strained juices, for when it comes to serving the fish, nobody wants little pieces of burnt fennel on his plate.

Adapted from Elizabeth David's *French Provincial Cooking*

Herb-Seared Tuna

The tuna is a warm-blooded fish and, as such, requires a lot of oxygen. To this end, it swims powerfully and constantly like a shark, so that it can extract the oxygen from the water that pours through its gills. This vigorous activity is what makes the flesh of the tuna fish dark, muscular, and meaty.

In east Asian, particularly Japanese, cooking, tuna is often eaten only very lightly cooked or even raw. It can be treated like—and, to some extent, resembles—prime beef filet. The best cuts from the best species, such as bluefin tuna, fetch correspondingly high prices at market.

Asian culinary traditions have exerted a huge influence on Western cooking in the last generation. Evidence of this is found in the technique of searing tuna, that is, cooking it for a very short time in hot oil so that the outer flesh whitens, but the center retains its deep red hue, just like a rare steak.

Cooked like this, with just a scattering of fresh herbs (cilantro, chervil, parsley, chives), it is one of the incomparable dishes of the entire fish repertoire.

Herb-Seared Tuna

Olive oil

4 (4 oz each) sushi-grade tuna steaks

Coarse sea salt

Freshly ground black pepper

1 cup finely chopped fresh herbs, such as basil, parsley, and chives

Rub a little olive oil over the tuna, and season with a generous amount of salt and pepper. Put the chopped herbs in a flat dish and press the sides of the tuna in the herbs to coat it. Put 2 tablespoons of olive oil in a large frying pan and heat it over medium-high heat. When the oil is hot, sear the tuna in the hot pan for approximately 1½ minutes on each side; as the tuna cooks, the red meat will become whiter. *Serves 4*

Skate Wings in Black Butter

The skate is a large flatfish (a member of the ray family). Common in European cooking, it is one of those species that has become dangerously overfished in recent years, as a result of its relatively slow growth cycle, and certain sub-species of it, such as the white skate, are now very rare.

This is a great pity because it makes superb eating, which is of course why it has been so exploited. The large wings with which it propels itself are the edible parts. Fried or steamed, they are combed off the "bone" (cartilage, in fact) with great ease, first from the top, then from the underside.

The most traditional accompaniment for skate is black butter. A generous quantity of butter is sizzled in the pan until it turns brown (not literally black—it shouldn't burn) and is then sharpened by the addition of capers and white wine vinegar. This recipe is referred to on French menus as *beurre noir*, but can be more attractively known as *beurre noisette* (hazelnut butter), not because it contains nuts, but because the correct shade of the finished sauce should be something like the skin of a hazelnut.

Skate Wings in Black Butter Sauce

4 cups water

2 tsp salt

$1/4$ cup white vinegar

1 medium carrot, diced

1 medium onion, chopped

Parsley sprigs

Thyme sprigs

2 (8-oz) skate wings

For the black butter sauce:

$1/3$ cup butter

1 or 2 tbsp chopped capers

1 tsp white wine vinegar

Being the water, salt, white vinegar, carrot, onion, parsley, and thyme to a boil in a large saucepan. Cut the skate into portions, and put it in the broth. Simmer for 15 to 20 minutes. Keep the fish warm on a serving dish.

To make the sauce, heat the butter until it is a deep golden brown—don't let it burn. Add the capers and vinegar and pour the sauce over the skate. *Serves 2*

Soused Herring

The herring is an enormously versatile oily fish that inhabits cool northerly waters, from the Baltic Sea to the western Atlantic. It lives in large shoals, making it an obvious target of the fishing industry, and its flesh is extremely tasty. Herring can be cooked fresh or cured by preserving in brine or any of a range of numerous traditional dressings. It can also be fermented in cans (a Swedish delicacy), or smoked, as kippers.

Soused herring is marinated in brine, in a process that matures the fish through the action of enzymes. They are traditionally kept in oak barrels for a few days, having been frozen first to kill off any parasites. The technique was developed in the Netherlands in medieval times and has become popular throughout Germany, Sweden, and England. In Dutch, they are known as *maatjesharing*, or "maiden herring," because they are caught in the spring before spawning.

Maatjes are usually eaten as a supremely healthy form of street snack, dressed with raw onion, and sometimes accompanied by a slice of rye bread. Alternatively, one simply tips one's head back and lowers the raw herring directly into the mouth, as though it were a bunch of grapes.

Soft-Shelled Crab Po'boy

The crab, which many people rate even higher among the crustacean family than the lobster, is a versatile and extremely flavorful beast. Although it looks utterly fearsome when fully grown, it has to develop its hard exoskeleton repeatedly. The shell itself doesn't grow, so the crab must continually shed it for another, bigger one throughout its life cycle.

For the brief period after each new shell has first formed (around 12 hours), it is very soft and pliable. Crabs caught at this stage may therefore be eaten whole. They are a popular ingredient in east Asian cooking and also in North America, where they have found their way into numerous recipes.

A po'boy is the New Orleans name for what others refer to as a sub roll or submarine sandwich, that is, a sandwich with the filling piled into a torpedo-shaped, firm bread roll.

It takes its name from the fact that it makes a sustaining, cheap meal for those short on funds. Filled with fried soft-shelled crab, cut up and dressed in mayonnaise, lettuce and tomato, it tastes more like the food of kings. Serve with a side of battered onion rings.

Spider Crab

Spider crabs are not one species but a name for a family of crabs that are all distinguished by their prickly shells, hirsute legs, and elongated claws. These are considered by many to be the best of all crab varieties and are found throughout European and Asian coastal areas.

There are many recipes for the spider crab. In France, they are often served simply as part of a seafood platter, having been boiled and served cold with a mixture of mustard and mayonnaise. In Spanish and Portuguese cooking, the meat is dressed with additions such as mustard and garlic, and then stuffed back into the shell. The females are especially sought after in case they contain the richly flavored roe.

The Japanese spider crab is the largest crab species of all, often up to 16 inches across. These are native to the Izu peninsula on the eastern coast of Japan and are caught by trawling. They are seasoned, steamed, and eaten in small portions. As this crab is becoming rarer, it is forbidden to catch it during spawning in the spring.

Sole Meunière

Sole meunière is a simple dish indeed. The sole is floured and fried, and then dressed in a meunière sauce, which is barely a sauce at all, but is made up of melted butter, lemon juice, and seasonings, with parsley to garnish. Some butter is used for frying the fish, and a further quantity is melted in the pan after the fish is removed, for pouring over it on the plate.

The origin of the name is quite simple too. A *meunière* is a lady miller, or miller's wife, a maker of flour, thus denoting the use of flour to coat the fish before cooking.

Many other ingredients can theoretically be subjected to the meunière treatment— *Larousse Gastronomique* suggests among them frogs' legs, scallops, brains, and soft roes—but these days, it is ubiquitously assumed to be a fish presentation and any other applications are rare.

Variations on the basic recipe include coating the fish with very finely diced shallot as well as flour, mixing white wine in with the butter and lemon juice, or spicing up the flour with chile flakes, cayenne pepper, paprika, or all three.

Sole Amandine

In the great days of French gastronomy, it tended to be assumed that fish always made for a delicate dish, often served as an intermediate course—after the soup and before the meat—with nothing more than a light sauce. These days, we tend to be more culinarily robust, but one or two of the classic recipes have survived, among them the amandine treatment.

There is nothing especially complex about the dish. It simply represented the discovery that flaked or slivered almonds make a good garnish for a delicate white fish. The fish is usually floured and fried, and then scattered with the browned, toasted almonds. It is dressed in lemon juice and parsley, and then given a final lubrication of melted butter, perhaps mixed with a drop of white wine vinegar.

Any of the gentler-textured fish is good for this dish. Fillets of sole work well with it, and so does freshwater trout, the kind with white flesh (as distinct from the pink-fleshed marine variety), when it is known as *truite aux amandes*. It should be simply accompanied by boiled new potatoes and a steamed green vegetable.

Sole Amandine

1¹/₂ lb sole fillets

4 tbsp butter

¹/₄ cup sliced almonds

1 tsp grated lemon peel

1 tbsp lemon juice

Chopped parsley to taste

Lemon wedges

Rinse the fillets with cold water and pat them dry. In a large frying pan set over medium heat, melt 2 tablespoons of the butter. Sauté the fillets for about 2 minutes on each side or until lightly brown. When each is done, transfer it to a platter and keep warm. Repeat with the remaining fillets. In the same frying pan, melt 2 tablespoons of butter, the almonds, lemon peel, and juice. Lower the heat and sauté for 1 minute, stirring. Pour the sauce over the fish, sprinkle with chopped parsley, and serve with lemon wedges.
Serves 4

Sole Véronique

Salt-Baked Bream

Of all the sole recipes in the repertoire of Auguste Escoffier (1846–1935), the French forefather of modern haute cuisine, Sole Véronique is the one that most merits preservation. Invented in 1903, it was named for the newborn baby of one of the master's sous-chefs.

Fillets of sole are lightly poached until just cooked, and then kept warm while a luxurious sauce is whipped up. This consists of the cooking juices, together with dry white vermouth and lemon juice, boiled until reduced. Thick cream is then added and, as a final touch, a handful of sweet green seedless (or seeded) grapes is stirred in.

Since the sole fillets are quite flat and thin, the usual trick is to enhance the presentation by cooking and serving them loosely rolled up. It is very important not to overcook them, though, or they will break up.

The grapes used should be the Muscat or Muscatel type, which have a lovely sweet flavor that complements the fish to perfection. Ideally, they ought to be skinned, which can be done by piercing them and blanching them in boiled water, as for tomatoes. Even if seedless, they should be cut in half.

A curious Mediterranean way of cooking a whole fish—classically a sea bream—involves submerging it in sea salt and baking it. The salt crust bakes hard around the fish and protects it from overcooking, and yet the final result is only very delicately salty.

A special receptacle for this treatment is a large, elliptical earthenware dish big enough to take a fairly mighty specimen, but a roasting dish will do just as well. The fish is given minimal cleaning and is literally buried in the salt. It cooks slowly and can safely be left for an hour or so in a moderately hot oven. When it is served, the salt crust pulls the skin away with it (which is why no descaling is necessary), leaving the gently cooked, opalescent flesh exposed.

The salt may not act to make the fish salty, but it does draw some of its water content out, so that the flesh is slightly firmer than it would otherwise be, and the flavor is correspondingly more concentrated. In effect, what you have done is give the fish the very beginnings of a drying treatment.

This is a specialty of Andalucía in southern Spain.

Stuffed Squid

Not the least obliging feature of the squid is that its body, once the innards have been removed, makes a very handy receptacle for encasing a stuffing. They can then be baked or even fried, and perhaps sliced across for serving or else presented whole.

The range of possible stuffings for squid is very wide, as the squid itself has a relatively mild flavor that makes a good neutral background for any number of other ingredients. As *calamares rellenos* (stuffed squid) in Spain, they may be filled with rice or bread crumbs, garlic, and some of the finely chopped tentacle meat. Raisins or currants and pine nuts are often included, along with onion, tomato, and chile flakes for a spicy preparation. Greek recipes for stuffed squid tend to be simpler, consisting just of rice with tomato, onion, and herbs.

Japanese cooks have recipes for stuffing squid too, again incorporating meat from the rest of the squid, but in combination with meat such as ground chicken seasoned with rice wine, soy sauce, and onion. Ground shrimp and pork might act as the stuffing in Chinese and Thai recipes.

Stuffed Squid

8 cleaned squid with tentacles (bodies should be 5 to 6 in long, 1½ lb total), rinsed

½ cup finely grated Parmesan cheese

½ cup fine bread crumbs

¼ cup chopped flat-leaf parsley

2 cloves garlic, minced

2 large eggs, lightly beaten

¼ tsp salt

¼ tsp freshly ground black pepper

1 (14- to 15-oz) can plum tomatoes

2 tbsp chopped fresh basil

2 tbsp oil

Finely chop the tentacles. Stir together the cheese, bread crumbs, parsley, garlic, eggs, salt, pepper, and tentacles. Stuff each squid body about half full with the bread-crumb mixture. The stuffing will swell as it cooks. Close the open end with a toothpick.

Heat the oil in a heavy frying pan over moderately high heat, then brown the squid on both sides, about 6 minutes in all.

Drain the tomatoes, reserving the liquid. Chop the tomatoes, and put them and the basil in the pan with the squid. Adjust seasonings. Simmer, covered, turning occasionally, until squid is tender, 25 to 30 minutes. Serve hot with the tomato sauce.

Serves 4

Red-Cooked Carp

Not much used in Western cuisines, other than those of the Danube basin in central Europe, the carp is a popular fish in China. It is a freshwater species that can grow up to a yard long and is at its best in the summer months. The disturbing-sounding "Fish Lips" of Chinese restaurant menus are just that, the most highly prized part of the whole revered creature.

Red-cooked Carp (*hongshao wanyu*) is a dish from the southeast of China, in which either a whole fish, or else belly fillets of it, are served in a sauce that starts by frying dried tangerine peel, garlic, scallions, and ginger, to which are added a blend of rice wine, yellow bean sauce, soy sauce, and broth. A mixture of exotic spices, including cassia, black cardamom, star anise, and fennel seeds, is also traditional.

Red-cooked dishes are a specialty of the Fujian region, to the south of Shanghai. The technique can be applied to any number of principal ingredients, from chicken to pig trotters, but always involves long simmering to produce a red-looking (or more accurately, reddish-brown) dish. Red is the color of good fortune in Chinese iconography.

Red-Cooked Carp

1 tbsp dried tangerine peel or citrus peel

1 (3-lb) firm, white-fleshed whole fish, cleaned

2 tsp salt

1/4 cup cornstarch

2 cups peanut oil

2 tbsp finely chopped garlic

3 tbsp minced gingerroot

1/4 cup finely chopped scallions

2 tbsp dark soy sauce

1 tbsp whole bean sauce (yellow bean sauce)

3 tbsp rice wine or dry sherry

6 tbsp chicken broth or water

Soak the tangerine peel for 20 minutes in warm water. Rinse it, then squeeze out excess liquid and finely chop it. Set it aside.

Make 3 or 4 slashes on each side of the fish. Rub the fish with the salt. Sprinkle the cornstarch evenly on each side of the fish. Pour the oil into a hot wok. When the oil is hot, deep-fry the fish on each side for 5 to 8 minutes until brown and crispy. Drain on paper towels. Pour the oil out of the wok, leaving 2 tablespoons. Reheat the wok. Add the chopped peel, garlic, ginger, and scallions and stir-fry for 30 seconds.

Add the remaining ingredients. Return the fish to the wok, spooning the ingredients over the top of the fish. Cover the wok. Cook over low heat for 8 minutes. Serve at once. *Serves 2*

Red Mullet

The red mullet has been esteemed since classical Roman times as an incomparable fish and remains a popular choice on chic restaurant menus today. It is unrelated to the less prized gray mullet and is distinguished by its silvery-pink sheen and pair of barbels underneath its chin. It inhabits the Mediterranean from one end to the other and is as sought after in Portugal as it is in Greece.

The best way to cook them is probably a quick broiling, but they can also be fried or baked. Nearly any place the fish is cooked, its liver is considered irresistible too and should never be wasted. In certain French and Iberian dishes, the liver is used in the sauce that accompanies the fish, in conjunction with parsley and lemon juice in one traditional dish of the Portuguese fishing port of Setúbal.

Another good treatment for red mullet is to cook it *en papillote*, in a sealed paper bag with lemon juice and herbs. The fish is brought to table in its package, which releases wonderfully appetizing aromas when torn open.

Rougets à la Niçoise

The Niçoise approach to cooking suits red mullet (*rouget*) perfectly. Niçoise means "in the fashion of Nice," the vibrant Riviera city on the Provençal coast of southeast France, right on the Mediterranean Sea where the mullet are plentiful.

Four principal ingredients are used in Niçoise preparations: tomatoes, anchovies, black olives, and garlic. The fish should be cleaned, seasoned, and brushed with olive oil, and then briefly broiled until the pink skin begins to brown. Meanwhile, some coarsely chopped deseeded tomato, with a little garlic, some pitted black olives, and perhaps a few capers are stewed down. When the fish is ready to be served, it is laid on the bed of tomato and garnished with plenty of anchovy fillets (it is quite normal to use salted ones, drained of their oil).

It isn't unusual for cooked red mullet to be eaten cold. The flesh is firm enough, and flavorful enough, to make an appetizing cold starter, for which a Niçoise dressing, again, comes into its own.

Swordfish with Tomato and Herbs

The swordfish is a highly successful species, having found its way into waters just about all over the world, although it is now on the critical list in European seas and parts of the Atlantic. Its prominent feature is the long, saber-like nose, which it brandishes as flamboyantly as D'Artagnan in order to stun its prey.

Swordfish is one of the meatier species, having a texture something like tuna, but with a much lower fat content. This means that more care than usual should be taken not to overcook it, which will cause it to quickly dry out.

Swordfish is common to many of the Mediterranean cuisines, from Portugal through to Greece. It can either be broiled or baked, and the preparation listed here is quite a common one. A fondue of stewed tomatoes is flavored with garlic, capers, bay leaf, even pine nuts and olives in some versions, and used as the dressing for steaks of the fish that are garnished with chopped fresh herbs at the end of cooking. It is generally served with rice. Swordfish is also widely eaten in North America, and US and Canadian cooks will have their own versions of this recipe.

Swordfish with Tomato and Herbs

4 (³/₄- to 1¹/₄-in thick) swordfish steaks

¹/₄ cup olive oil, plus some for frying fish

¹/₄ cup chopped shallots

3 cloves garlic, chopped

¹/₄ cup diced celery

3 medium tomatoes, chopped

1 bay leaf

¹/₄ cup pine nuts

2 tbsp capers

20 green olives, pits removed

Salt

Freshly ground black pepper

2 tsp fresh chopped oregano

1 tbsp chopped parsley

2 tsp fresh chopped rosemary

Preheat the oven to 400°F.

Over medium heat, in a frying pan, sauté the steaks in some oil. Remove the fish and set aside. Put the ¹/₄ cup of oil in the frying pan, then add the shallots, garlic, and celery and cook for 2 to 3 minutes, until soft. Add the chopped tomatoes, bay leaf, pine nuts, capers, and olives. Add salt and pepper to taste, then simmer for about 10 minutes. Add the fish to the sauce, cover, and bake for 20 minutes. Remove the bay leaf and sprinkle the chopped oregano, parsley, and rosemary overtop before serving. *Serves 4*

Surf and Turf

The term "surf and turf" has come into popular parlance to refer to any dish that combines fish and meat elements. There is no definitive recipe for it (we simply give one example here), although the common elements are a shellfish or crustacean with steak.

Combinations of meat and fish are not as thoroughly modern as they might sound. Spanish paella has always involved a mixture of chicken or rabbit and shellfish, while most versions of special chow mein, from mainland China to Singapore, have both pork and shrimp among the noodles.

Barbecue skewers might feature a mixture of steak and shrimp, or how about a juxtaposition of New York strip steak with chunks of lobster tail? The latter combination is said to have originated at Michael's House of Steaks Restaurant, in Buffalo, New York, in the 1960s.

Barbecued Surf and Turf

3 tbsp olive oil

2 cloves garlic, crushed

1 tsp paprika

$1/4$ tsp Tabasco sauce

$1/2$ tsp Worcestershire sauce

Salt

Freshly ground black pepper

12 tiger shrimp, peeled, deveined, heads removed

12 oz piece of sirloin or rump steak, 1-in thick, cut into 1-in cubes

4 (10-in) bamboo skewers, soaked in cold water for 30 minutes

2 small zucchini, sliced thickly

2 small onions, quartered

For the garlic and parsley butter:

$1/3$ cup butter

2 cloves garlic, crushed

2 tbsp chopped fresh parsley

Finely grated zest of a $1/2$ lemon

1 tbsp lemon juice

Combine the olive oil, garlic, paprika, Tabasco, Worcestershire sauce, salt, and pepper. Dip the shrimp into the marinade, then set aside on a plate. Stir the cubes of steak into the marinade and leave for 15 minutes. Turn the grill on to medium high.

Thread 4 pieces of steak and 3 shrimp onto each skewer, alternating the zucchini and onion chunks between them. Cook them on the grill until the steak is done to your liking and the shrimp are just cooked through (5 to 10 minutes). Turn the skewers as needed.

Meanwhile, put the butter and garlic into a small pan and set it to one side of the grill to melt. Add the chopped parsley, lemon zest, and lemon juice. As soon as the kebabs are cooked, put them on the serving plates, and spoon the garlic butter over them. *Serves 4*

Tandoori Shrimp

A tandoor is a type of compact clay oven used in Indian cooking. Any dish cooked in it is therefore described on menus as "tandoori." In recipes for tandoori shrimp, the shellfish are marinated in lemon juice, garlic, and ginger, before being coated in a curry mixture of onion, garlic, ginger, chili powder, turmeric, paprika, garam masala (a standard Indian spice mix), and yogurt, then cooked on a spit in the tandoor for a few minutes. Alternatively, they can be grilled on skewers to give something like the same result with the food exposed to the heat from charcoal embers at the bottom.

While cooking, the shrimp should be basted with ghee, the clarified butter that is the staple Indian cooking medium.

The correct shellfish to use for this recipe are black tiger shrimp, a large species with a lot of juicy flavor. Another ingredient that many recipes call for is ajwain seeds, ovoid gray seeds of a plant called bishop's weed. When roasted, their flavor resembles caraway seeds.

Tandoori Shrimp

1 tbsp cumin seeds

3 tbsp peeled and minced fresh gingerroot

3 tbsp minced garlic

3 tbsp toasted garbanzo-bean flour (besan) or all-purpose flour

1 tbsp paprika

1 tsp garam masala

$1/2$ tsp ground turmeric

$1/2$ cup fresh lemon juice

2 cups plain yogurt, drained through a strainer or filter for at least 1 hour

12 very large shrimp (about 2 lb), shelled

1 lemon, halved

Toast the cumin seeds in a frying pan over medium heat, shaking the pan, until lightly browned, 2 to 3 minutes. Grind 2 teaspoons of the seeds to a powder in a blender. Set aside the remaining whole seeds.

Stir together the ginger, garlic, flour, ground cumin, paprika, garam masala, and turmeric in a bowl large enough to hold the shrimp. Stir in the lemon juice and then the yogurt, a bit at a time, stirring after each addition. Add the shrimp and toss to coat with the marinade. Refrigerate, covered, for at least 2 hours.

Thread the shrimp onto metal or presoaked bamboo skewers and grill on a barbecue until they are firm and pink. (Alternatively, heat a large frying pan over moderately high heat. Sauté the shrimp in batches, turning once, until cooked through and golden, 3 to 4 minutes. Drain on paper towels and keep warm.)

Arrange the shrimp on a platter, sprinkle with the reserved toasted cumin seeds, and squeeze lemon juice over all. *Serves 4*

Ocean Trout

The trout is one of those fish that can live in
either fresh or salt water. Although much of
it is fished from rivers, its marine cousin is at
least as popular. These trout too spend part
of their lives in inland waters, where they go
to spawn like salmon, but the central portion
of their lives is spent on migrating to, and
living in, the ocean.

They are found from the top to the
bottom of Europe, from Scandinavian to
Mediterranean waters, and in North America.
The species is known as the *sewin* in Welsh
cooking, as the white trout in Ireland, and—
less widely—as the peal in southwest England.
Other, more common names for it are the
sea trout and salmon trout.

Salmon trout is not a misnomer in the
sense that the fish is related to the salmon
as a member of the Salmo family, sharing its
migratory and spawning habits, and also the
color of its flesh. This has the same attractive
orangey-pink hue as the salmon, from the
fish's diet of crustaceans.

Sea trout are best simply broiled or
poached, or served with a very light sauce.

Trout with Fennel

In this dish, freshwater trout is baked along
with slices of fennel in white wine and lemon
juice, and then served in a reduction of
the cooking juices with butter. Some of the
frondlike, feathery leaves of fennel can be
added to the sauce at the last minute. These
give a delicate, anise flavor to the whole
dish. If fennel leaves are not available, a good
substitute is fresh tarragon, the thin, spear-
shaped leaves of which also have a distinctive
anise scent.

The most commonly encountered species
of river trout found around the world is the
rainbow trout, so called because it has an
iridescent stripe along each flank. Much of
it is commercially farmed and can lack flavor.
Always choose a wild specimen if one is on
offer. The other species is the distinctly
dowdier-looking, but no less appetizing,
brown trout.

It is traditional to serve the trout whole,
the preparation involving just cleaning and
descaling. The fish has lots of tiny pin-bones,
though, and diners will need to watch out
for them as they eat.

Turbot with Fennel and Lemon

The turbot (*Psetta maxima*) is one of the most highly regarded of all marine fish species. It is a flatfish that lives near the sandy beds of Atlantic and Mediterranean waters, and also in the Black Sea. It is generally a dullish gray-brown in color with a stippling of white dots and, like other flatfish such as the sole, has the peculiar feature of having both its eyes asymmetrically positioned on the right-hand side of its body.

In religious times gone by, it was known as the King of Lent, because it was the kind of fish that nobody at all minded eating during the weeks when meat was forbidden. It has firm, relatively flaky white flesh with good flavor and can be adapted to a whole range of different culinary techniques, from simple hollandaise to the grandest lobster sauce.

Here, we find it paired with that vegetable, fennel, which might have been invented for fish, its aniseed flavor marrying well with the richness of the turbot. Turbot is perhaps best steamed, but is robust enough in texture to withstand frying, too.

Turbot with Braised Fennel and Lemon Butter Sauce

2 fennel bulbs

1½ tbsp olive oil

¼ cup dry white wine

Chicken broth to cover

1 turbot fillet, skin removed

1 tbsp flour

1 tbsp olive oil

For the lemon butter sauce:

3 tbsp butter

3 tbsp hot fish broth

Juice of 2 lemons

2 tbsp whipping cream

Cut off and discard the stalks of the fennel bulbs, then cut the bulbs in ½-inch thick slices, leaving the core intact. In a heavy frying pan over moderately high heat, heat the oil, then add the fennel slices, browning them well on both sides. Add the wine and broth, and bring to a boil. Reduce the heat to a simmer and cover the pan. Braise for 15 to 20 minutes or until tender. Drain the liquid and reserve the fennel.

Dip the turbot fillet in the flour and shake off any excess. Rub with the olive oil. Heat a heavy frying pan and sauté the turbot for 1 to 2 minutes on each side, or until completely cooked through.

Meanwhile, heat the butter in a small pan, add the hot fish broth and lemon juice and simmer until the liquid has reduced by half. Add the cream and heat gently, stirring to ensure a smooth sauce. To serve, place the fennel on a plate, set the turbot on it, then pour over the sauce. *Serves 1*

Tuna Ceviche

In keeping with the fact that very fresh tuna can be eaten raw, it is one of the fish that lends itself readily to the ceviche technique. This involves marinating uncooked fish in a mixture of citrus juices (mainly lemon and lime), which have the effect of denaturing the proteins in the fish flesh in the same way heat does. The fish doesn't have to spend too long in the ceviche marinade. Twenty minutes will do, and if it is of sashimi quality (that is, fresh enough to be used in a Japanese raw fish presentation), you will want to eat it as soon as possible anyway. It should be sliced no more than about 1/4-inch thick and will therefore tenderize more quickly.

Many recipes suggest adding soy sauce and/or ginger to the marinade, as though in distant homage to the sashimi tradition, while others spice things up with finely chopped fresh chile peppers such as jalapeños, which acknowledge the Central and South American origins of ceviche. Other regionally appropriate accompaniments might be chunks of cooked sweet potato and baby corn.

Whitebait

The whitebait is not a distinct species, but denotes the very young fish of various species, depending on where in the world it is served. In Europe, they tend to be young herring or sprat, fish that are sufficiently sustainable to withstand catching so young. On the eastern seaboard of North America, they are more typically the fry of the sand eel.

Whitebait have been a traditional food of London and the Thames estuary for about 400 years. They were served to both rich and poor in the riverside taverns and became a gastronomic fixation in the 1600s.

It has always been traditional to serve whitebait fried. They are given a quick dip in a light batter, or often just seasoned flour, and deep-fried for a few minutes. When ready, they are served piping-hot in steaming heaps, with lemon for squeezing over them, and bread and butter to accompany (and perhaps a pot of mayonnaise in the more highfalutin establishments). The fish are young and tender enough that it is possible to eat the whole thing—heads, bones, and all.

A whitebait festival takes place every September in the Essex port of Southend to bless the first of the new catch.

Fried Whitebait

1 cup seasoned flour

1 lb whitebait

½ cup milk

Oil for frying

Salt

1 lemon, cut into wedges

Put the flour on a plate. Dip the fish in the milk, then roll them in the flour, shaking off any excess. In a large heavy saucepan, heat the oil to 375°F. Fry the fish in several batches for 2 to 3 minutes until crisp and golden. Drain the fish on paper towels and sprinkle with salt. Serve immediately, garnished with lemon wedges. *Serves 4*

Chicken Kiev

Chicken Kiev is a well-traveled and much-loved dish. Despite its name, it was not originally a Ukrainian dish but was actually "invented" in the early 19th century by a French chef called Nicolas Appert.

There was great movement between France and Russia at the time, due to an 18th-century Russian Empress favoring French food and starting a fashion to hire French chefs. Versions of chicken Kiev that appeared in Russian cookbooks were called *cotelettes de volaille*. It is thought that it may have acquired the Kiev part of its name to please the many Russian émigrés.

Chicken Kiev is made by slicing skinned chicken breasts in half, then beating them out thinly. A mixture of butter, garlic, and herbs such as parsley and dill is beaten together and then chilled or frozen. Some versions include other spices such as paprika.

The thin chicken pieces are wrapped tightly around the butter mixture, then coated in bread crumbs and fried, resulting in a luxurious stream of flavored butter that gushes out of the chicken when pierced.

Chicken Forestière and Chicken Provençale

There is nothing more comforting than a well-flavored chicken casserole, the braised meat succulent in its aromatic juices, the crisp, golden skin glinting out from a delicious mixture of softened vegetables.

Every region has its own version, flavored with local or seasonal ingredients as well as reflecting something of the culture. In France, many of these flavorings have become standard restaurant terms that are not restricted to chicken and are seen on menus the world over. *Forestière* and *provençale* are two such terms. Poulet à la forestière is a dark, rich casserole made with mushrooms, ham, and some potatoes. In an ideal world, the mushrooms will be delicious forest varieties that change with the seasons. Poulet à la provençale is a bright, lighter dish where the chicken pieces are cooked in olive oil with garlic, tomatoes, and olives. Sometimes anchovies are added, infusing the dish with the flavors of the south of France. Although many people add bell peppers, this is neither necessary nor technically correct.

Other terms are *parmentier*, meaning that there will be potatoes, and *à la financière*, meaning a lavish dish with truffles, kidney, cockscomb, and peas, which were an early spring luxury in the 18th century.

Deviled Chicken

To devil food is an 18th-century term meaning to cook it with fiery spices, or condiments such as mustard; the equivalent in French cooking is *à la diable*. To make deviled chicken, the meat is slashed and generous amounts of cayenne pepper and mustard are rubbed into the slits before cooking; leftover turkey legs are excellent seasoned this way and thoroughly reheated in foil. Some like to use peppery Tabasco sauce as well. It certainly spices up a chicken that lacks flavor, but should not be overdone; in 1877, the preeminent British food writer E. S. Dallas wrote: "It is the great fault of all devilry that it knows no bounds... and ought to have no place in cookery, the business of which is to tickle, not annihilate, the sense of taste."

In Italy, cooking *alla diavola* simply means that it is grilled, the term referring to the heat of the grill. The chicken is split in half and fiercely grilled while being brushed with a rosemary sprig dunked in olive oil and seasoned with salt and black pepper—this is one of the best ways of cooking small chickens, so is traditionally a springtime dish.

Pollo a la Catalana

Catalonia proudly regards itself as distinctly un-Spanish; to reinforce its point, bull fighting is not practiced there. It is a vibrant region that has produced such original characters as Salvador Dali and Ferran Adrià, whose unique El Bulli restaurant has brought hundreds of disciples to the Costa Brava.

Traditional Catalan cooking is rustic in style, but it is certainly not meager. It is renowned for its variety of game and fungi and its rocky coast is well stocked with fish and seafood. The distinctive element of pollo a la Catalana is the finishing of the dish. Chicken pieces are browned in olive oil and removed. Then some previously soaked prunes and golden raisins are gently sweated in the pan, along with a generous dose of pine nuts (a favorite ingredient). Next, some onions are browned, and fresh tomatoes and broth added. These are cooked, sieved, and added to the chicken, fruit, and pine nuts, and simmered again. Meanwhile, a mixture of toasted almonds, more pine nuts, and toast that has been soaked in white wine is pounded together and stirred into the dish for the final minutes of cooking. This gives a wonderful rich thickening to the sauce.

Poulet Basquais

The Basque country straddles the border between France and Spain and, with it, the Pyrenees mountains. The Basque culture, which includes its own distinct language, goes back 50,000 years. Its cuisine, like its politics, is robust and fiery, influencing and being influenced by that of southwest France and Navarre. It was Henri IV of Navarre who, in the 16th century, is supposed to have expressed the wish that everyone should have a chicken in the pot every Sunday of the year. Like many country dishes, the traditional method for cooking poulet basquais is unsophisticated, simple, and delicious—a whole chicken is browned and simmered with ham or coarse spicy sausage, herbs, and orange peel. A ragout of bell peppers, garlic, tomatoes, and spices is cooked separately.

On the French side, goose fat is preferred for cooking both chicken and ragout; on the Spanish side, it is olive oil. The Basques have their own version of a hot chorizo called *loukenas*, and they also use *piment basquais* (a hot paprika) for seasoning. The chicken is carved onto a dish of rice that has been cooked in some of the chicken broth, and finished with the ragout and sausage—a moist, satisfying dish with a fiery kick from its spicy Basque seasoning.

Basque-Style Chicken

1 (4 lb) chicken

$1/2$ cup olive oil

8 cups roughly chopped green bell pepper

$1/2$ lb Bayonne ham, cut into strips

1 heaping tbsp roughly chopped garlic

$1^{1}/2$ cups roughly chopped onion

3 large tomatoes, peeled, seeded, and roughly chopped

Salt

Freshly ground black pepper

Cut the chicken into 10 to 12 pieces and season well with salt and pepper. Heat half of the olive oil in a Dutch oven over high heat and brown the chicken pieces on all sides. Reduce the heat, cover, and continue to cook the chicken for 15 minutes. Add the green bell peppers, ham, and garlic, and cook for a further 20 minutes. Heat the remaining oil in a frying pan, add the onions and fry over moderate heat for 15 minutes. Add the tomatoes and cook for 15 minutes more. Season to taste and serve hot, on a bed of rice. *Serves 6*

Roast Chicken

Exactly what constitutes classic roast chicken depends entirely on which country you come from, for nearly every country in the world has its own version of this famously comforting food.

The origins of chicken lie in north India and Burma; the Indian Game Fowl is the closest modern breed. But the ease with which chickens are kept and transported, and of course their usefulness as egg layers, meant that they rapidly spread throughout the world. Centuries of selective breeding have resulted in a huge variety of chickens to suit all tastes. But most people concur that for a dish as simple as roast chicken, nothing but the best-flavored free-range bird will do. Starting with that superb basic commodity, only small touches are needed. In France and Spain, garlic is added; in Greece and Italy, lemons and perhaps rosemary are used; in Asia, spices are rubbed into the skin. Sometimes nothing more than butter and salt is needed.

Formerly, chickens would have been roasted on a turning spit, but since most people use an oven, many now prefer to roast their chicken breast side down to ensure it remains as succulent as possible.

Roast Chicken

1 (6 lb) free-range chicken
1 lemon, quartered
3 tbsp chopped fresh oregano or thyme
2 tbsp extra-virgin olive oil
2 heaping tbsp chopped garlic
2 tsp grated lemon peel
1/4 cup dry white wine
1 cup water
2 tsp all-purpose flour
Salt
Freshly ground black pepper

Preheat the oven to 450°F.

Rinse the chicken and pat dry with paper towels. Season the cavity of the chicken with salt and pepper, and put the lemon quarters inside. Tie the chicken legs with string and place the chicken in a roasting pan. Combine the fresh herbs, olive oil, chopped garlic, and grated lemon peel in a small bowl. Reserve 1 tablespoon of this mixture, and rub the rest all over the chicken.

Roast the chicken for 20 minutes, then reduce the oven temperature to 375°F. Roast the chicken for a further 1 hour 15 minutes. Check for doneness: the juices should run clear when a skewer is inserted into the flesh at the thickest part. Empty the juices from the cavity into the roasting pan and remove the chicken to a serving plate—keep it warm by wrapping loosely with aluminum foil.

To make a gravy, tilt the roasting pan and spoon any fat from the top of the juices. Pour in the wine and, over high heat, deglaze the pan, reducing the liquid by about half. Add a cup of water to the pan. Combine the flour and remaining herb-lemon mix and stir this into the gravy. Boil the gravy, stirring continuously for 2 to 3 minutes. Season to taste and serve with the chicken. *Serves 6*

Coq au Vin

Coq au vin is a Burgundian dish, richly
flavored with salt pork, onions, mushrooms,
and brandy. Traditionally nearly a whole
bottle of Burgundy wine is used for its
voluptuous sauce. Like many excellent dishes,
it is not complicated, but relies on good
ingredients and careful attention to timing.
Cooked too long, the chicken becomes
overcooked and stringy; not cooked long
enough, the sauce is thin. The secret is using
an older bird, which tastes gamier and needs
longer to cook. If using a young chicken, it is
best to reduce the red wine and broth before
adding them to the cooking pot. Sautéed salt
pork—or thick pancetta—provides the fat to
brown the baby onions and the bird, cut into
pieces. In some recipes, when the chicken is
nicely colored, a glass of brandy is poured
over and set alight. Wine, chicken broth,
garlic, and herbs are added, simmered and
then reduced. When almost ready, baby
mushrooms are thrown in. The final touch is
whisking in *beurre manié*—flour and butter
mashed together—to thicken the sauce.
Traditionally, triangles of fried bread are
served with the stew.

Coq au Vin

1 (3 to 4 lb) chicken, cut into 10 pieces

6 slices slab bacon, cut into strips

8 to 10 baby onions

1 cup red Burgundy wine

1 cup chicken broth

1 clove garlic, crushed

1/2 tsp fresh thyme leaves

1 bay leaf

2 large sprigs of parsley

4 cups baby mushrooms

2 tbsp butter

2 tbsp all-purpose flour

Salt

Freshly ground black pepper

Season the chicken pieces with the salt and
pepper. Sauté the bacon strips in a Dutch
oven over medium heat to render the fat.
Remove the bacon, add the baby onions, and
brown in the rendered fat. Add the chicken
pieces, and brown well on all sides. Pour in
the wine, chicken broth, garlic, and fresh
herbs. Bring to a boil, stirring from time to
time, then reduce the heat and simmer,
covered, for 15 to 20 minutes. Add the baby
mushrooms and simmer, uncovered, for 30 to
45 minutes, or until the chicken is tender.
Remove the chicken and mushrooms with a
slotted spoon and transfer to a warm serving
dish. Combine the flour and butter and stir
into the cooking liquid to thicken, then pour
the sauce over the chicken pieces to serve.
Serves 4

Coronation Chicken

Coronation chicken is a cold dish of cooked chicken folded into a curried mayonnaise that is enriched with cream, tomato paste, onions, puréed dried apricots, and lemon juice. It was created for the banquet following the coronation of Queen Elizabeth II in June 1953. The Palace had to strike a balance between entertaining the foreign dignitaries and not being too lavish, since food in the UK was still rationed following the Second World War. However, 82 applications to roast an ox in celebration of Her Majesty were granted, provided applicants could prove that an ox had been roasted at previous coronations. The royal salad was created by Rosemary Hume, a professional Cordon Bleu cook and business associate of Constance Spry, the famous florist and designer. All the food had to be prepared in advance, and so one of Hume and Spry's suggestions was a dish of cold chicken in a curried cream and apricot sauce, served with a rice salad brightened with peas and fresh green herbs. It is highly likely their inspiration was the Jubilee Chicken that was served at George V's silver jubilee in 1935, also a curried mayonnaise chicken dish.

Coronation Chicken

1 (about 4 lb) free-range chicken, cooked, meat removed from the bones

1 cup chopped onion

1 tbsp vegetable oil

1 tbsp curry powder

1 tbsp tomato paste

$\frac{1}{3}$ cup red wine

$\frac{1}{2}$ cup water

1 bay leaf

A pinch of superfine sugar

A squeeze of lemon juice

2 cups good mayonnaise

2 tbsp apricot purée

3 tbsp whipped cream

Salt

Freshly ground black pepper

Sauté the onion in the oil for 2 to 3 minutes over medium heat. Reduce the heat, add the curry powder, stirring to coat the onion, and cook for 2 to 3 minutes more. Add the tomato paste, red wine, water, and bay leaf. Bring to a boil, then season with salt, pepper, sugar, and lemon juice. Reduce the heat and simmer the sauce, uncovered, for 5 to 10 minutes. Strain and set aside. When the sauce has cooled, fold in the mayonnaise, apricot purée, and whipped cream. Check the sauce for seasoning, fold in the cooked chicken, and serve with rice. *Serves 8*

La Poule au Pot à la Crème Normande

France raises more free-range poultry than any other European nation and this perhaps accounts for the many chicken recipes that are essentially very simple, since they rely on starting with a superbly flavored chicken.

The best chickens bear a *Label Rouge* mark, which means that they are reared slowly outdoors under strict quality control. A *poulet fermier* can be bought at most French markets; these are expensive, but their flavor and texture are exceptional. The ultimate is a *Poulet de Bresse*, which has its own *Appellation d'Origine Controlée*, just like a fine wine. Most recipes for poached chicken call for an older boiling fowl that has more flavor than a roasting bird, and the meat stays firm during the lengthy cooking.

In this simple recipe, the chicken is poached with herbs and vegetables, and cut into serving pieces. A sauce is made from melted butter and cream boiled together until thickened, with seasoning and freshly chopped parsley added at the end—a dish typical of Normandy, where dairy produce appears in many regional recipes.

La Poule au Pot à la Crème Normande
A boiling fowl, slowly simmered in water with vegetables and aromatic herbs, is served hot, cut into nice pieces, with the following sauce, made at the last moment when the dish is ready to serve.

In a heavy frying pan melt 6 tablespoons of unsalted butter, and when it is foaming (but it must not turn color) pour in 1 cup of thick cream. In a few seconds the cream and butter will have amalgamated, thickened, and started coating the wooden spoon with which you have been stirring and lifting the sauce. Taste for seasoning, add the smallest dusting of very finely chopped parsley and pour over the chicken. The process of thickening the cream takes hardly more than a minute, so long as a wide pan is used. *Serves 6*
Adapted from Elizabeth David's *French Provincial Cooking*

Pollo Rossini

In the 19th century, Gioacchino Rossini was almost as famous for being an epicure as a composer. He lived in Bologna and was particularly fond of the native white truffles of his region. For that reason, the description "Rossini" on a menu simply means that the dish contains truffles.

Although a luxury even then, truffles were common enough for people to roast large ones whole in the fire for a special treat. There has always been hot debate as to whether or not the white summer truffle is superior to the black winter truffle. Certainly when white truffles are in season, every restaurant is redolent of their powerful perfume—so much so that it is hardly necessary to actually order a truffled dish since the aroma will be breathed in anyway.

One of the best ways to enjoy pollo Rossini is to slip slices of truffle generously underneath the skin of the breast along with some butter or oil, which helps the perfume permeate the meat. A few shavings of fresh truffle scattered onto the plate just before serving will raise the dish from the delicious to the sublime.

Poulet en Papillotte

Cooking pieces of poultry in a sealed packet is an effective way of retaining moisture and infusing flavors, for the meat is partly steamed, partly baked. With a superb free-range young chicken or pheasant, all that is needed is to part-roast it so that the skin is nicely crisped, then split it lengthwise into two portions. The two pieces are laid onto sheets of parchment paper or foil, and seasoned delicately with salt, pepper, and a few drops of sweet wine or madeira. A thin slice of unsmoked bacon is laid over the breast, and the parcel is tightly wrapped up so that no juices can escape while the meat finishes cooking in the oven. They are served as soon as they are cooked, each person having the pleasure of opening a parcel.

That is the method, but of course the variations are legion. Many recipes call for just a chicken breast, but add vegetables like asparagus marinated in lime juice, or a mixture of julienne vegetables. Flavors such as garlic, lemon, and ginger are particularly good with chicken, releasing a mouthwatering aroma when the *papillote* is opened.

Jump-in-the-Pan Chicken

Jump-in-the-pan chicken is named for the method of cooking it. The chicken is beaten very thin and broken into shreds with the fingers. These little pieces are floured and sautéed—the French word *sauter* means "to jump"—in a frying pan with garlic and bay leaves. Instead of turning the chicken with a spatula, the pan is shaken and the pieces tossed so they jump around and don't stick together. White wine, capers, butter, lemon, and parsley are added and reduced to form a delicious lemon sauce that coats the chicken. Australian chefs love to take a classic dish and put their own light twist on it; this one is based on an Italian dish—*saltimbocca*—which translates as "jump-in-the-mouth." The original dish is made with veal that is pounded flat but, instead of being shredded, it has sage leaves and prosciutto placed on top of the slices. These are rolled up, gently browned in butter, and a glass of marsala or white wine is added to bubble into a sauce.

Jump-in-the-Pan Chicken

2 (8 oz) chicken breasts

2 tbsp all-purpose flour

2 tbsp olive oil

2 tbsp butter

1 clove garlic, crushed

4 bay leaves

1/2 cup dry white wine

2 tbsp capers, well-rinsed

Coarse sea salt

Freshly ground black pepper

A big squeeze of lemon juice

2 tbsp flat-leaf parsley leaves, picked from stem

Place each chicken breast between two sheets of plastic wrap, and use a meat mallet or pestle to flatten until very thin and almost breaking up. Tear the chicken into little pieces with your fingers, roughly 1 x 2 inches, and toss lightly in the flour.

Heat the olive oil and 1 tablespoon of butter in a large heavy-bottomed frying pan. When hot, add the chicken in bits and pieces so they don't clump together. Add the garlic and bay leaves. Rather than stirring, move the pan around on the heat, flipping the chicken and keeping it jumping in the pan until it is lightly golden on both sides.

Remove the pan from the heat and add the white wine, capers, sea salt, and pepper, then return to a high heat and let the wine bubble away, again keeping the pan moving. When there is only a little wine left, add the remaining butter, the lemon juice, and parsley leaves, jiggling the pan until the sauce comes together and looks creamy. Serve immediately. *Serves 4*

Adapted from Jill Dupleix's *Totally Simple Food*

Jambonette de Volaille

Jambonettes is a French term sometimes seen on restaurant menus, along with other names such as *crépinettes*, *paupiettes*, *andouillettes*, *rillettes*, *boulettes*, *gayettes*, and *croquettes*. The "ettes" suffix simply means "small." Jambonettes de volaille are so called because when whole chicken legs (thigh and drumstick) are deboned, the resulting plump little morsels are the same shape as tiny hams (*jambons*). Sometimes the whole leg is deboned, but more often, just the thighbone is removed so that the drumstick keeps the ham-like shape better. Completely deboned out jambonettes de volaille are covered with a sauce such as *forestière* (with mushrooms) or *crème ciboulette* (chive and cream sauce) the boneless meat making it easier to eat. More often, the cavity is stuffed, since this allows the chef more leeway to be creative. Sometimes the stuffed *jambonette* is encased in pastry for a more substantial dish. The different kinds of stuffing demonstrate their region and can include preserved lemons, celery and calvados, or cèpes and thyme.

Poulet Marengo

Great emperors spawn legends, and poulet Marengo is one such tale. In June 1800, Napoleon's dwindling army had pursued the Austrians to Marengo in northern Italy. As always, Napoleon ate nothing before the battle. Fortunately, reinforcements arrived and Napoleon was triumphant. Ravenously hungry, he demanded food, but since the supply wagons had been left behind, Dunan, his Swiss chef, had to scour the countryside, scavenging a chicken, eggs, some crayfish, tomatoes, onions, garlic, oil, and a frying pan. Using a saber, Dunan cut up the chicken, fried it in oil, and made a sauce with the vegetables and a splash of cognac from Napoleon's canteen. The crayfish and eggs were cooked separately and formed a garnish. Napoleon was delighted with the dish, demanding that it be served after every battle, and superstitiously refusing to allow any of the ingredients to be changed thereafter. The problem with this splendid tale is that Dunan did not enter Napoleon's service until 1805.

The proprietors of the famous Trois Frères Provençaux restaurant in Paris claim, instead, that their chef created this dish for Napoleon's victorious generals. However, chicken with crayfish is a specialty of the Jura, which is in Switzerland—Dunan's country. So the enigma remains.

Pollo alla Parmigiana

Dishes cooked *alla Parmigiana* are either cooked with Parmesan cheese, or in the style of Parma. One such is *melanzane*—eggplants baked with a mixture of soft mozzarella, thick, fresh tomato sauce, and grated Parmesan. In pollo Parmigiana the chicken replaces the eggplants. The two cheeses give a nice texture contrast, since the mozzarella melts easily into the sauce while the Parmesan stays grainy and crisp on top. Uniquely among cheeses, Parmesan does not form elastic strings when it melts. Parmesan is an ancient cheese—some claim it has been made for over 2,000 years. It was certainly well-enough known in the 14th century for Boccaccio to mention it in *The Decameron*, where one of his characters makes up a story about a mountain made entirely of Parmesan cheese that was scattered over macaroni and ravioli cooked in a capon broth—a bit of wishful thinking that developed into the legend of The Land of Cockayne. Lightly sparkling Lambrusco is the traditional red wine to accompany this dish.

Pollo alla Parmigiana

2 chicken breasts, skinned, boned, and halved

1 egg, lightly beaten

$1/2$ cup bread crumbs

1 tbsp butter

1 tbsp olive oil

1 ball (about 8 oz) fresh buffalo mozzarella, thinly sliced

2 cups tomato sauce

1 tbsp grated Parmesan cheese

Salt

Freshly ground black pepper

Preheat the oven to 350°F.

Place each chicken piece between two sheets of parchment paper, and pound gently with a rolling pin to flatten for even cooking. Dip the flattened chicken into the beaten egg and coat with bread crumbs. Heat the butter and oil in a frying pan over medium heat, and brown the chicken on both sides.

Transfer the chicken to an ovenproof dish. Layer slices of mozzerella over the chicken and pour the tomato sauce over the top. Sprinkle generously with Parmesan, salt, and pepper. Bake in the preheated oven for 25 to 30 minutes, until cheese is brown and bubbling nicely. Remove from the oven and serve.

Serves 4

Porkolt Csirke

Goulash—the best known of all Hungarian stews—was originally made by shepherds, who cooked their meat with onions and caraway seeds and dried it in the sun. When they were hungry they simply added water, lots for a soup and less for a stew. But the authentic *gulyas*—which comes from *ghaliyeh*, Arabic for stew or sauce—contains no paprika, bell peppers, or sour cream.

It is porkolt that uses bell peppers and paprika. *Porkolt* means "dry-stewed," and it is characterized by the generous quantity of onions used. These are browned in lard and then simmered in water with a liberal quantity of sweet paprika until they have melted down into a succulent purée that takes the place of sour cream. The chicken is cut into joints and added to the onions together with tomato paste, fresh tomatoes, green bell peppers, and garlic. The dish is then covered and the chicken cooks gently in its own rich juices and fat. There should not be much liquid, but the sauce that is left underneath the chicken pieces is a rich flame red with a punchy flavor. The porkolt should be served at once so that the chicken remains succulent.

Chicken with Yogurt

Thick Greek yogurt made from sheep's milk is a treat quite unlike the semi-liquid Western variety. If none is available, a workable substitute for cooking can be made by taking some plain, full-fat yogurt and straining it through cheesecloth. Squeezed and left to drip for several hours, it will reduce by half and thicken.

The best-known way of cooking chicken with Greek yogurt is to cut it into chunks, marinate it in yogurt and herbs, and then thread the pieces onto skewers as kebabs. Once grilled, the pieces are slipped into pita bread that has been stuffed with a tangy *tzatziki* of diced cucumber and garlic, dressed with yogurt, oregano, and lemon juice.

This Cretan way of roasting a chicken, however, has an interesting sauce. The chicken is rubbed with lemon juice and grated zest is rubbed into the cavity. This is left to infuse. Then the chicken is roasted, but before it is quite finished, a mixture of yogurt and eggs beaten together is poured over the chicken and cooked gently until it has set. The result is a wonderful light curd, scented with lemon.

Poulet aux Coings

Pollo Sofrito

The combination of quince and poultry is a great one. Quinces can be quite remarkably fragrant; try putting one in a covered jar for an hour or so and the perfume is heady. This extra perfumed element makes them much more special than the apples used in poultry recipes from Normandy, but quinces are a seasonal treat. Chicken, partridge, and quail are all particularly good with quince. The chicken pieces are fried with onions, covered, and cooked gently in their own juices; in Morocco, some ginger and cinnamon may be added. Quinces are quite hard to cut, so need simmering in water before being cored and sliced into segments. Once the chicken is cooked, it is removed to a dish, and the quince slices added to the pan, where they are cooked until tender with some honey and lemon juice—and sometimes some prunes— for a tart sweetness. The quinces and sauce are poured over the warm chicken and served, sometimes sprinkled with fried almonds.

Sofrito is a marvelous slow-cooked sauce associated mostly with Spanish cooking, though it is popular throughout the Middle East. In some places, the sauce could be made with plums, in others, lemon, garlic, and turmeric. The traditional Spanish version is made with garlic, onions, tomatoes, green bell peppers, salt pork, herbs, and gentle spices such as cardamom. These are cooked gently and slowly in olive oil until everything is tender. For a chicken sofrito, some lemon juice is added to give a citrus flavor, and a pinch of turmeric—or saffron for a touch of luxury—for color.

The cooking requires attention from time to time, as the water is only added very gradually so that it makes a voluptuous emulsion with the olive oil. The final touch is some tiny, diced potatoes that have been deep-fried until crisp; these are stirred in so that they absorb some of the sauce. Sofrito is much loved by the Jews living around the Mediterranean, though of course their versions might omit the salt pork.

Pollo al Limone

The combination of chicken with lemon, garlic, and pungent, sun-baked wild herbs from the terra-cotta countryside is redolent of Tuscany. The region has a rich heritage: stunning Florentine and Siennese architecture, powerful red Chiantis, and sweet Vin Santo wine. Vineyards and olive groves creep up the sides of hills topped with an ancient farmstead or a dense, scrubby wood concealing wild boar. The cuisine of Tuscany is simple and robust. Pollo al limone is typical, relying on straightforward ingredients that

have absorbed the flavors of their region: the chicken will have scratched about in the fragrant scrub, the lemons are ripe and juicy, their zest exploding with oil. The garlic will be intensified by the sun, as will the herbs. Soft supermarket varieties have no place here--Tuscan herbs are vigorous, wiry, and full of spicy oils. The chicken is jointed and marinated in the garlic, herbs, and lemon juice. Lifted out and fried in superb olive oil, it is then baked, with the marinade poured over the top.

Pollo al Ajillo

Chicken and garlic is such a fabulous partner-ship—one of those *umami* combinations of extra special deliciousness—that it appears in several countries' cuisines. In France, there is the famous *poulet à l'ail* where 40 cloves of garlic are roasted alongside the chicken until they are soft and sweet inside their papery skins. The cooked garlic cloves are sometimes served alongside the chicken so that guests can squeeze the garlic purée onto their bread; other times the purée is scraped out to add to the sauce. Such large amounts of garlic may sound surprising, but garlic loses much of its fire when cooked.

However, in Mexico, pollo al ajillo is all about fiery flavors. Here, the chicken is cooked with garlic and also *guajillo*, one of the most common of Mexican chile peppers, and is often served on chile-flavored rice as well. Finally, there is the traditional Castilian Spanish version of pollo al ajillo in which the chicken is jointed, fried, flavored with garlic, and gently simmered in dry white wine, or Fino (dry) sherry for a fuller flavor.

Pollo al Ajillo

$1/4$ cup extra-virgin olive oil

1 (3 lb) chicken, cut into pieces

3 medium potatoes, peeled and cut into large chunks

18 cloves garlic, peeled

$1^1/2$ cups Fino sherry

$1/2$ cup chicken broth

Salt

Freshly ground black pepper

2 tbsp chopped fresh parsley

Heat the olive oil over moderate heat in a large Dutch oven. Brown the chicken on all sides, then remove with a slotted spoon. Layer the potato chunks in the bottom of the Dutch oven. Scatter the garlic over the potatoes and place the browned chicken pieces on top. Pour in the sherry and chicken broth, and season well with salt and pepper. Cover and simmer over low heat until potatoes and chicken are cooked. This will take 45 to 50 minutes. Before serving, check for seasoning and stir in the chopped parsley.
Serves 4

Poulet aux Dattes

Chicken with dates is a dish that can be found throughout North Africa, though its roots probably go back to the medieval cooking of Persia. Typical of the area, the chicken is a wonderful concoction of spices and sweetness. In this dish, the dates are left whole so that they plump up in the juices, but the chicken is cut into pieces and fried with some onions. Then honey, cinnamon, nutmeg, mace, and saffron are all added, as well as a little water. About halfway through the cooking, the dates are added and cooked until they are plump enough. Finally, a generous amount of black pepper is ground into the dish, and lemon juice is also added to taste, to counteract the sweetness of the honey and dates.

Some recipes that combine dates and meat—chicken is regarded as meat in Jewish Kashrut laws—use a date paste instead. *Halek*, as this is sometimes called, is made by soaking pitted dates in a little water. When soft, they are boiled and then minced and pounded to a paste, which is strained and gently cooked until it is a thick purée.

Frango Piri-Piri

Frango piri-piri originated in Mozambique and Angola, both former colonies of Portugal. The name is a mixture of the two cultures, as *frango* is the Portuguese for chicken, and *piri-piri*—or *peri-peri*—is Swahili for "pepper-pepper," referring to the very hot little chile peppers that the Portuguese introduced to their African colonies from their explorations in South America. Another name for the dish is Frango à calfreal; *calfreal* is Portuguese for "grilled." Before being grilled, the chicken is soaked in a very hot marinade of cayenne pepper, minced hot chile peppers, salt, and some lemon or lime juice. The Portuguese colonials became so partial to this spicy, hot dish that they took it—and the chiles with which to make it—with them to other parts of their empire, notably Goa in India. It is so well known in Portugal that it is now regarded as a Portuguese dish, and piri-piri chiles are grown and made into a fiery array of sauces and condiments.

25 Favorite Poultry and Game Dishes

Roast goose with applesauce

Chicken wings and drumsticks

Roast grouse

Turkey mole poblano

Peking duck

Faisinjan

Pollo al ajillo

Chicken chow mein

Roast venison

Circassian chicken

Braised woodcock

Chicken korma

Kung pao chicken

Mojo chicken

Chicken fajitas

Fresh goose foie gras with figs

Chicken Divan

Spatchcocked quail

Chicken yakitori

Chicken Florentine

Guinea fowl with mushrooms, lemon, and
   herbs

Warm pigeon salad

Thai green chicken curry

Rabbit with garlic and rosemary

Fusion venison

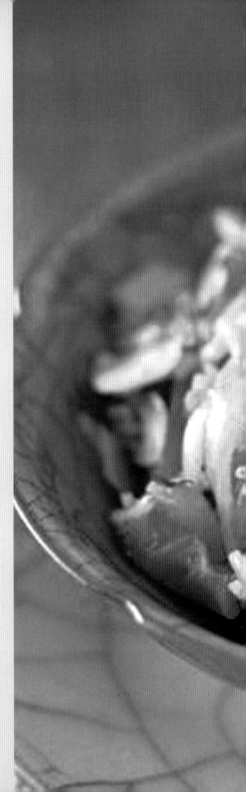

Thai Green Chicken Curry

Thai curries are delightfully distinctive, using tropical herbs and aromatics instead of the more usual Indian curry spices. Lemongrass is very well known, as is ginger or *galangal*, a variety of ginger that, depending on the variety, has a sour, peppery overtone or a pungent, eucalyptus-cardamom flavor. Makrut limes (also known as kaffir limes or "combavas") are used both for their leaves and also their knobbly sour skin. Thick, creamy coconut milk is used in lavish amounts for a wonderful richness. Fish sauce is added to many meat dishes and goes especially well with chicken, and a touch of sweetness comes from palm sugar—not unlike thick honey.

Thai curries are named for their colors: red from dried red chiles, yellow from curry powder, and green from green chiles. A paste is made out of lemongrass, garlic, onions, green chiles, galangal, and some spices such as cilantro root and cumin. These are sweated and thick coconut cream added. The chicken is cooked in this, together with fish sauce, palm sugar, some tamarind for a sour touch, and the whole is moistened with coconut milk. After it has cooked, the makrut leaves are strewn over the dish.

Mojo Chicken

A mojo sauce is made principally from oil, lots of garlic, and sweet, sharp citrus juice, such as bitter (Seville) orange and lime. Its origins lie in the Old World in the Spanish Canary Islands. It is sometimes also called "magic chicken," for the small red mojo bags that were used to contain charms. Cuban mojo sauce is made by toasting whole cumin seeds and then grinding them with crushed garlic, jalapeño chiles, and other spices to taste. Hot olive oil is poured into the paste, and the citrus juices stirred in. If bitter orange is not available, some orange or lime peel is added instead. The chicken is soused in this and left to marinate. It is then browned and either baked or broiled.

The classic accompaniment is a soothing avocado and mango salsa tossed in a sauce similar to the marinade and finished with cilantro; this contrasts well in flavor, color, and texture. Black beans and rice are the Cuban favorites, though plantain chips are excellent too.

Chicken Maryland

According to chef and food writer James
Beard, chicken Maryland or Maryland chicken
is a widely known name for a whole variety of
dishes; there seems to be no definitive recipe.
Indeed in Australia, chicken Maryland is not
a dish at all, but simply refers to the whole
chicken thigh and drumstick. Escoffier's last
cookbook, *Ma Cuisine*, published in 1934,
includes a recipe for "Chicken à la Maryland,"
but it goes much further back than that.
In fact it is, perhaps, an entirely appropriate
dish to include in a book with this title, since
"Chicken à la Maryland" appeared on the
very last menu for the first-class restaurant
on the *Titanic*.

Most versions of the dish are a variety of
southern-fried chicken, so the chicken is coated
in batter and bread crumbs and fried or baked.
Chicken broth and cream are boiled together
with the cooking juices to make a rich, creamy
gravy that is poured over the crisp chicken
pieces. The favorite accompaniments are hush
puppies and fried bananas.

Cajun Chicken

Cajun cuisine is often confused with Creole,
but the two are distinctively different.
Creole cuisine is urban with African, Spanish,
and Italian influences. Cajun, on the other
hand, is unsophisticated and influenced by
French rustic cooking. The word Cajun is an
abbreviation of "Acadian," which derives from
Acadia, the French-speaking area of Louisiana
that was populated by French-Canadian
refugees. The area was immortalized by
Kate Chopin's short stories: *Bayou Folk* and
A Night in Acadie.

Cajun cuisine is often thought to consist of
fiery chile pepper seasonings, and meat or fish
with a heavily scorched black crust. In fact,
authentic Cajun cooking does not use chiles
but relies on sweet bell peppers, celery, and
scallion tops as its main vegetables, and a salt
mixture spiced principally with red cayenne
pepper, paprika, and oregano. A very slowly
cooked roux is another distinctively Cajun
touch, which gives a delicious, brown, nutty
base to the sauce. Cajun chicken is prepared
by frying the vegetables and then adding flour
and broth to make a roux. The chicken is
cooked in this with the seasoning, and often
served with rice and another vegetable.

Chicken Divan

Chicken Divan was created at the Chatham Hotel in New York in the 1950s, where it was the signature dish of the hotel's Divan Parisien restaurant. The restaurant's name was chosen because the hotel's owners felt it added a touch of exotic elegance, "divan" sounding not unlike "divine" and "diva." Also, the Turkish word *divan*—meaning a couch or day bed—lends an air of Eastern mystery. Although the restaurant is now no longer, the dish has become a much-loved favorite of Americans.

The original dish was an elegant chicken casserole that had sprigs of fresh spring broccoli in it. This was served with a light béchamel sauce made with clear chicken broth and delicately seasoned with cheese. Browned slivered almonds were strewn over it for an attractive, crunchy finish. There are now countless variations; some use hollandaise sauce, others mayonnaise, and many recipes make use of canned soups and sauces. However, these bear scant resemblance to the subtle flavors of the original dish.

Chicken Goujons

Goujon is the French word for small, fried strips, originally of fish, since the "goujon" is a small European freshwater fish, about six inches long. They are delicious deep-fried, hence the culinary term, since the meat or fish is cut into strips the same size as the fish. In the gastronomic world, goujons are made from sole, and these have become a classic dish in their own right. They are dipped in egg and bread crumbs (homemade are best), then deep-fried and served with chunks of lemon and a salad. In Central America, however, a goujon is also the name of a species of catfish, so called because it resembles the European fish.

In culinary terms, strips of fish or chicken are dipped in a wonderfully light, thin batter that uses eggs, flour, sparkling water, and either sweet or hot paprika. Since the pieces of chicken are thin, they have the ideal proportion of spicy, crunchy batter to light, moist chicken. No wonder they are such a popular finger food.

Chicken Fajitas

Fajitas are an example of Mexican food that has been taken up by its close relation, Texas, and turned into a Tex-Mex dish; fajitas were introduced to America in Houston in the 1970s. They are simple and extremely good: marinated meat is quickly cooked and wrapped in tortillas—finger food at its best.

Here, the chicken is first sliced into strips and marinated for half an hour in a lively mixture of lime juice, oregano, a little sugar, some cayenne pepper, and ground cinnamon.

Meanwhile, onions are sliced thinly along with red, green, and yellow bell peppers. The marinated chicken is then quickly fried until tender, then the onions and bell peppers are added and fried until soft.

This mixture is laid onto tortillas and drizzled with sour cream and guacamole. The tortillas should be rolled up and eaten quickly so that the cool guacamole and sour cream contrast with the hot chicken and bell peppers.

Yakitori Chicken

The Japanese love to serve exquisite little nibbles with their drinks, and one of the most popular of these is yakitori—little chunks of chicken that have been grilled on bamboo skewers. However, these are not just any old barbecued chicken nuggets, they are a deep, rich, gleaming, sticky brown, having been coated with several layers of sweet-and-sour sauce. This is made from *sake* (rice wine), *shoyu* (soy), *mirin* (a sweet cooking version of rice wine), and a little sugar, all simmered together until they thicken.

The chunks of chicken are grilled on a rack, dipped into the yakitori sauce and grilled once again. This procedure is repeated twice more. Traditionally some scallions are gently grilled (without the sauce) to make a refreshing contrast. The coated chicken chunks and scallions are threaded alternately on skewers and grilled once more; again, only the chicken is brushed with the yakitori sauce.

The result is both delicious and attractive: the dark golden chicken lacquered with its yakitori sauce works visually as well as in flavor with the brilliant green of the gently softened scallions.

They take but a few seconds to savor and swallow.

Satsivi/Sherksiya

Circassian chicken—satsivi or sherksiyais—
a classic Georgian feasting dish; it seems to
combine the best of Eastern and Western
flavors. The sauce is a perfect balance of
sweet and sour, hot and soothing. The main
ingredient—walnuts—was brought over from
Persia and these, plus a dash of pomegranate
paste, display the influence of a once-vast
empire that used to include Georgia.

Walnut trees have always been highly prized,
and still are, in many parts of the world. Since
walnuts are attributed with aphrodisiac
qualities, it is not surprising that satsivi is a
popular wedding dish. The freshly shelled
walnuts are finely chopped and sweated in
chicken fat with garlic, onion, and spices such
as paprika, cilantro, allspice, cloves, and ground
chile. Then enough chicken broth is added to
make a thick sauce, which is sharpened with
pomegranate paste, tamarind, or vinegar. This
is poured over the chicken and left to cool.
Although it is commonly served with cold
chicken, it is also excellent with other roast
poultry such as duck, quail, or pheasant.

Chicken with Couscous Stuffing

Couscous is normally served steamed and
covered with steamed vegetables and meat.
This dish is a back-to-front version, made
especially delicious from the juices of the
bird trickling down to flavor the couscous.
First, the couscous is spiced with nutmeg,
cinnamon, mace, and saffron or turmeric.
Then it is softened with chicken broth and
fluffed up to separate the grains. Into this
is mixed some tart dried apricots, almonds,
pistachios, and pine nuts, and some mint
leaves, all finely chopped. A small amount of
sugar or lemon juice adjusts the sweet-and-
sour balance. This is stuffed into the chicken,
which is slowly roasted so the skin is lovely
and golden, and the meat and stuffing
moist and succulent. It is delicious as it is,
but if a sauce is needed, a caramelized onion
sauce goes well, and if a spicy condiment is
preferred, then it may be served with harissa:
a complex, spicy paste, the exact ingredients
of which are different in each kitchen. The
basic elements are seeded red chiles, garlic,
mint leaves, ground coriander, cumin, and
caraway seeds, all pounded to a paste with
salt and olive oil.

Jerk Chicken

Jerked meat is a popular street food in Jamaica, perfect for those who revel in hot seasonings. The elements that characterize the Caribbean jerk flavor are habaneros or Scotch bonnet peppers—one of the hottest of all—and allspice, the fruit of the Jamaican pimento, brought back to Europe by Christopher Columbus. Other spices such as cayenne pepper, cinnamon, cloves, and nutmeg are added with salt, herbs, and garlic; the perfect mix is a matter of debate. The dry marinade is rubbed into the meat before grilling.

Originally, the Carib-Arawak people of Jamaica would prepare their meat by piercing it, then pressing spices into the holes. A shallow pit was dug and a fire prepared using green allspice wood to produce a fragrant smoke. The meat was placed over a grid of branches, and allspice leaves covered the meat to intensify the smoke.

Early explorers' engravings show the Caribs preparing meat on such grids; it was an effective way of preserving the meat in a hot climate. Today, jerk sellers use oil drums fired with charcoal. Hard dough bread and Jamaican fried dumplings are offered as a good foil to the fierce spicing.

Jerk Chicken

1 (3 to 4 lb) chicken, cut into 10 pieces

Juice of 1 lime

A splash of rum

1/4 cup vegetable oil

10 scallions, finely chopped

4 cloves garlic, chopped

2 tbsp dried thyme

2 Scotch bonnet chiles, seeded and chopped

4 tsp ground allspice

4 tsp ground ginger

4 tsp ground cinnamon

2 tsp ground nutmeg

2 tsp salt

2 tsp freshly ground black pepper

2 tsp dark brown sugar

Put the chicken pieces in a large bowl, pour over the lime juice, and stir well to coat. Combine the remaining ingredients in a blender. Rub the blended mix all over the chicken pieces, then chill in the refrigerator for 3 to 4 hours or overnight, turning occasionally.

When ready to cook, remove the chicken from the marinade, sprinkle with salt and pepper, and grill, skin side down until the chicken is cooked through. Turn the chicken pieces two or three times during grilling.

Serves 8

Chicken Drumsticks and Wings

Even in the most sophisticated circles, people cannot resist a succulent roasted chicken drumstick; it's the perfect picnic food, and is also loved by children everywhere. Some maintain that the plain version cannot be improved; others like to marinate their drumsticks in satay sauce, grill them with lemon and herbs, coat them in bread crumbs, cover them in Cajun or jerk seasonings—even stuff them with Chinese sausage.

Their poor relation, the chicken wing, used to be reserved for the stockpot. But in 1964, its lowly status changed. Theresa Belissimo, owner of the Anchor Bar in Buffalo, New York, had to produce a late-night snack for her son and his friends. Having surplus chicken wings, she fried them and coated them in a hot, spicy sauce, serving them with a blue cheese sauce and celery. Such was their success that there is now an annual National Buffalo Wings festival, and they are popular food for competitive eating contests. In other words, these choice little morsels—known as hot wings or Buffalo wings—have become part of America's food culture.

Petti di Pollo alla Fiorentina

The name "Florentine" attached to a dish usually implies the inclusion of spinach in the ingredients, since it was Florentine cooks who were said to have introduced spinach to France in the 16th century. However, there is another version of chicken Florentine that is simply the skinned breasts of a small roasting chicken fried to perfection in butter—no more, no less. Such a simple dish obviously needs the sweetest butter and an immaculate chicken with the best possible flavor.

The more commonly known version is also made with chicken breasts. Sometimes these are browned and then baked between two layers of cooked spinach that has been folded into a very light cheese sauce with nutmeg grated into it. Other recipes stuff the chicken breasts with spinach and soft cheese and then bake them until golden brown and serve them with a creamy sauce, the whole combination producing a deliciously moist dish.

Chu Hou Chicken

Chu Hou was a chef who worked near Canton at the beginning of the 19th century. The invention of this famous bean paste is credited to him and so bears his name, as do several other poultry and seafood dishes that use his paste. It should not be confused with black bean sauce, which is a Hong Kong condiment made entirely for the Western market.

Chu Hou's bean paste was made from yellow soybeans, sesame seeds, flour, sugar, and lard. However, many modern versions, especially those exported to the West, use oil instead of lard. Chu Hou's bean paste is stir-fried along with some type of alcohol. Then broth is added and a chicken simmered in it. The chicken is removed from the broth, and the liquid is drained back into the pot and boiled again. The chicken is returned to the broth, simmered, and removed once more. This procedure is repeated five more times, by which time the chicken is cooked to perfection. The broth is reduced, slightly thickened, and poured over the chicken, which has been boned and cut into pieces. Chu Hou chicken can also be successfully made with duck, goose, pigeon, or pheasant.

Bang-Bang Chicken

Bang-bang chicken is a street vendor's dish from the Szechuan region of China. The name comes from the pounding of the chicken, which is both tenderized and shredded with a heavy wooden stick called a *bon*, hence its alternative name of bon-bon chicken. Like much street cuisine, it is speedy and simple. In the original version, the chicken is simply simmered and then pounded into shreds. While it cooks, the characteristic nutty flavored sauce is made by softening sesame paste with a little of the cooking broth and then blending in Chinese sesame oil, soy, rice vinegar, chili oil, and a touch of sugar. Savory sesame paste is strong, beautifully aromatic and much used in Szechuan cooking. However, many recipes substitute either tahini or smooth peanut butter, in which case extra sesame oil should be added to intensify the flavor—Chinese sesame oil is much more pungent than the Middle Eastern variety.

The dish is assembled by shredding lettuce leaves and strewing over them some carrot, red onion, and fine strips of scallion or cucumber. The shredded chicken is laid on top and the hot, slightly sweet-and-sour sauce is drizzled over the top.

Bang-Bang Chicken

9 oz chicken (breasts and thighs), skin on

1 tbsp soy sauce

1 tsp sesame paste

$1/2$ tsp sesame oil

2 tsp chili oil

1 tsp sugar

$1/8$ tsp ground Szechuan peppercorn

Lettuce leaves

1 scallion, cut into thin strips

Place the chicken in a saucepan, cover with water and bring to a boil. Reduce the heat and simmer, until cooked, about 10 minutes. Drain and set aside. Once cool, beat the skin side lightly with a rolling pin to loosen the fibers. Now remove the skin and shred the chicken meat with your fingers.

Make the sauce by combining the soy sauce, sesame paste, sesame oil, chili oil, sugar, and ground Szechuan peppercorn. Arrange the lettuce leaves on a serving platter. Sprinkle the scallion strips over the top and then the shredded chicken. Pour the sauce over the top and serve. *Serves 2*

Chicken Satay

Satays are part of a huge worldwide family that includes kebabs, *espedata*, *sosaties*, *brochettes*, *souvlaki*, *yakitori*, and more. They are a staple finger food throughout Southeast Asia, where a huge variety of meats are used, from the more usual pork, chicken, beef, and lamb, to venison, goat, snake, turtle, cow's udder, horse, and crocodile. In other words, whatever is available locally and enjoyed. The dipping sauces naturally vary from country to country and region to region, but the best-known are made from peanuts—popular in Malaysia—or from sesame paste, though other delicious Indonesian sauce ingredients include spiced pineapple, sweet soy sauce, or the licorice-flavored Nicola buds.

Some maintain that satays were brought out of China by emigrants to Southeast Asia, because satay sauce made with peanuts is said to have originated in the southeastern province of Fujian. Others think it was the other way around. In all cases, the meat is cut into bite-sized pieces and marinated in spices—turmeric is a popular one, as it colors the meat nicely. The marinated pieces are threaded onto bamboo skewers, grilled over a charcoal fire, and served immediately with their contrasting dipping sauce.

Chicken Satay

1 (4 oz) chicken breast

1 heaping tsp red chile, finely chopped

$1/4$ cup crunchy peanut butter

4 tsp soy sauce

1 tsp sesame oil

2 tsp toasted sesame seeds

Cut the chicken breast into bite-sized chunks, thread onto presoaked wooden skewers and broil until cooked through, turning occasionally. Place the chile, peanut butter, soy sauce, sesame oil, and sesame seeds into a food processor, add a tablespoon or so of water and blend until smooth. Lay the satays on a plate and serve the sauce alongside. *Serves 1*

Cantonese Chicken

There is no one particular dish called
"Cantonese Chicken;" rather, it is a style of
cooking particular to Guangdong province,
where Guangzhou, or Canton, is found. Its
cooking is known all over the world because
the majority of Chinese restaurants outside
China were run by Cantonese chefs. However,
their original fresh, lively dishes became
corrupted into a different kind of fast food
that nevertheless became immensely popular
in Western countries. In many parts of the
world "Cantonese chicken" is likely to be cubes
of chicken stir-fried with a sweet-and-sour
sauce thickened with cornstarch and sugar.

Traditionally, Cantonese cooking is
characterized by its fast cooking times:
shallow-frying or steaming is preferred
to preserve the aromas and fresh flavors.
Each dish should emerge from the wok
with its own special *wok-hay* or aroma.

Apart from *dim sum* (a series of small
snacks eaten mainly in the morning and
afternoon), chicken holds a special place.
Every part of the bird is used: the blood is
thickened and made into soup, the liver
is skewered with pork fat and grilled for a
delicacy called "gold coin chicken," and the
flesh is used in hundreds of imaginative ways.

Kung Pao Chicken

Although cashews do make a sumptuous
contrast to this popular Szechuan dish, the
original Chinese version uses peanuts, since
cashews do not feature anywhere in Chinese
cooking. This world-famous dish was
supposedly invented in the 19th century
by the chef to a court official named Ding
Baozhen. He was governor of Szechuan
province and his title, Gong Bao, meaning
"guardian of the palace," gave rise to the
name Kung Pao, which is one of the hottest
of Szechuan dishes.

The chicken is cut into small cubes and
marinated in soy, cornstarch, and salt. The
wok is heated and seasoned, and Szechuan
chiles of the hottest variety are quickly fried
to release their fiery, numbing effect.
Szechuan peppercorns add a fragrant,
floral note in contrast. The chicken pieces
are added and partly cooked. Then ginger,
scallions, bamboo shoots, and Shao Xing
rice wine are all added. Finally, a generous
handful of toasted peanuts is stirred in.

In America, Szechuan pepper was banned
from 1968 to 2005, during which time a milder
and sweeter version of this dish evolved,
using cashews, bell peppers, mushrooms,
oyster sauce, and hoisin sauce.

Salt-Baked Chicken

Baking food in a crust of salt is an excellent way of preserving its fresh taste. This rustic dish comes from southeast China. Some people have suggested that it is a version of another famous Chinese dish called "beggar's chicken," where a whole chicken is wrapped in clay and baked in wood ashes. A salt-baked chicken is first cleaned and blanched in boiling water. Then soy is brushed over the skin and the bird is hung up until completely dry. A marinade is made from gingerroot, scallions, star anise, and *mei kuei lu chiew*, a delicate, fragrant liquor made from rose petals steeped in sorghum spirit. This is stuffed into the cavity of the bird, which is then tightly wrapped in cheesecloth.

A Chinese clay pot is filled with coarse salt and heated, and the chicken is then completely buried in the salt and cooked over the fire. Once cooked, it is carefully removed from the cheesecloth so that the salt cracks off and the fragrant juices do not escape. It is served with a dipping sauce of ginger, scallions, and thick broth. Surprisingly, the finished dish is not particularly salty.

Szechuan Pepper Chicken

The Szechuan basin in southeast China is known as the land of plenty. Its warm, humid climate perhaps explains the preponderance of spices used in its cooking. Both the leaves and berries of Szechuan pepper are used to prevent gastric disorders and are also rubbed onto the skin as a pesticide. In culinary terms, it has a distinctively pungent flavor with a fantastically exotic floral aftertaste.

Although Szechuan pepper and chiles are the best-known spices for giving Szechuan dishes their characteristic fieriness, local chefs are renowned for producing extra-ordinarily complex dishes using the wide variety of ingredients available to them.

A typical Szechuan chicken dish will be made from pieces of chicken that are marinated in a mixture of soy and local Shao Xing rice wine, and then fried in a really hot wok until golden brown and crisp. The chicken is then removed, the heat lowered, and some garlic and ginger are gently fried, followed by the spices and chiles to release their aromas into the cooking oil. The chicken is returned to the wok, along with scallions, sugar, and some sesame oil, and these are stirred to coat the pieces in the fragrant, spicy liquid.

Drunken Chicken

Drunken chicken means different things to different people. In America, a chicken is placed upright onto a part-filled can of beer so that its cavity completely covers the opening. Then it is cooked slowly on a barbecue or in the oven. As the beer evaporates, its flavor permeates the chicken, and once the beer has evaporated, the chicken starts to wobble on top of its can and will eventually fall over in true drunken fashion. This indicates the chicken is done.

In China, there are two versions, one hot and one cold. In the cold version, the chicken is heavily seasoned and left to marinate overnight, then it is rinsed off and steamed or simmered. Next, it is quickly drained, dried off and submerged in rice wine or sherry for up to a week before being cut up and served.

The hot version uses no cooking liquid other than alcohol, so the aroma when the dish is brought to the table is intoxicating. The best golden-colored rice wine comes from Shao Xing and should come from Zhejiang—beware of imitations from other countries.

Drunken Chicken

1 (3 lb) chicken
1 cup salt
¼ cup black pepper
1 (12 fl oz) can beer
1 sprig of fresh rosemary

Preheat the barbecue. When the coals are hot and glowing, push them over to the sides of the grill, leaving an open space in the middle. Wash the chicken and pat dry with paper towels. Season the chicken liberally inside and out. Open the can of beer and insert the rosemary sprig. It may help to pour a little of the beer out first. Now stand the chicken over the beer can so that the top of the can is inside the cavity of the bird. Stand the can (and bird) on the barbecue, in the cleared space in the middle. Close the barbecue lid and cook until the chicken is done, turning the chicken as necessary. This will take 45 to 60 minutes. Test the chicken by inserting a skewer into the meat at its thickest part— the juices should run clear. *Serves 6*

Lemon Chicken

Sweet (Mandarin) oranges originated in China, but the origin of the lemon is less certain. Although its name comes from the Persian *limu*, it probably first grew in central India, once part of the Persian Empire.

The combination of lemon and chicken is such a classic one that it appears in cuisines all over the world. However, lemons are not widely used in China, which is curious since there are records of it being cultivated in the southern province of Canton in the 12th century. Nor can lemon chicken be found in restaurants in mainland China, despite it being one of the most popular Cantonese dishes outside China. It is a good example of the adaptability of those émigré chefs when they found themselves among people who thought their cuisine unfamiliar and puzzling.

For this dish, chicken fillets are marinated in rice wine and light seasonings, then coated in an egg-and-flour batter and wok-fried until deep golden.

Lemon sauce is practically always bought, so this is heated in the wok with oil and drizzled over the sliced chicken, which is served over shredded lettuce.

Oyako Don

This is the Japanese answer to the question "which came first?" and it is a typically Zen response. The dish is both delicate and immensely satisfying—one of the hallmarks of Japanese food. Oyako don means "parent and child," referring to the chicken and the egg. It is one of the *ten-ya-mono* type of Japanese dishes, which consist of warm rice with a *gu* (topping) poured over it. Typically, it is served in a deep ceramic bowl called a *don-buri*. The chicken is simmered with onions and perhaps some shiitake mushrooms in a delicate *dashi* (seaweed and tuna) broth, then a few leaves of *mitsuba* (a parsley-like herb) or mustard and cress are added for a tiny splash of color. Beaten eggs are poured over it and left to thicken but not completely set. This is scooped over the rice to serve. Those wishing a little more spice add a sprinkling of *shichimi-togarashi* (Japanese seven-spice powder), but it really doesn't need it.

Chicken Vindaloo

Some say the name "vindaloo" originates from a combination of vinegar and *aloo* (the Indian word for potato). Others maintain that it is a corruption of the Portuguese *vinho de alhos*, a wine-and-garlic marinade brought to Goa by the Portuguese when they colonized the island. It was certainly the Portuguese who introduced the tiny, fiercely hot chiles to Goa from their explorations in South America, and the vindaloo curry has now become renowned for being one of the hottest in the world. However, in Goa, it is not the heat of the chiles that makes it distinctive, but rather the use of the vinegar, as well as the particular vindaloo spices.

Dried red chiles, ground coriander, peppercorns, cumin, fenugreek, and garam masala may all appear with turmeric, garlic, fresh gingerroot, raw onion, and the vinegar. In Goa, this is made from either rice or coconuts, but the original may well have been made with Portuguese wine that had spoiled on its sea voyage. The vinegar is added to the curry after the chicken and spices have been browned; it lends its own particular tingle to the roar of the hot spices.

Chicken Madras

Southern Indian food is largely vegetarian and rice-based, and its curries are some of the hottest of all; only vindaloo curries are hotter. The word "curry" comes from the southern Indian Tamil word *kari*. However, "madras curry" is not really a dish known in India, but rather a style of curry that is particularly popular in Britain, a legacy from its time as ruler of India during the British Raj. Legend has it that in the 18th century, while in Madras, General Clive added some meat to his hot vegetarian *kari*, thereby creating the first madras curry.

The idea caught on among the expatriate community, who brought their much-loved colonial dishes back to Britain. Thus began the British people's special passion for curries. Good chicken madras will be made of small pieces of chicken cooked in liberal quantities of oils and spices. These will include fenugreek, tamarind, cilantro, cinnamon, cardamom, nutmeg, the herb "curry leaves," which is particular to south Indian cooking, and, of course, ginger, garlic, and both red and green chiles.

Murgh Makhani

Murgh makhani (butter chicken) is a traditional Mogul dish from Delhi. Delhi's cuisine has elements of many of her rulers, who were variously Arabs, Afghans, Rajpatis, and Moguls. Butter chicken is sumptuously rich, containing yogurt, sour cream, and a fragrant mixture of spices in its creamy sauce. Generous quantities of ghee are poured into the dish just before serving; *kaali daal* (black lentils) go especially well with it.

Although it is a popular restaurant food, and restaurants are now legion in Delhi, until the arrival of the Punjabis during the partition of India and Pakistan, orthodox Hindus would not dream of eating outside the home, considering such food unclean. But once the Punjabis started up their tandoori eateries, the locals soon changed their view and the restaurant capital of India was on its way. Being an original Mogul dish, however, butter chicken will be found at its most authentic in one of the legendary restaurants in Old Delhi, the Mogul Shah Jahan's city. Most of the oldest restaurants are owned by descendants of the royal cooks who served in the emperors' kitchens and prided themselves in preserving their traditional cuisine.

Tandoori Chicken Tikka Masala

A "tandoor" is the cylindrical clay oven that gives tandoori food its characteristic flavors. *Tikka* means "bite-sized," and *masala* is a spice mixture that varies according to region and use. The word *masala* originates from the Arabic for "interests," and was probably brought to India by the Moguls; it means the colorful, spiced nature of these dishes.

In this dish, the chicken pieces are marinated for at least 8 hours in yogurt and spices; these correctly include turmeric, which is bright yellow, and red chili powder or cayenne pepper to give the characteristic red, though often food coloring is used instead. The chicken is then threaded on long metal skewers, brushed with ghee and cooked in the tandoor where the temperature can reach up to 900°F by fanning the charcoal. This imparts a smoky flavor to the meat that complements the aromatic spicing and the hint of coconut in the creamy sauce.

Tandoori cooking has become immensely popular internationally, particularly in Britain where chicken tikka masala rivals pizza as the most popular takeout. Green cilantro chutney makes the perfect accompaniment.

Tandoori Chicken

1 (3 lb) chicken, cut into 10 pieces

$\frac{1}{2}$ cup natural yogurt

1 tsp garam masala

2 tbsp paprika

1 tsp chili powder

1 tsp ground cumin

2 tbsp lemon juice

2 tbsp vegetable oil

1 tsp salt

$\frac{1}{2}$ tsp turmeric

1 tbsp tomato paste

4 cloves garlic, crushed

2 tsp peeled and finely grated gingerroot

Wash the chicken well and pat dry with paper towels. Slash the skin a few times with a sharp knife. Combine the remaining ingredients in a bowl and rub the smooth paste all over the chicken, making sure some of it goes into the slits. Cover and refrigerate for 8 hours.

Preheat the oven to 350°F. Place the chicken in a roasting pan and cover with aluminum foil. Roast in the center of the oven for 1 hour 30 minutes, basting with the marinade halfway through. Remove the chicken from the oven and serve with green cilantro chutney. *Serves 6*

Balti Chicken

Baltistan is in northeast Pakistan, but as well as being a style of cuisine, a balti is also the name of the traditional cast-iron *karahi* that is used for cooking and serving these dishes. Similar to a wok with two handles, dishes are stir-fried, originally in ghee, though now oil is more common. Traditional balti spices originally tended toward the milder aromatic Kashmir mixtures, using *jeera* (cumin), fenugreek, and cardamom. Today, and especially outside India and Pakistan, many recipes call for *garam masala*—a hotter, more colorful spice mix—and chiles, reflecting the international desire for highly spiced food. Balti chicken, therefore, is made by cutting the chicken into *tikka* (bite-sized pieces) that are stir-fried in the *karahi* with onion, garlic, and the softly aromatic spices. Broth is added to make a thick sauce, and finally some cilantro.

This is finger food, so the sizzling curry is scooped straight from the balti with naan bread—and therein lies much of its appeal.

Chicken Korma

Most non-Indian peoples' perception of chicken korma is of a mild curry dish with a thick, turmeric-infused creamy sauce. This may be the case, but in western Indian cooking, chicken korma seems to be simply a contrast to the fierce "vindaloo" style of very hot curry.

Korma is a Mogul word originating from the Middle East, meaning to braise. In the Moguls' territory in northern India, there are a great variety of different kormas, but the word there implies a rich dish for celebratory banquets such as thanksgivings and weddings. The spicing, therefore, is fragrant and luxurious, with saffron (not turmeric), crushed cardamom pods, cinnamon, coriander seeds, white pepper, white poppy seeds, nuts, cloves, and just a hint of chile pepper. These are warmed in oil or ghee (clarified butter) to release their perfume, then onion is added, followed by the chicken, which is then braised with yogurt and saffron-infused broth. While it cooks, cashew nuts are pounded to a paste with cream and coconut milk and stirred into the juices. Finally, just a little garam masala is judiciously added during the last few minutes of cooking. The result is voluptuous in color, texture, and flavor.

Chicken Jalfrezi

Ex-colonials from the British Raj in India still become misty-eyed at hearing words like kedgeree, pish-pash, and jalfrezi, all reminiscent of the Indian kitchens of the British Empire. However, jalfrezi is not a traditional Indian dish, but rather a method of cooking. Jhal means "pungently spicy" and frezi means "dry-fry," that is, stir-fry. Some regard it as a form of Balti dish.

The colonials employed Indian cooks who sometimes fried leftover cold meat with onions and plenty of hot spices; chicken and lamb were the most popular meats and they appear in this guise in many Anglo–Indian cookbooks. But a jalfrezi can be made using fresh meat; sometimes this is cooked first and then immediately stir-fried, other times it is stir-fried from raw.

The common ingredients, other than chicken, are plenty of onion, garlic, some green bell peppers, and green chile. These are stir-fried with fresh gingerroot to make a vibrant sauce, which is much less liquid than many curries. It can be served with a garnish of fried potatoes, but rice is more common.

A Mogul Feast

In the early 16th century, the Mogul warrior tribe invaded India, forging disparate kingdoms and states into a powerful empire that lasted for nearly 300 years. Babar, the first Mogul king to rule in India, was displaced royalty from central Asia. He deplored the culture, climate, and food of his new state, and set about creating a more refined society, including a cuisine that combined Persian and Hindu sensibilities. The result of this fusion of cultures in the kitchen was Mogul cuisine, food of kings.

Mogul cooking made liberal use of cream, almonds and pistachios, saffron and other fragrant spices, sugar and syrup, chicken, lamb, dried fruits, and rice. The Mogul kings planted orchards in Kashmir so they could enjoy fruits that were not indigenous to India, including apples, peaches, apricots, and cherries. Sweets were very important to the diners so there would always be an array of tempting treats at the end of a meal. The feast itself could include dozens of different dishes, borne by a procession of servants. Today in Delhi, excellent traditional Mogul cuisine may still be found in private homes and some first-class restaurants.

Shahi Kofte
Chicken Balls in Tomato, Onion, and Sour Cream with Pistachios and Apricots

For the koftes:

1¼ cups chopped onions

1 clove garlic, chopped

¼-in piece gingerroot, chopped

¼ cup cilantro leaves

Salt

Freshly ground black pepper

10 raw almonds, ground to a powder

1 egg

2 slices of white bread, broken up

1 lb lean ground chicken

2 tbsp vegetable oil

For the sauce:

2 tbsp vegetable oil

½ tsp cumin seeds

1 clove garlic, grated

¼-in piece gingerroot, chopped

1¼ cups chopped onions

1 cup diced tomatoes

2 tbsp sour cream

¼ tsp cayenne pepper

½ tsp turmeric

1 tsp ground coriander

½ tsp ground cumin

1 tsp garam masala

Salt

Freshly ground black pepper

10 dried apricots, finely chopped

1 tbsp chopped raw pistachios

1½ cups water

In a food processor, mince the onions, garlic, and ginger. Add the cilantro, salt and pepper to taste, almonds, egg, bread, and mince again. Add the ground chicken and blend. Form the chicken into balls, about 25 in total. Warm the oil in a skillet over medium heat and place as many meatballs as will fit in a single layer. Brown lightly for about 2 minutes, turning once or twice for even cooking. Drain on paper towels and reserve.

To make the sauce, warm the oil in a skillet set over medium-high heat. Add the cumin seeds and toast for a few seconds before adding the garlic and ginger. Sauté for 30 seconds, then add the onions and sauté for 5 minutes. Reduce the heat and stir in the tomatoes, mashing them well with the back of a wooden spoon. Cook for 5 minutes until oil appears around the edges of the sauce. Mix in the sour cream and cook, stirring, for 3 minutes. Add the salt, spices, apricots, pistachios, and water, then bring to a boil. Gently slide in the browned meatballs, cover, and reduce heat to low. Cook for about 30 minutes, stirring occasionally. *Makes about 25*

A Typical Menu

- *Kashmiri Dum Alu* Baby potatoes in sautéed onion, tomato, and yogurt
- *Dhaniya Tamatar Moongodi* Mung bean dumplings in a tomato-herb sauce
- *Chane ki Dal Laukiwali* Yellow split peas with zucchini, tomatoes, and spices
- *Paneer Makhani Masala* Paneer, cashews, and mushrooms in a creamy sauce
- *Zafrani Paneer Kabab* Grilled chicken with yogurt, paneer, and cashews, tossed with sautéed onions
- *Murgh Kabab* Chicken marinated in herbs, sun-dried tomatoes, vinegar, eggs, and cream
- *Akhroat Murgh* Chicken breast morsels with portobello mushrooms, powdered walnuts, yogurt, mint, and spices
- *Bhindi Jhinga Masala* Shrimp stir-fried with okra and spices
- *Machali ke Tikke* Fish fillets marinated in yogurt, nuts, and spices, grilled
- *Mookal* Cooked, shredded lamb, stir-fried with onions, yogurt, and spices
- *Gosht Yakhni Biryani* Fennel-scented lamb curry, baked with rice
- *Shahi Kofte ki Biryani* Rice, layered and baked with a spicy meatball curry
- *Aam ki Kulfi* Ice cream made with thickened, sweetened milk, flavored with mangoes and pistachios

Roast Turkey

Christmas simply wouldn't be Christmas without turkey and all the trimmings. Their great size has made them prestigious feasting food: Spanish conquistadors in South America were lavishly entertained with turkeys, though they would have preferred red meat. Turkeys arrived in England about 100 years before the Pilgrims sailed for the New World to share their first Thanksgiving feast with the Native American Wampanoag, and the rest is history. Now turkey is eaten all year round as everyday food as well as for celebrations. Roast turkey was the first food eaten on the moon by Neil Armstrong and Buzz Aldrin.

As to the best stuffing and sauces to serve with the celebratory bird, sage and onion, apricot and prune, and cranberry are all popular, with chestnut stuffing a particular favorite. The chestnuts are peeled and gently cooked in butter with onion, parsley, seasoning, and broth before being stuffed into the cavity of the bird. But the most important thing is that this is not gourmet fare, it is family food, whose homey tastes become treasured childhood memories, along with the secret wish made on the wishbone. No ingredient is quite so satisfying as familiarity.

Roast Turkey

1 (11 to 13 lb) turkey

Salt

Freshly ground black pepper

For the herb butter:

3/4 cup unsalted butter, softened

1 tsp fresh thyme leaves

1 tsp chopped fresh rosemary leaves

2 tbsp chopped fresh parsley

For the stuffing:

1/2 cup butter

1/2 cup finely chopped onion

2 cups white bread crumbs

1 tsp fresh thyme leaves

1 tsp chopped fresh rosemary leaves

1 tbsp chopped fresh sage leaves

3 tbsp chopped fresh parsley

Grated zest of 1 lemon

1/2 cup pine nuts

Salt

Freshly ground black pepper

Preheat the oven to 375°F.

Wash the turkey inside and out and drain on paper towels. Season generously with salt and black pepper. Combine the ingredients for the herb butter and chill. Meanwhile, make the stuffing. Melt the butter in a frying pan and sauté the onion in the butter until softened. Add the bread crumbs and stir to absorb the melted butter, then add the chopped herbs, lemon zest, and pine nuts. Continue to cook for a few minutes longer, stirring well to combine.

Stuff the turkey, securing the opening with a metal skewer, and place the bird in a greased roasting pan. Smear with the chilled herb butter and cover with aluminum foil—this will prevent the tender breast meat from drying out while roasting.

Roast for 20 minutes per pound, basting the turkey every 30 minutes, and draining off excess fat. One hour before the end of the calculated cooking time, remove the foil, to allow the skin to get properly crisp and brown. Leave the bird to rest for at least 20 minutes before serving. *Serves 10–12*

Polpettone di Tacchino

Turkey Schnitzel

Polpettone is a terrine or meat loaf; it comes from the Latin *pulpa*, which means pounded boneless meat. Its poorer cousin, *polpetti*, is meatballs, a common way of using up leftover boiled meat quickly before the days of refrigerators: a family dish rather than one for entertaining. Many recipes for *polpetti* were given by the 18th-century writer Lorenzo Stecchetti in his book *The Art of Using the Leftovers from the Kitchen*. Polpettone, though, is made from raw meat and was far more highly regarded. Polpettone di tacchino is exactly the sort of dish that would have been produced by the great Renaissance master of cooking, Bartolomeo Scappi. At that time—the 16th century—turkeys were the height of fashion, being large, exotic birds and also having pale meat—an attribute considered more desirable than red meat to the civilized Renaissance diner. Sometimes the dishes were covered in gold leaf, and exquisite flavorings of herbs or bitter orange juice were sprinkled over the meat.

The word *schnitzel* is, of course, from Austria, home of the famous Wiener schnitzel. However, in Israel, the turkey schnitzel seems to have been adopted as a sort of national dish, one which binds together all of the many cultures that make up modern Israel, perhaps because it is a dish that cannot be claimed by any of the surrounding countries and therefore no one can be offended by sharing it. It is made in the same way as Wiener schnitzel: the skinned turkey breasts are placed between parchment paper and beaten out thinly. Then they are seasoned with salt, pepper, perhaps a little lemon zest, and some pulped garlic. The pieces are then dipped in beaten egg and, finally, in bread crumbs or, more correctly, matzo meal. They are fried at once until golden brown, in either oil or *schmaltz* (rendered chicken or turkey fat), and served with big wedges of lemon and some light, refreshing vegetables.

The matzo meal they are dipped in is made from ground matzo (crisp flatbread), which is made from flour and water and baked within 18 minutes, so that there can be no chance of yeast leavening it.

Mole Poblano

Mole poblano, a spicy red sauce, comes from the Aztec *molli*, meaning a concoction or sauce, and is thought to have originated in the 17th century in Puebla de los Angeles, Mexico.

   Naturally, innumerable versions abound, each family passing down its own definitive one, for fiesta food, is part of a Mexican's culture. Mole poblano is a complex combination of chiles, nuts, seeds, spices, vegetables, and chocolate, and requires lengthy preparation. If possible, use Mexican cinnamon, which has a delicate floral flavor. The ingredient most people think of—the chocolate—would originally have been toasted cacao beans, pounded to a paste.

Guajolote en Mole Poblano

The chiles:

Approximately $1/2$ cup lard

8 mulato chiles, seeded and veins removed

5 ancho chiles, seeded and veins removed

6 pasilla chiles, seeded and veins removed

1 tbsp reserved chile seeds

The giblet broth:

The turkey giblets

1 small carrot, trimmed and sliced

1 medium white onion, roughly chopped

6 peppercorns

Salt to taste

The turkey:

Approximately $1/3$ cup lard

1 (8 lb) turkey, cut into serving pieces

Salt to taste

The sauce:

2 cups giblet broth

$1/2$ cup tomate verde

3 cloves garlic, charred and peeled

4 whole cloves

10 peppercorns

$1/2$-in piece of cinnamon stick, toasted

$1/8$ tsp coriander seeds, toasted

$1/8$ tsp aniseeds

1 tbsp reserved chile seeds, toasted separately

7 tbsp sesame seeds, toasted separately

Approximately $1/4$ cup lard

2 tbsp raisins

20 unskinned almonds

$1/3$ cup hulled pumpkin seeds

1 small dried tortilla

3 small slices dry French bread

$1 1/2$ oz Mexican drinking chocolate

About 6 cups giblet broth

Salt to taste

Heat the lard in a skillet and briefly fry the chiles on both sides, taking care not to burn them. Reserve the lard. Drain the chiles and transfer to a bowl of cold water and let them soak for about 1 hour. Drain but do not attempt to skin. Preheat the oven to 325°F.

Put the giblets in a saucepan, cover well with water, add the carrot, onion, peppercorns, and salt, and bring to a simmer. Continue simmering for about 1½ hours, adding more water as necessary. Strain the broth and set aside.

Meantime, heat the lard in a Dutch oven, add the turkey pieces a few at a time, and fry until the skin turns a gold brown. Drain off the excess fat and reserve to fry the rest of the ingredients. Return all the pieces to the Dutch oven, sprinkle well with salt, cover, and braise in the oven until the meat is almost tender—about 40 minutes. This is not the traditional way of cooking a turkey for mole poblano—it is either boiled first or put raw to cook in the sauce—but the braising really enhances the flavor. Pour off the pan juices and add them to the giblet broth, then add water to make up to about 8 cups liquid.

Put 1 cup water in a blender and blend the drained chiles, a few at a time, to a slightly textured purée, adding only enough additional water to release the blender blades. In a heavy, flameproof casserole, heat the reserved lard and fry the chile purée over medium heat for about 10 minutes, scraping the bottom of the pan almost constantly to avoid sticking. Set aside. Put 1 cup of the broth into the blender, add the tomate verde and peeled garlic, and blend until smooth. Grind the spices together with the chile seeds to a finely textured powder. Then grind all but 4 tablespoons of the sesame seeds again to a textured powder. Add to the blender jar.

Melt the ¼ cup lard in a frying pan and separately fry the raisins, almonds, pumpkin seeds, tortilla, and bread, draining each ingredient in a colander before adding to the blender. Add another cup of the broth, or enough to release the blades of the blender, until you have a thick, slightly textured paste. Add the paste to the chiles in the casserole and continue cooking, again scraping the bottom of the pan well, for about 5 minutes. Break the chocolate into small pieces and add it to the mole with another cup of the broth and continue cooking for 5 minutes more. Dilute the mole with another 4 cups of the broth, test for salt, and continue cooking over medium heat until well seasoned and pools of oil form on the surface—about 40 minutes. Add the turkey pieces and cook for another 20 minutes. Serve each portion sprinkled with a little of the reserved sesame seeds. *Serves about 10*

Adapted from Diana Kennedy's *The Essential Cuisines of Mexico*

Canard à l'Orange

Turkey Stuffed with Birds

The ubiquitous duck in orange sauce served in chain restaurants and pubs has generally been prepared in factories and frozen or chilled for reheating on the premises. Such versions generally use sweet oranges and farm raised duck and bear little relationship to the original dish. The authentic version is made from wild duck and is served with *sauce bigarade—bigarade* is French for bitter or Seville oranges, whose sourness is an ideal counterpart to the richness of game meats, particularly wild duck. The orange peel is pared off its pith, cut into fine strips, and blanched to remove excess bitterness. Then it is simmered in butter and reserved. The sauce is made by caramelizing a pinch of sugar, and dissolving this in vinegar or lemon juice. This is thickened with potato flour and let down with game broth that has been enriched with curaçao. Finally, the softened orange peel is added. Meanwhile, the duck is roasted, and when done, the sauce is poured over the top so that the curls of orange peel decorate the dark brown skin of the bird. It is garnished with peeled and seeded orange segments.

The notion of stuffing creatures with other creatures has captured people's imagination for centuries. In medieval times, a *cockentrice* was made by sewing the front half of a capon to the back half of a suckling pig, but the record probably has to go to a 19th-century French dish. Called the *roti sans pareil* (roast without equal), it consisted of progressively smaller birds stuffed one into another—a bustard stuffed with a turkey, stuffed with a goose, then a chicken, duck, pheasant, guinea fowl, teal, partridge, woodcock, plover, lapwing, quail, thrush, lark, ortolan, and finally a warbler. A more modest version is known as a five-bird roast. Also known as a "Yorkshire Christmas pie," Queen Victoria's family was served a huge one for Christmas in 1857. Encased in pastry, it required four footmen to carry it to the table. In Louisiana, a "turducken"—a chicken inside a duck inside a turkey—has now become popular throughout America.

With all these creations, the conundrum is whether to preserve the spectacular look of the outside bird, or whether to stuff the meats in a roll so that everyone can taste all of the birds. Clearly only a very few slices of the *roti sans pareil* contained all seventeen birds.

Confit de Canard aux Lentilles du Puy

The rearing of duck for foie gras, once the province of Strasbourg and southwest France, is now ubiquitous throughout France. Some huge farms rear the birds under industrial conditions, but there still remain many small farmers who rear their ducks in less intensive ways. The word *confit* means "preserve," indicating the way in which goose, duck, and sometimes pork, was kept to provide filling meals for the winter months. The fattened duck is jointed into pieces, rubbed with a mixture of salt and spices, and left to marinate. Then the salt is brushed off and the pieces are completely immersed in duck fat and cooked for 3 hours over a slow wood fire that lends its smoky flavor. The pieces are then put into glass jars or cans and sterilized.

Puy lentils are good for soaking up the rich fat. They are grown in the Auvergne, where the volcanic soil around Le Puy gives a particularly fine earthy flavor to these tiny, slate-green lentils. Their color dulls when cooked, but they do not disintegrate like other lentils, retaining a pleasant crunchy texture. A purée of sorrel complements the lentils and warmed-up duck perfectly.

Magret de Canard aux Pommes Sarladaises

The ducks raised in southwest France today tend to be a cross, often between a Barbary (Muscovy) duck and the famed Rouen variety. This produces a particularly large duck suitable for fattening. The *magret* is the breast, which makes a substantial portion, weighing around 12 ounces before cooking, and it has a generous covering of fat.

The best way to cook *magrets* is to score the fat diagonally and cook the breasts, skin side down, in a frying pan. This renders excess fat and crisps the skin while gently cooking the meat from below. The other side is then quickly browned, and the *magret* is served *saignant* (rare).

Genuine *pommes sarladaises* are a superior version of the traditional dish of potatoes fried in garlic and parsley. The town of Sarlat holds a truffle auction every winter, and in the days when truffles were common, they were added to the sliced potatoes as they sizzled in rich duck or goose fat until crisp and golden. Some cooks break up the slices with a fork after adding the parsley and garlic, to produce extra crispness that complements the creaminess of the waxy potatoes.

Faisinjan

It is difficult to describe adequately the luscious texture and sweet-tart flavor of this sauce. Duck is the classic bird to use here, though pheasant is also excellent.

Walnut trees came from Iran and spread westward via Greece, where they were called "the Persian trees" and their rich, oily nuts reserved for the Gods. The Romans, too, thought walnuts were divine, calling them Jove's nut and attributing them with aphrodisiac powers. In England, they are called brain nuts because of the shape of the kernel, and in France, walnut trees often used to feature in people's wills. Faisinjan uses the Persian specialty called *robb-e anâr* (pomegranate syrup), which is made from the rich, tart, ruby-red pomegranates of the Middle East. Their tartness cuts through the duck fat and rich, oily walnuts.

Duck carcasses are used to make some broth and the meat is fried with onions. The walnuts are chopped fine, gently fried until dark, and then added to the duck with the broth and pomegranate paste to simmer gently, making a truly sumptuous Persian classic.

Faisinjan

1 duck, cut into quarters

2 to 3 tbsp light vegetable oil

1 onion, coarsely chopped

1³⁄₄ cups chopped or pounded walnuts

4 pomegranates

Juice of 2 lemons

1 tbsp sugar

¹⁄₂ cup water

Salt

Freshly ground black pepper

Brown the duck very quickly in hot oil in a large heavy pan. Remove the pieces and fry the onion in the same oil until it is a rich brown, stirring occasionally. Add the walnuts, which should not be too finely ground, and cook gently, stirring often, for about 2 minutes.

Cut the pomegranates in half, scoop out the seeds (discarding the pith) into a blender and blend a few seconds. Pour into a bowl through a strainer. There should be at least 1 cup of liquid. Pour into the pan and add the lemon, sugar, water, salt, and pepper. Bring to a simmer, stir, and add the duck pieces and cook gently for 1–1¹⁄₂ hours until they are very tender. Taste and adjust the delicate balance between sweet and sour by adding more lemon or more sugar. Remove as much fat as you can from the surface with a spoon before serving. *Serves 6*

Adapted from Claudia Roden's *A New Book of Middle Eastern Food*

Canard au Sang

This classic recipe typifies French restaurant cooking at its most theatrical. Not for the fainthearted, the dish is often prepared in front of the diner by the maitre d'. At the Tour d'Argent in Paris, where the dish was invented in the 1890s, diners are given a certificate afterward. The duck is not bled at slaughter, as this is what imparts the gamy flavor. To make canard au sang, the duck is part-roasted, leaving the meat very pink. Then it is brought into the restaurant where the breasts are skinned and lifted off, the legs are removed for a separate course, and the liver is taken out, puréed, sieved, and reserved. The remaining bones, meat, and crisp skin is put into a special duck press and crushed to extract the rich blood and juices, which are collected in a silver dish over a low flame. To this is added the liver, cognac, previously reduced red wine sauce, seasoning, a squeeze of lemon or lime, and some butter to finish the sauce as it thickens slowly over the low flame until is it is a deep, chocolate-brown. This is poured over the breasts and served.

Eight-Treasure Duck

Eight-treasure duck is a festive dish for the holidays, especially Chinese New Year. Sometimes it appears on a menu as "eight-jewel" or "eight-precious" duck (a duck represents fidelity in China). As its name suggests, it contains eight special ingredients made into a stuffing for the duck. These are chosen to symbolize good fortune, abundance, merriment, fertility, or whatever is appropriate to the occasion. Exactly which eight treasures are used for the stuffing vary from recipe to recipe, but common to all are the glutinous rice, the pork or ham, and the dried shrimp. Glutinous rice is auspicious in Chinese cooking, as the grains sticking together represent family unity. The other five

ingredients can include Chinese mushrooms, bamboo shoots, lotus seeds, giblets, Chinese chestnuts, or gingko nuts. The dried shrimp indicates Shanghai's style of using seafood in its recipes. Dried shrimps are sometimes called "sea rice" as the tiniest are only the size of a grain of rice. They are best presoaked in rice wine. This stuffing is particularly delicious, especially the glutinous rice, since it absorbs the flavors of the other treasures as well as the juices from the duck.

Eight-Treasure Duck

1 (6 lb) duck

1/2 cup glutinous rice, soaked

4 to 5 dried shiitake mushrooms, soaked and chopped

1/4 cup shelled chestnuts, diced

1/2 cup chopped lean pork

2 tbsp chopped smoked ham

1/2 cup chopped bamboo shoots

6 large raw shrimp, shelled and chopped

1/4 cup soy sauce, plus 2 tbsp

1 tbsp dry sherry, plus 2 tbsp

1/4 cup lotus seeds

2 scallions, cut into 1-in pieces

2 to 3 slices fresh gingerroot

3 cups duck broth

1 tsp salt

1 tbsp sugar

Wash the duck inside and out and pat dry with paper towels.

Cook the soaked rice in 4 cups of water, bringing the water to a boil first, then simmer, covered, for 5 minutes. Drain and rinse the rice under cold running water.

Put the rice, chopped mushrooms, chestnuts, pork, smoked ham, bamboo shoots, and shrimp in a large bowl. Add 4 tablespoons of soy sauce, 1 tablespoon of dry sherry, and the lotus seeds. Stir well to combine.

Stuff the rice mixture into the cavity of the duck and secure the end with a metal skewer. Put the duck in a large pan. Add the scallions and gingerroot, then the broth, the remaining soy sauce and sherry, and the salt. Bring to a boil, cover, and simmer for about an hour, turning the duck several times. Now add the sugar and simmer for another hour, again turning the duck every so often.

Remove the duck from the broth, scoop out the rice stuffing and arrange on a serving dish. Chop the duck into 2 to 4 pieces, arrange over the stuffing and serve. *Serves 6*

Aromatic Crispy Duck

Aromatic crispy duck is sometimes confused with Peking duck, as many people outside China serve aromatic crispy duck in the same way as Peking duck: wrapped in wafer-thin Chinese pancakes along with strips of cucumber and scallion and a tangy, dark plum or hoisin sauce. It seems as though Peking duck and a Szechuan crispy duck recipe have been combined. The main difference lies in the cooking methods. Whereas Peking duck is roasted in an oven, aromatic crispy duck is first marinated, then steamed, then cooled until completely cold and dry, and finally it is deep-fried in a wok; all much more typical Chinese cooking methods. The marinade usually includes five-spice powder, some beautifully aromatic Szechuan peppercorns, black peppercorns, star anise, and cumin or Chinese cinnamon. Ginger and scallion are placed inside the duck while it is steamed. Instead of being sliced, as is Peking duck, the aromatic meat and crackling skin are shredded with a fork before being brought to table.

The duck is eaten like a sandwich in a steamed bun with roasted salt and pepper. A selection of dipping sauces may be served alongside.

Peking Roast Duck

Peking, now known as Beijing, has long been a gastronomic center, with restaurants serving provincial food from all over China. Its signature dish turns out to have originated in Inner Mongolia, but was adopted by Pekingese restaurants in the 19th century and from there spread its fame all over the world as a Chinese banqueting dish. It is unusual in that the duck is roasted in an oven, which is a rarity in China. The original written version of Peking duck—15,000 words long—mainly featured instructions for building and using the oven, which was fueled by wood from the Chinese date tree.

What makes Peking duck sensational is the particular species of duck that is force-fed for the purpose. The method itself is simple. The duck is blanched in boiling water, its skin rubbed with malt sugar, after which it is hung up to dry. Then it is roasted in a sealed oven until the skin is crackling. The skin is sliced and the tender meat cut into strips and these are brought to the table where diners roll them up in wafer-thin Chinese pancakes with matchsticks of cucumber and scallion, and a plum sauce.

Aromatic Tea-Smoked Duck

Aromatic tea-smoked duck is a Szechuan specialty. Besides Szechuan, China has over a dozen tea-producing provinces, each of which produces about fifty different types of tea, so the choice of flavors and perfumes is vast. As with many Chinese classic duck dishes, tea-smoked duck is a lengthy process. First, the whole duck is marinated for twelve hours in ginger, sugar, onion, rice wine, and a mixture of toasted salt and ground Szechuan peppercorns. It is then steamed gently for several hours until cooked through and allowed to cool. After that, it is smoked in a large sealed wok, the smoking materials varying according to the chef. They could include star anise, cinnamon sticks, camphor, raw grains of rice, and brown sugar, though Szechuan peppercorns and black tea leaves are common to most recipes. Once the heat has released their aromas, the smoking takes about 20 minutes. Finally the duck is deep-fried to crisp the skin.

The combination of the marinade spices and the fragrant smoke impart complex flavors while the combination of poaching and fast-frying produces a wonderful contrast of crisp and succulent textures.

Soy Duck

Soy duck is a specialty of Shanghai and is not often seen in the West, unlike the soy-basted chicken that can be seen hanging in the windows of many Cantonese restaurants. Correctly, "soy sauce" should be called simply "soy," as it is a condiment rather than a sauce. For this recipe, the whole duck is blanched and the cavity salted. Cinnamon, ginger, scallions, and star anise are tied into a cloth and simmered to make a perfumed broth. Some like to add a few drops of red food coloring to the water. Both dark and light soy, rice wine, sugar, and salt are added to the broth with the duck, which is turned over from time to time as it cooks. It is left in the broth until nearly cool, then removed and the skin glazed with sesame oil. Once quite cooled, the meat is chopped into small pieces. The broth is reduced and thickened and then drizzled over the duck.

Foie Gras d'Oie aux Figues

Fattening geese with grain goes back to the ancient Egyptians but it was the Romans who singled out the liver. They fattened their geese with figs, and both the Italian and Spanish for liver (*fegato* and *higado*), still reflect this—*ficus* is Latin for fig. Both Romans and Jews spread their expertise throughout Europe, and centers of production emerged in Perigord, Hungary, and Strasbourg, where Jean-Pierre Clause famously produced "pâté de foie gras de Strasbourg" in the 18th and 19th centuries. Sealed in lard, it kept well and could be transported, even to America in the winter. This extraordinary delicacy is regarded by some as being cruel. Industrialized units mainly use ducks but, although many artisan duck producers still exist, foie gras from goose is preferable, not only for its superior flavor and texture, but also because industrialized geese are not commercially viable. Foie gras d'oie is one of life's gastronomic highlights. Freshly cooked, it melts into a semi-liquid. Preserved and served cool, it evokes Reverend Sydney Smith's 18th-century idea of heaven: "Foie gras to the sound of trumpets." The classic accompaniments are broiled fresh figs with their crunchy seeds, or fried apple, and chilled Sauternes wine.

Roast Goose

Roast goose, with its sensational frizzled skin and luscious dark meat, is savored with particular passion all over Europe, especially at Martinmas on November 11th, or the evening before. St. Martin, so the story goes, was betrayed by the cackling of geese when he hid to avoid being made a bishop.

The tradition of having a goose dinner goes back to the Middle Ages. With Christmas preceded by 40 days of Advent fasting, roast goose—in peak condition before the winter—was the preferred dish to bid farewell to meat. But November 11th is also the Feast of Bacchus, so hearty drinking and carnival spirits accompanied the succulent roast goose. In England until the early 20th century, it was served up at Christmas as well, and roast goose is traditional Hanukkah fare.

Its golden fat, so perfect for roasting potatoes, is released to crisp the skin, but even so, roast goose needs a sharp foil. Fluffy applesauce, and sage and onion stuffing make the perfect counterbalance.

Roast Goose with Caramelized Apples

1 (13 lb) goose, giblets and neck discarded

Salt

Freshly ground black pepper

3 cloves garlic, thinly sliced

8 Golden Delicious apples, peeled and quartered

$1/4$ cup fresh lemon juice

6 tbsp sugar

$1/4$ cup Calvados

$1^1/_2$ tsp ground cinnamon

Preheat the oven to 350°F.

Wash the goose inside and out and pat dry with paper towels. Season the bird generously with salt and pepper. Use a sharp knife to score the skin of the goose and insert slivers of garlic into the slits. Place the goose, breast side down, in a large roasting pan on the lowest shelf of the oven. Roast the bird for 2 hours 45 minutes, basting every 30 minutes or so, and draining the baking pan of excess fat.

Prepare the apples. Toss the quarters in lemon juice then place in a baking dish with 6 tablespoons drained goose fat and the sugar, Calvados and cinnamon. Stir well to coat the apple pieces and place the dish in the oven with the goose. Turn the goose over at this point so that it is breast side up and continue cooking for another 45 to 60 minutes. Check that the goose is cooked by inserting a metal skewer in the thigh at its thickest part. The juices should run clear.
Serves 8

Cassoulet

The origin of cassoulet remains hotly disputed. It has as many variations as places that claim its creation. But it is the variety of beans, the combination of meats, and the incredibly slow cooking that makes it so special. Renowned French chef Prosper Montagne recalls arriving at a Languedoc shoe-repair shop to find a notice saying "Closed because of cassoulet." The word "cassoulet" comes from *cassole* or *cassou*: the earthenware dish whose proportions are essential to the final cooking. It is crucial that the beans do not disintegrate on cooking and haricot beans are now favored, with connoisseurs preferring the Tarbais or Pamiers varieties. These are cooked slowly until soft. The meats are cooked separately, in goose fat. Toulouse cassoulet uses a combination of lamb and preserved goose, Castelnaudary's is all pork, Carcassonne's uses partridge, and many include Toulouse sausage.

The dish is usually assembled by placing half the beans over a layer of pork skin, then the meats on top, then the final layer of beans dredged with bread crumbs. This is cooked for at least three hours, during which time the bread crumbs and goose fat form a marvelous deep-brown crust over an unctuous interior infused with meat juices and fragrant with garlic.

Cassoulet

$3^2/_3$ cups dried white beans such as haricot or cannellini, picked over and rinsed

$1^1/_2$ lb boneless pork shoulder, cut into $^1/_2$-in thick slices

1 bouquet garni

1 cup chopped onions

1 medium carrot, cut into $^1/_2$-in pieces

2 tbsp finely chopped garlic, plus 2 cloves

2 tbsp olive oil

8 confit duck legs

3 sprigs of thyme

Salt

Freshly ground black pepper

1 lb cooked garlic pork sausage (not cured or dried), casing removed

For the bread-crumb topping:

2 tbsp olive oil

1 tbsp minced garlic

1½ cups coarse, fresh, white bread crumbs

Salt

Freshly ground black pepper

2 tbsp chopped fresh flat-leaf parsley

Cover the beans generously with cold water and soak overnight at room temperature. Drain and rinse. Fill a large, heavy pot with water (at least 16 cups), and simmer the pork shoulder with the bouquet garni for 1¼ hours. Skim the scum from the surface once or twice during cooking. Add the drained beans, onion, carrot, and chopped garlic and simmer, uncovered, for 45 minutes—the beans should be near tender, but not quite. Drain, reserving the liquid and discard the bouquet garni.

Preheat the oven to 375°F.

Heat 1 tablespoon of the olive oil in a roasting pan over high heat and brown the duck legs on all sides, working quickly to prevent burning. Set the duck legs aside, pour off excess fat from the roasting pan and cook the garlic cloves over low heat for 1 to 2 minutes. Remove from the heat.

Return the duck legs to the roasting pan, skin side up. Add the drained bean and pork mixture, spreading out in an even layer around the duck legs. Add the sprigs of thyme and 6 cups of the reserved cooking broth. Season generously with salt and pepper and bake, uncovered, on the middle rack of the preheated oven for 30 minutes.

Meanwhile, heat the remaining olive oil in a large skillet over high heat and quickly brown the garlic pork sausage on all sides. Once cool, cut the sausage crosswise into ½-inch slices. When the cassoulet has been cooking for 30 minutes, add the sausage slices and return to the oven for another 30 minutes.

To make the bread-crumb topping, heat the olive oil in a skillet over moderate heat. Cook the garlic for 1 minute, then add the bread crumbs and season to taste. Continue to cook for 4 to 5 minutes, to crispen the bread crumbs, then remove from the heat and stir in the parsley.

Remove the cassoulet from the oven and leave to stand for 10 minutes before serving with the bread-crumb topping. *Serves 8*

Woodcock and Snipe

Active at dusk and famously difficult to shoot, these birds have great cachet with the hunter—anyone who shoots two woodcock with a left and right shot is entitled to membership in the *Shooting Times* Woodcock Club. Unlike some other game birds, the custom is not to hang woodcock and snipe but to cook them fresh. They are plucked and the entrails are left inside the birds, though some people prefer to clean them.

Snipe are small and can be broiled, while woodcock are better roasted or, if serving them with the entrails, braised. After being browned, they are flambéed in brandy and simmered in a covered pot with shallots and white wine. When completely cooked and tender, the birds are removed and the entrails scooped out and mashed into the juices in the pan. This is reduced and the resulting pâté is spread on little croutons. Meat from the bird is placed on top and the combination of flavor, perfume, and texture, though difficult to express in words, is exquisite—quite out of this world and one of life's culinary triumphs.

Salmis de Sarcelles

Of all the game birds, many consider the teal—a tiny species of freshwater duck—to be the finest. Interestingly, the Catholic Church considered wild duck, and especially teal, to be *maigre* (lean) and therefore acceptable for fast days, perhaps because it is so lean compared to domestic duck, though it is hard to imagine anything so delicious constituting abstinence. A *salmis* is regarded as one of the best ways to serve teal, although it can be made from any game meat.

The essence of *salmis* is that the meat is first roasted but very undercooked. When it is warmed in its voluptuous sauce, it is crucial that the meat not be overheated, as this will make it rubbery.

To make the *salmis*, the teal are roasted to rare. The meat is removed and kept warm after being flambéed in cognac. Meanwhile, the carcasses are broken up and cooked with shallots, pepper, good red wine, and concentrated game broth. Once reduced, it is strained and thickened with butter. This is poured over the teal meat and served with a few slices of truffle and some cooked button mushrooms.

Spatchcocked Birds

The origin of the word "spatchcock" is slightly unclear but is thought to be an abbreviation of the Irish term "dispatch cock," which referred to a meal that had to be produced quickly—in other words, the hen was quickly killed, skinned, split, and roasted. A spatchcock is also a chicken of fewer than six weeks old, sometimes called a *poussin* or Cornish game hen.

Today, the word is associated with the method of splitting the bird down either side of the backbone and opening it out flat. Besides cooking more quickly than a whole bird, this techniques makes it easier to keep the breast meat moist. Very often the chef will stuff some softened vegetables, herbs, or cream cheese under the skin of the breast. In French, the method of flattening out is described as *à la crapaudine*, which means "like a toad." The birds are split down either side of the crown, then flattened out; they do indeed resemble a rather flat toad. The birds are broiled or grilled, and are ready in moments: delicious little morsels. Other small birds, such as pigeon and quail, are also successful spatchcocked.

Spatchcocked Birds

2 spatchcocked or butterflied chickens, Cornish game hens, or quail, marinated in: juice of 2 limes

2 tablespoons coriander seeds

Generous 1/3 cup peanut or vegetable oil

Good grinding of black pepper

To sprinkle over:

Maldon or other sea salt

Bunch of fresh cilantro, chopped

Set the birds in their marinade in a dish into which they fit snugly, cover with plastic wrap and leave in the refrigerator, preferably overnight or for 24 hours, though even a couple of hours would have an effect.

When the grill is good and hot, lift the birds out of their marinade and cook until the flesh has lost all raw pinkness but is still tender within and the skin is crisp and burnished and blistered. It's hard to be precise about times, since grills differ even more than ovens do, but on my grill—a gas-fired Outdoor Chef, which I love to distraction and, since it has a lid, I use even in the winter rain—the chicken takes about 35 minutes, the Cornish hens 15 and the quail about 7.

Along with sea salt, sprinkle freshly chopped parsley over the chicken and cilantro over the hens and quail, or use whatever other herb seems right for the marinades you've concocted. *Serves 4*

Adapted from Nigella Lawson's *Nigella Bites*

Quail

Quail are now reared in huge numbers, both for their meat and for their dainty, speckled eggs—another gastronomic treat, poached or hard-boiled. Initially, there was no need to rear them because astonishing numbers of migrating wild quail were regularly caught: Pliny wrote of a ship that overturned because of the numbers that rested on the rigging, and a 19th-century account mentions 40,000 being brought into Marseilles in just one boat. Quail are a popular restaurant choice, as they lend themselves to being boned out and broiled, spatchcocked and stuffed, truffled and perfumed with quince, and flambéed in brandy and braised. Many chefs love to wrap them in thin slices of bacon or pancetta, whose salty crispness complements the succulent flesh of the bird. Others surround them with piquant cherries, which nicely enhance their subtle flavor. They are remarkably resistant to drying out in the cooking, and are a favored lover's gift. One 18th-century recipe for a romantic dinner calls for a spirit lamp to cook the quail at the table, and enough champagne to simmer the quail and, presumably, intoxicate the diners.

Jugged Hare

There are two species of hare in Britain: the brown and the blue. It is the brown hare that fascinates people with its crazy spring mating behavior, and it has long been associated with witchcraft. However, in hunting and culinary terms, the brown hare was regarded as a noble beast, and its dense, lean, dark meat was formerly called venison. Jugged hare is a very ancient dish going back to the days before flour was used for thickening sauces.

The word "jugged" simply means meat that has been cooked in a lidded vessel or closed jar. The meat is jointed and slowly stewed with wine and a little dash of vinegar, some rich root vegetables, and some smoked bacon pieces. The distinctive characteristic of the dish is that the blood of the hare is collected and—along with the liver, which is pounded to a paste—is used to thicken the sauce at the end of the cooking time. The result is a very rich, dark stew; indeed the sauce is so dark that it almost looks as though the hare is coated in chocolate.

Hare in Chocolate Sauce

Serving game in a sauce enriched with chocolate is quite common in both Italy and Spain, where venison, pigeon, and partridge are similarly treated. When it arrived from the New World, chocolate was introduced as a rich, savory flavoring, as used in the mole sauces of Mexico. Consequently, any chocolate used in these sauces must be very dark, with little or no sugar. If bitter chocolate is not available, pure cocoa powder may be used instead.

There are two ways in which chocolate is served in a sauce. Sometimes the hare is stewed in wine and vegetables, with a small amount of chocolate melted in at the end, the chocolate adding the richness that the blood does in a civet. The other alternative is to reserve the saddle—the thighs can also be used if the hare is young. The forequarter is used to make a rich broth, which is concentrated by reducing it with wine. Shortly before serving, chocolate is melted into the sauce, but only a little, as it should not be apparent what has given the sauce its particular richness. The saddles are roasted and served pink, making this a much lighter way to enjoy a hare.

Lapin aux Pruneaux

Rabbit and prunes is one of those classic combinations that also works successfully with chicken, as in cock-a-leekie soup. The moist, sticky texture of the prunes and their tart sweetness are a perfect foil to both meats. In some recipes, the rabbit is soused in a sharp vinegary marinade before being slowly simmered. This produces a sweet-and-sour combination reminiscent of medieval dishes. However, the Belgians believe that the perfect rabbit and prune combination must include beer, for Belgium is famed for its hundreds of different beers. Many are slightly sweet, having been steeped with fruits, which makes them particularly suitable for cooking both sweet and savory dishes, adding a richness that is not cloying.

When substituting beer from other countries, care should be taken not to use one that is too bitter. If possible, find one that is slightly sweet, perhaps a white wheat beer. The rabbit pieces are gently browned with some onion and garlic, and then simmered in the beer. The prunes, previously soaked in beer, are added shortly before the end of the cooking time.

Rabbit in Garlic and Rosemary

Rabbits are native to Morocco and the Iberian Peninsula, and remained in the western Mediterranean until the 3rd century, when the Romans imported them to Italy as a source of meat. It was the Romans who perfected the use of warrens to contain them, although, as in Italy, when they were transported to other outposts of the Roman Empire, they eventually escaped and ran wild throughout the whole of Europe.

Originally a luxury, rabbit is now regarded as more lowly fare. Its meat is tender and white when young, and it is not unlike chicken, so many recipes can be adapted. Garlic and rosemary are one of the classic accompaniments. In Morocco, the rabbit, now usually domesticated, is cooked over a wood fire so that the skin is crisp and golden, aromatic with the scent of the herbs. In Italy, jointed pieces are baked in a large dish, scattered with garlic and rosemary, and drizzled with olive oil. Since this is very lean meat, it is crucial that rabbit cooked like this be served as soon as it is ready so that it does not toughen, but instead remains succulent and perfumed with sun-baked flavors.

Estouffade des Perdrix

Partridge with Sauerkraut

Lentils have been cultivated for at least 8,000 years. Known as *dhal* in India, they are as important a staple food as rice, and throughout the Middle East and Europe lentils appear in countless traditional dishes. Braised partridge with lentils—estouffade des perdrix—is especially popular in France and Spain. There are two species of European partridge: the red-legged or French partridge, and the gray or English partridge, which is thought to have a more interesting flavor. *Estouffade* means braised, so for this dish, the birds are first browned in oil and then they are simmered in broth with some nicely fatty smoked bacon. The Spanish add sherry and Seville oranges.

The correct lentils to use are the firm, greenish-gray Puy variety that keep their shape when cooked. They are simmered separately in broth with chopped garlic and onion, tomato paste, more of the smoked bacon, and a few cloves. Once the liquid has been absorbed, some lemon juice can be added to enliven the lentils. The broth from the partridge is degreased and reduced a little, and the partridges are served on top of the lentils.

The combination of partridge with cabbage is a dish that has crossed all European borders. One popular version makes use of both an old and a young partridge. The old one is very gently stewed with the cabbage and sometimes a pungent country sausage. Then, once it has imparted its flavor, the old partridge is removed and replaced with the tender young partridge, which has been freshly roasted.

Sauerkraut (called *choucroûte* in Alsace and Lorraine, France), with its slightly sour, fermented taste, is a wonderful accompaniment to game birds. Making sauerkraut is a lengthy process, but, fortunately, good sauerkraut is readily available for purchase.

For this dish, it is gently cooked in broth and smoked bacon, and the partridge is roasted separately or simmered in butter and served on top of a mound of this masterpiece. The two ingredients that lift the dish into the sublime are the addition of some crushed juniper berries and a dash of kirsch, which aids digestion.

Game Pâtés and Terrines

The complex flavors of game are particularly well suited to terrines and pâtés. To keep them moist, lubricating ingredients are introduced: butter, pork fat, or bread crumbs soaked in cream. The dishes' names indicate how finely the meats are cut. *Galantines* have chunks of meat bound with forcemeat and wrapped in bacon. *Terrines* are made from coarse-ground meat, fat, and seasonings, and, like meat loaf, are baked in a covered dish that replaces the pastry crust of old. *Rillettes* are shredded meat and fat pressed into a mold. *Pâtés* are the smoothest, their ingredients pounded to a paste as smooth and creamy as butter. An especially elaborate galantine of game was a favorite of Brillat-Savarin, the 19th-century "Philosopher in the Kitchen," and was often served by his mother, Aurore. A boned pheasant is stuffed with a whole goose liver and two magnificent forcemeats. One is made of wild rabbit, pheasant, pork, goose, and fat bacon. The other is made of woodcock, pheasant and chicken livers, mushrooms, and shallots, all pounded together. The stuffed pheasant is rolled up and cooked in a rich puff pastry, its plump square shape earning it the name *"L'Oreiller de la Belle Aurore"* (Fair Aurora's Pillow).

Pigeon Pie

Pigeons have been kept in dovecotes for hundreds of years, the plump, young squabs cooked for the table, and their droppings used in the manufacture of gunpowder. But abundant populations of wild pigeons provided cheap food for anyone who could catch them. Pigeon pie is one of those satisfying dishes associated with the rural idyll of the well-stocked farmhouse larder. Because it is dense and very lean, pigeon is best cooked very gently, submerged in liquid.

Mrs. Beeton's classic Epsom Grand-Stand recipe uses slabs of fat beef to line the pie dish. Each whole pigeon has a knob of butter placed inside and a layer of ham to cover it, then it is baked slowly, with broth, mace, and egg yolks, under a decorated puff-pastry crust. Other people prefer to bone the meat before baking the pie.

Completely different is *pastilla*—a favorite festive dish in Morocco. This sweet-savory pie is made from pigeon slowly simmered with onions, saffron, cumin, and ground coriander. The bones are removed and the meat is cooked in phyllo pastry layered with crushed, sweetened almonds, parsley, and hard-boiled eggs. Finally, it is dredged with powdered sugar and cinnamon.

El Hamam del Aroussa

The name of this dish translates as "the bride's pigeons." On their wedding night, Moroccan Jewish couples are traditionally served two plump little pigeons, stuffed with rich sweetmeats. This is to encourage a life full of love and sweetness ahead. But many think they are too delicious to be restricted to newlyweds. For the perfect dish, very young pigeons are needed for their delicate, tender flesh that has a fine coating of fat. Young pigeons are also called squabs or *pigeonneau*, though baby chicken or quail is also ideal.

As well as making it go further, stuffing a bird always turns it into a festive dish, particularly if it has been boned out first. These little birds are stuffed with a basic mixture of onion and cooked rice that has been enriched with ground beef or veal, chopped prunes, apricots, raisins, walnuts, and almonds. These are flavored with pepper, mace, nutmeg, ginger, and cinnamon. While they cook, a sauce is prepared from cooked onions seasoned with pepper and mace. Honey and lemon balance the sweet-and-sour element, and saffron adds its luxurious color and fragrance. The pigeons are garnished with fried almonds; in many cultures, almonds are fertility symbols.

Roast Pheasant with all the Trimmings

Until the 16th century, pheasants were raised like chickens for the table. Their tender, white flesh was particularly appreciated in the Renaissance—Henry VIII employed a French priest to supervise the pheasants for his banquets. A perfectly roasted brace of pheasant is one of life's gastronomic indulgences.

Like many simple treats, timing is everything, as overcooking dries out the meat. The skin is dredged with flour before cooking to produce a fizzled coating that covers a moist, succulent interior. The traditional trimmings are simple too. Strips of fatty bacon are either placed over the breast, or rolled up and cooked alongside the birds. Clear gravy is prepared from game broth. Good-quality bread crumbs are fried in butter until crisp and deeply golden. And finally, the bread sauce, which prompted the apocryphal French remark, "The English have sixty religions but only one sauce." This, however, denies the honorable ancestry of bread sauce, which goes back to the finest medieval cooking. The perfect example is a smooth, creamy sauce, with subtle but distinct flavorings of cloves, onion, mace, and bay leaf that cannot be bettered; it partners perfectly with pheasant.

Faisan Normand

As with many classic dishes, the variations on faisan Normand are endless, and it has been successfully adapted to chicken as well. Renowned French epicure, Brillat-Savarin, declared that of all birds, it is the pheasant that benefits most from delicate hanging; he called this maturing process *faisandage*.

Normandy is a lush region producing superb butter and cream, as well as many apple varieties that are used for cider and Calvados (apple brandy). In many Norman restaurants, one is offered *un coup Normand*, which is a shot of Calvados to settle the stomach before continuing with further courses. These are the constituents of faisan Normand.

To make the dish, the apples are peeled, cored, cut into segments, and browned in butter. Then the pheasant is jointed and browned. These are put in a casserole and seasoned, sprinkled with cream, and baked. The juices are strained off and flamed in Calvados, and then more cream is added. This marvelous rich sauce is reduced before pouring it over the apples and pheasant. Some versions serve the sautéed apples separately as a side dish.

Guinea Fowl with Lemon and Herbs

This is a delightfully refreshing way to enjoy guinea fowl and is also good with chicken. Some regard guinea fowl as game and therefore a winter dish, but the majority of guinea fowl are domesticated; the Belgians, always passionate about their food, rear huge numbers. The meat is a little firmer than chicken, and the drumsticks are free of the sinew that mars those of a pheasant.

Guinea fowl are available all year round, so this dish is a lovely summer one that makes use of all the fresh herbs that have soaked up the sun to yield their full flavor.

The bird is cut into joints and marinated with shallots, lemon juice, and sliced mushrooms. Then the joints are removed and browned in butter. Thick cream is added, and the pan is covered. When the meat is nearly cooked, the lemony mushrooms are added, along with three large handfuls of chopped fresh herbs. These can include thyme, lemon balm, marjoram, tarragon, parsley, chives, or chervil. The dish is ready within a few minutes, when the mushrooms are cooked, the herbs are softened but still fresh and bright, and the lemon-flavored cream sauce is a luscious golden brown.

Stuffed Guinea Fowl

Guinea fowl, with their beautifully speckled black plumage, originate from Ethiopia. The Romans imported them as opulent luxuries for their banquets. But Victorian gamekeepers in Britain made use of their loud alarm call to guard their pheasant coverts. It was the French who really took to guinea fowl (*pintade*), rearing them in great numbers ever since the 15th century, though today most come from Belgium.

The flesh of the guinea fowl is a perfect introduction to game; it is stronger in flavor than chicken but milder than pheasant. For that reason, its sauces and spicing can be gentler than for other game birds. Delicious examples include an orange and thyme stuffing that is bound with cream, egg, and fine bread crumbs; an asparagus and lemon stuffing; a bulgur wheat, juniper, and smoked bacon stuffing; or one made of softened shallots, mushrooms, ground walnuts, and apple. These are cooked inside the bird, which is often boned out for easier carving. However, stuffing may also be placed under the skin of the breast so that the flavors permeate the meat. Try one made of goat's-milk cheese and sage, or lemon, garlic, tarragon, and finely chopped mushroom.

Roast Grouse

The red grouse is unique to the United Kingdom, but it is a distant relation of the partridge, and similar species such as the willow grouse are found in Scandinavia. Red grouse feed on the growing tips of the purple heather that covers the Highlands of Scotland in summer. The other main population of grouse is found on the Yorkshire moors—also clad in heather. Many connoisseurs regard the flavor of grouse to be the best of all the game birds, and the heather tips undoubtedly lend a characteristic edge.

On the "Glorious Twelfth" of August—the start of the shooting season—there is a long tradition of rushing the first birds to restaurants in London and New York, where they are served that evening. This gimmick is a bit of a waste, as grouse is better hung for a day or two. The flesh is dark and filling, and its flavor unique, so it needs little adornment other than thin, clear gravy that is sometimes sweetened with heather honey and a dash of whisky. Watercress and game chips—deep-fried thin slices or matchsticks of potato—are the usual accompaniments.

Tjalknöl

The Swedes eat more venison that any other nation. Their most common species is the huge elk (known as moose in North America), but the smaller reindeer (caribou) is also popular. Tjalknöl is a great favorite for parties and is a traditional treat over the Christmas period. Large joints from the elk are perfect for large gatherings.

The name comes from *tjale*, which is the hard frozen winter soil, and *knoll*, which means a round lump. This is because the meat is cooked from frozen. A large joint of around 6 pounds is placed in a very low oven for 12 hours or so, until the temperature in the center reaches 150°F. Meanwhile, some brine is made; this is flavored with juniper, bay leaf, and pepper and left to cool. The hot meat is completely submerged in the brine and left to cool down and cure for about 5 hours. Then it is very thinly sliced and served as part of a huge buffet. Cold potato and onion salad and hot *gratin dauphinoise* are both favorite accompaniments, as are lightly pickled vegetables.

Venison Biryani

From 1834 onward, about 500,000 indentured Indians arrived in Mauritius, mainly from the northern regions of Bihar and Uttar Pradesh. In addition to bringing their language with them, they also brought their local dishes, and the biryani was one of these. But Mauritius is also a former French colony, and it was the French who introduced deer to the island for their gastronomic and hunting pleasure. Mauritians are particularly fond of venison and wherever they are in the world, they seek it out for their special celebrations.

In India, the best biryanis are delicate and subtly flavored. The meat is marinated in tenderizing ingredients like garlic or yogurt, and partially cooked. Then it is placed in layers with part-cooked rice, the lid is sealed, and it is cooked slowly and gently.

The secret lies in careful timing so that the meat is cooked through but the rice is not overdone. In Mauritius, as in South Africa, biryanis are much more robustly spiced, and tend to use potatoes rather than rice. The carefully cooked dish is brought to the table, where the lid is raised to release a burst of fragrant spicy aroma—a joyous dish indeed.

Roast Haunch of Venison

Originally the meat from royal forests, venison has long been held in the highest esteem. It was favored as a prestigious gift, as feasting food, and as a potent gift of lovers. Henry VIII sent some venison to Anne Boleyn when he was wooing her, making his intentions quite plain in his accompanying note. Roast haunch of venison, cooked on the spit in front of a brisk fire, was the choicest of dishes. Originally, a haunch included both the back and the hind leg, but now it means just the hind leg and the back is called the saddle. Of the two, the saddle is slightly more tender, but the haunch is bigger and perfect for entertaining large numbers. As with any lean game meat, venison should be served rare or medium, never well done. To achieve this, it should be part-roasted and then left to rest. Slowly braised venison joints are also delicious, but these should be larded to keep the well-done meat moist. Creamy sauces accompany venison really well, as do reduction sauces made with broth and wine. Fruits such as pears or red currants are often served alongside; their tart sweetness is a perfect foil to this sensational meat.

Fusion Venison

The worldwide renaissance of venison is in large part due to the zeal of deer farmers in Britain, America, and especially New Zealand. For the last twenty years, teams of New Zealand chefs have traveled the world to spread their culinary expertise. Eager to move venison away from its heavy traditional recipes, they have devised a fresh approach, using exciting combinations of Asian and European ingredients. Not surprisingly, international chefs have taken up the challenge to produce a raft of experimental dishes. Some of these fuse different combinations of cooking styles such as rare roast venison served with slowly braised osso buco. Others fuse cultures, such as chunks of sautéed venison with a green curry sauce. Yet others combine different meats: plump venison medallions with slivers of foie gras and a confit of celeriac perfumed with Szechuan pepper. Bright, refreshing flavors like slices of smoked venison with horseradish sauce, or carpaccio of venison with blackened asparagus, Parmesan, and truffle oil dressing, and unexpected textures such as venison haggis with red bell pepper and onion relish, are the hallmark of these innovative dishes.

Venison Casserole

This is one of the easiest and, consequently, most popular ways of cooking venison, especially when catering for large gatherings, since a venison casserole—or stew—is one of those dishes that only improves from being made the day before. There are endless permutations of venison casserole, but the most successful are those that use ingredients that complement venison's taste and texture. Flavors that go well with its richness fall into three categories: sweet—prunes, cider, carrots, wine; savory—celery, fennel, onion, walnuts, beer; and spicy—cumin, paprika, ginger, whole-grain mustard. Because a casserole is cooked long and slow, and venison is very lean with no fat, ingredients such as onions, eggplant, prunes, or mushrooms lend all-important luscious succulence to the dish. Eastern Europeans love to make fluffy dumplings to cook in the fabulous rich gravy. Others prefer to serve potatoes, perhaps roasted, perhaps in a creamy *gratin dauphinoise*, or perhaps as crisp hasselback potatoes (partly-sliced, drizzled with oil or butter, and roasted to produce a fan shape).

Venison Pasty with Cumberland Sauce

In the days before refrigeration, when people wanted to send a gift of venison, a pasty—a savory turnover—was often the safest way to send it. There are accounts of venison pasties being sent up and down the country, and even across the North Sea from England to Antwerp in the 16th century for a wedding.

The celebrated diarist Samuel Pepys mentions venison 76 times as opposed to only 40 references to beef. Of those 76 venison entries, 50 were for venison pasties. Fond of them as he was, he once describes feeling "cloyed, having been at five pasties in three days; viz two at our own feast and one yesterday and two today." Sometimes pasties were dish pies with pastry above and below the rich meat; these were served piping hot. Sometimes they were huge raised pies with immensely thick, inedible crusts to preserve the contents and withstand traveling. These were usually served cold, with a sharp sauce such as the classic Cumberland sauce, made from grated orange peel, port, sharp jelly, cinnamon, and ginger, all melted together and then allowed to cool and thicken before serving with the pasty.

Venison Steaks

The word venison—from the Latin *venare* (to hunt)—was used to describe the "noble" beasts of the chase. These included wild boar, hare, and deer, but now venison is reserved exclusively for the meat of deer. Populations of deer are increasing rapidly in many countries, including the United States, so venison is more widely available than it was. The efforts of deer farmers to promote this exceptionally delicious, lean, and tender meat have also borne fruit. Although often thought of as a winter food, it is a refreshing summer meat because it has almost no marbling fat. The best steaks for grilling, broiling, barbecuing, and frying come from the loin, though the haunch—back leg—is also excellent as long as the deer is young. Because of their leanness, venison steaks should not be cooked past the pink stage, otherwise they dry out. The easiest way to achieve this is to undercook the steaks then let them rest a moment. The meat is juicy and almost melts in the mouth. A tart jelly goes well with venison steaks, as does hollandaise sauce.

Warm Pigeon Salad

Pigeon meat is exceptionally dark and fine-grained, with no marbling of fat. Like other lean game meats, it is at its best either braised or stewed very slowly or served quite pink. Each method provides an excellent version of a warm pigeon salad.

The first manner of preparation is from Sicily, and is also a good way to treat partridge, wild duck, or pheasant if its age is unknown. The bird is immersed, breast side down, and simmered very slowly with vegetables such as onions or celery. Vinaigrette is prepared using good oil, mild vinegar or lemon juice, and herbs and spices suitable for the bird—mustard, thyme, orange peel. When cooked, the meat is slashed or pierced, and immersed in the vinaigrette until cool. The most tender meat is removed and scattered, with the vinaigrette and fried pine nuts, over mixed herbs and salad leaves.

The alternative method is to remove the pigeon breasts and briefly roast or fry them, leaving them to rest and cool so that they are really pink and juicy. They are then thinly sliced and served over a dressed salad with a little spiced chutney.

Boar's Head

With its ferocious tusks and muscular speed, the wild boar has always earned respect from hunters. Depictions of wild boar adorn Celtic bronze instruments, medieval paintings, Renaissance tapestries, and Asian hunting miniatures. And, like many respected savage creatures, they were made part of the ritual of the feast. Two English university colleges have traditional Christmas feasts in which a decorated boar's head is brought in as part of the ritual. The feast at Queen's College, Oxford, goes back to 1340 while St John's College, Cambridge, started theirs in 1604. Today, wild boar feasts are held all over the world. The boar's tusks are gilded, its head is decorated and garlanded with evergreens such as holly, bay leaves, and rosemary, and a golden orange is placed in its snarling mouth; all this supposedly represents the Christ child triumphing over sin, though the pagan origins are all too clear. As a general rule, the boar's head is not actually eaten, but in fact there are many choice pieces such as the tongue and the cheeks (sometimes made into Bath chaps), and a powerful headcheese can be made of the rest; all excellent winter fare.

Wild Boar Sausages

Despite the efforts of hunters and farmers, wild boar are increasing throughout central and southern Europe. The vast forests of central Europe accommodate them without trouble, but in many countries they cause great damage to crops and vineyards, plowing the soil with their razor-sharp tusks. Even in England, where wild boar have been extinct for some centuries—a friend of Henry III ate the last twelve from the forest of Dean in 1260 —wild boar are re-establishing populations with escapees from recently established farms. Such muscular and vigorous creatures need to be young to provide tender meat, hence the boar farms.

Traditional recipes either stipulate young boar (*marcassin* in French, *cingialetto* in Italian) or advise cooking the older *sanglier* and *cinghiale* very slowly in marinade ingredients (one Spanish recipe successfully uses Coca-Cola to tenderize it). The other option is to mince the meat and make it into sauces and ragouts, or into sausages. There are many splendid continental wild boar *saucisson*- and *salame*-style sausages, including punchy little *salamini di cinghiale* that are preserved in jars of brine or oil. And there are hosts of excellent fresh sausage recipes, the deep-flavored meat requiring robust spicing.

Short Ribs

Short ribs come from the forward quarter of the cow and therefore are subject to a lot of work (all that bending to chomp tuft after tuft of grass). As a result, they are tougher and fattier than other cuts.

Slow cooking, using low heat, takes care of the problem. There are two ways to go: wet or dry. The wet method, or braising, offers the opportunity to add a lot of flavor through the braising liquid. This includes broth, wine, crushed tomatoes, and seasonings. When short ribs are cooked dry, the flavor will be derived from the spices rubbed on the outside of the meat or, in the case of smoking, from the kind of wood chosen to burn.

Barbecued Beef Brisket

When you have lemons, you make lemonade. When you have beef brisket, you make barbecue. The brisket is a much maligned cut of the cow, generally quite fatty and tough if not cooked properly. Barbecuing is a popular method in the United States and, in particular, the state of Texas, where beef is an important part of the economy and culture.

There are two principal methods to achieving the barbecue effect, one with smoke, the other without. With the former, the cook must leave intact the thick layer of fat that covers one side of the brisket. This will baste the meat as it cooks slowly over a combination of coals and mesquite wood. Cooking time will run into several hours, during which time the meat will tenderize, the fat will render, and the smoke from the burning mesquite will penetrate deeply into the brisket, leaving its distinctive, unforgettable flavor. Additional flavor is imparted by applying a rub of spices before cooking and by basting hourly with seasoned liquid.

The same rub can be applied to the meat using the wet method. In this case, the brisket is trimmed of the outer layer of fat and cooked, covered, in a slow oven for several hours. Before serving, the brisket is sliced and then returned to the oven sodden with sweet barbecue sauce.

Barnsley Chops

Barnsley, a coal-mining town in northern England, gave its name to these succulent lamb chops when a local restaurant put them on the menu and thus entered the pantheon of prized foods named for a place (think New York strip steaks or Malpeque oysters).

The cut is taken from the loins, making for a single giant piece of meat, with the bone in the middle. They are prepared like a regular lamb chop: seasoned, then broiled or grilled with high heat, perhaps served with a slightly acidic sauce to offset the slight greasiness of the lamb. The bone adds weight and a convenient place to grasp the chop, first with tongs while grilling, then with fingers while eating. Traditional sides include that very English accompaniment, chips.

Barnsley Chops with Red Currant Sauce

½ cup red currant jelly

1 glass of port

4 Barnsely chops

Oil for brushing

Heat the red currant jelly in a saucepan over low heat until melted. Add the port and bring to a boil. After 5 minutes, reduce the heat while you prepare the chops. Brush the lamb with oil and broil for 8 to 9 minutes, turning occasionally, until brown on the outside but slightly pink in the middle. Serve hot with the sauce. *Serves 2*

Beef Bulgogi

Beef bulgogi, which translates as "fire meat" in Korean, begins with a simple marinade of readily available Asian ingredients: soy sauce, mirin, sesame oil, sesame seeds, garlic, ginger, and sugar.

The beef should be a tender cut such as sirloin or rib eye. Before spending several hours soaking up the flavors of the marinade, the beef receives a good pounding from the side of a heavy knife. This not only tenderizes the meat but, because the piece is flat,

ensures a relatively short cooking time. Some recipes suggest that the meat should be sliced thinly and then stir-fried. Others direct the chef to cook the meat on a very hot broiler and slice the meat after it is cooked. This second method produces more memorable results.

Although it's not strictly traditional to do so, the marinade can also be used as a dipping sauce. It is heated and reduced while the meat cooks and served warm, along with a mound of fragrant rice.

Beef Wellington

The connection with the Duke who defeated
Napoleon at Waterloo is somewhat nebulous
(some suggest it was a favorite dinner, others
point to an enterprising French chef looking
to cash in on someone else's celebrity). Either
way, the dish is not to be taken lightly. For
one, the ingredients—filet of beef, truffles,
foie gras—are among the most expensive in
their categories. But fear not, a poor man's
version—using pâté derived from duck, goose,
or chicken liver and wild mushrooms—still
makes for a spectacular meal.

The beef is slathered in pâté and stewed
mushrooms (or shaved truffles) and then
wrapped tightly in a sheet of buttery puff
pastry. In a medium-hot oven, the meat and
pastry will cook simultaneously, the latter
turning brown and crusty, the former to
perfect pinkness. Juices from the beef are
retained by the protective layer of the pastry
and mingle with the pâté and mushrooms
to provide a sublime flavor with a measured
addition of texture.

Beef Wellington

1 tbsp vegetable oil

1 tbsp butter

3 lb filet of beef

3 cups sliced button mushrooms

1/4 cup butter

3/4 cup liver pâté

13 oz puff pastry

1 egg, beaten

Preheat oven to 425°F.

Heat the oil and 1 tablespoon butter in
a large frying pan. Sear the beef in the hot
fat so it is lightly colored all over. Transfer
the beef to a roasting pan and roast for
20 minutes. After removing the beef from the
oven, let it cool down. Fry the mushrooms in
the 1/4 cup butter until they are soft, then set
them aside to cool. Mix them with the pâté.

Roll the pastry out into a rectangular
shape, about 1/4 inch thick. Spread the pâté
and mushroom mixture over the pastry to
within 1 inch of the edge. Set the meat on
top, centering it. Brush the edges of the
pastry with some of the egg.

Fold the pastry over the beef, turning
in the ends and folding the edges under
the meat. Set it on a baking sheet, with the
seamed side down. Brush with the remaining
egg. Bake for 50 to 60 minutes, covering
with foil after 25 minutes.

Let the cooked meat rest for 10 minutes
before serving. *Serves 8*

Red Beef Curry

One of the anchors of Thai cuisine, red beef curry is loved wherever Thai food is served. A hot bowl of it will bring aromas of pungent spice, rich creamy coconut, and fresh cilantro. Laden with sauce, the dish can be served over rice, allowing the flavor to melt into each grain. The color comes from the use of red chiles, which tend to be quite spicy on their own. They are ground into a paste with several other ingredients such as shallots, garlic, *galangal* (a relative of ginger with a pungent, earthy flavor), lemongrass, cilantro root, peppercorns, coriander, salt, shrimp paste, and kaffir lime zest—which mitigates the burn of the chili. As a result of the long list of ingredients and the time it takes to gather and prepare them, most curry pastes are purchased commercially. Coconut milk, another key ingredient, also tends to cool a paste down to edible levels. A final necessary ingredient is fish sauce, a strong-flavored, salty fermentation. Thinly sliced beef is quick-fried, then united with the sauce, forming a most delicious partnership.

Kobe Beef

Sizzling Beef

In Japan, Kobe beef fetches top dollar and is viewed as the pinnacle for beef lovers everywhere. It is tender and flavorful and delivers big doses of *umami*—a taste described as pungent, delicious, savory, and meaty.

What makes Kobe beef so special is the cow, the black Tajima-ushi breed of Wagyu cattle. They are raised primarily in the Hyogo prefecture of which the city of Kobe is the capital. Japanese beef production has always been low (beef was banned between 1603 and 1867, and was rare for several centuries before that). As a result, Japanese breeds have been raised in relative isolation and maintained characteristics that were bred out of more common and widespread breeds. Kobe cows are fed beer and given massages, the former to stimulate appetite, the latter to keep the cow relaxed. Their coats are brushed with sake to improve their appearance. The farming authorities of Kobe have tried to protect the brand, but Wagyu cattle are raised today around the world for domestic markets.

Regardless of cut, Kobe beef displays outstanding marbling—tiny granules of fat are distributed throughout the flesh that melt with the heat of cooking to keep the beef from becoming dry and to distribute flavor. Even the lowly meatloaf becomes an event when made with Kobe beef. A rib eye is worthy of celebration.

Living up to its tempting name, sizzling beef is an Asian-influenced dish with as delicious a bark as its bite. The beef used is a tender cut, either filet, rib eye, or strip loin. Sliced in bite-sized thin strips, it is marinated for several hours in a combination of flavors that will vary from kitchen to kitchen but should always have elements of sweet (from sugar, *char sui*—Chinese barbecue sauce—or oyster sauce), salt (soy or salt itself), and acid (wine or rice wine vinegar).

From there, the cook must work quickly. Thin slices of ginger, mashed garlic, and onions are stir-fried in a smoking-hot wok or pan, followed soon after by the beef. It will cook in seconds. So much for the steak, now the sizzle. This comes from a cast-iron platter heated in the oven before the beef goes into the wok. When done, the meat and other ingredients are transferred to the hot platter and then drizzled with some of the marinade. As the marinade hits the surface of the platter, it pops and sizzles in a most appetizing way.

Ulster Fry

The classic hangover breakfast, Ulster fry is a cornucopia of greasy food. This is no insult. Aficionados of the meal (of which there are many) wouldn't have it any other way. Demand for it is such that most restaurants that serve it keep it on the menu all day.

This classic breakfast offers the muddled mind an easy choice, as it contains all the elements to a fantastic, quick, and simple meal: salty bacon and savory sausage, fresh eggs, juicy tomato, and slightly dense fried potato sop up what doesn't make it to the fork. Even the most inept cook can make it, and all of it can be cooked in a single frying pan on a single element so even the most under-equipped kitchen is sufficient.

Boeuf à la Mode

This warm and comforting dish is given an especially French flair with the use of good, young red wine for both the marinade and the braising liquid. It begins with a piece of meat suitable for braising, a sirloin tip or rump roast, for example. The beef may spend a night in a marinade of red wine, olive oil, garlic, and seasoning. While this step is optional, the big, dense piece of meat must remain immersed for at least 12 hours to be effective, if not twice as long.

Another precooking option is larding, the practice of inserting strips of fresh pork fat into the meat that will baste the interior of the roast as it melts. Cooking the dish starts with browning the meat in hot oil, creating a lovely crust and plenty of flavor for the subsequent sauce. Then vegetables—carrots, celery, and onions—are added with wine and broth and the pot is deglazed (adding a liquid and boiling vigorously), releasing beefy goodness into the liquid.

The sauce may be enriched and given further body by the addition of cracked veal knuckle, split calf's foot, and pork rind. Classic aromatic vegetables—carrots, celery, onion— also go in the pot but are usually mushy and unattractive by the time the roast is cooked. A more appealing side dish is a big mound of buttery mashed potatoes.

Boeuf à la Bourguignon

Perhaps the highest form beef stew can take, this classic French dish was popularized by Julia Child when she taught Americans about mastering the art of French cooking.

It is a dish that fills a room with wonderful aromas as it slowly cooks in the oven and can be prepared well in advance of serving. For this reason, it is perfect for large dinner parties where the host's attention will be required outside the kitchen.

It begins with smoked bacon, which is first boiled and then browned. Then the cubed stewing beef is browned and some veggies are added, then the whole stew gets doused in beef broth and red wine. This is one of the times when the culinary adage about only cooking with wine that you would be happy to drink should be followed. Much of the flavor in the dish will come from the wine and so it ought to be good.

Meat on the Bone

Leaving meat on the bone provides structure that is otherwise left to several lengths of butcher string; they also add flavor in the same way that bones give flavor to water when preparing broths; and perhaps best of all, they make for delicious gnawing.

Roast beef and Yorkshire pudding is an English Sunday-lunch classic. A well-aged, well-marbled, multi-rib roast is a magnificent sight. The fat on the outer layer of the beef should be left intact or supplemented with a piece of suet as the melted fat eventually becomes the cooking agent for the puddings. These are made from a simple mixture of flour, milk, eggs, and salt. The hot fat is poured into a baking pan or a muffin pan and then heated in a very hot oven until it reaches the smoking point. When the batter hits the hot fat, it puffs up to three or four times its original volume.

While the Yorkies cook, the beef is sliced into thick slabs and put on the diners' plates. The pudding goes alongside and both are best when drizzled with pan gravy.

Osso buco, a dish with Milanese roots, is one of those dishes whose flavor benefits enormously from the presence of bones during cooking. The main ingredient is veal shank, cut into thick rounds with the bone in as the center. These are simmered in wine, stock, tomato paste, and seasoning until the meat is cooked through and falling off the bone. Traditionally, the dish is finished with a sprinkling of *gremolata*, a mix of grated lemon zest and finely chopped parsley.

It is not strictly necessary to leave the bone in a **leg of lamb**. Leg of lamb should be cooked rare, meaning the bone has little time to contribute to the flavor. Yet compare the look of both. A full leg of lamb has a noble aspect whereas a deboned leg resembles a well-worn balled up sweater. Lamb has a strong taste, especially in the skin, which, when liberally seasoned and cooked crisp, is a fabulous greasy treat.

Full-sized and tied in a ring, the regal **crown pork roast** is a spectacular sight. More modest cuts, say four ribs' worth, are nevertheless just as delicious. Cut from the loin, pork roast combines meat and fat in perfect proportions.

Osso Buco in Bianco

⅓ cup butter

3 tbsp olive oil

2 to 3 lb veal shanks

Salt

Freshly ground black pepper

Flour

2 cups chicken broth

1 cup dry white wine

Grated rind of 1 lemon

1 tbsp chopped parsley

In a large frying pan, heat the butter and olive oil until they begin to froth. Season the veal with salt and pepper and dip the pieces lightly into the flour, shaking off excess.

Put the veal pieces in the frying pan, and fry on both sides until they are golden.

Add about a cup of chicken broth and all the wine, then turn down the heat after the liquid has started to boil. Partially cover the pan and simmer gently. When the liquid has reduced by about half, turn the meat over and add a little more broth. Partially cover and leave on the heat for a further half hour. Check the liquid during cooking and add more broth if needed. After a total cooking time of 1 ½ hours, the meat should be very tender and the liquid a golden color. Transfer to a hot shallow serving dish and sprinkle with lemon rind and parsley (*gremolata*).

Serves 4

Irish Stew

This filling, hearty dish has always been a favorite, and pots full of Irish stew have been steaming somewhere on the island for several centuries. It is made from the meat of mutton, which has always been plentiful in Ireland due to the importance of the wool industry.

Using meat from the neck, the mutton is browned in a pot with hot fat. Traditionally, the only other ingredients are potatoes, onions, and water. With the migration of Irish to North America in the 19th century, the stew evolved depending on what ingredients were available locally. Beef sometimes substitutes for mutton and other root vegetables—carrots and parsnips; as well,

barley may be added to the mix (though traditionalists would object). Even the water has been subject to replacement, though certainly the choice liquid—a bottle or two of Guinness—will not diminish the flavor.

Irish Stew

1½ lb middle neck of lamb, cut into cutlets

½ cup unsalted butter

4 onions, sliced

1 lb potatoes, peeled and cut into 1-in dice

1 clove garlic

1 bouquet garni

5 cups chicken broth or water

½ lb carrots, diced

6 celery stalks, cut into 1-in dice

½ lb savoy cabbage, shredded

Salt

Freshly ground white pepper

2 tsp chopped fresh parsley

Put the meat in a large pan, cover with cold water, and bring to a boil. Drain off the water and run cold water over the meat. Drain well.

Melt the butter in a large braising pan and add the sliced onions, half the diced potatoes, and the garlic. Add the bouquet garni to the pan and sweat for 2 minutes. Add the lamb cutlets and cover with the chicken broth. Bring the broth to a simmer, cover, and cook for 30 minutes. The meat will be half-cooked and the potatoes will have started to purée and thicken the broth. Add the diced carrots and continue to cook for a further 10 minutes. Add the remaining potatoes and the diced celery, and cook for 15 to 20 minutes. At this stage we do not want to purée the potatoes but just cook them until soft. Add the cabbage and cook for a further 2 to 3 minutes until the meat and vegetables are tender. Season with salt and pepper, remove the bouquet garni, and serve in individual bowls or one large bowl. Finish with the chopped parsley. You now have a complete meal. *Serves 4*

Adapted from Gary Rhodes' *Rhodes Around Britain*

Pork and Beans

Pork and beans evoke a number of images: of the weather-beaten bum, camped below a railroad overpass, heating a can of pork and beans over an open flame; of the Boy Scout troop mixing up a batch deep in the woods; of soldiers in foxholes, getting some nourishment after a day in battle.

Pork and beans were among the first foods to take advantage of canning technology; the first cans were made for fishermen on lengthy forays to sea in 1875.

Today, many take advantage of the convenience of the canned product, but it is worthwhile preparing the dish from scratch, too. There are dozens of recipes, but all call for salt pork for meat. The beans are generally white or navy beans but this is by no means a regulation. The sauce in which both pork and beans cook is a combination of acidic tomatoes and sweet brown sugar or molasses.

Pork and beans benefit from a slow cooking and are tastier the day after they were made, making them a natural and most successful candidate for canning.

Cornish Pasty

Dating back to the Middle Ages, pasties have a long history in English cooking. Several different versions have been invented and evolved over those years but the basic formula of meat and vegetables baked inside a pastry shell remains constant. Cornish pasties, originating among the Cornish not only in England but also in places they migrated to over the years, are by far the best known of the lot. They began as food for miners; the crust in these early versions was too tough to eat and was used in a similar fashion to a Thermos to keep the insides warm until lunch while the miners dug out the coal.

Cornish pasties are marked by their oval shape and the pastry seam that runs the length of the pie. Traditionally, they hold meat, potatoes, and onions, all of which are uncooked when they fill the pastry. The juices from the meat and vegetables are released with the heat and form a rich gravy.

Cornish Pasty

1½ cups flour
A pinch of salt
½ cup mixture of lard and butter
Water
½ lb steak, cut into small cubes
2 large potatoes, peeled and thinly sliced
¼ cup diced rutabaga
1 onion, peeled and chopped
1 heaping tbsp chopped fresh parsley
¼ cup beef broth
Salt
Freshly ground black pepper

To make the pastry, sift the flour with the salt and cut in the fat. Add enough water to make a soft dough. Chill the pastry for half an hour. Preheat oven to 400°F.

Roll out the pastry about ⅛ inch thick. Cut out circles the size of a small plate.

In a bowl, mix the steak, potatoes, rutabaga, onion, parsley, broth, salt, and pepper. Divide this mixture among the pastry circles, spreading it over half of each circle, leaving about a 1-inch margin.

Dampen the edge of the pastry with water, and fold the pastry over to make a half-moon-shaped parcel with the filling in the center.

Patch any holes with a little extra pastry. Crimp the edges to make it look neater: fold the edge to make it thicker, then squeeze tightly every inch to make a pattern along the edge.

Put the pasties on a greased baking sheet. Brush the top with a little milk.

Bake for 30 minutes, then reduce the heat to 375°F and cook for another 30 minutes.

Makes 4 pasties

Classic Lamb Chop

The chop is one of the most prized parts of the young lamb; the meat is tender and flavorful and easy to cook. There are two cuts from which to choose. Rib chops are taken from the same place that produces a rack of lamb and are slightly smaller but have a higher meat-to-fat ratio than loin chops. The bones of rib chops are often frenched, that is, stripped of all the fat and meat.

The exposed bone serves as a convenient handle, negating the need for a fork and knife. Simplicity is the key to enjoying both.

They should be cooked over high direct heat and never overcooked, which results in unappetizingly gray and tough meat. Additional flavors may come from separately prepared sauces or relishes such as vinegar and mint sauce.

Leberkäse

Leberkäse is a Bavarian specialty, produced daily in butcher shops throughout the region. Food historians trace its roots back to the late 18th century, when a chef in the royal house invented the dish.

The word is a source of confusion in that it literally translates as "liver cheese," neither of which is included in the Bavarian recipe (although outside of Bavaria, liver makes an appearance). But the word is derived from old German, combining terms that translate roughly to "compact mass within a form."

Leberkäse begins as a mixture of finely chopped pork and beef along with water and scant seasonings. The chopping is so fine, in fact, that the loaf formed from the ingredients is uniform in color and texture, like a frankfurter or bologna.

It is baked in a medium oven and may be served hot as a main dish, accompanied by potato salad and cold beer. The less committed can also eat Leberkäse chilled, sliced thinly enough to serve as a sandwich meat or spread, like pâté on crackers.

Lechazo Asado

Lechazo asado is one of the greats of Spanish cuisine. Lechazo is a particularly young lamb, weighing no more than 15 pounds, slaughtered at about 30 days of age, while it still depends on its mother for milk (lechazo is similar to the Spanish word for milk, *leche*).

Asado literally translates as "roasted." To prepare, the lechazo is quartered and given a good rub of the fab four: salt, pepper, garlic, and olive oil. The traditional roasting vessel is made of clay, presumably because this material helps mitigate the effects of an uneven heat source such as a wood-burning oven. But with modern ovens, especially those with a convection fan, the need for clay is lessened. That said, the rusty-colored clay does give the dish an old-country quality.

Toward the end of the cooking, the heat is turned up to color and crisp the skin, arguably the best part of the lechazo. The meat underneath will be tender and mild for lamb and makes a terrific centerpiece to a large meal, punctuated by bottles of good Spanish red wine.

20 Superb Sausages

Hot Italian

Bratwurst

Kielbasa

Chorizo

Yorkshire

Calabrese

Genovese

Casalinga

Cumberland

Longaniza

Butifarra

Knackwurst

Bierwurst

Frankfurter

Bockwurst

Cacciatorino

Sardo

Peperone

Wild Boar

Wiltshire

Bangers and Mash

Bangers (sausages) and mash (mashed potatoes) are a cultural icon in the UK. For an authentic experience, make your own bangers.

The Perfect Bangers

17 slices of white bread

½ lb pork back fat (a single piece), rind removed

⅓ cup zwieback, in fine crumbs

½ tsp ground black pepper

½ tsp ground white pepper

¼ tsp ground nutmeg

½ tsp ground mace

¼ tsp ground ginger

1 tbsp corn syrup

1 lb ground pork, preferably from thigh, chilled

1 tsp table salt

4 ft of hog casings (1 ¼- to 1 ½-in diameter)

Peanut oil

Preheat the oven to 350°F. Soak oak chips in a bucket of water. Light the grill and leave for 20 to 30 minutes, until coals are white-flecked with glowing red spots.

Meanwhile, lay 16 bread slices on baking sheets. Put in the oven for 30 to 40 minutes until the bread is evenly dark brown. Break up the bread and put it into a large bowl. Fill the bowl with cold water and leave for 1 hour. Drain the oak chips and throw them on the grill. Once they begin to smoke, put the back fat in the center of the rack and

grill until blistered and charred and giving off a sausage smell. (The fat will catch fire: wear safety gloves and use large tongs.)

Remove the fat from the grill, allow it to cool, chill it in the refrigerator, then cut it into small cubes. Blitz the cubes, in 2 to 3 batches, in a food processor until smooth and paste-like. Scrape the fat into a bowl and set aside (not in the refrigerator) until required. Clean the food processor, and put the blade and bowl in the freezer.

Pass the zwieback and spices through a fine sieve into a bowl. Add the corn syrup. Drain the bread pieces, saving the water. Squeeze the bread to extract more water. Pour ¾ cup of the water into the bowl containing the spice mix, stir, and put in the refrigerator. Remove the food processor blade and bowl from the freezer. Blitz until smooth 1-cup batches of the chilled ground pork with the salt. If the meat is overheating, put the meat, bowl, and blade in the freezer.

Once all the pork is ready, put the meat, bowl, and blade in the freezer and chill to near freezing. Add the fat, chilled spice mix, and 1 slice of white bread to the pork. In small batches and not allowing to overheat, blitz the mixture in the food processor until smooth. Put the mixture in a large bowl, cover, and store in the refrigerator. Put the untangled casings in a bowl of warm water, and soak for a few minutes. Flush salt out of the interior by holding the casings up to the tap and rinsing with warm water. Leave them to soak in a bowl of warm water for 15 minutes until soft and pliable.

Scrape the sausage mix into a barrel of a sausage stuffer, packing it in firmly. Push the casing onto the stuffer's nozzle so it bunches up concertina-style. Extrude a bit of sausage meat and tie a knot in the casing, as close to the meat as possible, leaving 4 inches of casing dangling. Feed the sausage into the casing, applying uniform pressure. When finished, tie a knot in the other end of the casing. Form the sausages into a chain by pinching and twisting the stuffed casings every 6 inches. Turn the first clockwise, the second counter-clockwise, and so on to stop them unraveling. Heat a large pan of water to 150°F. Add the sausages and poach for 20 minutes. Remove them from the pan and pat them dry with a paper towel. Put a bit of oil into a large frying pan, and fry the sausages over medium heat until brown all over.

Serve with mashed potatoes and onion gravy. *Serves 4*

Adapted from Heston Blumenthal's *In Search of Perfection*

Andouille Sausage

From humble beginnings, the andouille sausage has risen to become a key ingredient in many classically Cajun dishes—gumbo, jambalaya, and étouffée among them. The origins are unclear—reports date back to the Middle Ages—but it is agreed that the first andouille sausages were made with tripe and other cuts from the gastrointestinal tract of a pig. More modern recipes may dispense with tradition in favor of the inclusion of butt or shank meat.

The roughly chopped meat is mixed with seasonings that vary from chef to chef (and may lean to the spicy) and then smoked slowly over smoldering sugar cane and pecan wood until fully cooked. The exact proportions of cuts of meat and spices differ depending on availability and local tastes so there are hundreds of variations, though common to each is that they are smoked. It can be served cold in slices on an appetizer plate or mixed in with the aforementioned hot dishes.

Black Pudding

Black pudding, also called blood pudding, is the Anglo name for a type of sausage common around the world. The key ingredient is the blood, which when cooked turns darkest red and solidifies. It is then mixed with minced fat and some form of cereal (usually oats) before being stuffed into sausage casing. The result is a mild-tasting sausage, flecked with chunks of white fat and oats that contrast sharply with the red-black blood. In England, it is often fried up as part of breakfast alongside eggs, bacon, and toast. In France, it is called *boudin noir* and is made with onions and cream. The Spanish version is *morcilla* and is used in regional stews. Italians make *sanguinaccio*, and the Germans make *Blutwurst* cooking it with smoke.

Blanquette de Veau

Blanquette de veau is a culinary rags to riches story. Developed several centuries ago, the dish was initially a means of getting rid of leftovers. By the time the first restaurants were opened in France in the 1800s, the dish had attained iconic status, a position it still holds today. Indeed, French restaurants around the world feature this simple, hearty meal.

The word *blanquette* evokes both whiteness and blanket and offers two clues about the final form the dish takes; the sauce is white and it envelops the veal and other ingredients. The recipe begins with less tender, fattier cuts of veal such as the breast or shoulder. Unlike many stews, the meat in a blanquette is simmered in cold water or broth, not browned. It is boiled slowly with aromatic vegetables until tender. Onions and mushrooms are sautéed in separate pans and then laid on a plate with the veal.

The dish is finished with a simple, roux-based sauce, made rich with veal broth (or the skimmed liquid used to simmer the meat), egg yolks, and thick cream.

Bockwurst

From the land of the 1,000 sausages, Bockwurst is one of the most popular. Invented in 1889 by Berlin restaurateur R. Scholz, it is a member of the *Bruhwurst* family.

The term refers to sausages that are made from raw meat, parboiled, intended to be eaten sooner rather than later, and heated before serving. It is sometimes known as *Weisswurst* (white sausage) although *Weisswurst* are often sold as a separate product. The moniker is deserved; Bockwurst are traditionally made with veal and are among the lightest-colored sausages in the land. Seasoning is limited to scant quantities of salt, pepper, chives, and sage, yielding a very mild flavor.

Cooking is a matter of boiling the sausages until they are done, although excellent results can be derived from the barbecue or stovetop. They are traditionally served with pungent mustard and ideally consumed with a Bock beer, a strong lager.

Bratwurst

Bratwurst is the best-known subgroup of the *Rohwurst* family of sausages. These are distinguished by the fact that they are purchased raw (as opposed to parboiled), air-dried, and sometimes smoked.

There are several types of "brats," often named for their place of origin. The original Bratwurst is said to come from Thüringen, in the middle of the country, but Bratwurst is enjoyed throughout Germany and in many places in the Americas where Germans migrated. They are made with a combination of pork and beef and sometimes veal. The meat is chopped finely but with quite a bit remaining in small chunks so that the finished sausage is dotted with evenly dispersed white specks.

There are a number of methods of cooking. The word *brat* means "roast" but grilling on a barbecue imparts a special, outdoorsy flavor. In Germany, Bratwurst is served as the main meat of a dinner, with sweet mustard. In the United States, where they are often called "brats," they are more often served on a long bun, with mustard and other condiments providing even more delightful eating.

Currywurst

The Berlin Currywurst Museum, opened in 2006, claims that Currywurst is as important to German history as the Brandenburg Gates. Well! The dish, first served in Berlin in 1949, is no more than a Bratwurst sausage, smothered in curried ketchup, then sprinkled with more curry. Yet it has achieved a lofty position in German society, enjoyed by citizens from all walks of life, lauded in verse, inspiring endless debates as to who makes it best.

The grease from the Bratwurst and the punch of the curry translate into a terrific late-night snack, especially after a night of drinking beer in the German capital.

It is served in two-bite slices on waxed paper or on a paper plate. More elegant establishments include an order of French fries and dinner rolls.

Chorizo

Distinguished by its bright reddish coloring, this sausage is fundamental to Spanish and Portuguese cuisine and is popular in various forms throughout South America.

It is made from pork and includes visible chunks of pork fat. The main flavor agent, however, is paprika, both sweet and hot—hence the red color. Chorizo (*chouriço*, in Portuguese) can be prepared both as a fresh sausage to be fried or included with stews or as a hard, dry sausage to be sliced and eaten piece by chewy piece. It is this latter form that is most prevalent on the Iberian Peninsula. In Spain, any tapas bar will serve a small plate of chorizo to accompany a mid-afternoon glass of wine or beer. In Portugal, slices of *chouriço* lie in wait at the bottom of the bowl of traditional soups like caldo verde.

Boerwors

This meat, being a farmer's sausage, is a long-standing tradition among settlers and their descendants in South Africa. The ingredients are simple: ground beef, chopped speck (firm pork fat from under the skin), spices, and, importantly, vinegar, all items that were readily available in the country when the dish was developed some 200 years ago. At the time, the sausages were either eaten fresh or dried and carried on long journeys.

Today, South African butchers offer a wide variety of boerwors flavored with garlic, chiles, and other seasonings. In all cases, however, they are made several feet long and then coiled (or hung to dry). Traditionally, boerwors are cooked outdoors over the hot coals of a *braai* (barbecue).

Devils on Horseback

Combining fruit and meat is all too uncommon, despite the undisputed success of a dish like this one. Devils on horseback combines the sweetness of a prune and the salty smokiness of a slice of bacon. The bacon is wrapped tightly around the prune, secured with a toothpick, then broiled under high heat until the bacon is cooked through and the prune has released some of its sweetness.

The name is rather puzzling, though obviously related to angels on horseback, which are scallops wrapped in bacon, prepared using the same method. So horseback clearly refers to bacon. From there, the gastronomical takes on a theological angle when we ask: Which came first, the angel or the devil? Either way, devils on horseback offer a splendid introduction to a larger meal, either as passed hors d'oeuvres or as an appetizer served on toast and topped with a pinch of grated cheese.

Back Bacon

As the name suggests, back bacon is cut from the back of the pork loin. In Canada, it is also known as Canadian bacon (in the US, Canadian bacon refers to a deli meat ground from pork that is often used as a pizza topping). Back bacon is an unsmoked version of the loin cut that is cured, pickled, and rolled in peameal or cornmeal, hence yet another of its names: peameal bacon (familiar throughout North America).

Back bacon bears little resemblance to the more common streaky bacon, which is cut from the belly and has a much higher fat content. Sliced back bacon can be grilled over high heat to make a fantastic sandwich filling. It can also be roasted and served as the main dish of a dinner.

Breakfast Bacon

The historical importance of bacon cannot be understated, as it sustained thousands of households through difficult times and long winters. In cooking, it is perhaps the most essential meat, used to provide flavor to countless dishes, from humble stews to noble filets. What's more, it's fantastic all on its own.

Bacon sold in grocery stores around the world today developed in Britain and Denmark in the 18th and 19th centuries and was a staple in both those countries. The famous Wiltshire cure is named for the city in England's southwest where the first large-scale bacon operation was founded. Bacon comes from the belly of the pig, a tender area with thick streaks of meat and fat.

What distinguishes bacon from other pork cuts is the curing process. Methods vary, but traditionally, the piece of meat would be preserved with salt and, after a number of days aging, smoked to impart additional flavor. It is generally sold in slices (called rashers in Britain) and cooked on the stovetop or under a hot broiler until just toothsome.

Fondue Bourguignonne

Frankfurter

The fondue trend reached its zenith in the seventies, which partially explains the frequent appearance of avocado-green and harvest-gold fondue pots at yard sales. But fondue has enjoyed a surge in popularity recently as a new generation has discovered this delightful way to share a meal.

Fondue literally means "melted" and *bourguignonne* means "butter." A good deal of butter, in fact, is melted over slow heat, perhaps supplemented with vegetable oil in order to raise the smoking point and prevent burning. Finely sliced meat, usually beef, may be marinated for several hours before cooking. It is threaded onto special long thin forks and then dipped into the hot butter where it cooks quickly, usually in only a few minutes. From the pot, the meat is dipped in any number of sauces, which should have an acidic edge to complement the butter. Lemon and sour cream make good bases for any number of dips.

German sausage makers invented the first frankfurter in the 1860s, naming it for their hometown of Frankfurt. Smaller than traditional sausages, these early versions were made from pork and had a mild taste, due to lack of seasoning.

In time, frankfurters became the preferred sausage for placing between the split halves of a bun. Although the sausage and bread combo was well-known before frankfurters came along, few people today think of anything but "franks" when they hear the term hot dog. Hot dogs have become a junk-food staple, especially in North America, where they are sold on street corners in nearly every city of size and in baseball parks and food courts in malls. The hot dog experience is often enhanced with the generous addition of any number of toppings: ketchup, mustard, onions, bacon, corn, potatoes—so many that in certain cases, the hot dog is no more than a vehicle for several servings of toppings.

Frankfurters (without the bun) have other fabulous uses, combining well with comfort foods like baked beans and macaroni and cheese.

Toad-in-the-Hole

What the frankfurter does for the hot dog bun, sausage does to Yorkshire pudding. For toad-in-the-hole is nothing more than traditional Yorkshire pudding batter with a hunk of sausage plunked in the middle. The batter cooks in a hot oven, rising to irregular puffiness, producing a golden crispy crust. But it is the sausage inside that generates the most excitement over this dish. And still, the question remains: Where did the name come from? Food encyclopedist Alan Davidson can only cite some early uses of the term, but is unable to pinpoint the reason behind the rather unsavory images it provokes.

Early recipes called for steak and kidneys, or other types of meat. But sausage is certainly the most traditional, and many recipes recommend Lincolnshire-style sausages, which are marked by the inclusion of sage.

Toad-in-the-Hole
8 pork sausages

1 cup milk

2 eggs

1 cup flour

Cook the sausages in a frying pan until they are just cooked. Set the sausages aside but keep some of the fat and juices in the pan. Preheat oven to 400°F.

In a bowl, mix together the milk, eggs, and flour—the batter should be thick with air bubbles in it.

Pour into a small roasting pan about 3 tablespoons of the fats and juices left over from cooking the sausages. Arrange the sausages in one layer on the bottom of the roasting pan and put it in the oven to heat the fat slightly.

Pour the batter mix over the sausages and return the pan to the oven.

Bake for 30 to 40 minutes until the batter has risen and is a golden brown. *Serves 4*

Merguez Sausage

Tourtière

Tunisians and Moroccans first produced this spicy sausage but it has since become a fixture in butcher shops and grocery stores around the western Mediterranean and even into Germany.

Merguez is usually made from lamb (shoulder) and, because it is packed in lamb intestines, is thinner relative to German sausages packed in pork intestines. Its distinct flavor comes from the liberal use of *harissa*, a fiery mixture of spices led by chile peppers and garlic. *Harissa* also contributes to the reddish color of the sausage. When fresh, the sausage is usually fried or grilled, producing smoky aromas while the outer skin becomes crisp from the heat.

It may be served at street-side stands, as a *meze* (appetizer or finger food) in a bar, or in larger quantities with couscous. Merguez can also be sun-dried and preserved in large jars of olive oil for later use.

Christmas Eve celebrations in French Canadian homes would not be complete without a fragrant homemade meat pie to enjoy after Midnight Mass. Every region of Quebec has its own version of this golden double-crust pie, which is made with the simplest of ingredients, including ground pork or beef that is browned with onions, thickened with mashed potatoes, moistened with broth, and flavored with cloves, savory, and a pinch of cinnamon. Lard is preferred for the flakiest pastry.

There are several theories surrounding the name of this satisfying dish. *Tourtes* were pigeon-like game birds that lived near the Gulf of St. Lawrence and may have been the original tourtière filling before they became extinct in the early 1900s, forcing Quebecers to substitute other meat and fowl. The name can also be traced to France, where tourtière was the name of a deep baking dish used to cook game birds.

Among the many versions made with ground pork or beef, Quebec's Saguenay-Lac Saint-Jean region has the most distinct, with its layers of cubed potatoes, onions, and meat all baked in a deep, pastry-lined casserole.

Melton Mowbray Pie

Controversy surrounds this not-so-humble pie. In 2004, a delegation representing the town of Melton Mowbray, in Leicestershire, petitioned authorities at the European Union to have their pie recognized and protected with geographical indication status, thereby making it impossible to make Melton Mowbray pie outside of a designated 1,800-square-mile area. Pie makers who fall outside the zone are, naturally, not happy. But whatever the courts decide, the pies will survive.

They resemble misshapen cylindrical cookie tins, the result of free-form baking that allows the pastry crust to fall wherever it sees fit. Inside, a combination of roughly chopped pork, seasonings, and natural pork gelatin cook together with the crust. The gelatin is necessary and desirable to help the pork hold its shape and make it much easier to cut a nice, thin slice to be placed delicately on a plate. Melton Mowbray pie is served chilled, usually at tea.

Pie Floater

The National Trust of South Australia, charged with recording and preserving the cultural heritage of that state, describes a pie floater as "a bowl of green mushy gruel with something solid sitting in it." Not a line you'd use in an advertising campaign, but fairly accurate nonetheless.

Pie floaters are most popular in Adelaide, where they are sold from open-air carts or trailers, a tradition dating back to the middle of the 19th century. The cart will have a kettle for the green mush (actually pea soup) and an oven for the solid something (a savory ground meat pie).

The preferred condiment is ketchup, which is liberally added to the surface of the pie crust and then mixed in with the pea soup as the dish is consumed. Eating pie floaters is something of a social event, albeit spontaneous and informal. The carts are often open late into the evening, making them a perfect gathering point for nighthawks looking to fend off hunger pangs.

Smoked Foods

Certainly one of the earliest flavor enhancers for food must have been smoke. It was never the original intention to use it this way, as smoke was no more than a by-product of cooking foods over a wood fire.

Later, smoking became a popular part of the process of preserving meat and fish, especially those with a high fat content. But it is the pungent, sweet flavor that survives the process, to the point where liquid, bottled smoke (essentially smoked water) is often used in recipes where true smoking is not convenient. The flavor comes from the tarry substances in the smoke that penetrate the food and deliver a deep, distinctive flavor.

The fire must be slow-burning and care must be taken to maintain the temperature at a relatively low level. The type of wood used is also very important. Hard woods, especially those cut from fruit trees, are preferred as these burn long and slow and deliver the best flavors. Softer woods such as pine tend to release resin as they burn, which can leave the food with a very unpleasant taste.

While the old method of hanging food over the fire certainly works, specially constructed smokers that regulate temperature and keep the smoke in a contained area (where the food will also be placed) are a more effective means of cooking and enhancing the taste of smoked foods. Several models are available, from a small home smoker that fits in a corner of the backyard to an industrial-sized smoker used by barbecue restaurants throughout the United States.

Any meat, from chicken to pork to beef and game meats, will benefit from a slow smoking, though care must be taken not to smoke mild meats for too long, as the flavor can easily cross the line from subtle to overwhelming. Pork is especially well-suited to the smoking process; one of the best ways to prepare baby back ribs is in a smoker filled with smoldering hickory wood chips. The meat becomes tender under the low temperatures and the smoky flavors are well-complemented by a sweet and tangy brush of barbecue sauce.

Fish is another popular candidate. Smoked salmon is a staple at cocktail parties. Smoked herring (or kippers) are a classic breakfast food. Certain cheeses, such as Cheddar, can reach heavenly heights when smoked gently over very low temperatures (so low, in fact, that the process is known as cold smoking).

It is not only food that uses smoke for flavor. Many spirits employ smoke in the distillation process to add substance to the bottle. A strong characteristic of several single malt Scottish whiskies, for example is peatiness, attained by roasting the barley over smoking peat.

Saltimbocca alla Romana

This recipe is so dear to the hearts of Italians that it was codified by authorities in 1962. Indeed, the colors involved, red from the prosciutto, white from the veal, green from the sage, echo those of the Italian flag. That said, so does a hot dog with green relish. The word *saltimbocca* means "jump in the mouth," and the method can be used to make similar lively dishes with chicken or turkey cutlets. Veal remains the classic and favored meat. Veal scallopini (or cutlets) are pounded flat into a near-translucent state and then lined with layers of prosciutto followed by fresh sage leaves. The whole bundle is rolled into a cylinder that is fastened with a toothpick.

Because the veal is so thin, cooking requires no more than a few minutes on each side in a hot pan with butter. Once removed from the pan, the dish is finished with a quick deglaze using dry white wine (from Italy, naturally). After a quick reduction, the sauce is poured over the saltimbocca and then served.

Veal Marsala

The delicate flavor of veal lends itself to the addition of complementary sauces, and marsala wine makes one of the best. Marsala is a fortified Sicilian wine, named for the town where it was originally produced (a name now protected by D.O.C. status— D.O.C. stands for *Denominazione di Origine Controllata*, which gives details about where the wine came from, the grapes used, and how it was produced).

There are many kinds of marsala wines, differing in sugar content and aging. It was originally produced with the hope of taking some market share from port and sherry, but has become better known as a key ingredient in cooking. Generally speaking, the sweeter marsalas are used for making veal marsala as they lend a fuller, fruitier taste to the final reduced sauce.

The recipe couldn't be easier. Veal scallops are dredged in seasoned flour and then sautéed in butter for a few minutes per side. The scallops are set aside and the pan is deglazed with marsala wine until it is reduced to a syrupy consistency. A whisk of butter adds a silky element to the sauce, which is spooned gently over the meat.

Veal and Ham Pie

A classic for picnics or outdoor luncheons, veal and ham pie is a simple dish to be prepared one day and eaten another.

The main ingredients, namely veal and ham, are sliced thinly and simmered slowly in water until cooked through and then allowed to cool. Meanwhile, a high-walled pan—suitable for meatloaf or one specially designed for meat pies—is lined with pastry. A layer of meat is placed at the bottom of the pan, followed by a shelled hard-boiled egg and then more meat is piled on top before the whole mound is covered by more pastry and a bit of broth, and baked.

After 30 minutes in the oven and several hours cooling, the pie is ready to be cut into thin slices, revealing the profile of the hard-boiled egg inside, like a gem lodged in rock.

Schweinebraten

The name of the dish, meaning roast pork, is vague and therefore wide open to interpretation. Indeed, there is very little agreement on how to properly cook a Schweinebraten, although most suggest that the roast should be basted frequently with a good German beer. Prior to that, it may be rubbed in a mélange of spices and seasoning, with garlic, paprika, onion powder, and sage making frequent appearances.

When the roast is done, the juices from the pork have mixed with the beer, which is thickened and reduced to produce a tasty gravy. A common accompaniment is *kartoffelknodel*, a type of potato dumpling that will soak up all the beery-porky goodness left in the gravy.

Choucroute Garnie à l'Alsacienne

This Alsatian classic blends economical and readily available ingredients into a single dish. The most important ingredient is time. The choucroute (braised cabbage or sauerkraut) must be prepared first. Slices of cabbage are braised in a combination of pork fat, goose fat, spices, broth, and dry, fruity wine. The fat is important as it will help limit the unpleasant sulfur smell that accompanies cooking cabbage. Together, these ingrdients need to braise for 4 or 5 hours until the cabbage has absorbed the liquid and the flavors of the spices. While it cooks, meat is added at different intervals, depending on the time needed to cook each type of cut. Pork hocks will likely be first. They are browned and then buried in the strands of now softening cabbage where they will cook and tenderize and pass their flavors to the choucroute.

Other cuts are added in sequence: pork chops, sausage, and bacon. This layering adds even more character to the choucroute so that when it is done, it is intensely flavored and almost as valued as the meat.

Sweet-and-Sour Pork

There are two distinct versions of sweet-and-sour pork. Both are associated with Chinese cooking, although one developed in China, the other in Chinese restaurants in the West. The difference lies in the sauce. While both rely on sugar for the sweet and vinegar to provide the sour, Western versions tend to add some manner of tomato, either in paste or ketchup, and additional sweetness with chunks of pineapple. The tomato produces the unmistakable bright red, shiny sauce that is the trademark of many a late-night Chinese takeout dish.

The punch and counterpunch of sweet-and-sour sauce finds no better friend than pork, which, when battered and deep-fried in oil adds remarkable crunchy texture to the mix. Other meats, such as chicken or fish, tend to get lost in the power of the sauce. Pork holds its own quite nicely.

Pork Schnitzel

The German version of the well-known and well-loved Wiener schnitzel (which is an Austrian legacy and is made with veal), pork schnitzel (*Schweineschnitzel*) follows essentially the same method. Pieces of pork cutlet are lovingly pounded into uniformly thin slices, no more than ¼ inch in thickness.

This process ensures a quick cooking time and also helps to break down any toughness in the meat. The cutlets are seasoned with salt and pepper and then taken through a three-stage dredging process: first flour, then egg, then bread crumbs (which also may be seasoned).

The order of operations ensures that the bread crumbs, which form a delightful light crust when cooked, adhere to the meat. Schnitzel is versatile. It can be served on its own as the main course alongside a mound of roast potatoes, or tucked inside a soft roll and topped with anything that might go in a sandwich. A squeeze of lemon juice also adds brightness to the finished dish.

Schnitzel has migrated to kitchens around the world, each adding its own variation. In Sweden, for example, it is served with gravy. In France, the famous Cordon Bleu cooking school invented a version that sandwiches slices of ham and cheese between the two cutlets.

Pork Schnitzel

6 boneless pork chops

½ tsp salt

⅓ cup flour

¼ cup dried bread crumbs

1 egg

1¼ cup milk

3 tbsp oil

Trim the fat from the pork chops, then place them between 2 sheets of waxed paper. With a meat mallet (use the smooth side) or a rolling pin, pound them to ⅛-inch thickness. Sprinkle both sides with salt.

Put the flour and bread crumbs into separate shallow bowls. Whisk together the egg and milk in a shallow bowl. Lightly coat each cutlet in flour, shaking off excess; dip each one in the egg mixture, then the bread crumbs, pressing to coat.

Heat the oil in large frying pan over medium-high heat. Cook the cutlets in batches in the frying pan, turning once, until golden brown, about 3 minutes per side. As each batch is finished, transfer them to a warm platter. *Serves 6*

Potée Lorraine

Potée Lorraine is a specific kind of pot-au-feu native to the eastern province for which it is named. Lorraine is known for its pork production, and it comes as no surprise that the meat included in potée Lorraine is almost exclusively pork.

Smoked sausage, shoulder, bacon, and hock may all be included. From there, the preparation is similar to that of pot-au-feu. The meats are browned and then cooked in white wine and chicken broth. Cabbage, potatoes, carrots, and onions are added later, followed by white beans. The whole stew is simmered on the stovetop until the meat has cooked through and is tender.

With a loaf of fresh bread for sopping up the flavorful broth, potée Lorraine is a comforting, uncomplicated, rustic dish that will satisfy even the most ravenous appetite.

Pulled Pork Sandwich

Inevitable cravings for pulled pork sandwiches must be strictly controlled as there are no short cuts to this barbecue classic. Four, six, even twelve hours of slow cooking are needed to take an otherwise inedible cut of pork (the butt or shoulder) and turn it into a tender mound of easy-to-shred meat.

There are a number of different slow cooking styles, though all begin with a generous rubdown with a mélange of dry spices: chili, cayenne, garlic, onion, salt, pepper, paprika, and brown sugar in combinations kept strictly secret by the legions of barbecuers who spend their summers hauling industrial-sized smokers from competition to competition. Smoking over a slow fire of aromatic woods like apple or cherry is a part of the United States tradition although credible pulled pork can be produced in a regular home oven. No less important than the cooking method is the sauce that bathes the meat.

Sauces generally fall into two distinct categories, the first sweet with molasses or brown sugar and the second made tangy by vinegar. Either one should be applied so generously that the bun can barely sustain the soaking, making a fork and knife a necessity for pulled pork sandwiches.

Pot-au-Feu

There is no way to make pot-au-feu for two. Its volume is more suited to a large, extended family dinner or a roomful of friends (and their friends). As such, pot-au-feu has particular cultural meaning in France for it is forever associated with family gatherings or special events.

The dish itself is not hard to make, despite the number and diversity of ingredients. It includes beef, sausage, chicken, and pork, using cuts that are particularly well suited to braising. There are also vegetables—carrots, onions, parsnips, celery, leeks—which are simmered together with the meat in a single, very large pot. Once everything is in the pot, there is little to do but wait for the meat to cook over the next few hours, leaving the host free to entertain the guests.

Service may be awe-inspiring as each piece of meat is carved into individual portions and the vegetables are separated and placed on a specific platter for passing. The braising liquid makes a terrific sauce, borrowing flavors from all the ingredients that had been immersed in it.

Cozido a Portuguesa

A national dish originating in Estremadura, cozido a Portuguesa has a little of everything: beef, chicken, sausage, and pork, all cooked together with starchy vegetables in a single pot in a slow oven.

In this respect, it resembles the French pot-au-feu. One important difference is in the sausage used. In Portugal, spicy red *chouriço* is the preferred choice. There also seems to be more flexibility with the preparation of cozido than pot-au-feu. Recipes vary in their ingredients. Some, for example, call for pig's feet and ears or *morcela* (blood sausage).

Regardless of the combination of ingredients, a cozido is cooked in a large pot with sufficient water to fully cover everything. As it cooks, the water will take on the flavors of the meats and turn into a rich and aromatic broth that is often served as a first-course soup before the meats and vegetables. The meat and vegetables come next and are often served with rice.

Cochinita al Pibil

From Mexico's Yucatán peninsula, this dish
has roots in the Mayan empire once centered
there. *Cochinita* translates as "small pig" and
pibil refers to the pit that served as the oven
in which the meat was cooked. While modern
methods call for modern ovens, the essential
elements of a good cochinita remain intact.
Foremost among these is the marinade,
a unique blend of bitter orange juice and
achiote paste. The latter is a simple mixture
of black pepper, oregano, garlic, onion, and
ground seeds of the achiote plant, a shrub
that grows throughout the Yucatán. The
seeds lend some flavor but are mostly
characterized by the vivid red color they
impart to all they touch. After several hours
in this marinade, the pork is no exception.
It is wrapped in large banana leaves, which
add an extra element of fragrance, and
cooked for several hours in a slow oven,
until the pork can be easily shredded with
a pair of forks. Traditionally, cochinita is
served in warm corn tortillas with onions
in *escabeche*, a quick pickled onion that
offers pungency and crunch.

Stuffed Loin of Pork

Many culinary traditions across cultures
have developed their own best methods
for stuffing a loin, the best cut of pork.

Although pork is available commercially
throughout the year, there was a time when
it was principally available in the late fall,
when the pigs had matured enough to
slaughter. Those cuts not suited to long-term
preservation, including the loin, were eaten
immediately while other cuts were destined
for curing, smoking, or sausages. As a result,
loins were traditionally stuffed with what
was available at that time of the year: fresh
fruit such as apples or pears; dried fruits
such as raisins, prunes, or apricots; or even
more pork in the form of sausage. All these
main ingredients may be supplemented
by bread crumbs and seasonings that
match the stuffing.

As the loin roasts, fat drippings fall to
the bottom of the pan and serve as the
foundation for any number of savory sauces,
later to be drizzled over a nice thick slice
of the pork, stuffing and all.

Petit Salé avec Lentilles

Petit salé is a simple, inexpensive dish from Auvergne, in the north of France, and is a staple among farmers of the region who looked to it to provide nourishment and warmth on cool evenings.

The meat involved is *gammon*, which is the hindquarters of a pig, cured but not cooked (unlike ham, which also comes from the hindquarter but is both cured *and* cooked.) The *gammon* is left in large chunks and cooks slowly in the same pot as the lentils. Of these, Puy lentils are considered the best as they carry a subtle flavor and maintain their texture better than cheaper varieties. Together, the meat and lentils make for a very satisfying dish, with lots of earthy aromas provided by bay leaves, onions, and carrots.

Petit Salé avec Lentilles

4 lb belly pork, in one piece, rind and bones intact

1 ⅔ cups Puy lentils

12 small carrots, peeled

20 button onions, peeled

12 tender celery stalks, cut into 3-in pieces

2 bay leaves

3 cloves

2 sprigs of fresh thyme

¼ cup butter

Salt

Freshly ground black pepper

2 tbsp chopped flat-leaf parsley

For the mustard sauce:

Dijon mustard

½ cup heavy cream

Soak the pork in brine for 3 days, then drain and place in a large pot. Cover with cold water, bring to a boil, and drain again. Put the pork back in the pot and cover with 3 pints of water. Poach gently for 30 minutes. Add the lentils, vegetables, herbs, and spices, and continue cooking on a very low heat, stirring from time to time, for a further 1 hour, or until the lentils and vegetables are tender.

Remove the pork and keep warm. Stir the butter into the hot lentils for added richness, check the seasoning, and stir in the parsley. Pour into a warmed oval serving dish, slice the pork, leaving the bones intact, and lay on top. Serve with a little mustard sauce, made by simply whisking the mustard into the heavy cream. *Serves 4*

Adapted from Simon Hopkinson's *Roast Chicken and Other Stories*

Pork Scratchings

Fat, some famous chef once quipped, is flavor. There may be no better example of this aphorism than pork scratchings. Produced when the skin of the pig is roasted apart from the meat, the result is an extraordinarily crisp, intensely flavored complement to any meal where pork is on the menu.

The texture is such that comparisons to candy are not out of place. A similar effect may be realized by leaving the skin on the pork. In this case, however, the result is something called "crackling." Confusingly, this is the same word used in the United States for what the English call scratchings. Beyond the Anglo-American axis, the names become more distinct, but the essence remains the same.

In many parts of South America, *chicharron* (prepared separately from the roast) is a popular snack food. Traditionally the pork skin (with some meat still attached) is cooked not by roasting but by deep-frying in a vat of oil or even lard. The fat will puff up in the deep fryer, creating an ironic lightness to the eventual snack. Commercially, the product is best known as "pork rinds" and is sold much like potato chips.

Crispy Roast Pork Belly

Better known as the cut of pork that produces bacon (which, through curing and smoking, is a different product), pork belly is a key secondary ingredient in many classic, slow-cooking recipes. That said, roasting a pork belly allows this cut's unique characteristics to shine all on their own. Of these, crisp, tawny skin is the most prized, and the crispier it is, the better. To attain peak crunch, the skin should be shocked with hot water straight from the kettle. This kick starts the breakdown of the leathery collagen.

Before cooking, the skin should be brushed with oil to aid in the transfer of heat to the skin. While the pork is roasting, the water in the skin vaporizes, helping the skin crisp until it is brittle. The meat itself will be basted by the streaks of fat that run through the pork and remain tender and full of flavor. The dish enjoys extraordinary popularity in China, where it is seasoned with Chinese five spice for a unique taste.

Katsu

Delightfully crispy, katsu is a Japanese dish of breaded, deep-fried pork or chicken. It came to Japan from the West in the late 19th century but today is clearly more Japanese than not. One Japanese touch is that the breading is made from crushed *panko*, a wheat-based bread that yields a lighter crust than bread crumbs made from more conventional, Western-based breads.

Essential to a good katsu is a top-notch *tonkatsu sosu*, sometimes called Japanese Worcestershire sauce. The comparison is misleading, though, for the Japanese version is made from fruit purées while English Worcestershire is distinguished by anchovy extract and tamarind. The Japanese sauce is also thicker than its counterpart.

When served, the pork or chicken katsu is sliced into two-bite pieces that are grasped between the points of the chopsticks and dipped delicately in the warmed *sosu*. As with its Austrian cousin, Wiener schnitzel, it is a popular filling for sandwiches.

Cuban Sandwich

From an island more known for post-repast cigars than the repast itself, the Cubano is an excellent contribution to the sandwich genre. They originated in the early 1900s when vendors and cafeterias began selling them to sugar mill employees and other workers.

Big enough to be eaten with two hands, the sandwich begins with a large, crusty roll called Cuban bread, which is similar to a loaf of Calabrese. The bun is split and filled with roast pork that has been cooked in a mojo sauce (a highly seasoned paste of peppers, garlic, salt, pepper, and oil). This is followed by ham, sour pickles, cheese, and, upon request, mustard. The now-bulging bun is heated and pressed on a two-sided, hinged *plancha* (like a panini press). This not only flattens the sandwich, making it easier to handle and more convenient to eat on the go, but also crisps the shell of the bread and warms the filling, releasing the juices from the pickle and melting the cheese.

Like many things Cuban, the sandwich has moved into the United States and different versions have developed. Those from south Florida, where the sandwich has a particular following, include the Key West Mix (with mayonnaise and tomatoes) and one that is made in the Tampa area that includes an additional layer of Genoa salami.

Cuban Sandwich

1 loaf crusty Italian or French bread

Prepared yellow mustard

½ lb baked ham, thinly sliced

½ lb roast pork, thinly sliced

8 dill pickle slices

½ lb Swiss cheese, thinly sliced

Slice the bread horizontally and spread a thin layer of mustard on the top and bottom halves. Arrange the ham, pork, pickle slices, and cheese slices in even layers on the bottom half of the bread. Cover the sandwiches with the top halves of the bread. Cut into 4 sections. Grill the sandwiches in a hot buttered sandwich press until the bread is browned and the cheese has melted. To serve, cut each sandwich in half diagonally. *Serves 4*

Best Barbecued Meats

The word "barbecue" is derived from *brabacot* and was one of the first Amerindian words to enter European vocabularies after Columbus crossed the ocean in 1492. It was used by the Arawaks and Caribs, the two major tribes of the Caribbean, to describe a cooking method using green sticks fashioned into a grill over a slow, smoky fire. The basic idea of outdoor cooking has changed very little in the intervening years and virtually any cut of meat will benefit from the smokiness that comes with grilling, although the method, fuel, and type of barbecue used will intensify or lessen the effect to a great degree.

Baby back ribs are the finest contribution to the barbecue from the pork family. Normally a tough cut, the pork between the bones turns tender when cooked slowly on a barbecue. Slathered with sweet, tomato-based barbecue sauce, ribs are messy and fun to eat and few foods go better during a North American summer, especially with fresh corn on the cob.

More meaty pork cuts, such as thick-cut **loin chops** are special indeed when they take on the smokiness of barbecued meats. In the morning, cured **peameal bacon**, sliced thinly and lightly grilled, is a fantastic, rustic breakfast. Of steaks, there are a number of cuts appropriate for barbecuing but the finest is the **rib eye or rib steak**. Wonderfully marbled, richly flavored,

this steak takes beautifully to a hot grill with no more preparation than a dose of salt and pepper.

Often, butchers will sell **beef ribs** cut from the bottom of a prime rib. There is no elegant way to eat these monster ribs, but the rewards far outstrip the potential breach of table manners. Sometimes hard to find, the **tri-tip** is worth the journey. The unique shape, thin on one end, thick on the other, makes serving guests with different preferences of doneness a breeze. Lean **flank steak or London broil** needs an overnight marinade, which helps intensify flavors that emerge even more once barbecued.

Lamb chops gain extra punch from the barbecue as the meat and fat gently caramelize to add a sweet element to the savory lamb. Larger cuts of lamb, such as the leg, can also be barbecued, requiring a spit to turn the meat slowly over the heat, ensuring even cooking and uniformly crisp and delectable skin. On the less expensive end, there is little more suited to the barbecue than the **hamburger**, a loosely packed disk of ground beef and seasonings and a self-basting barbecue dish; the fat bastes and flavors the meat as it melts away.

Most varieties of **sausages** can and should be grilled but those that are precooked via smoking seem to do best. Because they are already cooked, time on the grill is lessened, as is the risk that the casing will burst, releasing valued juices to the coals below.

Cholent

Cholent traces its roots to medieval France. Indeed, the word *cholent* is believed to be a composite of the old French words *chaud* (hot) and *lent* (slow). In the 14th century, the dish migrated to Germany, where the word *cholent* entered the Yiddish vocabulary and the dish took on a form more closely related to that which is familiar today. The traditional Sabbath midday meal, cholent includes meat, potatoes, barley, and beans.

The meat is usually beef (a fatty cut is preferred) but may also be chicken or lamb. It begins, as many stews do, with a browning of the meat in oil followed by the addition of the other ingredients, which are then covered in water and placed in a very slow oven overnight. This last step is key for observant Jews as it ensures that the prohibition of cooking on the Sabbath is not broken. The next day, the meat will be completely cooked and terrifically aromatic.

It may be served with kiske sausage or *knaidlach*—dumplings made from matzo meal or flour.

Cheeseburger

By now a staple on Western menus due to the ease of preparation, portability, and mass marketing, the cheeseburger is a relatively recent arrival on the gastronomic landscape.

The first versions to carry the label "hamburger" appeared in 1890 in Hamburg, Germany, and the popularity of the dish truly took off at the 1904 St. Louis World's Fair in the United States. Cheese was added by Californian Lionel Sternberger, who had his eureka moment in 1924. Grudgingly included on menus as a concession to fickle young diners, the cheeseburger can nevertheless reach great heights of tastiness when the three elements—the bun, the beef, and the cheese—work in tight tandem. Some clever chefs have created versions using costly Kobe beef and soft, aromatic cheeses like Brie.

More traditionally, less tender cuts (such as chuck) are ground and shaped into patties with or without the addition of fillings and flavorings. Direct heat is the most common form of cooking, either stovetop or on a grill. Further toppings make variations on the cheeseburger almost limitless and can range from iceberg lettuce for crisp texture to earthy truffles to a squirt each of ketchup, mustard, salsa, and relish.

Lamb Shanks

One of the least-desired cuts of lamb can, with a little patience, be turned into one of the most prized lamb dishes. Shanks have a loyal following among many cultures, most prominently in the Mediterranean, where Greek and North African cooks have taken a particular interest in including the shank in national cuisine.

The cut comes from the animal's forequarter and is quite fatty and crisscrossed with connective tissue. A long, slow braise renders the fat and breaks down the connective tissue, leaving tender meat that falls cleanly from the bone. The braising liquid goes a long way to determining the final flavor and generally includes stock (beef, veal, or chicken), red wine, tomatoes, aromatics, and seasoning. As the shank cooks, the flavors from the braising liquid and the lamb meld, creating an exquisite sauce that can be further reduced and then drizzled over the plated meat as well as the preferred starch (rice, potatoes, or, most deliciously, buttered couscous).

Lamb Shanks

4 (1½ lb) lamb shanks, trimmed

1 cup all-purpose flour, seasoned

2 tablespoons olive oil

1 cup diced onion

1 cup diced carrot

1 cup diced celery

4 cloves garlic

1 tsp black peppercorns

2 sprigs fresh thyme

1 fresh bay leaf

2½ cups dry red wine

Preheat the oven to 300°F.

Coat the lamb shanks in seasoned flour and brown on all sides in the oil. Use a skillet over medium-high heat and turn the shanks often to brown evenly. Transfer the lamb to a large roasting pan. Add the onion, carrot, celery, and garlic to the skillet and cook until soft. Pour the vegetables over the lamb shanks, adding the peppercorns and herbs. Pour in the wine, cover the roasting pan, and cook in the preheated oven for 2½ to 3 hours.

Transfer the lamb shanks to a serving dish. Strain the vegetables from the cooking liquid, reserving the liquid, but discarding the vegetables. Reduce the liquid by half, season to taste, and ladle over the lamb shanks to serve. *Serves 4*

Braised Oxtail

Virtually the only way to prepare the tough meat of an oxtail is to braise it. This is no loss, as the high bone and marrow content of the average oxtail, combined with slow cooking in savory liquid, allows a good deal of flavor to seep into the braise. The result is an impossibly rich gravy that can be reduced after the oxtails come out of the pot and poured in generous amounts over the meat and accompanying rice or egg noodles.

Meatloaf

There are few kitchens that have not produced meatloaf in their day. Surprisingly, the term is relatively new, appearing for the first time in the US in 1899, but there is little doubt that the dish enjoyed popularity well before that. And why not? It is easy to prepare, a simple matter of mixing ground meat (beef is most common) with bread crumbs and seasoning. The bread crumbs help bind the meat and, in lean times, help stretch supplies of the more expensive meat. Once mixed, the meat is shaped into a loaf and then topped with remaining bread crumbs, which toast in the oven and provide texture.

While commonly served as a hot meal with a tomato-based sauce for garnish, meatloaf is just as good the next day, served cold with sweet chutney or in a sandwich. Variations are endless; virtually any ingredient can be added to virtually any ground meat and, given the relatively inexpensive ingredients, experimentation is absolutely encouraged.

New England Boiled Dinner

Moussaka

New England boiled dinner (also called "Jiggs' dinner") consists of boiled corned beef, potatoes, and assorted winter vegetables. The dish arrived in the New World, together with the waves of Irish immigrants who crossed the ocean in the 19th century.

In Ireland, however, the dish was made with ham or bacon and, indeed, one can do so today. That said, it is more common to use corned beef. The switch came about with the predominance of Jewish butchers in New York City in neighborhoods that were also home to the Irish. In addition to meat, boiled dinners include potatoes, cabbage, onions, parsnips, and carrots—all vegetables that could be harvested late in the year and resist spoiling enough to be edible the following March.

Cooking is a simple process of simmering all the ingredients in a large pot with water. Seasonings are limited to salt and pepper. The result is a steamy and hearty dish, all from one pot. As with other meals involving corned beef, New England boiled dinner is often accompanied by a zippy mustard or hot horseradish.

Moussaka is a Turkish dish that has spread throughout the countries of the former Ottoman empire. Today, Turks, Greeks, Croatians, Bulgarians, and others all have their own versions of the recipe. In Romania, *musaca* is made with potatoes and is the national dish.

The variations that have had the most legs are those that belong to the migrating Greek and Turkish communities that have made the dish synonymous with their respective cuisines. Called a stew by some but more akin to a casserole, moussaka begins with ground lamb, followed by layers of eggplant and tomato sauce, and topped with a layer of creamy béchamel sauce, a rich flour, egg, and cheese sauce, seasoned with nutmeg.

The whole dish goes into the oven where the béchamel sauce becomes firm and turns a lovely golden color. When cooked, the loose elements in the pie acquire some adhesion, allowing individual portions to be served in a perfect square piece.

Butterflied Lamb

Butterflying a leg of lamb is a tricky business, and more than one otherwise lovely piece of meat has been mangled under the knife of an amateur. Fortunately, a good butcher will happily debone the leg, producing the splayed, butterfly effect.

The advantage of removing the bone is that the lamb is now more suited to grilling whereas with the bone in, roasting is about the only option available. There is also more surface area of the meat exposed, which provides an excellent stage for spice rubs and marinades to act their parts to the fullest potential. Indeed, leg meat is a bit tougher than other cuts used for grilling, so an acidy marinade (using vinegar or wine, perhaps) helps tenderize the meat. Of course, the more apparent use of a rub or marinade is flavor, and lamb takes to a wide variety, many of which have become classics: garlic and rosemary; cumin; mustard and thyme; olive oil, salt, and pepper are just a few.

Kashmiri Lamb Stew

Butterflied Lamb

¾ cup dry red wine

¼ cup red wine vinegar

½ cup extra-virgin olive oil

⅓ cup coarse-grained Dijon mustard

½ cup chopped fresh herbs of your choice
(rosemary, basil, thyme, oregano, parsley)

6 sprigs fresh rosemary leaves

2 large garlic cloves

1 (4- to 5-lb) leg of lamb, boned, butterflied

Salt

Freshly ground black pepper

Purée the first 7 ingredients in a blender
until all ingredients are completely blended,
about 3 minutes.

Trim excess fat from the lamb, to prevent
flare-ups when grilling. Put the lamb in a
shallow glass container. Pour the marinade
over the lamb, turning the lamb to be sure
it is well coated. Cover and chill for at least
8 hours or overnight. Turn the meat once or
twice so the marinade is well absorbed. Bring to
room temperature for 2 hours before cooking.

Remove the lamb from the marinade,
and sprinkle it all over with salt and pepper.

Grill the lamb over medium-high heat for
about 20 minutes, for medium-rare, turning it
occasionally, until it's brown and crusty on the
outside. Put the lamb on a serving dish, cover
with foil, and let stand for 5 to 10 minutes.

Serves 6

Kashmir, on the border between Pakistan
and India, is so distinct from either of those
countries that food writers give it special
attention. It is a particularly fertile area and
yields some legendary produce, some of
which is unavailable anywhere else in the
world. Lamb stew is just one of a number
of interesting dishes native to the area. It is
usually included in the traditional *Wazwan*,
a celebratory feast of astounding proportions
where up to 36 dishes are prepared by a
Vasta Waza, the head chef, and his crew.
Weddings are typical excuses for a *Wazwan*.

Kashmiri lamb stew has a lengthy ingredient
list. Many of these are spices and include
turmeric, cumin, ginger, garlic, coriander, and
cinnamon, all of which come into frequent
use in a Kashmiri kitchen. The body of the
stew comes from cubed lamb, potatoes,
tomatoes, peas, and cashews that have been
ground into a paste.

The heat of the spice mixture is quelled
somewhat by the addition of yogurt, which
also gives the stew a creamy consistency.

Souvlaki

Tough to prove, but meat on a stick cooked over fire has to be one of the earliest recipes concocted by hungry people. Lamb souvlaki is no exception. Modern versions call for meat from the leg, trimmed of most of the fat and cut into bite-sized pieces before being threaded on to a stick. From there, the meat may spend time bathing in a marinade of various savory flavors—olive oil, lemon, oregano, and garlic are among the most popular—before arriving on a hot grill.

When done, it makes a fine food-on-the-go, like a protein-laden lollipop. It also works well on a plate, and thousands of Greek restaurants around the world owe their survival to its popularity. As a dinner it generally comes with tzatziki—the cool garlicky yogurt sauce cuts the grease and improves the texture—as well as roast potatoes or rice, and a fresh salad.

Lamb Tagine

Tagine refers to both the dish and the vessel in which it is served. You can't have one without the other. It comes from North Africa and is a strong cultural symbol in Tunisia, Morocco, and Algeria.

Traditionally, a tagine is shaped from thick, red clay that is baked until hard and then painted and glazed with intricate and colorful designs. It makes a striking display on the table, but the conical shape of the upper half of the two-part dish has a practical purpose. It allows condensation from the cooking food below to gather and drip back into the stew, keeping it moist and preserving flavor.

Lamb tagine, or *mrouzia*, a dish made for celebrations, combines the savory taste of lamb with sweetness from raisins and honey. Almonds provide a healthy crunch. It is cooked slowly in the tagine with the sweet ingredients added toward the end of the process, ensuring that the flavors remain distinguishable. Couscous, which absorbs the juices from the stew, is the favored accompaniment.

Lamb Dopiaza

Dopiaza is a mild Indian curry with a double dose of onions. In fact, the word *dopiaza* means "two onions" and refers to the fact that onions are added to the dish in two stages, first to cook down with the lamb and spices, where they get soft and sweet and lose a great degree of pungency. More onions are added at the end of cooking for precisely the opposite effect: they are crunchy and zippy. The lamb is cubed and then marinated in a curry of several spices: ginger, garlic, chili powder, cardamom, cinnamon, cloves, coriander, cumin, and turmeric. The lamb is browned in ghee then cooked with onions and tomato and the curry.

In the final stages, yogurt gets added to give the dish a nice roundness and to lessen the impact of the spices. When served, the raw onions are scattered on top.

Lamb Dopiaza

4 onions, peeled

7 cloves garlic, peeled

1-in cube fresh gingeroot, coarsely chopped

2 cups water

10 tbsp vegetable oil

1-in cinnamon stick

10 cardamom pods

10 cloves

2½ lb boned lamb, preferably from the shoulder, cut into 1-in cubes (with most of the fat removed)

1 tbsp ground coriander

2 tsp ground cumin

6 tbsp plain yogurt, beaten lightly

¼ to ½ tsp cayenne pepper

½ tsp garam masala

Salt, to taste

Cut three of the onions into halves lengthwise, and then cut them, crosswise, into very fine rings. Chop the fourth onion finely. Keep the two types of onion separate. Put the garlic and ginger into the container of an electric blender or food processor. Add ½ cup of the measured water and blend until fairly smooth.

Put the oil in a wide, heavy pot and place over a medium-high heat. When hot, put in the finely sliced onions. Stir and fry for 10 to 12 minutes, or until the onions turn a nice reddish brown color. You may have to turn the heat down somewhat toward the end of this cooking period. Remove the onions with a slotted spoon and spread them on a plate lined with paper towels.

Put the cinammon, cardamom pods, and cloves into the hot oil. Stir them for about 5 seconds over medium-high heat. Now put in 8 to 10 cubes of meat or as many as the pot will hold easily in a single, loosely packed layer. Brown the meat on one side. Turn it over and brown the reverse side. Remove the meat cubes with a slotted spoon and put them in a bowl. Brown all the meat in this way, removing each batch as it gets done.

Put the chopped onion into the remaining oil in the pot. Stir and fry it on medium heat until the pieces turn brown at the edges. Add the garlic-ginger paste. Stir and fry it until all the water in it seems to boil away and you see the oil again. Turn the heat down a bit and add the coriander and cumin. Stir and fry for 30 seconds. Now add 1 tablespoon of yogurt. Stir and fry until it is incorporated into the sauce. Add another tablespoon of yogurt. Stir and fry, incorporating this into the sauce as well. Add all the yogurt this way, a tablespoon at a time. Now put in all the meat and any accumulated juices in the meat bowl with the remaining water, the cayenne, and the salt. Stir to mix and bring to a simmer. Cover, turn the heat to low, and cook for about 45 minutes or until the lamb is tender. Add the fried onions and the garam masala. Stir to mix.

Continue to cook, uncovered, for another 2 to 3 minutes, stirring gently as you do so. Turn off the heat and let the pot sit for a while. The fat will rise to the top. Remove it with a spoon. Fry the sliced onion in the remaining oil until brown, then add to the curry with salt to taste.

Simmer for a further 20 minutes, or until the lamb is tender. *Serves 6*

Adapted from Madhur Jaffrey's *Indian Cooking*

Lamb Navarin

Because of its strong flavor, lamb is particularly suited to stewing, a cooking method that tends to take the edge off. Lamb navarin is no exception, especially when made with the stronger tastes of mutton.

This traditionally French dish (*navarin d'agneau*) is sometimes made with tongue and neck meat (although most recipes suggest shoulder) as well as beans and root vegetables like potatoes, carrots, and turnips, all of which are harvested late in the growing season and can be stored long after.

As a result, the dish is most commonly associated with chilly winter days, although today it is possible to enjoy a good navarin any time of the year. After the meat is cubed and browned in hot oil, the vegetables are added, along with wine and/or broth to help cook the meat slowly and ensure the end result is fork-tender meat and vegetables within a rich gravy.

While there is no need for additional starch, a nice loaf of sauce-sopping crusty bread seems a natural accompaniment.

Lamb Pasanda

Kleftiko

Like many dishes from the rich culinary tradition of India, lamb pasanda begins with a lengthy list of ingredients. That said, it is sure to please a wide variety of tastes. Indeed, the word *pasanda* is derived from the Hindu and Urdu words for "like." Accordingly, pasanda does not contain strong or spicy flavors but instead delivers a smooth, mellow taste and unaggressive mouth feel.

The meat is sliced and pounded into thin strips and then marinated in yogurt and spices, including a dose of red chili. This marinade will flavor and tenderize the meat. The meat is then fried with juicy tomatoes and ghee, and the curry sauce is created from a variety of spices that include garam masala, coriander, and ginger, but no more additional heat. Lamb pasanda is a terrific introduction to curry for spice-averse palates.

In Greece, *kleftiko* refers to any dish that is sealed and baked. Although Greek is an ancient language, *kleftiko* is a relatively recent addition. It dates back to the early part of the 19th century, when Greece was struggling for its independence from the Ottoman Empire.

The Klephts were a group of men who, for one reason or another, were wanted by the Ottomans. Rather than face jail time, they fled to the mountains where they survived by nefarious means, hijacking travelers, raiding villages, and stealing whatever they could get their hands on (the root of the word *klepht* is the same that produces the English word "kleptomaniac").

Their position in history depends on the perspective taken. To the Turks, they were criminals. But their participation in the Greek wars for independence, culminating in 1829, made them heroes to their countrymen. Villains or heroes, they had to eat. Hence kleftiko, a dish made up of lamb stew (traditionally from a stolen lamb) cooked slowly in a sealed pot that was buried to prevent smoke from alerting authorities as to their position.

Lancashire Hotpot

Lancashire hotpot was born of necessity and evokes a certain sense of nostalgia. In the 19th century as industrialization swept across the north of England, women went to work in the cotton mills and were robbed of time and energy with which to prepare proper meals. Lancashire hotpot could be prepared in the morning and left to simmer unattended during the day. When work was over, dinner was ready. The specially designed stoneware hotpot also acted as an insulator, allowing the dish a degree of portability. Thus, it became a favorite lunch for miners in coal pits as well as for weekend picnickers.

There are several versions of the stew. Oysters were once a popular ingredient, though today most recipes call for lamb from the shoulder or neck, sliced potatoes, and onions. Some recipes call for the addition of other vegetables. The ingredients are layered and then covered in broth and cooked slowly in the oven until the lamb is tender and the onions and potatoes have been infused with the flavor of the broth and meat.

Lancashire Hotpot

2 lb lamb, from shoulder, neck, and shins, cut into pieces

1 tbsp peanut oil

Butter

4 lamb's kidneys, skinned, cored, and cut into bite-sized pieces

3 onions, cut into $\frac{1}{2}$-in wedges

1 tbsp flour

$2\frac{1}{2}$ cups hot chicken broth

Coarse sea salt

Freshly ground black pepper

1 bay leaf

2 sprigs of thyme

2 lb potatoes, peeled and sliced

Preheat oven to 325°F.

Trim the lamb of any excess fat and pat dry with a paper towel. Heat the oil and a small piece of butter in a large, heavy frying pan until very hot. Add the lamb, 2 or 3 pieces at a time, and fry until brown, turning as needed. Transfer browned pieces to a large casserole dish. Brown the pieces of kidney and add them to the lamb.

In the same frying pan, fry the onions over medium heat, adding a little more butter to the pan if necessary, until the onions are browned at the edges, about 10 minutes. Stir the flour into the onions, then add the hot broth, half a cup at a time, whisking until the flour and liquid are smoothly blended. Season with salt and pepper and bring to simmering point. Pour the liquid over the meat. Add the bay leaf and thyme. Arrange the potato slices on top in an overlapping pattern. Add more salt and pepper to taste, and scatter a few small pieces of butter on the top.

Cover the casserole with a tight-fitting lid and put in the oven. Cook for 1½ hours. Fifteen minutes before the cooking time is up, remove the lid and increase the heat to 400°F.

Remove the bay leaf and thyme before serving. *Serves 6*

Burgoo

This unusual dish has a loyal following, especially in the state of Kentucky and the surrounding area. It arrived there by sea, a strange circumstance given that Kentucky is landlocked. But historians insist that it came to America via the Atlantic Ocean, where sailors made a porridge that included bulgur wheat. (Burgoo is derived from the word.)

Today, it enjoys special status in Kentucky, where it is eaten annually at the Kentucky Derby. Preparing burgoo requires some commitment. Often, the pots used to make burgoo are enormous and are meant to serve hundreds, if not thousands, and the mixture needs several hours to cook. As such, burgoo is a popular dish served at community festivals.

The favored meats are mutton, chicken, and beef, but there are recipes that call for squirrel and other wild meats. The vegetables added are similarly at the discretion of the cook. Some recipes call for a thickening agent, such as cornmeal. Burgoo is cooked until thick enough to permit a spoon to stand upright.

Shepherd's Pie

Developed in the north of England and Scotland in the middle of the 19th century, shepherd's pie was a way to use up the leftovers from the Sunday roast. Its popularity grew with the invention of a machine to mince meat. Traditionally, said meat is lamb or mutton (not beef—this would be cottage pie), which is ground and then reheated with any leftover veggies (or fresh ones if none made it to Monday) as well as some liquid (either broth or watered-down gravy). This mixture forms the foundation of the pie. A layer of mashed potatoes (also ideally made from leftovers) sits atop the meat and forms a delicious thin crust when baked.

Among shepherd's pie's greatest advocates was Rolling Stone Keith Richards, said to have demanded the dish (along with healthy amounts of HP Sauce) wherever in the world the band was touring.

Rogan Josh

A northern Indian specialty, this curry is the one most associated with the Kashmir region. The word *rogan* translates as "oil" and *josh* is thought to be derived from the word for meat. Said meat is always lamb or mutton, taken from the leg, shank, or shoulder. Like many Indian dishes, the meat is first cooked in ghee, a clarified, evaporated butter that withstands the heat of India, although in the absence of this specialty ingredient, vegetable oil is perfectly acceptable.

From there, the seasonings will differ depending on the tastes of the cook. Pungent ginger, garlic, cloves, cinnamon, cumin, and paprika are often included. Cayenne pepper may also be added and determines the degree of heat the finished dish will have. The final result is a reddish, rich stew that is delicious on rice or as a dip for warm, flat naan bread.

Rogan Josh

5 cloves garlic, roughly chopped

1 onion, roughly chopped

1-in piece of fresh gingerroot, peeled and roughly chopped

1 tsp ground cinnamon

2 tsp ground cumin

2 tsp ground coriander

1 tbsp paprika

1 tsp chili powder

1 tsp salt

1 tbsp tomato paste

1/4 cup vegetable oil

2 lb lamb, cut into 1-in chunks

8 to 10 cardamom pods, lightly crushed

1 1/4 cups water

Put the garlic, onion, gingerroot, ground spices, salt, and tomato paste in a blender and blitz until smooth. Heat the oil in a flameproof casserole dish, add the lamb and cardamom pods, and fry over high heat to brown the meat on all sides. Add the paste and cook for 5 minutes, stirring frequently. Pour in the water and simmer, covered, for 1 to 1 1/2 hours until the meat is tender. *Serves 4*

Salumeria

A visit to an Italian salumeria, a place that sells cured meat (salumi), is more an event than a chore. These small specialty stores are packed from floor to ceiling with samplings of some of the finest products from a country that produces many fine products. The meat section, which is not only under glass but has its wares hanging from hooks wherever there is room, is no exception. It is hard to ignore the rich, smoky aromas of dried and spiced delicacies that meet you as you pass through the door.

There are two broad categories of salumi. *Insaccati* comprises those salumi that are finely chopped, mixed with seasonings and stuffed tightly into casing, then left to dry. The drying is part of the preservation as it reduces moisture content but there is also quite a bit of science at work. When the salted bits of meat are pressed together, harmless bacteria will feed on the potentially harmful microbes in the salty, oxygen-deprived interior. The process also alters the pH balance and makes the meat more flavor-intense.

The other category takes into account those meats that remain whole during the drying and curing process. **Prosciutto di Parma** is one of the most prominent and prized meats of this second group. It will be displayed whole, a leg from the hind quarter of the pig, often with the hoof attached. The cut is covered with a layer of protective fat, tawny colored on the outside, but creamy white on the interior. This gives way to soft and delicate, deep red meat that is sliced paper-thin. Good, well-aged (up to 16 months)

prosciutto can be eaten alone—it practically melts on the tongue as the flavors enter every corner of the mouth.

Speck is similar to prosciutto but gains its taste from heavy smoking over maple and beech woods, which also leads to a drier texture. **Culatello** is another solid, dry, aged ham-like salumi from the same hindquarter, but with the bone removed. **Coppa** follows the same basic process, only the meat is cut from the neck of the pig.

While prosciutto is prized, it is more expensive than more common *insaccati*, such as **casalingo**, **genoa**, **calabrese**, and **sopresatta**. Each of these is distinguished by shape and size (some as thick as a tree branch, others as thin as a finger), fat content (as high as 40% or more), seasonings (sweet fennel seeds for a touch of anise, dried chili for heat, black pepper for punch), and texture (coarse or fine chop). These salumi can be just as delicious as their more expensive counterparts and have the added advantage of being able to take on other flavors that get mixed with the mince.

A subcategory of *insaccati* are those that are cooked. Of these, **mortadella** is the most famous. Mortadella originated in Bologna, but similar versions are prepared in several places in Italy. Made from finely chopped, almost mashed pork, mortadella is marked by its uniform pinkness interrupted only by larding, where small chunks of raw pork fat have been distributed evenly throughout the meat. Unlike its North American cousin, bologna, mortadella is valued in Italy and it has gained Geographic Protection status from the European Union. Other cooked salumi include **zampone**, which is made from a mix of lean pork and minced skin and fat and is preserved in the hollowed leg of a pig.

Boiled and Baked Ham

A good-sized ham will last through several meals—breakfast, lunch, or dinner—and is versatile enough for all three and the snacks in between. It has been this way for centuries as farmers used ham from pigs slaughtered in the fall to provide meat throughout the winter. Ham is taken from the hind quarter and cured by salting and drying and (sometimes) smoking. There are several kinds, depending on the breed of pig, the curing process, the wood used for smoking, and how long the ham is left to age.

Cooking is a two-step process. The ham is initially immersed in simmering water with (surprisingly enough) hay. This helps reduce the salty taste left from the curing. While it is possible to eat the ham at this point (and many do), more flavor can be extracted by baking the ham with a sweet glaze and studding the fatty skin with cloves. When done, it can be sliced and served as a main course. The leftovers will last for days, providing meat for sandwiches, casseroles, omelettes, and any number of other dishes.

Braised Shin of Beef

What makes braised shin of beef so special is not so much the beef but the deep, rich, powerful gravy that is created when it simmers slowly in a big pot. The beef itself begins tough and heavy with fat and connective tissue. But as it braises, this connective tissue breaks down and thickens the sauce, giving it body and flavor.

Meanwhile, the meat tenderizes and will fall apart easily. Careful consideration must be given to the braising liquid. Dark beer, an ale or stout, adds even more body. A full-bodied red wine, preferably the same as the one being served with the meal, will add a degree of fruitiness.

Beef or veal broth complements the meat perfectly, especially when accompanied by juicy tomatoes or thickened with tomato paste. In a pinch, even water—supplemented by herbs and garlic—may be used, since the meat and vegetables from the stewing beef will release their flavors into whatever liquid surrounds them.

Braised Shin of Beef

2 tbsp olive oil

1 lb unsmoked pancetta, cut into large cubes

2 large onions, chopped

2 cloves garlic, sliced

½ lb button mushrooms

3 lb shin of beef, cut into large chunks

½ cup red wine

2 lb carrots, peeled and chopped

1 head of celery, chopped

1 can chopped tomatoes

1 bouquet garni

4 cups beef broth

Heat the olive oil in a frying pan, then add the pancetta. Fry until crispy, then transfer to a large casserole dish. Put the onions and garlic in the frying pan and cook until golden. Transfer to the casserole dish. Quickly toss the mushrooms in the frying pan, then put them in the casserole dish. Brown the shin of beef in the same oil and transfer to the casserole. Deglaze the pan with the red wine, and pour into the casserole dish. Set the casserole over low heat. Add the vegetables, tomatoes, bouquet garni, and enough broth to cover. Simmer, covered, for 3 to 4 hours, stirring occasionally. Add more broth if needed.
Serves 6

Chateaubriand

Named for François-René de Chateaubriand, who served in the governments of both Napoleon and Louis XVIII, this dish is the perfect centerpiece of an intimate dinner for two.

Chateaubriand can refer to the cut of meat, which is taken from the prized center part of the tenderloin and cut at least 2 inches in thickness, or to the finished dish involving rich béarnaise sauce. Either way, the simply seasoned meat must be cooked under a very hot broiler and is best served rare or, at most, medium rare. It is a lean cut and as tender as beef can be but the lack of fat means that it generally requires a boost of flavor. Some use bacon, though the béarnaise sauce, a warm, mayonnaise-like concoction spiked with tarragon, is a much better choice.

The sauce can be fickle to cook (eggs always seem to present challenges) but rewards patience and attentiveness with a smooth, rich result that perfectly complements a fine piece of meat.

Chateaubriand

A chateaubriand steak is cut from the center and thickest part of the filet, weighing about 12 oz, which is enough for two people. It is too thick to be broiled on an ordinary domestic stove, as the meat will be too near the broiling element and will dry up before it is sufficiently cooked. The best solution is, after painting the meat with olive oil and sprinkling it with a little coarsely ground pepper, to give it about a minute on each side close to the hot broiler and then to transfer it, standing on a rack, in a baking pan to a very hot oven (445°F) and roast it for 12 to 15 minutes. *Serves 2*

Adapted from Elizabeth David's *French Provincial Cooking*

Bresaola

From the Alpine regions of Italy, bresaola is dry-aged, salt-cured beef taken from a lean cut. Think prosciutto, only instead of pork, the meat used is beef. In this sense, it bears some relation to less celebrated versions of dried beef such as jerky or the South American *carne seca*, though it is not nearly as difficult to chew as either of these two examples. Part of the reason is that bresaola begins with a very lean piece (such as the inside round), which gives the end product a drier texture and a deep red, fall color. The flavor is not strong, but has a rich, round feel that makes for a good ingredient to a first course or as a midday snack. It is served in paper-thin slices, perhaps with shavings of Parmigiano Reggiano, a mound of arugula, a squirt of lemon juice, and a drizzle of good olive oil.

Calf's Liver with Onion Gravy

Smooth in texture and delicate in flavor when treated properly, calf's liver is an unfairly maligned delight. It is best when harvested from a relatively young animal.

The color of liver is important. Paler cuts have been taken from a calf raised more on milk than anything else and will be more tender when cooked. Simple preparations work best—a quick sauté in butter or oil or even bacon fat will create a crust and bring out this meat's best features. A hot grill will also do the trick nicely and leave tasty grill marks.

Onion gravy is a classic accompaniment. Onions are softened in butter or oil or bacon fat and turned into a gravy by the addition of flour, broth, and seasoning whisked together vigorously.

Calf's Liver with Onion Gravy

2 tbsp butter, plus 2 tbsp

4 cups thinly sliced onions

2 tbsp olive oil

1½ lb calf's liver, thinly sliced

¼ cup red wine

¼ cup beef broth

Juice of 1 lemon

Salt

Freshly ground black pepper

In a large frying pan over moderate heat, melt 2 tablespoons of butter, then add the onions. Cook, stirring, for 20 minutes or until the onions are soft and golden. Push the onions to the edge of the pan.

Add the remaining butter and oil and sauté the liver slices until the liver is browned lightly outside but still pink within—1 or 2 minutes. Remove the liver and keep warm.

Turn the heat to high, then stir in the wine, broth, and lemon juice. Reduce the pan juices until they are slightly thickened, stirring the onions into the gravy.

Season to taste. *Serves 4*

Char Siu

A calling card of Cantonese cuisine around the world, char siu literally translates as "fork roasted." This is but the beginning. Or the end, rather. Before the pork is cooked, it is seasoned with a combination of honey or sugar, soy sauce, and five-spice seasoning. Some chefs add food coloring, which leaves the crust of the roasted meat bright red. Modern methods call for the meat to be cooked in a medium oven, with frequent interruptions to turn and baste the meat with the marinade. The sugars caramelize and intensify the natural sweetness of the meat. When the meat is done, the outer edge of the interior also retains some of the redness from the marinade, leaving a distinctive mark that resembles smeared lipstick.

This simple dish is served either on its own or with a heap of steamed rice.

Steak and Kidney Pudding

Also known by the colloquial names "Kate and Sydney Pudding" or "Baby's Head," steak and kidney pudding is a well-known comfort food enjoyed in the UK and wherever British influence has been felt. Most pubs will include it on the menu.

Chunks of beef from chuck and kidney are browned and set aside. In the same pan, onions, carrots, and other wintery vegetables are added and browned, and then wine or broth is used to deglaze, pulling up all the flavor of the meats. This mixture also serves as the foundation for the gravy, and when the meat is returned to the pan, the gravy will begin to form its body, thickening as it is cooked.

True steak and kidney pudding calls for a suet crust rather than one made with vegetable shortening. The pastry envelops the thickened cooked stew and the whole package is left to steam in a double boiler. The final cooking is what distinguishes pudding from pie, as the latter is finished in the oven and results in a crispier, flakier crust.

Steak and Kidney Pudding

For the suet crust pastry:

2 ½ cups self-rising flour

Salt and freshly ground black pepper

6 oz (1½ cups) shredded beef suet or grated chilled butter

For the filling:

1¼ lb chuck steak

8 oz ox kidney after trimming, so buy 10 oz

2 tbsp flour, well-seasoned

1 medium onion, sliced

Cold water

1 tsp Worcestershire sauce

Salt and freshly ground black pepper

You will need a well-buttered pudding basin of 5 pints capacity and a steamer.

To make the pastry, first sift the flour and salt into a large mixing bowl. Add some freshly ground black pepper, then add the suet and mix it into the flour using the blade of a knife. When it's evenly blended, add a few drops of cold water and start to mix with the knife, using curving movements and turning the mixture around. The aim is to bring it together as a dough, so keep adding drops of water until it begins to get really sticky. Now abandon the knife, go in with your hands, and bring it all together until you have a nice smooth elastic dough that leaves the bowl clean. It's worth noting that suet pastry always needs more water than other types, so if it is still a bit dry, just go on adding a few drops at a time. After that, take a quarter of the dough for the top, then roll the rest out fairly thickly. What you need is a round approximately 13 inches in diameter. Now line the basin with the pastry, pressing it well all around. To make the filling chop the steak and kidney into fairly small cubes, toss them in the seasoned flour, then add them to the pastry-lined basin with the slices of onion. Add enough cold water to reach almost to the top of the meat and sprinkle in a few drops of Worcestershire sauce and another seasoning of salt and pepper.

Roll out the pastry top, dampen its edges, and put it in position on the pudding. Seal well and cover with a double sheet of foil, pleated in the center to allow room for expansion while cooking. Now secure it with string, making a little handle so that you can lift it out of the hot steamer. Then place it in a steamer over boiling water. Steam for 5 hours, topping off the boiling water halfway through. You can either serve the pudding by spooning portions straight out of the bowl or slide a knife round the edge and turn the whole thing out on to a serving plate (which is more fun!). *Serves 6*

Adapted from Delia Smith's *Winter Collection*

Faggots

A unique combination of offal, faggots are
a traditional Welsh dish with a reputation
throughout the United Kingdom, especially
in the industrial north (where they are
sometimes known as "savory ducks").

Coal miners played an important role in
solidifying faggots' presence in the annals
of English culinary history, as they were fond
of taking them underground for their midday
meal. During the rationing of the Second
World War, faggots found prominence
in a country eager for any kind of meat.
The name is derived from the Latin for
"bundle," which is somewhat appropriate,
given their presentation.

The dish begins with pig's liver and usually
includes another kind of pork—either more
offal or belly meat. With seasonings and
fillers mixed in, the meat is finely ground
and shaped into balls. To hold their shape,
faggots are wrapped in caul and then baked
in a slow oven. They are usually served with
onion gravy and mashed potatoes.

Deviled Kidneys

The use of the word "deviled" in the name
of this dish suggests something hot, and
indeed, deviled kidneys are relatively spicy,
especially by the standards of English cuisine.
But tradition states that they are served
at breakfast and so spicing is accordingly
moderate. They were a favorite in late-
Victorian and Edwardian England and though
their glory years may be behind them,
nostalgia demands that better butchers
supply them as needed.

The kidneys in this case come from lamb,
as these are tender enough to cook using dry
heat. They are fried on the stovetop for long
enough to create a fine, caramelized crust
but not so long that the flesh inside toughens.
When they are nearly done, spicy elements
such as mustard and Worcestershire sauce
get added to the pan and are then drizzled
over the kidneys when they are served on a
slice of toast.

Although they are considered a breakfast
dish, many commentators suggest a pint of
dark beer as an accompaniment.

Sweetbreads

Neither sweet nor bread, this ironic word describes the thymus gland and pancreas of a young calf or lamb. They are not, as is widely believed, calves' brains.

White and irregularly shaped, sweetbreads have a firm, dense texture and are extremely perishable—a perfect food to pick up at the market in the morning and bring home to prepare right away. Prior to cooking, a tough membrane must be removed and the pieces of sweetbread must be soaked in cold water for at least four hours with frequent changes of the water. The soaking removes much of the color, leaving the sweetbreads nearly white. From there, the pieces are blanched and then refrigerated until just before the final cooking. Traditionally, sweetbreads are simply broiled or breaded and fried in hot butter but in better restaurants around the world, top chefs have been using the meat in more sophisticated preparations.

Their mild flavor and pleasing texture lend versatility, and the meat takes well to a variety of sauces.

Welsh Cawl

In Welsh, *cawl* translates as both "soup" and "stew" and no one word could be more perfect. Cawl is a peasant dish with a history that stretches back to at least the 14th century. For many modern-day Welsh, it evokes nationalistic sentiments and, for those living abroad, memories of home.

Cawl is very simple. It begins with a cheap cut of lamb, which is simmered at length in water or broth. Vegetables such as carrots, parsnips, rutabaga, leeks, and potatoes are added, depending on what is available. The stew is simmered over low heat for several hours, in some cases overnight. The fat is skimmed from the top and the cawl is traditionally served in two stages, first as a soup and secondly as a stew.

Welsh Cawl

8 cups water

12 oz beef shank

2 large onions, chopped

2 large carrots, sliced

1 rutabaga, diced

Salt

Freshly ground black pepper

4 potatoes, peeled and quartered

2 leeks, sliced

1 small head cabbage, sliced

2 tbsp chopped fresh parsley

Place the beef shank in a large pan of water and bring to a boil. Turn down the heat and simmer for 1½ hours, then turn off the heat and allow to cool overnight.

Remove the meat from the water and pass the broth through a sieve. Cut the meat into chunks, removing any gristle.

Now reheat the broth. When it is boiling add the onions, carrots, and rutabaga. Season with salt and pepper and simmer for 1½ hours. Twenty minutes before the end of cooking time, add the potatoes. After another 10 minutes, add the leeks, cabbage, parsley, and beef chunks. The cawl is done when the vegetables are tender. *Serves 10–12*

Haggis

A traditional, if mostly ceremonial, haggis dish is strongly identified among Scots in both Scotland and in North America.

Its origins are ancient and rooted in the fact that the main ingredients, various offal from mutton or lamb, are perishable and needed ready preservation. This came in the form of salt, a tight packing in sheep's stomach, and quick boiling. In this way, the innards would remain edible for some weeks.

Haggis is enjoyed almost exclusively in Scotland and in Scottish communities and a sense of nationalism accompanies its serving. This is in no small part due to Robbie Burns' praise of the dish as the "great chieftain of the pudding race." On Robbie Burns Day (January 25), Scottish homes celebrate with a haggis, a piper, and a dram or two of Scotch whisky. In addition to offal (lungs, heart, and liver), the sheep's stomach is packed with oatmeal, suet, broth, and light seasoning. The suet lends richness and the oatmeal body.

Honey-Glazed Ham

A honey-glazed ham is a festive dish for more than one reason. First, the aesthetics. A coppery crust full of caramelized texture surrounds the entire piece of meat. When carved, it gives way to vibrant pink flesh.

Regardless of whatever else might be on the menu, the honey-glazed ham demands to be the center of attention. The juxtaposition of colors reflects a similar pairing of flavors. The sweetness of the honey penetrates the meat and offers contrast to the saltiness of the ham. Cut from the hindquarter of the pig and cured before cooking, it is better suited to being hidden between two pieces of sandwich bread. But with honey, the ham reaches its full potential.

There are many companies that will prepare a ham for you but the dish can also be prepared at home. The glaze will include not only honey, but also brown sugar (for extra crust) and butter (for extra flavor). As the ham bakes, it is basted with the glaze frequently. At the end of the cooking time, the ham spends some time under a hot broiler, which creates the distinctive brittle crust.

Döner Kebab

One of the world's most beloved late-night snacks originated in Turkey, traveled to Greece where it became *gyros*, and then set off to conquer the cravings of carousing youth in club districts of major cities around the world. In Germany, with its large Turkish population, döner kebabs are the most popular fast food.

Döner and *gyros* are essentially the same thing: meat (mostly beef and lamb) is ground to a very fine grade or sliced thinly and piled high on a vertical spit that rotates slowly in front of a heating element. As it cooks,

it is shaved in thin ribbons. Strictly speaking, this is all that is needed to create a döner (which means "turning roast"). In most places, however, the meat is used as the main ingredient in a sandwich or wrap. The bread is common flat or pita bread that is warmed on a flat grill and then stuffed with the freshly cut meat, salad-type vegetables, and a sauce.

The sauce is often the difference between döners and *gyros* in various places, most of which have a historically large Turkish or Greek migrant population. Greek places might use tzatziki while Turkish sauces can vary widely.

Bistecca Fiorentina

Bistecca Fiorentina has been the motivation behind countless pilgrimages to Tuscany, the region of Italy that produces this wonderful steak. It includes two of the most prized parts of the cow, the filet and the strip loin. Legend has it that the first ones were served during the San Lorenzo Festival, patronized by the infamous Medici family.

Although any cow can produce the cut, in Tuscany the breed must be Chianina, which thrives in the hills and valleys of the Chianti region. This is according to the Florentine Butchers Association, whose unusually strict rules also mandate the following: before butchering, the meat must be hung for five to six days. The steak must be cut from the loin through the sirloin with the bone intact, and it should be no less than 3/4 inch and no more than 1¼ inches thick. There's more. True bistecca Fiorentina must be cooked without seasoning over extremely hot coals, with the grill placed 8 inches from the fire. Each side is cooked for about 5 minutes, leaving the steak rare. When plated, it receives a drizzle of olive oil and salt and pepper. Nothing more. Nothing less.

Beef Olives

While there are no olives in the actual dish, with a little imagination, one can see the connection. Thinly sliced and pounded beef (sirloin is ideal) is slathered with stuffing and rolled tightly. The result is something resembling a pitted olive, cylindrical, fat in the middle, and open at the ends.

Sadly, this has nothing to do with the name, either. It is actually derived from a corruption of the old French word *alou* for "lark," with the thought that the bundles resembled the decapitated birds of the same name. In any event, the stuffing is a matter of choice, but most recipes call for some form of fatty pork (either bacon, sausage meat, or lard), bread crumbs, onions, herbs, and a binding agent (an egg or dollop of mustard). That said, there are no hard and fast rules regarding the stuffing, and beef olives invite experimentation.

Once rolled, the olives are browned and then baked in a hot oven until cooked through. Going to all this trouble yields its rewards. Each bite will contain a piece of beef and a quantity of the stuffing, making additional condiments unnecessary. Nevertheless, many recipes call for the addition of a sauce, with the pan drippings serving as the foundation.

Bowl of Red

"Bowl of red" is a term used in the southwestern United States for a dish more commonly known as chile con carne or just chili.

The origins are dim but chile peppers, which provide all the punch in a bowl of red, are an ancient and integral part of Mexican cuisine and so the theory goes that the beef version of the dish was developed in the southwestern United States when that region still formed part of Mexico. This, however, is the least of the controversies surrounding chili. For at least half a century, chefs have debated the place of beans in chili. In Texas and in official competitions, beans are an anathema. They are more accepted in the rest of the world, as is the other contentious ingredient: tomatoes.

With or without beans or tomatoes, bowl of red needs time and the inclusion of outstanding dried chili powder, of which there are hundreds of varieties, each with a unique character that will ultimately affect the finished dish. Spicing is a matter of taste and, in some parts, machismo, since some like it very hot indeed.

Tigua Indian Bowl of Red

1 cup chopped onions

2 cloves garlic, minced

2 tbsp vegetable oil

2 lb beef round, cut into ½-in cubes

1½ tsp salt

1 tbsp sugar

1½ tsp freshly ground black pepper

1½ tsp ground dried Mexican oregano

1 tbsp ground cumin

5 tbsp chili powder

1½ tsp red jalapeño powder

1 (15-oz) can tomato sauce

1 tbsp masa harina dissolved in ½ cup water

Cooked beans, rice, or bread

Sour cream

In a large skillet or Dutch oven, sauté the onions and garlic in the oil until soft. Add the beef and cook until browned. Add the salt, sugar, pepper, oregano, cumin, chili powder, jalapeño powder, tomato sauce, and 1½ cups water; stir well. Bring to a boil. Reduce the heat to a low simmering boil and cook, partially covered, for 1 hour and 10 minutes. Remove from the heat. Add the masa harina mixture. Return to low heat and cook, stirring occasionally, 5 minutes.

Serve with beans, rice, or bread on the side: all useful for muffling the heat. Also helpful is a tablespoon of sour cream. *Serves 6*

Adapted from Jane and Michael Stern's *Chili Nation*

Vindaloo

Vindaloo came to India when the Portuguese imported their favorite wine and garlic (*vinho* and *alho*) marinated pork dish to Goa, at the time a colony of the former empire.

Today's vindaloo bears little resemblance to this original, tame version. Goans added spices: ginger, cumin, cloves, cardamom, and, most importantly, chiles. Now more Indian than Portuguese, vindaloo caught on throughout the rest of the continent, and there are few Indian restaurants that do not have vindaloo dishes on the menu. Indeed, it is widely considered to be the hottest of the many hot curries in Indian cuisine.

While the Goans still insist on making their vindaloo with pork, chicken and lamb are certainly acceptable. The spice of vindaloo is intoxicating, one of those rare occasions where the body may undergo metabolic changes. Luckily, it is usually served with a loaf of naan and a serving of *raita*, a cucumber yogurt spread that neutralizes the burn.

Stifado

In a reversal of the norm, the Greek word comes from the Italian, *stufato*. Each means "stew." That said, contemporary preparations show some influence from Turkey. And so like the Greeks themselves, stifado is a dish that has adapted to survive. It traditionally comes from the mountainous northern region, where lower winter temperatures necessitate a hearty, warming stew at the end of the day. The meat in the dish is beef, taken from a less expensive cut and cubed. From there, variations are endless, depending on what is available, although potatoes, garlic, carrots, tomato purée (for body), and currants are common additions.

As with most stews, the meat is browned first and the vegetables are added along with a braising liquid—wine, broth, or, in the worst-case scenario, water. Seasonings come in the form of cinnamon and cumin. The whole lot cooks over a slow flame in a covered pot until the meat is cooked through and the harder vegetables are fork tender. As this happens, the flavors come together and the cumin and cinnamon produce wonderful, kitchen-filling aromas.

Sauerbraten

An ancient dish attributed by some (though not many) to Charlemagne, Sauerbraten (sour roast) is still enjoyed throughout Germany, although it is strongly identified with the Rhineland and surroundings. It was originally made with horse meat but today is almost always made with beef.

The sour in Sauerbraten comes from vinegar, which forms the basis of the marinade in which the meat bathes for two to three days before cooking. The meat used is typically a tougher cut and the acidic marinade, which will also include earthy aromatic spices such as peppercorns, juniper berries, cloves, and bay leaves, helps tenderize the whole roast before it cooks. In the Rhineland, sugar and raisins are added to give the dish some countering sweetness. Naturally, with such a lengthy stay in the marinade, the meat picks up quite a bit of flavor from the marinade ingredients.

Cooking follows the same method as any pot roast. It is browned and then roasted with the marinade in a covered dish in a medium oven. The marinade will continue to flavor the roast but as the meat cooks, its juices will also be released. When the roast is cooked, the marinade is strained and returned to a saucepan, where it is thickened with ground gingerbread, which brings both body and a unique zip to the sauce.

Steak au Poivre

There are few pairings that feature pepper so prominently as steak au poivre. This is the time to splurge on more expensive green, white, and red peppercorns, which add complexity to the taste and make for a more dramatic presentation. The peppers are crushed using the flat side of a big, heavy knife or a mortar and pestle. They should not be ground too finely but remain chunky enough to feel in the mouth. A piece of steak—any cut suitable for broiling will serve, though filet is preferred—is rubbed with the pepper and then seared in a hot pan, both creating a crust on the meat and leaving flavor in the pan, which serves as the basis for the sauce.

What makes steak au poivre unique is the use of brandy or cognac instead of red wine in the sauce. This liquid is reduced with beef broth and aromatics and may even be thickened with cream and butter. The result is a smooth, richly flavored accompaniment to the sharp taste of the pepper and pungent beef. When the sauce has reached the desired consistency, the steaks get a quick bath with it before plating and then the remaining sauce is drizzled on top.

Steak au Poivre

4 (6 oz) filet steaks

1 tbsp coarse sea salt

2 tbsp whole black peppercorns

1 tbsp vegetable oil

⅓ cup shallots, finely chopped

¼ cup unsalted butter

½ cup cognac

¾ cup heavy cream

Pat the steaks dry with a paper towel and season both sides with salt. Crush the peppercorns in a pestle and mortar and press the grains evenly onto both sides of steaks. Heat a large cast-iron skillet over medium to high heat until very hot. Now add the oil followed by the steaks. Fry the steaks for 3 minutes on each side then leave to rest while you make the sauce.

Brown the shallots in half the butter over medium heat. Increase the heat and add the cognac. Boil rapidly to reduce the liquid by half, stirring all the time. Now add the cream and continue to boil the sauce, stirring until reduced by half again. Turn heat to low and stir in the remaining butter, incorporating it fully, before pouring the sauce over the steaks to serve. *Serves 4*

Steak and Oyster Pie

There was a time when oysters were cheap and plentiful and the fare of the poor and downtrodden, and a dish like steak and oyster pie was a cheap means of basic nourishment. Like many of our best-loved foods, however, it has survived through the generations, despite the fact that oysters are now among the most expensive shellfish available. It is most closely associated with Ireland and has become a standard in pubs there but is also enjoyed in Australia and New Zealand, as well as the rest of the United Kingdom.

Many recipes suggest using Guinness, the iconic mealy dark beer of Ireland, as the braising fluid for the beef and the basis for the gravy that bathes the meat and oysters. This goes well with the rather heavy, lard-based crust that surrounds the stew and bakes until brown on top.

Steak Tartare

It is said that invading Tartars, who tore across Asia and Eastern Europe in the early centuries of the last millennium, tenderized beef by placing it between their saddle and the back of their horses. After a long ride, the meat was tender enough to enjoy raw. Today's versions are somewhat more refined. Good ground beef (filet or sirloin) is finely minced just before serving. The bright red beef is then mixed with onions, capers, gherkins, egg, and various seasonings.

In restaurants that offer steak tartare the server often prepares at tableside for maximum freshness. It is best served with toast or thin, crispy fries.

Steak Tartare

2 egg yolks
2 tbsp Dijon mustard
¼ cup olive oil
¼ cup onion, finely chopped
¼ cup capers, rinsed
4 sprigs of parsley, finely chopped
Freshly ground black pepper
1¼ lb fresh sirloin, finely chopped

In a large glass or stainless steel bowl, mix together the eggs yolks and mustard, then slowly whisk in the oil. Stir in the remaining ingedients. Shape into a large loaf or several small mounds. *Serves 6*

7 BEANS, CHEESE, AND EGGS

Adzuki Beans

These little red beans with the white stripe are eaten not only in Japan, but across the Far East. Adzuki or azuki beans are used as an ingredient in stews and porridge, served with rice and other grains, transformed into sprouts, made into sweet red-bean paste, or fermented into *miso* (a base for sauces and soups). They are low in calories and fat but high in nutrients, especially iron and potassium.

The red tint of adzuki beans lends a festive air even to simple dishes such as *sekihan* (Japanese red beans and sticky rice) and they figure in ceremonial meals from Korean weddings to Chinese Lunar New Year. According to legend, the Buddha ate a porridge of red beans, nuts, and rice to fortify himself on the journey to enlightenment.

One reason for their popularity is their subtle sweetness. A delightful way to eat adzuki beans is in *es kacang*, a sweet snack widely available in Southeast Asia. Created from shaved ice on a base of sweet corn, nuts, and adzuki beans and topped with evaporated milk, it has cooled and nourished many a weary traveler.

Black-Eyed Peas

Black-eyed peas originated in Africa and are grown in many countries around the world, making their way via the West Indies to the United States, where they have a very special place in the cuisine of the American South. Following the American Civil War, the noted black agronomist George Washington Carver, who also championed the peanut, encouraged the planting of black-eyed peas across the South to restore farmland that had been depleted by the cotton plantations.

They are not only nutritious to eat but, as legumes, they add nitrogen to the soil. The humble and hearty food of the American South eventually became the "soul food" of the 1960s.

In the same way that roast turkey is an essential part of an American Thanksgiving dinner, black-eyed peas, served with collard greens and corn bread, are a New Year's Day good luck tradition for Southerners. This tradition is said to date back to the civil war era when General Sherman's Union troops spared black-eyed peas during their scorched-earth campaign, believing them to be strictly animal fodder. Many Southerners survived on black-eyed peas and continue to celebrate this humble legume almost 150 years later.

Peas and Rice

Jamaica boasts several iconic dishes, from ackee and saltfish to jerk chicken and curried goat, but rice and peas has a special spot on every table. It has a place of honor at Sunday lunch and at celebrations, and every home has its own recipe.

Red pigeon peas or kidney beans are traditional through the year but at Christmas and New Year's, green pigeon peas are a must. Like the pace of island life, cooking rice and peas is a leisurely affair. The beans are cooked slowly in a rich broth of coconut milk and seasonings. Scallions, fresh thyme, garlic, and Scotch bonnet peppers provide the traditional flavor. Some cooks add a pig's tail to enrich the broth. Rice is added last, in just the right amount to absorb the cooking broth.

Scotch bonnet peppers have a well-deserved fiery reputation. For a touch of warmth, just rest the whole Scotch bonnet on top of the rice and let it steam. For an eye-watering encounter, chop the Scotch bonnet and add it to the pot. Yah mon!

Peas and Rice

$1\frac{1}{2}$ cups cooked red kidney beans, liquid reserved

2 cloves garlic, chopped

$1\frac{1}{4}$ cup unsweetened coconut milk

Water

1 cup uncooked rice

2 scallions, crushed

1 or 2 sprigs fresh thyme

Salt

Freshly ground black pepper

Put the beans in a large saucepan and add the chopped garlic. Pour the reserved bean liquid into a large measuring cup. Add the coconut milk and enough fresh water to make $2\frac{1}{4}$ cups of liquid. Pour over the beans and garlic. Add the rice, crushed scallions, thyme, and salt and pepper to taste. Stir, and bring the mixture to a boil. Reduce the heat and cook, covered, for about 20 minutes or until all liquid is absorbed. *Serves 4*

Marrowfat Peas and Vinegar

Pisum sativum is the plant family that provides the large and very diverse family of peas that has now traveled around the world. Centuries ago, experiments with smooth yellow peas and green wrinkly peas helped Gregor Mendel develop his theory of dominant and recessive genes. Until immature peas—known variously as garden peas, English peas, or green peas—became popular in 16th-century France, most peas were allowed to grow to full maturity in farmers' fields, then harvested, dried, and stored.

Marrowfat peas are a legacy of that time when peas were a hearty staple. Large, green, smooth, and filled with energy, they can be made into the classic British dish "mushy peas," eaten as a side vegetable, or made into soup. But there is a special place in the hearts—and stomachs—of people in Scotland and the north of England for a helping of hot marrowfat peas dressed in vinegar.

Malt vinegar, an assertive, dark vinegar made from malted barley and grain, is the perfect foil for the fat, starchy, green marrowfats.

Bean Sprouts

By the time it reaches us much of our food has been separated from its life-support system and is losing nutrients. In contrast, bean sprouts are a "living" food. Like a tiny food factory, they have just unpacked the storehouse of energy, enzymes, and vitamins in dried mung beans and are busy making it all available to us in a sweet, crunchy, ready-to-eat package.

Looking at a bean sprout, it's hard to believe it has much, if any, nutritional content, but from the tip of its tiny root to the pair of emerging yellow-green leaves at its other end, a sprout provides part of our daily need for vitamins B6 and C, plus thiamin, riboflavin, and niacin.

Chinese cuisine has enjoyed lightly cooked mung bean sprouts for thousands of years in crispy egg rolls and spring rolls, in stir-fries and soups. As a *yin,* or cooling food, they help balance the *yang,* or hotness, of spicy ingredients. Their crunchy texture and mild, sweet flavor are a great addition to Western-style foods, such as salads and omelettes.

Dried mung beans produce roughly six times their weight in sprouts, just with the addition of water, making them appealing to the pocketbook as well as the stomach.

Flageolet beans

Flageolets, the *Chevrier vert*, are small and kidney-shaped, and are pale green in color. Developed in a suburb of Paris in the late 19th century by a grower named Gabriel Chevrier, flageolets are a classic accompaniment to roast lamb, dressed with rosemary, garlic, and mustard. Their subtle taste and creamy texture absorb and amplify other flavors without distortion. Flageolets are best when prepared simply, with a *mirepoix* of carrots, onions, and celery, in chicken broth, or cooked slowly in a cassoulet.

Flageolets are harvested before the pods reach maturity and that is the secret to their unique taste and tint. Left to ripen fully on the plant, they would become rather ordinary white beans. Flageolets are eaten when freshly picked, if available, but are often dried for storage. They may also be available frozen and in cans. Dried beans must be soaked before using.

Perhaps it is the labor-intensive hand-picking and drying process that lends them their air of exclusiveness or, perhaps, it is having their very own annual festival, the *Foire aux Haricots*, in Arpajon, near Paris, that gives flageolets their prestigious title "the caviar of beans."

Butter Beans

Butter beans and lima beans come from the same wild ancestor but were domesticated at different times. They are native to the Western hemisphere and traveled from their likely origin in modern-day Peru into Central and North America and then around the world. The larger form is popularly known as the lima bean and its smaller version as the butter bean or baby lima.

Butter beans have a starchy yet buttery texture and a delicate flavor. Although fresh butter beans are difficult to find, they are worth looking for in the summer and fall when they are in season. They are available dried and canned year round.

Butter beans are very high in molybdenum, a component of sulfite oxidase, an enzyme that helps to detoxify sulfites. With so many preserved foods containing sulfites, adding butter beans to your diet is a healthy choice. And there are many ways to do that: puréed with garlic and fresh herbs, they make a great dip for bread or vegetables; they combine well with winter vegetables to make a hearty soup; and they are essential to succotash, a Native American classic combining butter beans and corn (maize), often served at an American Thanksgiving meal.

Cannellini Beans

Beans have a solid history as peasant fare, dating back to Roman times, but their nutritious merits have made them popular in contemporary Italian cuisine. With their long, leisurely cooking times, they epitomize many of the virtues espoused by the Slow Food Movement of northern Italy.

Cannellini beans appear so often in Tuscan cuisine that people of the region are affectionately known as *mangiafagiole*—bean eaters. But who can blame them? These beans, also known as white kidney beans, are so versatile, they can go almost anywhere.

They stay whole and firm when cooked, so they are wonderful in salads, say, mixed with tomato quarters, fresh mozzarella, torn basil, olive oil, slices of red onion, salt, and some freshly ground black pepper. They are the familiar bean found in minestrone soup. Puréed in a blender with some roasted garlic, a little olive oil, and fresh lemon juice, cannellini beans make a creamy dip for chunks of fresh or toasted bread. Just sprinkle with a little chopped parsley before serving or sauté with fresh herbs and some olive oil for a simple, flavorful side dish. *Buon appetito!*

Dal Masala

Dal is to an Indian cook as oatmeal porridge is to the Scots or rice to the Chinese. It is a dish prepared more by intuition than logic. Eaten daily from childhood, dal is on the table at almost every meal. The term "dal" encompasses many different split pulses, among them *masoor dal* (red lentils), *moong dal* (husked mung beans), and *toor dal* (pigeon peas). Their popularity varies from region to region and dal masala takes many different forms as well, depending on which type of dal is favored and which spices are preferred.

One of the easiest ways to make dal masala is with masoor dal, which turns a golden-yellow color when cooked. The lentils need only be washed and drained before cooking and they cook very quickly. To flavor the dal, fry onions, garlic, and ginger until soft and add a dash of turmeric. Lightly fry the lentils in the mixture, and simmer for about 15 minutes. Add salt to taste and your chosen *masala* of roasted and ground spices—coriander, cumin, cardamom, cinnamon, cloves, peppercorns, or nutmeg. It is the masala that makes this dish your own. Simmer until the dal is a soft, fragrant purée.

Chana Masala

Garbanzo beans have many aliases—chickpeas, Egyptian pea, ceci beans, and kabuli chana among them. No matter what they are called, they are beloved in many cultures for their firm, crunchy texture and nutty flavor. One of the earliest domesticated foods from the Fertile Crescent, they have been included in many cuisines for around 10,000 years. They are a staple of Mediterranean cooking, found in a number of signature dishes such as hummus and falafel.

The knobbly little legumes are perfect nutritional partners for Indian flatbreads and star in classic vegetarian dishes from northern India, such as chana masala—a rich stew of garbanzos with a supporting cast of spices and herbs. A treat is in store from the moment toasted cumin seeds leap to fragrant life in the pot and chopped onions begin to brown. Mashed gingerroot, garlic, and chiles blend with chopped tomato to make a rich sauce flavored with coriander, turmeric, and garam masala—a cook's choice of spices. When the sauce is blended, it is ready for the chana to begin absorbing its rich flavors. Topped with fragrant fresh cilantro leaves, eaten with rice, chapati, or crispy *bhatura* (fried bread), chana masala is comfort food in any language.

Edamame

Edamame are immature soybeans, picked when still green, rubbed with salt, and boiled, in the pod, in salted water for about 10 minutes. Tossing them into cold water stops them from overcooking. They can be eaten warm, at room temperature, or chilled. There are reputedly more than 200 kinds of edamame, with diminutive names like "Don't Tell," "Green Pearls," and "Beer Friend." They come in many different flavors and are priced according to how desirable they are.

Edamame are a very popular snack food in Japan, in the same way that peanuts in the shell are a popular snack in North America. It's not just the sweet, nutty taste and delicious texture that attract people. There is something contemplative and inherently satisfying about popping those little pearls out of their pods and into one's mouth and then reaching for the next pod.

Eating edamame, you can imagine yourself in a Tokyo baseball park calling a roving vendor to bring you a glass of Japanese beer; or sharing a bowl of edamame with friends and family catching up with all the gossip; or at a bar enjoying edamame with chilled sake.

Fermented Bean Curd

Fava Beans

Fermented bean curd, or *fu yu*, takes soybean cake or tofu to the next level. Made with dried, firm bean curd that has been allowed to ferment as the result of the action of fungal spores or bacterium, it is preserved in brine and rice wine. The liquid is flavored with different ingredients, such as chiles or sesame oil. One variety is tinted red with the addition of red rice. *Tempe*, widely available in Indonesia, is also a form of fermented bean curd, produced by a different fungus.

Fu yu is salty, pungent, and smooth. It's sometimes called Chinese cheese and compared with Camembert or Stilton; that tells you something of its pungency! Small cubes of *fu yu* are packed into jars or cans along with their brine.

Fermented bean curd is a condiment— a little goes a long way. It is often added to *congee* (rice porridge) or stir-fried with green vegetables, like beans, bitter melon, or various leafy greens. It makes a great marinade for pork and chicken, along with a little of the brine. It can also be spread thinly on crackers, like a cream cheese, or added to dipping sauces.

Fava beans are not a true bean but are a cousin to peas. Like peas, they are a cool-season vegetable, so they are one of the first fresh crops of the temperate growing season. Only the very youngest pods are tender enough to eat. When mature, the flat beans sit comfortably in the fuzzy interiors of tough pods. They originated in the Mediterranean thousands of years ago and fava is the Italian name for them.

In season, simple preparation is all that is needed. Steam young favas for about 5 minutes, then brush with butter or olive oil and salt lightly. Their fresh flavor is a spring treat. Fava beans pair well with the saltiness of pancetta or bacon. Try garnishing with some crumbled feta or pecorino, or add them to a risotto or soup.

According to folklore, if you want luck to follow you, try planting fava beans on Good Friday; if you never want to go hungry, a dried fava bean in your pocket should help; and if you ever want to get away from it all, someone named Jack can tell you about a beanstalk with a fabulous view (but watch out for the giant).

Ful Medames

A dish whose origins are so ancient that even the pharaohs must have eaten it, ful medames is a staple of Middle Eastern cuisine for rich and poor alike. Fava beans form a moist and hearty base to which are added fresh ingredients: the pungency of finely crushed garlic, the piquancy of lemon juice, the smoothness of olive oil, and the fresh flavor of chopped parsley. Crushed lightly and scooped up with a piece of warm flatbread or stuffed into the pocket of a pita, ful medames taste of traditional hospitality and the warmth of a shared meal.

Often eaten before sunrise during the fasting month of Ramadan, ful medames may be garnished with a hard-boiled or fried egg to make a long-lasting breakfast. The name, partly adopted from ancient Coptic, means "buried beans," indicating that ful medames may have been prepared by burying them in the earth with hot coals—a kind of pre-modern slow-cooker.

Ful Medames

1 medium onion, chopped

3 cloves garlic, minced

1 tbsp olive oil

2 medium tomatoes, chopped

3 cups fava beans, rinsed and drained

1 tsp ground cumin

$1/4$ tsp cayenne or pepper

3 tbsp lemon juice

$1/4$ cup freshly chopped parsley

In a large, nonstick frying pan, sauté the onion and garlic in the olive oil for about 5 minutes. Add the tomatoes and cook for another 5 minutes. Stir in the fava beans, cumin, and cayenne, and cook on medium-low heat for about 10 minutes.

Remove the pan from the heat and mash the fava beans lightly until most of the beans are crushed. Spoon the mixture into a serving bowl, and stir in the lemon juice and parsley. Serve with warm pita bread. *Serves 4*

Feijoada

Feijoada is Brazil's national dish. To call it a bean stew is an understatement. Black beans are the essential element in feijoada. Their strong, earthy flavor has the assertiveness to hold its own with the other boisterous ingredients, which may include smoked ham hocks, pepperoni or chorizo sausage, *carne seca* (sun-cured salt beef), spare ribs, back bacon, hot chile peppers, bay leaves, chopped onion, and garlic. Feijoada emerged from the melding of Native, Portuguese, and African cultures. Variations of feijoada using different beans and ingredients can be found in Portugal, Angola, and São Tomé. A popular, possibly unreliable, myth traces the origins of feijoada to the colonial farms of Brazil, where it was a luxury meal for slaves. In homage, it's customary to find various recognizable animal parts hidden in its creamy depths—pig's ears, tail, feet, or snout.

Feijoada is a festive dish, served on special occasions or for Saturday lunch. Hotels and lunch counters also offer it as a daily or weekly special. It's traditionally served on rice, accompanied by sautéed greens, *farofa* (fried cassava meal), and orange slices.

With *caipirinhas*—a strong Brazilian cocktail made from cane liquor, lime juice, and sugar—to wash it down, it's the perfect prelude to a Saturday afternoon nap!

Lentilles de Puy

Puy lentils grow in the rich volcanic soils around the medieval city of Le Puy in the Haute Loire, a department of the Auvergne region of central France. In recognition of their long history and unique character, Puy lentils have their own *appellation contrôlée*, recognized throughout Europe. These lentils are smaller than most and are dark blue-green in color. In texture, they are less starchy and, therefore, remain firm after cooking, making them suitable for many uses, including salads.

What makes them unique is their peppery flavor, perhaps a hint of the volcanic heat that created the soil that nurtures them. The Auvergne is not a region of haute cuisine; its specialties are hearty peasant dishes, and Puy lentils play their part in many a soup and as an accompaniment for rich meats, goose, and duck. A popular pairing with Puy lentils is sausage, especially the seasoned chorizo sausage of Spain and Portugal. Chorizo has a rich, smoky taste. It is seasoned with roasted paprika, which gives it a characteristic reddish tint. Lightly grilled or fried, then sliced on a bed of Puy lentils, this dish is peasant cuisine at its most satisfying.

Mung Beans

This little green legume appears in many guises in Asian cuisine. Moistened and left in the dark, mung beans become bean sprouts; skinned and split, they become yellow moong dal; skinned, cooked, and pulverized they become bean paste; when mung bean starch is extracted, it is used to make cellophane noodles and jellies. It is hard to imagine Asian cuisine without it.

Mung beans are usually available dried and must be soaked before cooking. Eaten whole, they have a creamy texture and a taste somewhere between a garden pea and a lentil. Here is a quick sampling of their versatility: warm your insides with a hearty mung bean soup; bite into a plump spring roll bursting with mung bean cellophane noodles; for a luscious dessert, scoop up a refreshing spoonful of shaved ice and sweetened mung beans cooked with coconut; enjoy the crunch of bean sprouts atop a mound of lightly cooked vegetables and peanut sauce in a serving of *gado-gado*; bite into a plump moon cake and enjoy the sweet mung bean paste filling; savor the rich mixture of garlic, ginger, onions, and fragrant Indian spices in a meal of moong dal and rice.

Moong Dal

Moong dal is derived from mung beans that have been skinned of their green coats and split in two, revealing their yellow interiors. The advantage is that moong dal cooks faster than the whole bean; long soaking is not required. Moong dal is also easily digested. Ayurvedic practice recommends moong dal for children, the elderly, and convalescents. It is the equivalent of chicken soup in a Jewish household—good for whatever ails you!

Moong dal is very versatile and plays a part in a multitude of dishes from comforting soups to hearty stews with tomatoes and vegetables. Moong dal also features in sweet dishes, such as those eaten during Sankranthi, a traditional harvest festival celebrated in January in Tamil Nadu, south India. In a classic Sankranthi sweet, toasted moong dal is cooked with rice in milk or coconut milk, seasoned with cardamom, and topped with raisins, cashews, and palm sugar. Food of the gods, indeed!

Frijoles Refritos

Corn, beans, and squash form the trinity
of foods originating in the New World and
refried beans—*frijoles refritos*—are a staple
of northern Mexican and Tex-Mex cuisine.
The proper translation is not refried, implying
a second frying, but "well fried." The purpose
of frying the beans is to take what might
be a rather sloppy serving of beans and dry
it out until it holds its shape. Refried beans
don't just sit passively on a plate beside
huevos rancheros; they are combined with
their sister corn in a number of ways,
especially with flat corn tortillas. Refried
beans are rolled in tortillas to make burritos
and chimichangas (deep-fried burritos), spread
onto tostadas and scooped up in nachos.

Refried beans start with dried beans,
such as pinto beans, but can also be made
with other beans including red kidney or
black beans. The beans are soaked overnight,
simmered until tender, and mashed. The
mashed beans are fried in oil until they are
dry enough to hold their shape. Sometimes
other ingredients are added to flavor the
beans: onions, garlic, herbs, and a little hot
chili sauce to taste.

Red-Bean Paste

Red-bean paste is made from adzuki beans,
beautifully dark red and already subtly sweet.
The cooked beans may be puréed or just
mashed, depending on whether the ultimate
texture is to be smooth or somewhat crunchy.
The beans are sweetened with sugar or honey.
Gula melaka (palm sugar) lends a rich and
full-bodied sweetness to the paste but brown
sugar, white sugar, or honey will do. The
mixture is cooked with a little shortening
and salt to achieve the desired consistency.
It must be thick enough to spread on the
surface of the pancake.

Chinese pancakes are made from a simple
flour-and-hot-water dough that is kneaded
until smooth and elastic and rolled into
flat circles. The traditional technique calls
for cooking a double-sided pancake. Two
pancakes are layered together with a brushing
of toasty sesame oil to keep them from
sticking too tightly. The outer sides are
browned on a greaseless griddle, resulting
in pancakes with a beautifully golden outer
side and a soft inner side. Each pancake is
spread with a dollop of red-bean paste and
then rolled several times, making a delicately
layered, mouthwatering treat.

Boston Baked Beans

The dish that gave Boston its "Beantown" nickname was very likely adapted from the indigenous people who lived in Massachusetts before the Pilgrims arrived. Pea beans soaked in water and combined with bear fat and maple syrup eventually evolved into the classic Boston baked beans, flavored with salt pork, molasses, and mustard. In the 18th century, Boston became a storehouse for a great deal of molasses, a by-product of the so-called triangular trade. The first side of the triangle brought cane sugar from the Caribbean and turned it into molasses in the process of producing rum. Rum was shipped back across the Atlantic. Once empty, cargo ships picked up human cargo in West Africa for delivery to the Caribbean.

The cans of baked beans in modern supermarkets are a pale imitation of the original. Boston baked beans, cooked for hours in the oven at a very low temperature in a classic bean pot, are a rich, dark brown. Every bean is suffused with the salt-sweet of its simple ingredients.

Boston Baked Beans

1³⁄₄ cups dry beans (haricot, Great Northern, Navy, yellow eye or similar)

1 tbsp oil

1 large onion, sliced

1 tsp dry mustard

2 tbsp molasses

²⁄₃ cup tomato juice

1 tsp Worcestershire sauce

2 tsp brown sugar

1¹⁄₄ cups unsalted vegetable broth

Soak the beans, then drain and rinse them. Put them in a pot and cover them with fresh water. Bring them to a boil, then lower the heat. Cook them until they are almost tender, about 45 minutes, and drain them again.

Preheat the oven to 275°F. Heat the oil in a flameproof casserole and add the onion slices, sautéing them for about 5 minutes, then add the rest of the ingredients, including the drained beans, and bring the mixture to a boil. Cover the casserole and put it in the oven. Cook for about 4 hours, stirring occasionally. Add more water if the beans become too dry. *Serves 4*

Borlotti Beans

Borlotti beans—sometimes called Romano beans—have distinctive reddish-brown-to-pink streaks on a white background. In season, you may be lucky enough to find fresh borlotti beans at an Italian market just before they begin to mature, for they are widely used in Italian cooking. If you can't find them, they are available in cans or dried. The dried beans must be soaked before use.

Their creamy texture and slightly sweet flavor make them very versatile in casseroles and hearty salads. Their starring role, however, is in the classic Venetian soup known as *pasta e fagioli* or *pasta fazool*. Like so much of the best Italian cooking, *pasta e fagioli* combines simple, locally available ingredients such as borlotti beans, potatoes, celery, carrots, and onions for the soup base. There are many local variations, perhaps as many as there are Italian cooks! Pieces of medium-sized pasta are added to this hearty base to cook until tender. Topped with freshly grated Parmesan cheese and garnished with good-quality olive oil, *pasta e fagioli* can take its place, and often does, at five-star restaurants as well as in humble trattorias.

Four Strong Cheeses

Limburger

Originally made in the Belgian province of Limburg, the production of this cheese of strong, pungent smell and milder flavor, migrated into Germany sometime in the 1800s and became a specialty of the Bavarian district of Allgäu in the south of that country. It is a soft cow's-milk cheese with a creamy yellow paste and a brine-washed rind that usually looks tawny-brown. The cheeses are matured for around three months until they have developed the bloom of mold on their surface that is their distinguishing feature.

Limburger nearly always has a decadently pungent aroma, but it should look dry rather than oozy, and the paste shouldn't be in a liqueous state.

Surprisingly, the flavor of even the most richly scented cheeses is never quite as strong as the smell suggests. Limburger should be eaten with dark rye bread and accompanied by a good Belgian beer.

Stinking Bishop

This English soft cheese has been made only since 1972. It is the creation of the family firm of Charles Martell and Son at Laurel Farm in Dymock, Gloucestershire. A soft, full-fat, cow's-milk cheese with pale yellow paste and a darker, orange-yellow rind, it is reputed to have one of the most singularly pungent aromas of all English cheeses.

The name is actually that of a variety of pear and denotes the fact that the cheese's rind is washed in perry, or pear cider, made from those pears. No salt is added during the initial phase of the cheese's development, so that air bubbles form in the paste, creating shallow holes in its texture. It is made in five-pound wheels, mainly using the milk of a cattle breed, Gloucesters, that were almost extinct when the cheese was first invented.

If a comparison can be made, Stinking Bishop is perhaps closest in style to Epoisses, as they are similarly pungent.

Stilton

The best-loved blue cheese of England, Stilton is one of the few British cheeses to have had its zone of production strictly regulated by law. It may be made only in one of the neighboring counties of Nottinghamshire, Derbyshire, or Leicestershire. It is named for a village of the same name where, in the 18th century, a tavern called the Bell Inn became famous for selling it.

Made of cow's milk and molded with the same strain of penicillin culture used for France's Roquefort, the cheeses are matured for around four months, until they have developed a hard, brown, stubbly crust. The interior should show intricate veins of greenish-blue mold in a pale yellow paste. Celebrated brands include Cropwell Bishop and Colston Bassett.

In the UK, Blue Stilton is a traditional Christmas cheese, which is when cheeses made with the summer's milk will have matured to peak condition. Its customary table partner is a glass of port, either ruby or tawny.

Epoisses

Epoisses is made in the heart of one of France's premier wine-growing regions, Burgundy. Epoisses is one of the strongest soft cheeses produced anywhere. It is a cow's-milk cheese with an alcohol-washed rind, sold in small, round nine-ounce boxes, usually in an advanced stage of ripeness. The aroma of a ripe Epoisses can be so overpowering that it is forbidden to carry this cheese on public transport in Paris.

The washing agents that, between them, produce the orange rind are, first, a salty brine, then white wine or *marc*, a powerful, rustic spirit produced from the grapeskins left over from winemaking. These washings take around three weeks each. The paste is pale yellow, with a gently melting texture and a rounded flavor that echoes the aroma. Bulk-produced versions of the cheese are not washed at all, only colored artificially, but handmade Epoisses is significantly superior.

Gorgonzola

Italy's preeminent blue cheese, Gorgonzola was being made as far back as the ninth century AD, after it was discovered that a batch of white cheeses that had been stored in a cool, damp cellar had developed a natural blue mold that conferred an incomparable flavor on it.

Gorgonzola can be very different in character, depending on how long it has been aged before sale. It is the product of pasteurized cow's milk, generally of two milkings, to which a culture of *Penicillium glaucum* is added (although some producers are now resorting to the *P. roqueforti* widely used in other blue cheeses). Its original homeland was in the Lombardy region around Milan, where a village called Gorgonzola lays (disputed) claim to being its ancestral home.

Sold wrapped in foil, Gorgonzola should be a supremely creamy cheese with pale yellow paste and even blue veining, aged for an optimum period of around four months. Longer aging doesn't necessarily improve it, but can result in a drier cheese with an offputting gritty texture.

Gubbeen

It is only in modern times that the Republic of Ireland has become noted as a producer of pedigree cheeses, but its progress has been startling. Much of the production is in the hands of small artisan producers, among which the Ferguson family's Gubbeen is a prime example. The name derives from a Gaelic word meaning "small mouth" or "small mouthful," suggesting that the cheese is of such quality that a little will go a long way.

Made at Schull in the west of County Cork, Gubbeen is a cow's-milk cheese with a washed rind and a delicate, semi-soft yellow paste. Although it is ripened for only two to three weeks, it has a gently gamey flavor, which varies according to the time of year each batch has been produced. The winter cheeses have a firm, drier texture compared to the creamy, yielding quality of those made from spring milk. It is sold in two-pound wheels. The rind is characteristically wrinkly and develops a light farmyard aroma.

As well as the principal cheese, a smoked version is also produced by the traditional method of smoking over oak chippings. Smoked Gubbeen is wax-coated and matured for three months.

Caerphilly

Cheddar

Caerphilly cheese has been made in south Wales since the early part of the 19th century. It is a semi-hard cow's-milk cheese with a yellowish-white paste and loose, crumbly texture. There is a saltiness and sharpness to its flavor, as with many cheeses that are traditionally made quickly for selling young, but in recent years, some specialist producers have been making an unpasteurized version that is aged for longer, acquiring a slightly firmer texture in the process. The difference between a Caerphilly sold within a week of its production and one aged for around three months is very pronounced.

While it is traditionally a Welsh cheese, dairy farming has never been subject in the British Isles to anything like the geographical protection that prevails in France, and hence much Caerphilly comes from just over the border in the West Country of England. As it is known for being a young cheese, it proved itself an attractive commercial proposition for Cheddar makers, who customarily had to wait many months for their cheeses to mature. Some English Caerphilly today can rival the best Welsh products for quality.

The best-known named cheese in the world, Cheddar originated in the county of Somerset in England's West Country, in and around a stretch of dramatic landscape known as the Cheddar Gorge. It was traditionally matured, in centuries past, in the region's limestone caves, where it gained a reputation for incomparable flavor.

The name Cheddar came to be applied to the way the cheese was made, which involves cutting the slabs of soft curd into bricks that are turned and stacked on top of each other to express much of the remaining whey. Cheddar is sold in mild, medium, mature, and vintage versions, depending on the length of time it matures. Vintage Cheddar is typically 18 months old and has a mouth-filling, buttery richness that owes its character to the milk of Friesian cows on which much of it is based.

Fine Cheddar has a firm, unyielding, deep-yellow paste and an aroma that combines buttermilk with a note of mustardy spice in the older cheeses. Younger and (literally) paler imitations are often of much poorer quality.

This cheese is now made all over the world and may have many other flavoring ingredients added, including artificial flavors to produce "smoked" versions.

Chaumes

A semi-soft French cheese with a vivid orange rind and a mild, buttery flavor, Chaumes was a creation of the early 1970s. It is made from pasteurized cow's milk and comes from the Périgord region of western France, famous for its black truffles. The texture of Chaumes is springy as the cheese is sold quite young, usually after no more than a month's maturation. Small holes are usually visible in the paste. It is made in large, flat wheels weighing around five pounds.

Chaumes is not a geographical name but comes from the French word for "stubble," denoting the texture of its rind, which forms after the crust of the cheese has been subjected to several washes. Its lighter flavor makes it quite a useful cheese in cooking, and it is sometimes used in the preparation of toasted cheese. Perhaps just because it has a relatively unchallenging flavor, even when at its ripest, Chaumes is one of the biggest-selling cheeses in France.

Cornish Yarg

Cornwall's flagship cheese is a richly flavored, semi-hard cheese made of cow's milk and sold under a coating of nettle leaves. It is an uncooked cheese that is pressed in the manner of English crumbly cheeses such as Lancashire, but it is ripened in molds over a period of a month to six weeks, so that it has something of the firmer texture of young Cheddar at the edges, but remains delicately crumbly in the center.

Cornish Yarg (never just Yarg) has become a fashionable ingredient in the new English cuisine. A favored recipe is to melt a slice of it at the bottom of a bowl of earthy soup, such as leek. However, it is also a fine cheese board item, as the faintly grassy tang that it picks up from its nettle wrapping makes it an interesting partner to aromatic dry white wines such as Sauvignon Blanc or to traditional English beers.

The nettles are gathered locally from hedgerows by the cheese's producers. While the cheese matures, the wrapping attracts mold cultures, producing an attractive, varicolored surface by the time the Cornish Yarg is sold.

Ricotta

One of those delicacies that began as a mere by-product in ancient times, ricotta is a whey-based cheese that was traditionally made from the runoff produced during the manufacture of other cheeses. Most cheese is made from the creamy curd of the milk, once it has separated from the whey. The whey itself is often fed to farm animals (pigs, mainly), but a light cheese product can be made from this too.

Its Italian name means "recooked," denoting the fact that the whey is subjected to a further heat treatment at high temperatures to precipitate out from it what remains of its protein content. An acid agent such as vinegar is the catalyst in this procedure.

Ricotta, like cottage cheese, is very white, with a mild taste, and usually made in a hemispherical mold. Specialty versions are made using sheep's whey, and some products have whole milk added to them for a richer flavor. Ricotta has become a standby of those looking to reduce their weight, as it is so low in fat. Combining it with spinach has become a classic preparation as a filling for other foods.

A Sicilian product, ricotta infornata, is baked until the paste turns brown.

Cottage Cheese

The nursery rhyme character Little Miss Muffet was a devotee of something very like cottage cheese, except that she called it "curds and whey." It is a curd cheese product that isn't pressed, so that not all of the whey is expelled from it. Neither is it aged in any way, the result being a snow-white, soft substance with a very mild flavor and a semi-liquid texture. It is usually lightly salted and sold in its natural state, its low fat content making it a favorite choice for people on weight-reduction regimes. Washing of the curd removes much of the lactic acid, but there is generally a faintly sour tang to good cottage cheese.

As well as being low in fat, cottage cheese is rich in the milk protein casein. This makes it an unexpected standby for bodybuilders, as it helps to bulk up muscle tissue.

There are many different qualities of cottage cheese, and the one sold in your local convenience store may not be the best available. Many of the big-name brands produce versions with additions such as chives, onion, or pineapple.

Cream Cheese

Dating from the late 19th century, cream cheese is an American invention. It is one of those products that has become widely associated with one particular brand—in this case, Philadelphia cream cheese—and it is referred to in many countries as Philadelphia cheese (*queso filadelfia* in Spanish-speaking Latin America).

Cream cheese is a fresh, unaged white cheese that contains a minimum of one-third dairy fat. When first produced in New York State in the 1870s, it had cream as well as milk added to it, resulting in a richer, denser flavor than most fresh cheeses have. The texture is soft but firm, not unlike a young goat cheese, but there is much less acidity in it. Indeed, cream cheese is often described as "sweet."

As well as its time-honored role in being spread on crackers as a party snack, cream cheese is also combined with smoked salmon as a filling for bagels, and it is the indispensable ingredient in classic New York cheesecake. Value-added commercial cream cheese may have other flavoring ingredients added, such as chives or garlic.

Cheese Soufflé

Usually served as a first course, a cheese soufflé relies on the air-bearing properties of beaten egg white, which, when incorporated into a flavored batter of other ingredients, causes the mixture to rise majestically above the rim of its dish. A soufflé must be served as soon as it leaves the oven, before it has time to deflate.

Any strong, hard cheese makes a good basis for a soufflé; the two most commonly used are Gruyère and Cheddar. The dish should always be buttered and sprinkled with finely grated Parmesan to accentuate the flavor before the mixture is loaded in. It can be served with a sauce, but some believe that the airy simplicity of the dish needs no adornment.

Soufflé au Fromage

Prepare the basic mixture by stirring one generous tablespoon of flour into 2 tablespoons of butter melted in a heavy saucepan. Gradually add just under 1¼ cups of warmed milk, stirring until your mixture is quite smooth. Let this sauce cook very gently, stirring frequently, for close on 10 minutes. Now stir in ¼ cup of finely grated Parmesan cheese and then the very thoroughly beaten yolks of 4 large eggs. Remove the mixture from the fire, and continue stirring for a few seconds. Now add a seasoning of salt and quite a generous amount of freshly ground black pepper, plus, if you like, a scrap of cayenne. This basic mixture can be made well in advance. When the time comes to make the soufflé, preheat the oven to 400°F. Have the shelf placed fairly low in the oven and a baking sheet on the shelf. Butter a 3¾-cup capacity soufflé dish.

Whisk the whites of the eggs, plus one extra, in a large, scrupulously dry and clean bowl, until they will stand in peaks on the whisk and look very creamy. Tip half the whites on top of the basic mixture. With a flat spatula, cut them into it, slowly rotating the bowl with your left hand, lifting rather than stirring the whole mass. Add the remainder of the whites in the same way. All this should take only a few seconds and as you pour the whole mixture, without delay, into the dish, it should look very bubbly and spongy. With the flat spatula, mark a deep circle an inch or so from the edge, so that the soufflé will come out with a cottage-loaf look to the top. Put it instantly into the oven.

As to the timing, it depends so much upon the size and type of both the oven and the dish, that it is misleading to give precise details. I can only say, as a general guide, that in the oven of a representative domestic gas cooker, this soufflé is perfectly cooked in 23 to 25 minutes. *Serves 4–5*

Adapted from Elizabeth David's *French Provincial Cooking*

Chile con Queso

A specialty of that crossover cuisine known as Tex-Mex, which blends influences from the southwestern states of the US with the cooking of Mexico, chile con queso (chile with cheese) is more Tex than Mex. Nothing quite like it occurs in the Mexican kitchen, for all that its reliance on chile peppers marks it out as a fiery Latin preparation.

It is a cheese-based dip served warm like fondue, normally consisting of a blend of hard cheeses melted and combined with diced tomatoes and chopped chile peppers, both mild (such as Anaheim) and red-hot (jalapeño). In some versions, cooked ground beef is also incorporated to give an even more substantial result. As well as being used for dipping tortilla chips into, chile con queso can be used as a relish for Tex-Mex main dishes such as fajitas and enchiladas.

The cheeses used in the dip are usually a combination of a processed cheese such as Velveeta and Monterey Jack or American Cheddar. The variant traditional to the state of New Mexico is hotter than Texas queso, owing to its higher proportion of green or red chile peppers.

Chile con Queso

5 tbsp vegetable oil

1½ cups thinly sliced white onions

1 cup thinly sliced tomatoes

15 green Anaheim chiles, charred, peeled, and cut into strips

Salt to taste

¾ cup milk

3 tbsp water

8 oz Chihuahua, asadero, or Muenster cheese, thinly sliced

Heat the oil in a deep skillet and cook the onion over low heat until translucent—about 2 minutes. Add the tomatoes with the chile strips to the pan with salt. Cover and cook over medium heat for 5 minutes. Add the milk and water and let the mixture cook for a few minutes more. Just before serving, add the cheese to the chile mixture. Serve as soon as the cheese melts. *Serves 6*

Adapted from Diana Kennedy's *The Essential Cuisines of Mexico*

Quesadilla

A quesadilla is a variant on the traditional Spanish tortilla. As its name implies, it should involve some cheese element (*queso* is Spanish for "cheese"), but there are many different regional variations on the basic idea.

In its most obvious form, in Mexico, a soft tortilla is folded around grated or sliced cheese and then broiled, or deep-fried, until the filling has melted. Alternatively, the prepared tortilla may be sprinkled with grated cheese, and then another tortilla layer is laid over it, before it is cooked on both sides.

In still another variant, the cheese is sprinkled on to the tortilla as it is cooking on a griddle.

The name has come to be widened beyond its original application, in that a quesadilla may now be any kind of filled tortilla, prepared in turnover fashion, and then cooked. Other fillings might include chorizo, ham, mushrooms, bell peppers, beans, olives, tomatoes, and onions. Where cheese is used, the favored types are Monterey Jack or Mexico's *queso Chihuahua*, for their excellent melting qualities.

Four Sheep's-Milk Cheeses

Lanark Blue

Sometimes hailed as Scotland's riposte to Roquefort, Lanark Blue needs no such reflected glory. It has become a classic modern cheese in its own right. A blue-veined, full-fat creation with an off-white paste, it is made on a Lanarkshire farm on the western fringe of the Pentland hills by its inventor, Humphrey Errington, using unpasteurized sheep's milk and a vegetarian rennet.

The flavor of Lanark Blue varies according to the time of year and the sheep's diet. It is creamy and relatively mild in the spring, and much more pungent and classically "sheepy" in the winter. The mold culture introduced is the same as that used for Roquefort, *Penicillium roqueforti*, and the cheese is brined, which gives it something of the saltiness of its French antecedent.

Lanark is matured for three to four months before sale.

Feta

Feta is a generic sheep's-milk cheese originally produced in Greece and Cyprus. Traditionally made from sheep's milk, It is a milk-white, brine-cured cheese with a soft, friable texture, good for crumbling into salads, especially the classic Greek salad, or diced and mixed with marinated olives as an appetizer nibble.

After the initial fermentation, both the curds and whey are reheated in combination, before draining and a light pressing follow. The cheese is then cut into slabs and immersed in brine, which results in a sharply acidic, pointedly salty flavor.

Feta has been made in much the same way right back to classical times. There are records of cheese being produced in this way during the Byzantine period, although it acquired its present name only in the 17th century—oddly enough from an Italian word, *fetta*, meaning "slice," from the way it was traditionally served.

Pecorino Romano

Pecorino is the generic name for sheep's-milk cheeses produced all over Italy (from the Italian word for a sheep, *pecora*). The most celebrated of these is Pecorino Romano, traditionally made in Lazio, although much production now takes place on Sardinia. It is off-white in color, with a close-grained, crumbly texture, and a sharp, salty flavor.

Produced between winter and late spring, Pecorino is matured for a minimum of eight months. It can be used in much the same way as Parmesan, but has a sharper flavor.

Pecorino has an ancient lineage. It is known to have been sold overseas as early as the first century AD and was issued as a standard ration to Roman legionaries. It is traditionally eaten as a May Day food by modern Romans, when it is seen as the perfect partner to the new season's fava beans. Older pecorino is often paired with ripe pears and honey as a dessert dish.

Roquefort

Roquefort is traditionally matured in caves in the Combalou region of southern France, where it develops its fine veining of greenish-blue mold. Brining gives the cheese an intensely salty flavor that is wonderful when offset with sweet fruits.

The mold, known as *Penicillium roque-forti*, is sprinkled onto the curd and then encouraged in its development by the insertion of steel skewers into the ripening cheese. Roquefort has virtually no rind, as it is foil-wrapped toward the end of the maturation. The ripening typically takes three months, with the cheeses at their best between spring and late fall.

In prime condition, Roquefort should look pale creamy-white and should smell fresh, with no trace of ammonia. The combination of creaminess, saltiness, and the pungency of the mold means that only a little ripe Roquefort goes a long way.

Dolcelatte

Danish Blue

Dolcelatte was invented by the Galbani cheesemaking company of Italy as a gentler alternative to that country's more famous blue cheese, Gorgonzola. Its name means "sweet milk," denoting the relative mildness of the cheese. Very often, it has only the faintest trace of blue veining, and a gentle, creamy flavor.

Made from cow's milk, Dolcelatte is always produced from a single batch of milk, rather than the successive milkings typical for other cheeses. It is a full-fat cheese, with around 50% dairy fat, and is matured for eight to twelve weeks to mellow and allow its flavor to develop. The texture is always soft, and the cheese may be used as a salad ingredient, alongside prosciutto, or as a garnish for a dessert plate of fruit. In Italy, it is very popular as an accompaniment to fresh figs.

The name Dolcelatte is a registered trademark of the Galbani company, but similar cheeses are made by rivals under different names. One such is Dolceverde. Galbani also makes a Dolcelatte product called Cremoso, which is a soft, creamy dip for crudités.

France's Roquefort, king of blue cheeses, has had many imitators over the years, and none more explicit than Danish Blue, or Danablu as it is known on its home territory. First created in the early years of the 20th century by one Marius Boel, it was an attempt to produce a readily accessible version of a creamy, mature blue cheese at an affordable price.

That said, the flavor of Danish Blue is nothing like Roquefort, for one simple and obvious reason, namely that it is made from cow's milk rather than sheep's. The paste is normally very white, and the veining starkly blue, in contrast to the softer greenish-blue tone of Roquefort mold. It is sold after two to three months' maturation and is wholly edible, including the very light rind. The flavor is creamy and assertively salty, but the molding is less concentrated on the palate than that of Roquefort.

It has to be said that Danish Blue hasn't traditionally enjoyed the same level of reputation among gastronomes as most of the cheeses in this section. Nothing in its production suggests that it should be any less favored, though, and it is wonderful when crumbled into a salad.

Edam

Gouda

Once the world's favorite cheese, Dutch Edam, from the town of the same name in the province of North Holland, was exported in enormous quantities during the 17th and 18th centuries. It kept well during travel, and while it is often unfairly thought of as having next to no flavor, was sufficiently mild in character to gain widespread favor.

In the export markets, Edam is noted for its bright red coating, which is made of paraffin wax, although on its home territory, it is usually sold with its coat removed. Beneath, there is a thin golden rind, enclosing a similarly colored paste with a chewy, homogenous texture and a delicate, slightly lemony aftertaste. Most Edam is sold at about six weeks old. Though there are more mature versions, aged for six months or more, which develop a correspondingly more assertive flavor, even this is never particularly pungent, and the cheese remains relatively non-aromatic.

The fat content of this cow's-milk cheese is lower than many others, although not quite as low as its inclusion in many diet plans would suggest. Flavored Edams containing peppercorns or cumin seeds make interesting variations on the basic formula.

Like Cheddar, Gouda is one of those cheeses that is now made in various countries, but the genuine article comes from the Netherlands. Most of it is produced in the province of North Holland, where it accounts for around two-thirds of all Dutch cheese production, although the town of Gouda after which it is named lies in the neighboring province of South Holland.

Gouda is a hard cow's-milk cheese usually sold in a yellow paraffin-wax coating. It has a firm, deep-yellow, often dryish-textured paste scattered with shallow holes, and comes in hugely varying degrees of maturity. The very youngest cheeses may be no more than a month old, but the best will have had two to three years' aging. These are darker in color and have a strong, buttery, even mustardy flavor. Unpasteurized cheeses have the word *Boeren* ("farmer") impressed on the rind.

A particularly rich variant of Gouda known as Roomkaas has cream added to the milk during its production, driving its fat content up to a fairly heady 60%. Others have flavoring additions such as mustard seeds, peppercorns, herbs, or garlic.

Gruyère

Gruyère is one of the world's most widely used culinary cheeses. At its best, it makes an excellent addition to a cheese board, but it is also the indispensable ingredient in many a cheese sauce, in cheese soufflés, or as the enriching component in the potato dish *gratin dauphinois*.

It originally hailed from the town of Gruyère in the canton of Fribourg in Switzerland, where records of its manufacture go back to the 12th century. Although much of it was traditionally produced in France, it has been an *appellation contrôlée* (a protected name) since 2001. Made from the milk of Swiss cows, it often has its country of origin stamped all over the rind (whether as "Switzerland," "Suisse," or "Schweiz").

A firm-textured, pressed, cooked cheese, it occasionally has very small holes in it, but quite often none at all (certainly nothing like Emmenthaler). The flavor is delicately sweet, but with a pronounced savory nuttiness underlying it, and it has a clean, springy texture in the mouth. It is sold at anything between four months and a year old.

Emmenthaler

Synonymous with Swiss cheese the world over, true Emmenthaler (sometimes known as Emmental) should come from the Emme Valley in the canton of Bern, near the Swiss capital. As yet, it has not been subjected to the same rigorous protection as its compatriot Gruyère, and so much Emmenthaler comes from France or Germany.

Emmenthaler is instantly recognizable as a cheese style from its appearance. It's the one with the holes, its gently firm, deep-yellow paste evenly scattered with relatively large, gaping cavities. These are formed when one of the bacterial strains used in its production consumes the lactic acid. This in turn leads to an evolution of carbon dioxide gas, causing bubbles in the setting curd. The Swiss like to say that while the holes may be copied elsewhere, the cheese itself remains inimitable.

Made from cow's milk, its flavor is quite mild, but delightfully buttery. In Switzerland itself, it finds its way—much as does Gruyère —into fondues and gratinéed dishes. It is marketed at anything between four and ten months old, but even the more mature specimens retain that pleasant creamy mildness.

Fontina

A firm-textured cow's-milk cheese from the Valle d'Aosta in the far northwest of Italy, Fontina has become highly fashionable in recent years. It has something of the sweet, nutty character of good Swiss Gruyère, with a light scattering of small holes in the springy yellow paste.

The best Fontina is made from the summer milk of cows that are put out to pasture in the high alpine meadows. Cheese production itself takes place in wooden chalets in the mountains, making this a scene that looks almost undisturbed by the march of technology. Only one milking is used to make each batch of cheese, without pasteurization, and the cheeses are pressed, lightly cooked, and then matured for an average period of three months. Look for the stamp of the local Consorzio, with its logo of the Matterhorn mountain, to distinguish true alpine Fontina from similarly named cheeses made elsewhere in Italy.

It can be used in much the same culinary contexts as Gruyère and Emmenthaler (the younger cheeses work well in fondues), or there is a dish known as *fonduta*, in which the cheese is melted in milk and eggs and used as a dressing for pasta.

Goat's-Milk Cheeses

Chèvre de Montrachet

Goat cheeses are produced in many regions throughout France, all going under the generic name of chèvre (the French word for goat). The Montrachet chèvre comes from the department of Sâone-et-Loire in the Burgundy region of eastern France. Generally around three ounces in weight, it is a small, log-shaped cheese with the chalky-white paste of most goat cheeses, and sold very young—after about a week's storage. Montrachet undergoes its brief maturation inside a leaf wrapping, which can be either a vine leaf or chestnut leaf, and is often sold with a layer of salty ash covering its surface.

Although the characteristic flavor of young goat cheeses is an acid tang, they are at least 45% butterfat. The texture is pasty, and the cheeses usually have a long aftertaste, as does Montrachet, which also gives its name to the most celebrated of Cardonnay white wines.

Crottin de Chavignol

Granted *appellation contrôlée* status in 1976, Crottin de Chavignol is one of the most uncompromising styles of goat cheese made in France or anywhere. It comes from the eastern end of the Loire Valley.

Crottin is traditionally aged for longer than is usual for goat cheeses, which results in a firmer, drier texture and a mold-infected rind that looks brownish-black. This explains the first part of its name, *crottin*, which—unappetizingly enough—means "dung," and this is indeed what the more mature cheeses visually resemble. The second part of the name denotes the geographical area of production, which is concentrated around the tiny hamlet of Chavignol. The cheese is known to have been produced in these parts since at least the 1500s. Like other goat cheeses, Crottin is especially delicious if served warmed on dressed salad leaves.

Pantysgawn

Within the British Isles, Wales has developed an unrivaled reputation as a region for premium goat cheeses. This one was originally made on a small farm but the operation has moved to a larger facility. Nothing has been lost, however, in the care with which its maker, Anthony Craske, approaches its production.

Pantysgawn is made from pasteurized goat's milk and sold as small rounds or in larger two-pound logs, at an average of around three weeks old. The flavor is creamy and gentle, delicately salty with a faint lemon tang.

Variations include a covering of mixed herbs or crushed black peppercorns.

Valdeteja

Valdeteja, an assertively "goaty" cheese, comes from the León region of northern Spain. It is a full-cream cheese of 72% fat with a semi-hard consistency and a classic white paste.

There is a pronounced degree of lactic acid sharpness in the flavor, making it a good choice with crisp, white wines such as Spain's own Rueda.

Valdeteja is usually ripened for at least four weeks, giving it a chance to develop an orangey-brown, stubbly rind. Unpasteurized milk is always used, contributing to its slightly feral animal flavor, and most of the production is still in the hands of small artisan cheese-makers. It is sold in rounds of two pounds.

Brie

One of the most famous and most imitated soft cheeses in the world, Brie is of very ancient lineage. There are records of it under that name dating back to the 1200s, and it is a much more venerable cheese than its equally famous sibling, Camembert.

Cheeses named Brie are made in various countries (England's Somerset Brie enjoys something of a reputation), but the best examples come from its ancestral home in northern France, in the department of Seine-et-Marne. It is a soft cow's-milk cheese with an off-white rind, made in the form of a large, flat wheel. The paste should look pale yellow and shiny and should be pliable but not oozingly runny, a state that would indicate the cheese is probably past its best. Brie receives a very modest maturation period of about a month before it is released for sale. It should taste creamy, but also tangy and fresh.

Brie comes in many different versions, even within France itself. There are blue-veined Bries, as well as cheeses that have had other ingredients added to them, such as herbs, peppercorns, or—most luxuriously of all—slivers of black truffle.

Camembert

This cheese, like Brie, is virtually synonymous with the image of French cheeses around the world. It, too, is a soft cheese made of cow's milk, but its name doesn't extend as far back in history—no more than around 300 years. Produced in the Normandy region of north-west France, it accounts for a massive 20% of all of France's annual cheese production.

Although Camembert of one sort or another is made internationally, the best specimens are Normandy cheeses made from unpasteurized milk. They are produced from the spring through to the early fall each year. Ripe Camembert should have a soft creamy-white rind with a tinge of orange, enclosing a glossy, non-runny paste. Mature cheeses should have a pronounced farmyardy aroma, but with no hint of ammonia, which is the sign of an over-mature cheese.

Much Camembert is sold in small wheels packed into light wooden boxes. Look for the geographical designation Pays d'Auge on the label. This is the best enclave for the cheese in Normandy, the same region where much of France's apple brandy, Calvados, is produced.

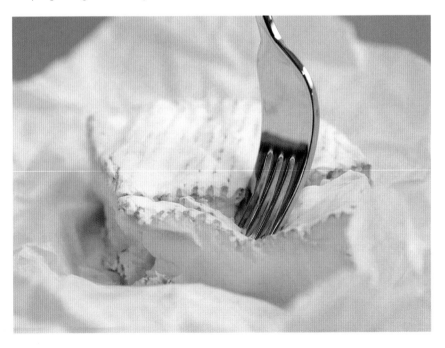

Halloumi

A semi-hard white cheese made with either sheep's or goat's milk, halloumi originally comes from Cyprus, although much of it is also made in Greece. Despite being brine-cured in much the same way as feta, it has a noticeably less salty attack on the palate, and the texture tends to be a little more homogenous, compared to the crumbliness of a good feta.

Traditional Cypriot production involves rolling out the cheese like pastry dough, mixing chopped mint into it and then cutting it into bars. It can be sold almost at once or aged a little, but hardly ever for more than about four weeks. These days, there is a tendency among bulk producers to cut costs by adding a preponderance of cow's milk to it, but this isn't the traditional method.

The stringy, mozzarella-like texture of halloumi makes it suitable for grilling and serving as an appetizer. It should be rinsed before use to wash away some of the excess salt. On Cyprus, its customary summer partner is watermelon, but it is also eaten as a component of various meat dishes.

Deep-Fried Halloumi

Vegetable oil, sufficient for deep-frying

5 oz halloumi, cut into rectangular cubes

1/3 to 1/2 cup flour

2 eggs

Milk

1/2 to 3/4 cup bread crumbs

Put enough oil in a large pan to fill it about a third and heat it. Dip the halloumi rectangles in the flour. In a bowl, whisk the eggs and a bit of milk together. Dip the floured halloumi in the egg mixture.

Put the bread crumbs in a bowl. Coat the halloumi with the bread crumbs.

Deep-fry the breaded halloumi in the hot oil for 3 to 4 minutes, until golden. Using a slotted spoon, take the halloumi out of the hot oil and drain on paper towels.

Arrange the slices on a serving plate and serve with chili sauce, tomato sauce, or a salsa. *Serves 2*

Leerdammer

A brand name for one of a class of Dutch cheeses known as Maasdam, Leerdammer is a semi-hard cheese made from cow's milk. It is usually compared to Switzerland's Emmenthaler, as it has a similar texture, but the flavor is a little sweeter, and it has an aftertaste suggestive of walnuts. Leerdammer also has a higher moisture content than Swiss cheeses, although the fat quotient is the same (around 45%).

It is one of those cheeses that Dutch people like to eat at breakfast, alongside cold meats and bread, but it also melts well for use in toasted cheese and to make a gratinéed cheese topping for various savory dishes. Aging is longer than for other Maasdam cheeses, which can be sold at a mere month old. Leerdammer is always at least three months old, and the most mature versions can be up to a year, when the flavor takes on a richer, rounder character.

The Leerdammer brand is owned by Groupe Bel, which has been marketing it since 1984. Other examples of Maasdam cheese brands are Meerlander, Westberg, and Fricotal.

Mascarpone

Italy's mascarpone is only just cheese by any conventional definition. It is the whipped, slightly fermented, full-fat product of the cream of cow's milk, a staggering 85% dairy fat that is as soft as creamed butter. It originated in Lombardy in northern Italy, but is now made all over the country, even appearing in a buffalo-milk version as a counterpoint to traditional mozzarella.

Mascarpone is effectively a dessert ingredient and is used as an accompaniment to ripe fruits of summer, which is when mascarpone itself was traditionally produced (these days, it is a year-round affair). It has many culinary uses as well, though, standing in for butter, for example, in certain risotto recipes where a particularly rich result is required. It is also an essential ingredient in the classic Italian dessert tiramisú, where it combines with marsala, eggs, and coffee to make a stimulating confection whose name means "pick-me-up."

The origins of mascarpone's name are disputed. A favorite theory has it that it was derived from the Spanish phrase *más que bueno*, meaning "better than good," but it may well also have been named for a Lombard family in the late 16th or 17th century

Mozzarella

Many people may be familiar with mozzarella cheese only from its time-honored role as a pizza topping, but it deserves consideration in its own right. The different qualities of mozzarella depend on the provenance of the milk from which it is made. Cow's-milk mozzarella, known in Italian as *fiordilatte*, is a very bland commercial product, with barely any cheese taste and quite suitable for melting on those pizzas.

The premium version is *mozzarella di bufala*, made from the milk of the Italian water buffalo. Among these, the most highly sought-after is the *mozzarella di bufala campana*, from the buffalos of Campania in the southwest. All versions are sold virtually immediately after production, as they have only very limited keeping qualities.

Because it is always so fresh, the flavor of even the best grades is very modest, but consists of a delicate creaminess, with a slight overtone of hay. Sliced fresh into rounds, it is classically partnered with ripe plum tomatoes and fresh basil.

Provolone

Although Provolone was originally native to the southern regions of Italy, most production of this cheese is now concentrated in the north, around the Po Valley. It is a firm-textured, cow's-milk cheese with a homogenous, Cheddary texture and a flavor that varies according to the age of the cheese.

The younger cheeses, known as *dolce*, are mild and buttery and have a thin rind, being matured for only around two to three months. When aged for up to two years, the cheese is known as *piccante*, partly because of its more concentrated and spicier flavor, but also because these older cheeses are traditionally set with goat's rennet, as opposed to the normal calf product.

Provolone is noted for the many varied, usually huge, forms in which it is sold. Whether in fat sausages, in truncated cones, or in pear shapes, it always looks distinctive in the delicatessen, where it is customary to hang the cheeses up. (Provolone cheeses often have a little nodule at the top expressly for this purpose.) Some of the older cheeses, bound in raffia, are smoked.

Raclette

The generic name for a group of Swiss cheeses originating in the canton of Valais, raclette is a semi-hard cheese widely made by small producers from unpasteurized cow's milk. It has a relatively firm texture sparsely scattered with air bubbles, and an appealing, fresh, buttery flavor. The name of the cheese is generally stamped into the rind.

Raclette is the French word for any kind of abrading implement (from the verb *racler*, "to scrape"), and denotes the classic manner in which the cheese is eaten in its native regions. The whole cheese is cut across into two halves, which are then heated—sometimes in a special utensil, but traditionally in front of an open fire—and the half-melted cheese is then scraped onto diners' plates, where it is mixed with baked potatoes, pickled onions, gherkins, mushrooms and other vegetables, and sometimes cured meats. The dish probably has its origins among mountain herdsmen, who would have eaten it in this way with bread, while gathered around an open fire.

Like many another Swiss cheese, raclette is also made in eastern France, chiefly in the regions of Savoy and Franche-Comté.

Quark

A light, semi-liquid curd cheese originating in Eastern Europe, quark is somewhat similar to what is known in English-speaking countries as cottage cheese. It is sold young and fresh, spooned into tubs, with a fair bit of the whey still in it, and has a very mild, slightly acidulous flavor. Like other forms of curd cheese, it is high in the milk protein casein, making it a very nutritious standby when other sources of protein are scarce.

Quark may be made from skimmed cow's or sheep's milk, along with a starter culture and rennet, and is traditionally made in countries such as Bulgaria, Poland, and the Czech Republic by being hung in a cheesecloth, until some of the whey has drained out of it. It is made very widely in Germany as well, where it finds its way into numerous dishes, from salads to desserts, as well as being used as a spread on crackers and bagels.

Such a simple product naturally has a very ancient lineage and was probably being produced in northern Europe as far back as the 6th or 7th century BC. Its name is the German word for "curds."

Parmigiano Reggiano

The most famous Italian cheese of them all, Parmigiano is made in the regions of Parma, Modena, Mantua, Bologna, and Reggio Emilia, in strictly controlled zones of production, the last giving its name to the type under consideration here. It is made from cow's milk and may be produced only between the beginning of April and mid-November each year.

During its production, the curds are minced down into minuscule grains using a special skewer and then cooked in the whey. The cheeses are shaped in molds and brined, before being matured for anything from one to four years, the four stages of its maturity known, in ascending order, as *giovane*, *vecchio*, *stravecchio*, and *stravecchione*.

Known in the English-speaking world as Parmesan, the cheese is used for grating or shaving over pasta and risotto dishes, and on to minestrone soup, but when younger, it makes an excellent cheese board cheese too. As it ages, it takes on a gloriously spicy flavor, tasting quite hot on the tongue, and there is always a close-grained, salty texture to it. This texture is what makes it the best-known of a family of Italian cheeses known as *grana* (its near-neighbor, Grana Padano, is very similar in character).

Cheese Fondue

The Swiss tradition of cheese fondue remains abidingly popular among skiers in the Alpine resorts. It requires special equipment to prepare it, in the shape of an earthenware pot in which a mixture of Swiss cheese, white wine, and seasonings is warmed until it is in a melting, creamy state. The pot is then kept warm over a gentle burner, while the diners gather around and use long toasting forks to dip pieces of bread into it.

Almost any of the traditional cheeses of Switzerland can be used for fondue—Tilsit, Appenzell, and Gruyère are favorites—and a number of different flavoring ingredients may be added. In the Jura, they add the cherry spirit, kirsch, along with garlic and nutmeg. Other versions use dried mushrooms or shallots.

Fondue traditions also crop up in the neighboring regions of the Savoy and Franche-Comté in France, and in the Aosta Valley in northwest Italy (where priceless minced white truffle might be included), but in the international gastronomic Hall of Fame, cheese fondue remains as proudly Swiss as the cuckoo clock.

Cheese Fondue

1 clove garlic

1 tbsp cornstarch

2 tsp kirsch

1½ cups dry white wine

2 cups shredded Emmenthaler cheese

2 cups shredded Gruyère

Cut the garlic in half crosswise. Rub the inside of a medium heavy pot with the cut sides of the garlic, then discard the garlic.

Mix the cornstarch and kirsch together in a small bowl and set aside.

Pour the wine into the pot and bring it just to a simmer over moderate heat. Do not let it boil. Lower the heat under the pot and gradually add the cheese in batches. Cook, stirring constantly in a zigzag or figure-8 pattern to prevent the cheese from forming a ball, until the cheese is melted and creamy. Do not let it boil. Stir the cornstarch mixture again and add to the fondue. Bring the fondue to a simmer and cook, stirring, until thickened, 5 to 8 minutes.

Transfer to a fondue pot set over a flame and serve with bread for dipping. *Serves 6*

Mont d'Or

The best version of a family of cheeses going under the generic name Vacherin, Mont d'Or is made in the Joux valley in the west of Switzerland. It is a full-fat soft cheese traditionally made from the milk of cows that have fed on the last hay crop of the season. As such, it has always been a Christmas specialty in its region of production.

It is molded in a strip of spruce bark and then matured for around three months before being packed in a light wooden box. It has become traditional to eat the cheese from this box too. The wrinkly, tan-colored surface rind must be carefully removed, and the luxuriously creamy cheese can be eaten with a spoon. The soft, semi-liquid center has a distinct resiny taste from its bark wrapping.

Vacherin Mont d'Or may be served as it is or else baked in the oven as one of the most sensational examples of comfort food the cheese world has to offer. Traditionally it should have a glass of (ideally Swiss) dry white wine poured over the pricked surface, before being baked in foil for about 25 minutes in a moderately hot oven.

Morbier

Morbier from the Franche-Comté region of eastern France is one of the most distinctive-looking cheeses on the board. It is sold in rounds, its mid-gold paste divided halfway down by a black or dark brown layer. This peculiar appearance derives from the fact that it is the product of two milkings, the morning and the evening milk. Once upon a time, after the morning milk had coagulated in the mold, a layer of ash or soot was spread over it to protect it from developing the beginnings of a rind, before the evening milk was poured on.

It is made of unpasteurized cow's milk and has a semi-soft, but very mild-tasting, character. Some of it is released at only six weeks old, while even the most mature versions are aged for only about three months. The outer rind is grayish-yellow, the inner paste pliable. Morbier hardly ever develops a very pronounced aroma, and it is sweetish and even slightly fruity to taste.

The ash layer may look a little unnerving to some, but it doesn't contribute any taste of its own to the cheese. Today, it is generally derived from vegetable matter rather than wood.

Mutter Paneer

This is one of the most popular side dishes of Indian cooking, a specialty of the northern regions, including the Punjab. It consists of a stewed mixture of mutter (fresh peas) in onions, ginger, garlic, and spices, mixed with yogurt and paneer, India's very own cheese product.

Paneer is best thought of as a kind of south Asian cottage cheese. It is a protein-rich curd product made from cow's milk, acidulated with lemon juice or vinegar, and then pressed and drained. It is generally cooked with vegetables.

After cooking, it gives a mildly flavored, stringy result, not unlike cooked Italian mozzarella, but in most versions of mutter paneer, it is fried first and then added back close to the end of the dish, so that it remains in whole pieces.

Paneer is usually sold in rectangular slabs, looking a little like feta. Cut into cubes, it can withstand an initial frying in ghee (clarified butter) before the other ingredients of the dish are added. Production of paneer is very common in Indian homes, and the cheese is always used soon after it is made.

Welsh Rarebit

This traditional British savory dish or snack consists of a melted hard cheese such as Cheddar or Gloucester, mixed with milk and eggs and sometimes beer, seasoned sharply with mustard or Worcestershire sauce, and then spread on toast and broiled. It is the original of which buck rarebit is a variation.

In times gone by, the proper name for the dish was Welsh rabbit. Despite its name, it is an English creation. The "Welsh" tag derives from a 17th-century racial slur, in which anything of inferior or shoddy status was known in derogatory fashion as "Welsh." During the more cultured Georgian era, in the later 18th century, such derogatory usages began to be frowned on in polite company, and the second part of the name became "rarebit," as though it now denoted some choice morsel. Why the dish was originally known as "rabbit" remains unclear.

In many British homes today, Welsh rarebit has become little more than cheese on toast. No preparation of the cheese is undertaken, other than laying slices of it on a piece of bread and toasting it under the broiler—not the real thing at all.

Welsh Rarebit

2 tbsp unsalted butter

2 tbsp all-purpose flour

$^1/_2$ cup brown ale

$^1/_2$ cup milk

1 tsp Dijon mustard

1 tsp Worcestershire sauce

$^1/_2$ tsp salt

$^1/_2$ tsp freshly ground black pepper

6 oz (approximately 1 $^1/_2$ cups) shredded Cheddar

4 slices lightly toasted bread

Preheat the broiler.

In a medium saucepan, melt the butter over low heat, then stir in the flour. Stir for 2 to 3 minutes, being careful not to let the flour brown. Whisk in the beer and milk gradually, stirring constantly to prevent lumps. Add the mustard, Worcestershire sauce, salt and pepper to taste and whisk until smooth. Add the cheese, stirring constantly, until the cheese melts and the sauce is smooth, 4 to 5 minutes. Pour the cheese mixture over the toast and put it under a hot broiler until the cheese mixture is bubbling. *Serves 4*

Buck Rarebit

Once a savory dish enjoyed at the end of a meal in Victorian times, buck rarebit has become a breakfast food, a lunchtime treat, an anytime dish in fact. It consists of a thick slice of toast with a coating of bubbling melted cheese. Served as simply as that, it is known as Welsh rarebit. Buck rarebit is basically the same thing, but with the addition of a soft-poached egg to each slice.

The cheat's way of making rarebit is just to cover the piece of toast with thinly sliced or grated hard cheese (ideally Cheddar), and then melt it under the broiler. To do the dish justice, however, requires melting the cheese with butter and seasonings in a pan, and then spreading this mixture over the toast before broiling.

It should generally have some other flavoring ingredient in it, traditionally a splash of English ale and a spoonful of mustard or else several drops of Worcestershire sauce, the sharp, brown English condiment made from anchovies, vinegar, and spices. The final broiling slightly browns the cheese and also helps to dry any excess water off the poached egg.

Grilled Cheese Sandwich

The North American version of Britain's
Welsh rarebit and France's croque-monsieur
is the grilled (or toasted) cheese sandwich.
As its name announces, it is a toasted bread
envelope enclosing a filling of mainly melted
cheese, although other ingredients may be
added. What is misleading about its name
is that the sandwich is hardly ever grilled.

Classically, the dish should be made in a
frying pan or griddle. The sandwich is made
up in the normal way, and then the outside
surfaces of the bread are buttered too. It is
cooked on both sides until the bread surfaces
have browned, and the cheese inside is
thoroughly molten. It could be cooked under
a broiler with the same results, but almost
never is in North American homes. What has
taken the place of the griddle pan in many
cases is the patented toasted sandwich maker,
but purists tend to frown on these as not
producing the authentic result.

An important technique in the preparation
of the grilled cheese sandwich is that it should
be pressed down firmly with a spatula as each
side cooks, giving a compressed final article,
a quality the scorned electric sandwich maker
is at least capable of replicating.

Eggs en Cocotte

The French have one of the highest rates of
egg consumption in the world—255 eggs per
capita in 2005. Of course, some of these
eggs find their way into rich sauces such as
mayonnaise and hollandaise, or wonderful
desserts like crème caramel, but many are
broken gently into French white buttered
ramekins and baked "en cocotte." Eggs cooked
in this style are seasoned lightly and baked for
about 10 minutes. Their creamy consistency,
with firm whites and runny yolks, makes a
perfect starting place for your imagination.
Put a combination of finely cut herbs in the
ramekin before adding the egg or moisten the
egg with a spoonful of cream. Lightly sautéed
mushrooms or vegetables from artichokes
to zucchinis are also good companions. For a
hearty luncheon or supper dish, garnish with
chopped ham or a robust grated cheese and
serve with a salad.

Deviled Eggs

The "devil" in a deviled egg refers to the condiments used to give the blandness of a hard-boiled egg a spicy personality. Originally, deviling was a cooking technique applied to meats, and deviled ham is still widely available but, in contemporary home-cooking, it refers to a way of preparing cold, stuffed eggs. Eggs are hard-boiled, cooled, peeled, and sliced in half. A lengthwise cut gives a more stable shape but the halves resulting from a horizontal cut (around the middle) can be stabilized by lightly trimming the rounded ends. The yolk is scooped out without breaking the white. The yolks are mashed with an ingredient that moistens the yolk to a smooth consistency: mayonnaise, salad dressing, sour cream, vinegar, or lemon juice. The deviling comes from adding ingredients like Worcestershire sauce, mustard, cayenne pepper, or fresh herbs. The deviled mixture is returned to the white halves, elegantly with a piping bag, or less so with a spoon or fork. A dash of the devil's cooler cousin, paprika, may be sprinkled on top or the eggs can be garnished with anchovies, olives, capers, or anything you wish.

Eggnog

The "nog" or "noggin" was a serving cup common in old English inns; an eggnog, sometimes called an egg flip, is a historical term for an alcoholic drink containing a beaten egg. Some might say that's a terrible waste of a good drink but, for many, a punch bowl of eggnog is an essential part of a Christmas or New Year's party. Nonalcoholic, commercially prepared eggnog is widely available in North America where eggnog is very popular during the winter holiday season but it's easy to make at home. The basic ingredients include egg yolks beaten with fine sugar, cream or milk, a little vanilla, and a spirit such as rum, brandy, or sherry. The egg whites are beaten until stiff and are folded gently into the mix, giving it a rich but airy texture. A sprinkle of grated nutmeg is the traditional topping. There are many favorite variations. Bourbon is the spirit of choice in the American South; Puerto Rican *coquito* uses coconut milk and white rum; and, since no one counts calories during the holidays, why not top off your eggnog with a big dollop of sweet whipped cream and some cinnamon sugar!

Oeufs Mornay

In the classic French sauce family, Mornay sauce is daughter to the mother sauce, béchamel. A Mornay sauce starts as a basic béchamel sauce—a roux of melted butter and flour to which milk is added. Mornay sauce is sometimes enriched with an egg yolk and may be flavored with a shallot, a pinch of mustard, or some nutmeg. After the mixture thickens, grated cheese is melted into the sauce. Gruyère and Parmesan are traditional, but sharp white Cheddar or Emmenthaler also pair well.

With such a simple sauce, the outcome very much depends on the quality of the ingredients and the sensitivity of the technique. If your only encounter with eggs Mornay is the result of your fumbling efforts as an adolescent in a school cooking class, you should definitely give this dish another look. Eggs Mornay is a wonderful way of serving hard-boiled eggs. The eggs are halved, covered in sauce, then dusted with a little extra grated cheese and placed under the broiler until the topping bubbles and browns to a light and delectable crust.

The next time you're doing the same old thing for breakfast, surprise everyone with a serving of eggs Mornay.

Egg Bhurji

A bhurji is a *masala* or mixture of tasty ingredients, so there is quite a bit of latitude in its creation. An egg bhurji is a scrambled omelette made with onions and potatoes and a fragrant mixture of chiles and spices that gives you a taste of India. Here is one way to make an egg bhurji for two, using whatever ground spices you have at hand.

Lightly beat five eggs. Add a dash of milk or some coconut milk. Dice two medium onions and two medium potatoes. Chop some ginger, chiles, and garlic; the amount depends on your taste. Heat two tablespoons of oil in a large skillet. Lightly brown the diced potatoes, then add the onions and sauté them with the potatoes until just translucent. Add the ginger, chiles, and garlic and cook until soft. Add ground spices, such as cumin, coriander, turmeric, and garam masala, according to your taste. Stir to coat the mixture.

Pour the beaten eggs into the pan and let the egg begin to set. Stir occasionally to gently break up the egg and mix it with the spicy ingredients. It's a great last-minute dish for unexpected company; serve it with Indian flatbread and some green mango pickle.

Torta

An Italian torta is a delectable tart or pie made with a pastry of flour, eggs, and olive oil. The most elaborate tortas divide the pastry into several parts, roll each part very thinly, and layer them together with brushed olive oil to create a very flaky crust on both the bottom and top. The top layer may be latticed or elaborately decorated.

A sweet torta is a rich mixture of ricotta and eggs combined with spices and dried fruit and topped with nuts. It is sometimes compared to cheesecake. A savory torta is a rich mix of onions, one or more cheeses, and ham or sausage set in an egg custard. Spinach, asparagus, peppers, olives, sun-dried tomatoes, and fresh herbs may be added to the mix. Italian cheeses offer a wonderful range of taste and texture from the sweet softness of ricotta to the richness of asiago, provolone, or groviera, to the sharpness of freshly grated Parmesan. Whole eggs may be gently set between layers of filling to be revealed when the pie is sliced. There are many regional variations and every family has its favorite recipe, especially for the *torta pasqualina* or special Easter pie.

Frittata

A frittata is the Italian version of the French omelette. Instead of folding the eggs around the filling, the fillings in a frittata are combined with the egg mixture and the result is an open-faced omelette. Cheese, mushrooms, sautéed vegetables, and ham all make tasty combinations. Even a simple frittata can sound impressive and taste outstanding: *frittata con le cipolle* is an onion frittata; and *frittata di aglio e prezzemolo* is made with garlic and parsley.

A frittata also lets you show off your manual dexterity. Have an additional oiled frying pan at hand. When the frittata is almost set, cover the first frying pan with the second like a lid, flip the frittata into the second pan, and return it to the heat to finish cooking the top surface. If you're not ready for this feat, don't fret; you can just slide the frittata under a hot broiler and achieve almost the same result. No one need ever know! Cut the frittata into wedges and serve hot or cold.

Green Veg Frittata

2 lb Swiss chard (silver beet)

6 free range eggs, plus 2 extra egg yolks

$1/2$ cup light cream

$1/3$ cup freshly grated Parmesan or Gruyère cheese

Coarse sea salt

Freshly ground black pepper

$1/2$ tsp grated nutmeg

1 tsp butter

2 tsp olive oil

First, cook the veg (if you don't, they will release their juices, making the frittata too watery). Cut the stems from the Swiss chard and roughly chop. Cook in a large pot of simmering salted water for 10 minutes. Wash the leaves well, roughly chop, and add to the pot. Cook for 3 or 4 minutes until wilted.

Drain well and cool, then squeeze out any excess water. Beat the eggs, egg yolks, cream, Parmesan, salt, pepper, and nutmeg in a bowl. Heat the butter and oil in a nonstick frying pan, and pour in the eggs. Arrange the drained greens in the pan, jiggling them so they settle into the egg.

Cook over moderate heat until the eggs have set on the bottom and are lightly golden. Heat the broiler, wrap the frying pan handle with aluminum foil and place under the broiler for a few minutes until lightly golden and just set in the middle. If it's still runny, cover the pan and give it another couple of minutes over moderate heat. Cut into big wedges and serve. *Serves 4–6* **Adapted from Jill Dupleix's** *Totally Simple Food*

Poached Eggs

Coddled Eggs

According to French tradition, the chef's hat, or *toque blanche*, has 100 pleats to signify the chef's ability to prepare eggs in 100 different ways. Surely, poaching has a pleat of honor on every hat. It is such a simple task, yet so hard to perfect. All you need is a pan of water heated just to the boiling point and a fresh egg, preferably not straight from the refrigerator. The older the egg, the more tips and techniques you must employ to get the result you want. Salt or vinegar in the water is often recommended; immersing the egg in boiling water for 10 to 15 seconds to coagulate the white of an elderly egg is a Julia Child tip; cracking the egg first into a cup instead of directly into the water is another. The perfect poached egg has a compact shape and the yolk is nicely encased by the white on all sides. Somewhere between two and four minutes after immersing the egg in water, you will know whether you have earned your pleat.

To poach an egg add a little vinegar to the water to help the egg set more quickly and keep its shape. An egg poacher lets you easily lift the eggs out of the water. while rings, similar to muffin rings, can be set in the pan to give the eggs a uniform shape. Cook the eggs until they are just firm enough to lift out without breaking the yolks. Serve on slices of hot buttered toast set on a hot dish.

Coddling is one of the gentlest ways to prepare eggs. Strictly speaking, coddling an egg means immersing it, in the shell, in boiling water for a minute, removing it promptly and cooling it to prevent further cooking. Eggs coddled in this way are used in Caesar salad.

The term "coddled egg" also refers to an egg broken into a buttered egg coddler and seasoned with salt and pepper. Around 1890, Royal Worcester introduced egg coddlers just for this purpose—cup-shaped containers made of earthenware or fine porcelain, with metal lids. Once the coddler is filled, the metal lid is lightly screwed down and lowered into a pan of simmering hot water that reaches almost to the coddler's rim. After seven or eight minutes, the egg is ready to eat. Served in the coddler, it makes a very elegant breakfast.

Coddled eggs have a reputation as a food for invalids. As Jane Austen's fuss-budget Mr. Woodhouse says in her novel, *Emma*, "An egg boiled very soft is not unwholesome."

Quail Eggs

The eggs of Japanese quails are speckled and mottled in shades from dark brown to golden and from blue-gray to white. They are tiny, only about a fifth as large as a standard hen's egg but somewhat similar in taste and nutritional content. Marinated in soy sauce, pickled, or simply hard-boiled, nestled among ramen noodles, collected on a skewer, or tucked into a child's bento box with a parsley "tail" and a sesame seed "eye," their diminutive size suits the ambiance of Japanese cuisine with its tradition of small, perfectly presented individual servings. They also have a place in the cuisine of China and Korea.

Outside of Asia, quail eggs are very often associated with gourmet cuisine. Their size makes them a favorite ingredient in inventive canapés. Who could resist half a tiny quail's egg topped with crème fraiche or an equally tiny dollop of caviar?

To find fresh quail eggs, you may have to visit an egg market that specializes in a wider range of eggs than your local grocery store. Shelling quail eggs can be quite labor-intensive, but they are available cooked and shelled in jars and tins in specialty stores.

Four Children's Favorites

French Toast, Eggy Bread, Pain Perdu

People have been dipping stale bread into an egg and milk mixture and frying it since medieval times. But opinion is divided on exactly how to make it or even what to call it. The British tend to call it eggy bread, while French toast is the norm across the Atlantic, and the French term is pain perdu, with reference to using bread that might otherwise go to waste. Thereafter, the consensus is hard to find. Shall it be sourdough bread, crusty white, or brioche? Should the bread be thickly or thinly sliced? What about adding sugar or vanilla, salt or pepper? And then there is the question of the toppings: jam, sugar, syrup, or even tomato sauce. In fact, the setting sets the rules. A gourmet kitchen may produce an exquisite pain perdu whereas a Boy Scout troop simply fries up a hearty French toast over a campfire. The universal result? A contented expression and full stomach.

Soft-Boiled Egg with Toast Soldiers

A soft-boiled egg will nourish the body while being gentle on the digestion and soothing to the spirit. The ideal soft-boiled egg has a firm white and runny yolk. Place eggs in a pan and cover with at least an inch of cold water. Bring just to a boil on high heat. Reduce the heat and cook for three to four minutes. The timing depends somewhat on the size of the eggs and whether they were at room temperature. While the eggs are cooking, make the soldiers. Toast the bread, butter lightly, and cut very carefully into strips— too wide and they won't fit into the yolk; too narrow and they won't stand up to the weight of the yolk (with the potential for telltale stains on the necktie). When the cooking time is up, set the egg in an egg cup, small end up, and remove the top. Dip the toast soldiers into the yolk and march them smartly into your mouth. Scoop up the remainder with a spoon.

Sunny-Side Up Eggs

Sunny-side up eggs are a staple of the classic Full English Breakfast. When perfectly cooked, the runny yolk complements the crispy toast and oozes its way among all the other items on the plate. It can be challenging to make the perfect sunny-side up egg.

Try these tips. Break the egg into a teacup or small bowl before sliding it gently into the pan. Preheat the pan to medium heat but lower the heat immediately after adding the egg so that the bottom of the egg doesn't overcook. Tip the pan slightly and spoon some of the hot butter or oil onto the surface of the egg, or cover the pan briefly with a lid and let the surface steam slightly. Trapped in a drizzly climate, Britons named this dish after the sun, perhaps as a surrogate for the real thing. In sunny Indonesia, on the other hand, it has the evocative name *telur mata sapi*—an egg like the eye of a cow.

Egg-in-the-Hole

What a comfort it is to know that dietary cholesterol does not lead directly to coronary heart disease; otherwise, our health-guilt might stop us from indulging in an old-fashioned egg-in-the-hole now and then. Butter a slice of bread on both sides and cut a circular hole in the center. Place the bread and the cutout circle in a frying pan over medium heat and lightly brown one side. Turn both over and break an egg into the hole. Cover the pan and continue cooking until the white is firm and the yolk is still slightly runny, then serve. Fast, nutritious, uncomplicated, egg-in-the-hole has many aliases, from cowboy eggs to frog-in-the-hole. Best known as a favorite in the nursery, the campsite, and the student kitchen, egg-in-the-hole has made occasional appearances in films from *Moon over Miami* to *Moonstruck* to *V for Vendetta*.

Bacon and Egg Pie

If, as the saying goes, "Real men don't each quiche," there is a manly-man alternative in this down-under favorite, egg and bacon pie. It's a double-crust pie, filled with slices of smoky bacon and whole raw eggs arranged very gently between the bacon layers. Some chopped parsley, chives, and other vegetables might not go amiss. Sliced and served, either hot or cold, along with a side of warm vegetables or a cool salad, this is a hearty dish fit for a big appetite.

Bacon and Egg Pie

8 oz shortcrust pastry

6 eggs

1 cup milk

4 strips bacon, chopped

$1/3$ cup grated aged Cheddar cheese

2 tbsp chopped chives

1 tbsp chopped dill

2 tsp Dijon mustard

cracked black pepper

6 thin strips bacon, rind removed

Preheat the oven to 350°F.

Roll out the pastry on a lightly floured surface until $1/8$ in thick. Place the pastry in a 10-inch pie dish and trim the edges. Refrigerate for 30 minutes. Prick the base of the pastry and line with nonstick parchment paper. Fill the shell with baking beans and bake for 5 minutes. Remove the weights and paper, and cook for a further 5 minutes. (This process keeps the pastry crisp when adding wet ingredients to the pastry shell.) Place the eggs and milk in a bowl and whisk to combine. Add the bacon, Cheddar, chives, dill, mustard, and pepper and mix to combine. Pour the mixture into the pastry shell, top with thin bacon, and bake at 315°F for 35 to 45 minutes or until the pie is set. Serve hot or cold with a peppery arugula salad. *Serves 6* **Adapted from Donna Hay's** *The New Cook*

Oeufs Florentine

The title of this dish hints at its lineage. Although part of French cuisine, its name connects it to Florence, the principal city of the Italian region of Tuscany. When the future Henry II of France married Caterina de Medici of Florence in 1533, she came with a retinue that included Florentine cooks. The Tuscan influence is sometimes credited with profoundly influencing medieval French cuisine and contributing to its pre-eminent status today. In contemporary times, the term Florentine often tells you that the dish you are about to eat has spinach as one of its main ingredients.

Eggs Florentine is sometimes prepared as a meatless version of eggs Benedict, with a layer of spinach replacing slices of bacon. Spinach has a great affinity for cheese, so this dish is traditionally prepared with a Mornay sauce—a béchamel sauce flavored with onion and made richer by the addition of an egg yolk, a little cream, and freshly grated Gruyère or Parmesan cheese. A poached egg nestles on a bed of wilted spinach, covered in a savory layer of Mornay sauce, garnished with a dusting of bread crumbs and Parmesan and lightly browned under a broiler. It's like a little Tuscan holiday.

Oeufs Florentine

½ lb fresh spinach

Salt

Freshly ground black pepper

4 eggs

4 tbsp light cream

A pinch of grated nutmeg

2 tbsp freshly grated Parmesan cheese

Preheat the oven to 450°F.

Wash the spinach and tear roughly. Put the wet leaves in a saucepan over low heat and cook, stirring, until just wilted—a matter of minutes. Season to taste. Transfer the spinach to two shallow gratin dishes and use a spoon to make two hollows for the eggs. Break an egg into each hollow and spoon 1 tablespoon of cream over each. Season lightly and sprinkle with nutmeg. Bake in the preheated oven for 15 minutes. Sprinkle with Parmesan cheese and return to the oven for 1 to 2 minutes more, or until the cheese melts.

Serves 2

Hamine Eggs

Hamine eggs (in Arabic *beid hamine*) are eggs simmered for a very long time, along with the skins from yellow onions. Skins from two medium onions will color about half a dozen eggs. A little olive oil helps to slow evaporation. Over the long cooking time—from 6 to 24 hours, depending on the method and tradition—the onionskins leave their warm glow on the shells, in swirls of gold and deep brown. The color and flavor seep through the shell to tinge the egg whites a creamy yellow, with a creamy texture to match. Slow cooking can be done on a stovetop, in an oven or, as a modern innovation, in a slow cooker. Hamine eggs are frequently served atop Egypt's national dish, ful medames.

Eggs are intricately linked with the rituals of the spring equinox in many cultures, Easter eggs being a familiar example. In Egypt, hamine eggs are a traditional part of *Cham el Nessim*, an ancient spring festival during which families celebrate renewal in the natural world with picnics and visits to the country. Likewise, in the mix of Moorish, Spanish, and Judaic culture that emerged from Andalusian Spain, *huevos haminados* have become integral to celebrating Passover in Sephardic households.

Eggs Benedict

Eggs Benedict and the weekend brunch tradition stand as New York's culinary gifts to the world. There are differing accounts of the origin of this dish. In one, a Wall Street broker named Benedict, breakfasting at the Waldorf, needed a hangover cure and requested this unusual combination for a late breakfast; in another, a couple named Benedict, eating at Delmonico's, wanted to try something different for lunch.

Many of the ingredients are immigrants: English muffins, Canadian bacon, and hollandaise sauce, although outsiders would say the muffins aren't really English, the bacon isn't really Canadian, and the sauce isn't really Dutch. Eggs Benedict is a unique creation of the American melting pot.

A classic eggs Benedict consists of a layer of tangy hollandaise sauce spooned over two poached eggs resting on slices of back bacon on top of a split, buttered, and toasted English muffin. The quality and freshness of the lemon-accented hollandaise sauce is the key to success. Though variations abound with smoked salmon, asparagus, and the like, the classic eggs Benny has held its ground on brunch menus for more than a century.

Eggs Benedict

Vinegar

4 eggs

2 English muffins

4 slices cooked back bacon

Ready-made hollandaise sauce

Fill a large, shallow pan with water, about 1 inch deep, and bring it to a simmer. Add some vinegar (1 to 2 tablespoons per 4 cups of water) to help the eggs hold their shape.

To further help the eggs retain their shape in the pan, break each egg individually into a cup. Carefully slide the eggs into the simmering water and poach for 2 to 3 minutes.

Slice the muffins in half and lightly toast them. When the eggs are poached, remove them with a slotted spoon and drain them.

Place the back bacon on top of the muffins, set the egg on the spinach, and drizzle hollandaise sauce over the eggs. *Serves 2*

Pancakes

Pancakes may have been around since
Neolithic humans domesticated einkorn
wheat, ground it into flour, mixed it with
birds' eggs and goat's milk, and poured the
batter on a heated rock. Perhaps because of
this ancient lineage, pancakes are associated
with cultural rituals in many countries—
Shrove Tuesday, Candlemas, and Chanukah
to name a few.

The pancake family tree has two branches,
depending on the leavening process used.
From early days, pancakes relied on eggs as
the leavening agent. The French *crêpe* and the
Dutch *pannekoeken* are made this way. The
batter must rest before being exposed to
heat. *Crêpes* and their cousins are thin and
delicate and often stuffed with fillings of fish,
eggs, or vegetables, or dusted with sugar and
fruit. Later, the use of leavening agents like
baking powder became more common.

The United States adopted the pancake
during colonial times. New Englanders called
them flapjacks in honor of the custom of
flipping them in the pan with a flick of the
wrist. American pancakes are leavened with
baking powder, and a "stack of pancakes"
is a breakfast staple. Fluffy, thick, and
smothered in butter and maple syrup,
a pancake breakfast keeps hunger at bay
for the rest of the day.

Pancakes

2 cups all-purpose flour

$2^1/_2$ tsp baking powder

$^1/_2$ tsp salt

$1^1/_2$ cups milk

1 egg

2 tbsp unsalted butter, melted

Additional melted butter

Whisk the flour, baking powder, and salt
in a large bowl to blend. Whisk the milk and
egg in another medium bowl to blend. Make
a well in the center of the dry ingredients.
Pour the milk mixture into the well. Add
the 2 tbsp melted butter and whisk the
ingredients together until just blended.
The batter should be lumpy.

Heat a nonstick griddle or large nonstick
frying pan over medium heat. Brush
generously with additional melted butter.
For each pancake, ladle about $^1/_4$ cup of
batter onto the griddle. Cook the pancakes
until bottoms are brown and the batter has
set and is bubbly, about 3 minutes. Using
a spatula, turn the pancakes over and cook
until bottoms are brown and pancakes are
cooked through, about 2 minutes. Transfer
to plates. Serve with butter and maple syrup.
Makes about 20

Lemon Curd

As English in spirit as William Wordsworth's "host of golden daffodils" and just as brilliant in color, lemon curd is one of those treats that make English expatriates homesick. Lemon curd is not strictly speaking a preserve, although it is sold commercially in jars, like jam. It's a creamy egg-based spread made with sugar, butter, and lemons. Slow cooking is the secret to its smooth texture; lemon zest gives it its sharp flavor. It's simple to make at home. If your friends or family like lemon meringue pie, try substituting lemon curd for a standard cornstarch-thickened lemon pudding mix.

Lemon curd is very versatile. Make a lemon curd tart, spread it on toast, use it as a filling in layer cakes and pastries, as a topping on cheesecake, or spoon it straight from the jar (but don't let the children see you). Best of all, lay the table for an English cream tea and bake some scones fit for your lemon curd.

Lemon Curd

3 egg yolks

Finely grated zest of 1 lemon

$1/4$ cup lemon juice

$1/2$ cup superfine sugar

$1/2$ cup unsalted butter, cut into small pieces

Put the yolks, zest, juice, and sugar in a heatproof bowl and whisk together until smooth. Set the bowl over a saucepan of simmering water, making sure the bowl does not touch the water. Stir for 8 to 10 minutes, or until thickened slightly. Remove from the heat and whisk in the butter, one piece at a time, until smooth. Cool. *Makes about 1 cup*
Adapted from Bill Granger's *Bill's Kitchen*

Selsig Morgannwg

Now that more vegetarians are around the
breakfast table, a dozen "poor-man's sausages"
make a popular substitute for the meat-based
sort. Selsig Morgannwg in Welsh, Glamorgan
sausages consist of roughly equal quantities
of grated cheese and fresh white bread
broken into crumbs, mixed with a chopped
onion and a small amount of dry mustard,
herbs, and seasonings. The mixture is bound
together with the yolks of two eggs plus the
white of one and is shaped into sausages.
Each sausage is dipped into the second egg
white, rolled in dried bread crumbs, and fried
in hot oil or lard.

For the true Welsh flavor, choose a semi-
hard Welsh cheese such as Caerphilly and
substitute leeks for the chopped onion.
The consistency of the sausages depends a
lot on the type of cheese and the moisture
content of the bread, so play with the amount
of each ingredient until you find a mixture
that holds well together in the pan. Even
pork sausage devotees will be scooping
these onto their plates.

Mayonnaise

Food historians have been debating the
origins of mayonnaise since the 18th century.
Does it celebrate the French victory at
the Battle of Mahón? Is it derived from
moyeunaise, a word that refers to the yolk of
an egg? Is it named for the Duc de Mayenne?
No matter. There is no doubting the staying
power of this classic French mother sauce.
If vinaigrette is a short-term relationship
between oil and vinegar, mayonnaise is
a rewarding long-term marriage. Lecithin,
a component of egg yolks, is the secret.
Oil is drizzled into egg yolk and beaten until
it stabilizes at between 65% and 85% fat
content, then flavored with fine vinegars
or lemon juice and mustard. Most of the
mayonnaise flavoring today's sandwiches,
potato salads, and deviled eggs, or spread
on hamburgers, or used as a garnish for
French fried potatoes, is now commercially
prepared, saving the arm strength of aspiring
chefs for other tasks.

While lower-fat alternatives are available—
salad cream, Miracle Whip, low-fat yogurt—
only mayonnaise has the clear, tangy richness
that contrasts with, yet complements, eggs,
fish, and potatoes. Many a weight-loss diet
has been abandoned at the bleak prospect
of living without mayonnaise.

Huevos Rancheros

After doing their early morning chores, ranch hands—*rancheros*—tucked into a hearty second breakfast of eggs served with tortillas. Today, huevos rancheros is a popular hearty breakfast or brunch dish all over the Americas, even though very few morning chores may be involved. The eggs may be prepared any style—sunny-side up, scrambled, poached, or even baked. What gives this dish its unique taste are the ranchero sauce and the accompaniments.

Ranchero sauce is a mixture of sautéed onions, garlic, green bell pepper, and chiles, combined with chopped tomatoes. It is hot but the best ranchero sauce is also flavorful. The heat depends on which chilies are used (habaneros are reckoned to be the hottest) and whether the cook has a heavy hand with the chili powder. The traditional accompaniments—refried beans, slices of fresh, cool avocado, sour cream, and fried potatoes—cool down the taste buds. A sprinkling of Monterey Jack, a cheese first made in the Spanish missions around Monterey, California, provides the final flourish. Served with warm tortillas, huevos rancheros will keep you going for many hours, no matter what chores are on your list.

Huevos Divorciados

A serving of huevos divorciados lets you savor some of the classic flavors of Mexican cuisine. In this breakfast dish, two fried eggs form the base. They are separated—*divorciados*—by a row of chilaquiles, a mixture of broken pieces of stale tortilla, broth, and tomato sauce. On one side, the egg is garnished with *salsa roja*, a red sauce made with tomatoes, garlic, onions, chiles, and freshly chopped cilantro; on the other, the egg is garnished with *salsa verde*, a green sauce made with tomatillos, spinach, onions, garlic, and green chiles.

From their home in Latin America, tomatoes have colonized most of the world's menus but their smaller cousin, the tomatillo, has been more of a stay-at-home. Salsas date back to Aztec times. The Aztecs domesticated both tomatoes and tomatillos but the Spanish adopted only the familiar red tomato and carried it back to Europe. Hispanic emigrants have introduced tomatillos to the United States. Tomatillos are harvested before they ripen. Inside their loose paper husk, they are green and have a tart taste. Imagine a chopped green tomato garnished with lime or lemon and you may have a hint of the astringent taste of *salsa verde*.

Huevos Divorciados

1/2 lb plum tomatoes

1/2 lb fresh tomatillos, husks discarded and tomatillos rinsed

2 fresh jalapeño chiles

1 wedge of large white onion (about 1 inch)

2 cloves garlic

2 tsp salt

3 tbsp chopped fresh cilantro

1/4 cup water

4 to 8 tbsp corn or vegetable oil

8 large eggs

8 (6- to 7-inch) corn tortillas

Heat a griddle or cast-iron frying pan over moderate heat until a bit of water dropped on it evaporates quickly. Roast the tomatoes, tomatillos, jalapeños, and onion, turning with tongs, until charred all over, 10 to 15 minutes. Core the roasted tomatoes. Discard jalapeño stems and half the seeds from each chile.

Coarsely purée the tomatoes, 1 jalapeño, 1 clove garlic, and 1 teaspoon salt in a blender or food processor. Transfer to a bowl.

Coarsely purée the tomatillos, remaining jalapeño, remaining clove garlic, remaining teaspoon salt, cilantro, and 1/4 cup water. Transfer to a bowl.

Heat 2 tablespoons of oil in a small nonstick frying pan over moderately low heat until hot. Gently break 2 eggs into a cup (this is one serving), keeping the yolks intact, then pour them into the frying pan and cook, covered, for 5 minutes, or to desired doneness. Season with salt and pepper. Fry the tortillas while the eggs cook. Make more eggs in the same manner, adding oil as needed.

While each serving of eggs is cooking, heat 2 tablespoons of oil in another small nonstick frying pan over moderate heat until hot but not smoking. Stack 2 tortillas in the frying pan. Cook the bottom tortilla for 30 seconds on the first side, then flip the stack with tongs. While the second tortilla cooks on the bottom, turn the top tortilla over with tongs, then flip the stack again.

Continue until both sides of both tortillas are cooked but not brown or crisp. Fry more tortillas, adding oil as needed.

Put the tortillas on a plate, overlapping them slightly. Top with the eggs and spoon salsas on one egg each. *Serves 4*

Strata

Strata is a popular make-ahead choice on the American "bed and breakfast" menu and finds its way to many a celebratory brunch table. Its name reflects its layered construction. It's made with cubed bread, preferably a day old or more, layered with other ingredients. Ham and a sharp cheese, such as Monterey Jack, are often used, but there are other tempting options, including mushrooms, sausage, broccoli, sun-dried tomatoes, basil, and spinach. Once the ingredients are layered in a baking dish, the casserole is filled with an egg and milk mixture and refrigerated overnight.

The key to its light yet rich texture is to avoid excess moisture in the layers. Use stale bread, lightly buttered, and avoid ingredients that bring too much moisture into the mix. Some strata aficionados recommend weighing the strata mixture down overnight with a small bag of dried beans or rice to improve its texture—and no wonder. When this casserole goes into a hot oven after returning to room temperature, it almost takes flight, emerging transformed into an airy, flavorful treat. It feels so light, you can almost convince yourself it's calorie-free.

Dashimaki Tamago

As delicate as a mille-feuille pastry, with a sweet-salty flavor, dashimaki tamago—a Japanese rolled omelette—is typical of Japanese cuisine. The ingredients are simple: beaten eggs, thinned with a mixture of a little sugar, Japanese soy sauce, and a pinch of salt, all dissolved in a quantity of *dashi*, or fish broth. The magic of this dish is in the way it is made. The traditional, rectangular Japanese omelette pan makes the perfect tool for the job but a round omelette pan will do.

The egg mixture is cooked progressively in very thin layers on low heat so that the mixture does not brown too darkly. When set, the first layer is rolled to the edge of the pan but not removed. A second layer is poured into the pan and the first roll is lifted up so the next layer can attach itself to the first. When the second layer is set, it is rolled around the first. Layers are added until the mixture is finished and the omelette has three to six layers. When the rolled omelette is complete, it is turned onto a bamboo mat or cloth, rolled firmly, and left to rest for a few minutes, before serving cut into four to eight pieces.

Chawan Mushi

Chawan mushi is the only Japanese food traditionally eaten with a spoon. Unlike the sweet, firm egg custards usual in Western cuisine, Japanese egg custard is loose in texture and flavored with *dashi* fish broth, soy sauce, and sake or rice wine, making it an ideal soup course or a warming winter snack. Chawan mushi is steamed and served in special glazed cups with lids.

When you lift the lid, you never know what you will find in a chawan mushi cup, as the cook is free to extemporize. In the soft, velvety custard, you may find chopped mushrooms, small prawns or shrimps, slices of *kamaboko* fish sausage, cubed chicken, oysters, a little grated carrot or turnip, water chestnuts, or tofu.

Chawan Mushi

$2\frac{1}{2}$ oz chicken breast, cut into bite-sized pieces

2 tsp light soy sauce, plus 3 tbsp soy sauce

2 large eggs

$1\frac{1}{2}$ cups *dashi* (fish broth)

4 fresh shiitake mushrooms (discard stems)

1 tbsp parsley stalks, cut into 1-in pieces

4 sprigs fresh parsley for garnish

Sprinkle the chicken with 2 teaspoons soy sauce and set aside. Break the eggs into a bowl and mix gently. Add the broth and 3 tablespoons soy sauce. Mix well and strain. Divide the mushrooms, parsley stalks, and chicken among 4 ramekins with lids and pour in the egg mixture.

Put about an inch of water into a steamer and bring to a boil. Lower the heat to medium and put the ramekins in the steamer. Steam for 10 minutes. Serve garnished with parsley sprigs. *Serves 4*

Quiche Lorraine

The Lorraine region of northeastern France was a Germanic kingdom in medieval times; hence, the *kuche* became the *quiche*. The origins of quiche Lorraine can be traced to 1586 but it likely dates from much earlier. A classic quiche Lorraine is a rich, open pastry tart filled with a mixture of beaten eggs, fresh cream, and small pieces of precooked smoky bacon, seasoned with salt, pepper, and nutmeg. In the late 20th century, quiche became wildly popular and the classic recipe was left behind as ingredients stretched to include onions, cheese, mushrooms, spinach, leeks, anchovies, and olives, to name just a few. Quiche is easily reheated and can serve as an hors d'oeuvre, as part of a hearty lunch, or as a light supper.

Quiche Lorraine is a specialty of the town of Nancy, a noted center of the Art Nouveau movement. The stunningly beautiful city center of Nancy has been designated a UNESCO World Heritage site, so if you visit you can feast the mind and heart as well as the body.

Quiche Lorraine

1 (9-in deep-dish) pie shell, baked and cooled

1 tbsp butter

1 onion, chopped

$1/3$ cup finely chopped ham

1 cup shredded Gruyère cheese

4 eggs

$1^1/_2$ cups milk

A pinch of salt

A pinch of grated nutmeg

Preheat the oven to 350°F.

Melt the butter in a frying pan, then add the onion and sauté until soft and golden.

Spread the ham, cheese, and onion over the pie shell.

In a bowl, whisk the eggs, milk, salt, and nutmeg together, then pour into the pie shell. Bake for 35 to 40 minutes. Let stand for 5 or 10 minutes before cutting. *Serves 4–6*

Scotch Eggs

A Scotch egg has a peeled, hard-boiled egg at its center. The egg is lightly dusted with flour, wrapped in a layer of forcemeat or sausage, rolled in bread crumbs, deep-fried until crisp, and then served, usually at room temperature. It's ideally paired with a pint of ale or lager in a fine old pub. True, it compresses lots of calories into a small package but sometimes you just need that! Originally popular in Victorian-era picnic hampers, Scotch eggs are ubiquitous now in public houses, at soccer matches, and in convenience stores.

Don't let a bad experience with a pre-packaged, mass-produced Scotch egg put you off. There are treasured pubs all over the United Kingdom still serving the real thing and you will surely taste some fine pints in the course of your search for the best. As to their roots, it's not certain where Scotch eggs originated. They were first sold by London victualler Fortnum & Mason in the 18th century but they do improvize creatively on homespun ingredients like those other Scottish classics, haggis and Scotch broth.

Pickled Eggs

Thousand-Year-Old Eggs

The origin of vinegar is lost in the mists of time. It is the product of secondary fermentation of juices. First comes the alcoholic fermentation, then the acidic fermentation; hence the common name *vin aigre* or sour wine. Vinegars are also made from other fruits and grains, such as rice, barley malt, sugar cane, and apple cider. From medieval times, and even earlier, vinegar was essential in preserving food. What better way to manage all the eggs produced during the Lenten fast than to turn them into delicious pickled eggs to be consumed after Easter.

Eggs for pickling are hard-boiled, cooled, and shelled. It's traditional to make them in a big clear glass jar, the better to tantalize you into tasting one. The pickling process is much the same as in medieval times. A quantity of vinegar mixed with whole spices such as cloves, mustard, peppercorns, allspice, and cinnamon sticks is brought to boiling point and cooled. This vinegar mixture is poured into the jar to cover the eggs.

After about two weeks, the eggs are a beautiful brown color, firm and succulent—the perfect accompaniment to a pint of bitter.

Although thousand-year-old eggs may look like something from an ancient burial site, they are only about four months in the making. Most cultures have devised ways of preserving eggs during times of plenty but the Chinese have developed a process that transforms preserved eggs into a truly unique food experience.

Wood ash, quicklime, and salt are all dissolved in an infusion of tea to make a paste. Each egg is coated in the paste, then rolled in rice chaff and stored in a jar or basket. After about four months, the eggs are ready to eat. (A modern short cut disdained by connoisseurs calls for soaking the eggs in salt and lye for ten days and aging them for several weeks in plastic—plastic indeed!).

When they are ready, the clay coat is broken open, revealing an amber shell. As the shell is cracked, a characteristic ammonia-like smell is released. Inside is a dark, blue-brown transparent jelly surrounding a variegated green yolk. The yolk has a taste somewhat akin to ripe cheese and is the tastiest part. Thousand-year-old eggs are often quartered and eaten cold along with other condiments, or you may find them cubed and stuck into congee, a popular rice porridge.

Scrambled Eggs

Wholesome and versatile, scrambled eggs are a welcome dish at any time of day. Their mild taste combines beautifully with the boldest of ingredients, but they're also delicious plain or with a sprinkle of fresh herbs.

Julia Child, along with her co-authors Simone Beck and Louisette Bertholle, is credited with transforming the North American approach to cooking with the 1961 publication of *Mastering the Art of French Cooking*. Her television kitchen is a popular exhibit in the Smithsonian Institute in Washington, DC.

Imagine being immortalized for the ability to make perfectly scrambled eggs. Simple dishes can be easily ruined and Julia's careful instructions helped aspiring gourmet cooks to achieve scrambled egg perfection: gently cooked, soft curds that melt in the mouth and taste of the simple ingredients from which they were made.

Scrambled Eggs

8 eggs

Salt

Freshly ground black pepper

4 tsp water

2 tbsp butter, for cooking

2 tbsp softened butter or whipping cream

Parsley

Beat the eggs in a bowl with the seasonings and water for 20 to 30 seconds, just to blend the yolks with the whites. Smear the bottom and sides of the cooking pan with butter. Pour in the eggs and set over moderately low heat. Stir slowly and continually, reaching all over the bottom of the pan. Nothing will seem to happen for 2 to 3 minutes as the eggs gradually heat. Suddenly they will begin to thicken into a custard. Stir rapidly, moving the pan on and off heat, until the eggs have almost thickened to the consistency you wish. Then remove from the heat, as they will continue to thicken slightly.

Just as soon as they are of the right consistency, stir in the softened butter or cream, which will stop the cooking. Season to taste, turn out onto a platter, decorate with parsley, and serve. *Serves 4*

Adapted from Julia Child, Louisette Bertholle, and Simone Beck *Mastering the Art of French Cooking*

Scrambled Eggs with Smoked Salmon

Smoked salmon is a treasured delicacy. Its rich, intensely smoky flavor is the perfect complement to creamy scrambled eggs. Scotland, with its clear streams and long coastline, is home to some of the best salmon. It is the perfect place to try this combination, but smoked salmon is so widely available that you can make it easily in your own kitchen. Scrambled eggs with smoked salmon make an elegant breakfast or brunch for a special occasion.

Scrambled Eggs with Smoked Salmon

8 large eggs

3 tbsp milk

2 tbsp chopped fresh chives, plus 3 tbsp

5 tbsp butter

3/4 cup chopped yellow onion

6 oz thinly sliced smoked salmon, cut into strips

Beat the eggs with the milk and 2 tablespoons of chopped chives. Melt the butter in a large skillet over medium heat. Add the onion and sauté until golden, about 15 minutes. Add the egg mixture and cook until almost set, stirring occasionally. Stir in the smoked salmon strips and cook for 1 minute more—the eggs should still be moist. Season to taste and serve sprinkled with the remaining chopped chives. *Serves 4*

Scrambled Eggs with Chèvre and Chives

Chèvre is the French word for goat but also the name of the cheese produced from goat's milk. It's a soft cheese with a mild flavor and light texture. In regions where goats are common, chèvre is an artisanal cheese, so there are many varieties.

Chèvre spreads easily, so it is often found rolled in cracked peppercorns or mixed with chopped herbs. Plain chèvre is frequently sold in the form of small *bûchettes* (logs) or disks.

To make a rich, tangy addition to scrambled eggs, scatter small pieces of chèvre on top of the scrambled eggs a moment or two before they are finished cooking. The heat from the eggs will be enough to begin melting the chèvre into the mixture. Serve immediately, topped with a sprinkling of chopped chives.

Tea Eggs

Tea eggs are a popular snack food across Southeast Asia and in Chinese neighborhoods all over the world. They are cooked in their shells in a broth of tea leaves and dark soy sauce. The broth is flavored with Chinese five-spice, a combination of ground star anise, fennel, cinnamon, cloves, and hot Szechwan pepper.

Once the eggs are brought to a boil and cooked just long enough to solidify the egg white, they are removed from the broth and very gently cracked all over with a spoon, then returned to the pot. As they continue to simmer, the broth seeps into the eggshell. Every tea egg, like every snowflake, is unique —a treat for the eyes as well as the taste buds.

Tea Eggs

6 eggs

3 tbsp soy sauce

1 tsp salt

1 tea bag

4 pieces star anise

1 small stick cinnamon

Bring the unshelled eggs to a boil in a saucepan of cold water and simmer for 3 to 4 minutes. Remove the eggs and cool until you can handle them. Gently crack the shells in two or three places. Put the eggs back in the saucepan with the remaining ingredients. Simmer for at least an hour, adding more water if necessary. Drain and serve hot or cold. *Serves 6*

Asparagus

Kids will be pleased to learn that it's perfectly polite to eat asparagus with their fingers. Parents might want to take advantage of this hands-on approach as asparagus is a highly nutritious vegetable.

The name of this harbinger of spring comes from the Persian *asparag*, which means sprout or shoot. Valued for its delicate flavor and diuretic properties, asparagus has been cultivated for centuries. It is even featured in the oldest surviving book of recipes by Apicius, which dates back to the 3rd century AD.

While most people are familiar with green asparagus, it also comes in white and purple varieties. White asparagus is literally kept in the dark to prevent the formation of chlorophyll, which gives plants their green color. Preferred by Europeans, it has a sweet, nutty taste when eaten raw. Purple asparagus was developed in Italy and commercialized under the exotic name Violetto d'Albenga.

The long, elegant asparagus stalks are easily boiled, steamed, or roasted once the end is snapped off, and require only a sprinkling of sea salt and a drizzle of olive oil to provide a delicious feast.

Pomegranate

The "seeded apple" *(Pomum granatus)* is a storied fruit. According to Greek mythology, Persephone, the daughter of Demeter (goddess of the harvest) was kidnapped by Hades and taken to the underworld. As Demeter mourned her daughter, the earth's fertility dwindled. Zeus commanded Hades to return Persephone but, as she had eaten the seeds of the pomegranate while in the underworld, she could never completely escape. As punishment, the legend continues,

Persephone must return to the underworld for part of each year, during which time the earth's fertility declines.

Pomegranates originated in Persia but were cultivated widely in ancient times around the Mediterranean, across Asia, and into Europe. Inside their tough, reddish skin lie pockets of brilliant, juicy, red seeds, nestled in a white membrane.

To eat a pomegranate, score the skin several times, peel it back, and break the seed clusters from their tight confines. Eating a pomegranate is a contemplative affair, as the seeds are squeezed gently in the mouth, releasing their pulp and juice.

Now-trendy pomegranate juice is a refreshing drink. Its derivative, grenadine, flavors and colors cocktails and mixed drinks. Fresh pomegranate seeds garnish hummus and tahini, while its molasses-like syrup is used as a flavoring in Persian cooking.

Peach

Closely related to nectarines, peaches originated in China and were introduced to the Mediterranean area around 2000 BC. They're a juicy fruit with a yellow or whitish flesh depending on their variety. Low-acid white-fleshed peaches are more popular in Asia, while North Americans adore the yellow-fleshed varieties.

In China, peaches were said to be the food of gods, who ate them to remain immortal. Their Feast of Peaches, which was held every 6,000 years, took place in the celestial palace of Xi Wangmu. Luckily, mere mortals don't have to wait that long to enjoy peaches, which ripen toward the end of summer. They can be enjoyed fresh in salads, baked in cobblers, and preserved in any number of ways from chutneys and liqueurs to jams.

The famous dessert peach Melba was created in 1892 by Auguste Escoffier at London's Savoy Hotel. When he heard that Australian opera singer Nellie Melba would be a guest, he decided to create an ice cream dish that wouldn't harm her sensitive vocal chords. By adding a sauce of raspberries, red currant jelly, sugar, and cornstarch, he presented her with a new way to enjoy ice cream that has remained popular to this day.

Pear

Curvaceous pears, with varieties now numbering in the thousands, are related to apples and originated from two wild species that once covered Europe and Asia. There is evidence that people tended them in the neolithic period. Pears are also mentioned in early Greek writing, and they are certainly known to have been cultivated by the Romans.

Today there are two distinct categories of pear—European and Asian. European pears have been bred to be more fragrant with a smooth texture, while Asian pears tend to be crisp with a milder taste. Pears are popular anytime, anywhere. They can be teamed up with Gorgonzola cheese to create a new twist on bruschetta, or with salsas and salads to add sweetness and texture. Their lightness and acidity also work well with pork, lamb, and shrimp dishes.

It's at dessert time, however, that pears shine. They can be poached, caramelized, brandied, and used in puddings, cakes, squares, and pies. A perfect digestif to accompany your dessert might be Poire Williams, a light brandy made in Alsace and Switzerland from the popular Bartlett pear, which the French call William's Bon-Chrétien.

Plum

Plums are the world's second most popular fruit after apples, and they grow on every continent except Antarctica.

They can be divided into three families: damson, European, and Japanese. The damson, whose name derives from "plum of Damascus," grew in ancient Mesopotamia. Today it tends to be small and slightly tart in flavor, making it the perfect choice for cooking and preserving.

Denser European plums are ideal for drying as prunes. They have a delicate blue to purple skin and are sometimes called prune plums. Plum pudding—which has never included plums—derives its name from earlier recipes that called for prunes.

Originally from China, Japanese plums can be crimson to deep red and are extremely juicy; perfect for eating fresh. There is no need to peel plums before eating. Like other tender fruits, they're delectable in baked goods such as cobblers, pies, tarts, and cakes.

On the savory side, this delicate fruit shines in Asian plum salad with spinach, water chestnuts, onions, cilantro, and crispy wonton strips in a tangy ginger dressing. To accompany it, you might try a plum-tini, which combines vodka, shaved ice, and plum wine.

Aloo Gobi

Take two humble vegetables, mix in a few pungent herbs and spices, and you have a sensational golden curry that's a staple in Indian restaurants worldwide.

Aloo means potato in Hindi, while *gobi* means cauliflower. This dry curry is made with garlic, ginger, onion, cilantro stalks, and cumin. A touch of turmeric gives it a distinctive yellow color.

Aloo gobi is associated with north Indian and Punjabi cuisine as their cooler climates support the cultivation of root and cruciferous vegetables. The dish gained prominence with the release of the popular British film, *Bend it Like Beckham*. One of the DVD extras shows director Gurinder Chadha preparing aloo gobi, prompting the phrase: Why cook aloo gobi when you can "bend it like Beckham?"

Not only is this delectable dish entirely vegetarian, but it's enjoyed by many who normally shun cauliflower. Even so, some restaurants will omit the "gobi" in deference to those who might agree with Mark Twain that, "Cauliflower is nothing but cabbage with a college education."

Snow Peas

These flat emerald pods, with their edible shell, bear an Asian pedigree. Peas are one of the most ancient food crops, likely emerging in southwest Asia and domesticated around 8500 BC or earlier. They fall into three broad categories: split peas, left to ripen in the field and prized for their starchy fullness; garden peas, the classic green peas shelled from their pods early in their development and beloved for their tiny freshness; and edible pod peas, such as the snow and sugarsnap pea, with pods so tender and crisp that the tiny peas inside are almost incidental. Snow peas grow in cool weather, hence their name. The French call them *mangetout*, or "eat-all."

They require very little, if any, cooking. Many home gardeners have a hard time just carrying them from the garden to the kitchen without eating them all, for their pods are never sweeter than when just picked from the vine. If preparing them for a stir-fry or salad, trim the stem and blossom ends lightly, string, if necessary, and rinse. Steaming is a gentle enough process for them and tossing them in oil for less than a minute in a wok intensifies their bright green color.

Garlic

The "stinking rose" is one of the oldest cultivated crops. There are references to garlic in Egyptian and Indian culture dating back 5,000 years. At that time, it grew wild in a vast region from China to Egypt. Garlic has a sharper taste than its cousins—onions, shallots, and leeks—due to its high concentration of sulfur compounds. Although we've learned to love it, birds and insects avoid garlic precisely because of its acrid scent.

In the kitchen, garlic may add a mellow or intense flavoring to dishes. It is often paired with onion, tomatoes, and ginger. Roasting and braising give it a soft, nutty taste, while sautéing preserves more of its distinct flavor.

Raw garlic whisked into dressings and dips adds both heat and pungency, which can linger for hours afterward.

In addition to the tightly packed cloves that form the head, garlic leaves and stems (scapes) can be eaten when immature and tender. In Vietnam and Cambodia, the leaves are often stir-fried with eggs, meat, and vegetables. The Chinese pickle young garlic bulbs, while Russians eat pickled shoots as appetizers. In Lebanon, garlic sauce is widely used in salads.

Along with its full-bodied flavor, garlic has long been prized as a powerful antibiotic and for preventing the common cold.

Beet

The earliest written mention of beets comes from Mesopotamia dating back to the 8th century BC. Long before that, there's good reason to believe that prehistoric people were harvesting them, as charred beets were discovered at the neolithic site of Aartswoud in the Netherlands.

Although the remains found were undoubtedly those of wild beets, they were the precursors of the varieties we enjoy today. Now a range of cultivated forms of "blood turnip" flourish, including sweet sugar beets, which are processed for their natural sugars, and chard, which is a beet bred for its broad edible leaves.

Beets not only store well, but they have a variety of uses. They can be steamed, boiled, pickled, shredded, and used in soups. Borscht, a hearty beet soup popular in Eastern Europe is Ukraine's national soup while, in Australia, it is not unusual to see a hamburger topped with sliced beets.

The beet's distinctive red color is due to a combination of purple and yellow pigments that tend to "bleed" when a beet is cut. In fact beet juice is often used as a coloring agent.

Marinated Beets

18 baby beets, peeled and trimmed

2 cups white wine vinegar

1 cup water

½ cup sugar

1 tbsp coriander seeds

2 tbsp orange-rind strips

2 tbsp dill sprigs

Place the beets in a saucepan of boiling water and cook for 6 minutes or until they are tender, then drain and peel.

Place the vinegar, water, sugar, coriander seeds, and orange-rind strips in a non-reactive saucepan and bring the mixture to a boil. Remove the pan from the heat and add the beets and dill.

Allow the mixture to cool. Store the beets and marinade in sterilized jars in the refrigerator.

Marinated beets are great served with washed-rind cheese and bread.

Makes 1 medium jar

Adapted from Donna Hay's *Entertaining*

Coconut

These nuts are the ultimate survivors. Fossil records from New Zealand show small, coconut-like palms growing there 15 million years ago. Similar fossils have been found in regions of India as well.

While we'll never know how they were used in that vast stretch of time, we do know they have proved invaluable since our arrival. From the tops of their fronds to the tips of their roots, humans have discovered a range of uses for this tree, described in ancient Sanskrit as "the tree which provides all the necessities of life."

Most people are familiar with the fruit we call a coconut. It has two layers—a fibrous husk and a hard "stone," which houses the rich, white flesh and highly nutritious coconut water. At the end of the stone are three distinctive hollows, which the Portuguese felt resembled the wizened face of "Coca," a scary witch of legend.

What isn't scary is the coconut palm's versatility. Its fruit is eaten fresh or dried, sap from its flowers is fermented to produce palm wine, while buds of adult plants are eaten as "palm-cabbage."

Outside the kitchen, fiber from the husk is used to make rope, mats, and brushes while the leaves are woven into baskets and roofing thatch. Its roots are ground for medicine and eco-friendly palm wood is growing in popularity.

Pistachios

Pistachio trees thrive on stony ground in hot, dry climates with cool winters. They take about 15 to 20 years to mature and survive for centuries. Perhaps that is why pistachios are as precious and desirable to us today as to our ancestors who first harvested them in Asia Minor, about 9,000 years ago.

Pistachios form in clusters inside a fleshy fruit. When mature, the ivory shell splits open to reveal a bright green seed. When a shell fails to open, the seed inside did not mature. In the United States, the shells are sometimes dyed a vivid pink, possibly the result of a sales gimmick used by an early importer.

Pistachios are related to cashews and have a similar mouth-feel—nutty, rich, and satisfying. Their distinctive green color makes them stand out in any recipe, especially pistachio ice cream.

In the Middle East, pistachios play many roles from mains to desserts. They are added to stuffing for meat or chicken dishes, mixed with dried apricots, raisins and grains, folded into whipped cream flavored with orange blossom water, and sprinkled on pastries. In honey-drenched *baklava*, ground pistachios are layered between buttery sheets of paper-thin phyllo pastry. Yet even when served in a bowl, lightly-salted pistachios in the shell symbolize the hospitality of the table and the home.

Pine Nuts

Most pine nuts come from the fat cones of the stone pine *(Pinus pinea)* whose characteristic umbrella shape dots the Mediterranean landscape. Our Stone Age ancestors harvested them for millennia as a rich source of fat and protein. The trees themselves, which have been cultivated for at least 6,000 years, trace the trade routes of the ancient world. The slim nuts were also reputed to have aphrodisiac properties.

Cones take about three years to mature. Harvested and dried, their fat seeds are shaken loose, revealing a dark shell. The shell must be removed before the nuts can be eaten. The shelled nuts are so rich in oil that they should be refrigerated to prevent them from going rancid.

Pine nuts are added to stuffing for meat and vegetables and they are an essential ingredient in Italian pesto—the paste of ground pine nuts, chopped basil, and olive oil flavored with garlic and Parmesan cheese. Pasta mixed with a teaspoon of pesto makes a quick, nourishing meal. Toasting pine nuts brings out their natural richness and smoky essence. Scattering a few over a spinach and orange salad or a rice pilaf lifts these dishes from good to exceptional.

Ratatouille

When eggplant comes into season, ratatouille takes pride of place on the menu. It is at the heart of this peasant stew made with zucchini, peppers, tomatoes, and fresh herbs. While ratatouille is associated with the traditional cuisine of Provence in the south of France, it draws its principal ingredients from both the orient and the New World, and has links with the Basque region.

Eggplant likely emerged from India or China and eventually migrated to Spain with Arab traders. The Spanish brought tomatoes from South America. In a delightful collision of the two, ratatouille emerged sometime in the 17th century.

Ratatouille

1 large eggplant
Salt
3 onions
3 red bell peppers
4 summer squashes
5 tomatoes
6 to 12 cloves garlic
Extra-virgin olive oil
Hot pepper flakes, optional
1 large bunch fresh basil (about ½ lb)

Cut the eggplant into ½-inch cubes. Salt it liberally and leave it to drain in a colander. Peel and cut up the onions, and cut up the peppers, squashes, and tomatoes, keeping them all separate. Everything should be cut into pieces about the same size as the cubed eggplant. Smash and peel the garlic and chop it coarsely. Press down on the eggplant to extract more water and dry it.

In a heavy-bottomed pot, heat some of the olive oil and gently fry the eggplant until golden. Drain and reserve. Add more olive oil to the pot, and over medium-low heat start sautéing the onions. When they are soft and translucent, add the garlic, optional hot pepper flakes, and a bouquet garni consisting of the bunch of basil wrapped tightly with string, reserving a handful of the basil leaves for a garnish. Stir for a minute, toss in the peppers, and cook for a few minutes; next add the squash and cook a few minutes more, and then add the tomatoes. Cook for about 10 minutes, stirring occasionally. Finally add the eggplant, and cook 15 to 25 minutes more, until everything is soft and the flavors have melded together. Remove the bouquet of basil, pressing on it to extract all its flavors, and adjust the seasoning with freshly chopped basil leaves, salt, and a bit of fresh extra-virgin olive oil and fine-chopped garlic, if needed. Serve warm or cold. The dish tastes even better the next day. *Serves 8*

Adapted from Alice Waters' *Chez Panisse Vegetables*

Bok Choy

Bok choy (or pak choi) has been a staple vegetable of Cantonese cuisine for thousands of years. While Asian markets sell more than 20 varieties, North Americans will find the familiar, sturdy, white stems and dark green leaves attached to a bulbous base. Bok choy is a member of the *brassica* (cabbage) family. It has a slightly mustardy taste and is, like many of its cousins, packed with vitamins and minerals.

To prepare, the stalks are taken apart and washed carefully, and any coarse parts are cut away from the leaves. Some prefer to trim away most of the leaf, leaving a green fringe on the white stalk. The stalks take longer to cook than the leaves, which need only be wilted, so stalks are generally added first when steaming or stir-frying.

Miniature baby bok choy is more expensive but easier to use. The stalks and leaves are cooked whole or cut into two or three pieces.

Bok choy can be added to soups or stir-fried with a little oil, garlic, and soy sauce. It also makes a nice change of pace for Western-style pork and chicken dishes. Flavor with a few drops of soy or oyster sauce and you'll have an easy, great tasting, and good-for-you dish.

Parsnip

In one respect, the parsnip has come down in the world. It used to be a staple carbohydrate of the European diet until that interloper from the Andes, the potato, came along in the 1500s. Parsnips are related to parsley, carrots, and celery; hints of these flavors grace every dish of cooked parsnips. They resemble carrots in shape and size but are creamy white and usually more tapered.

Parsnips do well in regions with short growing seasons. They are one of the few vegetables that need a touch of frost to bring out their full flavor, and are the last vegetables harvested from home gardens.

Scrubbed and peeled, parsnips are usually cut into pieces and boiled or steamed for 15 minutes or less if you plan to roast or fry them. Remove and discard any hard woody core before cooking.

Mashed parsnips with butter and seasonings make a great side dish for a roast. Boiling one or two with potatoes and garlic cloves also makes a sensational mash. Hearty winter soups taste even better with sweet parsnip chunks. They are equally delicious oiled, seasoned, and roasted on a baking sheet with other root vegetables.

Lemonata Potatoes

There's a favorite saying regarding Greek cuisine: you can add olive oil, lemon juice, and oregano to sawdust and it will taste good. Fortunately, potatoes are easier to digest. This is a classic Greek side, one that goes with virtually any main. It is dead easy to make, too. Potato wedges are tossed in a combination of olive oil, lemon juice, and oregano before being oven-roasted. Lemon juice adds a zesty sparkle and prevents the potatoes from becoming too crisp. The result is a warm, soft potato dish that overflows with flavor.

Lemonata's versatility as a side dish reflects the versatility of its ingredients: fish takes to lemon as easily as to water, while meat of all sorts (veal, chicken, beef, or pork), benefits from the addition of oregano. As well, there are few foods that cannot be improved with a drizzle of green-gold olive oil.

Bombay Potato

This dish is a perfect example of the maxim, "less is more." Consisting of potatoes, onion, and spices, it's a simple recipe that can be served alongside any number of south Asian dishes. Standard spices include turmeric, cumin, and mustard seeds. Other variations include ginger, garlic, chiles, coriander, and masala, a popular spice mixture.

For those who might feel that "less is less," further enhancements can run to chopped tomatoes and yogurt. Adventurous types can take the original chopped, spiced potatoes a step further and create soft patties to pan-fry and serve with chutney. There is some debate as to which potatoes are best; some prefer new potatoes while others opt for firmer, waxier types.

The Portuguese brought potatoes to India in the 1500s. When they arrived in the region of Mumbai on the west coast, they called the area various names, finally settling on Bombaim. When the British arrived in the 1600s they changed it to Bombay. The ancient goddess Mumbadevi, for whom the city was originally named, didn't think much of their potatoes and eventually set things right: the name was officially changed back to Mumbai in 1995.

Eggplant

The versatile eggplant hails from southern India and Sri Lanka. Like its relative the tomato, it has seeds and an edible skin. It has been cultivated in Asia since prehistoric times.

Despite cultivation and crossbreeding, which reduced its original bitterness, this glossy vegetable was slow to gain acceptance in Europe. It was believed to cause a range of ailments—including madness—which is why the English initially used it only for decoration. Its identity crisis didn't end there. The name eggplant, popular in North America and Australia, is derived from the fact that some are white and resemble hen or goose eggs.

One of the eggplant's early American boosters was President Thomas Jefferson, who experimented with it in his Virginia garden. Today it comes in many varieties, from the slim, purple Japanese eggplant and the small, round green Thai variety to the large, shiny Black Beauty found in North American grocery stores. This adaptable vegetable can be fried, baked, mashed, and stuffed with meat, rice, and other fillings. It's no wonder southern Asians call it the king of vegetables.

Melanzane alla Parmigiana

Olive oil for frying

2$\frac{1}{2}$ lb ripe tomatoes, peeled and chopped

Half a small onion, minced

A large bunch of basil

4 lb eggplant

Salt

$\frac{3}{4}$ lb fresh mozzarella

$\frac{1}{2}$ cup grated Parmesan

2 eggs

Heat a little olive oil in a pan and cook the tomatoes with the minced onion and a sprig of basil. When soft, drain and push through a sieve.

Peel the eggplant and cut into $\frac{1}{4}$-inch slices. Place in a colander and sprinkle generously with salt to eke out the bitter juices. Leave for 30 minutes to an hour and pat dry. Heat the oil until smoking and fry the eggplant in a single layer—you may need to do this in batches. Once brown on both sides, remove from the pan and drain on paper towels. Shred the remaining basil and cut the mozzarella into strips.

Preheat the oven to 350°F.

Spoon some of the tomato sauce over the base of an ovenproof dish. Layer one-third of the eggplant slices over the tomato sauce, overlapping them slightly. Sprinkle generously with one-third of the Parmesan, torn basil, and mozzarella strips. Now beat the eggs with $\frac{2}{3}$ cup of tomato sauce and spoon one-third into the dish. Repeat the layers twice more, then bake the dish for 35 to 40 minutes. Serve at room temperature. *Serves 6*

Imam Bayaldi

As befits a culture rich in anecdotes and proverbs, this Turkish dish has a classic story. According to folklore, Imam bayaldi—translated as "the Imam fainted"—acquired its name either because the Imam was overcome by the sublime taste of these stuffed eggplants or stunned by the amount and cost of the olive oil consumed in making them! Given the popularity of Imam Bayaldi, it was more likely the wonderful stuffing made from rich tomato, onion, garlic, parsley, and olive oil, cooked in the shell of a tender eggplant, that brought on his sudden weakness.

With its shiny, light-mauve to deep-purple skin and voluptuous shape, eggplant is a favorite vegetable in Mediterranean cuisine. Before cooking, it is necessary to tease out the bitter juices. The eggplants are cut in half lengthwise or slit whole, then sprinkled generously with salt and left to drain. Alternately, the cut eggplants can be weighted down in salted water for at least 30 minutes. Once rinsed and patted dry, they are ready to be stuffed with this hearty and delicious filling, prepared with a generous amount of olive oil.

Imam Bayaldi

2 tbsp olive oil for sautéing

2 medium onions, chopped

2 cloves garlic, crushed

3 medium tomatoes, peeled and chopped

3 tbsp chopped parsley

Salt

Freshly ground black pepper

2 medium eggplants, stem end removed

2 tsp sugar

3 tbsp lemon juice

1/2 cup olive oil

Preheat the oven to 350°F. Heat the oil in a large pan and sauté the onions, garlic, tomatoes, and parsley until soft. Season with salt and pepper. Make 3 slits down the length of each eggplant, and submerge the eggplants in salted water for 30 minutes. Pat dry, and spoon the onion mixture into each slit. Arrange the eggplants in a baking dish and sprinkle with sugar, lemon juice, and the 1/2 cup of oil. Cover and bake for 40 minutes. Serve at room temperature with Greek yogurt. *Serves 6*

Hash Browns

Hash is derived from the French verb *hacher* (to chop) but hash also implies making a mix or mess of something. Hash browns, or more precisely hashed brown potatoes, are a comfort food with so many variations that it is hard to choose just one. A week's worth of breakfast specials on an American road trip might offer a good sampling of the genre.

Some cooks swear that grated, raw potatoes make the best hash browns, while others prefer coarsely chopped, cooked, leftover potatoes. Some prefer to peel the potatoes, while others savor the skins. All agree, however, that hash browns are fried,

but there the debate begins again. Should they be pressed into patties or cooked in one large mass in the frying pan and divided up when it comes to serving them.

Commercial brands of frozen hash browns come as little cubes of potato, slightly pre-cooked, pre-oiled, and pre-seasoned. These generally fall so far short of anyone's idea of good hash browns that a new variety of hash brown comfort food has been invented for them: the hash brown casserole. This is a mix of frozen hash browns, a little onion, canned cream of chicken or mushroom soup, sour cream, and cheese, all baked in the oven.

Pommes Anna

In the days when consuming butterfat was a mark of social distinction rather than a failure of willpower, pommes Anna was a dish fit for a king. Created at the court of Napoleon III in honor of a beautiful woman, pommes Anna is a crispy cake of melted butter and potatoes with a crunchy outside and a rich, soft center.

A heavy pan is essential for achieving the crisp, browned finish. Cooks normally use a tablespoon of butter per potato. The classical recipe uses clarified butter. To make this easy dish, potatoes are peeled, washed, thinly-sliced with a mandoline, and stored in cold water. When ready to cook, the slices are patted dry and carefully arranged in a buttered pan with seasoning to form six layers. To compact the "cake," a heavy pan or plate is laid on top to weigh it down before baking.

Cooled and sliced, this delicate cake makes a most impressive and delicious side dish.

Pommes Gratin Dauphinoise

A dish prepared *à la Dauphinoise* is baked with cream and, usually, garlic. This potato dish from the classic French repertoire is not without controversy, however, mainly about whether or not to include eggs and cheese.

While the great Escoffier favored adding both, a more modern authority named Pomaine omitted them and emphasized the garlic. The revered Julia Child split the difference—cheese, if you like, but no egg. As this is comfort food, the "correct" way is whatever comforts you and your guests.

Most people begin by arranging half the thinly sliced potatoes in a shallow casserole dish that has been buttered and rubbed with garlic. The potatoes are showered with grated Swiss cheese and a little butter, salt, and pepper before the second layer is added and seasoned. Warm milk or cream is poured over all, and the dish is brought to a simmer then baked until meltingly tender.

Served with ham, roast chicken, turkey, or veal, this luxurious cold-weather dish is sensational. It also makes a heavenly hot buffet item.

Crash Hot Potatoes

This is one of those wonderful recipes that, once tried, is immediately incorporated into your own repertoire. It's like a crisp, roasted potato, only better, and all you have to do is boil a few small potatoes, smash them flat and blast them in a hot oven until they're terminally crisp. Serve with lamb, pan-fried fish, grilled sausages, or topped with smoked salmon and crème fraîche, with drinks.

Crash Hot Potatoes

16 small, round potatoes

1 tbsp extra-virgin olive oil

1 tsp sea salt

Freshly ground black pepper

1 tbsp fennel or caraway seeds

1 tbsp fresh thyme or rosemary leaves

Heat the oven to 450°F. Don't peel the potatoes. Just put them in a pot of salted water, bring to a boil, and simmer for around 15 minutes until a skewer goes in without too much resistance. They should be just about cooked, without being soft. Drain and arrange on a lightly-oiled baking sheet. Use a potato masher to squash each potato flat, until it is twice its original diameter. Brush the tops with olive oil and scatter with salt, pepper, fennel seeds, and thyme. Bake on the top rack of the oven for 20 to 25 minutes until very crisp and golden. Serve hot. *Serves 4*
Adapted from Jill Dupleix's *Totally Simple Food*

Potato Latkes

A staple of Eastern Europe and, by association, the Ashkenazi Jewish home—this quick and filling comfort food has calories to spare. Latkes—a Yiddish term—are very popular in the United States, where they traveled along with Jewish immigrants from Russia and Eastern Europe in the 19th century. Latkes are a favorite food during Chanukah, the Festival of Lights, commemorating the miracle of the small flask of oil that kept the menorah alight for eight days.

Like many comfort foods, there is no hard and fast recipe beyond peeling and grating raw potatoes. If the result is very wet, the excess liquid is drained off. Eggs, chopped onion, salt, and some matzo meal (crumbs of unleavened bread) are added to achieve a thick, pancake-like batter.

The batter is dropped by spoonful into a generous amount of oil and cooked until golden. The trick is not to overcrowd the pan. Once the second side is browned, the thin, lacy cakes are served immediately with sour cream and applesauce. One can never make too many latkes.

Potato Latkes

2 cups peeled and shredded potatoes

1 tbsp grated onion

3 eggs, beaten

2 tbsp all-purpose flour

1½ tsp salt

½ cup vegetable oil

Place the shredded potatoes in a piece of cheesecloth and wring, extracting as much moisture as possible. In a medium bowl, stir the potatoes, onion, eggs, flour, and salt together.

Heat the oil in a large heavy-bottomed skillet over medium-high heat. When hot, add a few large spoonfuls of potato mixture, pressing down to form patties ¼- to ½-inch thick. Brown patties on one side, then turn and brown the second side. Drain on paper towels and serve hot. *Serves 4*

Pommes Frîtes

Rösti

Pommes frîtes, or French fries, symbolize today's fast-food culture. If one is going to put on weight, however, it is a pity that so many people go through life believing that dry, undercooked, or soggy fries represent the real thing.

Despite its French name, which is not used in France, Belgium claims to have invented this deep-fried treat. Anyone who has eaten frîtes served in a paper cone from a *frîture* or *frietkot* (the Belgian equivalent of a British chip wagon in both official languages) would be inclined to agree. These frîtes really sing. How do they do it?

The secret is to start with the right potatoes—Bintjes or Yukon Gold are creamy yellow-fleshed potatoes perfect for frîtes— and then apply the two-step cooking technique. The washed, peeled potatoes are cut into sticks. On the first round, the sticks are submerged in vegetable oil, beef or duck fat for 5 to 7 minutes at 320°F. Drained and cooled, they are fried again at 350°F. This method ensures beautiful golden-brown frîtes with moist, tender insides cooked to perfection. Dipped in mayonnaise or peanut sauce, they are worth the weight!

Rösti (also written as röschti and pronounced rush-tee) is a favorite in the Swiss-German-speaking cantons of Switzerland. Along with fondue and raclette, it is one of Switzerland's best-known dishes. It even has its own special tool called a rösti grater.

The rösti served in Bern is made from potatoes cooked in their skins. To ensure they are properly cooked, it is customary to use day-old potatoes, much as one would use day-old rice for fried rice. In this version, the potato is grated, salted, then fried and tossed in clarified butter or lard until the strands turn a beautiful golden color.

Experienced cooks fry rösti undisturbed until it forms a crust. At the right moment, the chef sets a plate on top of the pancake and flips it over to continue browning. Rösti is sliced and served with bacon or topped with a slice of Gruyère or Emmenthaler.

Swiss cuisine tends to reflect its heritage of hardworking farmers. After eating rösti, you may have to climb a few hills to prepare for your next meal.

Preserved Lemons

Tangy salt-preserved lemons, also known as *citrons confit*, are a popular condiment across North Africa. They are simple to prepare using lemons, limes, or Meyer lemons.

First, at least two tablespoons of kosher or pickling salt are put in the bottom of a wide-mouthed sterilized jar. The lemons are carefully washed and trimmed of enough rind to expose the flesh, then sliced into wedges, stopping short of the base. The cook spreads apart the wedges and sprinkles them liberally with salt before packing the lemons in the jar and adding more salt on top. Once the jar is full, the lemons are pressed down to release their juice. For an authentic touch, a very clean rock is used as a weight. If needed, more juice is added to fill the jar to the top.

Within three to four weeks, the rind and pulp will be soft and intensely flavored. It helps to turn the jar periodically to ensure that the salt and juice are well distributed. Slivers of these preserved lemons add a piquant saltiness to chicken dishes, stews, and vegetable salads.

Radicchio

Radicchio is the popular name for Italian chicory, a slightly bitter leafy vegetable. The shape of the head depends on the variety—some are loose and lettuce-like (radicchio di Verona), while others are tight and endive-like (radicchio di Treviso).

Since antiquity, radicchio has been part of the Mediterranean diet. Modern varieties were developed in the late 1800s by the Belgian agronomist who also whitened Belgian endive by bringing it to maturity in the dark. Depriving radicchio of light sharply reduces chlorophyll in the leaves and accentuates the remaining red pigment.

The late-season Treviso variety has deep-red leaves with strong white ribs and tastes even more bitter. The unique character of Treviso and radicchio variegato di Castelfranco qualifies both for protected status in Italy.

Radicchio is intertwined with the cuisine of the region around Venice but is widely available across Europe and North America. Served raw, it adds its unique bitterness to salads. The flavor is gentled by cooking, however, whether sautéed with herbs and onions, garnished with cheese or cream, added to a creamy risotto, or paired with chicken or fish.

Four Dried Fruits

Dates

Date palms have been grown for their small, exquisitely sweet fruit for thousands of years— possibly as early as 6000 BC in Mesopotamia and prehistoric Egypt. Over time, cultivation spread to northern Africa and from there to Spain. Spaniards introduced them to California in 1765.

Small and cylindrical, dates measure about 2½ inches long and 1 inch across. They are smaller when dried, but not by much as their water content is low. When unripe, they range from bright red to bright yellow.

There is an astonishing number of varieties grown mostly in Egypt, Iran, Saudi Arabia, and the United Arab Emirates. Their Arabic names are exotic and evocative: *barhee* (hot wind), *deglet noor* (translucent) and *khalasah* (quintessence). The large, meaty *medjool* is considered the Cadillac of dates.

These delicacies have inspired cooks for centuries. They can be used in a variety of sweet and savory dishes.

Black and Red Currants

Unlike Greek Zante currants, which are dried grapes, black and red currants grow on shrubs further north in Europe. While they may share the same name—derived from the city of Corinth—they're entirely unrelated.

Black currants are jam-packed with nutrients and often end up in jam along with lots of sugar, given the berry's renowned pucker power. Cassis, the French liqueur, is made from black currants and added to white wine to make the elegant cocktail known as Kir.

Red currants will grow anywhere—hedgerows, ditches, and gardens. They can be used for jam, jelly, glazes, and purées. In Scandinavia, they're often used in fruit soups and summer puddings while in Germany, red currants can be found in custard or meringue tarts. They also complement wild game.

Cultivated red currants date back to the 1400s in Belgium and France. Over the centuries, they've been prized for their antiseptic properties and their ability to soothe burns.

Raisins

Nature gave us an ideal snack when grapes dried naturally on the vine. Not only are they sweet, but they have a long shelf life and make a great go-anywhere treat.

It's believed that people first discovered naturally-occurring raisins around 1500 BC and cultivated them in vineyards between 900 and 120 BC.

Raisins transport well as they lose close to 95% of their moisture when dried in the sun or, more recently, by mechanical heat. Their high sugar content—60% by weight—serves to preserve them, as well as making them tasty.

Spanish missionaries brought grapes to California in the 1700s, to produce wine. A blistering heat wave in 1873 withered the grapes on the vine, leading one resourceful San Francisco grocer to advertise the shriveled grapes as "Peruvian delicacies." Now Fresno, California, is the world's raisin capital.

Apricots

Resembling a small peach, this blushing fruit is native to China and made its way west through the Persian Empire before reaching the Mediterranean, where it flourished.

A cousin of the plum, it matures much earlier in the summer, earning its Latin name *praecox*, meaning early or precocious. The French *abricot* and English apricot share the same root.

Impressed with the tender sweet fruit, Roman General Lucullus imported apricot trees from Armenia in the 1st century BC. They've thrived in Italy ever since. The flavorful kernels are used in the production of Amaretto liqueur and biscotti.

Apricots made their way to North America by way of Spanish explorers, who introduced them south of San Francisco in 1792. Today, nearly 95% of US production comes from California.

The orange fruit can be eaten fresh, dried, or used in jam and pastries. Apricots can also be made into wine or brandy.

Durian

This ungainly tropical fruit is renowned for its custard-like flesh and unique odor. There are 30 species of durian, often called the "king of fruits" in Southeast Asia. The tough husk covered in ferocious-looking spikes inspired the name *duri*, meaning thorn, in Malay.

While the soft fruit inside tastes nutty and sweet, its smell is notably otherwise. Travel and food writer Richard Sterling describes it as "turpentine and onions garnished with a gym sock." Other descriptions are even less flattering. For this reason, durians are banned in hotels, airports, and on public transportation throughout the region. While some people shun the fruit, animals are drawn to it—even from a distance of half a mile. Among those who consider durian a delicacy are pigs, orangutans, elephants, and even carnivorous tigers.

Humans have devised a number of uses for durian, whose flesh can range from orange to bright red, depending on the variety. The creamy fruit can be used for both sweet and savory dishes, and is common in Malay candy, cookies, ice cream, and cake. Savory dishes include curries, side dishes, and an Indonesian fish soup called *sajur*. The seeds, which are the size of chestnuts and have the consistency of yams, can be boiled, roasted, or fried.

Dragon Fruit

This prehistoric-looking fruit with the hot pink leathery skin is native to Mexico, and Central and South America. About the size of a grapefruit and adorned with soft spikes, it grows on cactus vines in dry, tropical climates. It's also called *pitaya* and strawberry pear.

Though this dragon may look intimidating, its pink or white flesh, peppered with small black edible seeds, tastes like melon. To enhance its mild flavor, chill the fruit, scoop out its flesh, and sprinkle with lemon or lime juice. It's also good with ice cream or blended into a refreshing drink. A good test for ripeness is a gentle give when the exterior is pressed.

Although native to the Americas, this gorgeous fruit is now cultivated in Southeast Asia, southern China, and Israel. Even its plant puts on a good show. It flowers exclusively at night, producing large white flowers called Moonflower or Queen of the Night.

A famous hedge planted in Honolulu in 1836 is about three football fields long and blooms from July to October. It's a popular draw for travelers who visit at night to take in the spectacular sight.

Lychee Fruit

The fruit of the lychee tree is renowned for its sweetness. In season, clusters of red fruit dangle temptingly from handsome evergreen trees with dark-green leaves. Inside a thin, crisp skin, firm, translucent white flesh surrounds a long, dark seed. No wonder it is a symbol of romance. One variety is even called "the imperial concubine's laugh." Lychee fruit is sometimes compared to a grape and, indeed, the fruit is sometimes made into fruit wine.

Lychee trees thrive in subtropical climates. The fruit sets in cooler weather, but it cannot tolerate freezing temperatures. The province of Guangdong, where the fruit has been cultivated for more than 2,000 years, is known as the Kingdom of Lychee. The trees have spread from China across Asia, to Hawaii, Australia, and Florida.

Lychees are best when eaten by the dozen, fresh from the stem. Peeled and pitted, they add their tropical perfume to fruit salads, ice cream, and drinks. Honey harvested from hives near lychee groves is said to capture the fragrance of lychee juice.

Out of season, they are available as lychee nuts, not a true nut but a dried fruit in the manner of a raisin or a prune. Lychees are also preserved in syrup and canned.

Mango

Paleobotanists believe the mango originated in northeastern India and spread into Southeast Asia when the Asian and Indian tectonic plates collided. With this ancient pedigree, it is no wonder that mango fruit is woven tightly into the cultural fabric, featuring in art and ritual as well as cuisine.

Depending on the variety, mango has hints of peach, pineapple, plum, or cantaloupe, but tastes always and uniquely of itself. Most mangoes are sweet and fleshy with a large pit in the center. The skin color varies from green through yellow and orange to red, and the shape from round to kidney-shaped. There are hundreds of cultivars, but many grow in only one region.

The Tommy Atkins is the most common shipping mango. Opinion is divided on which mango is the best. From the sweet Julie mango of the West Indies to the creamy Alphonso of India, to the luscious Mamuang of Thailand, no two mango fanciers will agree.

Eating a mango requires technique; the "hedgehog" is one of several. Slice off the cheeks of the mango and score the flesh both ways. Bend the skin back and eat the cubed fruit right off the skin. Accept the fact that juice will flow!

Meyer Lemons

The next time someone dares you to bite into a lemon, chose a Meyer and have some fun. As a cross between a lemon and a mandarin orange, they're much sweeter and have an edible skin.

Originally from China, they were brought to the US in 1908 by Frank Meyer, who worked for the Department of Agriculture. He became the namesake of this citrus fruit with the fresh, sweet scent.

It was considered an ornamental fruit until the early 1980s, when it was discovered by top California chefs. Today, Meyers are popping up in drinks, desserts, savory dishes—any recipe that calls for lemons.

One juicy squeeze complements salmon, marinated tuna, crab, and scallops. Vegetables such as asparagus and artichokes sing with a quick spritz of Meyer lemon, which also gives creamy aïoli dips a richer flavor. For a lemonade that surpasses all others, include fresh Meyer lemon along with lime juice, kaffir lime, and bay leaves.

These lemons come into their own when added to almond waffles, sherbet, pot de crème, fluffy mousses, and puddings.

Cantaloupe Melon

In the United States, cantaloupe melons are small and instantly recognizable by the netted pattern on their khaki-colored skin. When ready to eat, a cantaloupe has a very fragrant, tempting smell. Inside, orange flesh, rich in beta-carotene, surrounds a hollow center filled with abundant seeds. Split it in half, scoop out the seeds, and prepare to be refreshed.

Cantaloupe can be eaten by the slice, cut into cubes, or shaped into rounds with a special tool called a melon-baller and added to fruit salads. When ripe and sweet, cantaloupe needs no enhancements other than, if you like, a squeeze of lemon or lime juice.

Honeydew Melon

In Europe and North Africa, where it originated, the honeydew is known as White Antibes. Larger and sweeter than its cousin the cantaloupe, with a pale yellow skin and light green flesh, honeydews are not highly scented. In some shops, you may be able to find a hybrid with orange flesh, similar to a cantaloupe. Honeydew continue to ripen after being picked. When unripe, their skin is slightly downy, however this downiness disappears when the melon is ripe.

For an elegant appetizer, serve a slice of honeydew with some thinly-sliced prosciutto. The melon's subtle sweetness contrasts deliciously with the saltiness of the ham.

Watermelon

"When one has tasted [watermelon], he knows what the angels eat. It was not a Southern watermelon that Eve took; we know it because she repented." (Mark Twain)

Watermelons have been cultivated since prehistoric times around the Mediterranean and in Asia Minor. Archaeologists reported watermelon seeds in the tomb of King Tut. In China, where watermelons became available toward the end of the first millennium, this monster melon is often pickled rather than eaten fresh. By the 17th century, watermelons were being cultivated in North America.

Over time, watermelons have been bred in various shapes and sizes: large ovals, compact, round, easily stored "ice-box" shapes, even cube-shaped! Red is the most popular flesh color but yellow and white are also common.

Four Exotic Fruits

Papaya

When Europeans encountered the papaya for the first time, with its intense orange-to-red flesh and its mild, sweet flavor, they called it a "tree melon." They wasted no time in carrying it from its native Central America and southern Mexico to other tropical regions around the world.

The shape of a papaya depends on whether the fruit-bearing plant carries hermaphrodite flowers (with both male and female organs) or has only female flowers. The fruit of female-only plants is rounder and has a thinner wall, whereas the fruit of hermaphroditic papayas tends to be elongated, with thicker flesh.

A papaya is ripe when its green skin is tinged with yellow. To eat a fresh papaya, cut it in half lengthwise and scoop out the round black seeds, which resemble large peppercorns and have a peppery taste. Slice into serving sizes and garnish with lemon or lime. It's perfect just like that.

Pineapple

The Carib Indians of the West Indies called the pineapple *anana* (excellent fruit) for its juicy, intense sweetness. By the time European adventurers reached the New World, this fruit from Brazil and Paraguay was widely cultivated. The French and Dutch still keep the old Carib name: *anana*; the English named it for its resemblance to a pine cone.

Peeling a pineapple demands a certain respect for nature. Spiral your way round the fruit both ways, cutting out the sharp little eyes before peeling away the rough skin.

In the 18th and 19th centuries, pineapples were regarded as symbols of friendship and hospitality. Take a look at older buildings and furniture and you will often see the characteristic shape and leaf pattern worked into doors, mantelpieces, furniture, windows, and gateways.

Delicious fresh or canned, pineapple is widely used in fruit salads and juice, upside-down cakes, and atop pizza.

Passion Fruit

This exotic fruit grows from a large, fragrant flower on a vigorous climbing vine native to southern Brazil, Paraguay, and northern Argentina. Spanish missionaries believed the marks on its flower resembled signs of the crucifixion, evoking the passion of Christ.

Passion fruit comes in two main forms. The larger variety, has firm, smooth, yellow skin and is more acidic than the more popular purple form, which is small, round, juicy, and sweet.

When ripe, purple passion fruit dents easily and the leathery skin appears rumpled. Inside, its seductively aromatic pulp contains numerous edible black seeds. It can be cut in half and eaten with a spoon like a soft-boiled egg.

Passion fruit makes flavorful jams and sorbets, and adds its sweet-tart flavor to juices and cocktails. In Australia, where it grows prolifically, passion fruit is scooped fresh from its skin to top pavlova.

Star Fruit

This intriguing fruit is beloved for its shape, which resembles a pale yellow or white star when sliced crosswise.

Star fruit may have originated in the Moluccas, the Spice Islands of present-day Indonesia, which also gave the world nutmeg and cloves. Currently, they are grown across Southeast Asia and China and in tropical locations around the world.

The deeply ridged skin is slightly waxy, like an apple, and edible. The fruit itself turns from light green to yellow or light orange as it ripens. It grows 4 to 5 inches long. Thin-ribbed varieties tend to be tart, while thick-ribbed varieties are generally sweet. There are a few small seeds inside. The flesh is translucent and the flavor is delicate—depending on the cultivar, star fruit tastes a little like grapes or apples. With no peeling or deseeding required, this fruit is usually eaten fresh in its characteristic star-shaped slices.

Almonds

Sweet almonds grow on trees and are related to peaches. They've been valued for thousands of years and now enjoy international popularity.

Egypt's King Tutankhamen stored almonds in his tomb for his journey to the afterlife. Other cultures have also prized almonds. In the Bible they're referred to as *shaqued*, meaning the "awakening one," likely because almonds are one of the first trees to flower in Israel in the spring. On the tree, this familiar nut is protected by a husk and wrapped in a velvety cloak.

California now produces 80% of the world's almonds. The sweet, crunchy, heart-healthy nuts can be smoked, salted, and toasted for savory dishes or ground into paste for marzipan. Menu items marked *amandine* give a clue to their garnish.

In case you need another reason to eat almonds, scientists suggest that eating one ounce of almonds and other nuts a day may reduce the risk of heart disease.

Chestnuts

The eight types of chestnut tree producing edible nuts grow in warm, temperate regions of the northern hemisphere. China seems to have led the chestnut charge by growing them in 4000 BC. Instead of the water chestnuts popular in Chinese cuisine, however, they were growing a variety of sweet chestnuts from the Castanea group. Water chestnuts, though deliciously edible, are from another family.

A chestnut is about the size of a walnut and covered by a thin, rigid, brown shell that is easily removed. Trees will only start producing nuts at 15 years but will continue for decades, reaching their peak at 50.

The Romans, who were cultivating chestnuts by 37 BC, are believed to have introduced them to Britain. Throughout the Dark and Middle Ages, these rich nuts were an important source of food in Italy, Spain, Portugal, and France. Those who could afford little else would visit the forest and collect fallen chestnuts, often consuming between 2 and 5 pounds a day!

Today, we have the privilege of using them with other foods in a variety of ways. They can be candied—the French *marrons glacés*—boiled, roasted, puréed, added to stuffing, and ground into flour. Even the leaves can be used to wrap specialty cheeses.

Hazelnuts

These nutritious, low-fat nuts grow on shrubs in clusters, each encased in a husk. They are native to Europe and Asia. While the names filbert and hazelnut are used interchangeably, there is actually a difference: hazelnuts are partially housed by their husk while filberts are entirely encased. The taste is almost the same, however.

The hazelnut has grown for centuries in hedgerows, the traditional field boundaries in lowland England. Over time, it moved beyond its rustic roots and is now cultivated in Europe, China, Australia, and Turkey, which accounts for nearly 75% of the world's output.

Used extensively in confections, hazelnuts have also gained prominence as a salad oil, a liqueur, and a scrumptious spread. They're especially popular as a coffee flavoring, providing a sweeter, less acidic taste. Ground hazelnuts are an essential ingredient in Vienna's hazelnut torte and in Piedmont's dark and delicious *gianduia* chocolate.

Brazil Nut

Despite its name, most Brazil nuts now come from Bolivia and Peru, where they are harvested as nature intends. For, unlike the vast majority of food crops, Brazil nuts resist cultivation. The tree that produces them—one of the tallest in the Amazon rainforest —only produces nuts in forests undisturbed by human activity. This is due to the tree's complex and mysterious relationship with wild orchids. The flower's scent attracts bees, which then pollinate the tree's fruit.

Indigenous Amazon tribes have valued these nutritious nuts for millennia. In addition to their rich, earthy taste, one nut contains a day's worth of selenium, a trace mineral essential to good health.

Calling them *almendras de los Andes*— almonds of the Andes—the Spanish and Portuguese brought Brazil nuts to Europe in the 1500s, where they remain popular to this day.

They can be sliced, chopped, or ground, and are used in sweet or savory dishes such as cookies, cakes, salads, and stuffings. One great advantage of choosing Brazil nuts is that their harvest is sustainable and provides employment for local inhabitants without damaging the Amazon rainforest.

Macadamia Nuts

These ivory, rich-tasting nuts were named after John Macadam, an Australian chemist, teacher, and politician. The honor was bestowed on him by his friend Ferdinand von Mueller, the botanist who first described the genus. Other names given to macadamias, which are native to Australia and Indonesia, include bush nut and maroochi nut. Indigenous Australians call them *kindal kindal* and *jindilli*.

Macadamia trees wait a good seven to ten years before bearing commercially viable quantities. Harvesters are then faced with a shell that puts up a good fight. It can take pressure of up to 300 pounds per square inch to break the shell containing the delicate nut. Some approaches include using a metal-working bench press, PVC pipe cutter, and boiling the stubborn shells to produce cracks large enough to be pried open.

Nutritious and blessed with "good" mono-unsaturated fats, macadamias are delicious raw, roasted, or in cakes. Their delicate flavor, versatility, and crunchy texture make them a delight to eat.

Gigantes

This side dish is popular in Greece and Turkey, where it's served with meals or as part of an assortment of appetizers called *mezes*. The preparation is simple, rustic, and very satisfying. The main ingredients, apart from beans and tomatoes, are celery, carrots, onion, garlic, oregano, parsley, and dill. Some recipes call for honey in addition to salt and pepper, which balances the flavors.

The Greeks call this dish *koukia yahni* or simply *gigantes* in reference to the large lima or butter bean. The name is evocative of ancient myth, which holds that a race of giants, the Gigantes, rose up against the Olympians in an attempt to end their reign. The stronger Olympians vanquished the rebellious Gigantes and banished them to the Netherworld.

Bubble and Squeak

Bubble and squeak is an English dish made from the leftovers of a roast dinner. It typically includes potatoes and cabbage, though carrots, peas, and Brussels sprouts may be added.

The name comes from the sound it makes while cooking. Often served on a Monday following the weekend roast, the ingredients are mixed together, and can be flattened and pan-fried until browned on both sides or just fried together and served. Considered a comfort food, and often served on Boxing Day, bubble and squeak is a clever way to get kids—and adults—to eat their cabbage. Frozen and canned versions are also available.

The Irish call their version colcannon, while the Scots prefer rumbledethumps.

Bubble and Squeak

2 tbsp butter

1 medium onion, finely chopped

1$^3/_4$ cups cooked and mashed potatoes

2 cups cooked and finely chopped cabbage

Salt

Freshly ground black pepper

Heat the butter in a frying pan over medium heat. Add the onion and cook until soft. Add the potatoes and cabbage; mix well and season. Fry until golden brown, about 15 minutes.
Serves 4

Double Happiness Beans

A feast for the eyes and the taste buds, this popular side dish blends two kinds of beans: fine green beans and salted black beans.

The strong-tasting black beans are actually small fermented soybeans preserved in salt. They're also known as Chinese black beans, available in cans or bags in Asian food stores.

To prepare the dish, the black beans are soaked in cold water for ten minutes while the green beans are cut in half lengthwise, blanched, and drained. Meanwhile, ginger, garlic, red pepper, and a small red chile sizzle in hot oil. Rice wine, soy sauce, and sesame oil form the sauce, which is thickened with a water-cornstarch mixture. Add the beans and happiness results.

The symbol for happiness in Chinese is often referred to as "double happiness." At the bottom of the character is a mouth, wide open and ready to shout for joy. At the top is the symbol for drums, beating in jubilation. The character is used during Chinese New Year and is commonly seen on wedding or anniversary gifts, given its "double" nature.

Double Happiness Beans

2 tbsp salted black beans

10 oz fine green beans, halved lengthwise on the diagonal

1 red bell pepper, seeded

2 tbsp vegetable oil

1-in piece gingerroot, peeled, cut in thin matchsticks

1 clove garlic, crushed

$\frac{1}{2}$ small red chile, finely sliced

1 tbsp rice wine or dry sherry

2 tbsp soy sauce

1 tsp sesame oil

1 tsp cornstarch mixed with 1 tbsp water

Soak the black beans in cold water for 10 minutes. Meanwhile, cook the green beans and red pepper in a pan of simmering, salted water for 3 minutes, then drain and refresh under cold water. Drain again and pat dry with a clean towel.

Heat the oil in a wok; add the ginger, garlic, and chile, tossing well. Add the green beans and red bell pepper and sauté for 2 minutes over high heat. Add the drained black beans, rice wine, soy sauce, and sesame oil and toss well for 1 minute. Add the cornstarch mixture and stir until the sauce thickens and coats the vegetables. Serve hot. *Serves 4*
Adapted from Jill Dupleix's *Totally Simple Food*

Dill Pickle

It so happens that the pickle—staple of delis and lunch specials—has a distinguished history. It traces its ancestry back to 4400 BC Mesopotamia, where it was first introduced to brine. From there, it made its way to ancient Greece, Egypt, and Rome and into the *Old Testament* books of Numbers and Isaiah.

Dill pickles, which include fresh dill in their brine, are called pickled cucumbers outside North America. They're still made at home, with one bundle of dill flavoring four dozen small cucumbers. The other ingredients are simple: water, vinegar, salt, and garlic. The boiling-hot mixture is added to small, crisp "cukes" in jars then sealed for four to five weeks to develop their flavor.

In addition to their crunchy good taste, dill pickles help us absorb iron and contain lots of Vitamin C plus good bacteria to aid digestion. These benefits weren't lost on the world's great thinkers. The philosopher Aristotle praised pickles for their health benefits, Napoleon carried them for his army, and George Washington grew a prized collection of 476 varieties. So next time you add a pickle to your burger, consider yourself in good company.

Endive

Lettuce sing the praises of three varieties of endive: curly endive, escarole, and frisée. Belgian endive is literally an offshoot of endive, discovered when the roots were left in soil in a dark cellar.

Like its mates, curly endive is grown like lettuce. Its curly, narrow, outer leaves are crisp and slightly bitter, while the milder inside leaves are pale green or creamy white. Tossed in salad with milder greens, endive provides color and "bite."

Escarole is milder with wider leaves. Since the leaves tend to hold dirt, they require a good swish in cold water before being braised or added to salads and soups. Escarole cooks very quickly, so add it at the last minute. It pairs deliciously with tomato-based recipes.

Frisée is the fun endive, its spiky fronds resembling a frilly tutu. Eating frisée raw has been compared to chewing on a hedgehog. For this reason, it stands up well to warm dressings that soften its edges and reduce its bitter taste.

Braised Belgian Endive

This simple dish is the result of a happy accident. Under normal conditions, endive is a green, slightly bitter salad green. But in 1830, when the head of the botanical gardens in Brussels left some roots covered in soil in a cellar, a new vegetable was born. Left to grow in the dark, the roots produced pale, tight, cone-shaped heads. Further cultivation produced the torpedo-shaped Belgian endive we know today.

Braised endive—the Belgians call it *witloof*—is an enduring component of the country's cuisine. The preparation is very simple: the endive is cut lengthwise in half, with the bitter root removed. It's browned lightly in butter and seasoned with salt and pepper before a small amount of water, broth, or white wine is added. A pinch of sugar compensates for its slight bitterness. When served as an appetizer or side dish, the remaining sauce is spooned over the heads.

In Europe, Belgian endive is mainly served cooked. North Americans tend to use it raw for dipping, filling, or in salads. Its mild bitter taste comes from intybin, a substance that stimulates the appetite and aids digestion.

Braised Belgian Endive

8 heads Belgian endive

2 tbsp peanut oil

1 medium onion, finely chopped

4 tsp lemon juice

Salt

Freshly ground black pepper

1 tsp sugar, optional

Cut each endive in half lengthwise. Heat the oil in a large pan and fry the endives until brown on all sides—you may need to work in batches. Return all endive to the pan, add the onion and lemon juice, and season to taste. Simmer, covered, until tender, about 50 minutes. Turn the endive occasionally during this time. Add sugar, if preferred, to counter any bitterness in the endive. *Serves 4*

Braised Fennel

Fennel is a highly aromatic herb that resembles an oblong celery with delicate dark-green fronds. It has a distinct flavor similar to anise so if you like licorice, you'll love crunchy fennel.

Braised fennel, typically served as a side dish, consists of browned fennel bulbs simmered in broth and seasoned with salt and pepper, which mutes its strong flavor.

Originating in the Mediterranean and Asia, fennel is now grown around the world. One of the more popular varieties is Florence fennel, valued for its mild flavor and sweetness. It grows mainly in India and Egypt, and was one of three ingredients used to make absinthe, the notorious alcoholic beverage that gained prominence in the late 1800s for its supposed psychoactive properties. The drink is often associated with European cultural icons such as Vincent van Gogh and, especially, Henri de Toulouse-Lautrec.

These days, fennel is found more often in kitchens than cafés. In China, fennel is used in five-spice powder. South Asians chew the seeds to freshen their breath, while Germans use it in salads tossed with chicory and avocado. Italians find it the perfect complement to sausages, while northern Europeans enjoy it with rye bread.

Cauliflower Bhaji

Brinjal Bhaji

This dish is similar to brinjal bhaji (right) in that it's curry-based. The spices used are standard Indian aromatics—cumin, coriander, mustard seed, and ginger. Some recipes call for the mustard and cumin seeds to be dry-fried first, which adds to the fragrance and taste of this simple classic. It can be served as a side dish, or as a main course with basmati rice.

Traditional recipes are low in fat and suitable for vegetarians. Following the addition of onion and garlic, the star ingredient—cauliflower—is added, along with tomatoes and water, which form the sauce. Some cooks will also add potatoes, corn, peas, or yogurt.

Cauliflower goes back to at least 400 BC in Egypt. It gets its name from the Latin *caulis*, which means cabbage, and *floris*, meaning flower. It was once called *cole florie* before evolving into the word we use today.

This traditional dish can be prepared very simply or made more elaborate with the addition of spices, yogurt, tomatoes, and okra. Streamlined preparations call for sautéing brinjal (eggplant) in oil with red chili powder, turmeric, salt, and pepper. In this version, the eggplant is cut into rounds—not too thick and not too thin, as some recipes warn—and fried in hot oil. It can be served as a side dish, or rolled in Indian roti.

Curry-based recipes call for onion, garlic, and ginger in addition to tomatoes, which produce a sauce when simmered with water. The brinjal is cubed for faster cooking and served with fluffy flavorful basmati rice.

Confusion may arise over the word *bhaji*. In south Asia, it typically means a simple vegetable curry. In the West, it has come to refer to a type of fritter such as small onion bhajis, served as snacks or appetizers.

Four Juicy Fruits

Clementine

Like other mandarin orange varieties, clementines have a loose skin that is easily removed. They're sometimes known as "zipper" oranges. They're similar to tangerines in this respect, but tend to be sweeter and have fewer seeds.

Although their name comes from Father Clément Rodier, who discovered them in the garden of his orphanage in Algeria, this delightful citrus fruit is believed to have originated in Asia as the Canton mandarin.

Medium-sized with glossy orange skin, clementines are a children's favorite. Their eight to fourteen sections are easily separated and extremely juicy.

Most clementines come from Spain, especially the Valencia and Castellón regions. Other producers include Morocco and California, which grows clementines from mid-November to January. For this reason they're sometimes referred to as Christmas oranges.

Nectarine

Contrary to popular belief, smooth-skinned nectarines are not a cross between a peach and a plum. Instead, they're a variety of cultivated peach that grew in China at least 2,000 years ago.

As they're so closely related to peaches, their flavor and uses are similar. The special appeal of nectarines is their edible skin. Even easier to eat is the "freestone" type whose pit pulls free of the flesh. Its "clingstone" cousin boasts a more tenacious pit.

Within these two categories, there are more than 150 varieties that vary slightly in shape, taste, size, and color. When selecting nectarines, think of the three "F's"—fragrant, firm (but not hard), and fetching. Once they're ready to eat, there's no end to the ways you can enjoy them. They can be eaten out of hand, with cream, baked in pies and cobblers, or preserved in jams and jellies.

Tangerine

Tangerines are one of the many members of the mandarin orange family, which has its roots in Southeast Asia. Like others of its tangy kin, the tangerine is smaller than an orange and has a peel that's very easy to remove.

These "Egyptian" oranges got their name from Tangier, Morocco—the port from which they were first shipped to Europe in the 19th century. Today's main producers are China, Spain, and Brazil.

Tangerines have recently been discovered by Western chefs, who use their juice and zest in marinades for broiled meats and seafood. They're also popular in salads, dressings, custard sauces, and cocktails. Tangerine flavoring is often added to bottled juices and soft drinks.

They're a great lunchbox addition and will keep at room temperature or refrigerated for about a week.

Pomelo

Ancestor of the grapefruit, the pomelo has a number of aliases: pummelo, shaddock, Chinese grapefruit, and jabong. Whatever you call it, you might want to show some respect to this largest member of the citrus family, which ranges from 8 to 11 inches in diameter and can weigh more than 20 pounds.

Originally from Malaysia, the pomelo was brought to the West Indies in the 17th century by English Captain Shaddock, which accounts for one of its names. It has remained popular there ever since, particularly in Jamaica. It is also cultivated in the Middle East, China, and the United States.

The pomelo can be round or pear-shaped, with yellow to deep-red pulp, and is eaten like any sweet citrus. In fact, it's sweeter than a grapefruit. Though the thick layer of skin and the large segments may take a bit of work to separate, the peel is easy to remove.

Figs

Fiddleheads

Soft, voluptuous figs are truly an ancient fruit. In the original Olympic games, victors were crowned with fig wreaths and plied with figs to eat. Figs are frequently mentioned in the Bible while, further east, Siddhartha Gautama is said to have experienced enlightenment while sitting under a fig tree, leading to the founding of Buddhism.

There's evidence that neolithic people cultivated figs 11,400 years ago in the greater Mediterranean region. Today, there are close to 800 species, though not all are edible. Because fig trees are hardy and produce delicious fruit, their cultivation spread to areas with suitable climates. In the 16th century, Spanish and Portuguese missionaries brought them to the New World.

Fresh figs are about the size of a small plum with green or purplish-black skin. Though the skin is edible, some prefer to peel figs and eat only the soft inner flesh, which can range from light to dark pink. Dried figs are sweet and chewy.

In addition to the popular Fig Newton cookie, figs can be cooked into pies, puddings, cakes, and jams. Greece, Turkey, and California are leading producers.

So named for their resemblance to the rounded tip of a violin, fiddleheads grow wild in the northeastern United States and eastern Canada, particularly in the province of New Brunswick, where they are a symbol of regional pride and where their brief harvest in spring is celebrated with festivals.

Fiddleheads are the young, still-curled shoots of the ostrich fern, and were part of the native diet before North American colonization. They are not farmed, but gathered by foragers in (often secret) places in forests. The most common way to cook fiddleheads is simply by boiling them in salted water and then tossing in butter and salt.

Crunchy and brimming with flavor, they make a perfect side dish with anything that would normally take asparagus, particularly regional specialties such as Atlantic salmon.

Apples

There are few things more satisfying than biting into a crisp, juicy Red Delicious apple. From homey pies and sophisticated tarts to baby's first applesauce and a pint of cider at the bar, this naturally sweet fruit has been a favorite for more than 4,000 years.

There are now more than 7,500 varieties of apple, with new ones cropping up every year bearing names such as Fuji and Honey Crisp. The world's top apple producers are China, the United States, Turkey, Poland, and Italy.

Modern apples are sweeter than those first produced by Mother Nature, although some hardy souls still prefer tart varieties such as Granny Smith. Apples pair deliciously with meat dishes, particularly pork.

Any teacher who's received an apple from a student knows they get top marks for nutrition as they contain Vitamin C, disease-fighting antioxidants, and a range of phytonutrients.

Given their versatility, flavor, and health benefits, it's no wonder that apple myths and legends abound. One Irish tale, for example, claims that if a woman peels an apple in a continuous ribbon and throws it behind her back, the shape of her future husband's initials will appear.

Key Lime Pie

Key limes get their name from the Florida Keys where they thrived until 1926, when a hurricane wiped them out. Most key limes are now imported from Mexico and Central America.

Unlike the more familiar Persian limes, these limes are smaller and rounder—about the size of a walnut. While they may have a thin skin, more seeds and grow on thorny evergreen trees, they make up for it with their juicy, fragrant flavor.

When it comes to making key lime pie, some people insist on the real deal. The filling in this popular pie consists of lime juice, eggs, condensed milk, and sugar. Condensed milk was originally used as fresh milk wasn't widely available in Florida before modern refrigeration. Earlier recipes didn't require baking—the acid from the lime juice was thought to be enough to "cook" the eggs and thicken the mixture. Today's pies are sometimes baked for a short time before being topped with meringue and browned.

Frozen Key Lime Pie

For the crust:

1½ cups graham cracker crumbs (10 crackers)

¼ cup sugar

6 tbsp (¾ stick) unsalted butter, melted

For the filling:

6 extra large egg yolks, at room temperature

¼ cup sugar

1 (14-oz) can sweetened condensed milk

2 tbsp grated lime zest

³⁄₄ cup freshly squeezed lime juice (4–5 limes)

For the decoration:

1 cup (1½ pint) cold heavy cream

¼ cup sugar

¼ tsp vanilla extract

Thin lime wedges

Preheat the oven to 350°F.

For the crust combine the graham cracker crumbs, sugar, and butter in a bowl. Press evenly into a 9-inch pie plate, making sure the sides and bottom are even thickness. Bake for 10 minutes. Allow to cool completely.

For the filling beat the egg yolks and sugar on high speed in the bowl of an electric mixer fitted with a paddle attachment for 5 minutes, until thick. With the mixer on medium speed, add the condensed milk, lime zest, and lime juice. Pour into the baked pie shell and freeze.

For the decoration beat the cream on high speed in the bowl of an electric mixer fitted with a whisk attachment until soft peaks form. Add the sugar and vanilla and beat until firm. Spoon or pipe decoratively onto the pie and decorate with lime. Freeze for several hours or overnight. *Serves 8*

Adapted from Ina Garten's *Barefoot Contessa's Family Style*

Satsuma

Satsumas are named for the province of Satsuma, one of the nine that once made up the present-day island of Kyushu on Japan's southern tip.

The Japanese call this small, mild mandarin-type orange *unshu mikan* after its birthplace in Wenzhou, in southeast China. It came to the West in the 1800s, and is beloved for its almost seedless nature (one to two seeds per fruit) and its soft, easy-to-peel skin. This makes it one of the more popular oranges with young and old alike.

For citrus fanciers, satsumas have another attractive quality—they can be grown in a container as they are generally small. In locations with sufficient sun, enthusiasts may be able to enjoy the fragrance of satsuma blossoms and watch the tiny fruit swell on their very own tree!

Champagne Grapes

The facts surrounding these tiny black grapes would make anyone giddy. While you might assume they're grown for making champagne, you'd be off the mark. They actually got their name in the early 1980s when all things small were big in the food industry. And these grapes are small—each about the size of a pea with a stem so delicate it's edible.

So a new grape, perhaps? Not at all. These tender sweet grapes with black skin and white flesh were first grown near the city of Corinth, Greece, more than 2,000 years ago. At that time they were grown for juice, wine, and eating. When dried, they're known as Zante currants, the name "currant" derived from Corinth.

So why the champagne moniker? Chalk it up to clever marketing. Because these grapes are so small, a cluster is said to resemble champagne bubbles. The whimsical association does have merit, however: they're beautiful draped over the edge of a champagne glass and can be dropped singly into the bubbly for a great visual effect.

Not stopping there, this seedless grape mingles well with food. It's an elegant addition to fruit bowls, goes well with cheese, is great in salads, and can garnish roasts and decorate cakes. On especially hot days, champagne grapes straight from the freezer are a sweet and nutritious way to cool down.

Roasted Butternut Squash

Butternut squash is a wonderfully versatile winter squash available when so many other vegetables are finished for the season. Its deep-yellow flesh has a natural sweetness. When roasted, it is superb.

Butternuts have a round bottom, a gently elongated neck, and thin beige-to-yellow skin. To roast, split the squash in half lengthwise and scoop out the seeds and fibers. Score the flesh lightly. Place some crushed garlic and butter in the hollow and sprinkle with salt and freshly ground black pepper. Place on a baking tray in a slow oven and roast for an hour or so, depending on its size, brushing with butter periodically. Scooped from the shell, roasted butternut squash is ambrosia.

Another option is to stuff the squash before roasting. The quickest way to roast squash is to peel and cut it into chunks. Toss the pieces in oil with similar-sized pieces of zucchini, onion, fennel, and celery root. Roast and serve with crumbled goat's-milk cheese for a sublime fall dish.

Puréed roasted squash adds sweetness to soups and casseroles. One of the best pairings is squash and roasted red peppers. The smoky-sweet combination is irresistible.

Roasted Butternut Squash

1 (1½-2 lb) butternut squash

Olive oil cooking spray

⅛ tsp allspice

⅛ tsp salt

¼ tsp freshly ground black pepper

Preheat the oven to 350°F.

Cut the squash into four wedges and remove the seeds. Spray each wedge with oil and dust with allspice, salt, and pepper. Bake for 40 minutes or until tender. *Serves 4*

Celeriac

While this knobby root will never win a beauty contest, its pronounced celery flavor has been admired for centuries, enriching soups and stews. Also known as celery root, it is about the size of a potato with light mottled skin and pale white flesh.

It hails from a celery variety bred over centuries to produce a flavorful root. Europeans, especially the French and Germans, have embraced this misshapen vegetable and don't seem to have any problem peeling it. Some use a knife to cut away the irregular skin, while others prefer a potato peeler. Either way, the exposed white flesh darkens quickly when exposed to air. If the root is to be used raw in a salad, the cut pieces should be soaked in a bowl of water and lemon juice for at least 15 minutes to preserve their color.

A further hidden beauty of celeriac is its durability. It can last for months in a cool, dry space. As with all root vegetables, it's a good idea to look for those that feel heavy and hard with no soft spots. For a burst of flavor, try mashing celeriac with potatoes using three parts potato to one part celeriac.

Cashews

The evergreen tree that produces cashew nuts is native to Brazil but can be cultivated in any region with a warm, humid climate. Called *caju* in Portuguese, these kidney-shaped nuts grow in an individual shell containing an extremely caustic oil. Removing the shell can be a tricky business if not handled properly. Portuguese colonizers in Brazil studied the technique used by indigenous Indians, who roasted the shells over a fire to burn off the toxic covering.

Once the Portuguese had mastered the technique, they introduced this rich, delicious nut to India in the 16th century. India is now one of the leading producers of cashews, along with Vietnam, Brazil, and Nigeria.

Roasted cashews are a popular ingredient in savory Asian dishes. High in oil, they can also be ground into a spread much like peanut butter. Although cashews don't find themselves invited into candy boxes as often as other nuts, they're delicious teamed with milk chocolate or with savory herbs such as rosemary and thyme.

Whether you call them *cashu, casho* or *caju,* they're a healthy and delicious treat.

Haricots Verts

The aristocrats of the bean family, these French beans are long and slim with a sweet delicate flavor. Their skins are thinner, their seeds are smaller, and they have less water than regular green beans, which gives them a desirable crispness. Not only are there a wide variety of French beans, but there are endless ways to prepare them. They can be served as a side dish with roasted meats, included in salads for extra flavor and texture, or served with raw vegetables and dip.

An especially vivid variety to use raw is Purple Teepee, with its brilliant purple pod and flavorful zing. Once immersed in boiling water, the pods become a dazzling emerald.

Like all green beans, French beans are the unripe fruit of a bean picked before it reaches maturity. If left too long on the runner or bush, the beans become woody and tough. When selecting them, look for young bright fresh pods with a crisp look. Any green bean recipe is enhanced by the addition of haricots verts.

Glazed Carrots

This sweet and simple dish was a long time coming. Originally from Afghanistan, carrots left their wild roots behind to become the popular root vegetable we know today. Prehistoric carrots were forked, thin, and colored red, purple, or black.

After cultivation began around 3000 BC, they eventually made their way west to Rome and Greece where they were taken up and grown in kitchen gardens. The Romans brought carrots to England, but it wasn't until the 1600s that the Dutch developed the modern orange variety. Queen Elizabeth is reputed to have cooked carrots in butter after receiving them as gifts. Glazed carrots awaited only the addition of a sweetener.

Today we can glaze carrots with anything, including sugar, honey, corn syrup, maple sugar, orange juice—even ginger ale. The preparation is simple: simmer sliced carrots in a mixture of butter and sweetener until tender. They are typically served with roasts or other main dishes.

Lately, carrots have been discovering their roots as purple varieties make a comeback. Unlike their ancestors, these carrots are large, sweet, and juicy. Even so, they might not have appealed to American actress Mae West who once claimed, "The only carrots that interest me are the number you get in a diamond."

Glazed Carrots

$1\frac{1}{2}$ tbsp brown sugar

1 tbsp unsalted butter

$\frac{1}{2}$ cup chicken broth

$\frac{1}{2}$ cup water

$\frac{1}{2}$ tsp salt

$1\frac{1}{4}$ lb carrots, cut into 2- by $\frac{1}{4}$-in sticks

1 tsp fresh lemon juice

2 tsp finely chopped fresh parsley

Salt

Freshly ground black pepper

Put the brown sugar, butter, broth, water, and salt in a pan and bring to a boil, stirring to dissolve the sugar. Add the carrots, cover, and simmer for 4 to 5 minutes. Remove the carrots with a slotted spoon and continue to cook the liquid, over high heat, to reduce to about 2 tablespoons. Return the carrots to the pan, stir to coat in the glaze and sprinkle with lemon juice and parsley. Season to taste before serving. *Serves 6*

Four Less Popular Veggies

Broccoli

Although some scholars believe broccoli was cited by the Roman writer Apicius, there's little evidence of it in Europe before 1560, when it was first mentioned in France. Its name comes from the Latin *brachium*, which means strong arm or branch.

Despite France's adoption of this particular member of the cabbage family, its big break-through took four centuries. In 1922, Italian brothers Stephano and Andrea D'Arrigo began cultivating the tree-like vegetable in San Jose, California. When they shipped a few crates to Boston's North End, home to a thriving Italian community, broccoli found favor at last. The popular Andy Boy brand, named for Stephano's son Andrew, dates back to this time.

Broccoli's current popularity may be due in part to its calcium content and cancer-fighting antioxidants. Steam or stir-fry, as its nutrients dissolve in water.

Brussels Sprouts

This unjustly maligned vegetable is related to the wild cabbage and grows on long thick stalks from which it is picked by hand. The common green Brussels sprout, along with its purple cousin, resembles a perfect miniature cabbage. This should endear them to small children, but it hasn't happened yet.

The name comes from the Belgian capital, its original place of cultivation. Although they were also grown in Italy in Roman times, they only became popular in the 1500s.

Fans of Brussels sprouts believe they're at their best in mid to late winter, when cooler temperatures bring out their flavor. In the UK, they're often served at Christmas.

Cooking them lightly is the key to preventing the release of unpopular sulfur compounds. Traditionally, the base of the sprout was cut with a cross—to keep the devil out—and boiled at length. Now it is just as likely to be roasted or sautéed.

Cabbage

When most people think of Vitamin C, they think of oranges. How unfortunate for the cabbage. Not only can it make the same claim, but is versatile enough to make an orange green with envy.

Cabbage can be eaten raw in salads, cooked in soups and stews, and made into cabbage rolls. Fermenting cabbage, a technique used to make German sauerkraut and Korean kimchi, helps keep its crunch and preserves it well.

There are a great many varieties of this cool-season crop. While pale green cabbage has traditionally been used for coleslaw, tastier varieties such as red and savoy are gaining in popularity.

Cooked shredded cabbage is a popular European side dish. Adding a bay leaf or splash of vermouth to the cooking water will keep your kitchen smelling fresh. When cooking a red cabbage add a dash of vinegar.

Okra

Although used around the world as a vegetable, okra is technically a fruit. Also known as "lady's finger," its name comes from *okuru* in Igbo, a West African language. It grows wild in Africa, Asia, and Australia but does well in any tropical, subtropical, or warm temperate region. The soft green fruit, measuring between 2 to 8 inches in diameter, contains round white seeds and is picked when immature.

In the Middle East, okra is typically used in meat and vegetable stews. In India, particularly in the south, it's sautéed or added to sauces. Gumbo, synonymous with the southern US, is thickened with okra. The Japanese adopted okra toward the end of the 20th century, and now serve it with a soy dipping sauce or lightly battered and deep-fried as tempura.

Okra is one of the world's most heat- and drought-resistant plants. Aside from cooking, crops can be pickled or dried, either whole or sliced.

Stewed Okra

Okra holds a revered place in the Cajun cooking of Louisiana. In 1763, French-speaking Acadians, shortened to Cajuns, were expelled by the British from their settlements in Nova Scotia and fled to Louisiana. These migrants of French heritage mingled with the rich cultural potpourri of the thriving port of New Orleans to create a unique culture and cuisine.

Okra is widely associated with the African slave trade, and is the essential ingredient and natural thickener in New Orleans's famous gumbo, a rice stew based on fish, fowl, or meat. Shellfish from the Gulf of Mexico are popular ingredients, as are Cajun sausage and smoked pork. Onion, celery, and bell peppers are also traditional ingredients. During Lent, restaurants often prepare gumbo z'herbes (*gumbo aux herbes*), with a mixture of local greens.

Stewed Okra

1 lb fresh okra, washed, trimmed, and sliced

1 (14.5-oz) can stewed tomatoes

1 cup chopped green bell pepper

2 tbsp finely chopped onion

Salt

Freshly ground black pepper

Put the okra in a saucepan with enough water to cover. Bring to a boil and cook for 5 minutes. Drain the okra, discarding the water. Return the okra to the pan with the tomatoes, bell pepper, and onion. Simmer the mixture for 15 minutes, or until the okra is tender. Season to taste before serving. *Serves 4*

Bhindi Bhaji

Okra (*bhindi* in Hindi,) is a green, ridged pod
filled with round, cream-colored seeds. Its
mallow family tree includes the hibiscus and
hollyhock. When okra is fresh, breaking the
pointed tip of the pod releases some of the
thick, slimy liquid inside. A pod past its prime
will not break cleanly, and the flesh of the
okra will be woody, stringy, and unpalatable.

Since okra pods must be picked within a
few days of forming, timing is everything.
This African native has found a comfortable
niche in the cuisines of south Asia, the
southern US, and Brazil, where it was
reputedly carried during the slave trade.

Bhaji, meanwhile, translates as a vegetable
side dish (hence *aloo bhaji* made with
potatoes, *piaz bhaji* made with onions, and
palak bhaji made with spinach). Bhindi bhaji—
okra pods fried in a mixture of spices—is a
favorite vegetable side dish. The natural
sweetness of the okra blends perfectly with
spices. It is often served with curries and
plain rice or bread.

Bhindi Bhaji

2 tbsp sunflower or vegetable oil

1 medium onion, chopped

1/2 tsp ground cumin

1/2 tsp ground coriander

1/2 tsp chili powder

1/4 tsp ground turmeric

1 medium tomato, chopped

1 lb okra, cut into 1-in pieces

Salt

Freshly ground black pepper

Heat the oil in a large frying pan. Add the
onions and spices, stirring to coat evenly.
Sauté until the onions are transparent, about
5 minutes. Now add the tomatoes and cook
for a further 1 to 2 minutes before adding
the okra. Simmer until the okra is cooked
and tender—8 to 10 minutes. Season with
salt and pepper. *Serves 2*

Crispy Seaweed

This whimsical name denotes a tasty and popular dish found in Chinese restaurants. While it may resemble nori, the Japanese seaweed, it's really cabbage—or other leafy greens—deep-fried until crispy.

The best way to prepare this dish is to roll up the leaves of a green or savoy cabbage and slice it thinly into long strips. Bok choy, kale, or brussels sprout tops can be used as well. Once cut, the strips are deep-fried in oil at 350°F until crispy but not brown. They're best removed with a slotted spoon and served with salt or garnished with ground fish. They can be eaten on their own, or sprinkled over soup.

It seems seaweed appeals to more than just food connoisseurs. Stephen Hillenburg, marine biologist and animator of the television character SpongeBob SquarePants, gave seaweed its due in an episode titled "Plankton!" In it, a character called Karen probes deep into the heart of seaweed, declaring it, "50% sea, 50% weed."

Zucchini

This slim summer squash, which got its start in North America, headed to Europe to find itself. Once there, it underwent a transformation in Italy toward the end of the 19th century through spontaneous mutation, more commonly known as a "sport of nature." The Italians named it zucchini (little squash), the name now used in Australia and North America. The British prefer the French *courgette*.

Although they can grow up to 3 feet long, zucchini are best eaten when young, at 6 to 8 inches long. They range in color from yellow to dark green and resemble a thin cucumber with denser flesh and soft, edible skin.

While zucchini can be served raw in salads or with crudités, they're most often cooked. They can be steamed, boiled, broiled, baked, fried in oil, or sliced into soups and stews. Their delicate yellow flowers are especially valued. In Japan, they're deep-fried as tempura, in Italy they're stuffed with ricotta cheese, while in Mexico they're used as a filling for broiled quesadilla sandwiches.

Having returned to the Americas transformed, zucchini were taken up by gardeners who marveled at their hardiness and output. Gardeners now fret over how to give away huge unwanted zucchini to friends who already have more than they can use.

Four Mushrooms

Shiitake

This flavorful mushroom gets its name from the Japanese *shii*—the type of tree it grows on—and *take*, which means mushroom. Native to China, it has been cultivated for more than 1,000 years.

In the wild, the shiitake leads a fascinating life. Fruiting mushrooms release spores that drift until finally settling on a tree branch. There they lie dormant until the limb eventually dies and falls to the ground, which "wakes up" the spores. Only then do they start growing to produce the mature mushroom whose complex flavor has been prized for centuries.

In Japan, shiitakes are served in miso soup, or simply fried and served as a side dish. The Vietnamese slip them into crispy spring rolls with a host of other fresh veggies.

Shiitake mushrooms can also be dried, which connoisseurs claim brings out their essential *umami*, a flavor best described as meaty and savory.

Portobello

The most notable feature of the portobello mushrooms is its wide cap—4 to 6 inches across—with dark gills beneath.

As they mature, portobellos lose moisture, which intensifies their earthy flavor and gives them a meaty texture. Their size and texture make them ideal for stuffing, with combinations ranging from spinach, cheese, and bread crumbs to crab with bell peppers and shallots.

Given their size and consistency, they're perfect for the grill. A zesty marinade will bring out their flavor, whether the cook chooses simple soy sauce or a more dramatic sauce of aged balsamic vinegar, olive oil, fresh basil, and onions. Portobellos are excellent in creamy stroganoffs, gourmet pizzas, and casseroles. They make a scrumptious vegetarian burger.

As for the name, mushroom marketers simply made it up. One theory has it named after fashionable Portobello Road in London, England.

Cremini

These tan mushrooms are the midway point between a white button and a portobello. They're somewhat larger than their button counterparts with a denser texture and rich flavor. They also go by the names "portobellini" and "Swiss brown."

Creminis enhance any dish. They can be added to soups, salads, and pasta and are mild enough to include on vegetable platters. Cooks who like experimenting with international cuisine will want to have creminis on hand as they're suitable for any mushroom recipe.

Try creminis with spinach, artichoke hearts, and smoked cheese in a warm quesadilla. Asian dishes gladly make room for this flavorful mushroom in quick stir-fries. Broiling brings out their deep flavor, especially when marinated in onion, garlic, and olive oil. A quick dusting of grated cheese and parsley makes for a tasty side dish.

Oyster

Oyster mushrooms come by their name honestly: their velvety texture, pearly finish, and delicate aroma are reminiscent of oysters from the sea. Unlike other mushrooms (and oysters), however, they're at their best when cooked and should not be eaten raw.

There are several varieties of oyster mushrooms ranging in color from brown, gray, pink, yellow, and white. They have a robust meaty flavor when cooked, which makes them a great addition to vegetarian meals.

Originally cultivated in Asia, they're known as *ping gu* or "flat mushroom" in Chinese. They're now grown around the world and appear in a variety of cuisines. A simple Italian antipasto may include oyster mushrooms marinated in balsamic vinegar, parsley, garlic, and a little good olive oil. The French take a simpler approach, sautéing oysters in butter with a pinch of salt for a juicy, flavorful side dish.

Poutine

At one time, poutine seemed to be available only to late-night revelers searching for snacks on the streets of Montreal. No more. Poutine has spread across Canada and is also available in select locations in the US.

The recipe is simple. French fried potatoes are sprinkled liberally with fresh cheese curds and the whole plate is smothered in steaming beef gravy, leaving the curds a stringy, gooey mess. The origins of the dish date back to the 1950s, when a certain Fernand Lechance, responding to a customer's request for the concoction, reportedly said that it would be a *maudite poutine,* a hell of a mess.

Since then, many variations have developed, from the simple (spaghetti sauce instead of gravy) to the sophisticated (foie gras instead of cheese curds). The authenticity of these departures from the traditional is often a point of controversy, with purists insisting that there is only one true recipe for poutine.

Regardless, portions of this combination of starch and fat are generally large and leave a heavy, lasting impression on the stomach.

Mushy Peas

No genuine meal of English fish and chips can really be complete without a serving of mushy peas. Their name says it all. Big, starchy, dried marrowfat peas are soaked overnight in water and baking soda. This secret ingredient breaks down the pea's rather tough coat and, incidentally, disperses the natural gases that build up during soaking.

Brought to a rapid boil, then left to simmer for an hour or so, the peas develop the familiar mushy consistency and gray-green color that are their hallmark. A dash of salt and a pat of butter complete this icon of English cuisine. Yorkshire caviar at its finest!

Mushy Peas

2 tbsp olive oil
1 medium bunch scallions, chopped
1 tsp chopped fresh mint
1 lb frozen green peas, thawed
2 tbsp butter
$1/2$ tsp coarse sea salt
Freshly ground black pepper

Heat the oil in a skillet over medium heat. Add the scallions, mint, and peas. Cover, and cook for 3 to 4 minutes, until tender, then mash peas with a potato masher. Stir in the butter, and season to taste. *Serves 4*

Champignons à la Grecque

The French lexicon has a multitude of dishes cooked "in the style of," including *à l'Alsacienne, à l'Américaine,* and *à la Florentine.* These often honor regional specialties or classic techniques. A dish prepared à la Grecque promises a hint of the sunny Greek islands. The basis of these dishes is a *court bouillon,* a light broth made with olive oil and lemon juice, flavored with a bouquet garni of fresh herbs. Court bouillon is prepared in advance, since it is important not to overcook the ingredients—including mushrooms, leeks, endives, and artichokes—prepared in this way.

For Champignons à la Grecque, trimmed and cleaned mushrooms are simmered briefly in the *bouillon* and removed. The remaining broth is reduced to an intense, concentrated syrup and poured over the waiting mushrooms, usually in a shallow dish.

Champignons à la Grecque are a typical deli offering, but are easy to make at home. This dish makes an attractive addition to a cold buffet table or an easy first course for dinner.

Champignons à la Grecque

1 cup water

2 tbsp olive oil

1 tbsp white wine vinegar

Zest of 1 lemon, lime, and orange

A pinch of salt

5 oz mushrooms

Place all of the ingredients, except the mushrooms, in a saucepan and bring to a boil. Add the mushrooms and simmer for 5 minutes. Remove the mushrooms with a slotted spoon and arrange in a shallow serving dish. Reduce the broth to about ¼ cup by boiling rapidly, then pour over the mushrooms. Allow to cool before serving. *Serves 2*

Jerusalem Artichoke

The North American delicacy known as
Jerusalem artichoke is overshadowed by its
companions—corn, beans, and squash—the
three sisters of the New World diet. This
humble food is the Cinderella of roots and
tubers. Known to native people as the "sun
root" *(Helianthus tuberosus)*, its true name
evokes the jaunty but modest sunflower that
marks its presence in a garden or a sunny
field. In the 17th century, however, it acquired
the name Jerusalem artichoke because
the French explorer Samuel de Champlain
compared its flavor to an artichoke, to which
was added a clumsy English pronunciation
of *girasole*—the Italian word for sunflower.

   Early settlers in Canada and the
northeastern United States appreciated sun
roots as a food source and cultivated them in
kitchen gardens. They are now grown mainly
as an alternative crop for specialty markets.
Many industrial farmers consider them a
weed because they tend to spread rapidly.

   Jerusalem artichokes have a beige/pink skin
and resemble a gingerroot or a gnarly new
potato—a challenge to peel! When raw, they
have a slightly nutty flavor and a crunch
similar to a water chestnut. Try them in a stir-
fry, add them to soups, cook them alongside
a roast, or toss them raw into a salad.

Potato and Jerusalem Artichoke Soup with Thyme, Mascarpone, and Hazelnuts

2 knobs butter

2 cloves garlic, finely chopped

1 medium onion, finely chopped

1 lb Jerusalem artichokes, peeled and chopped

2 cups peeled and chopped potatoes

1 good handful thyme leaves, picked

5 cups chicken or vegetable broth

$5^1/_2$ oz mascarpone cheese

Salt and freshly ground black pepper

$1^1/_2$ cups hazelnuts, toasted and broken up

In a large pan, melt the butter and slowly fry
the garlic, onion, artichokes, potatoes, and
thyme. Add the broth, then bring to a boil
and simmer for about 30 minutes until the
potatoes and artichokes are tender. Blend in
a blender or food processor just enough to
leave it chunky or blend until a purée. Reheat,
adding the mascarpone and correcting the
seasoning. Serve sprinkled with the hazelnuts.
Serves 4–6

Adapted from Jamie Oliver's *The Return of the Naked Chef*

Lotus Root

Fried Plantains

The lotus blossom has powerful spiritual resonance for Hindus and Buddhists. It floats serenely on still water, a symbol of purity and detachment. The Buddha is often depicted sitting within a lotus blossom. But deep down in the mud at the bottom of the pond is an earthly treasure—the lotus root.

The rhizome of the water lily or lotus is thick, like a sweet potato but with a brownish-white skin. The rhizome can grow up to 3 feet long, with a series of linked swellings. Like a new potato, its skin should be scraped away. A little lemon juice helps retain its fresh creamy color.

The real delight of a lotus root happens when it is sliced, revealing a lacy rosette. The flesh is interspersed with a pattern of spaces reminiscent of a snowflake. Its decorative quality, apart from its taste, appeals to anyone who wants to create food pleasing to all the senses.

Even when simmered for hours in a pork soup, its delicate tracery does not break down. In a stir-fry, it cooks to crunchiness in just a few minutes. It can be deep-fried in batter or added raw to a salad.

In the Caribbean and in South American countries lying close to the equator, a typical midday meal consists of meat or fish, rice, beans, salad, and a few strips of fried plantain. The latter is often the best part of the meal. Plantains are related to the banana, but are much larger and less round. Another important difference is that plantains cannot be eaten raw.

Only the ripest plantain can be fried successfully. At its peak sweetness it is slightly soft, with skin more black than yellow. Pan-fried in vegetable oil, the cream-colored slices form a glistening brown crust that offers a perfect light crunch when eaten. The warm insides turn just mushy enough to be cut with the side of a fork. The sweet flavor is reminiscent of bananas, but is distinct unto itself.

Four Bountiful Berries

Blackberries

Blackberries are a small, soft fruit similar to a raspberry with purple-black flesh. They grow on shrubs, called brambles in England, which thrive in forests, scrublands, and hillsides. They don't mind poor soil and will soon put down roots in wasteland and even building sites.

This small, juicy fruit is used in desserts, jams, jellies, and occasionally wine. Its blossoms produce ample amounts of nectar which can be made into a dark, fruity honey.

Blackberries grow around the world from Europe to the US, New Zealand to Chile. Breeding has produced an array of large, firm varieties bearing names such as Black Diamond, Nightfall, and Obsidian. These cultivars have been bred for taste, yield, and also to produce thornless shrubs for ease of picking.

Blueberries

Along with blue cheese and blue corn, blueberries belong to a select category of naturally blue foods. They don't start out that way, how-ever. At first blush, they're pale green, moving to reddish-purple before finally turning blue.

Blueberries are native to North America and eastern Asia and are related to other fruits from shrubs such as cranberries, bilberries, and cowberries.

Hybrid varieties now grow around the world. While most are cultivated highbush species, some are picked wild. Wild blue-berries are smaller and more expensive, but are prized for their intense flavor and color. Canada's First Nations peoples harvest them from low scrubby bushes and sell them on the side of the road in summer.

Whether highbush or lowbush, blueberries make excellent jams and jellies and are popular in baked goods such as pies and muffins.

Raspberries

Raspberries aren't really berries at all: they're what is known as an aggregate fruit consisting of drupelets or beads formed around a central core. Unlike blackberries, which stay attached to the core, raspberries have a distinctive hollow center. For this reason they require gentle handling.

While the fruit is delicate and sweet, the canes they grow on are extremely hardy. In the wild, they're found in forest clearings and fields.

Commercially-raised raspberries come in two types: summer-bearing, which produces fruit in mid-summer, and ever-bearing, which bears fruit into the fall. While most are red, they also come in golden, amber, and purple.

Raspberries are as delicious as they come, but also feature in jams and tarts, pies and muffins, even gourmet vinegars. Since they spoil easily, they should be kept as dry as possible and eaten within two or three days of purchase.

Strawberries

Strawberries originated in the Americas from the species "fragaria," meaning fragrant. Anyone who has cut into a ripe strawberry knows the tantalizing scent of the fresh fruit. Madame Tallien, a figure from the French Revolution, was apparently so taken with them that she floated strawberries in the bath to keep her skin scented and radiant.

The English had a more prosaic interest: they contented themselves with naming them. The word we use today comes from *streawberige*, which means either "straw" or "strew" berry. Some believe it denotes the straw-like appearance of the plant's runners; others claim that the berries are strewn among the leaves. Whichever side of the debate you come down on, it doesn't seem as much fun as bathing in them, or devoting a weekend to sampling them.

Broiled Grapefruit

Once known as the "forbidden fruit," grapefruit is a newcomer to the fruit world. While coconuts date back 15 million years, grapefruit is a hybrid that appeared less than 300 years ago. A recipe containing grapefruit and coconut would be the ultimate May to December dish.

Grapefruit was first documented in 1750 in Barbados, where it developed from a pomelo and a sweet orange. Given its tart, acidic taste, it was not immediately embraced. Over time, however, sweeter varieties were developed, some with brilliant red pulp, leading to the patented name "Ruby Red." The name of the fruit itself comes from its tendency to grow in clusters, like grapes.

Recipes for broiled grapefruit add both sweetness and warmth, which enhance the fruit's flavor. Although grapefruit can be peeled and broiled in sections, the traditional approach has a certain elegant simplicity.

After being cut in half crosswise, the juicy fruit is topped with sugar, honey, or maple syrup before being run quickly under the broiler. Some cooks place a maraschino cherry in the center before serving, while others add a dash of cinnamon, nutmeg, or cloves.

Served for breakfast, broiled grapefruit is a refreshing and healthy way to start the day.

Gooseberries

Although native to Europe and western Asia, there are now two types of gooseberries—American and European. Some are red to purple, while others are light green. They grow on bushes with thick spines and prefer cooler temperatures. Since the flavor of this small juicy fruit is said to improve the further north it goes, bushes growing in Norway close to the Arctic Circle would likely win the taste test.

There's no evidence that these berries are eaten by geese, or that they taste like geese. The odd name probably comes from the Dutch *kruisbezie*, the German *Krausbeere* or possibly the French *groseille*.

However their name evolved, the English took to these berries in a big way. In colonial days, gooseberry wine, pies, and puddings were very popular. By the end of the 1700s, gooseberry bushes were a favorite among cottage gardeners.

The versatile fruit is now making a comeback, no doubt because of its great taste—a tangy blend of pineapple and strawberry. The berries are sold fresh in specialty stores and farmer's markets, or canned. Gooseberries will stay fresh in the refrigerator for about two weeks, becoming pinker and softer as they age. They're delicious cooked with apples or ginger, added to salads, used to garnish sweet and savory dishes, or prepared the good old-fashioned way and turned into jam.

Rhubarb

The first crop of rhubarb is a rite of spring. Whether you cut the slender stalks from your garden or choose a bundle at the market or grocery store, there is a shiver of anticipation about the first rhubarb of the season.

When rhubarb first emerged on the European stage from China, it was treasured for its medicinal properties, especially its purgative qualities. Various attempts were made to control the trade in this valuable commodity. The medicinal variant of rhubarb is still a popular herbal remedy.

By the 1600s in Europe, rhubarb was being planted as a food crop. To temper its natural tartness—try chewing a raw stalk—it is fortunate that a plentiful supply of affordable sugar was available from the West Indies.

Rhubarb leaves are rich in toxic oxalic acid, and must not be consumed. Stewed rhubarb is a treat. Rhubarb also pairs deliciously with strawberries for an old-fashioned pie, cobbler or jam. But the queen of desserts must be a rhubarb tart with fresh cream.

Rhubarb Tart

For the crust:

$1^2/_3$ cups all-purpose flour

$1/_4$ tsp salt

$1/_2$ cup chilled unsalted butter, cut into small pieces

$1/_4$ cup sugar

2 large egg yolks

2 tbsp (or more) ice water

3 tbsp apricot jam

For the filling:

1 cup sugar

$1/_3$ cup water

3 (3 x $1/_2$-in) strips lemon peel (yellow part only)

$1/_2$ cinnamon stick

2 lb fresh rhubarb, trimmed, cut on the diagonal

Mix flour and salt in a food processor. Add butter and pulse until the mixture resembles coarse crumbs. Add sugar and yolks and process briefly to blend. Add 2 tablespoons of water and process just until moist clumps form. If the dough is dry, add more water by teaspoonfuls to moisten. Gather dough into a ball and flatten into a disk. Wrap in plastic and refrigerate until the dough is firm enough to roll, about 30 minutes. (Can be prepared one day ahead and refrigerated. Let dough soften slightly at room temperature before rolling.)

Roll out the dough disk on a floured surface to a 12-inch circle. Transfer to a 9-inch tart pan with a removable bottom. Trim crust overhang to $1/_4$-inch. Fold in overhang, creating double-thick sides. Freeze for 15 minutes.

Preheat the oven to 350°F. Line the chilled crust with foil and fill it with dried beans or pie weights. Bake until the sides are set, about 20 minutes. Remove the foil and beans.

Continue baking until the crust is golden brown, about 15 minutes, piercing with a fork if bubbles form. Brush the crust with jam and bake until the jam sets, about 5 minutes more. Transfer the pan to a rack to cool. Combine sugar and water in a large heavy frying pan over low heat. Stir until the sugar dissolves. Add the lemon peel and cinnamon stick. Increase the heat and bring to a boil. Add rhubarb, bring to a boil then reduce the heat to medium-low. Cover and simmer until the rhubarb just begins to soften,

about 5 minutes. Remove the pan from the heat. Let stand, covered, until the rhubarb is tender, about 15 minutes. Uncover and cool completely.

With a slotted spoon, remove the rhubarb from the cooking liquid and arrange in concentric circles in the crust. Strain cooking liquid into a small saucepan and boil until reduced to 1¼ cups, about 5 minutes. Cool, then spoon over rhubarb. This tart can be prepared 6 hours ahead. Serve at room temperature. *Serves 8*

Daikon

This large root vegetable stars in many Asian dishes. In India it's known as *mooli*, in China it's *loh-bak* or Chinese turnip, and the Japanese use the name daikon. Whatever its name, it can grow to be more than 12 inches long and 3 inches wide.

A Punjabi classic is *mooli paratha*, a fried Indian flatbread stuffed with grated, sautéed daikon, chiles, and chopped cilantro leaves. Crisp, fragrant, hot, and sweet, all in one, it is an irresistible accompaniment for raita or curry.

Daikon is a staple vegetable in Japanese cuisine, used in everything from garnishes to pickles. The sweetest part, near the leaves, is often used raw. The bottom third is the hottest part, adding spice to stir-fries and soups. Daikon is also sculpted into decorative birds and flowers, adding visual delight to many dishes and bento boxes.

One of daikon's most illustrious roles is in *loh bak gao*, a savory turnip cake traditionally served during Lunar New Year celebrations and a dim sum favorite. Grated daikon is simmered until tender, combined with rice flour, scallions, shiitake mushrooms, dried shrimp, and Chinese sausage, and steamed to perfection. When cool, slices of the crisp, salty flavorful cake are fried and served to symbolize prosperity for the coming year.

Corn on the Cob

Hot buttered corn on the cob is one of the most satisfying hands-on foods around. There's nothing like rolling up your sleeves and sinking your teeth into the 300 to 400 tender kernels on a cob of roasted, boiled, or grilled corn.

Not all corn, however, lends itself to this popular summer tradition. Only sweet corn will do, bred to produce more sugar and less starch. It's actually a recent hybrid of an ancient plant domesticated in Mesoamerica at least 9,000 years ago.

Corn and the Americas go together like kernels on a cob. Its domestication is of great interest to archeologists, who have studied the central role corn played in ancient civilizations. The Mesoamericans were sustained by corn and believed it to have spiritual significance. Other cultures gradually learned about its cultivation so that by the first millennium AD its use had spread from Mexico to the rest of the Americas and the Caribbean.

Native Americans developed an ingenious method for growing corn, beans, and squash together. Known as the "three sisters," this arrangement allows the beans to use the corn stalk for support while the low-lying squash provide ground cover to prevent the growth of weeds.

Today we eat sweet corn fresh, canned, or frozen. In Britain, it's occasionally served on pizza. Special varieties are grown to make popcorn. Cereal made from corn is called cornmeal mush, or polenta if you're Italian. It's not to be confused with the corn mash used to produce bourbon!

How to Cook

Fantastic stuff. Buy young, proud, explicit cobs with their sheath still on, and plump, tightly packed kernels underneath. Size matters.

Avoid anything withered. Peel off the papery skin, then throw them whole into boiling salted water and cook at an excited boil till a tested kernel comes away easily. It could take anything from 5 to 15 minutes, depending on size and freshness. It should be as sweet as a nut. Smother the cob with melted butter and eat immediately, holding it in your hands, the butter dribbling down your chin. A feast.

Adapted from Nigel Slater's *Real Cooking*

Pomodori Secchi

People crave the sweet acidity of tomatoes, one of the most successful and influential of New World crops. Before the advent of modern canning, people either preserved tomatoes at home or, as the Italians do, cut them in slices and spread them in the sun to dry.

Even if you don't live in a sunny climate, the low heat of an oven or food dehydrator puts these delicacies within reach. Fleshy tomatoes are best—Principe Borghese is traditional but Roma or plum varieties will do. It takes from 8 to 15 hours to dry tomatoes to perfection, depending on the weather, the technique, and the moisture content of the slices.

Sun-dried tomatoes should be leathery but tender, not crisp. If they are stored in olive oil, they do not need to be reconstituted. Dry slices can be stored in airtight containers and soaked in warm water, broth, or white wine for 20 to 30 minutes when ready to use.

A burst of concentrated flavor will remind you of warm summer days even on the darkest winter night. Use sun-dried tomatoes to garnish fish and chicken, add zip to sauces, dips, and salad dressings, and to make the scrumptious classic, sun-dried tomato focaccia bread.

Pico de Gallo

Pico de gallo is an essential condiment at any Mexican table. The spiritual inspiration behind jarred salsa, which has overtaken ketchup as the condiment of choice in the United States, it consists simply of cubed tomato, onion, chile pepper, and cilantro.

With a sprinkle of lime juice and a dash of salt, these basic ingredients combine to produce a refreshing accompaniment to grilled meats and fish, tacos, or any tortilla-based dish. Pico de gallo goes especially well with the distinctive taste of corn tortillas, providing a fresh counterpunch to the roasted corn flavor. It is possible to find pico de gallo commercially, but because freshness is important to the taste and texture, a homemade batch is always a better option.

Sweet Potato Fries

Sweet potatoes belong to the morning glory family. Their vines are often used as decorative plants. The edible part of the plant is a not a true tuber, like a potato, but a storage root. At the market, sweet potatoes stand out with their orange-to-red skin, hinting at the beta-carotene within.

Sweet potatoes are often touted as the healthy alternative to potatoes, but that depends a great deal on how you prepare them. Boiled and mashed, they are low in calories and high in nutrients. Start adding butter or oil, however, and the calories will quickly add up. Oven roasting brings out the sweet potato's natural sugars. The "healthy" method calls for cutting the sweet potato into chunky chips or fries, tossing them in oil with garlic and other seasonings and spreading them on a baking sheet. In a very hot oven and turned halfway through the baking time, these fries cook in about half an hour.

For the ultimate indulgence, sweet potato fries can also be cut into strips and deep-fried. Enjoy either type of fries with a sour cream or mayonnaise dip, flavored with curry. You may never return to standard potato fries.

Baked Sweet Potato Fries

3 lb sweet potatoes

3 tbsp extra-virgin olive oil

1 tbsp coarse sea salt

1 tsp Spanish paprika (mild)

Preheat the oven to 450°F and place a baking sheet in the oven to warm. Peel and cut the sweet potatoes into $\frac{1}{2}$-inch sticks about 3 inches long. Toss with olive oil, salt, and paprika. Remove the baking sheet from oven. Spread the sweet potato fries in a single layer on the baking sheet and cook for 20 to 30 minutes, stirring gently every so often, until the fries are cooked through and browned.
Serves 6–8

Squash Flowers

Edible flowers of all sorts are turning up in the world's salad bowls, from nasturtiums to pansies. But the queen of edible flowers must be squash blossoms. The flowers are sold either on "baby" vegetables, which have just started to fill out, or on stems. They have a delicate flavor that hints of the fruit to come. In beautiful shades of yellow and orange, they are a special treat. As flowers, they are, of course, ephemeral, and only available for a short time, so they are somewhat of a luxury. Enjoy them while you can.

Once the pistils and stamens have been removed, the flowers are washed and gently patted dry. The French make *beignets de fleur de courgette* (zucchini flower fritters), dipped lightly in a batter of milk, flour, and eggs, and quickly deep-fried to a delicate crispness. The Italians, meanwhile, stuff and bake the flowers with a savory mixture of bread crumbs, ricotta, grated Parmesan, beaten egg, garlic, and fresh herbs.

Hobby gardeners always end up with too many zucchini in the fall. Perhaps it's time to encourage them to cull their crop early by offering to take a few flowers off their hands.

Zwiebelkuchen

When new grapes are pressed in the wine-growing regions of south-central Germany, it is time to make this traditional onion cake or pie. The fall treat is a rich accompaniment to *Federweisser*, a light and bubbly new wine still in the fermentation stage.

Zwiebelkuchen is a single-crust pie made with yeast. The uncooked base is filled with simple ingredients: sour cream, eggs, and a little flour for thickening added to a rich mixture of cooked bacon and lightly sautéed onions. The pie is then sprinkled generously with caraway seeds—a traditional aid to digestion—baked at a high temperature until golden, then sliced and served warm. If you are fortunate enough to be touring Swabia, Franconia, or Rheinessen in September or October, look for small family-run wineries offering *Federweisser* and Zwiebelkuchen for sale on the spot. Just remember, the light, sweet-tasting wine may be stronger than you think!

French Apricot Tart

This tart is known in France as *abricots à l'ancienne* and features fresh or dried apricot halves poached in sugar syrup. A slightly dry sponge cake is placed in a cake pan, then drenched with syrup laced with rum (as for rum baba). A layer of sweetened applesauce is spread on top, followed by the poached apricots and coarsely chopped slivered almonds.

The tart is drizzled with melted butter and baked in a hot oven until the almonds are browned, 10 to 15 minutes. It is served with a sauce of sieved apricot jam thinned with apricot liqueur or brandy.

In a simpler version, ripe apricots are arranged in a pie shell and sprinkled with sugar before baking. To prevent the crust from becoming soggy, sweetened cream cheese may be brushed on the pastry before the fruit is added.

Banana Split

This North American summer staple consists of a banana sliced in half lengthwise with three scoops of ice cream in between, drizzled with topping. It was apparently created in 1904, in a small town in the foothills of the Allegheny Mountains, by a trainee pharmacist named David Strickler. Those were the days when pharmacists also operated snack bars and ice-cream parlors.

While it may seem like a simple dessert, an entire book has been devoted to the subject: *The Banana Split Book: Everything There is to Know About America's Greatest Dessert* by Michael Turback.

The absolute classic split contains a scoop of vanilla ice cream drizzled with pineapple, a scoop of chocolate drizzled with chocolate syrup, and strawberry ice cream with strawberry topping. Oh, and don't forget the blizzard of chopped nuts, the dollop of whipped cream, and a maraschino cherry! It is often served in a special boat-shaped dish.

Banana Flambé

Bananas do not normally lend themselves to cooking as they can become mushy. The exception is banana flambé. The dish is said to have originated variously in the West Indies, the French Antilles, and in France. Since it is simplicity itself, it was probably thought up in all three places simultaneously!

The bananas are peeled and sliced in half lengthwise, then fried in melted butter. Some recipes advocate first cooking them in a vanilla-flavored sugar syrup, but this will make the bananas mushy.

The butter is drained from the pan, leaving the fruit to be sprinkled lightly with soft brown sugar. A tablespoon of rum warmed gently in a saucepan is poured over the bananas.

The liquor is set alight, preferably using a taper rather than a match as it tends to flare up suddenly. The bananas are kept on the heat, shaken lightly until the flames die down of their own accord. The bananas are then ready to eat.

When flambéing food, the alcohol should always be gently warmed beforehand or it cannot be set alight.

Angel Food Cake

This ethereal sponge cake, also known as angel cake, takes its name from its pure white color. It is baked in a special pan with deep sides and a central funnel, and must be inverted after baking to prevent it from collapsing. Angel cake may be of Pennsylvania Dutch origin, and is the ideal way to use up surplus egg whites, as most recipes require ten or more at room temperature. Since it requires a reliable oven, it must have been created after the 1870s. Some recipes contain baking powder, but most rely on a large quantity of egg white, stiffened with cream of tartar, to keep the cake light. Like all classic sponge cakes, angel cake contains no fat. The only other ingredients are sugar, flour, and vanilla extract.

Angel Food Cake

1 cup flour

1½ cups sugar

12 egg whites

½ tsp cream of tartar

2 tsp grated lemon rind

½ tsp vanilla extract

Berries to serve

Sift the flour and half the sugar into a bowl and set aside. Place the egg whites and cream of tartar in a bowl and beat until soft peaks form. Gradually add the remaining sugar to the egg whites and beat until the egg whites are thick and glossy. Fold the lemon rind, vanilla, and flour mixture into the egg whites. Pour the mixture into a non-greased 9-inch angel food cake pan and bake at 375°F for 30 minutes or until the cake is cooked when tested with a skewer. Invert the pan and allow the cake to cool. Run a knife around the edge of the pan to release the cake. Serve with mixed berries. *Serves 8*

Adapted from Donna Hay's *The New Cook*

Baked Cheesecake

The cheesecake is of central European origin and was brought to the English-speaking world by Jewish refugees between 1820 and 1920. It is made from cottage or cream cheese. Since the batter is very soft, it is added to a firm base. This often consists of crushed shortbread cookies or graham crackers mixed with butter or margarine, but can also be made from other cookies (such as gingersnaps) or crushed cereal.

Hungarian cheesecakes consist of a pastry base and lid with the cheese mixture sandwiched in between. The batter consists of four to six eggs, usually separated, as a cheesecake is raised with eggs rather than baking powder or yeast. The soft cheese may be replaced entirely with yogurt or sour cream and either of these may be added to the cheese mixture. The cake is usually flavored with lemon or vanilla but new flavors such as coffee, chocolate, and even savory smoked salmon are gaining popularity.

Cheesecakes are baked in a springform pan (with sides that can be loosened) because they are difficult to unmold from a standard cake pan. The cake is left to cool in the oven after baking to prevent it from sinking in the middle. America's most famous cheesecakes are baked by Lindy's and Junior's, both New York restaurant/bakeries.

Baked Cheesecake

1¼ cups graham cracker crumbs

¼ cup sugar

⅓ cup butter, melted

2 (8 oz) packages cream cheese, softened

1 (14 fl oz) can sweetened condensed milk

3 eggs

¼ cup lemon juice

Preheat the oven to 300°F.

Put the graham cracker crumbs and sugar in a large bowl and pour in the melted butter. Stir to combine well, then press the mixture into the bottom of a 9-inch springform cake pan.

In another large bowl, beat the cream cheese until fluffy. Add the condensed milk and beat until smooth. Add the eggs, one at a time, and the lemon juice, beating well after each addition. Pour the filling on top of the graham cracker base.

Bake the cheesecake for 50 to 55 minutes. It should be springy to the touch. Cool to room temperature and then keep in the refrigerator until ready to serve. *Serves 6*

Spumoni

This elaborate ice-cream cake, a specialty of Naples, is sold mainly in the winter though it is available year-round outside Italy, where it is known as "Neapolitan."

There are many variations, but it generally consists of bars of contrasting colors of ice cream occasionally lightened with whipped cream or beaten egg whites. A layer of whipped cream, flavored with rum or liqueur and laden with toasted nuts and candied fruit, is sandwiched between and around the striped ice cream and the whole refrozen inside an elaborate mold.

Other versions of spumoni are made in a bombe mold with the colored ice-cream layers surrounding a central core of sorbet. Spumoni is rarely made at home due to the elaborate preparation required.

When sold commercially, it is usually pre-sliced with waxed paper inserted between the slices.

Bakewell Tart

This rich, delicious tart hails from the picturesque Derbyshire village of Bakewell, where it was known as Bakewell pudding until the 20th century. It consists of a pastry crust spread with a layer of jam and filled with a thick egg and almond mixture. The tart is said to have been invented in the mid-19th century in the village of Bakewell when the cook at The White Horse Inn (now known as the Rutland Arms) accidentally put the jam in the bottom of a strawberry tart and the egg mixture on the top. This story is still touted by The Original Bakewell Pudding Shop, but there are records of a similar dessert dating from the Middle Ages. In some, the jam is replaced with mincemeat. All the leading British cookbook writers of the 1800s, including Mrs. Beeton, give recipes for Bakewell tart or pudding.

A modern commercial variation, known as a cherry Bakewell or Bakewell cake, tops the almond mixture with a thick layer of white icing garnished with a halved glacé cherry.

15 Apple Desserts

Amber pudding

Apple brown Betty

Apple Charlotte

Apple crumble

Apple dumpling

Apple flan

Apple fritters

Apple pandowdy

Apple pie

Apple snow

Apple strudel

Baked apple

Gâche malée (Guernsey apple gâche)

Swedish apple cake with vanilla sauce

Tarte Normande (French apple tart)

Apple Brown Betty

While nobody is quite sure who Betty is, both the United Kingdom and the United States claim the recipe, which appeared sometime after the mid-1800s. The ultimate fall comfort food, this simple dessert consists of sliced and sweetened apples layered in a buttered baking dish with cake or shortbread cookie crumbs and baked for about 45 minutes. There are many variations.

The British use Bramley apples, which tend to soften and break down during cooking, while Americans prefer varieties such as Gala or Golden Delicious, which stay firm. Health-conscious cooks may substitute rolled oats for the cookie crumbs, making the dish more of a crumble. The topping mixture is usually flavored with sweet spices such as cinnamon, allspice, and nutmeg.

Similar apple recipes alternating the fruit with a cake or grain mixture are known variously as crisp, crumble, slump, pandowdy, or cobbler.

Apple Brown Betty

3 tbsp unsalted butter

$3/4$ tsp cinnamon

$1/8$ tsp salt

1 tbsp light brown sugar, plus 2 tbsp

3 cups coarse fresh bread crumbs

4 large crisp apples such as Granny Smith or Gala

$1^1/4$ cups water

Preheat the oven to 375°F.

Melt the butter in a large nonstick frying pan and remove from the heat. Stir in the cinnamon, salt, and 1 tablespoon brown sugar, then stir in the bread crumbs. Sprinkle one-third of this mixture over the bottom of a 1-quart baking dish. Peel and coarsely chop 2 of the apples. Put in a large saucepan with the water and the remaining 2 tablespoons of brown sugar and cook, covered, over medium heat for 10 minutes, stirring occasionally. Purée the mixture in a blender and set aside.

Peel the remaining 2 apples and cut into wedges $1/4$-inch thick. Arrange the wedges over the crumbs, then pour the hot applesauce on top. Sprinkle with the remaining crumbs. Bake on the middle rack until the top is golden brown and the apples are tender, about 40 minutes.

Cool on a rack for 10 minutes before serving. *Serves 6*

Apple Fritters

While many fruits can be battered and deep-fried, apples are the clear favorite. The word "fritter" comes from the French *friture*, the batter used to deep-fry foods. Firm, tart varieties such as Granny Smith are sliced into rings and dipped into a thick batter of flour, eggs, milk, and a little sugar. They are then deep-fried in vegetable oil heated to 350°F. When cooked, the fritters are drained on paper towels and dusted with a mixture of sugar and cinnamon before serving. They may also be served with a raspberry or strawberry coulis, made by puréeing the fruit, straining it to remove the seeds, then adding a little powdered sugar.

In the north of England, apple fritters are served with wedges of cheese. Yorkshire fritters are a round yeast-raised variation, studded with currants, raisins, and grated apple. The cooked fritters are drained and served sprinkled with fine sugar and warm sherry.

In the US, apple fritters are more commonly known as a doughnut. The apples are chopped into small pieces and mixed into the dough. The dough is then formed into balls, deep-fried, and either glazed or sprinkled with powdered sugar.

Apple Strudel

This beloved dessert is associated mainly with Austria but is enjoyed throughout Eastern and central Europe. In the United Kingdom and the United States, it is often associated with the large Jewish immigration from central Europe, which began in the late 19th century and lasted until the end of the Second World War.

Thinly sliced apples are tossed with sugar, cinnamon, and bread crumbs—some cooks add nuts, raisins, and lemon rind. The filling is rolled up in a log of paper-thin phyllo pastry like a jelly roll and baked. The results are always crisp and delicious.

Apple Turnover

Turnovers are baked in many countries under different names. They are known as *calzone* in Italian and *chausson* in French. The English call them pasties or puffs. They consist of rounds of dough folded over a precooked filling. The edges are sealed with water or an egg wash to ensure that no filling escapes.

While most countries fill turnovers with a savory mixture, in Britain, France, and the US a stewed, spiced apple filling is traditional. The British prefer regular piecrust dough while the French make their *chausson* with puff pastry. The latter are glazed with honey or jam before baking, and the result is roughly triangular in shape. The English apple turnover is more rounded and usually glazed with egg wash. Both are baked for about 40 minutes in a hot oven or deep-fried in oil.

It is easy to see why turnovers are a popular way to make a pie as they do not require a special dish or even an oven, but can be baked on a griddle or browned in a frying pan.

Apple Pie

The expression "as American as apple pie" is misleading, as apples are not native to the US. Since arriving with white settlers in 1620, however, apple pie encased in a golden crust has held pride of place in the hearts and stomachs of North American dessert lovers.

The first English recipe for apple pie appears in *A forme of Curye*, compiled around 1390 by the cooks to King Richard II. Since sugar was rare and expensive at that time, figs and raisins sweetened the apples.

Variations on the traditional deep-dish, double-crusted pie include those with a lattice crust, a crumbly German-style streusel topping, or no top crust at all, as in the glamorous *tarte Normande* from France, made by arranging firm apple slices in overlapping circles and brushing them with glaze before baking.

The choice of apples for pie is a personal one. Macintosh apples are popular, as they break down during cooking, but some cooks prefer firmer apples, such as Northern Spy or Gala, which keep their shape.

Most apple pies contain sweet spices, especially cinnamon. Several traditional English recipes add chopped candied peel, raisins, and almonds, while others add berries (such as blackberries), pumpkin, and even tomatoes. Quince and apple pie is another variation, with the quince precooked until tender.

Baked Apple

This is the simplest of desserts, made with cooking apples such as Granny Smith, Northern Spy, or Golden Delicious. The apples are cored, without peeling, and placed on a baking dish in which a little liquid may be added, perhaps fruit juice or even ginger beer. The center is filled with raisins, candied peel, and sweet spices, then drizzled with honey or sprinkled with sugar. Filled apples are baked at 350°F until extremely tender.

The skin ensures that the apples keep their shape. They can also be cooked in the microwave, for 4 to 5 minutes, depending on the power of the oven. Encased in pie dough, the same recipe becomes an apple dumpling. Apples can also be enclosed in flaky pastry or even phyllo sheets before baking.

Baked Apples

4 large tart apples

$1/2$ cup brown sugar

$1/4$ cup butter

$1/4$ cup raisins

2 tsp ground cinnamon

Preheat the oven to 350°F.

Scoop out the core through the top of each apple, leaving a hole. Do not cut all the way through. Mash the brown sugar with the butter, add the raisins, and stuff each apple with 2 tablespoons of the mixture. Put the apples in a shallow baking dish and sprinkle with cinnamon. Bake for 30 minutes, until the sugar begins to caramelize and the apples are very tender. *Serves 4*

Mincemeat Pie

This traditional English fare for Christmas and New Year takes the form of a large tart or dainty tartlet of pastry filled with mincemeat —without the meat. Today's mincemeat consists of currants, raisins, sultanas, apple, and candied fruits, all chopped finely and laced with brandy, rum, and Madeira. It may also contain suet (kidney fat), which is optional in these heart-healthy times. The top crust is sometimes topped with a pastry cut-out to represent the Star of Bethlehem.

The original mince pie, which had its heyday in 16th-century England, consisted of a huge pie filled with ox tongue, hard-boiled eggs, liver, and chicken plus sugar, lemon peel, dried fruits, and spices.

As tastes changed and the mixing of savory and sweet flavors became unpopular, the meat and eggs were eliminated. In Victorian times, and even today, some ground meat may still be added to the mixture. Mincemeat filling can be made well in advance and stored in jars as a preserve.

Christmas Pudding

This is probably the only suet pudding still consumed extensively. It is made with flour and chopped suet (kidney fat) to which almonds, raisins, currants, glacé cherries, and brandy are added. On Christmas Day, the pudding is steamed in a pudding cloth or basin for several hours, although modern versions are even cooked in a microwave oven. Traditionally, silver sixpences and other trinkets are baked into the pudding to surprise the guests. Before being brought to the table, it is decorated with sprigs of holly.

Christmas pudding is served with hard sauce—a mixture of butter, sugar, and brandy—or a brandy-flavored white sauce. A tablespoon of brandy is warmed, then poured over the pudding and set alight, the blue flames making an attractive contrast to the glistening brown pudding.

Christmas pudding was once known as "plum pudding" due to its high fruit content. In 1664, it was banned by the Puritans in an attempt to suppress Christmas celebrations. King George I reinstated it as part of the Christmas feast in 1714. Though Christmas pudding is not eaten in Scotland, a version of the mixture, wrapped in pastry and known as "black bun," is eaten for Hogmanay, the last day of the year.

Banoffee Pie

The name of this decadent dessert is the clue to its contents—bananas and toffee. However, it is not toffee at all, but caramelized milk, which can be created in several ways; the easiest is to boil condensed milk in the can for 3 to 5 hours.

Banoffee's creation is claimed by a chef named Ian Dowding, who invented it in 1974 (as a variation on an American dish) at a restaurant in East Sussex called The Hungry Monk. It was published in the book entitled *Secrets of the Hungry Monk*.

Though variations have sprung up, basically the pie consists of a layer of crushed chocolate cookie crumbs topped with boiled condensed milk. While cooking the can of milk, you must ensure that the water around it does not evaporate or the can will explode.

A less dangerous method is simply to use ready-made Mexican *dulce de leche*. Indian sweet shops sell a similar concoction. The toffee layer is covered in sliced bananas and the whole generously coated in whipped cream. Easy to make at home and utterly delicious!

Blancmange

This classic dessert, which seems to have gone out of fashion, has ancient ties to England, and was even mentioned by Geoffrey Chaucer (1343–1400) in the prologue to *The Canterbury Tales*. Though the name means "white food" in French, pink appears to be the preferred color today, achieved with a drop of red food coloring.

In the Middle Ages, blancmange was even more gaudy, decorated and flavored with saffron, sandalwood, and gold leaf. The dish almost certainly originated in the Middle East (though similar milk puddings are known all over northern Europe) as it originally included rice and cow's milk or almond milk (the latter being less likely to sour), sugar, and flavorings such as cinnamon and rosewater. The original blancmange recipe may also have included finely shredded chicken or game meat, even fish. A similar dish known as *tabuk gogsu kazandibi* is still eaten in Turkey.

At some point, blancmange earned a reputation as a suitable food for invalids, one that persisted well into the early 20th century, though the meat or fish was omitted after the 17th century. The pudding was originally thickened with arrowroot or sago, replaced in the late 19th century by cornstarch and eventually gelatin.

Lemon Meringue Pie

The crust for this tart classic is usually a basic pastry or crumb crust made from cookie crumbs combined with melted butter. The pie is filled with a layer of sharp lemon curd and topped with meringue. It was invented in the United States, though it is now equally popular in the United Kingdom. The Quakers can take credit for inventing a lemon curd pie in the late 18th century but Elizabeth Coane Goodfellow, a pastry chef and founder of the Philadelphia Cooking School in 1806, turned the lemon pie into a classic when she replaced the pastry lid with a fluffy meringue topping. No doubt the idea came about because the lemon base uses up to five egg yolks, and there was nothing much else to do with the whites. Citric acid may be added to the lemon filling to make the flavor a stronger contrast to the sweet meringue.

In California, lemon meringue pie is often served at Thanksgiving instead of the traditional pumpkin pie, as it better represents the local harvest.

Lemon Posset

Linzertorte

A posset belongs to the family of English desserts known as syllabubs, in which cream is the main ingredient. It dates back to at least the Middle Ages. Cream or milk is whisked with a contrasting flavor, in this case lemon, along with white wine or ale, beaten egg whites, and sugar. Originally, the syllabub was made with fresh milk straight from the cow. This produced a semi-liquid posset, considered suitable food for invalids and the elderly. Special pots with lids were designed for drinking the posset, many of which are very elaborate and were displayed with the family china. Tall versions date from the 1400s and are usually made of pottery or porcelain. The froth from whisking rose to the top of the pot. The spout allowed drinkers to suck the liquid from below while the lid kept the posset warm.

This luscious tart takes its name from the Austrian town of Linz and is reputed to be the oldest pie or cake recipe in the world, dating from 1696. The recipe itself can be found in the Vienna State Library. The modern linzertorte begins with a sweet piecrust mixed with ground almonds and hazelnuts, flavored with lemon and cinnamon, and fitted into a shallow tart pan. The pastry is spread with raspberry jam and topped with a lattice made from the reserved dough. The top is brushed with a glaze of sieved, thinned apricot jam. Early recipes contained much more butter, the pie was baked in a silver bowl, and it was filled with stewed fruit instead of jam.

Lemon Posset

3 cups heavy cream

1¼ cups sugar

Juice of 3 lemons

3 tbsp heavy cream for topping

In a saucepan, stir together the cream and the sugar. Bring to a boil and cook for 2 to 3 minutes, until the sugar is dissolved. Stir in the lemon juice. Pour into serving glasses and refrigerate until set, about 5 hours. Just before serving, pour a little more cream over the top of each glass. *Serves 4*

Summer Pudding

This popular English dessert is made in a bowl or mold lined with slices of stale, crustless bread and filled with a mixture of berries. Black currants, blackberries, blueberries, raspberries, and strawberries may all be used, along with stewed fruit. The mixture is then sealed in with more bread slices and covered with a tight-fitting lid. It is then steamed or oven-baked in a *bain-marie* (a tray of warm water). The pudding is cooled, refrigerated until set, and unmolded onto a plate. The rich red color is enhanced by a garnish of whipped cream or vanilla ice cream. Summer pudding was once called "hydropathic pudding" and served at spas, since it was considered a light alternative to traditional suet pudding. In the 1700s, Dr. Samuel Johnson mentions a rhubarb version layered with bread dough and cooked in a bowl. Wakefield pudding is similar, but consists only of rhubarb and gooseberries inside a bread-lined bowl. The name summer pudding did not come into use until the early 20th century.

Summer Pudding

3 to 4 cups prepared fruit (black currants, blueberries, gooseberries, mulberries, strawberries, raspberries, red currants, rhubarb)

$^1/_3$ cup water

$^1/_2$ cup sugar

6 to 8 large slices bread, crusts removed

Stew the fruits gently in the water and sugar until they are soft but retain their shape. Remove from the heat and allow to cool slightly. Cut a circle of bread to fit the base of a 1-quart ceramic bowl and line the sides, overlapping the bread slightly.

Carefully pour the fruit into the prepared bowl, reserving 3 tablespoons of the liquid. Shake the bowl slightly to ensure the fruit fills it evenly. Cut the remaining bread to form a lid and cover the fruit. Cover with foil, then place a plate on top that just fits inside the bowl. Place a weight on top of the plate. Allow to cool, then refrigerate overnight. Run a knife around the edge of the bowl before turning the pudding out to serve. Serve with cream, if desired. *Serves 8*

Steamed Treacle Pudding

This sweet dessert is also known as "Rochester pudding" and even "patriotic pudding." The latter name dates from the time of the Continental blockade imposed by Britain on imports from Europe during the Napoleonic Wars in the early 19th century, since all the ingredients came from the colonies.

It is made with self-rising flour, butter, sugar, an egg, and milk. The batter is sweetened with corn syrup or black strap molasses, then transferred to a greased metal or china bowl and steamed for up to 2 hours. It is then unmolded and served with warmed corn syrup or custard.

A modern commercial version is sold in its own plastic pudding basin and cooks in just a few minutes in the microwave.

In one variation, marmalade replaces the treacle and the sauce is made of warmed marmalade. Yet another variation is the Scottish "urney pudding": red jam replaces the treacle and is folded into the mixture to give the finished sponge a marbled effect.

Shoofly Pie

This pie is typical of the Amish (Pennsylvania Dutch) community centered in Lancaster, Pennsylvania. Since this devout Protestant community eschews modernity, home cooking is still very much in vogue and the pie is a popular dessert.

Shoofly pie is the Amish version of a treacle tart. It is made with molasses and there are wet or dry versions depending on the thickness of the filling. The pie filling, consisting of molasses mixed with egg, baking soda, and water, is poured into a prebaked shell and sprinkled with a mixture of flour, butter, and brown sugar. The pie is baked on high heat then lowered to medium to simulate the cooling of the bread ovens in which the pies were originally baked. Some "modernists" pour a chocolate topping over the filling.

Shoofly pies can be bought ready-made from Amish bakers. The name may derive from shooing flies away from the pie, while another theory claims it is a corruption of the French "choux-fleur," because the pie's lumpy surface resembles a cauliflower.

Divinity

Also known as "divinity candy" or "divinity fudge," this sweet is a cross between fudge and marshmallow: a fudge mixture is combined with egg whites beaten with sugar. The history of divinity is not clear, although it probably emerged in the US at the same time as fudge, in the late 19th or early 20th century. It was customary at the time to exchange recipes between friends and families, so it spread very fast.

The name implies that it tasted divine and some may associate the food with southern cooking, because it is the sort of name that might appeal in the Bible Belt. It is unlikely to be exclusively Southern in origin, however, because recipes for divinity appeared all over the United States at around the same time. There is even a record of one in the *New York Times*.

That divinity is American is indisputable, because the recipe uses corn syrup—an essential ingredient that was available only in the United States until recently. Although now made commercially, the candy is very much a home-cooked food, which explains why recipes for divinity feature in so many Junior League and other community cookbooks.

Mississippi Mud Pie

As its name suggests, this incredibly rich pie is a favorite in the southern US—in fact, it is the state food of Mississippi. The dense layered cake gets its name from the color of the brown mud of the Mississippi Delta. The pie is actually more like a cake since it has no top crust and is usually baked in a cake pan. It consists of a white cream cheese layer, followed by a chocolate custard layer, and a rum custard or sweetened cream cheese layer. It may be decorated with whipped cream and chocolate shavings.

It is thought that the Mississippi mud pie was conceived after the Second World War because the ingredients were easy to find and no complex utensils were necessary. The crust is often made from crushed graham crackers or chocolate cookies mixed with butter. The custard layer can be made from an instant chocolate pudding mix.

Chess Pie

The name of this classic American pie, popular in the southern states, is a corruption of the word "cheese," though it does not contain any cheese. Without a top crust, it resembles a tart. Chess pie is a variation on the traditional British custard pie. The type of filling used, containing milk, eggs, sugar, and buttermilk or cream, was typical of the "cheesecakes" of the 18th and 19th centuries, which contained no cheese but had the consistency of a soft cheese (slightly firmer than custard). Flour was added to firm the texture; this has been replaced by cornstarch. According to the *Oxford Encyclopedia of Food and Drink in America*, the earliest reference to a chess pie in America dates from 1866.

Chess pies of the past were flavored with lemon, vanilla, and even vinegar. Today, they can also be flavored with chocolate. Chess pie is one of the recipes in the classic 19th-century cookbook *The Virginia House-Wife* by Mary Randolph.

Cherry Pie

Cherry pie can be enjoyed year-round thanks to the availability of canned and frozen cherries. The cherries should be ripe and preferably of the Morello or Bing varieties, which are juicier than the pale red-and-yellow Rainier variety. Cherries for a pie should always be pitted; a stainless steel pitter can be bought in good cookware stores, or you can use a tool made for pitting olives.

The cherries are first cooked on gentle heat until soft, which makes it easier to remove the pits. The juice is strained, then a little of it is mixed with cornstarch, arrowroot, or potato flour, returned to the heat and stirred until thickened. The cherries and thickened juice are then combined and left to cool while the pastry is made and rolled out thinly to line a pie plate.

The filling is added and covered with the top crust. A funnel or slits in the crust will draw off steam. The pie is brushed with glaze and baked in a hot oven for 40 minutes or until golden brown.

Chocolate Mousse

This dessert is simplicity itself to make and is thus a dinner party favorite. When served in individual ramekins or coffee cups, it is called *petit pots de chocolat*—little chocolate pots. Only the finest ingredients are used, such as a bittersweet chocolate with a high percentage of cocoa butter. In some recipes the chocolate is melted (try the defrost setting on a microwave oven), then mixed over gentle heat with sugar, vanilla extract, and egg yolks. The egg whites are whipped separately into stiff peaks with more sugar. The chocolate mixture is then folded into the beaten egg whites and the mixture transferred to a soufflé dish or individual ramekins and chilled for at least two hours. Since the eggs are barely cooked, chocolate mousse went out of fashion during the salmonella scare in the 1990s, but it is regaining popularity. In some newer recipes, the eggs are cooked sufficiently to avoid salmonella and whipped cream is used to give the mousse an airy texture.

Like similar dishes, it originated in the late 19th century when better kitchen equipment, such as metal whisks, made it possible to whip egg whites to stiff peaks.

A new variation is the chocolate mousse cake, often found on restaurant menus.

Chocolate Mousse

2 cups heavy cream, chilled

4 egg yolks

3 tbsp sugar

A pinch of salt

1 tsp vanilla extract

7 oz bittersweet chocolate (not unsweetened), chopped

Heat ¾ cup of the cream in a heavy saucepan until hot. Remove from the heat. Whisk together the yolks, sugar, and salt in a metal bowl until combined well, then add the hot cream in a slow stream, whisking until combined. Transfer the mixture to the saucepan and cook over moderately low heat, stirring constantly, until it registers 160°F on a candy thermometer. Pour the custard through a fine-mesh sieve into a bowl and stir in the vanilla. Meanwhile, melt the chocolate in a double boiler or a metal bowl set over a pan of simmering water, stirring frequently. Whisk the custard into the chocolate until smooth. Beat the remaining 1¼ cups cream in a bowl with an electric mixer until it just forms stiff peaks. Whisk a quarter of the cream into the cooled chocolate custard to lighten it, then fold in the remaining cream gently but thoroughly. Spoon the mousse into 8 ramekins and chill, covered, for at least 6 hours. Let stand at room temperature for about 20 minutes before serving. *Serves 8*

Chocolate Fondue

Coconut Barfi

This gloriously rich dessert requires only a fondue pot filled with good-quality chocolate broken into pieces. The pot is heated over a small burner placed in the middle of the table. Guests are provided with dipping sticks (cocktail sticks or wooden kebab skewers) and a selection of sliced fresh fruits such as banana, kiwi, orange segments, pineapple chunks, or strawberries. Everyone skewers a piece of fruit on their stick and dips it into the bubbling chocolate. One must be careful not to burn one's mouth on the hot chocolate. Other dipping ingredients may include cookies, marshmallows, and coconut macaroons.

The latest variation on chocolate fondue is the chocolate fountain, a big hit at parties and weddings, which lets guests dip their fruit into a continuous cascade of melted chocolate. The fountain can be rented or purchased outright. The chocolate used to "fuel" it comes in buttons known as *callets* which contain a high proportion of cocoa butter for easy melting and pouring.

Barfi, or burfi, is a soft Indian sweet with a texture similar to fudge. The main ingredient is *khoya*, made by reducing fresh milk to a thick paste by continuous stirring over low heat. Fortunately, ready-made *khoya* is also available, or you can boil a can of condensed milk in water as for banoffee pie. To make nariyal burfi, the *khoya* is mixed with grated or shredded coconut and fried in ghee (clarified butter) on low heat. Sweet spices are added, such as cardamom, cinnamon, and nutmeg, and the mixture is combined with sugar syrup. When smooth, the mixture is poured into a tray of chopped or grated mixed nuts, scored into squares or diamonds, and left to set. It may be decorated with gold and silver leaf for special occasions.

There are many flavors of barfi, such as pistachio and besan or garbanzo. Barfi is not always square. Pink and white chum-chum barfi, for example, is shaped like a small cylinder. This delectable sweet is popular throughout India and is traditionally eaten at festivals, especially Holi.

Clafouti

This French custard comes from the Limousin region of south-central France, its name derived from a local Occitane word meaning "to fill." It consists of a rich, thick pancake-type batter of flour, sugar, eggs, and milk poured over sweetened cherries. Although the fruit is arranged in the buttered pie plate or flan pan before the batter, it rises to the surface while baking. The dessert should be cooled to lukewarm and dusted with powdered sugar before serving. The cherries should be the juicy, dark variety typical of the region.

Clafouti can also be made with other fruit, such as plums, prunes, apples, and berries, in which case the dish is known as *flognarde* or *flaugnarde*.

Clafouti

3 cups pitted black cherries

1¼ cups milk

⅔ cup granulated sugar

3 eggs

1 tbsp vanilla extract

⅛ tsp salt

½ cup flour*

Powdered sugar, for dusting

* When measuring the flour, scoop the dry-measure cup directly into your flour container and fill the cup to overflowing; do not shake the cup or pack down the flour. Sweep off excess so that the flour is even with the lip of the cup, using a straight edge of some sort. Sift only after measuring.

Preheat the oven to 350°F. Place the milk, ⅓ cup sugar, the eggs, vanilla extract, salt, and flour in a blender and blend for 1 minute. Pour a ¼-inch layer of batter into a 7- to 8-cup capacity, 1½-inch deep, fireproof baking dish. Set over moderate heat for a minute or two until a firm batter has set in the bottom of the dish. Remove from the heat. Spread the cherries over the batter and sprinkle on the remaining sugar. Pour on the rest of the batter and smooth the surface with the back of a spoon. Place in the middle of the preheated oven and bake for about an hour.

The clafouti is done when it has puffed and browned, and a knife plunged into its center comes out clean. Sprinkle the top with powdered sugar just before bringing it to the table. *Serves 6–8*

Adapted from Julia Child, Louisette Bertholle, and Simone Beck *Mastering the Art of French Cooking*

Cranachan

This traditional Scottish dessert is made from the pure ingredients for which Scotland is famous—cream, whisky, honey, berries, and oatmeal. The oatmeal is toasted, mixed with whipped cream, and flavored with heather honey and Scotch whisky. Blackberries or raspberries are added. When the Scottish cream cheese known as "crowdie" is added, the dish is called cream crowdie.

Cranachan was once a harvest treat, but it is now eaten year-round, particularly at special occasions such as weddings. Bowls of each ingredient are traditionally brought to the table so that guests can serve themselves.

It may also be served in a tall glass. Another variation is ale crowdie, in which ale is added to the cream and the honey is replaced with treacle or corn syrup. When a ring is placed in the mixture, whoever finds it will be the next to marry.

Cranachan

1 cup rolled oats

1 cup heavy cream

1½ cups fresh raspberries

1 tsp Drambuie

Toast the oatmeal in a frying pan over high heat until lightly brown. Let cool. Whisk the cream until soft peaks form and stir in the toasted oatmeal, raspberries, and Drambuie. Spoon into glass dishes to serve. *Serves 4*

Ambrosia

Almost unknown outside North America, this dessert is named for the food of the Greek gods. It varies in its ingredients, though it always contains miniature marshmallows, fruit, and chopped nuts and is usually topped with strands of sweet shredded coconut. Peaches, pears, and canned pineapple chunks are popular ingredients, as are chopped apple and sliced banana. The base is usually made from instant pudding, sweetened sour cream, or whipped topping.

The basic ingredients, minus the coconut, are combined and refrigerated for a few hours or overnight to blend the flavors. Coconut is added at the last minute, and the dish may be sprinkled with cinnamon.

This mixture may also be served on lettuce leaves as an appetizer or side dish. Though you won't find ambrosia on the menu in a fancy restaurant, it is nevertheless extremely tasty and an excellent choice for a homemade dessert at a dinner party.

Eaton Mess

Custard Tart

This rather unappetizing-sounding dessert hails from Eton College, the United Kingdom's most prestigious boys' school, which includes members of the Royal Family among its graduates. The "mess" of strawberries and bananas mixed with ice cream or whipped cream was first served in the school's candy shop in the 1930s. Meringue was a later addition. It then became popular at award ceremonies, laced with generous amounts of alcohol to put the parents in a good mood. The name "mess" derives from the fact that all the ingredients are stirred together. Chocolate mousse is included today, and the whipped cream is sweetened and colored with a liqueur such as cherry brandy.

For special occasions, Eton mess is often presented with an extra topping of sliced strawberries and sweetened whipped cream. It remains a favorite British dessert, no doubt because it is so easy to make and assemble, and tastes delicious.

The custard tart is an English classic with many variations. It may have emerged in the Middle Ages. A pie plate or flan tin is lined with pastry then blind-baked (baked before the filling is added) for about 15 minutes in a fairly hot oven. This step firms up the pastry so that the liquid filling does not make it soggy during baking. The custard ingredients —eggs, milk or cream, sugar, and flour or cornstarch—are sometimes cooked together until the custard begins to thicken. In other recipes, they are merely combined and left to thicken and solidify in the oven.

The filled tart is dusted with nutmeg and baked in a moderate oven for about 20 minutes or until set and the pastry is golden brown. Individual custard tarts can be made in tartlet pans.

Coeur à la Crème

Sweetened cream cheese made in a special
heart-shaped mold is an obvious favorite
for Valentine's Day. The mold is pierced with
holes to allow the whey to escape and the
cheese mixture to firm up. One large mold or
individual molds may be used. Cheesecloth is
required to line the molds. To make the coeur,
cream cheese is softened with sour cream
or thick yogurt and sweetened with vanilla
and powdered sugar. A little lemon juice and
a pinch of salt are beaten into the mixture,
which is then strained through a sieve. The
cheesecloth should be large enough to hang
over the edges and cover the top of the
filled molds. The hearts are refrigerated on
a cake rack placed in a tray to catch the
whey as it drips.

Candied fruit can be beaten into the
mixture before chilling, making it similar to
the Russian *paskha* dessert eaten at Easter.
The coeur can also be topped with fresh fruit
before serving. It keeps well in the refrigerator
for several days.

Crème Caramel ▷

This favorite dinner party and restaurant
dessert is also known as egg custard or
caramel custard. A mixture of eggs, sugar,
vanilla, and milk or cream is cooked until
it begins to thicken, then poured into a
large mold or individual ramekins coated
with a caramelized sugar syrup. The custard
or custards are then baked in a *bain-marie*
(a tray half-filled with water) in a fairly hot
oven for about 30 minutes. When cooled
completely, they are chilled until firm. Just
before serving, the mold or ramekins are
overturned on a dish and heat is applied
in the form of a damp cloth rinsed in hot
water. The custard should unmold whole,
surrounded by a layer of liquid caramel.
This dessert is extremely popular in Spanish-
speaking countries and in the Philippines,
where it is known as *flan*. In these countries
it is often flavored with coconut.

Crème caramel probably originated in
southwestern France and the Catalonia region
of Spain since both Toulouse in France and
Vitoria in Spain claim it as a specialty.

Crêpes with Nutella

Crêpes or French pancakes are a feature of
Brittany and other parts of northern France.
The batter, consisting of flour, eggs, and milk,
should be the texture of thick cream. It
should always be allowed to rest for at least
20 minutes after beating, to allow the gluten
to relax so the pancake will not be tough and
leathery. Crêpes should be made on a griddle
or in a crêpe or omelette pan, a small, flat
frying pan just large enough for one crêpe.

A little butter is melted in the pan until
hot but not browned, then the batter is
added and swirled until it covers the base
completely. The trick to making crêpes is
to add just the right amount of batter to
the pan—not too much and not too little.

Nutella is a scrumptious spread of ground
hazelnuts and chocolate. It was invented
by Pietro Ferrero, who founded the Ferrero
company in the 1940s in Piedmont, Italy.
He wanted to make a chocolate cream, but
chocolate was in short supply due to the war
so he added hazelnuts, which are plentiful
in the region. Nutella is delicious spread on
warm or cold crêpes.

Crêpes Suzette

This is the epitome of the fancy French dessert
—thin pancakes soaked in a sweet, warm
orange-butter sauce and set alight with
liqueur. Several French chefs claim to have
invented the dish in the late 19th century.
Foremost among them is Henri Charpentier,
who claimed in his memoirs to have served
them to England's Prince of Wales (later
Edward VII) at the Café de Paris in Monte
Carlo. The prince's companion was apparently
named Suzette. The crêpes are traditionally
soaked in a sauce of butter, sugar, fresh
orange juice, grated orange zest, and an
orange liqueur such as Grand Marnier.

Before serving, they are folded into
quarters and set alight with more liqueur.

Croquembouche

Translated as "crunch in the mouth," this cone-shaped tower of small, filled cream puffs is reserved for festive occasions. The choux paste for the puffs is made by bringing water, milk, and butter to a boil. Flour is added all at once and the mixture is beaten vigorously until it comes away from the sides of the saucepan. It is then ready to shape into puffs, also known as *profiteroles*, and baked. The baked puffs are filled with pastry cream and dipped in sugar syrup cooked to the hard-crack stage (300°F to 310°F). This "glue" holds the balls together as they're arranged around an 18-inch cone shape. Candied fruit and sugared almonds are often inserted between the choux balls, and the whole tower is covered in spun sugar.

Other decorations may include chocolate, flowers, and ribbons. The French serve croquembouche at family occasions such as christenings, first communions, and particularly at weddings, where each guest gets one or more of the filled puffs.

Croquembouche

For the pastry cream:

⅔ cup sugar

⅓ cup all-purpose flour

2 cups whole milk

4 egg yolks

5 oz bittersweet or semisweet chocolate, finely chopped

For the cream puffs:

½ cup water

¼ cup whole milk

¼ cup unsalted butter

2 tbsp sugar

½ tsp salt

¾ cup all-purpose flour, plus 2 tbsp

2 tbsp unsweetened cocoa powder

4 eggs

For the glaze:

10 oz bittersweet or semisweet chocolate, chopped

This simplified version uses chocolate to "glue" the choux-paste balls together and creates individual desserts rather than one tall cone.

Whisk the sugar and flour in a heavy medium saucepan to blend. Gradually whisk in the milk, then the egg yolks. Whisking constantly, cook over medium heat until the cream thickens and boils, about 10 minutes. Remove from the heat. Whisk in the chocolate until it is melted and smooth. Transfer to a medium bowl and press plastic wrap on the surface. Chill the pastry cream until cold and firm, at least 3 hours and up to 2 days.

Preheat the oven to 375°F. Line 2 large baking sheets with parchment paper. Combine the water, milk, butter, sugar, and salt in a medium saucepan. Bring to a boil, whisking until the sugar dissolves and the butter melts. Remove from the heat. Add the flour and cocoa all at once; whisk until smooth and blended and the dough forms a ball. Continue stirring over low heat until the paste leaves a film on the bottom of the pan, about 2 minutes. Transfer the paste to a large mixing bowl and cool to lukewarm, about 8 minutes.

Using an electric mixer, beat in the eggs one at a time. Drop the batter by teaspoonfuls onto the prepared baking sheets to make at least 64 scant 1-inch mounds. With moistened fingertips, smooth any pointed tips. Bake the puffs for 20 minutes, then reduce the heat to 350°F and continue baking until the puffs are firm and beginning to crack and dry on top, about 23 minutes longer. Transfer the puffs to a rack. Using a small knife or chopstick, poke a hole in the side of each puff near the bottom to allow steam to escape. Cool the puffs completely. Spoon the pastry cream into a pastry bag fitted with a ¼-inch plain round tip and pipe a little through the hole in the side of each puff.

For the glaze, put the chocolate in a small microwave-safe dish and microwave on high at 15-second intervals just until it begins to melt. Remove from the microwave and stir until completely melted and smooth.

Dip the bottom of 4 filled cream puffs into the glaze. Arrange the puffs about ¼-inch apart in a square on plate. Dip the bottom of 3 more puffs in the glaze and arrange in a triangle on top of the first 4 puffs, pressing down slightly so the chocolate holds the puffs in place. Dip the bottom of 1 more puff into the glaze and place on top. Drizzle the mound of puffs with some of the glaze. Repeat with the remaining cream puffs to form 8 desserts. Refrigerate until the glaze sets and holds the puffs together, at least 1 hour and up to 1 day. *Serves 8*

Jam Roly-Poly

Many English people associate this comforting dessert with school, where it was often served. The pastry, traditionally made of suet, flour, lemon juice and zest, an egg, and sugar, is rolled out flat then spread with jam (raspberry, strawberry, blackberry, or blackcurrant) and rolled up from the short side. It is wrapped in plastic wrap and in aluminum foil to retain its shape when steamed for several hours. The roll can also be brushed with an egg wash and baked in a moderate oven for 45 minutes or until browned. Crisp on the outside and oozing with jam inside, it is always served with custard made from custard powder. This satisfying dessert was once known as "shirtsleeve pudding" because a shirtsleeve was considered the most suitable cloth in which to steam it.

The jam roly-poly had its heyday from the 1850s to the 1950s, when winters were cold and heating sparse. Mrs. Beeton's *Household Management*, first published in 1861, contains a recipe for Roly-Poly Jam Pudding.

Chocolate Lava Cake

When a diner cuts into this decadent flourless chocolate cake, chocolate oozes out of it like molten lava. The liquid center can be achieved by placing a ball of ganache (chocolate truffle) in the middle of the sponge batter, which melts as the cake bakes. The cake can also be made by simply melting butter and chocolate together, whisking in eggs (which may be separated) and sugar to a thick paste, and baking for a short time.

Famous New York chef Jean-Georges Vongerichten claims to have invented the molten chocolate cake in 1987 when he pulled a chocolate sponge cake out of the oven before it was done. The dish is now popular in high-end restaurants. Lava cakes are usually baked in individual molds and served with vanilla ice cream and a rich chocolate sauce.

Marshmallows

These soft, fluffy sweets, occasionally coated with toasted, dessicated coconut, were originally thickened with the root of the pink-flowered plant known as marsh mallow or common mallow, and may date back to ancient Egypt. Since the marsh mallow has healing properties, 19th-century doctors prescribed it mixed with sugar and egg white to soothe coughs. The modern marshmallow consists of corn syrup, sugar, and egg whites beaten until fluffy then cooked and thickened with gelatin.

Marshmallows are popular all over the English-speaking world, and the miniature version may be found sprinkled on hot cocoa. Marshmallows roasted on the end of a stick in the flames of an outdoor fire are a popular treat at summer camp. In the 19th and early 20th century, marshmallows were promoted as a substitute for whipped cream.

Americans still use them to top soft creamy pies such as sweet potato pie and pumpkin pie, for which recipes appeared in the early 1930s.

Marshmallows

3 packages unflavored gelatin

$^1/_2$ cup water, plus $^1/_2$ cup

$1^1/_2$ cups sugar

1 cup light corn syrup

$^1/_4$ tsp salt

1 tbsp vanilla extract

Powdered sugar for dusting

$1^1/_4$ cups water

Combine the gelatin and $^1/_2$ cup of the cold water in the bowl of an electric mixer fitted with the whisk attachment and let it sit while you make the syrup.

In a small saucepan, combine the sugar, corn syrup, salt, and remaining $^1/_2$ cup water and cook over medium heat until the sugar dissolves. Raise the heat to high and cook until the syrup reaches 240°F on a candy thermometer. Remove from the heat.

With the mixer on low speed, slowly pour the hot sugar syrup into the dissolved gelatin. Put the mixer on high speed and whip until the mixture is very thick, about 15 minutes. Add the vanilla and mix thoroughly.

With a fine mesh sieve, generously dust an 8- × 12-inch non-metal baking dish with powdered sugar. Pour the marshmallow mixture into the pan, smooth the top, and dust with more powdered sugar. Allow to stand uncovered overnight until it dries out.

Turn the marshmallows onto a board and cut them in squares. Dust with more powdered sugar. *Makes about 96 pieces*

Crème Brûlée

This classic dessert superseded chocolate mousse as the ultimate dinner party dessert of the 1990s. France, Spain, and England all claim credit for inventing this recipe, which is called *crema catalana* in Spanish and translates as "burnt cream" in English. The classic crème brûlée consists purely of heavy cream beaten with egg yolks and vanilla and stirred on low heat until thick. No sugar is added to the mixture in the original recipe, all the sweetness coming from the generous layer of fine sugar sprinkled on top. Instead of caramelizing the sugar under a broiler, which can be tricky, home cooks can now buy a small blowtorch, once available only to chefs in fancy restaurants and pipe-welders, to caramelize the sugar to an amber crust that must be cracked with a spoon.

Crème Brûlée

2 cups cream

1 vanilla bean

3 tbsp superfine sugar

5 egg yolks

⅓ cup sugar

Preheat the oven to 350°F.

Place the cream and vanilla bean in a saucepan over low heat. Simmer for 3 minutes, and then let stand for 20 minutes to allow the vanilla to infuse into the cream. Add the egg yolks and sugar to the cream and stir over low heat until the mixture thickens enough to coat the back of a spoon. Remove the vanilla bean from the custard.

Pour the mixture into four ¼-cup capacity ramekins. Place the ramekins in a baking dish and fill the baking dish with enough water to come halfway up the sides of the ramekins. Place the dish in the preheated oven and bake for 20 minutes or until custards are just set.

Remove the ramekins from the baking dish and refrigerate for 1 hour or until they are cold. Place the ramekins in a tray and sprinkle the tops with sugar. Put ice cubes in the tray around the ramekins and place the tray under a preheated hot broiler for 1 minute or until the sugar melts and is golden. *Serves 4*
Adapted from Donna Hay's *The New Cook*

Fruit Cobbler

Cobbler, crisp, crumble, and grunt are the folksy names used to describe a fruit compote with some type of crisp crust or topping. Cooks in the United Kingdom and Canada favor crisps with a crust of rolled oats, butter, cinnamon, and brown sugar, while US cooks love their cobbler, slump, or pandowdy with a cake-like topping of flour and butter mixed with buttermilk and baking powder. The thick batter is dropped over the fruit in clumps, creating a cobblestone effect.

Apples and tart rhubarb from the garden tend to be favorite fruits for this simple family dessert, though any seasonal fruit can be used, including peaches, pears, or plums. The cobbler and slump are of 19th-century origin, while the crumble and crisp emerged in the late 20th century.

Fruit Compote

Compote is simply the French name for gently cooked or stewed fruit. Many fruits are suitable for stewing, especially dried fruits such as prunes, apricots, pears, and raisins, as this is the best way to reconstitute them. Stewed fruit can be served at breakfast, lunch, or dinner as is, or "dressed up" for a special occasion. The fruit is simmered in plenty of water with sugar until soft but not disintegrated. Flavorings include vanilla, lemon juice, cinnamon, and allspice, and the mixture may be thickened with cornstarch, arrowroot, or potato starch if necessary. The cooked fruit is chilled and served with cookies such as gingersnaps.

Popular fresh fruits for stewing are apples, rhubarb, plums, and peaches. Stewed fruit may be served as a family dessert with custard or ice cream.

Fruit Compote

2¼ cups diced dried fruit

3 cups water

2 tbsp sugar

1 tsp cornstarch

1 tsp lemon peel

1 tsp cinnamon

¼ tsp nutmeg

1 tbsp honey

¼ cup orange liqueur or 2 tsp orange extract

Bring the dried fruit and water to a boil in a medium saucepan and simmer for 10 minutes. Drain the fruit, reserving 1 cup of the liquid and set the fruit aside. Add the remaining ingredients to the liquid and bring to a boil; reduce the heat and simmer until thick. Pour the liquid over the cooked fruit. Serve warm or cold. *Serves 4*

Tarte au Citron

Luscious lemon is beloved as a filling for tarts or tartlets. A classic French tarte au citron consists of a *pâte sablée* ("sandy" shortcrust dough) filled with a mixture of grated lemon juice, grated rind, sugar, and eggs. For this type of tart, the crust can either be partially baked, filled with lemon filling, and returned to the oven, or it can be prebaked and filled with filling that has been cooked on top of the stove. Decorations may include candied lemons and whipped cream.

Lemon Tart

For the pastry:

¹⁄₃ cup almonds

1¹⁄₄ cups all-purpose flour

3 tbsp sugar

¹⁄₄ tsp salt

¹⁄₃ cup chilled unsalted butter, cut into ¹⁄₂-inch pieces

2 tbsp or more ice water

For the filling:

²⁄₃ cup fresh lemon juice

2 tsp finely grated lemon zest

¹⁄₂ cup sugar

3 tbsp sour cream

4 eggs

Lemon slices (optional)

Grind the almonds finely in a food processor. Add the flour, sugar, and salt and process until blended. Add the butter and process until the mixture resembles coarse crumbs. With the machine running, add the ice water, 1 tablespoonful at a time, and blend until moist clumps form, adding more water if dry. Gather the dough into a ball and flatten into a disk. Wrap in plastic and chill for at least 1 hour or up to 1 day.

Preheat the oven to 375°F. Roll out the dough on a floured surface to a 12-inch round. Transfer to a 9-inch tart pan with a removable bottom. Fold in the excess dough and press to form double-thick sides. Pierce the dough all over with a fork. Freeze 20 minutes then bake about 30 minutes, until the crust is light golden; pierce again with a fork, if it bubbles. Remove from the oven (don't turn it off!) and transfer to a rack to cool for 15 minutes.

Meanwhile, whisk the lemon juice, zest, and sugar in bowl to blend. Whisk in the sour cream then add the eggs, 1 at a time, whisking until blended. Pour this mixture into the cooled crust and bake until the filling is set, about 35 minutes; cover the edges of the crust with foil if it browns too quickly. Cool the tart completely on a rack in the pan, then refrigerate until cold, about 2 hours. To serve, remove the pan sides and garnish the tart with lemon slices, if desired. Cut into wedges and serve. *Serves 6*

Sachertorte

The original recipe for this rich chocolate cake continues to be jealously guarded by the Hotel Sacher in Vienna, where it was created in 1832. The ingredients, however, can easily be guessed at, and many a sachertorte has been made in home kitchens and in Viennese patisseries.

The secret is to use the finest ingredients. A dense chocolate sponge is baked in a springform cake pan, then sliced in half horizontally. One half is spread with warmed, strained apricot jam, the two halves are sandwiched together and the cake is glazed all over with more jam. This step prevents the cake from becoming soggy and ensures that the chocolate icing to come remains glossy. The icing is made by melting baking chocolate in sugar syrup boiled to the thick thread stage. The syrup is then reheated and worked repeatedly on a marble slab with a palette knife to turn it into a fondant. When the icing reaches the correct consistency, it is poured over the cake to cover it completely. The chocolate should dry to a glossy finish.

Queen of Puddings

The original recipe for queen of puddings, crowned with heavy suet pastry, was developed by Queen Victoria's chefs at Buckingham Palace in the 17th century. Today's lighter version starts with a custard of eggs, milk, butter, and sugar, flavored with vanilla and grated lemon rind and thickened with bread crumbs. This is baked in a moderate oven. A layer of warm raspberry jam is poured over the cooked custard, followed by whipped egg whites and sugar. The pudding is returned to the oven for 15 minutes and baked until the meringue is set and has lightly browned.

Queen of puddings can be served hot or cold with a custard or jam sauce. Manchester pudding is identical except that it omits the jam layer and is always served cold.

Pumpkin Pie

Pumpkin pie is served all over North America on Thanksgiving, which is celebrated in October in Canada and in November in the US. It consists of a prebaked crust filled with a thick custard of cooked, puréed pumpkin blended with eggs, cream, and sugar. Flavorings include cinnamon, nutmeg, and allspice. Pumpkin pie is technically a tart since it doesn't have a top crust.

Thanksgiving was proclaimed a national holiday to mark the day on which the pilgrims, who landed on Plymouth Rock in 1620, celebrated their first harvest. Although pumpkin pie was not served at the original feast, it did include boiled pumpkin.

The pilgrims soon found that the local pumpkins, grown by Native Americans, were far superior in flavor and consistency to the European varieties and their sheer size meant that they could feed a large number of people. Early pumpkin recipes called for discarding the seeds and fibers in the center and replacing them with milk, honey, and spices before baking.

Pumpkin pie recipes did not appear in American cookbooks until the 1800s.

Cannoli

These typical Sicilian pastries from Palermo consist of deep-fried pastry tubes (the name itself means "little tubes") filled with a rich mixture of sweetened sheep's-milk ricotta cheese and candied fruit. The pastry can be as small as an inch wide; larger cannoli are common in the south of Sicily.

Cannoli were historically prepared as a treat during carnival season and probably date back to the time of the Saracen conquest in the 7th century. Thanks to the huge influx of Sicilian immigrants to the United States in the 1800s and 1900s, cannoli are also considered an American dessert. In the US, the filling is more often mascarpone rather than ricotta, or even milk custard dotted with chocolate chips and nuts (often pistachios). Fresh fruit such as cherries or strawberries is sometimes used to "plug" the tube at either end.

The secret to making good cannoli is to ensure that the tubes are filled only when completely cooled and at the last moment. This ensures the perfect contrast between the crunchy pastry and the soft, creamy filling.

Galaktoboureko

Galaktoboureko is the Greek version of
the custard pie or tart. It translates as "milk
pie." The same cake is known as *sütlü börek*
in Turkey. The lemon-flavored custard is
thickened with semolina (durum wheat) then
poured over buttered phyllo sheets layered
in a round shallow pan. More phyllo is piled
on top before baking and the dough is lightly
scored into small 4-inch squares or diamonds.
When cooled, the cake is served in individual
pieces drizzled with a sugar syrup flavored
with orange, ouzo, or Greek brandy. It may
also be heavily dusted with powdered
sugar before serving.

As with similar rich Middle Eastern cakes,
galaktoboureko is rarely eaten after a meal,
but rather is enjoyed as an afternoon snack
with strong, sweet coffee and a glass of water.

This refreshing custard is best eaten on
the day it is made, preferably while still warm.

Halva

Written variously in English as halva, hulwa,
or halwa, this traditional candy or cake derives
from the Arabic for "sweet" or "good." It is
found in many countries, from Eastern Europe
and the Balkans to the Middle East and India,
yet each country has its own version. In India,
it is a firm, cardamom-scented custard
thickened with semolina, or it may be a milk
pudding made with carrots or pumpkin and
served with sugar syrup. In the Middle East
and the Balkans, it is a solid block of ground
almonds, sesame seeds (and, more recently,
peanuts) and/or pistachio nuts originally
sweetened with honey or sugar. The Turkish
version is made of spun sugar and almonds
with the consistency of candy floss. In Israel
and throughout the Jewish world, halva is
thickened with saponaria (soapwort) instead
of flour so that all the ingredients are not
only "pareve" (neither milk nor meat) but also
kosher for Passover.

Galette des Rois

This is the French version of "twelfth night cake," which has been baked in various forms all over the Christian world since the Middle Ages. It marks the twelfth day after Christmas, the day the Three Kings are reputed to have arrived in Bethlehem to find the Christ Child.

A design is cut into the top of the galette, representing the Three Kings or other symbols, and a bean, coin, or ceramic figure is pressed into the dough before baking. Whoever finds the prize, which symbolizes the Christ Child, becomes king or queen for the evening.

A more elaborate version of the galette des rois is made from two rounds of puff pastry sandwiched together after baking with frangipane, an almond-flavored paste.

Galette des rois is a favorite in New Orleans, with its French Creole tradition, where it has evolved into an oval-shaped braid of rich puff pastry decorated with cinnamon sugar in the Mardi Gras colors of gold (for power), green (for faith), and purple (for justice). The bean or coin is replaced by a tiny plastic baby.

Ice Cream

The idea of freezing a sweet liquid and eating it cold in hot weather has been around for at least 2,500 years. The Chinese, the Greeks, and later the Romans brought ice and snow from the highest peaks and mixed it with milk and fruit juices, to be served to the Emperor himself. It was later discovered that salt has a lower freezing temperature than water, which led to the invention of the ice-cream machine. Ice and salt were mixed in a wooden bucket with a metal pot of cream and fruit juices inserted in the center. The mixture inside the metal pot was churned for a long, long time by hand, to break down the large ice crystals, until the contents froze.

Ice cream continued to be the dessert of the wealthy, though a few ice-cream parlors opened in Paris, the most famous being Procope in 1686. In the mid-1800s, ice-cream making machines were perfected and refrigeration became cheaper so more ice-cream parlors opened, especially in the United States. Ice cream gradually became as popular and widespread as it is today.

Vanilla Ice Cream

2 cups heavy cream

2 cups whole milk

1 vanilla bean, split

3/4 cups sugar, plus 1/2 cup

9 egg yolks

Place the cream and milk in a medium sauce-pan. Scrape the vanilla seeds from the bean into the cream mixture, add the bean and the 3/4 cup of sugar, and bring to a rolling boil over medium-high heat, stirring occasionally.

Meanwhile whisk the 1/2 cup of sugar with the egg yolks until well mixed. Temper the yolks by gradually whisking in about 1/2 cup of the hot cream mixture. Whisk the tempered yolks into the remaining cream mixture and strain the mixture through a fine sieve into a metal bowl or pot set over ice (this prevents the yolks from overcooking).

Chill the ice-cream base thoroughly, then process it in an ice-cream maker according to the manufacturer's directions. Transfer the ice cream to a container and let it firm for at least 2 hours in the freezer before serving.
Makes about 1 1/2 quarts
Adapted from Tom Colicchio's *Craft of Cooking*

Kulfi

This aromatic ice-cream-like dessert is made of dense *khoya* (milk reduced and thickened by long boiling and stirring), *ghee* (clarified butter), and spices, particularly ground cardamom, which is often frozen in conical molds. Kulfi comes in many flavors, the most traditional being pistachio, mango, cardamom, and saffron. Throughout the Indian subcontinent, it is sold in the streets by vendors called *kulfi wallahs* who freeze the mixture in metal molds, kept buried in a metal pot of ice and salt, then unmold and serve a portion of kulfi on a plate garnished with chopped pistachio nuts, ground cardamom, and rice noodles. Kulfi is popular in Indian restaurants in the West as a cooling counterbalance to hot curries.

Kulfi

$1/4$ cup evaporated milk

14-oz can sweetened condensed milk

16-oz container frozen whipped topping, thawed

4 slices white bread, torn into pieces

$1/2$ tsp ground cardamom

Combine the evaporated milk, condensed milk, and whipped topping in a blender and blend in pieces of bread until smooth. Pour the mixture into a 9- × 13-inch baking dish or into plastic ice cube trays. Sprinkle with cardamom and freeze for 8 hours or overnight. Serve like ice cream. *Serves 24*

Fruit Gelatin

This shimmering dessert, often refered to by the brand name Jell-O in North America, is peculiar to the English-speaking world. Most French, for example, dislike it. Sweet gelatin came into its own with the invention of a flavorless gelatin that was easy to use. Previously, food had been gelled with isinglass, a substance obtained from swimbladders, the sac in a fish's abdomen (particularly the Beluga sturgeon), that helps it float. In 1795, William Murdoch invented a cheaper substitute using the more plentiful cod. In 1845, American Peter Cooper obtained a patent for powdered gelatin derived from the bones of geese. Gelatin is now made from collagen derived mostly from pigs. (Gelatin made from calves is reserved for processing photographs!)

Fruit gelatin had its heyday in Victorian England, when intricate copper molds held elaborate layers of different colors. In the United States, the fashion for gelatin salads reached its peak in the 1950s, thanks mainly to advertising. Today, neat packets of flavorless gelatin powder are easy to use, while instant powder is sold in a rainbow of fruit flavors to which more fruit (except raw pineapple or kiwi, which interfere with the setting process) can be added.

Pomegranate and Apple Gelatin Desserts

Vegetable oil

2 tbsp gelatin powder

⅔ cup pomegranate juice

2 tbsp lemon juice

⅓ to ¼ cup sugar

⅔ cup apple juice

Brush four 1-cup molds with oil and wipe out the excess oil with a paper towel. Put 3 tablespoons of water in a large bowl and sprinkle half the gelatin over top. Leave for a minute or two until it softens and swells. Meanwhile, put the pomegranate juice, 1 tablespoon of the lemon juice, and half of the sugar in a saucepan. Heat gently until the sugar dissolves completely. Stir into the gelatin mixture until the gelatin dissolves.

Put 3 tablespoons of water in another large bowl and sprinkle the remaining gelatin on top. Pour the apple juice into a saucepan with the remaining lemon juice and sugar and heat until the sugar dissolves. Add the hot liquid slowly to the gelatin, stirring constantly until it dissolves.

Divide half the pomegranate mixture between two of the molds. Put the remaining mixture to one side but do not refrigerate. Divide half of the apple mixture between the other two molds and put the remainder aside.

Refrigerate the molds for about 3 hours or until the desserts are almost completely set. Carefully spoon the remaining apple mixture on top of the pomegranate gelatin and vice versa, so that each dessert has two layers. (If the new gelatin has already started to set in the pan, heat it just until liquid. Let it cool completely and then pour over the set layer.) Refrigerate the molds for at least 4 hours or overnight, until the desserts are set. *Serves 4*
Adapted from Tessa Kiros' *Apples for Jam*

Knickerbocker Glory

Though the English claim this ice-cream extravaganza, its origin may actually be American. It consists of vanilla ice cream layered with raspberry or strawberry jam and topped with raspberry or chocolate syrup, whipped cream, a glacé cherry, and chocolate sprinkles. Halved strawberries, whole raspberries, and peach slices are often layered in between and the whole concoction is served in a sundae glass. While most sources claim this glorious dish was named after the striped stockings, known as knickerbockers, worn by women in the 1920s and 1930s, other sources claim that it was named after Diedrich Knickerbocker, the fictitious author of Washington Irving's *History of New York* (1809). More likely is the fact that "knickerbockers" is a Dutch name for "breeches" and is also a genuine American surname. Furthermore, a recipe for knickerbocker glory appears is an American recipe book of ice-cream sundaes and parfaits published in 1915.

Knickerbocker Glory

2 tbsp butter

2 tbsp brown sugar

4 plums, chopped

$1/2$ tsp cinnamon

$1/2$ vanilla bean

3 scoops vanilla ice cream

For the garnish:

2 tbsp sliced almonds, toasted

2 tbsp chocolate, grated

2 tbsp rolled oats, toasted

Melt the butter and the brown sugar in a medium saucepan on high heat. Add the plums, cinnamon, and vanilla bean, and simmer for 4 minutes on low heat. Remove from the heat. When completely cool, remove the vanilla bean. Spoon a little of the stewed plums into a sundae glass, then add a scoop of vanilla ice cream. Repeat the layers until the glass is full. Sprinkle the almonds, chocolate, and oats on top. *Serves 1*

Boston Cream Pie

Bread Pudding   ▷

Proclaimed the official Massachusetts State Dessert in 1996, Boston cream is not a pie at all but a rich cake. No one really knows why it is called a pie, though the dividing line between pies and cakes in the mid-19th century, when it originated, was rather blurred and the colonists did bake their cakes in pie plates.

A yellow sponge or white cake is sliced in half crosswise and filled with a generous layer of thick yellow custard "cream." A glaze of liquid chocolate icing is poured over the cake, and it is served in wedges, like a pie.

The Parker House Hotel in Boston claims its creation, having served it from the day the hotel opened in 1856. It was then called a chocolate cream pie. Though Boston cream pie is usually made as one large cake, some 19th-century recipes baked individual "cream cakes" in muffin rings.

This thick "pudding" must be made with chunks of bread at least a day old—eggy challah bread is ideal—with the crusts removed. It is mixed with fat (originally suet), eggs, sugar, corn syrup, and mixed dried fruits, including currants. Bread pudding is popular in Britain, but is also well known in Belgium, the US, and France. In New Orleans, it is made with a splash of bourbon whiskey. Cinnamon, nutmeg, and allspice are favorite spices. The mixture is then transferred to a deep dish and baked at 350°F for about an hour. Bread pudding is usually served with a whiskey or rum sauce, but it can also be served with a caramel sauce or a sweet, white vanilla sauce to contrast the rather drab brown color of the pudding itself. It is delicious hot or cold; when served cold, it is usually sprinkled with sugar.

There are endless variations, some calling for additional fruits such as banana, stewed apple, and coconut.

Loukoumades

Also called *lokma* in Turkish, these popular yeast-raised doughnuts are deep-fried in peanut or sunflower oil and drenched in sugar syrup or cinnamon-flavored honey. They may also be rolled in sesame seeds before frying or coated in sugar syrup containing sesame seeds. In Greece and Cyprus, they are often thickly dusted with powdered sugar and cinnamon after frying. Loukoumades are called *zvingous* or *zvingoi* (names of German origin), and *bimuelos* or *burmuelos* (names of Spanish origin) by Greek and Turkish Jews who serve them for Hanukkah in December, a festival at which deep-fried foods are traditional to commemorate the miracle in the Temple of the day's supply of oil burning for eight days.

In Turkey, *lokma* are served at funerals and distributed to the poor. In both Turkey and Greece, loukoumades and *lokma* are sold by street vendors during religious festivals and at Christmas. In these hot countries, loukoumades are considered a winter food.

Marzipan

This firm paste is made of ground almonds or apricot kernels cooked with egg whites and sugar or sugar syrup. It is not quite the same as almond paste, which is softer and does not contain eggs. Marzipan has also been known as "marchpane," and comes from the French *massepain* or the Italian *marzapane*. The mixture is as old as the hills; there are records of the Egyptians making it in 1800 BC. Marzipan was eaten in the Middle East but probably did not reach Europe until the time of the Crusades and was not known in England until the 1500s. Its ability to be creatively shaped is one of its great advantages. At the court of Elizabeth I of England (1558–1603), it was colored and shaped in hoops. Today, marzipan is rolled out in a sheet and used as a "liner" for wedding cakes to prevent the icing from soaking through the rich fruitcake beneath. It is also eaten as a sweet during holidays such as Easter, shaped and colored to represent miniature fruits, vegetables, bunnies, and such.

Fudge

The exact origin of this popular confection is not known, but it may have originated from a "fudged" batch of toffee. It is beloved throughout the English-speaking world, and is made simply by boiling sugar with butter and milk until it reaches the soft-ball stage (235°F to 240°F) and adding flavoring. Fudge was first made in the United States sometime after the mid 1800s and popularized through the women's colleges, particularly Vassar. It was first sold by a female college student in Baltimore in 1886; the first American candy store devoted exclusively to fudge opened two years later. The recipe gradually crept into early 20th-century cookbooks.

A slab of fudge is a popular tourist souvenir in vacation spots throughout the United Kingdom and North America. It is now produced in every imaginable flavor, from rum and raisin to peanut butter and chocolate mint. The first sumptuous hot-fudge sundae, made with fudge so liquid it could be poured over ice cream, was served in 1906 at C.C. Browns, an ice-cream parlor in Hollywood, California.

Fudge

8 cups sugar

1 cup unsalted butter

1¹⁄₂ cups evaporated milk

¹⁄₃ cup water

1 tsp vanilla extract

Put the sugar, butter, evaporated milk, water, and vanilla extract in a saucepan. Heat gently until the sugar dissolves completely. Bring to a rapid boil and cook to the soft-ball stage, 238°F to 245°F on a candy thermometer.

Remove from the heat and allow to cool for 2 to 3 minutes, then beat rapidly with a wooden spoon until the mixture thickens and becomes rough in texture. Pour the mixture into an 8-inch square pan lined with waxed or parchment paper.

Let cool a little before lightly marking into squares with a knife. Leave in a cool place to set, cut into squares and store in an airtight container. *Makes about 64 pieces*

Cassata

True cassata, the traditional dessert from Palermo, is a layered sponge cake moistened with cherry or orange liqueur, filled with ricotta or cream cheese and mixed with candied peel and raisins. It is very similar to the filling for cannoli.

Some of these cakes are also covered with marzipan or chocolate icing or topped with whole candied fruits. The word *cassata* may stem from the medieval Arabic *kas'at*, referring to the circular pan used to mold it, or the Latin *caseata*, meaning a dish made with cheese. Cassata may have been introduced to Sicily under the Saracens, who conquered the island in the 9th century and ruled for two hundred years. It may be even older, however, since it is traditionally served at weddings.

A second form of cassata, better known outside Italy, is layered ice cream consisting of an outer shell of vanilla ice cream, sometimes frozen into elaborate shapes and decorated with whipped cream. The inner layer is filled with softer ice cream in contrasting colors, some blended with candied fruit.

Bavarian Cream ▷

This jiggly custard is made with gelatin and set in individual molds. It is occasionally refrigerated until set and then topped with a band of clear jelly of a contrasting color. The original dessert is said to have originated in the late 17th or early 18th century, created by French chefs working for the Wittelsbach family, who then ruled Bavaria.

The recipe was exported to France, where the famous chef Antonin Carême (1783–1833) included a recipe for *bavaroise* in his book. Carême, who worked for the Rothschild family in England at one time, brought it with him across the Channel, where it often appeared at the tables of the wealthy, being an attractive dessert for the large banquets served *à la russe* with all the dishes for the course displayed on the table at once. Today, the mixture is often used as a cake filling and for filled doughnuts.

Neenish Tart

Neenish or nienich tart is a pastry tartlet filled with jam and Bavarian cream and topped with two-toned frosting, usually chocolate brown and white, or chocolate brown and pink. The origin of the name is uncertain, but two sisters claim it was named for a friend of their mother's who first made the tart in 1913. According to one source, Ruby Neenish came from the East End of London before the First World War to marry an Australian. She apparently added white frosting after running out of chocolate. The name "nienich" suggests a German origin, but it was noted after the neenish name had become popular.

The earliest printed recipe for the tart is in *Miss Drake's Home Cookery* published in Glenferrie, Victoria, in 1929. It calls for a Bavarian cream (set with gelatin) filling and pink and white icing. A 1932 recipe in *Miranda's Cook Book* (published in Melbourne) calls for custard filling topped with chocolate and vanilla frosting.

Nougat

Derived from the Occitane French word for nut, *noga*, nougat is a confection made with toasted almonds or walnuts, egg whites, and sugar syrup cooked to the small-crack stage. In this respect, it is like a hard version of marzipan, though the nuts are chopped rather than ground and some whole nuts are included. In France, orange flower water is added to the mixture, which is cooked on the stove then poured onto thin sheets of edible rice paper. More rice paper is placed on top and the mixture is pressed with a heavy weight until cold. Nougat is generally made by craft confectioners in rectangular blocks; the small French town of Montelimar near the Spanish border is famous for its nougat.

The Spanish and Italian equivalents, known as *turrón* and *torrone* respectively, are sometimes made with brown sugar and honey, which makes for a softer consistency. Any kind of nuts can be used for this toothsome treat, including hazelnuts, pistachios, and pine nuts.

Peach Melba

This ice-cream sundae is named for a famous Australian performer, Dame Nellie Melba (1861–1931). Peach Melba was created in the opera singer's honor by the famous French chef Auguste Escoffier, who served it to her in 1892 when she stayed at the Savoy Hotel in London. Melba reputedly loved ice cream but feared that the cold might affect her vocal chords. Since it was only a small part of peach Melba, Escoffier hoped she would not consider it too dangerous for her voice. The sundae is made with fresh or canned peach halves, the hollow filled with vanilla ice cream. The peach and ice cream are drizzled with raspberry sauce, which may be thickened with red currant jelly and cornstarch. This delicious dessert was originally served to the diva in a swan-shaped ice sculpture.

Peach Melba

2 tbsp sugar, plus 1 tbsp
1 cup raspberries, puréed
1 tbsp fresh lemon juice
2 peaches, peeled and sliced
4 individual meringue shells
2 cups premium vanilla ice cream
Fresh raspberries, for garnish

Stir 2 tablespoons of the sugar into the raspberry purée and set aside. Mix the remaining tablespoon of sugar with the lemon juice in a bowl. Stir in the peaches and let stand for 15 minutes. Place the meringue shells on 4 dessert plates. Scoop the ice cream into the shells and place the peach halves pit-side down over the ice cream. Drizzle with the raspberry purée and garnish with raspberries. *Serves 4*

Pavlova

This festive meringue from down under may have been invented by Herbert Sachse, chef of the Hotel Esplanade in Perth, Western Australia, to celebrate the visit of the great Russian ballerina, Anna Pavlova (1881–1931) who toured Australia and New Zealand twice in the 1920s.

Others claim it was invented by a chef at a New Zealand hotel during the ballerina's visit. The white meringue is said to be a tribute to her swan costume, worn during the famous dance of the Dying Swan, set to a cello solo by Saint-Saëns.

The Pavlova meringue is a mixture of stiffly beaten egg whites, fine sugar, vinegar, and cornstarch piped or spooned in a ring on a baking sheet lined with nonstick parchment paper. The Pavlova must be baked slowly until it is crunchy on the outside and soft and moist on the inside.

The central hollow is then filled with fruits of contrasting colors, such as peaches, pomegranate seeds, or raspberries, folded into whipped cream. In Australia, Pavlova mixes are available that require only the addition of water and sugar.

Mixed Berry Pavlova

13 egg whites

$1/4$ tsp salt

$2^1/2$ cups superfine sugar, plus $1/2$ cup

$1^1/2$ tbsp cornstarch

$1^1/2$ tbsp distilled white vinegar

6 to 8 cups strawberries, halved or quartered if large

3 tbsp fresh lime juice

$1/4$ cup sugar, plus $1^1/2$ tbsp

2 cups blackberries

$2^1/2$ cups chilled heavy cream

2 tsp vanilla extract

Preheat the oven to 250°F and line 2 large baking sheets with parchment paper.

Swirl the egg whites in a metal bowl set over a saucepan of simmering water until they are barely warm to the touch. Remove the bowl from the heat.

With an electric mixer, beat the whites with the salt until they form soft peaks. Beat in 2 cups of the superfine sugar and continue beating until the mixture forms stiff, glossy peaks. Stir together the remaining $1/2$ cup sugar and the cornstarch. Beat into the meringue, then beat in the vinegar.

On each lined baking sheet, spoon the meringue into 8 mounds of about $1/2$-cup each and 2 inches high, set 1 inch apart. Divide any remaining meringue among the mounds. Bake in the upper and lower thirds of the oven, switching the sheets halfway through baking, until crisp but still soft inside, 1 to $1^1/4$ hours total. If the meringues are still not crisp, turn off the oven and let them cool with the oven door slightly ajar for 1 hour more. Transfer the cooked meringues from the parchment paper to racks to cool (they will stick if cooled completely on paper).

Just before serving, toss the strawberries with the lime juice and ¼ cup sugar and let stand 10 minutes, tossing occasionally, until the sugar dissolves. Add the blackberries and toss to coat.

With clean beaters, beat the cream with vanilla and the remaining 1½ tablespoons of sugar. Tap the meringues gently with the back of a spoon to create indentations in the center, then mound some whipped cream and berries onto each. *Serves 8*

Pasteles de Nata

This Portuguese specialty, which is also popular in the Philippines, consists of little tartlets filled with a baked cream mixture. The name simply means "cream pastries," though it is often translated as "egg pastries." The tiny pastry cups, about 2 inches in diameter, are filled with a rich custard mixture of eggs, whipping cream, and sugar, sometimes flavored with cinnamon, baked in a hot oven until the tops are covered in brown blisters. Pasteles de nata are usually bought in small bakeries rather than being made at home. They are eaten with coffee as a snack rather than as a dessert after a meal.

The finest pasteles de nata in Lisbon are reputed to come from the Pasteleria Belem in the Belem district, but excellent tarts can bought in Portuguese and Filipino bakeries wherever significant numbers of immigrants have settled, such as in Montreal and Toronto, Canada. The little custard tarts are also popular in Malaysia, where they belong to the category of cookies and small pastries known as *kuih*.

Pear Bavarois

This dish consists simply of poached pears chilled and arranged around a mold of Bavarian cream—a custard thickened with gelatin. Both pears and peaches are popular in this dish, which is increasingly being offered in the United Kingdom for special occasions such as weddings and bar mitzvahs. The bavarois or Bavarian cream itself may be made with cooked, puréed pears combined with lemon juice, cream, and gelatin. It is poured into a fancy mold or individual molds with the poached pears arranged around it.

The pears are poached in sugar syrup flavored only with vanilla to keep them white. Pear bavarois is usually served with a white sauce flavored with vanilla and brandy, a rich chocolate sauce, or a red coulis (uncooked sauce) of crushed raspberries, strawberries, or black currants.

It is sometimes served on a base of flake pastry layers brushed with a pear liqueur such as poire William.

Pears Poached in Red Wine

This is another classic dinner party dessert. The best pears to use are long and firm. Very ripe pears are difficult to peel and may disintegrate during cooking. The peeled pears are poached in a light sugar syrup mixed with red wine, a strip of citrus peel, a vanilla bean, and a few whole cloves, which flavor the syrup and enhance the color. The pears are transferred to a serving bowl and refrigerated with the strained syrup poured over top.

This simple and sophisticated dessert is usually served with whipped cream or vanilla ice cream. Poached pears can also be drained and arranged in a prebaked flan shell on a bed of frangipane cream mixed with crushed macaroons. This dish is called pear bourdaloue.

Even the most cast-iron of pears are soft and delicious using this method. Peel the pears, leaving on the stems, then place them in a tall ovenproof dish or earthenware crock. Add about 3 ounces of sugar per pound of pears. Half cover with red wine. Fill to the top with water. Bake in a very slow oven between 5 and 7 hours, until the pears are quite tender and the juice greatly reduced. From time to time, as the wine diminishes, turn the pears over.

A big dish of these pears, almost mahogany-colored by the time they are ready, served cold in their remaining juice with cream or creamed rice separately, makes a lovely sweet. The best way to present them is to pile them up in a pyramid, stems uppermost, in a shallow bowl. **Adapted from Elizabeth David's** *French Provincial Cooking*

Panna Cotta

Though "cooked cream" may not sound terribly
appetizing, this attractive custard-like pudding
from Piedmont, in northern Italy, makes a
light-tasting and refreshing dessert. Baked in
one large mold or smaller individual molds,
panna cotta consists of cooked heavy cream
sweetened with sugar and solidified with
gelatin. It is served cold. In Italy, the mixture is
often flavored with orange flower water and
the finished puddings are decorated with
candied citron peel. Panna cotta has become
popular for dinner parties as it is easy and
quick to make and can be served with a variety
of colorful accompaniments such as a raspberry
or strawberry coulis or tropical fruit.

Chocolate and other versions of panna
cotta are starting to emerge. The original
dessert probably used milk streamed straight
from the cow into a pail containing fish
bones, which gelled the mixture. Honey
would have been used as a sweetener. In
this respect, eggless panna cotta is closer
to a syllabub or posset than to a custard,
and it is closest of all to a Bavarian cream.

Baked Alaska

This wondrous hot-and-cold dessert consists
of ice cream placed on a layer of sponge
cake, then covered in stiffly beaten egg whites
whipped with sugar. The confection is frozen
until just before serving, then placed under
a broiler long enough to brown the meringue
without melting the ice cream, about
5 minutes. Kitchen torches are now available
that will brown the meringue perfectly.

The idea of "cooking" ice cream appeared
in the early 1800s. A guest at a White House
dinner in 1802 described a similar dessert
in which the ice cream was covered in pastry.
Benjamin Thompson (Count Rumford), famous
for other culinary inventions, claimed to
have created it in 1804, calling it "omelette
surprise" or *omelette à la norvégienne*.

The first baked Alaska was served in 1876,
at New York's Delmonico's restaurant (the
dessert was named to honor the territory
of Alaska, which the US had just acquired).
A customer who ordered the dessert in
the 1880s described the ice cream as being
"surrounded by an envelope of carefully
whipped cream which, just before the dainty
dish is served, is popped into the oven, or
is brought under the scorching influence
of a red hot salamander (portable broiler)"

Pecan Pie

This classic American pie, a specialty of the Deep South, is decorated with pecans, a member of the walnut family native to the United States. Pecan trees grow as far south as Mexico, but Texas is the largest producer. Its name derives from the Algonquin word *pacan*. The oval, reddish-brown nut is milder and sweeter than the walnut. Pecan pie consists of a prebaked pastry filled with a sweet filling, usually a mixture of corn syrup and sweet spices, topped with a layer of pecans. In the 1800s, the filling was usually a custard mixture, sometimes thickened with puréed pumpkin.

In Britain, the corn syrup is replaced by more readily available golden syrup. Hickory nuts, closely related to pecans, can be baked in a pie in the same way.

Pecan pie is another favorite dessert for US Thanksgiving and Christmas.

Peppermint Creams

These sweet, round patties are rarely made at home anymore, but their creamy centers can be made from fondant powder, or powdered sugar and liquid glucose, flavored with a few drops of peppermint oil. The commercial version consists of light corn syrup flavored with peppermint oil and thickened with cornstarch and guar gum.

Both versions are dipped in dark chocolate and left to harden. After Eight is one popular commercial brand, as are York Peppermint Patties in the US and Fry's Peppermint Cream Bar in the United Kingdom.

Pralines

This scrumptious candy is made from sugar and whole or chopped toasted nuts stirred in a heavy-bottomed copper pan over low heat until the sugar starts to color, by which time the nuts should be roasted. The mixture is then transferred to a marble slab or buttered metal tray and left to cool. The now-brittle praline may be broken into jagged shards, called nut brittle, or crushed with a rolling pin and stored in an airtight container for sprinkling over cakes and ice cream.

The original French *pralin* is simply a nut coated in caramelized sugar. César duc de Choiseul, comte du Plessis-Pralin (1712–1785) claimed to have invented the mixture. The New Orleans or Creole praline, meanwhile, is a soft caramel, similar to fudge, containing butter, cream, and chopped pecans. Now sold on every street corner, these mouthwatering disks were probably first made by Ursuline nuns who arrived in New Orleans in the 18th century.

Turkish Delight

This delightful sweet is known in Arabic and Turkish as *rahat loukoum,* meaning "rest for the throat." The pale, jelly-like cubes are made of sugar syrup thickened with gum Arabic and flavored with essences, mainly rosewater in the United Kingdom, but orange flower water, peppermint, and lemon in Egypt and Turkey. The mixture is boiled, poured into rectangular trays and left to cool. Then it is scored, cut into cubes, and dusted heavily with powdered sugar mixed with cornstarch to prevent the pieces from sticking together. The exotic jellies are also popular in Greece and Cyprus, where they are known as *loukoumia.*

At one time, true Turkish delight was made in London by the Politi family from Crete, who came to the United Kingdom in the late 19th century. Cheaper versions are made with corn syrup and thickened with cornstarch. One brand is even coated in chocolate.

Cannelés

Swiss Roll

These delightful little molded pudding-cakes are a specialty of Bordeaux, where nuns are said to have created them in the early 19th century using flour salvaged from the holds of sailing ships anchored in the port.

They are made in tall, individual, fluted molds (*cannelé* means "fluted"), which are coated on the inside with a mixture of butter and beeswax. This makes it easier to unmold the cakelets and gives them their distinctive crunchy crust.

The batter is very rich and thin, consisting of milk, powdered sugar, eggs, yolks, and rum. After the batter is beaten smooth, it should rest in the refrigerator for a full 12 hours before being brought to room temperature. Filled three-quarters full, the molds are baked in a fairly hot oven for 45 minutes. The inside of the cakes is white and creamy, their slightly liquid center contrasting with the dark, crisp exterior.

The best way to eat cannelés is drizzled with warm butterscotch sauce and served with a cup of strong coffee.

This delightful and versatile dessert consists of a thin, light sponge cake rolled around a sweet filling. It is baked in a rectangular pan with slightly raised sides lined with waxed or parchment paper so the sponge can be removed easily. Immediately after baking, before it has time to firm up, the cake is spread with jam, chocolate spread, lemon curd, or buttercream filling and rolled up quickly along the short side. If the sponge is chocolate-flavored, the filling should be white, for contrast. The Swiss roll is cut into thick slices for eating.

It is known as a jelly roll in the United States, in France as a *gâteau roulé*, in Germany as *Biscuitrolle* and in Spanish as *brazo de gitano*. Why the cake, which originated in the mid-1800s, was named "Swiss" in the United Kingdom is a mystery. The roll has spread, via the former British Empire, to the Far East and especially Hong Kong. Light versions are popular in China and Japan.

Rice Pudding

Rice pudding, made with short-grained rice and milk, appears in different forms throughout the English-speaking world and in Asia. In England, rice pudding generally consists of raw rice placed in a metal pudding basin to which milk and sugar are added. The pudding is baked in a medium oven until the milk is absorbed and a skin forms on the surface. Raisins and cinnamon are sometimes added to the mixture, which can be eaten warm or cold after cooking.

In the Middle East and the Indian subcontinent, the rice is stirred constantly as it cooks over low heat, and the pudding is usually eaten cold. Various flavorings are added, particularly essences such as rosewater, orange flower water, and pandanus (screwpine). Raisins and nuts may also be used. When the rice has swollen and cooked, the mixture is cooled, poured into small cups and chilled.

Moroccan rice pudding is strewn with rosebuds, while the Lebanese decorate it with gold- and silver-colored sugared almonds. It is particularly popular at weddings, the rice symbolizing fertility.

Rice Pudding

5 tbsp butter

$1/3$ cup superfine sugar

$1/3$ cup round-grain rice

$41/2$ cups whole-fat milk

$1/2$ vanilla bean, split lengthwise

$1/2$ cup heavy cream

A pinch of salt

Preheat the oven to 275°F.

Melt the butter in a flameproof casserole and add the sugar. Stir around and heat gently until gooey, like toffee. Add the rice and continue stirring until the rice looks puffy, pale golden, and sticky with sugar. Add the milk, which will seethe, and the rice/butter/sugar mixture will set into lumps. Fear not. Feel around with a wooden spoon and disperse the lumps because as the milk heats it will dissolve all in its path. Add the vanilla bean and squash it around a bit to release its little black seeds. Add the cream and the salt, and bring to a boil.

Place in the oven and cook for 3 to 4 hours or until just starting to set and still *slightly* liquid-looking; as the pudding cools, it will finish cooking in its own heat. Serve very lukewarm, or cold if you like, but never hot. *Serves 4*

Adapted from Simon Hopkinson's *Roast Chicken and Other Stories*

Ricotta and Pine Nut Tart

Though not a traditional Italian recipe, this blend of typical Italian ingredients has lately gained popularity in Italy and in Italian restaurants around the world. The crust is prebaked, then filled with a smooth, cooked ricotta cheese mixture sweetened with powdered sugar and flavored with cinnamon and rosewater. The pine nuts, which are first toasted in a dry frying pan, may be incorporated into the mixture or scattered on top. The pie is then chilled and served cold.

In other versions, the ricotta is mixed with chopped candied fruit and topped with a dense layer of pine nuts, then the tart is baked until lightly browned.

Ricotta and pine nut tart may be served with ice cream or with a strawberry or raspberry coulis for contrasting color.

Some restaurants serve it with a black currant sorbet.

Rum Baba ▷

Originally a Polish cake, rum baba or *baba au rhum* as it is known in French, was exported to France via Count Stanislas Lesczinski (1677–1766), the King of Poland who was exiled to Lorraine, bringing many Polish courtiers with him. The Polish baba or *babka* is a sponge cake containing raisins and baked in a fluted mold that is said to resemble the skirts of an old lady (*baba* is "grandmother" in Polish). The Count's cook transformed the cake into a luscious dessert by lacing it with a generous amount of rum.

Today, the baba is baked in individual ring molds. Its rather dry sponge mixture is well aerated so that it will absorb the syrup with which it is liberally doused when removed from the oven. It is then decorated with cream, pieces of angelica, and glacé cherries.

Rum baba is rarely made at home but is often bought from a patisserie. It should be eaten very fresh, when the sponge is meltingly tender.

Lamington Cake

Likely named for the popular Baron
Lamington who governed the then territory
of Queensland at the turn of the last century,
Lamington cake is a popular café treat
and dessert in Australia and (in somewhat
different forms) New Zealand. Hardcore
republicans claim that the confection is
the only positive contribution from an
English governor in the history of Australia.
Nevertheless, it is a mainstay for scout or
guide groups looking to raise money for
camp trips and new uniforms. The recipe
for the cake itself is quite basic: flour, sugar,
eggs, butter, cornmeal. It is the icing that
gives Lamington cake its place in the culinary
mythology of the continent. A square of
cake is dunked in a vat of sweet chocolate
and then sprinkled with dried coconut
shavings. Often, two squares are stacked,
one on top of the other, and joined with
a sweet adhesive—fruit jam or jelly.

Semifreddo

This Italian word simply means "half-cold."
In culinary terms it refers to partially frozen
desserts including cassata and custard.
The Spanish equivalent is known as *semifrío*.
Semifreddo usually includes ingredients that
do not actually freeze, or that taste better
when not fully frozen such as honey or
nougat, or those that are simply too delicate
to freeze, such as soft fruits. It begins with
a custard base of sugar, egg yolks, and liquid,
which is thickened on the stove and then
cooled. Whipped cream is folded in along
with any additions, which may include sponge
cake, cookie crumbs, nuts, small pieces of
fruit, nougat, or caramel. Egg whites may
also be folded in. The final delectable result,
which is chilled in the freezer in a loaf pan,
has a smooth mousse-like texture. It may be
unmolded and served in slices with fresh fruit
or drizzled with chocolate sauce.

The greatest advantage of a semifreddo
for the home cook is that it is as luscious
as ice cream without requiring an expensive
ice-cream maker.

Sorbet

This water ice is simply ice cream without the cream. It is actually more difficult to prepare than ice cream since there is no milk to break down the large ice crystals. Thus sorbets have to be either made in an ice-cream machine or frozen in a tray and beaten several times as the mixture begins to freeze in order to keep the crystals small. Sorbets can be made of any fruit purée mixed with thick sugar syrup. Because freezing tends to dull the flavor of food, the fruit purée itself should be intensely flavored and the sugar syrup very sweet. Popular sorbet flavors include lemon, raspberry, black currant, melon, and peach. The sorbet is also known as sherbet in the United States. Both words derive from the Arabic *sharaba*, "to drink," due to the semi-liquid nature of the iced dessert. The French and Eastern Europeans serve a sorbet during a banquet to cleanse and refresh the palate and hopefully revive the appetite for subsequent courses. This custom is known in France as the *trou normand* or "Norman hole."

Strawberry Sorbet

¾ cup sugar

⅓ cup water

¼ tsp salt

6 cups fresh-picked strawberries, hulled

3 tbsp lemon juice

In a saucepan over medium heat, combine the sugar, water, and salt. Cook, stirring, until the sugar and salt dissolve, about 3 minutes. Let cool for 15 minutes. In a blender, purée the strawberries with the cooled syrup and lemon juice, in batches if necessary, until very smooth. For a smoother texture, strain through a fine-mesh sieve. Cover and refrigerate until chilled, at least 4 hours or overnight. Churn in an ice-cream maker according to the manufacturer's directions. *Serves 6*

Floating Islands

This classic dessert, translated as *ile flottante* or *oeufs à la neige* (snow eggs) in French, consists of a meringue "island" or islands floating on a sea of custard sauce (*crème anglaise*). The meringue is made by whipping stiffly beaten egg whites with sugar. Two soupspoons are used to shape the mounds and transfer them to simmering milk or water to poach. The cooked meringues are drained on paper towels and refrigerated before being served on the custard sauce, sprinkled with caramel sauce, crushed praline, or chopped toasted almonds. Floating islands originated in the mid- to late-19th century (Mrs. Beeton's *Household Management* contains a recipe) when meringues could be whipped with a wire whisk. Before that, egg whites were beaten with a bundle of wooden twigs, which could take hours.

Floating Islands

For the meringues:

8 egg whites

A pinch of salt

3/4 cup sugar

For the custard sauce:

4 egg yolks

1/4 cup sugar

A pinch of salt

2 cups milk

1 tsp vanilla extract

1/4 tsp finely grated lemon rind

To serve:

Caramel sauce

To make the meringues, beat the egg whites with the salt until they form soft peaks. Add the sugar slowly, beating well after each addition, and continue beating until the egg whites are very stiff. Bring a large saucepan of water to a boil, then reduce to a simmer. Scoop up a large tablespoonful of the egg-white mix and slide it into the hot water. Poach for 2 minutes, turn it over and poach for 4 minutes on the other side, then remove and set aside. Repeat, making 12 meringues.

To make the custard, beat the egg yolks lightly, then add the sugar and salt. Scald the milk and add it to the egg mixture in a slow steady stream, whisking to prevent the yolks from curdling. Cook the custard in a double boiler, stirring constantly, until it begins to thicken and coat the back of a spoon. Remove from the heat and cool slightly before adding the vanilla extract and lemon rind. Chill thoroughly until ready to use.

When ready to serve, cover the base of a deep dessert plate with a layer of custard. Float two poached meringues on each pool of custard, and drizzle with caramel sauce. *Serves 6*

Caramelized Oranges

Popular in French and Italian restaurants throughout the United Kingdom, this dessert is extremely quick and easy to make at home. Since the oranges need to be juicy, it is best to serve them when they are in season.

The fruit is peeled, sliced crosswise, and seeded. The sugar for the sauce is cooked, or caramelized, in a saucepan and may be flavored with cinnamon sticks and whole cloves. This amber liquid is poured over the peeled orange slices. The zest of the oranges is sometimes parboiled in several changes of water then shredded finely and used as a garnish. The dish is wonderful with ice cream or custard and makes an excellent accompaniment to a bitter chocolate mousse or a hot orange soufflé.

Caramalized oranges served on their own at room temperature, or chilled, are especially refreshing after a heavy meal.

Sticky Toffee Pudding

Unlike many other puddings, this sweet steamed pudding of brown sugar, butter, cream, and dates appears to be a relatively new and well-documented creation.

Although a number of restaurants since the 1960s claim to have invented a similar mixture, the official sticky pudding has been trademarked by a restaurant in Grange-over-Sands, whose owners took over a village bakery in northwest England from which they now sell their ready-made puddings to gourmet grocers in London and the world.

The recipe for the pudding is a standard sponge mixture for steamed puddings (which are now oven-baked) and, of course, the suet has been replaced by butter and cream.

The magic ingredients are pitted and puréed dates, treacle, and corn syrup. The result is a gooey and sticky dark-brown mixture that melts in the mouth.

Sticky toffee pudding is served with a thick sauce, also containing treacle and corn syrup, and goes well with vanilla ice cream.

Easy Sticky Toffee Dessert

For the cake:

Scant $^1/_2$ cup dark brown sugar, packed

1 cup plus 7 tbsp self-rising flour

$^1/_2$ cup whole milk

1 egg

1 tsp vanilla extract

$^1/_4$ cup unsalted butter, melted

$^3/_4$ cup, plus 2 tbsp chopped, rolled dates

For the sauce:

$^3/_4$ cup dark brown sugar, packed

Approx. 2 tbsp unsalted butter, in little blobs

$2^1/_4$ cups boiling water

Preheat the oven to 375°F and butter a $1^1/_2$-quart capacity pudding dish.

Combine the sugar with the flour in a large bowl. Pour the milk into a measuring cup, beat in the egg, vanilla, and melted butter and then pour this mixture over the sugar and flour, stirring—just with a wooden spoon —to combine. Fold in the dates then scrape into the prepared pudding dish. Don't worry if it doesn't look very full: it will do by the time it cooks.

Sprinkle over the sugar for the sauce and dot with the butter. Pour over the boiling water (yes really!) and transfer to the oven. Set the timer for 45 minutes, though you might find the dessert needs 5 or 10 minutes more. The top of the dessert should be springy and spongy when it's cooked; underneath, the butter, dark brown sugar, and boiling water will have turned into a rich, sticky sauce. Serve with vanilla ice cream, crème fraîche or heavy or light cream as you wish. *Serves 6–8*

Adapted from Nigella Lawson's *Nigella Bites*

Syllabub

The syllabub has been transformed since Elizabethan times from a drink meant for invalids to a proper dessert. Early recipes consisted of sherry or wine mixed with lemon juice, grated zest, and sugar.

Today, it is mixed with whipped cream. In an early version, the ingredients were poured into a pail and the cream was achieved by milking a cow straight into the mixture.

The first alcohol added was probably cider. Syllabub is always served in tall glasses so the liquid and cream separate and the alcohol can be drunk through the cream. In the 16th and 17th centuries, the cream was whipped with lemon juice to make a firm curd.

As with posset pots, special syllabub glasses were devised to allow the cream to rise and separate more easily.

Tapioca Pudding

This uniquely English creation is made by
boiling tapioca starch, which is produced
from dried cassava root. It is similar to sago,
another starchy substance made from the pith
inside the bark of the sago palm (*Metroxylon
sagu*), which comes from South America.

Cooked tapioca forms delicate jelly-like
rounds, which has led to the pudding being
known in schoolboy slang as "frog's spawn."
It is poured into a pie plate with milk, sugar,
and flavorings such as cinnamon. The pudding
is then baked until a skin forms on the top
and the starch is cooked.

A fancier version, called Colchester
pudding, calls for boiling the tapioca in milk
on the stove with sugar and lemon zest.
The cooked pudding is layered over stewed
fruit in a pie plate and covered with another
layer of tapioca or egg custard, all topped
with meringue. The pudding is served
with custard sauce.

Spotted Dick

This plain suet sponge is also known as plum
duff and, in Sussex, as hunt pudding. It is
typical boarding school fare, being cheap
to make and very filling.

Many ex-public-school boys and girls
remember it fondly, which is why it is still
served at English gentlemen's clubs. Its firm
suet dough consists of flour, baking powder,
spices, sugar, chopped or shredded suet,
and milk, "spotted" with raisins or currants.

The mixture is traditionally covered with
a floured cloth and steamed up to 3 hours.
Today, it can be cooked in a metal or china
pudding bowl sealed with a cloth or covered
in foil held in place with string.

Sweet haggis is a similar pudding containing
raisins, currants, and spice. It is enjoyed in
Scotland, where oatmeal replaces much
of the flour.

Tarte Tatin

This classic French apple tart was allegedly invented by the Tatin sisters, who ran a hotel-restaurant in Lamotte-Beuvron in the Sologne region. It uses an interesting technique that requires great care. The apples, which should be firm, tart, and uniform in shape, are peeled, sliced, and arranged in concentric circles in a heavy frying pan or a deep, buttered pie plate. They can be caramelized on the stove and then baked with the pastry lid, or cooked in butter and sugar as the crust bakes. The cooked tart is removed from the oven. A plate is inverted over the tart and the whole thing quickly turned upside down so the pastry is on the bottom. The apples should be slightly crisp and caramelized.

Tarte tatin is a specialty of Maxim's restaurant in Paris though, of course, it is widely available in restaurants and patisseries.

La Tarte des Demoiselles Tatin

4 lb firm cooking apples, such as Golden Delicious

$1/3$ cup sugar, plus $1/2$ cup

1 tsp cinnamon, optional

2 tbsp softened butter, plus 6 tbsp melted butter

For the pastry:

$2/3$ cup flour*

1 tbsp granulated sugar

$1/8$ tsp salt

4 tbsp chilled butter

$1^1/2$ tbsp chilled vegetable shortening

$2^1/2$ to 3 tbsp cold water

* When measuring the flour, scoop the dry-measure cup directly into your flour container and fill the cup to overflowing; do not shake the cup or pack down the flour. Sweep off excess so that the flour is even with the lip of the cup, using a straight edge of some sort. Sift only after measuring. Preheat the oven to 375°F.

Quarter, core, and peel the apples. Cut into lengthwise slices $1/8$-inch thick. Toss in a bowl with $1/3$ cup sugar and the optional cinnamon. You should have about 10 cups of apples.

Butter a 9- to 10-inch diameter, 2- to $2^1/2$-inch deep baking dish heavily with the softened butter, especially on the bottom. Sprinkle half the remaining sugar in the bottom of the dish and arrange a third of the apples over it. Sprinkle with a third of the melted butter. Repeat with a layer of half the remaining apples and butter, then a final layer of apples and butter. Sprinkle the rest of the sugar over the apples.

To make the pastry, place the flour in a large mixing bowl. Mix in the sugar and salt, then add the butter and vegetable shortening.

Rub the fat and flour together rapidly between the tips of your fingers until the fat is broken down into pieces the size of oatmeal flakes. Add the water and blend quickly with one hand, fingers held together and slightly cupped, as you rapidly gather the dough into a mass. Then press the dough firmly into a roughly shaped ball. It should just hold together and be pliable, but not sticky.

Roll out the pastry to a thickness of about ⅛ inch. Cut it into a circle the size of the top of the baking dish. Place it over the apples, allowing its edges to fall against the inside of the dish. Cut 4 or 5 holes about ⅛-inch long in the top of the pastry to allow cooking steam to escape.

Bake in the lower third of the preheated oven for 45 to 60 minutes. If the pastry begins to brown too much, cover lightly with aluminum foil. The tart is done when you tilt the dish and see that a thick brown syrup rather than a light liquid exudes from the apples between the crust and the edge of the dish.

Immediately unmold the tart onto a serving dish. If the apples are not a light caramel brown, which is often the case, sprinkle rather heavily with powdered sugar and run under a moderately hot broiler for several minutes to caramelize the surface lightly.

Keep warm until serving time, and accompany with a bowl of heavy cream. *Serves 8*

Adapted from Julia Child, Louisette Bertholle, and Simone Beck *Mastering the Art of French Cooking*

Tiramisu

The name tiramisu translates as "pick me up," which accurately describes the strong espresso coffee in this rich calorific dessert. There are several ways to make it, the simplest involving beating egg yolks with sugar and vanilla until thick and fluffy. In the cooked version, a little milk is added and the mixture cooked in a double boiler until it thickens. Heavy cream is whipped with mascarpone cheese and folded into the egg-yolk mixture. Eggs may be omitted altogether, though this makes the dessert heavier. To assemble, some of the mascarpone mixture is spread in a serving dish and Savoiardi cookies (sponge or lady fingers) are dipped in a mixture of coffee and coffee liqueur and arranged in a layer on top.

The layering continues until the ingredients are used up, then the dessert is refrigerated until well chilled. Just before serving, it is generously sprinkled with cocoa powder.

Tiramisu has gained universal popularity in recent years and is served in many restaurants. It has even spawned variations such as tiramisu-flavored ice cream and tiramisu cake.

Toffee Apples

Also known in North America as caramel apples, these sweet and crunchy treats have been sold at fairs and other outdoor gatherings in England since the early Middle Ages. They are especially popular in the fall and winter in England, and are often served on Bonfire Night, November 5th.

Round juicy apples such as Cox's Orange Pippin are skewered with lollipop sticks and dipped in a toffee mixture usually made from brown sugar, butter, molasses, and a little vinegar. In North America, brittle candy apples are also popular, dipped in a sugar and cream of tartar mixture cooked to the hard-crack stage (300°F) and colored with bright red food coloring.

Toffee Apples

8 small apples, stems removed

1 cup water

2 cups sugar

Wash and dry the apples well. Put the sugar and water in a microwave-safe bowl and cook on high for 5 minutes. Stir until the sugar has dissolved then continue cooking on high until golden, 15 to 20 minutes. Meanwhile, insert a 5- or 6-inch skewer into each apple. Remove toffee from the microwave and let stand for 2 minutes. Dip the apples in the toffee, hold over the bowl to catch any drips and stand on parchment paper to harden. *Serves 8*

Treacle Tart

This English tart is a staple of the boarding-school dinner and remembered with affection. For some reason, it has never traveled to North America except, perhaps, in the form of shoofly pie or Quebec's sugar pie. In England, the piecrust may or may not be prebaked. The main ingredient is golden syrup, which, like treacle and molasses, is made from refined sugar cane. The syrup is thickened with bread crumbs, cake crumbs, or a crumble mixture of flour, butter, and brown sugar. Some recipes include a top crust or pastry lattice.

In Yorkshire, the treacle is mixed with chopped dried fruit and grated apple, while in Suffolk, two eggs are beaten with the treacle and poured into the pie crust for a treacle custard tart.

Treacle Tart

12 oz pastry

9 tbsp golden syrup or molasses

9 tbsp fresh white bread crumbs

Grated zest and juice of 1 lemon

1 tsp ground ginger

Egg wash (1 egg beaten with 1 tsp water)

Preheat the oven to 375°F.

Roll out two-thirds of the pastry and use it to line a 10-inch pie plate or flan tin. Warm the syrup over low heat and add the bread crumbs, grated lemon zest, 1 tablespoon of the lemon juice, and the ginger. Pour into the pastry shell.

Roll out the remaining pastry and cut into strips to create a lattice design on top of the tart. Press the strips to the bottom crust with a fork to create a decorative edge and seal them well. Brush the crust with the egg wash and bake for 25 to 30 minutes or until the pastry is crisp and golden. *Serves 6*

Turròn

White Chocolate Mousse

This Christmas candy, made from honey and sugar mixed with chopped walnuts, pine nuts, or hazelnuts, is also known as *jijona* for the town of Jijona (Xixona) in Alicante where it is made as a specialty. It is called *turró* in Valencia and Catalonia. The nut mixture, which may contain sweet spices, is boiled until thick, then spread on greased sheets and left to harden. It is almost certainly of Arab origin and there is a 16th-century recipe for it. The sugar-and-nut mixture varies considerably depending on where it is made. In Catalonia, for example, turròn is made with coarse brown sugar and contains only hazelnuts, while in the Basque region, turròn is a simple almond paste colored red and rolled into small balls.

A French version called *touron* is made in the French provinces bordering Spain. In Bayonne, it is made into a checkerboard of different colors and flavors. In the Philippines, *turrone*s is made with peanuts or cashews and sandwiched between two wafers.

The Italian version, *torrone*, is a specialty of Cremona.

This variation on a classic dark chocolate mousse is made from melted white chocolate blended with milk, whipping cream, and liqueur such as crème de cacao. Egg whites are folded in to lighten the mixture. White chocolate consists of cocoa butter, milk solids, and sugar, and contains no cocoa solids or chocolate.

It was invented in Switzerland by Nestlé in the early 1920s and became popular in France before being introduced into the United Kingdom in 1937. It finally reached the United States in 1984. White chocolate mousse is one of several white desserts (panna cotta, crème brûlée) that have become popular in recent years and are often featured on restaurant menus. It may be garnished with curls of dark chocolate and sprinkled with powdered sugar.

Waffles

Although waffles are inextricably linked to Belgium and northern France, the batter and cooking technique have been known since ancient times. The French name *gauffre* and the English name "waffle" both derive from the same medieval French word for this thick batter of flour, milk, and eggs.

Before the invention of ovens, the only way to make a cake or cookie was to bake the batter on a hot metal plate, which the Greeks are known to have done. In the 13th century,

a Flemish baker had the idea of hinging two metal plates and adding a grid pattern to facilitate cooking, thus inventing the now-familiar waffle iron. Handmade waffle irons were popular in the 15th century, some designed in elaborate fan-shaped patterns still used today.

Modern electric waffle irons have nonstick coatings. Waffles are served with syrup for breakfast or topped with ice cream, whipped cream, and fruit for dessert.

Zeppole

Zeppole are fried or baked to celebrate St. Joseph's Day on March 19. They have several names, including *cavazune* and *le sfinge di San Giuseppe*. Savory versions consist of deep-fried balls of sweetened bread dough filled with various mixtures such as garbanzos (*ceci*) or cheese and anchovies. They never contain meat, since the day usually falls during Lent.

Another treasured family recipe consists of a deep-fried choux paste doughnut cut in half crosswise and filled with a mixture of ricotta cheese and chopped candied fruits, the same filling used for cannoli. Jam-flavored zeppole are also sold in the streets on the saint's day in Rome, Naples, and throughout Sicily.

In countries with a large Italian population, St. Joseph tables are set up in churches and homes. Each table, covered with a lace tablecloth, is blessed by a priest and presided over by a statue of St. Joseph. Lilies and votive candles decorate the feast table. Traditional foods for the day, including pasta Milanese and zeppole, are placed on the table as an offering to the saint.

Zabaglione ▷

Zabaglione is a classic southern Italian dessert. This frothy sauce or custard is made from egg yolks, sugar, and sweet Italian wine, traditionally marsala, though other sweet wines can be used. It is said to have been invented in the 16th century and brought to France (where it is known as *sabayon*) by the cooks of Marie de Medici, who became Queen of France in 1600 and introduced many new foods to her adopted country. Semi-liquid desserts of this type, known variously in English as caudle, posset, or syllabub, were extremely popular at that time.

Zabaglione should be made just before serving or the foam on the surface will disappear. Egg yolks are whisked with sugar and cooked in a double boiler until thick enough to coat the back of a spoon. The sweet wine is then beaten in. Zabaglione can be served hot, as a dessert or sauce, or cooled and frozen into ice cream.

For a different texture, the egg whites can be whipped and folded into the finished custard before serving.

Blueberry Muffin

American muffins bear no resemblance to the teacake known in the US as an English muffin. The American baked good was christened by the Thomas bakery in New York, and the word appears to be derived from the Low German *muffe*, meaning "cake." The American muffin looks something like a large cupcake, but has a rounded top instead of a flat one and is never frosted. Blueberries, a fruit native to North America, are a popular inclusion in the American muffin, as are other fruits, nuts, and chocolate. The flour used for muffins may be white or whole wheat, and bran is sometimes included. Traditionally, the mixture is yeast-raised, but homemade muffins often use baking powder as the leavener.

Muffins are popular in the United States at breakfast time or mid-morning, usually eaten with coffee. It is an odd fact that the English muffin, or teacake, which had been sold in the streets for centuries, disappeared from Great Britain in the 1930s, but was reintroduced from the United States in the 1980s and is now regularly sold in supermarkets, as is the American-style sweet blueberry muffin.

Baguette

Is there anything more delicious than a warm, crisp baguette? The term "baguette" is the generic name for the traditional "French bread" or "stick," which in France is more often known as *ficelle* (the thinner one) and *flûte* (the thicker one). Baguettes known as *épis* are baked to resemble a wheat grain. Somewhat surprisingly, as it is so strongly associated with France, the baguette originated in mid-19th-century Vienna, where steam ovens were first used.

The secret of the baguette, with its crisp crust and very airy inner texture, is the use of French flour and the long rising time that starts with the *levain*, the mixture of flour and water to which yeast is added to make a very liquid dough. The bread may be left to rise in a cool place for as long as 24 hours.

The shape is the result of a law passed in France in October 1920, which stipulated that bakers were not allowed to start work before 4 a.m. This meant that loaves could not be ready for the 6 a.m. French breakfast. The slender baguette solved the problem, since it could be shaped, proofed, and baked within 2 hours.

Rye Bread

Rye bread is popular in Europe, especially in central and eastern regions, but less so in France. In the United Kingdom and the United States, it is largely associated with Jewish bakers, many of whom came from Eastern Europe. Rye has a low gluten content and does not react as well with yeast, which means that bread made exclusively from rye takes a very long time to rise—up to 12 hours. For this reason, rye is usually leavened from a sourdough starter, which lowers the pH level of the dough, causing the starch to gel and enabling it to trap gas bubbles. For the same reason, rye has a much denser interior and is heavier than wheat bread. Light rye bread is made from rye mixed with wheat. Rye bread is often flavored with caraway seeds or molasses. Rye was introduced to Britain by the Saxons and Danes, and the bread was a staple until the late Middle Ages. It remains the most popular bread in the Baltic countries, Denmark, and Finland. Rye is higher in fiber and lower in gluten content than wheat bread.

Baklava

One of the oldest known pastries, baklava may have been invented by the Assyrians who lived in the 8th century BC. It consists of layers of paper-thin phyllo or strudel dough, with chopped nuts sandwiched between, over which a sweet syrup is poured. Baked in huge trays, the assembled pastry is cut into triangles, lozenge shapes, or other patterns before baking, so the pieces are easy to separate for serving.

Baklava is popular in Europe and Asia—spreading from the Balkans in the west, via Turkey, to as far east as the Indian sub continent. This means that some of the ingredients vary with local availability. In Greece, walnuts are the nut of choice; in the Middle East, a mixture of almonds and pistachios is used, as well as a pistachio topping to add color. Sugar syrup is sometimes flavored with rosewater, but the best baklava is made with honey. Once the food of the wealthy (there is even a Turkish proverb to this effect), it is now enjoyed by all, often at weddings and other celebrations.

Biscotti

Biscotti are Italian rusks, the name meaning "twice baked." Originally, slicing and drying bread in a slow oven was a way of stopping it from going moldy when times were hard and even bread was scarce. Nowadays, biscotti can be a sweet or savory cookie. The mixture may be yeast-raised or consist of a *pan di spagna*, a light sponge mixture containing butter and eggs.

Biscotti are flavored differently in various parts of Italy. In the south, aniseed or aniseed liqueur is the preferred flavor; in the north, almonds are popular. There are even chocolate-flavored biscotti.

Biscotti are baked, cut into bars while still warm, and then baked again in a slow oven until crisp and golden. As a finishing touch, they may be dusted with powdered sugar or coated with a crumbly frosting. Biscotti have always been popular in Italy for dunking into morning coffee.

Chocolate-Hazelnut Biscotti

$^3/_4$ cup chocolate chips

$^1/_3$ cup butter

$^3/_4$ cup sugar

2 tsp baking powder

A pinch of salt

2 eggs, beaten

$^1/_2$ tsp vanilla extract

2 cups all-purpose flour

$^1/_2$ cup hazelnuts, coarsely chopped

Heat the oven to 350°F and lightly grease 2 baking sheets.

Melt the chocolate chips in a bowl over simmering water. Remove from the heat and leave to cool. Beat together the butter and sugar until light and fluffy. Beat in the baking powder and salt. Add the eggs, one at a time, and the vanilla extract, beating well between additions. Fold in the flour. Divide the dough in half, then stir the cooled chocolate into one half and the chopped hazelnuts into the other.

Divide each half into 4 equal parts and shape each portion into a long, thin strip, about 10 by 1 inches. Take a strip of each dough and interlace them to make a twist. Place on the baking sheet and flatten slightly.

Repeat with the remaining dough. Bake for 25 minutes, then remove from the oven and allow to cool slightly. Lower the oven temperature to 300°F. When the dough twists are cool enough to handle, cut each one, across its width, into about 10 biscotti. Return to the baking sheet and crispen in the oven for 20 to 25 minutes. *Makes about 40*

Paratha

A paratha is an unleavened Indian flatbread.
Like most such breads, it originated in what
is now Pakistan. It is brown in color because
it normally contains all or some whole-wheat
flour. The dough, which includes oil for
suppleness, is mixed then left for 20 to 30
minutes for the phytin to develop. It is then
rolled out into thin pancakes that are folded
into squares or triangles and baked on a
bakestone or griddle.

Parathas are traditionally eaten hot, with
chutney and yogurt, to accompany curry
or on their own with vegetables or ghee.
The shape of the bread lends itself to
stuffing, and stuffed parathas are eaten as
a snack between meals or as an appetizer.
The stuffing usually consists of vegetables,
such as boiled potatoes and cauliflower,
and/or *paneer* (Indian curd cheese).

The *kerala porota* is a paratha made in
an oval shape. The dough is left to proof for
4 hours to ensure softness. In another type
of paratha, the flour is kneaded and rolled
with ghee to make a dough that resembles
the Western flake pastry. Both types of
paratha are popular in the West, and the
paratha is eaten throughout India and
the Indian diaspora. A very large paratha
is eaten in Trinidad and Tobago.

Paratha

4 cups wheat flour

3 tbsp melted butter

1 tsp salt

1¼ cups water

Oil for brushing

All-purpose flour for dusting

Place the wheat flour, melted butter, and salt
in a large bowl. Create a well in the center
and pour in the water. Bring the ingredients
together, kneading to make a reasonably
soft dough. Knead for approximately 5 to 8
minutes. Cover with a clean towel and leave
for 20 minutes.

Form the dough into 2-inch diameter balls,
then roll the balls into circles, about 4 inches
in diameter. Brush each dough circle with
oil and dust with a little flour. Fold in half,
brush with oil and dust with flour. Fold in
half again. You should now have a triangular-
shaped piece of dough. Roll out each triangle
until it is about $\frac{1}{8}$-inch thick.

Preheat a griddle pan. Place a triangular
piece of dough onto the pan and cook for
30 seconds. Turn over and brush the cooked
side with oil. Continue frying until crisp and
golden brown in color. Cover the cooked
parathas in foil to keep them warm while
you cook the rest. *Makes 12*

Pita

This flatbread is baked throughout the Arab countries and in recent years has been imported to the West, where it is often known as a pita pocket. Despite its current popularity in the United Kingdom and the United States, it was unknown in both countries until the early 1950s.

This type of dough, which is leavened, sometimes with a sourdough starter, was shaped into rounds and baked on a flat stone over an open fire. This method was used all over Asia (from the Near East to India), North Africa, and the Balkans. The original word is from Hebrew and Aramaic, where it simply means "bread."

The Italian word "pizza" is from the same root. In the Balkans and Greece, *pitta* is the name for a cake or pie, thus *yaortipitta*, a Greek cake made with yogurt, and *spanakopita*, a spinach pie.

What distinguishes pita bread from most breads is the high temperature at which it is baked, which causes the dough to "balloon" as steam builds up inside. The interior separates, leaving a hollow center that is perfect for fillings, such as falafel with salad vegetables, moistened with tahini.

Pretzel

The pretzel or bretzel is a twisted rope of shiny yeast-raised dough made from white flour. It can be crisp or soft and is often sprinkled with salt crystals. Prior to baking, the shaped dough is dipped into a solution of sodium hydroxide, which gives it its typical shiny brown crust. The word "pretzel" comes from *bracellus*, the Latin for "crossed arms." The Roman attitude of prayer is that of standing with the arms crossed, hands on shoulders, and the pretzel was originally baked as a Roman ritual bread, but there are many other stories about the origin.

Known as *brezl* or *brezn*, the soft pretzel is eaten throughout Germany and also in the United States, where they are bought fresh from street vendors or frozen from supermarkets.

Americans have reinvented the pretzel, miniaturizing it and even coating it in dark and white chocolate. Because their salty coating promotes thirst, pretzels are traditionally served in bars, inns, and taverns to encourage patrons to drink more beer.

◁ Croissant

The deliciously flaky, crescent-shaped roll always associated with France is believed to have originated in Vienna. Stories exist of its invention to symbolize the defeat of the Ottoman army at the Battle of Vienna in 1529, or its introduction to France by the Austrian-born Marie Antoinette, but these have been dismissed as fables. Food historians claim that the croissant was unknown until the 19th century. Nevertheless, there is a strong possibility that flake pastry (known in French as *viennoiserie*) was created by Viennese pastry cooks, who are famous for their technique and ingenuity.

The croissant is made from a yeast dough enriched with copious amounts of butter, using a technique of repeatedly rolling out the dough and constantly folding it in three, chilling it, then refolding and rolling it out again—making the dough for a croissant can take several days. The croissant is traditionally eaten for breakfast in France where it is bought fresh early in the morning. Since the popularity of the croissant has spread, short-cuts have been invented. However, dough made and rolled in bulk and sent out, frozen, to restaurants and retail bakeries for baking cannot compare with locally made produce.

Crumpet

This round, flat circle of dough dotted with small holes on the top side is an English teatime specialty. The strange texture and unusual flavor are achieved by making a soft yeast batter containing milk. To ensure that the mixture is light and full of holes, soda water is sometimes added to the batter, before it is baked in hoops or rings on a heated baking sheet or griddle. When served, crumpets are toasted before being spread with melted butter and possibly jam or a savory spread. Once only available commercially in the winter, they are now eaten year-round.

Crumpets are known as "pikelets" in northern England and Wales. The Scotch crumpet is a thin pancake, about 7 inches in diameter and studded with raisins. It is also spread with butter and eaten at teatime. English and Scottish crumpets are also popular in Australia and New Zealand. The crumpet certainly has a long history, since similar words for teacakes appear in literature as far back as 1382, when John Wycliffe mentioned "crompid cake." The first printed recipe was by Mrs. Elizabeth Raffald, whose *The Experienced English Housekeeper* was published in 1769.

Beer Bread

Beer, due to its yeast content, is often used to raise dough or lighten batter. The ancient Egyptians, said to have been the first beer brewers, made a barley bread. They began by combining barley flour, sprouted barley grain, and water (making a beer-like substance) and letting it ferment. The natural yeasts in the atmosphere made it foam and converted the sugar content to alcohol. This very liquid mixture, still used in making certain breads today, is called the leaven. The process is speeded up when actual beer is used in the leaven. Many modern beer breads do not require the lengthy kneading, rising, and proofing of traditional breads. In fact, beer bread has a very long tradition, since the earliest forms of yeast did not come in compressed form or as dried granules, but were the liquid drawn off as a by-product of beer making. The beery liquid used to make breads was known as "barm," hence the expression "barmy" for someone perceived to be light-headed. The term persists in northern England, where bread rolls are known colloquially as barm-cakes.

Butter Tarts

One of the few truly indigenous Canadian foods, the butter tart has long been a staple in Canadian kitchens, where they are served at teatime or as a dessert. Even today, no rural bake sale would be complete without a tray of butter tarts on offer.

The first recorded recipes date back to 1915, though historians suggest that tarts were a part of the cooking repertoire of pioneer households for many years before, no doubt favored because they will keep for weeks in a tightly sealed tin. The formula is simple: butter, eggs, and brown sugar are beaten together and then scooped into flake-pastry shells, where they are baked until brown. Some cooks add raisins to the mix, though this is a matter of no small controversy. The proportion of the three main ingredients determines the texture of the tart (runny versus not runny), which is the other major butter tart controversy.

Brioche

The brioche has a special place in history because Marie Antoinette is alleged to have answered *"Qu'ils mangent de la brioche!,"* loosely translated as "let them eat cake," when told that the people of Paris had no bread. The brioche owes its light crumbly texture to a rich, yeast-raised dough containing eggs and milk. It is usually eaten for breakfast and can be spread with jam.

The name "brioche" comes from two Old French words—*bris* meaning "to break" and *hocher* meaning "to stir," referring to the kneading movement required to make the dough rise and to shape it. The most common shape for a brioche is a large, round ball with a smaller ball on top, known as a brioche *à tête*. It may be baked in this shape or as individual smaller rolls. There is also a column shape, known as a brioche *mousseline,* which contains more butter. In the brioche *nanterre,* the dough is shaped into small balls that are baked in a loaf pan. During baking, the balls of dough fuse together and form a pattern on the surface. The brioche *en couronne,* where the dough is formed into a crown or wreath shape before baking, is often filled with raisins and then frosted, to be served on special occasions. It is similar to the brioche *des rois,* the Provençal version of the kings' cake, served on Epiphany (Twelfth Night).

Pumpernickel

Sourdough Bread   ▷

This German black bread is made from various grades of rye flour, using a sourdough rye starter. Associated with Westphalia, the first written reference to it dates from 1450. Classic Westphalian pumpernickel is almost impossible to bake at home. As rye reacts so slowly with yeast, it needs several days in which to rise and proof. The bread is then baked in a square loaf pan with a lid (to prevent a crust from forming) for between 16 and 24 hours in a low (250°F) oven. When it emerges, the bread is the typical dark brown or black color.

American pumpernickel bread is totally different. It is merely a dark rye bread, the color being achieved not from slow baking but from the addition of a dark flavoring such as molasses or unsweetened chocolate. The bread usually contains wheat flour and yeast to make the rising process quicker, and it is baked in the traditional way, in trays or in a loaf pan and at the normal high heat.

True pumpernickel is imported into the United Kingdom and the United States, where it is sold pre-sliced and packaged, and is often eaten with toppings, such as cheese or ham, as an open-faced sandwich.

A sourdough is a natural leaven created by mixing flour and water into a very liquid dough and allowing it to ferment naturally when a combination of *lactobacilli* and yeasts from the air come into contact with it. The starter has to be "fed" with more flour and water every few days for about ten days, when it should be foaming and ready for breadmaking.

San Francisco sourdough became famous because the quality of the wild yeasts was so good that it made the best bread, in recognition of which the dominant strain of *lactobacillus* in sourdough starters has been named *Lactobacillus sanfranciscensis* (the yeast strain is usually *Saccharomyces cerevisiae*). Instead of making a sourdough leaven from scratch, most bakers make the first leaven and preserve a little of it for the next batch of bread. San Francisco sourdough bread uses sourdough leaven added to a white flour mixture. The flavor of the resulting bread is distinctly sour, but very pleasant. It has remained in continuous production for nearly 150 years, with some bakeries able to trace their starters back to the beginning of permanent white settlement in California.

Garlic Bread

Garlic bread is simply fresh bread rubbed with garlic and butter or margarine, and broiled or baked. The tastiest garlic bread depends on the freshness, quality, and type of bread used. The bread should preferably be French or Italian, such as a ciabatta or short French loaf. There are different ways of making garlic bread: the loaf may simply be sliced in half lengthwise and thickly buttered, then rubbed with cut garlic cloves or sprinkled with chopped garlic. Or bread slices may be dipped in melted butter and fried with garlic and possibly parsley. Another method, which keeps the bread soft, is to slice a ciabatta or French loaf and spread the slices with a mixture of melted butter, chopped garlic, chopped parsley, and grated cheese. The bread is then "reassembled," wrapped in foil, and baked at 350°F for 30 minutes.

Garlic bread seems to be an American invention that has spread throughout the English-speaking world. It is mainly eaten as an accompaniment to Italian and French meat or vegetable stews and is a feature on the menu of most pizzerias. The Italians claim it is simply a variation on the Tuscan bruschetta.

Granary Bread

It is not often realized that Granary is a proprietary name. It is used for an English bread-making flour mixture containing fermented and sprouted wheat (malt). Other ingredients may vary, but it often includes seeds such as linseed and sesame. The basic recipe has existed for centuries. In the 14th century, the Benedictine monks of Burton-on-Trent are said to have invented a malting process for brewing the ale for which the locality is famous and, almost by accident, discovered that malted wheat could add greater flavor to their bread.

The exact Granary formula is a closely guarded secret, now owned by Rank Hovis (Premier Foods). However, the magic ingredient in Granary flour is the maltose from the sprouted wheat that is left to ferment for ten days. (The ambient temperature and precise timings are decided by the master maltster.) The malted wheat grains are then pressed between metal rollers to crack them and flatten them into flakes.

After flaking, the wheat is taken to a huge kiln where it is roasted for two days. The roasting dries out the wheat, stops the germination, and caramelizes the maltose. The grains are then blended with brown flour to produce the unmistakable Granary malted flour.

Ciabatta

Extremely popular outside its native Italy
in recent times, this soft, moist, white loaf
has a light-brown floury crust and very porous
interior. The loaf is long and flat, sinking
slightly in the middle, with roughly square
ends. This shape is how the loaf got its name:
ciabatta means "slipper," from the Turkish
word *cabat*. The ciabatta is baked and eaten
in every province of Italy. Sometimes it is
baked plain, but other varieties are flavored
with herbs, as in Rome, where marjoram is
added to the dough. In some parts of Italy,
the crust can be firm and shiny and there are
even ciabatta breads baked using whole-wheat
flour. The dough is soft due to the addition
of olive oil, the use of a starter or leaven,
and the long rising time, normally 6 hours.
The soft, dry crust is achieved by dusting the
loaf with finely ground durum wheat flour
and baking it in an oven containing a bowl
of water so that steam rises and envelops
the dough during baking. In modern bakeries,
steam ovens are used to bake ciabatta. The
toasted sandwiches made from ciabatta rolls
are known as panini.

Challah

The challah is a braided loaf of rich yeast
dough that is eaten by Ashkenazi Jews on
the Sabbath (Friday evening to Saturday
afternoon). It is usually finished with an egg
or sugar-and-water wash and topped with
poppy seeds or sesame seeds. The challah
dough always contains eggs but never milk,
as Orthodox Jews may not eat milk and meat
at the same meal.

The tradition of braiding a bread for festive
occasions dates back at least to Roman times
and probably earlier. Braided loaves are found
in many cultures, especially in Eastern Europe
where the challah probably originated. The
name challah comes from the Hebrew word
lekhalot meaning "to divide," because it was
the custom in biblical times to donate some
of the dough to the high priest. Today, this
portion is ceremonially burned; this is done
whether the challah is baked at home or
in a commercial bakery, otherwise the challah
is not kosher. The challah is known as *barches*
among Jews of German origin (derived from
the Hebrew word for a blessing). It was one
of the few types of bread that was permitted
to be baked in Britain during and after the
Second World War, when bread and eggs
were rationed.

Irish Soda Bread

Hot Cross Buns   ▷

The damp climate of Ireland is the reason
for the popularity of soda bread. In the days
when only home-grown flour was available,
the cool, wet summers meant that the grain
might not be ripe, so yeast would not act
upon it. The cold, damp climate also inhibited
the yeast's action. The essential ingredients,
apart from the wheat, which may be white,
wheatmeal (80% whole), or whole wheat,
are baking soda and buttermilk or soured
milk. Fresh milk can also be used, but a pinch
of cream of tartar must be added. The only
other authentic ingredients are a pinch of
salt and sugar added to the dough.

   The bread can be baked as a loaf in the
oven or cooked as flat cakes on a griddle.
The bread is shaped straight after kneading,
and it must not rest for more than 15 minutes
or the soda loses its effect. A deep cross cut
in the surface of the loaf ensures even baking,
and easy breaking into four pieces.

These sweet, sticky buns, commemorated
in a song, are baked in England for Easter
("Give them to your daughters, give them
to your sons, one a penny, two a penny, hot
cross buns"). The buns certainly have a very
long tradition in England and were possibly
introduced by Christian missionaries
especially to commemorate Good Friday,
the Day of the Cross. The yeast-raised dough
contains mixed spice, dried fruit, butter, and
sugar. A large cross is made on the surface
by piping a flour-and-water paste on the raw
buns just before they are baked. After baking,
the buns are glazed with honey or corn syrup.
According to food historian Elizabeth David,
the buns were seen by Elizabeth I, a militant
Protestant English monarch, as a dangerous
vestige of Catholic practice in England. She
passed a law permitting bakeries to sell them
only at Easter and Christmas. Similar buns are
baked for Easter in other Christian countries,
but none are as distinctive as the English hot
cross bun. It is also a tradition in England to
buy the buns from street vendors or bakeries
rather than make them at home.

INDIA

Roti and Chapati

The generic Indian flatbread is the roti, the word for "bread" in Hindi and Urdu (known as a chapati in southern India). This bread is always unleavened but, nevertheless, is light and supple because the flour and water are mixed into a dough, kneaded well, shaped, and left for a few hours or overnight. An enzyme in the flour known as phytase "digests" the dough and makes it supple, so the effect is similar to that of having added yeast. The final round of preparation consists of flattening the dough again, coating it with oil, and cooking it in hot oil on a sheet of iron. The ideal roti is flat, fluffy on the inside, but crisp and flaky on the outside.

Traditionally, roti is served with dal, curried lentils, or garbanzos.

The chapati is made in the same way as the roti but using different types of flour—generally atta flour, whole-wheat durum, and sometimes added millet or cornmeal. The chapati measures about 4³/₄ inches in diameter. If held in an open flame, it can also be made to puff up like a balloon with steam inside; it is then known as a *phulka*.

Finished chapatis are brushed with ghee and usually served with vegetable curries.

ITALY

Foccacia

Like all flatbreads, the foccacia is of very ancient origin, probably from the Etruscans or ancient Greeks. It is a specialty of Liguria and, according to British chef and restaurateur Antonio Carluccio, the best foccacia is made in Camogli, a fishing village. Foccacia has become extremely popular in the United Kingdom and the United States in recent years. In those countries, slits or depressions are cut into the surface of the dough before baking and these are sprinkled with olive oil and salt, and stuffed with sprigs of rosemary.

In Italy, foccacia is often spread with tomato paste before baking. It may be baked on an oiled baking sheet or fitted into a large square or oblong pan. In one variation, the dough is divided in two and rolled out like a strudel. The bottom layer is placed in a pan and covered with stracchino cheese, then the top layer is added and drizzled with olive oil.

There are also variations in which the top is sprinkled with sliced olives or hazelnuts.

Tortilla

The Mexican tortilla is not to be confused with the Spanish tortilla, an omelette stuffed with vegetables. In Mexico and the southwestern United States, several of the states having once belonged to Mexico, the tortilla is a staple food. The corn tortilla is made from *masa harina* dough, maize that has been slaked in lime and then ground. It has a diameter of about 6 inches. The dough is simply mixed with water, then rolled out as thinly as possible, using a short, light rolling pin. They are then baked on a flat griddle. Since cornmeal does not keep and must be eaten fresh, these tortillas are brought to the table wrapped in a warmed cloth and sometimes inside a woven basket, so the steam in them is retained. These tortillas are sometimes filled and rolled, in which case they are called tacos.

The flour tortilla is often twice as large as the corn tortilla and is made of white flour, *harina de trigo*. It is prepared and cooked in the same way as the corn tortilla, but keeps better. It can be folded more easily, so it is often wrapped around fillings, in which case it is known as a burrito or enchilada.

Tortilla "Sandwich"

12 tortillas

6 oz cooked ham, thinly sliced

6 oz Chihuahua cheese or Cheddar, finely sliced

Vegetable oil for frying

3/4 cup sour cream

3/4 cup salsa de tomate verde or guacamole

1/2 cup finely chopped white onion

1 1/2 cups finely shredded lettuce

6 radishes, cut into flowers or sliced

Lay 6 of the tortillas out flat; spread each one with some of the ham and cheese. Cover with another tortilla to form a sandwich, then secure each pair of tortillas together with toothpicks, one on each side. Heat the oil and fry each sandwich on either side until just beginning to get crisp, not hard. Drain well, then top with the sour cream, sauce or guacamole, and chopped onion.

Decorate each plate with the lettuce and radishes, which will serve as a foil for the richness of the tortillas. Serve immediately.
Makes 6
Adapted from Diana Kennedy's *The Essential Cuisines of Mexico*

Knackebrød

This is the Danish and Norwegian (Bokmål) name for crispbread. Crispbreads are popular throughout Scandinavia, as well as in the United Kingdom, where Ryvita is the leading brand. The leading Scandinavian brand is Wasa. The main difference between Ryvita and Wasa is that Ryvita does not use yeast. The crispbread, made from wheat or rye, was first invented because grains often do not ripen in the harsh Scandinavian climate. Unripe wheat and rye will not rise when yeast is added to them, so they were baked as flatbreads. They differ from Indian flatbreads, such as chapati and roti, because they have to be hard, crisp, and dry or the damp that also prevents fermentation of the yeast will turn a soft bread moldy, whether leavened or not. The dryness means that the bread will keep for a very long time. In Scandinavian homes, the breads were baked as round cakes with a hole in the center (some crispbreads are still sold in this shape) and strung on strings or poles high above the kitchen fire, where they would keep well all winter. The holes pricked in the crispbread are the secret, as they prevent it from softening.

Matzo

Matzo is the unleavened bread that Jews eat for the eight days of Passover to commemorate when the Israelites had to leave Egypt in such a hurry that their bread did not have time to rise and it was baked on their backs in the hot sun. Matzo (plural: matzos or matzot) can also be eaten at other times of year. Under religious law, no more than 18 minutes must elapse between the time the water touches the flour and the time the cake of matzo is placed in the oven. The dough is not kneaded but beaten, then rolled flat, always using a metal rolling pin, in case wood contains fungal spores that might leaven the dough. Before baking, it is pricked with a regular pattern of holes to allow for quick baking and to ensure the dough does not rise, as for crispbread.

Matzos were once shaped and baked exclusively by hand. The first matzo-baking machine came into use in the mid-19th century, and now most matzos are kneaded and baked in a production-line process, untouched by human hand. Traditionally, matzo contained nothing but wheat flour, water, and salt. Today, whole-wheat matzos, egg matzos, and even chocolate-dipped matzos are kosher for Passover.

Churros

Corn Bread

On a sun-blasted Sunday morning in Spain, it's easy to find the nearest *churreria*. Just follow the locals carrying clear plastic bags full of grease-stained paper. The crunchy, ridged sticks of deep-fried pastry contained within are made for munching with *café con leche* (espresso with milk) or pudding-thick hot chocolate, another Spanish specialty. Named for the curved horns of the Churro sheep, churros are wildly popular throughout Spain and Mexico from breakfast until late at night, among people of all ages. They're now appearing in much of North America.

The churro maker presses the addictive snacks from a large tube (picture a giant cake-decorating nozzle) into the hot oil below. The choux-paste dough, made with cooked flour and eggs, may be extruded in a large spiral or in individual lengths. After frying, they are drained briefly on butcher paper and sprinkled with sugar.

At home, ridged churros can be pressed from a star-tip nozzle on a cookie press, while fatter *porras*, or clubs, require a round nozzle.

The corn in this case is cornmeal, made from maize or sweet corn that is slaked, dried, and ground into a flour or meal ranging in consistency from fine to coarse. In Europe, corn bread is made only in the Balkans, where cornmeal has come to replace durum wheat as a crop. The best-known and tastiest corn breads come from the southern United States. They may be made with white or yellow cornmeal. Only cornmeal breads containing a high proportion of wheat flour can be leavened with yeast and baked like wheat bread. Plain cornmeal does not react with yeast, so the mixture is lightened with baking powder and eggs, or very often with butter-milk combined with baking soda and/or cream of tartar. The mixture is not a dough but a batter so it cannot be baked frees-tanding on a sheet; it must be poured into a loaf pan. It can also be made into cakes or patties and fried in a cast-iron frying pan or baked on a greased griddle. Corn bread or corn cakes are eaten as an accompaniment to hearty stews, sometimes with a green vegetable, such as collard, turnip, or mustard greens, or served for breakfast along with broiled sausages or ham.

Danish Pastry

The Danish pastry, or "Danish" for short, is not one pastry but a whole range, all made from the same type of yeast puff dough used for the croissant. In Denmark (and throughout Scandinavia), these pastries are called *Vienerbrød*, meaning "Vienna bread." In the late 19th century, when Danish bakers went on strike, they were replaced by Viennese bakers who made these light, fluffy creations. In Germany and Austria, they are called *Kopenhagener Gebäck*, which translates to "Copenhagen breads."

Danish pastries are always sweet and take many forms. They may be the sugared, looped whorls known as palmiers; folded pastries containing fruit, such as apple, plum, and apricot; or pastry wrapped around chocolate or almond cream and topped with flaked almonds and powdered sugar.

The Danish pastry is hugely popular in English-speaking countries, especially in the United States, to which it was introduced in 1915. A Danish baker made a large Danish pastry, possibly a kringle, for the wedding of US President Woodrow Wilson in December of that year. The baker then supplied the pastries to the owner of a chain of restaurants in New York City and the rest, as they say, is history.

Doughnut

The doughnut comes in two shapes, a round ball and a ring. The jam or jelly doughnut, depending which side of the Atlantic you're on, is a ball of dough with jam inserted in the center. The ring doughnut is made either by joining the ends of a long strip of dough into a ring, or by using a doughnut cutter that leaves a hole in the center. This smaller piece of dough (called a doughnut hole) can be cooked or incorporated into the dough to make more doughnuts. Doughnuts are made from either a yeast-based dough, in which case they are called raised doughnuts, or a richer dough with baking powder added. After deep-frying or baking, doughnuts are often frosted or sprinkled with powdered sugar or a mixture of cinnamon and sugar.

Most countries and cultures have their own version of the doughnut. For example, they are called *Berliners* in Germany, *ponchiki* in Poland, and *yo-yos* in Tunisia.

Doughnuts

$1^{1}/_{2}$ cups all-purpose flour
2 tsp baking powder
2 tbsp cinnamon
$^{1}/_{4}$ tsp salt
$^{1}/_{8}$ tsp nutmeg
1 tbsp unsalted butter
$^{1}/_{2}$ cup milk

1/3 cup sugar

1 egg

1 tbsp canola oil

1 tsp vanilla extract

To finish:

1/4 cup powdered sugar

1 1/2 to 2 tsp hot water

2 tbsp sugar

1/2 tsp cinnamon

Preheat the oven to 350°F.

Sift the flour, baking powder, cinnamon, salt, and nutmeg into a large bowl. Melt the butter in a large saucepan over low heat, then whisk in the milk, sugar, egg, oil, and vanilla extract. Beat the mixture until smooth, then add the flour mix, a spoon or two at a time, and continue to beat until well blended.

Spoon the dough into the molds of a greased doughnut pan, filling them about 3/4 full. Bake in the preheated oven for 8 to 10 minutes. While the doughnuts are still warm, brush them with a thin syrup made from the powdered sugar and hot water. Combine the sugar and cinnamon in a shallow dish and roll each doughnut in this to finish. *Makes 18*

Naan

Eaten in northern India and over much of the subcontinent, in Afghanistan, Iran, Uzbekistan, Tadjikistan, Myanmar, and Iran, this is a yeast-raised flatbread. It was brought to India by the moguls who ruled there from 1526 to 1862, who ate it for breakfast as they still do in Myanmar today.

Most flatbreads, whether yeast-raised or unleavened, are very plain since they are baked on a unidirectional heat source, such as a flat stone heated on an open fire or on a griddle. Naan is different because the yeast dough is quite rich, containing milk or yogurt, and it is baked in a very hot tandoor, or clay oven. When home-baked, the naan is cooked under a preheated broiler, and turned once during cooking. The top is usually dimpled, brushed with oil or ghee and sprinkled with salt and black onion or nigella seeds. Naan is browned all over through oven baking.

Naan is often stuffed with other mixtures. Peshwari naan, for example, is filled and topped with a sweet mixture of grated coconut, jaggery (palm sugar), and raisins. It can also be flavored with rosewater, vetiver, and the screwpine essence known as kevra. Naan bread is extremely popular outside India and is always a staple on the menu at Indian restaurants.

Naan

| ¼ oz package active dry yeast |
| 1 cup warm water |
| ¼ cup sugar |
| 3 tbsp milk |
| 1 egg, beaten |
| 2 tsp salt |
| 4 ½ cups bread flour, sifted |
| ¼ cup butter, melted |

In a large bowl, dissolve the yeast in the warm water. Leave for 10 minutes, until frothy.

Add the sugar, milk, egg, salt, and sufficient flour to form a soft dough. Knead the dough until smooth—6 to 8 minutes. Place in an oiled glass bowl and cover with a clean, damp tea towel. Leave to rise for 1 hour.

Punch the dough down, then make 14 balls about the size of a golf ball. Place them on a platter, cover with the clean, damp tea towel, and leave to double in size—30 minutes.

Place a griddle over high heat and brush with oil. Roll a dough ball out into a thin circle, place on the griddle and cook for 2 to 3 minutes, or until nicely puffy and a light brown color. Brush the uncooked side with a little melted butter and turn over. Now brush the cooked side with butter. Brown the uncooked side for 3 minutes and remove from the griddle. Repeat with the remaining dough, and serve. *Makes 14*

◁ # Bagel

The bagel has been described as tasting like "a doughnut dipped in cement," which seems an odd description, as they are delicious. They are made using an ancient technique of first briefly boiling the yeast-raised dough and then baking it. If the dough is not boiled, it is not a true bagel. The origin of the ring-shaped roll is obscure; one story credits Jewish bakers of Warsaw with making bagels in honor of the victory of King Jan Sobieski at the Battle of Vienna in 1683.

The meaning of the word is equally obscure, but it is connected with the French word *bague* meaning "ring" and the German word for a stirrup, *beugel*. Bagels are now more popular in the US and England than in their native Eastern Europe. In addition to the basic bagel, choices include egg, whole-wheat, and pumpernickel varieties. They are sometimes sprinkled with poppy seeds, sesame seeds (popular in Israel), and chopped onion. Also popular are thoroughly modern bagels with raisins, blueberries, or chocolate chips in every bite.

Pain au Chocolat

A popular snack in France, pain au chocolat simply means "bread with chocolate." Originally, it was simply a narrow bar of chocolate inserted into a large chunk of French bread and eaten as a snack, generally by children coming home from school. From this evolved the bakery item we know today. The dough is of the croissant type, but sweetened and rolled out in a rectangle. The chocolate, usually a slab of high-quality baking chocolate, is placed in the center and wrapped in the dough. As the dough bakes, the chocolate melts.

The pain au chocolat is known as a "chocolatine" in French-speaking Canada and in certain regions of France. Like all puff-dough products, the pain au chocolat should be eaten as soon as possible after baking. It has become a staple of the French, English, and American bakeries that sell the yeast-raised, buttery, puff-dough morning goods known in France as *viennoiserie*. Pain au chocolat can be made at home very easily: roll out and wrap ready-made dough around a stick of good-quality chocolate, then bake it in a hot oven for 15 minutes.

20 Chocolate Treats

Black Forest cake

Chocolate Yule log

Chocolate fudge cake

Chocolate Swiss roll

Chocolate syrup sponge

Chocolate truffle cake

Devil's food cake

Mohr im Hemd

(Austrian chocolate hazelnut cake)

Chocolate chip cookies

Bourbon cookies

Chocolate graham crackers

Chocolate muffin

Chocolate cupcakes

Chocolate brownies

Chocolate éclair

Chocolate fancies

Chocolate cheesecake

Chocolate mousse

Death by chocolate

Profiteroles

◁ # Eclair

This delicate French pastry, whose name means "flash of lightning," is made with choux paste. This type of dough is made by heating water and butter in a saucepan, adding flour and sugar to the hot liquid, then vigorously beating the mixture with eggs to form a shiny paste. This dough can be piped into various shapes, including the oblong shape of the éclair. The filling is inserted into the hollow shape, either by making a hole at one end or by splitting the dough lengthwise and spreading one half with filling. In France, the éclair is filled with confectioner's custard (crème pâtissière), which is sometimes flavored with chocolate, and topped with chocolate or coffee frosting. In England and the United States, the éclair is always frosted, but more frequently filled with sweetened whipped cream.

The éclair is supposedly an invention of Antonin Carême (1784–1833), the famous pastry chef who worked for French royalty and the Rothschilds. The Oxford English Dictionary traces the first use of the word "éclair" in English to 1861, although choux paste was invented at least 200 years earlier. However, it would have been very difficult to bake an éclair before a regulatable oven was invented in the early 19th century.

Jaffa Cake

This light little cake, a British specialty, is a cross between a cake and a cookie and was the subject of a major court case in 1991. The brand leader and inventor of the formula in the late 1940s, McVitie's (part of United Biscuits), had to fight a battle with the tax man to prove that they are cakes, because chocolate-coated cakes, as a food, bore no Value Added Tax (VAT), but chocolate-coated cookies are considered a luxury item and thus subject to VAT. The baker won, which must have saved the British taxpayers millions of pounds in view of the popularity of the jaffa cake.

The jaffa cake measures 2 inches in diameter and is $1/4$-inch thick from knob to base. It is a flying saucer-shaped sponge mixture with a knob or protrusion on top, filled with a sharp orange jelly; the top is glazed with semisweet chocolate. The name is derived from the orange filling, since most sweet oranges were shipped from the port of Jaffa, in Israel, at the time it was invented. The original recipe, created over 60 years ago, is a trade secret, but the name was not registered as a trademark, so there are lots of imitators.

Chocolate Fudge Cake

This is a rich chocolate confection invented in post-war United States, when rationed ingredients became easily available once more. The cake is also known as chocolate velvet cake and is said to have originated at New York's Four Seasons restaurant in 1959. The rich, moist batter can be baked in two or three pans, and the layers sandwiched together with a buttercream chocolate frosting, or in one large pan, and the single cake cut in half crosswise to hold the frosting. A chocolate fudge cake is always frosted, either with the same buttercream frosting or with a boiled frosting containing butter, powdered sugar, and cocoa. The frosting is always swirled, never smooth, and it should glisten. Coffee can be added to the chocolate flavoring and sometimes the recipe includes nuts.

Chocolate Fudge Cake

For the cake:

$2^2/_3$ cups all-purpose flour

$3/_4$ cup plus 1 tbsp granulated sugar

$1/_3$ cup light brown sugar

$1/_4$ cup best-quality cocoa powder

2 tsp baking powder

1 tsp baking soda

$1/_2$ tsp salt

3 eggs

$1/_2$ cup plus 2 tbsp sour cream

1 tbsp vanilla extract

$3/_4$ cup unsalted butter, melted and cooled

$1/_2$ cup corn oil

$1^1/_3$ cups chilled water

For the fudge icing:

6 ounces bittersweet chocolate, minimum 70% cocoa solids

1 cup plus 2 tbsp unsalted butter, softened

$1^3/_4$ cups confectioners' sugar, sifted

1 tbsp vanilla extract

Preheat the oven to 350°F.

Butter and line the bottom of two 8-inch cake pans.

In a large bowl, mix together the flour, sugars, cocoa, baking powder, baking soda and salt. In another bowl or wide-necked measuring cup whisk together the eggs, sour cream and vanilla until blended. Using a standing or handheld electric mixer, beat together the melted butter and corn oil until just blended (you'll need another large bowl for this if using the hand mixer; the standing mixer comes with its own bowl), then beat in the water. Add the dry ingredients all at once and mix together on a slow speed. Add the egg mixture, and mix again until everything is blended and then pour into the prepared tins. And actually, you could easily do this manually; I just like my toys and find the KitchenAid a comforting presence in itself.

Bake the cakes for 45–50 minutes, or until a cake-tester comes out clean. Cool the cakes in their pans on a wire rack for 15 minutes, and then turn the cakes out onto the rack to cool completely.

To make the icing, melt the chocolate in the microwave—2–3 minutes on medium should do it—or in a bowl sitting over a pan of simmering water, and let cool slightly.

In another bowl beat the butter until it's soft and creamy (again, I use the KitchenAid here), and then add the sifted confectioners' sugar and beat again until everything's light and fluffy. I know sifting is a pain, the one job in the kitchen I really hate, but you have to do it or the icing will be unsoothingly lumpy. Then gently add the vanilla and chocolate and mix together until everything is glossy and smooth.

Sandwich the middle of the cake with about a quarter of the icing, and then ice the top and sides, too, spreading and smoothing with a rubber spatula.

Serves 10. Or 1 with a broken heart.
Adapted from Nigella Lawson's *Nigella Bites*

Black Forest Cake

The *Schwarzwälder Kirschtorte*, to give it its original German name, is a chocolate sponge sandwich filled with whipped cream and cherries and decorated on top with whipped cream, cherries, and chocolate flakes and curls. This elaborate cake was almost *de rigueur* at any celebration in the late 1950s and 1960s, when food rationing had ended and all the luscious ingredients of this cake again became available. It has fallen out of favor somewhat, no doubt due to its rather clichéd image and poor imitations made from inferior ingredients.

The cake is said to have been invented in 1915, when Josef Keller served it at his café Agner in Bonn, Germany. It became popular throughout Germany, Austria, and Switzerland, where the batter always included lavish amounts of *Kirschwasser*, a potent, colorless liqueur made from distilled cherries, which is often omitted from the modern recipes used in the United Kingdom and the United States. It is vital that the cherries used should be pitted morello cherries, preferably canned or brandied; one reason for the cake's decline in popularity is that inferior bakers replaced them with cocktail or candied cherries, which cannot compare with the soft, moist texture of real cherries.

Black Forest Cake

4 eggs

$^1/_2$ cup superfine sugar

$^3/_4$ cup self-rising flour, sifted

$^1/_4$ cup cocoa, sifted

2 tbsp cornstarch

2 (15-oz) cans morello cherries

3 to 4 tbsp kirsch

2 cups heavy cream, whipped

$^1/_4$ cup flaked almonds, toasted

Semisweet chocolate flakes and curls, to decorate

Preheat the oven to 350°F. Line a deep 9-inch round cake pan with parchment paper.

Whisk the eggs and sugar until pale and thick, then fold in the flour and cocoa. Pour into the prepared pan and bake for 40 to 45 minutes. Turn out onto a wire rack.

Heat the cornstarch on medium and stir in the juice from the cherries. Bring to a boil, stirring, until the mixture thickens, then simmer for 2 minutes. Remove from the heat. Pit the cherries. reserving a few, and add to the juice with the kirsch.

Cut the cake into 3 layers. Sandwich them together with $^3/_4$ of the cream and all of the cherry mix. Spread cream over the sides of the cake and cover with almonds. Pipe cream around the top of the cake and decorate with chocolate flakes and cherries. *Serves 8–10*

Florentine

The florentine is described as a type of cookie, although it contains no flour or raising agent. It could be called the cookie for people who do not like cookies but love anything sweet.

A mixture of coarsely chopped hazelnuts and almonds, candied peel, and brown sugar is combined with honey or corn syrup in a saucepan. Whole hazelnuts and almonds are often added. When the sugar has melted, the mixture is transferred by spoonfuls to a buttered or oiled baking sheet and baked in a slow oven until the mixture sets. The baked nut clusters are cooled then brushed with melted chocolate in a way that leaves a pattern of wavy lines on the surface.

The origin of this biscuit as applied to Florence is obscure, but certainly recent, possibly 19th century. Although nut clusters are a popular sweet throughout Italy, eaten especially during Advent, all the ingredients are typically Florentine, and Florence is alleged to be the first place where chocolate was sold and eaten in Italy.

Gingerbread

This is the name given to cakes or cookies that contain ginger, usually in powdered form. All are ginger to dark brown in color. Gingerbread baked as a cake is usually moist, like the Yorkshire Parkin or the French *pain d'épices*, and contains honey or corn syrup. Some dry versions of the soft dough contain no fat and soften during lengthy storage. Polish gingerbread is an example.

Gingerbread has been a favorite snack in England for centuries, and was decorated with sprinkles and even gold leaf (hence the expression "the gilt on the gingerbread") and sold at fairs. As a cookie dough, it is used to make the firm, round, ginger cookie with cracks on its surface. Alternatively, the dough can be rolled out thinly like the gingersnap or the Dutch and Belgian *speculassje*.

Gingerbread Cookies

$1/4$ cup maple syrup
$1/2$ tsp ground ginger
1 tsp ground cinnamon
A pinch of ground cloves
$1/2$ tsp ground cardamom
Scant $1/2$ cup whipping cream
$1/2$ cup superfine sugar
7 tbsp butter, softened
1 egg
2 cups all-purpose flour
1 tsp baking powder

Put the maple syrup, ginger, cinnamon, cloves, and cardamom in a small saucepan over low heat, stirring to dissolve all the spices. Remove from the heat and allow to cool a bit, then stir in the cream with a wooden spoon. Mix well, making sure that nothing is left stuck on the bottom.

Beat the sugar and butter together for a minute or two, until the sugar dissolves. Add the egg. Mix in the flour and baking powder alternately with the maple syrup cream. Mix well with a wooden spoon until the mixture is thick and smooth. Cover the dough with plastic wrap and leave in the refrigerator for at least 3 hours or even overnight.

Preheat the oven to 375°F and line two baking sheets with parchment paper. Take lumps of the dough and roll out on a floured surface with a floured rolling pin to about 1/4 inch thick. Add extra flour as you roll if you find the dough too soft to handle. Cut out shapes with your cookie cutters. Put about half the shapes on the baking sheets, leaving just a little space between them for spreading. Bake one sheet at a time for 12 to 15 minutes, or until the cookies are golden with a deeper gold around the edges.

Lift them onto wire racks to cool and use the same sheets to bake the rest of the cookies. These will keep in a cookie jar or plastic bag for up to 2 weeks. *Makes about 35*

Adapted from Tessa Kiros' *Apples for Jam*

Chocolate Brownie

One of the all-time classic chocolate indulgences, the brownie is an American chocolate creation, baked in a square or oblong pan and cut into squares or bars. If frosted, it is covered with a thick chocolate fudge, in which case it is known as fudge brownie. Some brownies are moist and chewy in the center, others more dry and crumbly; some contain chopped pecans or walnuts. All kinds of variations of the chocolate brownie have been produced, including the "blondie," a brownie without the chocolate, and a white chocolate brownie.

Popular in the United States since the 19th century, the first published recipe was in the 1897 Sears, Roebuck catalog. By far the most famous brownie recipe of all time was the so-called "haschich fudge," which appeared in *The Alice B. Toklas Cookbook* published in 1954 in the United Kingdom (the American editors spotted it and cut it out of the US edition!), and which contained a generous tablespoon or so of cannabis resin. The recipe was recommended, tongue-in-cheek, for ladies' bridge club meetings or reunions of the Daughters of the American Revolution.

Coffee and Walnut Cake

Most popular in England, this delicious confection was the signature cake of Fuller's, a chain of tea shops. The chain flourished in southern England during the first half of the 20th century, but it sadly disappeared sometime in the late 1950s. The way Fuller's made it, the cake was a light-brown Victoria two-layer sponge dotted with chopped walnuts and sandwiched together with a sweet, coffee-flavored buttercream filling. The frosting was traditionally white and decorated with walnuts.

Other versions of this cake, especially those that come from the United States, tend to have darker, coffee-flavored icing, sometimes with added chocolate flavor and walnut decorations. American variations add bananas, cinnamon, and chocolate to the walnuts and coffee. Walnut wafer cakes are also popular in countries in which walnuts grow abundantly, such as Austria and Switzerland; there is a famous walnut cake from the Engadine. For the coffee, most food experts recommend using instant coffee granules rather than strong, fresh coffee made from beans, as the former produces a stronger flavor. The combination of bitter coffee, bittersweet walnuts, and the soft, melting, sugary combination of sponge cake and frosting is irresistible.

Flapjack

The name flapjack is given to two completely different types of sweet snack. The first is a thick, sweetened pancake, eaten cold, either with syrup or jam or on its own. The term "flapjack" means to flip, as in flipping a pancake. This was the original meaning of the word, which according to the Oxford English Dictionary dates from the early 17th century. The flapjack is even referred to by Shakespeare in *Pericles*, when he talks of "puddings and flapjacks." The original meaning has been retained in North America, where pancake-type flapjacks are made with baking powder so that the batter is light and fluffy.

It was not until 1935 that the term was first used in the United Kingdom to mean an oatmeal bar baked with butter, brown sugar, and corn syrup. The bar may be soft and chewy or light and crisp, and because it contains oatmeal, a grain that reduces cholesterol, flapjacks are deemed to be "healthy," regardless of the rest of the ingredients. Cinnamon is sometimes added, and there are new, light versions that cut out some of the fat and sugar.

Flapjack

6 tbsp butter

$\frac{1}{2}$ cup light brown sugar

1 tbsp corn syrup

2 cups quick-cooking oats

Preheat the oven to 350°F.

Melt the butter, sugar, and corn syrup in a saucepan over low heat, stirring all the time. Add the quick-cooking oats and stir well to combine. Press the oat mixture into a well-greased 8-inch baking pan. Bake for 25 minutes—the flapjack should be a rich, golden-brown color. Remove from the oven and leave in the pan while you mark it into squares with a sharp knife. Allow to cool completely before removing from the pan.
Makes 16

Carrot Cake

The carrot was brought to America by European immigrants and by the mid-19th century had developed into the familiar, orange-colored conical root we know today. Since the carrot is naturally sweet, it came to be used in puddings in both England and Ireland. This use spread to America, but carrots did not become popular as a cake ingredient until the mid-20th century. In 1983, the Pillsbury Company staged a competition to find the first published recipe for carrot cake in the United States. The winner was a recipe printed in *The Twentieth Century Bride's Cookbook* published in 1929 by a

women's club in Wichita, Kansas, followed by a recipe printed in 1930 in the *Chicago Daily News Cookbook*.

Carrot cake came into vogue as part of the health craze for macrobiotic and other high-fiber foods that swept the English-speaking world in the 1960s.

Carrots are only a minor ingredient in the cake, the rest consisting of flour, sugar, and butter. Recipes vary, from those that contain delicious orange-juice-soaked raisins, to those that are coated with a rich buttercream frosting. A good alternative is a low-fat cream cheese frosting.

Oatcake

Oatcakes are a British specialty, since oats are the only cereal that will grow well in the cool, damp climates of Scotland, Ireland, and northern England. Originally very much a regional food, they are now sold in health food shops and supermarkets throughout the United Kingdom and United States, since oats have been found to reduce cholesterol.

Oatcakes have been baked in Scotland since Roman times and have always been a staple of the Highland diet. The standard Scottish oatcake is a flat biscuit containing oatmeal, salt, water, and a raising agent, usually baking soda. However, each locality has its own version. Bannock, baked in Scotland, combines oatmeal, buttermilk, and baking soda. For Derbyshire oatcakes, yeast is added to lighten the mixture, though oats cannot be leavened in the same way as wheat; made into small patties, they are griddle-baked or fried.

North Staffordshire oatcakes are a flat pancake made of a mixture of yeast-raised flour and oatmeal that can even be bought online!

Throughout Ireland, the pratie oaten is a small, triangular cake made from mashed potato and fine oatmeal. It is spread with butter before eating.

Four Little Cookies

Raspberry Thumbprints

Like many other cookies and cakelets, these are popular at Christmas. The little round cakes are mainly found in the United States, though they are also a feature of European patisseries in the United Kingdom.

The dough includes rolled oats as well as whole-wheat flour, almonds, eggs, flour, sugar, and/or corn syrup. The mixture is shaped into a small drum shape, rolled in chopped almonds or grated coconut, and a depression is made in the center with the baker's thumb. The depression is then filled with raspberry (or, sometimes, loganberry) jam.

The cakes are almost certainly of Austrian or German origin and made the transition through the large number of immigrants from central Europe who arrived in America during the mid-to-late 19th and early 20th centuries.

Macaroons

Macaroons are eaten in many parts of Europe. The name comes from the French *macaron*, although the recipe is said to have been invented in an Italian monastery in 1792. During the French Revolution, two Carmelite nuns, hiding in the town of Nancy, baked and sold macaroons and became known as the "Macaroon Sisters." In Italy, they are known as *amaretti*, are always made with ground almonds, and tend to be smaller than British and American macaroons, which are sometimes made with coconut and measure about 2 inches in diameter.

The rest of the ingredients are just sugar and egg whites whipped into stiff peaks. The secret of the macaroon is in the baking, which should leave the cookie crisp on the outside and soft and chewy on the inside.

Kourabiedes

Kourabiedes are found at every celebration
—weddings, birthdays, christenings, and
especially at Christmas and Easter. The word
is pronounced "koo-ra-bi-ETH-es," the plural
of the word *"kourabies"* (kou-ra-bi-ES). It comes
from the word for a boat, because the original
shape of the cookie was that of a boat.

The dough contains white flour, large
amounts of butter and powdered sugar, and
sometimes almonds. In Greece the cakes
often contain alcohol, usually brandy or ouzo,
but not those made in Cyprus. The finished
cakes are heavily dusted with powdered sugar.
Legend has it that these buttery shortbreads
were crescent-shaped during the Turkish
occupation of Greece. After Greece regained
its independence the shape was once again
that of balls or little pears.

Lebkuchen

These heart-shaped German and Austrian
cookies, which can vary in size from tiny
to huge, are made of a gingerbread mixture—
flour, honey, spices, candied fruit, and
chopped almonds—and are either glazed
with a transparent frosting or coated with
chocolate. They are a Christmas specialty,
probably invented by monks in Franconia in
the 13th century, but are popular year-round.

The dough is raised with traditional
hartshorn (potassium carbonate), rather than
baking soda, and placed on rice paper before
baking—an ancient tradition predating the
invention of nonstick paper. As they contain
no eggs or butter, they keep very well.

No one seems to know what the word
leb means, but it may derive from the Hebrew
word *lev* for "heart," which could also explain
the cookie's shape.

Fortune Cookie

There is nothing remotely Chinese about the fortune cookie; both the ingredients and the baking technique are totally foreign to Chinese cuisine! A small, round cookie is baked in a little metal mold. A series of these molds run vertically on a conveyor belt over a gas flame. Before the baked cookie has time to harden, it is removed from the mold and a piece of paper containing the "fortune" (a prophecy or piece of Chinese wisdom) is placed in the center. The cookie is then swiftly wrapped around the paper as the batter stiffens.

San Francisco and Los Angeles both lay claim to having invented the fortune cookie— one alleging it was served at the Japanese Tea Garden in San Francisco in 1909; the other claiming it was invented by the Hong Kong Noodle Company in Los Angeles in 1918. Whatever the truth, the Chinese fortune cookie is a bit of fun that people look forward to as the typical ending to a Chinese meal in the United States. Fortune cookies are now being baked in Canada and the United Kingdom. The "fortune" can even be inserted to order.

Dundee Cake

This fruitcake is named for the port of Dundee on the east coast of Scotland, a town that is also famous for its marmalade. The dried fruits that are such an important part of the cake—raisins, golden raisins, almonds, candied peel, candied cherries— would first have come to the shores of Britain via Dundee. The cake is not of very ancient origin, dating from the heyday of the port's activity at the end of the 19th and into the 20th century.

Dundee cake is often eaten at Christmas instead of the richer, heavier English Christmas cake, which often contains large amounts of alcohol, something that would not have been permitted in a Dundee cake, as Dundee was a Presbyterian city. Traditionally, the cake is not frosted; the top is sprinkled with slivered almonds, added after the cake has been baked for an hour, so that they are nicely browned but not overcooked. Fruitcakes are always baked in a very slow oven so that the raisins do not burn. The cake may additionally be topped with candied cherries and it may be glazed with a transparent sugar syrup after baking.

Mohnkuchen

Mohnkuchen, poppy-seed cake, is extremely popular throughout central and Eastern Europe, less so in France, and almost unknown in the United Kingdom. Black poppy seeds are usually ground and softened in milk or milk and water, then cooked with sugar, sweet spices, and butter. The mixture is cooled, then spread on the dough. Raisins are often added, as is brandy or kirsch. The cake may be baked in a large square or oblong pan, as for Polish *mazurek*, and covered with a pastry lattice, or rolled up like a strudel. The poppy-seed strudel, known in Polish as *makoviec*, is frosted and served at Christmas. The Greeks are said to have combined poppy seeds with curd cheese and eggs in a cheesecake traditionally served at weddings.

Poppy seed is such a popular filling in Austria that supermarkets often have two grinders available for customers: one for grinding coffee, the other for poppy seeds. In the United States, poppy-seed filling can be bought ready-made in a can. A poppy-seed mixture is also used in the triangular pastries that Ashkenazi Jews eat at Purim (mid to late March), known as *Hamantaschen* (Haman's pockets or Haman's ears).

Pound Cake

Although the name "pound cake" is used on both sides of the Atlantic, the British pound cake is very different from its American namesake. Both cakes get their name from the fact that they use a pound of each of the ingredients. The English cake is a rich fruit cake containing eight eggs and a pound each of butter, superfine sugar, all-purpose flour, and mixed dried fruit. A little chopped candied peel, lemon rind, spices, and a drop of brandy are usually added.

In the United States, a pound cake contains a pound each of butter, flour, and sugar and usually only six eggs. The mixture is raised with baking powder and buttermilk.

The pound cake is particularly popular in the southern states of America. The easy-to-make cake is usually home-baked for parties and picnics. It is almost certainly based on the French version, known as *quatre quarts*, as each of the four ingredients—eggs, butter, flour, and sugar—are used in equal quantities.

It is the custom to weigh the eggs first, then use the weight of the eggs to determine the weight of the other ingredients.

Palmier

These distinctive-looking pastries are made from the same type of buttery, yeast-risen puff dough that is used for croissants, pain au chocolat, and other similar delicacies. They first appeared in Paris in the early 20th century. As with other such pastries, the dough is folded, rolled out several times, and left to rest. It is then sprinkled with granulated, superfine, or powdered sugar, and rolled out a few more times, resting in the refrigerator, wrapped in plastic wrap, in between. Finally, it is rolled into a thin sheet and sliced into narrow strips that are then shaped into two whorls to resemble palm leaves. They are baked in a hot oven for 10 minutes or until the sugar caramelizes and the pastry is golden-brown. They must then be turned over so the sugar can caramelize on the other side. Palmiers are best eaten soon after baking, but they can be stored for a few days in an airtight container. They are usually eaten at teatime or with coffee, as they are too rich and sweet for breakfast.

Panforte

Dating from the 13th century when the first spices were imported from the eastern Mediterranean, this rich concoction is a specialty of Siena. It is mentioned in city archive documents dating from 1205. Panforte was once only eaten at Christmas, but it is now eaten year-round.

Panforte, which simply means "strong bread," is based on a honey cake known as *pan melato*. The mixture contains no raising agent and only a small amount of flour—just enough to hold the ingredients together—mixed with powdered sugar, honey, nuts, and spices, as well as candied peel. The traditional mixture includes candied pumpkin and candied citron, both of which are hard to find outside Italy, although panforte is now made all over the Italian diaspora and in every part of Italy. The honeyed batter is poured into a round pan or mold lined with rice paper and baked at a low temperature for 30 minutes. It is left to cool in the pan and sprinkled with sifted powdered sugar. Since it contains no eggs or fat, panforte will keep for a very long time, though that is unlikely to be necessary as it is so delicious!

Pannetone

Pannetone, or panneton in Milanese dialect, is traditionally eaten at both Christmas and New Year's. The rich dough, started with a sourdough leaven, has to be raised and proofed many times over several days, during which time candied peel is incorporated into the mixture.

Pannetone are generally made commercially in Italy but only in October and November, in the run-up to the festive period. Like all yeast-raised doughs, the keeping qualities of the cake are not very good and it is important to eat it as fresh as possible.

Literally translated, the name means "big bread." It is baked in various shapes including a tall cylinder, a dome shape on a cylindrical base, and sometimes on an octagonal base. As the cake is rather dry, it is always served with coffee or hot chocolate or with Asti, a dessert wine. The cake seems to date back to Roman times, and it features in a painting by the 16th-century artist, Pieter Brueghel the Elder. Bartolomeo Scappi, a chef to Popes Pius IV and V, included a recipe for pannetone in his *Opera dell'arte del cucinare,* one of the earliest cookbooks, written in 1570.

Stollen

This classic German Christmas cake, shaped to resemble the baby Jesus in swaddling clothes, is a specialty of Dresden. The original stollen was rather flavorless and hard because only Lenten ingredients could be used during Advent, when the cake was made. In 1647, the Elector Ernst and his brother, Duke Albrecht, persuaded the pope to permit the use of richer ingredients, such as butter. The true Dresden stollen is distinguished by a seal depicting the city's famous king, August the Strong. The "official" stollen may only be baked by 150 Dresden bakers who have special permission. It is still a feature of the local Christmas market, the *Striezelmarkt*.

Stollen is made from a yeast-raised dough containing candied peel, including citron peel, dried fruit, almonds, and sweet spices. The dough contains little sugar but the finished cake is liberally sprinkled with powdered sugar. The dough is folded so that one half lies over the other, the lower fold being thinner than the upper.

The stollen is traditionally baked to weigh about 5 pounds, but miniature stollen are now also produced.

Babka

This cake is baked in a special fluted tin that flares out from the bottom in a wide funnel shape. When unmolded it is supposed to represent a grandmother's wide skirts, hence the name "babka" or "baba," meaning "grandmother" in Polish. The cake is popular throughout central Europe, starting from Lorraine in eastern France, where Polish culinary influence persists because this French province was ruled by a former king of Poland, Stanislas Leszczynski, in the 16th century.

The batter is yeast-raised and enriched with eggs and butter, like another favorite cake of the region, the *gugelhupf*, which is baked in a different-shaped fancy mold. Candied fruits and raisins are usually added to the dough and a fruit-flavored frosting coats the baked babka, which is traditionally eaten in Poland on Easter Sunday. The cake is also popular in Jewish cuisine. Unfrosted, but with a dusting of powdered sugar, it is served on the Sabbath afternoon. Rum baba is a plainer French version of this cake, baked in a ring mold then soaked in a rum-flavored syrup, more closely resembling an Asian pastry.

Brandy Snaps

These delicate, lacy cookies are virtually unknown outside England. They are cylindrical and hollow and often filled with cream. The mixture, which may or may not contain a tablespoon or so of brandy, consists of equal quantities of flour, butter, and brown sugar. (In the recipe here, a slight variation on the traditional approach is used, with the inclusion of superfine sugar and corn syrup.) The batter is dropped by spoonfuls onto a well-buttered baking sheet and baked in a medium oven for about 10 minutes. As the batter spreads, holes appear in it. The trick is to quickly wrap the cookies around a long, narrow wooden or metal cylindrical object, such as a thin rolling pin, before they harden. This gives them their distinct "cigar" shape.

Brandy snaps are a very old tradition and may have been mentioned in the writings of Geoffrey Chaucer (1340–1400). In those days, long before ovens had been invented, hot pokers or similar-shaped irons, with a long handle to protect the baker, were dipped in the batter and held briefly over a fire until the mixture solidified.

Brandy Snaps

¼ cup butter

¼ cup superfine sugar

¼ cup corn syrup

1 tsp lemon juice

½ cup all-purpose flour, sifted

1 tsp ground ginger

1 tsp brandy, optional

Preheat the oven to 350°F.

Grease 2 baking sheets. Place the butter, sugar, and syrup in a pan, and heat, on medium, stirring every now and then until the sugar dissolves. Stir in the lemon juice, then remove the pan from the heat.

Add the flour and ginger to the sugar/syrup mixture and stir until smooth. If you are using the brandy, add it now.

Drop teaspoons of the mixture onto the prepared baking sheets, spacing each spoonful a couple of inches apart to allow the mixture to spread. Bake for approximately 10 minutes (keep an eye on them though, as you do not want them to overcook) until brown and perforated in texture. Allow to cool slightly.

While still warm, remove the snaps from the baking sheets, one by one, with a flat spatula and wrap aound the handle of a wooden spoon or similar object. Let the snap firm up before removing. *Makes 12–18*

◁ Tuilles

Toasted Teacake

A specialty of French pâtisseries, the name for these thin, curved cookies derives from the French word for a "tile," since their shape is reminiscent of the curved red roof tiles seen on older buildings in France. The name is also given to mixtures shaped into baskets or bowls to hold a soft pudding or stewed fruits. The mixture always contains flour, sugar, eggs, and salt, and it is baked in thin rounds in a very hot oven, so the edges are lightly browned and the centers pale. The curved shape is achieved by quickly rolling the baked, hot wafers around a rolling pin or the handle of a wooden spoon.

There is a multitude of variations on the recipe, the shape of the finished cookie is often all they have in common. Sweet versions are made with orange juice and Grand Marnier liqueur and savory versions are flavored with Parmesan cheese. Most often, the sweet cookies are served as an accompaniment to ice cream, mousse, or other desserts, or they may be filled with whipped cream. In one variation the tuilles are left flat and sandwiched together with a meringue mixture; these are called *mignons*.

Made with a sweet, yeast-raised dough, the inclusion of a few currants is what distinguishes a teacake from a plain roll or bun. About 4 inches in diameter, the teacake is split, toasted, buttered, and served at teatime. In certain parts of Yorkshire and Lancashire, the teacake does not contain currants. In fact, "teacake" is a generic name for a bun or roll, known elsewhere in northern England as a "breadcake" or "barm cake" and even eaten with fries. In Yorkshire, the true teacake is known as a "fat rascal."

In America, teacakes are very popular in the South, but a teacake there is just a little cake flavored with vanilla and spices. There is a huge variety of recipes for American teacakes. Tunnock's Teacakes, a Scottish commercial product, is not a teacake at all, but a chocolate-marshmallow cookie. Teacakes in Australia are actually pound cakes, sometimes sprinkled with sugar and cinnamon and so called just because they are eaten at teatime. In Ireland, the Irish brack teacake is a rich fruitcake, similar to barm brack, but raised with eggs and baking powder instead of yeast.

Battenberg Cake

Uniquely British, this distinctive-looking cake consists of four small oblongs of Victoria sponge cake: two colored pink to contrast with two that are either yellow or white. The oblongs are sandwiched together with apricot jam and covered with a layer of marzipan. No one knows who invented the cake, but it was created in the late 19th century to celebrate the marriage of Princess Victoria of Hesse-Darmstadt, granddaughter of Queen Victoria, to Prince Louis of Battenberg in 1884, and the marriage in the following year of Queen Victoria's daughter Beatrice to Prince Henry of Battenberg. The four squares are said to represent the two couples.

The cake is not often made at home as it appears to be difficult to create the checkered appearance. In fact, this is easily achieved. Two identical sponge batters are required, one plain, one colored pink. A square pan is divided down the center with a piece of card wrapped in foil, and the batters are poured into each half of the pan. The baked cakes are cut in half crosswise and then sandwiched together using apricot jam. The cake is then coated with jam so that the marzipan covering will adhere.

Although the Battenbergs later anglicized their name to Mountbatten due to anti-German feeling during the First World War, the cake has retained the original name.

Scones with Cream ▷

The scone, an invention of the British, especially popular in England and Scotland, is traditionally eaten with Devonshire or Cornish clotted cream. This is particularly the case in the West Country, from Bristol and Avon right down to the tip of Cornwall, where the cream is pale yellow and particularly rich. The cream tea is the backbone of country fare in southwest England, which involves one or two scones per person, served with clotted cream and a cup of tea. Strawberry or raspberry jam is added and there is much debate as to whether the scone should be spread first with the jam or with the cream.

The English scone is made from a white flour dough raised with baking powder and buttermilk, soured milk, or even fresh milk. The dough is shaped into small round cakes about 2 inches in diameter, sometimes shaped by hand, sometimes cut with a dough cutter, which may or may not be fluted. This makes it very similar to the American biscuit, which in some recipes is identical. Scones are traditionally baked on the griddle but most are now oven-baked. In Scotland, scones may also contain oatmeal or even rye flour and may be cooked as a round cake, scored into triangles before baking

Shortcake, Shortbread, Shortening Bread

These are all names for what was once the same thing; the nomenclature varying depending which side of the Atlantic you are on. The "short" refers to the lightness of the dough, which is always achieved by adding a large proportion of fat to flour. The fat in question would have been lard originally, and is now either a cooking fat or cooking margarine or butter, or a mixture of the two. Some American recipes for shortcake, which is actually a type of sweet scone or teacake, use as much as half the volume of fat to flour.

American shortcakes are baked exclusively to be filled with cream and fruit, the best known version being strawberry shortcake. Scottish shortbread is very different; it is a hard, plain cookie, though the dough is very buttery. Its keeping qualities make it popular with commercial bakers in Scotland and it is exported worldwide as a typical Scottish delicacy.

Shortening bread ("short'nin' bread" as in the song) is a specialty of the Deep South in the US. It is what is known as a "quickbread," whose basic ingredients are fat, flour, sugar, and baking powder. The bread is cut into bars before baking. It is often eaten for breakfast with bacon.

Rugelach

Strawberry Shortcake

$7^1\!/_2$ cups strawberries, hulled and quartered

$^1\!/_3$ cup sugar, or to taste

1 cup heavy cream

$^1\!/_4$ cup sour cream

$1^1\!/_2$ to 2 tbsp powdered sugar, or to taste

$^1\!/_2$ tsp vanilla extract

6 shortcakes

Place the strawberries in a bowl. Sprinkle over the sugar and set aside for 5 minutes. Using the back of a spoon, gently press the strawberries to release some of their juice. Don't crush them completely. Set aside for approximately 1 hour, stirring occasionally.

Put the heavy cream, sour cream, powdered sugar, and vanilla extract in a bowl. Beat until the combined mixture is thick and smooth, but it should not be stiff.

Carefully cut the shortcakes in half. Top each half with the strawberries and a good dollop of the cream mixture. *Makes 12*

Rugelach are small pastries that are an Eastern European Jewish specialty. The name is a Yiddish diminutive, meaning "little rolls," because the dough is cut into a triangle and then rolled up into the shape of a croissant or, in some cases, rolled up and sliced into miniature strudels. A wide variety of rugelach recipes exist although, strangely, they do not feature in many Jewish cookbooks. The tradition seems to be that the family recipe is handed down from mother to daughter.

One thing that all true rugelach recipes have in common is that the dough contains butter and cream cheese or sour cream, which means they must be eaten at a non-meat meal, as Orthodox Jews are not allowed to eat milk and meat at the same meal. There are recipes where the dough contains margarine and no cream cheese, but they cannot be called true rugelach. These rich, sweet pastries are very much a Sabbath teatime treat, accompanied by tea or coffee. The fillings vary but usually include chopped nuts, raisins or golden raisins, sugar, and sweet spices. A variation uses a combination of cocoa and sugar and the top is drizzled with chocolate frosting.

Simit

Simnel Cake   ▷

Simit is the Turkish word for "sesame seed." These sesame-topped breads are sold in one form or another in many parts of the Middle East. In Greek, they are known as *koulouri*, and in Arabic, as *kayik* (from which the English word "cake" is derived). Simit are baked in a variety of shapes, but the most familiar is the ring shape, like a bagel but thinner and bigger. The yeast-raised dough is fairly plain—milk, sugar, salt, yeast, and sometimes oil to improve the keeping quality. Traditionally, the dough has to be baked until it is the color of a gold coin.

In Turkey, most simit is eaten on the run, bought in the street from vendors who replenish their stock as often as five times a day. A good tip is always to buy from a vendor with many simit on his barrow, as this means he has just brought in a new supply. Some commercial bakers sell simit in other shapes, such as sticks or even a lattice inside a large ring; these breads are twice-baked, like rusks, to improve their keeping qualities, and will keep for many months in an airtight tin.

This special cake, traditional in England and Ireland, is baked for Mothering Sunday, the last Sunday before Easter. This tradition comes from a time when female servants were allowed to go home to visit their families and they would take a cake with them. The name is probably derived from the Latin word *simila*, meaning "fine," a reference to the fine flour used in the recipe. The mixture is that of a light fruitcake, containing white flour, butter, sugar, sweet spices, dried fruit, and candied peel.

When baked, the whole cake is covered in marzipan and 11 marzipan balls are placed around the edge to represent the apostles (Judas is not included). Sometimes, the decoration on the top of the cake features a single ball in the center of the cake to represent Jesus. There is a story that the cake was invented by the English pretender to the throne, Lambert Simnel (1477–1534), who after being deposed, was given work in King Henry VII's kitchens.

The Irish also bake a simnel cake decorated in the same way, but with the addition of crystallized violets, representing the posies of spring flowers that daughters would also give their mothers.

Madeira Cake

Mille-feuille   ▷

The heavy, sweet wine produced on the island of Madeira was a great favorite in 18th- and 19th-century England, and this cake was baked especially to be served with the wine as a mid-morning snack. Today, it is eaten at teatime. Madeira cake is a plain sponge cake raised without baking powder, which date-stamps its origins before artificial raising agents were available. It is flavored with grated lemon rind and never frosted, but topped with pieces of candied citron and baked in a loaf pan for approximately 2 hours. The citron peel is added after the cake has been baking for 30 minutes. The citron, a citrus fruit which looks something like a lemon but which has a very thick, fragrant skin, was the first citrus fruit known outside Asia. It is only grown in a few places commercially. In England, candied citron peel is usually imported from Italy; in the United States, it comes from Puerto Rico. Madeira cake has poor keeping qualities and should be eaten fresh, but if it goes stale, it can be spread with jam, soaked in hot custard, and eaten as Madeira pudding.

There are many names for this flake or puff pastry confection. The technique for rolling, folding, and chilling the dough several times is the same as for croissants and Danish pastries. The cake is usually baked in a square pan, and the dough scored into bars before baking. The commonest name in England, mille-feuille, is the French for "thousand leaves," reflecting the way the dough splits into individual flaky layers as it bakes. In other countries, especially the United States, it is known as a "Napoleon," not for its association with the French emperor, but because it is said to have originated in Naples.

The pastry is usually split in half after baking and topped with vanilla frosting, when it is known as a vanilla slice. A cream or custard slice is filled either with whipped cream or confectioner's custard (crème patissière), or with jam, or both. The mille-feuille is usually glazed with royal or fondant (boiled) frosting with chocolate frosting strips, the latter dragged with a fork to make a spider's web effect. The top may also be sprinkled with powdered sugar. Savory mille-feuilles may be filled with white or yellow cheese, spinach, or a mixture of both.

Victoria Sandwich

The Victoria sandwich or Victoria sponge cake is one of several dishes named after Queen Victoria. Like all sponge cakes, it requires intense and prolonged beating of the butter-and-sugar mixture and of the eggs to ensure that the texture is as light as possible. Today, this task is considerably eased with a handheld electric whisk or electric food mixer.

After the death of her husband, Prince Albert, in 1861, the Queen was encouraged to give tea parties during her stays at Osborne House on the Isle of Wight, and the cake was served at these gatherings. The cake soon became popular throughout England. It is known as a sandwich because the batter is divided between two cake pans and then baked in a medium oven. The two cakes are then sandwiched together with a filling consisting of whipped cream, buttercream, or strawberry jam.

The classic topping for a Victoria sandwich is a sprinkling of sifted powdered sugar, but the cake can be left plain or frosted. Victoria sponge cakes are often entered into baking competitions at English village fêtes and they are used by manufacturers to test their ovens.

Victoria Sandwich

1 cup butter, softened

1 cup superfine sugar

4 eggs, beaten

2 cups self-rising flour

2 tsp baking powder

To finish:

$1/4$ cup strawberry jam

Powered sugar for sprinkling

Preheat the oven to 350°F. Grease 2 8-inch cake pans and line with parchment paper. Beat together the butter and sugar until light and fluffy. Add the eggs, one at a time, and beat well between additions. Fold in the flour and baking powder.

Divide the mixture evenly between the prepared cake pans and smooth the surface with a knife. Bake in the center of the pre-heated oven for about 25 minutes, until well risen and golden.

Leave to cool in the pans for a few minutes, then turn out onto a wire rack to cool completely. Place one cake on your serving plate, spread its surface with jam, and put the second cake on top. Sprinkle with powered sugar to serve. *Serves 6–8*

Absinthe

One of a group of anise-flavored drinks originating in France, absinthe contains the leaves of the medicinal shrub, *Artemisia absinthium*, or wormwood.

Around the time of the First World War, in the era that saw the first formulation of laws to prohibit the use of various narcotics, absinthe was banned throughout Europe. It was held to be responsible for mental derangement in those who drank it regularly, a finding that had some basis in medical fact, as the active component in wormwood— thujone—has been linked with the formation of cortical lesions in the brain.

In the 1990s, absinthe was reintroduced in most European countries, although it remains illegal in France. This has led to its production in various Slavic regions, principally the Czech Republic, where it is often bottled at up to 80% alcohol by volume.

The traditional way of taking absinthe is to pour it over a sugar lump through a perforated spoon balanced across the top of the glass. The sugar, which may be set alight, is then dissolved in the drink. Water is added to mitigate its potency.

Amarone

The name of Amarone is derived from the Italian word for "bitter," *amaro*, which could hardly be a more apt description of this classic red. It is made within the delimited area for Valpolicella, in the Veneto region of northeast Italy. Valpolicella itself is a straightforward, everyday red wine, but it comes in a range of specialty versions, of which Amarone is the most renowned.

Produced from a blend of three native grape varieties—Corvina, Molinara, and Rondinella—the wine is made from grapes that have been allowed to dry out on straw mats in the broiling heat of the late summer sun. As the moisture content in the grapes decreases, their natural sugars, and thus their potential alcohol, are heightened. Amarone is then fermented all the way out to full dryness, meaning that not only does it acquire that characteristic bitterness, but it is also toweringly strong (as much as 15 to 16% alcohol), putting it on a par with many a fortified wine.

These wines are not drunk in Italy as table wines, but are classed as *vini da meditazione*, wines to mull over at the end of a meal, perhaps with a handful of freshly shelled nuts.

Barolo

Made in the Piedmont region of northwest Italy, Barolo is often considered the king of Italian wines. That reputation rests partly on its fame as a quality wine, but also because it is—in old-fashioned wine parlance—an indubitably masculine style of wine.

It is made exclusively from a local red grape variety, Nebbiolo, which gives a massively full-bodied, alcoholically heady wine with heavy-duty tannin (the substance extracted from the skins and pips of the grapes, and which contributes to that feeling of mouth-furring astringency when the wine is young). Red wines can normally be expected to lose their tannin after the first few years in the bottle, but Barolo jealously hangs on to its toughness well into middle age.

The reward, for those who wait, is a powerful, dense, concentrated wine, with an array of complex aromas and flavors. These typically include dark chocolate, tobacco, and molten tar, all overlaid with an unexpectedly delicate floral top layer like rose petals.

Barolo is much exported, as befits a wine that falls within Italy's highest quality designation, DOCG (*denominazione de origine controllata e garantita*). Notable producers of the wine include Mascarello, Voerzio, Ceretto, and Conterno.

Primitivo

Rioja

⊳

The name of a grape variety native to the southeastern region of Puglia, the heel of Italy, Primitivo has attracted much inter-national attention in recent years, not least because it has been identified as the same grape that is hugely important in Californian viticulture as Zinfandel.

Primitivo is a fascinating variety, producing wines of great concentration and intensity. Its flavors usually evoke dark-skinned fruits such as black plums and blueberries, and there is often an herbal edge to it that reminds some tasters of tea leaves. As well as these characteristics, it generally has a distinctly sweet aftertaste, which is carried through on a supporting raft of powerful alcohol (Primitivo wines are typically in the 13.5 to 14% range).

In Puglia, its main denomination is Primitivo di Manduria, a muscular, slow-maturing red known in the regional dialect as *mirr test*, "hard wine." It is the specific clone of Primitivo grown in the Manduria district that has been found to be identical with Zinfandel. The latest theory has it that the grape possibly originated in Croatia.

Rioja is made in a region of that name in northern Spain, around the river Ebro. It can be a red, white, or rosé wine, but it is the red that is the most widely known around the world. It became popular on export markets in the 1970s, and remains Spain's most important table wine.

The red wines are blends of up to four grape varieties, the most important of which is Tempranillo, a fine variety grown all over Spain. There are various quality categories, depending on the lengh of aging, from simple unoaked Joven, through Crianza, Reserva, and Gran Reserva. In the case of the last three categories, the wine has already undergone maturation in both barrel and bottle before it is released onto the market, meaning that it doesn't have to be cellared.

The white wines are based on the Viura grape and come in much the same categories, though there is a tendency these days to give them much less oak-aging than in the past.

American oak, with its sweet, vanilla-scented taste, was once the traditional wood used, but many producers now use French oak or a mixture of the two.

Rioja

DENOMINACION DE ORIGEN CALIFICADA

Reserva Especial

Cosecha 1991

Super-Tuscan

The Tuscany region of north-central Italy was once pre-eminently known for Chianti, but a movement that began in the 1970s, and gathered momentum over the following decade, reoriented international perceptions of Tuscan wine.

Super-Tuscans, as these modern-classic wines came to be generically tagged, were wines conceived outside the scope of the local regulations, often marginalizing (or else completely eschewing) Italian grape varieties in favor of the internationally recognized likes of Cabernet Sauvignon, Cabernet Franc, and Merlot. These were wines that aimed explicitly to compete with the best wines of France, especially Bordeaux, and sold for comparable prices.

An irony for many years was that, although these were undoubtedly among Italy's greatest red wines, they were only entitled to the humblest quality description, *vino da tavola* (table wine), because they were being made outside the designated stipulations for Tuscany. That is now changing as regulations are redrawn to accommodate them. The Bolgheri denomination, for example, created in 1994, now encompasses some of the super-Tuscans.

Wines to look out for include Sassicaia, Ornellaia, Tignanello, Sammarco, and Solaia.

Beaujolais

Made at the southern end of the Burgundy region in eastern France, Beaujolais is one of the world's unique wine styles. The vast majority of the production is a featherlight red wine made from the regional grape, Gamay, a variety not much seen anywhere else in the world.

The wine's singular characteristics of a very light body allied with a high alcohol content (around 13%) owe much to a traditional vinification procedure called *macération carbonique* (carbonic maceration), in which the grapes are not crushed mechanically, but sit on top of each other in a closed fermenting vat until the ones at the bottom are burst by the pressure of those above them, thus initiating the fermentation.

The relative lack of tannin in young Beaujolais is compensated for by lively, fresh acidity and a simple red-fruit palate suggestive of strawberries. Wines from any of ten named villages within the region are officially the best, and have their own respective appellations. These are Moulin-à-Vent, Morgon, Fleurie, Chénas, Juliénas, St-Amour, Chiroubles, Brouilly, Côte de Brouilly, and Régnié.

A third of all Beaujolais is sold within weeks of its production, as Beaujolais Nouveau. There are also small quantities of rosé and white Beaujolais.

Green Tea

In contrast to the black tea popular elsewhere, the tea commonly drunk in east Asia is made from leaves that are only heated before being rolled and dried. They are neither fermented nor oxidized, meaning that the flavor is much more pungently aromatic than tea made from black leaves. These teas, perhaps most familiar to Westerners in the form of the pots usually served free in Chinese restaurants, are at first an acquired taste. They have neither milk nor lemon added to them, only hot water.

There are many types of green tea, from different varieties of the tea plant, and from different regions. One of the most celebrated green teas in China is Longjing (Dragon Well) from Hangzhou in the eastern province of Zhejiang. Japan's green teas include Gyokuro (Jade Dew), which is always an intense, bright green color after infusion.

More than any other hot beverage, tea is still subject to highly ritualized methods of preparing and drinking it in many countries. The most famous of these is *chanoyu*, the Japanese tea ceremony. This is an extremely formal occasion that may last several hours, but which has at its heart the studied appreciation of the drink itself.

White Tea

Black Tea

White tea is essentially a variant of green tea in that it is unoxidized, but is based on the smaller leaves and buds of the plant in the early stages of the growing cycle. Because the leaves are not yet fully developed, the resulting dried tea has a less green appearance than its more mature cousin.

This is a specialty of the southeastern Chinese province of Fujian. The best grade is Bai Hao Yinzhen (Silver Needle), so called because it consists of the long, white unopened buds of the spring plant. It is traditionally harvested between mid-March and mid-April. The second-best grade is Bai Mu Dan (White Peony), which is comprised of buds and some of the immature, downy leaves. Other white teas are produced in India and Sri Lanka.

Interestingly, white tea turns out to be higher in both antioxidants and caffeine than green tea, making it useful both as an inhibitor of cell damage and as a stimulant. The phrase "white tea" has also been used for centuries in China as a polite way of referring to a simple cup of hot water, which was often all that very poor families could offer guests.

Black tea is the form in which tea is most widely drunk in the Western world, so called because the leaves are fermented before undergoing the drying process, becoming blackened and oxidized. This results in a totally different flavor from the green teas traditionally drunk in China.

Both types of tea are derived from the leaves of the *Camellia sinensis* plant, which is native to China. Legend has it that one day in ancient times, a Chinese peasant stopped to rest under a tea bush. Some of its leaves fell into the pot of water he had boiled, and the result was a strangely satisfying and restorative brew.

Tea first arrived in Europe with the Portuguese, who brought it back from their settlement in Macao in the 1500s. By the following century, the English had become history's most dedicated tea importers. The beverage found favor at the court of the restored monarchy under Charles II, whose wife was Portuguese. Initially, England's tea was imported from India, where the East India Company eventually established its own plantations, but China has always been an important source too.

Today, the British, along with the Irish and Turks, remain the most avid consumers of tea outside its native regions.

Bourbon

Bloody Mary   ▷

Bourbon is made mostly in the US state of Kentucky, from a grain base that must legally be a minimum of 51% corn. It is matured in new oak barrels, the inner surfaces of which are heavily toasted so as to impart a characteristic smoky flavor to the spirit.

Although bourbon can technically be produced anywhere in the United States, in practice most of it—including leading brands Jim Beam and Maker's Mark—is made in Kentucky. Bourbon has been made in these parts ever since the Independence era, when it was an obvious way of using surplus grain from the abundant harvests. Wheat, rye, and barley may also be used in its production, but do not tend to account for much more than about a third of the customary mix.

Traditional ways of drinking bourbon involve either pouring it over ice ("on the rocks"), or tempering its strength with spring water, often known as branch water, hence "bourbon and branch." It is the basis of many a whiskey cocktail, including the simple Whiskey Sour, where it is mixed with lemon juice and sugar, and the Old-Fashioned, with sugar and bitters.

A Bloody Mary is renowned both as a fine aperitif and, perhaps even more so, as a quick-fix drink for many a gruesome morning after.

Recipes vary according to the individual maker, but the common elements are tomato juice, spiced up with Worcestershire sauce and black pepper, lemon juice, usually celery seasoning, plenty of ice, and as generous a slug of vodka as you feel you deserve. The mix should always be stirred well; a Bloody Mary with its alcohol floating on a sea of tomato is not at all correct.

It is served in a tall glass, usually garnished with a stick of celery and a slice of lemon. The reputed inventor of the drink was Ferdinand Petiot, a bartender at Harry's in Paris, who created it in the 1910s in honor of one of his regular customers.

Bloody Mary

4 cups chilled tomato juice

1 cup chilled vodka

⅓ cup fresh lemon juice

1½ tbsp Worcestershire sauce

½ tsp celery salt

¾ tsp Tabasco

¾ tsp freshly ground black pepper

Combine the ingredients thoroughly in a large pitcher. Pour into ice-filled glasses and garnish with celery sticks and lemon slices. *Serves 6*

◁ # Rum

Calvados

Rum is a global drink with inextricable links to the history and culture of the Caribbean. Distilled using molasses made from the sugar cane that was farmed in abundance in the colonial era, rum formed part of a trading triangle that helped spread it around the world. Molasses traveled north to New England and Nova Scotia where it would be distilled and then sent to Africa, where it was traded for slaves who, in turn, were brought back to the Caribbean to work the cane fields.

The early versions of this drink were harsh tasting and appropriately associated with traders and pirates. In the middle of the 19th century the process for distilling rum became more refined. Rums were now more pure and more palatable. Distillers began to age rum, further mellowing the taste. Today there are a few large players responsible for most of the rums that make it into bar cocktails. But there are also hundreds of small distilleries located on islands throughout the Caribbean, each producing relatively small batches that have their own unique characteristics.

Produced in the Normandy region of northern France, calvados is a type of brandy distilled from pressed apples. It is effectively the European antecedent of America's applejack. The apples used are always a balanced blend of sweet and sour varieties.

Many different grades of calvados are produced, from the youngest and fieriest spirit to products labeled *Hors d'Age* (literally "beyond age"), which are matured for many years in oak casks. Within the delimited area of its production, there is an enclave called the Pays d'Auge, commonly held to be the source of the finest calvados. It is all bottled at the standard spirit strength of 40%.

Calvados is only occasionally drunk with a mixer in France (although it marries surprisingly well with tonic water), but is more often drunk as it is. In its native region, it is customarily drunk not at the end of a meal, but in between the first and main courses, a tradition known as the *trou normand* ("Norman hole"). The idea is that the spirit punches a hole in the food that has already been consumed, aiding digestion and preparing the stomach for the principal dish.

Café au Lait

Three popular ways of drinking coffee are featured on these pages. Originating in North Africa, the coffee plant has been the source of a stimulating beverage since ancient times. Legend has it that its sublimely invigorating properties were first discovered when an African goatherd noticed one of his animals bounding about more friskily than usual after nibbling the berries of the coffee bush, *Coffea arabica.*

Arabica is still the best variety of the coffee plants. Commercial coffees made from the beans of the *C. canephora robusta,* or from a mixture of the two, are much less refined in quality.

What the French people know as café au lait—a form in which they hardly ever drink it themselves—is essentially a white coffee made by adding milk, *lait*, to a strong cup of black coffee. It is perhaps a more digestible form in which to drink coffee first thing in the morning. Under the influence of Italian modes, this kind of coffee has recently come to be known as "caffe latte," or just "latte," and now contains a higher proportion of milk than the traditional café au lait.

Cappuccino

Italian cappuccino has become one of the world's favorite styles of coffee. It is based on a strong shot of espresso, to which is added hot milk and a frothy crown of milk foam, traditionally decorated with a sprinkling of powdered chocolate or cinnamon. Its name is derived from the monastic dress of the Capuchin friars—a brown robe surmounted by a white hood, just like the drink.

The preparation of a good cappuccino requires a special skill. The milk must be correctly steamed so that it retains the right amount of froth, which is buoyed by the mass of minuscule air bubbles whisked into it. The less fat it has, the better it will froth, so skim milk is generally preferred for a cappuccino. Home cappuccino makers who possess a cafetière can achieve the correct degree of frothiness by plunging the hot milk until it forms a foamy head. The finished drink should be equal thirds coffee, milk, and froth.

When the milk is poured, a spoon is used to hold back the froth, which is added at the end. A brown rim of coffee should be visible around the circumference of the froth.

Espresso

Strong black coffee served in small quantities, the espresso was invented in the mid-19th century, when a French technologist called Edouard Loysel de Santais went to the Paris Exposition with a machine for brewing coffee that was capable of producing no fewer than 2,000 cups an hour.

Espresso is so called because the hot water in it is forced, under pressure, over the finely ground coffee. The low ratio of water to coffee results in a short shot of black coffee that combines caffeine-rich strength with a flavor that should ideally be balanced between mellow roundness and mordant bitterness. It is a fine pick-me-up when taken at the end of a long meal, or in the course of a morning's or afternoon's work.

In Italy, most espresso is drunk as a small shot called a *solo*. A *doppio*, or double, is increasingly popular in the coffee bars and restaurants of North America. One of the distinguishing characteristics of a good espresso is that it should have a thin surface layer of tan-colored foam, known technically as the *crema*, which consists of natural oils and sugars present in the coffee.

Chablis

Chablis was so internationally renowned that in some English-speaking countries, it became a generic name for any light, dry white wine. In fact, it should properly be associated only with a white wine made in a region to the north of Burgundy, France. It is a Chardonnay wine, made in a style that combines fairly high alcohol (around 13%) with lightness of body and steely acidity, as befits a wine grown in a cool northerly climate.

Although certain growers use a modicum of oak-aging to round out their wines, the great majority use no wood at all. The popular image of Chablis is of a fresh, clean white wine with a keen edge of acidity, and only a little fruit content—perhaps a touch of green apple splashed with lemon.

Chablis is divided into four quality categories, entirely dependent on the respective vineyard locations. In ascending order these are Petit Chablis, Chablis, Chablis Premier Cru, and Chablis Grand Cru. With the exception of the first, all are capable of aging for several years in the bottle, taking on, as they do so, a creamy richness that is altogether remarkable for an un-oaked wine.

Campari

Campari is one of a group of alcoholic drinks collectively known as bitters. Made in Italy, it is a bright-red product, bottled at a strength of 25%, and flavored with a range of bitter herbs, spices, and orange peel. Like other such drinks, it is intended to be drunk as an aperitif, its bitterness exercising a powerfully stimulant effect on the appetite. It mixes well with orange juice, on account of the bitter orange in it, and also with soda water.

The drink is named after its original inventor, one Gaspare Campari, who first formulated it in 1860. As with all proprietary drink brands, the precise ingredients remain a matter of commercial confidentiality.

It is possible to buy a premixed version of Campari and soda, but it doesn't taste as good as the one you can make freshly at home. Campari is also the essential ingredient in a great aperitif cocktail called a Negroni, where it is mixed with gin and sweet red vermouth. This drink was invented by a customer of that name at a bar in Florence in the early years of the 20th century. The Negroni formula soon became all the rage.

FRANCE

Champagne

ENGLAND

Buck's Fizz

The story is that champagne was invented when a blind monastic cellar master, Dom Pérignon, one day tasted a batch of wine that had started re-fermenting. "Come quickly," he called to his cohorts, "I am drinking stars!" Like most such legends, it is pure bunkum, and has now been superseded by the theory that it was the wine's English importers who discovered that the fizzy state that re-fermented wine went into made it a far more interesting drink.

Champagne has enjoyed a virtually unrivaled reputation ever since as a wine of partying and celebration. Based on the thin, acidic white wine of the Champagne region of northern France, it is given a second fermentation in the bottle. As the yeasts produce more alcohol, they also produce carbon dioxide, which remains trapped in suspension until the bottle is broached.

Although champagne has many rivals, nothing quite achieves the same combination of lightness, elegance, and richness in maturity that the real thing does. It comes in many styles, including vintage, rosé, and demi-sec. It is the non-vintage wine of each house, however, upon which its reputation depends, and that inspires loyal followings.

Star of many a wedding day, drunk at luxurious breakfasts, or sometimes as the last resort to disguise a less than scintillating sparkling wine, Buck's fizz—a mimosa in the US—is a mixed drink combining an effervescent wine and fresh orange juice.

Invented in 1921 at Buck's Club in London by a barman named McGarry only two years after the club itself had been founded, the drink was intended as an exotic way of taking champagne. The original proportions were two-thirds champagne to one-third orange juice, the color made a little more vivid by the addition of a teaspoon of grenadine, a bright red, usually nonalcoholic pomegranate syrup. These days, it tends to be mixed half-and-half, without grenadine.

For the best results, a name-brand pressed orange juice from a carton should be used, not one made from fruit concentrate. Squeezing your own juice may sound like a good idea, but tends to produce an overly thin-textured drink. If you don't want to use the best champagne, a quality sparkler from elsewhere makes an acceptable alternative.

Cider

The drink made from fermented apple juice comes in many guises throughout the world, and—it's fair to say—covers a multitude of sins. When showing at its best, though, it is an incomparably refreshing glassful, teeming with the flavor of ripe fall apples, either still or slightly sparkling, bone-dry or gently sweet.

The commercial products of the big drink companies are not generally likely to excite, and cider is still best made by small, artisan farmhouse producers selling it from their own premises. This remains a thriving tradition in parts of England, especially the West Country of Somerset, Gloucestershire, and Hereford-shire. Cloudy with yeast cells in suspension, still and potent, this is one of the great unreconstructed drink styles, sometimes known by its English dialect name of "scrumpy."

In centuries past, cider was as highly regarded in England as vintage wines are still. Particular varieties of apple were much sought after, notably the now vanished Redstreak, but the tradition of paying farm laborers partly in cider—and the effect it inevitably had on them—helped to set it on the road to reputational ruin. It is only now recovering.

Cognac

Long synonymous with fine brandy, the Cognac region of western France produces some of the finest such products in the world. They start life as thin white Charente wines, which are then double distilled and aged in casks, often for many years.

Cognac was accidentally discovered when the light white wines were heat-treated to preserve them on sea voyages, and found to be much improved. During distillation, they acquire complex characters that are further enhanced during barrel maturation, which also gives the spirit most of its color.

The various grades of cognac form a strict hierarchy of quality. The basic VS (three-star) cognac can be a drinkable, if rough-and-ready, product. Above that is VSOP (five-star) which represents a noticeable step up in terms of richness and mellowness. Then comes XO, which denotes a cognac aged for a minimum of seven years (usually much longer) until it achieves a luxurious, velvety softness.

Cognac is best enjoyed on its own, without ice, at the end of a meal and should be served in narrow glasses, rather than the traditional old brandy balloons. Among the famous-name producers are Rémy Martin, Hine, Hennessy, Martell, and Courvoisier.

Homemade Lemonade

The lemonade you make at home will bear no relation to any commercial products, with their colorings, artificial sweeteners, and flavorings. All you need is lemon juice, sugar, and good spring water. Allow about 1¼ cups of sugar to the juice of 4 lemons. Mix them in a pitcher to dissolve the sugar, and top up with 4 cups of either still or sparkling water, as you wish. Some recipes call for a sugar syrup to be made first. Lemonade is generally best made immediately before it is needed. It can be enjoyed on its own, with ice, or as a mixer with vodka, white rum, or whiskey.

Versions of this drink are made across Europe and in the US. The drink is particularly popular in India, where it is known as *nimbu paani* ("lemon water"). It is sold at street stalls for the relief of throats parched by the heat.

Lemonade

1¾ cups superfine sugar

8 cups water

1½ cups freshly squeezed lemon juice

Pour the sugar into a saucepan and add 1 cup water. Bring to a boil over high heat, stirring all the time. Once the sugar has dissolved, leave the liquid to cool, then cover and chill thoroughly in the refrigerator. Pour the lemon juice into a pitcher, add the chilled liquid and top up with the remaining water. Stir well to mix before serving. *Serves 8–10*

Coke Float

The textbook Coke float consists of just two ingredients—Coca-Cola and vanilla ice cream. You put your ice cream into the glass and top it up with the Coke, the bubbles of which keep the ice cream in suspension, hence the name. A Coke float can either be sipped through a straw (difficult), or eaten with a spoon (much the best recourse), depending on how vigorously the ice cream has been stirred in.

Coke float can be made in individual glasses, or made up in a large pitcher for serving at summer parties. If you're going down the pitcher route, allow about 2 cups of Coke to each scoop of ice cream.

The ice cream of course makes the drink very smooth and creamy and, traditionally, it should be stirred energetically enough to produce a head of froth, a little like a cappuccino. Variations on the basic recipe involve using other soft, fizzy drinks, such as root beer, or replacing the vanilla ice cream with another flavor. Some prefer coffee ice cream, which has a natural affinity with the taste of cola.

The original float drink in the United States was probably the version made with root beer, but Coke float has a much greater international following.

Elderflower Wine

Much concocted in rural England, elder-flower wine was the very taste of summer to a certain generation. It is a thoroughly refreshing drink on the kind of baking-hot day for which English summers are more renowned than they were when the drink was better known.

To make it, you will need to gather a mass of fully opened elderflowers by snipping them off the stems neatly with scissors. When you have enough to fill the best part of a pint glass, they should be put in a demijohn and covered with 16 to 20 cups of boiling water. Add the juice of three lemons, around 1¼ cups of chopped raisins, and 6 cups of sugar.

When the liquid is cooled down to body temperature, a yeast and nutrient culture is added, and the mixture is left to begin its fermentation and infusion. After four days or so, the wine is poured off its solid components and left to clarify. Once a clear liquid emerges, it is stored for a further two months before it can be bottled. Homemade wines like these were often more potent than ordinary commercial wine, so caution was advisable when offered a second glass.

Dry Martini

For many the very definition of the perfect cocktail, a dry martini consists of gin, dry vermouth (whether Martini or any other brand), and perhaps a green cocktail olive. Inevitably, for such a simple drink, its precise origins are lost to collective memory, but it may well have been named a Martinez in the 1870s by the great bartender Jerry Thomas, for the California destination to which his first customer was traveling.

In truth, the basic formula of gin and vermouth is certainly much older. It was originally made with sweet red vermouth. Hence, at one time, if the customer asked for only a very little vermouth, the drink would be referred to as "very dry."

Dry vermouths became more popular in the first decade of the 20th century, and the modern-day dry martini became the classic preparation. Everybody has his or her own preferred proportions, but true purists favor as little dry vermouth as possible—often no more than the residue that remains after a dribble has been poured into the glass, swooshed around, and tipped out.

And, despite what James Bond insists, the martini should be stirred (in a pitcher with ice, which is then strained out), not shaken.

◁ Lager

Pilsener

Lager is the generic name for any beer made by the process of bottom-fermentation. Beers made in this style ferment after the yeasts introduced to them have sunk to the bottom of the mash, where they cannot crossbreed with any wild yeasts in the atmosphere, as top-fermenting beers do. Once the yeasts have sunk, the beers can be stored (or "lagered") in cool cellar conditions until they are ready. The risk of spoilage is virtually eliminated in bottom-fermentation.

Beer experts hold the view that top-fermented beers are nearly always more complex and interesting than bottom-fermented styles, which is one of the reasons that commercial lagers in particular have not exactly enjoyed a reputation as premium products in the modern era. Certainly it was the lighter style of lager that began to make it popular in Europe from the 1960s on.

Not all lager is bland and forgettable, though. The best lagers of Germany, the Netherlands, and Alsace have a degree of crisp, malty character, and may be deep reddish-brown, in contrast to the light golden lagers of Britain and North America. Strengths vary enormously, with export products often being in the 6 to 7% range.

The premium name among lager styles of beer is pilsener. It is one of those geographical designations that, through lack of protection, has been allowed to travel the world, so that pilseners, pilsners, or just pils, are produced all over. Originally, the name derives from the town of Pilsen in the province of Bohemia in the Czech Republic, prime beer-making country.

Czech pilsener (or *Pilsner Urquell*, literally "original pilsener") is still a reliable product, and one that may be enjoyed for remarkably little cost, as tourists to Prague are often delighted to discover. Outside the Czech Republic, the best producer of pilsener is Germany. German brewers market their beers under the designation pilsner. They are made in as close an approximation as possible of the style of centuries gone by from malted barley, hops, yeast, and water.

Good pilsener should have a bright amber color and a crisp, dry, rounded taste, allied to a light-bodied texture. There should be a good frothy head on the beer, which is often served in a huge glass called a stein. It is moderately strong in alcohol, and the aftertaste is distinctly hoppy, even floral.

Weizenbier

Guinness

The German term Weizenbier, or its alternative Weissebier, means wheat or white beer. Most beer is made from malted barley, but one made using a high proportion of wheat gives a paler brew. These are top-fermenting beers that often have a noticeable haze to their appearance from the yeast sediment left in them.

Of these, Berliner Weisse, made in the German capital, is perhaps the most renowned, seen as a quality product despite its relatively low alcohol content (usually around 3%). In the southern regions of Germany, wheat beers of more typical strength are the norm. If the prefix "Hefe" appears on the label, it denotes a beer that is being sold on its sediment. All styles share a fruitiness of flavor, and a tendency to leave a sweet aftertaste on the palate. The Bock (extra-strong) version of wheat beer is often drunk as a Christmas specialty.

Weizenbier is made in Austria too, and there is a significant production of it in Belgium, where the correct term is Witbier. The style has also been taken up by micro-breweries in North America, where its light-ness attunes it to the regional taste in beer.

Guinness is the most famous brand of stout ale in the world, and one of Ireland's premier products. Made under license in many other countries, aficionados of the "black stuff" claim that there is nothing to compare to the taste (and texture) of a pint of freshly drawn Guinness in one of Ireland's numerous pubs.

The beer is practically jet-black in color, and should be served with a deep, creamy, white head. Despite its color and relative density of texture, it has a light, dry, fruity flavor that is supremely refreshing and nutritious to the extent that it was once prescribed by doctors in the British Isles to patients who lacked essential nutrients in their diet.

Guinness began life in the disused brewery of a Dublin abbey in 1759, when Arthur Guinness, the son of a clergyman's estate manager, set up his own brewing business. The beer's color is obtained simply by the high roasting of the malted grains that go into it.

Different styles of Guinness are made for different markets. The bottled product on sale in North America is unusually stronger than Irish Guinness (around 6%, compared to the gentler 4% of Dublin draught).

Hot Chocolate

Chocolate first came to European notice during the Spanish voyages of conquest in the 16th century. Among the native peoples, it was drunk as a bitter infusion in hot water, and highly revered for its restorative properties.

Surprisingly, chocolate didn't immediately catch on in Europe. It wasn't until it was mixed with sugar that it became palatable to European tastes. The first establishment devoted to serving hot chocolate in England was opened in 1657 in the City of London, after which its rise to popularity was swift and sure, and went in parallel with the equally novel beverages of tea and coffee.

Hot Chocolate

⅔ cup best-quality semisweet chocolate

2 cups milk

½ cup heavy whipping cream

1 tsp powdered sugar

Unsweetened cocoa powder or ground cinnamon, to serve

Heat the chocolate and milk in a heavy-based saucepan over medium heat, stirring constantly with a wooden spoon. Bring it to just below boiling point and whisk with a wire whisk to make sure it is completely smooth. Meanwhile, whisk together the cream and powdered sugar until quite thick but not stiff—just dense enough to sit on top of the hot

chocolate. Pour the hot chocolate into cups and gently spoon the cream over the top, dropping it first onto the back of a spoon and letting it slide onto the top of the chocolate. Sieve a tiny amount of cocoa powder or cinnamon over the top and serve at once.

This can be drunk as it is so the chocolate streams through the cream, or the cream can be stirred through first. *Serves 4*
Adapted from Tessa Kiros' *Apples for Jam*

Irish Coffee

The preparation of Irish coffee requires care and attention to detail, but is always worth it. It is best served as an after-dinner drink, in the place of a normal coffee, but is also appreciated when served on its own on a cold winter's afternoon.

It consists of a glass of strong black coffee sweetened with soft, brown sugar and fortified with a good slug of (traditionally Irish) whiskey, on top of which is floated a layer of thick cream, so that the end result looks something like a glass of Guinness. The story goes that the drink was created in the 1940s by Joseph Sheridan, a chef at an airport near Limerick in the west of Ireland, as a warming drink for transatlantic travelers awaiting their connecting flights.

The secrets of a good Irish coffee are many. It must be sweetened to help the cream to float. The coffee, sugar, and whiskey are best warmed (not boiled) together in a pan, before being decanted into a reinforced glass mug with a handle. Some people whip the cream to enable it to float, while others pour it slowly over the back of a spoon.

Spanish Coffee

There are many variants on the Irish coffee formula, essentially depending on what type of liquor is added to the black coffee. Another favorite is Spanish coffee, in which a half-and-half mixture of Tia Maria and dark rum goes into the hot coffee, which is then topped with a layer of cream in the prescribed manner.

The pedantically minded will note that neither of the alcohol products in this coffee is actually Spanish, at least not these days. Tia Maria is from Jamaica, while rum can come from anywhere around the Caribbean or South America. This was, of course, the route that the Spaniards took in the 16th century on their voyages of discovery and conquest.

Tia Maria, a liqueur flavored with Jamaican Blue Mountain coffee beans, has an obvious affinity with coffee, while the rum helps to give an extra kick to the drink. For those who find a traditional Irish coffee a touch too bitter, Spanish coffee may well be the answer.

Irn-Bru

Orangina ▷

A highly popular nonalcoholic Scottish drink, Irn-Bru is made by a company called AG Barr in Glasgow. Its advertising slogan—"Made in Scotland, from girders"—indicates that the product is intended to be seen as anything other than a soft drink, despite its absence of alcohol. It is a glaring orange-yellow in color, and tastes something like a sweet citrus cordial with a backnote of sea air to it.

It was first marketed in 1901, when it was known as Iron Brew, but legal niceties eventually forced a change of spelling on it because the drink is not technically "brewed" at all, in the way that a beer is. The variant spelling has been in use since 1946.

The original drink has had many imitators, demonstrating the immense and enduring popularity of the product in Scotland. For many years, it has outsold the principal brands of cola. So inextricable an element of Scottish culture is it that, when McDonalds first opened branches in Scotland, it was forced by popular pressure to revoke its original decision not to stock Irn-Bru.

The drink may be taken on its own, with ice, or used as a mixer with vodka or even Scotch.

Marketed as a high-quality soft-drink product that bridges the gap between real pressed orange juice and orange soda, Orangina was first produced in French-occupied Algeria during the colonial period. After independence in 1962, its production was shifted to France itself, where generations of tourists discovered it as a respectable alternative to the many garden-variety sweetened soft drinks on the market. French parents gave it to their children as a more nutritious variant on such products.

Its flavor is derived from a mixture of orange and tangerine (the latter element telling of its North African origins), a little of the juice and pulp of which are added to sweetened carbonated water. It has always been packed in a highly distinctive flask-shaped bottle made of mottled glass, to resemble the surface of an orange.

Orangina is now owned by the Schweppes company, and is made under license in various foreign territories. In Scotland, it is made by AG Barr of Glasgow, makers of Irn-Bru. In North America, production has moved from Canada to Florida, home of the orange.

A spin-off product, Orangina Sanguine, is made from blood oranges.

◁ # Kir Royale

Kir is a wine cocktail made by adding a spoonful of cassis (black currant liqueur) to a glass of dry white wine. The recipe originated in Burgundy, where it was named for a mayor of the city of Dijon, Félix Kir, who used to serve it to visitors at international receptions in order to promote two of the great products of the region. To be absolutely correct, the wine used should be Bourgogne Aligoté, one of the lesser-known white wines of Burgundy, and one of the few that isn't made from the Chardonnay grape.

There are many different variants on the recipe, but the use of champagne instead of white wine is the one that most obviously changes its character. It is possible to use other types of fruit liqueur, such as *framboise* (raspberry), *mûre* (blackberry), or even *pêche* (peach). The drink is made by putting the liqueur into the glass first, and then topping it off with champagne. It should not be stirred, as this would risk flattening the sparkle.

Madeira

Along with port and sherry, one of the three classic fortified wine styles of Europe, Madeira is the one with the strangest history. Made on the tropical island of the same name, it is a product of the days of the great sailing ships, when it was accidentally discovered that a batch of the island's light white wine that had undergone a particularly torrid journey through the pitching seas and sweltering heat of the tropics was found to be positively improved by the experience.

During the 18th century, this is how all Madeira was made. It was loaded in casks into the holds of cargo ships, where it took its chances in whatever conditions it encountered, generally undergoing the round trip from Madeira to the East Indies and back.

It was eventually determined that the heat was the telling factor, and the conditions were more economically re-created in the winery, by means of hot-water pipes or through simple exposure to the sun.

Rising from the lightest and driest to the sweetest and richest, there are four styles of madeira—Sercial, Verdelho, Bual, and Malmsey. It is an utterly unique wine, rounded and intense in flavor, tasting of nuts and toffee.

Sherry

Although the name was once also used for similar products made elsewhere, such as Cyprus, true sherry now comes only from a delimited area of southern Spain around the towns of Jerez de la Frontera, Puerto de Santa María, and Sanlúcar de Barrameda.

Sherry—*jerez* in Spanish—is a white, fortified wine made principally from a grape variety called Palomino. Its method of production is quite unlike that of port. It is fortified only after the base wine has completed its fermentation, and then left to develop a layer of natural yeast, called *flor,* on its surface. This protects the wine from the effects of too much oxygenation, and helps to create the lightest and driest style of sherry, known as *fino.* Manzanilla is another type of fino from around the town of Sanlúcar.

The sweeter and darker styles are made when *flor* doesn't develop, or else breaks up and sinks into the wine, or when the fortification is undertaken to a higher level of alcohol, which prevents its development.

Not all pale sherries are dry, and not all dark ones are sweet, but in typical ascending order of sweetness, the wines are *fino, amontillado, palo cortado,* and *oloroso.*

Port

Portugal's other world-famous fortified wine, port, is made in the north of mainland Portugal, in an area called the Douro Valley. *Oporto* in Portuguese, it is a complex blend of many different red (and some white) grape varieties that, at its best, has a balance of natural sweetness and grape tannins that enables it to age superbly for many years.

The sweetness in port is derived from the fact that a proportion of the natural grape sugars are still present in the base wine when its fermentation is interrupted by the fortification agent. At one time, cognac was used, but as that came to be seen as interfering too much with the flavor of the wine, a neutral grape spirit is now the preferred medium.

The origins of port, as of many such products, lie in sea voyages, when British merchants would fortify the rough red wines of the Douro to preserve them on the journey back to England.

Many different styles of port are made, from basic ruby all the way up to vintage port, which is the product of a single year, released at two years old and intended for long cellaring.

Pastis, Ouzo, Raki

All around Europe, there are examples of a clear spirit made either from grain or vegetables, but always strongly flavored with aniseed or licorice. Famously, these are drinks that go cloudy when any other ingredient—including water—is added to them.

The most well-known manifestation of this class of drink is France's pastis, typified by the two big brands, Pernod and Ricard. These are bottled at just short of 40% alcohol and find mixing partners with a whole range of soft drinks, from lemonade to black currant cordial. In France itself, they are typically drunk with nothing more than ice, and perhaps a little water, as a means of whiling away a lazy sunny afternoon.

Greece's answer to pastis is ouzo, which tends to be a little stronger than pastis, but has the same piercing anise flavor. Raki is the Turkish or Balkan equivalent, some of which is cask-aged until it takes on a light golden hue.

It will be noted that absinthe, too, is basically a form of pastis, albeit a highly concentrated one. Pernod was originally conceived as a substitute for it in the era that saw absinthe banned.

Mulled Wine

Mulled wine is still considered by many to be the authentic taste of Christmas. There are many different recipes for it, but most rely on the basics of red wine with sweet spices, sliced orange or apple, and sometimes honey, gently warmed and served in mugs, often with a stick of cinnamon to act as a stirrer.

In the era before wine was sold in a micro-biologically stable state, it was more prone to spoilage, and it is possible that, in some areas, mulling was a way of disguising the off-tastes in spoiled wine. Mostly, though, it developed as a cold-weather way of making wine taste more comforting and luxurious at a time of year when feasting and celebration were mandatory. Cups of mulled wine would be handed to wassailers, the ancestors of today's carolers, who came to your door in the depths of winter to spread good cheer.

The practice of mulling wine penetrated as far south as the German-speaking parts of northern Italy, but essentially it is a German and Slavic tradition. In these regions, it is customary to add a dose of something stronger too, such as grape brandy, or the Jewish digestif, *slivovitz*.

Prosecco

Prosecco is one of the traditional sparkling wines of Italy, a dry or just off-dry style made in the northeast of the country in a region called the Veneto. The designated area for the best Prosecco possesses the unwieldy name of Prosecco di Valdobbiadene, as Prosecco is the name of the grape variety as well as that of the wine.

At one time, Prosecco was generally only of very modest quality. Although it is essentially a dry wine, it often had a kind of confected tutti-frutti flavor to it, which didn't exactly encourage connoisseurs to take it seriously. In recent years, quality has improved enormously, and the wine has become a popular aperitif, both within Italy and increasingly outside it too.

The wine is not made by the traditional method used for champagne, but gains its sparkle from a procedure known as the Charmat method, in which the second fermentation is induced in bulk in a large tank, before the wine is bottled under pressure.

Prosecco is the base ingredient for the widely known aperitif cocktail, Bellini, a regional specialty of the bars of Venice. It consists of Prosecco mixed with peach juice.

Sangria

Much beloved of vacationers to Spain, Sangria is essentially a wine-based cocktail made for drinking on the beach in the summer sun. It consists of red wine, to which is added a heady mix of brandy or rum, citrus juices (usually orange and lime), and sugar. It is mixed in a large glass pitcher and served with plenty of ice and slices of citrus fruits.

Not the least appealing aspect of sangria is that it is a great use for cheap red wine of very humble quality. By the time it is sweetened up, and the other ingredients added, a multitude of rough-and-ready sins may be hidden.

A variant on sangria made in southern Spain is called *zurra*, and is garnished with peach and nectarine, rather than citrus fruits. There is also a white wine version, *sangria blanca*, made with either still white wine or sparkling *cava*, but as the name of sangria is derived from the Spanish word for "blood," red is really its natural color.

Sake

Sake is sometimes erroneously thought of as a spirit, but is in fact more comparable to a strong wine—or perhaps a beer, as it is a grain product. It has been made since ancient times as a way of using up surplus rice whenever there had been a bountiful harvest. It is thought that the technique of making a fermented drink from rice probably originated in China, but sake is Japan's very own version.

Whereas most rice wine made in China tends to be for cooking, sake is very much a quality product in Japan. The various regions produce their own special versions, and certain individual brands have come to be highly prized. Different styles depend on the degree to which the rice is polished, and whether the resulting brew is cask-aged or not. Cedarwood, as opposed to the oak traditional in grape wines, is the preferred medium.

Sake is customarily drunk slightly warm, but in cold weather it can be served as hot as tea. In the summer months, it is increasingly normal to drink it cold. A ceramic cup called a *choko* is the traditional drinking vessel.

Sambuca

Schnapps

The name for a generic liqueur traditionally produced in and around Rome, sambuca is a clear, potent drink, flavored with a mixture of European black elderberries (*Sambucus nigra*) and aniseed. It has a sweet, pungent taste and oily, viscous texture.

What distinguishes sambuca as a drink from the host of other Italian liqueurs is the ritual that has come to be associated with its consumption. In Italian restaurants, you will quite likely be asked whether you would like your sambuca *con la mosca* (literally, "with the fly in it"). These are not real insects, of course, but two or three coffee beans, which are floated in the drink. It is then set alight as it is served to you.

The skilled sambuca drinker blows out the flame and knocks back the drink in one shot, crunching up the soaked coffee beans at the end. As long as you don't burn your nose in the process, this is easier than it sounds, not least because the fire burns away some of the alcohol, making the drink seem less fiery in the other sense of the term.

If a burning drink doesn't appeal, sambuca is a very versatile cocktail ingredient.

Schnapps is the term for a family of clear, ardent spirits of grain, fruit, or vegetable origin, made in Germany and the Scandinavian countries. They are essentially another version of aquavit, in that they are colorless, untreated distillates of their primary ingredient, bottled at spirit strength, and intended for drinking neat.

The name schnapps comes from an old Nordic word, *snappen*, meaning "to snatch," and refers to the method of consumption that is traditional for these drinks. They are served in small glasses, and usually snapped up in a single gulp (after which you may well decide to hurl your glass at the fireplace, assuming the company isn't too formal).

These are typical drinks of cold northerly climates, intended to warm the blood in the winter months especially. In Scandinavia, they are customarily drunk with cured herring, or the array of foods at a smörgasbord, rather in the manner that cold vodka is drunk in Poland and Russia.

Fruit-flavored liqueurs of half strength are now common in the North American market. They might be labeled "peach schnapps," for example, but they are not to be confused with true north-European schnapps.

Rye

As its name suggests, this is a whiskey made predominantly from rye, as opposed to corn or barley. It is a specialty of the United States, where regulations stipulate that it must be made from no less than 51% rye.

It was traditionally a product of the eastern states, especially Pennsylvania, Maryland, and Virginia, where much of the country's crop of rye was grown. Of all the styles of American whiskey, this was the one that was most damaged by the era of Prohibition (1919 to 1933), when it was illegal to trade in, or consume, alcohol. Manufacture of rye is limited now to a few specialist producers, such as Old Overholt and Heaven Hill, although bourbon maker Jim Beam also produces a rye.

Rye has a much more assertive-tasting spirit than corn or barley, with a spicy flavor that is further enhanced by aging in oak casks. Some have compared it to the taste of Canadian whisky. Some of the classic whiskey cocktails of the Prohibition era call for rye rather than any other type. Not many people are aware that rye is the true base of the famous Manhattan cocktail.

Vanilla Milkshake　▷

Just occasionally, when all the serious drinking is done, it's good to revert to the tastes of our childhood.

A sumptuous mix of whole milk and vanilla ice cream, perhaps with a dash of vanilla syrup added to boost the flavor, and a regal topping of whipped cream, a milkshake is one of the most enticing beverages of all. Usually made in a blender these days, shakes were very often whipped up entirely by hand in a mixing cup, with all the attention lavished on them that the most assiduous bartender brought to the task of mixing cocktails.

The first known reference to a "milkshake" dates from 1885, when the drink really was a cocktail, and resembled something more like a whiskey-laced eggnog. The modern ice-cream milkshake really got going in the 1920s, with the invention of the electric blender. After vanilla, a whole world of exotic flavors opened up in the form of strawberry, chocolate, banana, and malted milk. Life would never be the same again.

Vanilla Milkshake

2 large scoops vanilla ice cream

1 cup whole milk

1 tsp vanilla extract

Combine the three ingredients in a blender, pour into tall glasses, and serve. *Serves 2*

◁ Scotch Whisky

Scotland's most celebrated export, and one that firmly bolsters its economy, is Scotch whisky (spelled without an "e"), the precise taste of which has proved quite inimitable wherever else in the world whiskey is made.

Scotch comes in varying styles, depending on whereabouts in Scotland it is produced. The four main regions are the Lowlands, Highlands, Campbeltown, and Islay, the last including the western isles of Jura, Mull, and Skye. Islay whiskies are distinguished by their pungent peatiness, while the Lowlands whiskies are the mildest and sweetest in flavor.

At the top of the quality tree for Scotch sit the single malts, the unblended production of individual distilleries, which all have their own particular styles within the overall regional idioms. These whiskies are sometimes bottled at cask strength—up to 60%—the intention being that the drinker finds his or her own preferred level of dilution (with good Scots spring water, naturally).

The bulk of the market is accounted for by blended whiskies, many of impressive quality, from producers such as Teachers, Johnnie Walker, Bell's, J&B, and Whyte & Mackay.

Irish Whiskey

The chief distinguishing characteristic of Irish whiskey is that, whereas most other whiskies go through a double distillation to achieve mellowness and roundness, Irish whiskey is triple distilled. This is held to result in its particularly easy-drinking, gentle style. Indeed, it was only toward the end of the Victorian era, at the turn of the last century, that the demand for Irish whiskey began to be eclipsed by that for Scotch.

Other factors account for its distinctive taste. No peat is used in the kilns in which the grains are malted, so there is none of the pungency associated with Scotland's whisky. Furthermore, Irish is always based on a mixture of malted and unmalted grains, and not on malted grains alone. The whiskey is then cask-aged—traditionally in oak barrels— for six to eight years.

Other than that, the grades of Irish are broadly comparable to those for Scotch. There is single malt, single grain, and blended whiskey, just as in Scotch, as well as products bottled at cask strength. Producers include Jameson's, Paddy, Bushmills, Murphy's, and Tullamore Dew.

Tequila Slammer

The tequila slammer will forever be associated with the most reckless style of drinking. It is messy, hedonistic, and can be a great deal of fun in the right company.

The formula could hardly be simpler. You pour a measure of ice-cold silver tequila into a small glass, and add an equal amount of something fizzy. This can be sparkling lemonade, soda water, even champagne. You then cover the glass with one hand, bang it down hard a couple of times on the tabletop or bar counter, and then throw it down in one gulp before the foaming drink overflows the top of the glass.

Slammers became enormously popular among young professionals in the 1980s. They are a kind of competitive drinking (how many can you handle?), and as such, not really the sort of thing that is officially encouraged any more.

On the other hand, tequila has always been about this kind of drinking. The traditional way of drinking it in Mexico, which involves lime biting and salt licking from the back of the hand, has its own air of what-the-heck heedlessness, a spirit the slammer undoubtedly salutes.

Vermouth   ▷

Vermouth is one of a class of drinks known in the European regulations as "aromatized wines." That is to say, it is a fermented (and fortified) wine that has ingredients other than grape juice in it. In the case of vermouth, its flavoring components are a mixture of dried herbs and roots, indicating that it was once a medicinal drink that has become popular in its own right.

There are broadly three main styles of vermouth: dry (typified by France's Noilly Prat); sweet red (as in Italy's Martini Rosso), and a sweetened white version (the most famous of which is Cinzano Bianco). In addition to these, a small amount of rosé vermouth is made, and there are such products as France's Chambéryzette, a vermouth flavored with strawberries.

Vermouths may be drunk with mixers, such as tonic water or lemonade, but they are also indispensable elements in the cocktail cabinet. A dry martini would be nothing without its whisper of dry vermouth, and the Perfect Manhattan blends sweet and dry versions with rye whiskey.

The name vermouth originally indicated the presence of wormwood in the drink, but this is now restricted to absinthe.

Riesling

One of the great white grape varieties in the world of wine, Riesling originated in Germany, where it remains the sole ingredient of the vast majority of all the finest wines. It is grown over the border in the French region of Alsace, throughout central Europe, and is also a popular varietal in New Zealand, South Africa, and the cooler regions of Australia and California.

Riesling is prized for its versatility. Almost never vinified with oak, it is capable of a diversity of different styles, from the steely-dry wines of Alsace to the luscious dessert wines of Germany's Rheingau and Pfalz regions. It is susceptible to "noble rot" in the right conditions, but is also superb at making very appealing off-dry wines with just a touch of residual sweetness in them.

When vinified dry, the wines have an unmistakable tang of fresh lime juice or lime zest in the flavor, shading to peach with higher sweetness, and then orange marmalade and honey in the richest versions. What unites all these styles is the pronounced acidity the wines always have, which helps to make the dry wines more appetizing, and balances out the intense sweetness of the rotted styles.

Gewürztraminer

Wines made from the Gewürztraminer grape variety are among the most peculiarly aromatic in the vinous world. The grape is grown quite widely these days in the newer wine-producing countries outside Europe—Chile, South Africa, and New Zealand are having particular success with it—but its prime heartland is the Alsace region of northeastern France.

Technically a white variety, Gewürztraminer has a pinkish skin, but its most singular characteristic is the aroma of its juice. There is an often eerily precise evocation of lychees about it, backed by Turkish delight, floral scents that encompass roses, violets, and jasmine, acerbic citrus fruits such as pink grapefruit, and a range of sweet culinary spices, including cinnamon, ginger, and cloves. The first part of its name, *Gewürz*, is the German word for "spicy."

The wines are generally round and full-bodied to taste, with relatively low acidity, and are best drunk quite young to catch them in their first aromatic flush. As well as making dry wines, growers in Alsace also make luscious dessert wines from Gewürztraminer, either by harvesting the grapes late, or by leaving them to develop "noble rot" on the vine. Sauternes is one such wine.

Sauternes

These are among the most labor-intensive wines in the world. They are made from grapes affected by "noble rot" (*Botrytis cinerea*), which develops naturally in the damp mornings and warm days of fall. As the fungus attacks the grapes, it shrivels them up, drying the water content out of them, and thus concentrating their sugars.

The result is that, when pressed, the rotted grapes exude a sticky, viscous juice with very high sugar. This ferments slowly, eventually reaching a natural halt when the alcohol level in it will support no more fermentation (usually around 15%), but leaving plenty of unfermented sugar in the wine.

Not every vintage delivers ideal conditions for the formation of botrytis, so that Sauternes made in good years fetch extremely high prices. It is exquisitely rich and concentrated at its best, full of dried apricot fruit, and with a silky layer of vanilla running through it from oak-aging. The principal grape variety in Sauternes is Sémillon, with a little Sauvignon Blanc and Muscadelle for acid balance.

Feuerzangenbowle

The name means "fire-tongs bowl," and denotes an elaborately ceremonial festive punch traditional to Germany. Similar in conception to *Glühwein* or mulled wine, it is prepared like fondue in a bowl suspended over a flame. Red wine, citrus fruits, and spices are gently warmed in it, and then the *Zangen*, or tongs, are laid across the top of it, supporting a loaf of sugar.

The sugar loaf is doused in strong rum and set alight. As it burns with a tall blue flame, it dissolves into the pot below, encouraged as it does so by further libations of rum. When all the sugar has melted into the bowl, the drink is ladled out into cups and served around.

Feuerzangenbowle is a winter specialty, and is very often prepared at Christmas gatherings, or to see in the New Year. Nothing has ever matched the 38 cups that were prepared in a colossal copper pot in Isartor, near Munich, at Christmas 2005.

The drink also gave its name to a comic novel of the 1930s by Heinrich Spoerl, in which a man relives his childhood by going back to school in student disguise after ingesting a little too much Feuerzangenbowle.

Rum Punch

Rum punch is the kind of cocktail that seems to slip effortlessly down in a mellow style that is the direct antithesis of the tequila-slamming ethos.

There are many different recipes for rum punch, as different Caribbean rums blend in different ways with other ingredients. What is essential is a good measure of rum—usually golden, the style in between white and dark—mixed with various fruit juices, perhaps a dash of angostura bitters and plenty of ice.

The best fruit juices to use in a rum punch are pineapple, orange, and lime. A century ago, the ingredients were simpler, just lemon juice with sugar syrup and rum, while in the 1800s, this was a hot drink, in which the rum was blended with brandy and topped with lemon juice, syrup, and boiled water. It is hard to imagine that being a popular option now on the beach in Barbados!

An old rhyme elucidates the basic formula: "one of sour, two of sweet, three of strong, four of weak." That might translate as a measure of lime juice, two of syrup, three of rum, and four of pineapple.

Contributors

The original entries were written by the specialist contributors listed below; subsequent versions of the entries may have been altered.

Josephine Bacon – Breads, Cakes, and Pastries; Desserts
Josephine Bacon has been a food writer for thirty-five years, contributing to newspapers and magazines in Cyprus, the US (where she wrote regularly for the *Los Angeles Herald-Examiner*) and the UK. She is the author of fourteen cookbooks and numerous translations, the latest of which is *A Sprig of Dill*, a Romanian memoir with recipes. She was also a contributor to the *Oxford Encyclopedia of Food and Drink in America*.

Mario Batali is the co-owner and operator of award-winning restaurants in New York, Las Vegas, and Los Angeles, and is known for his seamless combination of traditional principles with intelligent culinary adventure. Batali is the author of five cookbooks (the most recent of which, *Molto Italiano*, won the James Beard Award for Best International Cookbook), has hosted three TV programs, and has appeared on many others. Since 2003, Batali has served on the board of the New York City Food Bank and has participated in numerous hunger awareness campaigns.

Hilary Bell – Beans, Cheese, and Eggs; Fruits, Nuts, and Vegetables
Hilary Bell is a Toronto-based writer and editor. Raised on solid English-Canadian fare as a child, she later set out to see the world as a community development consultant, sampling the delights of roadside food stalls, markets and restaurants across Southeast Asia, Africa, and the Caribbean, with extended stays in the US, Europe, and the UK. She counts herself lucky to live in Toronto—a city with inexpensive restaurants from every corner of the world.

Mark Bittman is the author of seven cookbooks, including *The Best Recipes in the World* and the classic best-seller *How to Cook Everything*, which has sold more than one million copies. He is also the coauthor of Jean-George Vongerichten's *Simple to Spectacular*, and *Jean-Georges: Cooking at Home with a Four-Star Chef*. Now ten years running, Bittman's weekly "The Minimalist" column in the *New York Times* is followed by more than two million readers. His new PBS series, *The Best Recipes in the World*, premiered in April 2007.

Heston Blumenthal has been described as a culinary alchemist for his innovative style of cuisine. His work researches the molecular compounds of dishes to enable a greater understanding of taste and flavor. His restaurant The Fat Duck, in Berkshire, England was awarded three Michelin stars in 2004, and voted the Best Restaurant in the World by an international panel of 500 culinary experts in *Restaurant Magazine*'s The World's 50 Best Restaurants 2005 awards. He also owns the Hinds Head Hotel, a village pub in Bray.

Massimo Capra was born in Cremona, Italy, where he learned his craft in his mother's kitchen. Chef Capra owns the wildly popular Mistura Ristorante in Toronto, where he is famous for his risottos.

Julia Child attended the Cordon Bleu in Paris and opened L'Ecole des Trois Gourmandes with Simone Beck and Louisette Bertholle in 1951. In 1961, the three coauthored *Mastering the Art of French Cooking*, which is a cookbook classic. Her many TV cooking shows include *The French Chef*, *Julia Child and Company*, and *Julia and Jacques Cooking at Home* with Jacques Pépin. She was an active member of the International Association of Culinary Professionals and a co-founder of The American Institute of Wine and Food. She died in 2004.

Samuel and Samantha Clark not only work together but are husband and wife, and have both cooked at leading restaurants such as the Eagle gastro-pub and The River Cafe. Sharing a passion for the Moorish regions, they joined forces to open Moro in London in 1997. Since then, the restaurant has enjoyed unequalled reviews and accolades. Their first book, *The Moro Cookbook*, was published in 2001 to widespread acclaim.

Tom Colicchio is a self-taught chef, who worked his way up through restaurants in his native New Jersey and then New York City at hot spots such as the Quilted Giraffe and Rakel. He landed his first posting as executive chef at midtown Mondrian. Tom eventually struck out on his own with Craft (New York), Craftbar (New York), Craftsteak (in Las Vegas and New York), and 'wichcraft (multiple locations), along with other consulting projects and three cookbooks. He is currently the star of Bravo's *Top Chef*.

Elizabeth David continues to be one of the most influential food writers in the world. She discovered her taste for good food and wine when she lived with a French family while attending the Sorbonne. Keeping house in many countries, she aspired to learn the local cuisine, and her books (*Mediterranean Food, French Country Cooking*, and many others) led readers to view food as more a way of life than sustenance. In 1977, she won the Glenfiddich award for *English Bread and Yeast Cookery*. She died in 1992.

Jill Dupleix is an Australian-born food writer currently living in London, where she was the food editor of the *Times* for six years. She is the author of fourteen cookbooks, is a popular guest chef on television, likes drinking Campari, and cannot live without Parmigiano Reggiano.

Terry Durack is an Australian-born restaurant critic and food commentator, and author of several books including *Yum, Hunger*, and *Noodle*. He has twice won the prestigious Glenfiddich Restaurant Critic of The Year Award, in 2005 and 2007. He currently lives in London.

Nichola Fletcher – Poultry and Game
Nichola Fletcher leads three lives: she is a food writer and historian, an active designer-goldsmith, and she runs an upmarket venison business. Nominations, short listings, and awards include Slow Food, BBC Food Awards, Gourmet Voice at Cannes, Guild of Food Writers, and Royal Society of Arts. Nichola has written five books on the preparation and cooking of venison and game birds, and one book on the history of feasting. She divides her time between Scotland and Perigord, France.

Ina Garten left her job as a budget analyst in the White House in 1978 to pursue her dream: operating a specialty food store in the Hamptons in New York. Twenty years later, Barefoot Contessa is celebrated for its stylish charm as well as its delicious food, and Ina Garten is now a best-selling cookbook author and TV personality. Ina lives in East Hampton, New York, and Southport, Connecticut, with her husband, Jeffrey.

Bruce Geddes – Meats
Bruce Geddes' food writing includes Lonely Planet guides on Mexico and the Caribbean and work for *Toronto Life* magazine. His mother was a terrible cook (may she rest in peace). As a result, his interest in food developed in his adult years. An avid cook, he credits much of his culinary education to the combination of long bouts of unemployment and the advent of the Food Network. He lives in Toronto, happily within blocks of much of the best beef in town.

Bill Granger is a leading Australian food writer who has always been passionate about cooking, and takes pride in presenting delicious food that is simple, fresh, and irresistible. Granger is a self-taught cook who gained his knowledge from eating, reading, and experiencing food. Bill has published numerous books that have topped international best-seller lists. His Sydney restaurant, bills, is famous for its delicious breakfasts. Bill appears frequently in both Australian and international media and writes regularly for British and Australian newspapers and magazines.

Donna Hay is an Australia-based food stylist, author, and editor. Though a home economics diploma at the local technical college may not sound like the obvious starting point for international success, mastering the skills needed for domestic cooking enabled Hay to create a brand that is accessible to anyone with a kitchen. Hay has published eight phenomenally successful cookbooks, won a host of prestigious international food awards, and continues to inspire cooks of all levels each season with fresh, modern recipes from *donna hay* magazine.

Marcella Hazan, the godmother of Italian cooking in America, has written five remarkable cookbooks, including *The Classic Italian Cookbook, Essentials of Italian Cooking*, and *Marcella Cucina*. She lives with her husband, Victor, himself an authority on Italian food and wine, in Longboat Key, Florida.

Ken Hom is regarded as a leading authority on Chinese cuisine. He was eleven when he started working after school at his uncle's Chinese restaurant, and he paid his way through college by teaching at the Culinary Academy in Chicago (Charlie Trotter was a student). Ken's first cookbook, *Ken Hom's Chinese Cookery*, has sold over 1.5 million copies worldwide. The book accompanied the wildly popular BBC TV series of the same name, which is internationally syndicated.

Simon Hopkinson is one of Britain's most highly regarded food writers. He has won the prestigious Glenfiddich Award for Cookery Writing three times, and his book *Roast Chicken and Other Stories* was voted the most useful cookbook of all time in a 2005 survey of food writers, chefs, and restaurateurs.

Madhur Jaffrey is regarded by many as the world authority on Indian food, and is an award-winning actress and best-selling cookbook author. Her first book, *An Invitation to Indian Cookery*, was published in 1973 and her series for BBC television *Madhur Jaffrey's Indian Cookery* made her a household name. She has appeared in more than twenty films, including Merchant Ivory's *Heat and Dust*, and has written fifteen cookbooks, including *Madhur Jaffrey's Ultimate Curry Bible*.

Diana Kennedy moved to Mexico in 1957 to marry Paul P. Kennedy, the foreign correspondent for the *New York Times*. In 1969, at the suggestion of Craig Claiborne, Diana began teaching Mexican cooking classes and in 1972 published her first cookbook. She has been decorated with the Order of the Aztec Eagle, the highest honor bestowed on foreigners by the Mexican government. She lives much of the year in her ecological adobe house in Michoacan, Mexico, which also serves as a research center for Mexican cuisine.

Tessa Kiros was born in London to a Finnish mother and a Greek-Cypriot father. She has lived in South Africa, London, Sydney, Athens, and Mexico and is now based in Tuscany, Italy. Her cooking is influenced by her childhood experiences and a life of travel and exploration in various parts of the world. Tessa has collected and created her unique recipes over many years and continues to share special memories and moments with her readers along with wonderful, eclectic food.

Anne Langdon – Fruits, Nuts, and Vegetables
Anne Langdon is a writer living in Toronto. She has written for print, radio, theater, video, television, and film. She is currently working to establish an edible landscape community food garden in her local park, which will promote the value of local food production and encourage home owners to include some food in their landscape.

Nigella Lawson is the author of *How to Eat, How to Be a Domestic Goddess* (for which she won the British Author of the Year Award), *Nigella Bites, Forever Summer*, and *Feast*. Her unique hosting style on television has spawned many imitators and legions of fans. She has been profiled in the *New York Times Magazine, Gourmet*, and many other publications. She lives in London with her two children.

Jamie Oliver is one of the world's best-loved chefs. He has inspired people to spend more time cooking and his television programs have been broadcast in more than fifty countries. His accompanying cookbooks are best-sellers not only in the UK but across the world, having been translated into twenty-six languages. Jamie lives in London and Essex with his wife, Jools, and their two daughters.

Martin Picard has worked around the world as a professional chef since the early 1990s. In 1993, Picard was heavily involved in the opening of the internationally-recognized Montreal restaurant, Toqué!, and in 2001 he opened his own restaurant, Au Pied de Cochon. Picard is known for his extensive knowledge of French cuisine and his warm sense of hospitality.

Gary Rhodes is a British restaurateur, food writer and chef, known for his love of British cuisine. He has hosted numerous television shows for the BBC, is the owner of four restaurants, and is the author of many best-selling cookbooks.

Claudia Roden was born in Egypt. Her books include *The New Book of Middle Eastern Food, Mediterranean Cookery, The Food of Italy – Region by Region, The Book of Jewish Food*, and *Arabesque: A Taste of Morocco, Turkey and Lebanon*. She has won many awards, including six Glenfiddich awards and a James Beard Best Cookbook of the Year award, the Premio Orio Vergani of Italy, and the Prince Claus Award for Culture in the Netherlands.

Rose Gray and Ruth Rogers opened the River Cafe on the banks of the Thames in Hammersmith, London, in 1987. They have trained some of the biggest names in cooking, and are best-selling cookbook authors. They have won a Michelin Star and many other awards.

Nigel Slater is one of Britain's best-known food writers, whose first book, *Real Fast Food*, was shortlisted for the Andre Simon Award. Other books include *The 30 Minute Cook*, *Real Good Food*, *Real Cooking*, and *Appetite*, which won the Andre Simon Award for Cookbook of the Year. His autobiography, *toast—the story of a boy's hunger*, won six major awards, including the British Biography of the Year. Nigel also writes an award-winning weekly column in the *Observer*.

Delia Smith is Britain's top-selling cookbook author, having sold over 15 million copies of her books. After spending several years researching traditional English recipes in her spare time, Smith became the food writer for the *Daily Mirror's* magazine in 1969. Since then, she has written more than twenty cookbooks and starred in several television series.

Diana Steedman – Noodles and Rice
Diana Steedman is a writer and editor who has worked on dozens of general reference books with many leading writers. Educated in the Bahamas, she pursued a successful career in medical research, newspapers, and publishing before focusing her attention on the world of cooking, craft, and garden writing. Passionate about adventure and great-tasting, fresh produce, she makes her home in the rural countryside of England, growing flowers and vegetables and cooking for friends.

Rick Stein, OBE, is one of the UK's favorite chefs. For more than twenty-five years he has run The Seafood Restaurant in Padstow, Cornwall, which is known internationally. His other Padstow restaurants include St. Petroc's Bistro and Rick Stein's Café. Rick has also won many awards, including the Glenfiddich Trophy in 2001 for his commitment to food quality, and, in 2005, the James Beard Foundation KitchenAid Book of the Year for *Rick Stein's Seafood*. *Rick Stein's Mediterranean Escapes* is his eighth BBC television series.

Jane and Michael Stern are the authors of more than twenty books about America, including *Eat Your Way Across the U.S.A.*, *Chili Nation*, and *Roadfood*. They write the "Roadfood" column in *Gourmet*, which has won three James Beard Awards for Best Magazine Series, and the "Wish You Were Here" postcards for Condé Nast's Epicurious.com. In addition, they serve as regular contributors to the Food Network's show *In Food Today* and to NPR's *The Splendid Table*. They live in Connecticut.

Eric Vellend – Soups and Salads
Eric Vellend is a Toronto-based food writer and chef. After graduating from George Brown Chef School in 1994, he worked at a number of restaurants before becoming the executive chef at a boutique catering company. He has been the food columnist at the *City Centre Moment* since 2004, and his work has appeared in *City Bites*, *Toronto Life* magazine, the *Globe and Mail*, and the *Toronto Star*, among other publications. In thirteen years of professional cooking, he has made soups and salads for thousands of people.

Stuart Walton – Appetizers; Fish and Seafood; Beans, Cheese, and Eggs; Beverages
Stuart Walton is a British food and wine writer and cultural historian. His books include *The Right Wine with the Right Food*, *Out Of It: A Cultural History of Intoxication* and *Humanity: An Emotional History*, and he is a major annual contributor to the *Good Food Guide*, the UK's premier restaurant guide. He has contributed to many reference works on food and drink, and was a senior writer on *ICONS: A Portrait of England*.

Alice Waters has been a well-known and influential chef since the 1970s. An advocate for locally-grown, organic foods, she has been recognized as the creator of California cuisine and has written several books on the subject, including *Chez Panisse Cooking*. Waters has founded two restaurants, Chez Panisse and Café Fanny, where she uses in-season, small-farm products, because she believes shipping produce around the world is harmful to the environment and results in lower-quality foods.

Index

Picture Credits

Every effort has been made to correctly attribute all material in this book. We will be pleased to correct any errors in future editions.

Corbis
pages 10, 41, 60, 61, 80, 84, 85, 179, 216, 313, 331, 343, 390, 403, 422, 425, 500, 522, 554, 589, 593, 625, 738, 742, 743, 793, 807, 821, 828, 863, 870, 877, 943

Food & Drink Photos
pages 38, 253, 326, 408, 413, 441, 705, 749, 750, 763, 789, 801, 802, 910

Sian Irvine
pages 8, 29, 34, 53, 65, 83, 95, 115, 117, 122, 261, 301, 407, 811

Jupiterimages
pages 90, 105, 108, 118, 133, 143, 144, 145, 163, 180, 191, 192, 225, 244, 276, 333, 336, 462, 467, 481, 544, 558, 578, 591, 615, 649, 699, 774, 819, 856

Gareth Morgans
pages 6, 13, 14, 15, 17, 18, 19, 21, 23, 31, 35, 37, 43, 47, 49, 55, 59, 67, 70, 72, 73, 79, 96, 99, 106, 111, 113, 121, 124, 131, 135, 136, 139, 147, 149, 150, 152, 155, 169, 170, 173, 184, 187, 194, 203, 205, 206, 209, 211, 221, 226, 239, 247, 268, 275, 279, 283, 302, 305, 314, 338, 346, 350, 353, 357, 358, 367, 373, 377, 381, 387, 393, 415, 452, 455, 465, 468, 471, 474, 475, 477, 483, 485, 486, 494, 497, 499, 503, 507, 511, 513, 515, 516, 527, 533, 537, 540, 549, 551, 552, 557, 571, 572, 578, 579, 581, 583, 584, 586, 595, 597, 600, 601, 602, 605, 607, 619, 621, 637, 644, 647, 655, 657, 659, 675, 676, 677, 682, 683, 691, 701, 711, 716, 717, 722, 723, 727, 729, 735, 741, 759, 765, 791, 799, 813, 817, 823, 832, 837, 851, 854, 855, 859, 869, 879, 880, 883, 884, 890, 899, 903, 906, 909, 914, 917, 918, 921, 922, 925, 929, 933, 934, 937, 941

Ian Garlick
pages 22, 32, 33, 57, 63, 76, 77, 87, 93, 100, 103, 127, 140, 158, 164, 175, 176, 183, 236, 256, 263, 266, 281, 286, 292, 295, 299, 307, 317, 321, 341, 361, 384, 397, 431, 444, 456, 459, 473, 488, 492, 504, 521, 525, 531, 538, 539, 543, 547, 563, 567, 568, 575, 576, 579, 608, 611, 626, 626, 627, 627, 629, 630, 633, 663, 664, 666, 669, 670, 684, 684, 685, 685, 688, 697, 698, 699, 703, 704, 719, 731, 747, 766, 797, 803, 827, 835, 849, 861, 864, 867, 868, 870, 871, 871, 887, 889, 895, 904, 913, 926, 931, 938, 945

Getty Images
pages 81, 197, 365, 378, 394, 430, 560, 598, 599, 635, 650, 652, 653, 654, 661, 680, 686, 687, 708, 710, 711, 715, 725, 732, 736, 754, 809, 872, 874, 900

StockFood UK
pages 25, 44, 51, 69, 75, 167, 199, 213, 215, 219, 229, 232, 243, 249, 250, 254, 265, 271, 289, 297, 308, 311, 325, 335, 349, 363, 382, 383, 389, 398, 418, 427, 429, 434, 437, 439, 443, 446, 449, 451, 478, 491, 509, 519, 534, 564, 592, 593, 603, 612, 617, 643, 679, 695, 706, 712, 716, 717, 745, 753, 769, 770, 773, 777, 781, 782, 785, 787, 795, 814, 824, 841, 844, 847, 852, 876, 892, 897, 930

Recipe Credits

Mario Batali
Bucatini all'Amatriciana from MOLTO ITALIANO by
Mario Batali, copyright © 2005 Mario Batali. Reprinted
by permission of HarperCollins Publishers.

Mark Bittman
Crostini and Drunken Shrimp from THE BEST RECIPES
IN THE WORLD: MORE THAN 1,000 INTERNATIONAL
DISHES TO COOK AT HOME by Mark Bittman,
copyright © 2005 by Doubleday B Publishing, Inc.
Used by permission of Broadway Books, a division
of Random House, Inc.

Heston Blumenthal
Bangers and Mash from IN SEARCH OF PERFECTION
by Heston Blumenthal, © Heston Blumenthal,
published by Bloomsbury, 2006.

Julia Child
Clafouti, Scrambled Eggs, and Tarte Tatin from
MASTERING THE ART OF FRENCH COOKING by
Julia Child and Simone Beck, copyright © 1961 Alfred
A. Knopf, a division of Random House, Inc. Used
by permission of Alfred A. Knopf, a division of
Random House Inc.

Tom Colicchio
Vanilla Ice Cream and Green Olive Tapenade from
CRAFT OF COOKING by Tom Colicchio, copyright
© 2003 by TC Enterprises. Used by permission of
Clarkson Potter Publishers, a division of Random
House, Inc.

Elizabeth David
Chateaubriand, Cheese Soufflé, Chicken Normandy,
Langoustines, Pears Poached in Red Wine, and Sea
Bass with Fennel from FRENCH PROVINCIAL
COOKING by Elizabeth David, published in 1960 by
Penguin Books Ltd.

Jill Dupleix
Crash Hot Potatoes, Jump-in-the-Pan Chicken, Double
Happiness Beans, and Green Veg Fritatta © Jill Dupleix.

Terry Durack
Pho Bo and Chicken Chow Mein from NOODLE
by Terry Durack, published by Allen and Unwin,
Australia, 1998.

Ina Garten
Key Lime Pie from BAREFOOT CONTESSA FAMILY
STYLE by Ina Garten, copyright © 2002 by Ina Garten.
Used by permission of Clarkson Potter Publishers,
a division of Random House, Inc.

Bill Granger
Lemon Curd from BILL'S OPEN KITCHEN by Bill Granger,
© Bill Granger, Murdoch Books Australia, 2003.

Donna Hay
Bacon and Egg Pie, Angel Food Cake, and Crème Brulée
from THE NEW COOK by Donna Hay, © Donna Hay,
Murdoch Books Australia, 1997.

Marinated Beets from ENTERTAINING by Donna Hay,
© Donna Hay, Murdoch Books Australia, 2007.

Marcella Hazan
Pasta e Fagioli and Bolognese Sauce from ESSENTIALS
OF CLASSIC ITALIAN COOKING by Marcella Hazan,
copyright © 1992 Alfred A. Knopf, a division of Random
House, Inc. Used by permission of Alfred A. Knopf,
a division of Random House, Inc.

Simon Hopkinson
Rice Pudding and Petit Sale avec Lentilles From ROAST
CHICKEN AND OTHER STORIES by Simon Hopkinson,
published by Ebury Press.

**Madhur Jaffrey, Rick Stein, Delia Smith, Rose Gray
and Ruth Rogers, Samantha and Samuel Clark,
and Ken Hom**
Lamb Dopiaza from INDIAN COOKING by Madhur
Jaffrey, published by BBC Books; Cullen Skink from
FRUITS OF THE SEA by Rick Stein, published by BBC
Books; Steak and Kidney Pudding from DELIA SMITH'S
WINTER COLLECTION by Delia Smith, published
by BBC Books; Hot and Sour Soup from CHINESE

COOKERY by Ken Hom, published by BBC Books; Moors and Christians from MORO: THE COOKBOOK by Samantha and Samuel Clark, published by Ebury; Panzanella from THE RIVER CAFE COOKBOOK by Rose Gray and Ruth Rogers, published by Ebury. Reprinted by permission of The Random House Group Ltd.

Diana Kennedy
Arroz a la Tumbada, Chiles con Queso, Guacamole, Tortillas, and Turkey in Mole Pablano from THE ESSENTIAL CUISINES OF MEXICO by Diana Kennedy, copyright © 2000 by Diana Kennedy. Used by permission of Clarkson Potter Publishers, a division of Random House, Inc.

Tessa Kiros
Gingerbread Biscuits, Hot Chocolate, Pomegranate and Apple Jelly from APPLES FOR JAM by Tessa Kiros, © Tessa Kiros, Murdoch Books Australia, 2006.

Nigella Lawson
Bagna Cauda, Easy Sticky-Toffee Pudding, Chocolate Fudge Cake, and Spatchcocked Chicken from NIGELLA BITES by Nigella Lawson. Copyright © 2002 Nigella Lawson. Reprinted by permission of Hyperion. All rights reserved. UK edition published by Chatto and Windus. Reprinted by permission of The Random House Group Ltd.

Jamie Oliver
Potato and Jerusalem Artichoke Soup, Fish Pie, and Seared Scallops from THE RETURN OF THE NAKED CHEF by Jamie Oliver (Michael Joseph, 2000) Copyright © Jamie Oliver Ltd 2000. Reproduced by permission of Penguin Books Ltd.

Martin Picard
Ploye à Champlain courtesy of Martin Picard, owner, Restaurant Au Pied de Cochon, Montreal, Quebec.

Gary Rhodes
Carpaccio and Irish Stew from RHODES AROUND BRITAIN by Gary Rhodes, published by BBC Books.

Claudia Roden
Fattoush and Faisinjan from THE NEW BOOK OF MIDDLE EASTERN FOOD by Claudia Roden, published by Penguin Books Ltd. in 1986.

Nigel Slater
Corn on the Cob, Crab Cakes, Fennel, Watercress, and Orange Salad, Old-Fashioned Fish Cakes, and Greek Baked Fish from REAL COOKING by Nigel Slater, 1997. Copyright © Nigel Slater. Reproduced by permission of Penguin Books Ltd.

Jane and Michael Stern
Bowl o' Red from CHILI NATION by Jane Stern and Michael Stern, copyright © 1998 by Jane Stern and Michael Stern. Used by permission of Broadway Books, a division of Random House, Inc.

Alice Waters
Ratatouille from CHEZ PANISSE VEGETABLES by Alice Waters. Published by HarperCollins. Copyright © 1996 by Alice Waters. All rights reserved. Reprinted by permission of HarperCollins Publishers.

Project Editors: Anna Southgate, Anna Stancer

Editors: Cynthia David, Eleanor Gasparik, Clare Hubbard, Bridget Jones, Wendy Thomas

Permissions and Photograph Research: Hannah Draper

Index: Ruth Pincoe

Art Direction: Richard Dewing

Design: Ian Hunt, Luke Jefford, Lucy Parissi

Color Separation and Proofing: Colourscan
Printing and Binding: Imago Productions (F.E.)

Produced by Madison Press Books

Diana Sullada, Art Director

Sandra L. Hall, Production Manager
Susan Barrable, Vice President, Finance and Production

Alison Maclean, Associate Publisher
Oliver Salzmann, President and Publisher